TRIAL MANUAL 8
FOR THE DEFENSE OF CRIMINAL CASES 2023 EDITION

Anthony G. Amsterdam and Randy Hertz

TRIAL MANUAL 8 FOR THE DEFENSE OF CRIMINAL CASES
by Anthony G. Amsterdam and Randy Hertz

The *Trial Manual 8 for the Defense of Criminal Cases* is a guidebook for criminal defense lawyers at the trial level. It covers the information a defense attorney has to know, and the strategic factors s/he should consider, at each of the stages of the criminal trial process. It is organized for easy access by practitioners who need ideas and information quickly in order to jump-start their work at any given stage.

The allocation of material among the four volumes of the book is intended to facilitate defense attorneys' use of the book:

- *Volume One* (Chapters 1-16) provides an overview of criminal procedure and then focuses on the issues a defense attorney is likely to confront, and the steps s/he will need to take, at the early stages of a criminal case, including: the first steps to be taken to locate, contact and protect a client who has been arrested or summoned or who fears s/he is wanted for arrest; arguing for bail or other forms of pretrial release; conducting the initial client interview; developing a theory of the case; dealing with police and prosecutors; planning and overseeing the defense investigation; conducting the preliminary hearing; grand jury practice; handing arraignments; and plea bargaining. This volume also addresses the additional considerations that may arise when representing a client who is mentally ill or intellectually disabled.

- *Volume Two* (Chapters 17-27) begins with a checklist of matters for counsel to consider between arraignment and trial, and then focuses extensively on pretrial motions practice. In addition to discussing strategic and practical aspects of drafting motions and handling motions hearings and non-evidentiary motions arguments, this volume covers the substantive law and procedural aspects of each of the types of motions that defense attorneys commonly litigate in criminal cases: motions for discovery (along with a discussion of all other aspects of the discovery process); motions to dismiss the charging paper; motions for diversion or for transfer to juvenile court; motions for a change of venue or for disqualification of the judge; motions for severance or for consolidation of counts or defendants; and motions to suppress tangible evidence, to suppress statements of the defendant, and to suppress identification testimony. These chapters provide detailed information about federal constitutional doctrines and a large number of state constitutional rulings that confer heightened protections.

- *Volume Three* (Chapters 28-40) starts with the immediate run-up to trial: issues relating to the timing of pretrial and trial proceedings; interlocutory review of pretrial rulings; and the concrete steps that counsel will need to take to prepare for trial, including working with expert witnesses where appropriate. It then begins the book's coverage of the trial stage, discussing the decision to elect or waive jury trial; jury selection procedures and challenges before and at trial; general characteristics of trials; opening statements; evidentiary issues and objections; techniques and tactics for handling prosecution and defense witnesses; and trial motions. Issues, procedures, and strategies unique to bench trials are discussed in tandem with the parallel aspects of jury-trial practice.

- *Volume Four* (Chapters 41-49) concludes the coverage of the trial by discussing the renewed motion for acquittal; closing arguments; requests for jury instructions; objections to the court's instructions; and jury deliberations. This volume then discusses posttrial motions and sentencing and concludes with a short summary of appellate and postconviction procedures and a précis of the first steps to be taken in connection with them.

The structure and presentation of material are designed to facilitate the conversion of text into defense motions and other types of briefing. Three of the documents in the text are available for direct downloading from the ALI website: section 2.5's flow-chart of procedures in summary, misdemeanor, and felony cases; section 4.5's questionnaire for obtaining information pertinent to bail from the client; and section 6.15's checklist for interviewing the client. The bail questionnaire and the interview list are in Word format that can be edited and thus customized to an individual user's practice and/or turned into a form for use in taking notes in real time during client interviews. **The downloadable versions of these documents are available at www.ali.org/trial-manual.**

The conventions the book uses for gender pronouns are designed to be fully inclusive. As societal conventions for gender pronouns change, the book's terminology is updated.

ABOUT THE AUTHORS

Anthony G. Amsterdam is a University Professor and Professor of Law *Emeritus* at the N.Y.U. School of Law. He previously taught at the University of Pennsylvania and at Stanford. Throughout and following his fifty years of law teaching (which were preceded by a stint as an Assistant United States Attorney in the District of Columbia), he has engaged in extensive *pro bono* litigation in criminal, civil-rights, and civil-liberties cases. He has also served as counsel, as a consultant, or as a member of the board of directors or advisors for numerous public-defender and civil-rights organizations.

Randy Hertz is the vice dean of N.Y.U. School of Law. He has been at the law school since 1985, and regularly teaches the Juvenile Defender Clinic, 1L Criminal Law, Criminal Procedure, and a simulation course titled Criminal Litigation. Before joining the N.Y.U. faculty, he worked at the Public Defender Service for the District of Columbia, in the juvenile, criminal, appellate and special litigation divisions.

TABLE OF CONTENTS
VOLUME ONE
PART ONE: INTRODUCTION AND OVERVIEW
Chapter 1
Introduction

Chapter 2
Outline and Flow-Chart of a Criminal Case

PART TWO: INITIAL STAGES OF THE CASE THROUGH ARRAIGNMENT

Chapter 3
The Lawyer's Entrance into the Case – First Steps

Chapter 4
Bail

Chapter 5
State-Paid Assistance for the Defense: Obtaining State Funding for Counsel's Time and for Defense Services

Chapter 6
Interviewing the Client

Chapter 7
Case Planning

Chapter 8
Dealings with the Police and Prosecutor

Chapter 9
Defense Investigation

A. *General Aspects of Defense Investigation*

B. *Locating and Interviewing Defense Witnesses*

C. *Interviewing and Taking Statements from Adverse Witnesses*

Chapter 10
Summary of Things to Do Before First Court Appearance

Chapter 11
Preliminary Hearing

Chapter 12
Defensive Procedures Between Bind-over and
the Filing of the Charging Paper

A. *Matters Relating to the Grand Jury*

B. *Other Defense Activity During the Pre-filing Stage*

Chapter 13
Defense Procedures After the Filing of the Charging Paper and Before Arraignment

Chapter 16
Representing Clients Who Are Mentally Ill or Intellectually Disabled
A. Introduction and Overview

VOLUME TWO

PART THREE: PROCEEDINGS BETWEEN ARRAIGNMENT AND TRIAL

Chapter 17

Defense Procedures and Considerations Between Arraignment and Trial

A. *Checklist of Matters for Counsel to Consider Between Arraignment and Trial*

B. *Selecting and Drafting Pretrial Motions: Strategic and Practical Considerations*

C. *Resisting Prosecution Attempts to Freeze a Defendant's Assets*

Chapter 18
Pretrial Discovery; The Pretrial Conference

A. *Introduction*

B. *Informal Discovery*

C. *Formal Discovery: Mechanisms and Legal Bases*

Chapter 19
Motions Practice in General

Chapter 20
Motions to Quash or Dismiss the Charging Paper

Chapter 21
Removing the Case from the Criminal Court's Docket:
Motions for Diversion, ACD, or Stetting; Transfer to Juvenile Court

A. *Motions for Diversion, ACD, Stetting*

Chapter 22
Motions for a Change of Venue or for Disqualification of the Judge

A. *Motions for a Change of Venue*

B. *Motions for Recusal or Disqualification of the Judge*

Chapter 23
Motions for Severance or for Consolidation of Counts or Defendants

A. *Motions Challenging the Joinder of Counts*
or Seeking Consolidation of Counts

Chapter 24
Suppression Hearings

Chapter 25
Motions To Suppress Tangible Evidence

C. *Police Entry and Search of Dwellings or Other Premises*

Chapter 26
Motions To Suppress Confessions, Admissions, and Other Statements of the Defendant

Chapter 27
Motions To Suppress Identification Testimony

VOLUME THREE

Chapter 28
Defense Motions To Advance or for a Continuance; Motions To Dismiss
for Want of Prosecution; Speedy Trial Motions

Chapter 29
Defense Trial Preparation

A. *Organizing the Defense Preparation*

B. *Selecting, Subpoenaing and Preparing Defense Witnesses to Testify at a Suppression Hearing or Trial*

Chapter 30
Retaining and Working with Expert Consultants and Potential Expert Witnesses

Chapter 31
Interlocutory Review of Pretrial Rulings by Means of Prerogative Writs

PART FOUR: TRIAL
Chapter 32
Election or Waiver of Jury Trial; Pretrial Matters
Relating to the Jury

Chapter 33
Selecting the Jury at Trial: The *Voir Dire*

Chapter 34
Trial: General Characteristics

Chapter 37
Handling Prosecution Witnesses

A. Cross-Examination Generally

B. Cross-examination in Particular Types of Cases or of Particular Types of Witnesses

C. Responding to Common Prosecutorial Gambits

Chapter 38
Motion for Acquittal

Chapter 39
Presenting the Case for the Defense

A. *General Aspects of the Defense Case*

B. *Planning and Presenting the Testimony of a Defense Witness*

C. *Testimony by the Defendant*

Chapter 40
Objections to Evidence; Anticipatory Objections;
Motions *in Limine* or to Preclude Prosecutorial Evidence or Practices;
Motions to Strike; Motions for Mistrial; Proffers;
Rulings on Evidentiary Questions

VOLUME FOUR

Chapter 41
Renewed Motion for Acquittal

Chapter 42
Instructions to the Jury; Defense Requests to Charge

Chapter 43
Closing Arguments

Chapter 49
Post-Sentencing: Motion for Reduction of Sentence; Appeal and Postconviction Proceedings; Probation and Parole Revocation Proceedings

PART ONE: INTRODUCTION AND OVERVIEW

Chapter 1

Introduction

1.1. *The Nature and Purpose of the Manual*

This *Trial Manual* is a how-to-do-it guidebook for handling criminal cases from beginning to end. It provides a compact guide through the stages of an ordinary criminal case, from arrest and investigation to appeal. Its focus is upon the key points at which defense counsel must make decisions and take actions. Options and factors to be considered in each decision, and steps that can be taken to assert a client's rights and protect the client's interests at each stage, are laid out.

Of course, no criminal case is "ordinary" in any but a highly artificial sense. Every criminal charge is intensely personal to the accused. Every accused person is a complex and unique individual. Every prosecution of an accused is unique in facts and in law, and makes unique demands on the skills of the defense attorney. Every defense attorney has his or her own style. There is no such thing as conducting a criminal defense generally. What is right or advisable in one case or situation is wrong in another. The most important attribute of the good criminal defense lawyer is perceptive selectivity – the ability to determine the precise requirements of each case and to respond to them in a highly specific manner best suited to the particular circumstances. In cases of women or transgender clients charged with serious crimes, counsel will find additional valuable guidance in CORNELL CENTER ON THE DEATH PENALTY WORLDWIDE, DEFENDING WOMEN AND TRANSGENDER PERSONS FACING EXTREME SENTENCES: A PRACTICAL GUIDE (2021).

No book can capture or instill that quality. All that is attempted here is a listing of available options for the lawyer; an identification of the major strategic considerations that may affect choice among the options; an introductory description of the prevailing legal principles and potential legal arguments, procedures, and practical techniques that defense counsel may encounter or may wish to employ; some warnings about common problems; and some suggestions of ways to avoid them or to cope with them. Counsel will have to cull all these things according to his or her own lights and the needs of the particular case and client in making the ultimate decisions what to do, when, and how.

The *Manual* should communicate enough information to dispel the edge of uneasiness that a lawyer without much criminal experience naturally feels when s/he is retained or appointed in a criminal matter. Having at least a general notion of what is coming and what can be done about it rightly inspires some confidence, and confidence is no less important in dealing with a criminal defendant than with any other client. Confidence should not get out of hand, however. Criminal practice *is* a specialty, and the lawyer with relatively little specialized experience must be careful not to bite off more than s/he can chew. In difficult matters s/he should consider the practicability of consulting (formally or informally, and on a limited or extended basis), associating with, or withdrawing in favor of, a more experienced criminal practitioner.

1.2. *The Structure of the Manual*

The *Manual* proceeds more or less chronologically, moving step-by-step through the process of handling an individual criminal case. It begins with the earliest stages at which defense counsel may enter a case, then advances through the pretrial stages, trial, sentencing and post-trial proceedings.

To make this *Manual* easy to use during court proceedings, we have abandoned various conventions of manual-writing. We take up topics in the order in which they become relevant at each particular stage of a typical prosecution, even when this format requires dispersing substantively related material among different chapters. For example, the topic of suppression of illegally obtained evidence is covered in five different chapters. A section on drafting suppression motions is found in the chapter on motions that need to be filed shortly after arraignment; a later chapter spells out techniques for handling suppression hearings; then come three substantive chapters covering, respectively, motions to suppress tangible evidence, incriminating statements, and identification testimony. The latter chapters summarize the voluminous federal and state law on their respective subjects.

Where judicial opinions are cited to illustrate basic propositions accepted in a majority of state and federal jurisdictions, we have not multiplied citations but have chosen a case or two reported with headnotes that target the proposition in point. By using these headnotes to access the national data bases, attorneys in all jurisdictions can zero in efficiently on the relevant local caselaw. We cite some unpublished opinions, for one or another reason. (Unpublished opinions are commonly issued in cases that judges regard as controlled by indisputably settled law. Thus they illustrate propositions that counsel can expect to be particularly well established, and these opinions often collect the leading precedents in compact form. Conversely, some courts use unpublished opinions to resolve cases in which unusual factual records cause the judges to stretch legal rules to the breaking point and sometimes beyond it. We cite these cases to illustrate the extent to which, in regard to some issues, judges are susceptible to factual persuasion in the teeth of the law.) Counsel considering including in briefs and motions references to opinions cited in the *Manual* should be careful to heed the restrictions that some courts place upon citation of unpublished opinions.

Citation form in the *Manual* has also been adapted to the realities of trial practice. Thus, for example, a short-form ("*supra*") citation to a case will only refer back to cases cited within a page or two before the *supra*, so that attorneys consulting the text when arguing a point in a trial or hearing will not need to search far afield for the full citation.

1.3. *The Attorney-Client Relationship*

"Defense counsel have the difficult task of serving both as officers of the court and as loyal and zealous advocates for their clients. The primary duties that defense counsel owe to their clients, to the administration of justice, and as officers of the court, are to serve as their clients' counselor and advocate with courage and devotion; to ensure that constitutional and other legal rights of their clients are protected; and to render effective, high-quality legal representation with integrity." AMERICAN BAR ASSOCIATION, STANDARDS FOR CRIMINAL JUSTICE MONITORS AND MONITORING, DEFENSE FUNCTION (4th ed. 2017), Standard 4-1.2(b), *Functions and Duties of Defense Counsel*. The duties of a defense attorney, which "run throughout the period of representation, and even beyond," include: "(a) a duty of confidentiality regarding information relevant to the client's representation which duty continues after the representation ends; ¶ (b) a duty of loyalty toward the client; ¶ (c) a duty of candor toward the court and others, tempered by the duties of confidentiality and loyalty; ¶ (d) a duty to communicate and keep the client informed and advised of significant developments and potential options and outcomes; ¶ (e) a duty to be well-informed regarding the legal options and developments that can affect a client's interests during a criminal representation; ¶ (f) a duty to continually evaluate the impact that each decision or action may have at later stages, including trial, sentencing, and post-conviction review; (g) a duty to be open to possible negotiated dispositions of the matter, including the possible benefits and disadvantages of cooperating with the prosecution; ¶ (h) a duty to consider the collateral consequences of decisions and actions, including but not limited to the collateral consequences of conviction." AMERICAN BAR ASSOCIATION, STANDARDS FOR CRIMINAL JUSTICE MONITORS AND MONITORING, DEFENSE FUNCTION (4th ed. 2017), Standard 4-1.3, *Continuing Duties of Defense Counsel. See also* AMERICAN BAR ASSOCIATION, MODEL RULES OF PROFESSIONAL CONDUCT, Rules 1.1 (competence), 1.2 (scope of representation and allocation of authority between client and lawyer), 1.3 (diligence), 1.4 (communication), 1.6 (confidentiality of information) (2015); AMERICAN BAR ASSOCIATION, CODE OF PROFESSIONAL RESPONSIBILITY, Canons 4 (preservation of client confidences and secrets), 6 (competent representation), 7 (zealous representation) (1980). *Cf.* Charlie Gerstein, *Dependent Counsel*, 16 STAN. J. CIVIL RIGHTS & CIVIL LIBERTIES 147 (2020).

"Certain decisions relating to the conduct of the case are for the accused; others are for defense counsel. Determining whether a decision is ultimately to be made by the client or by counsel is highly contextual, and counsel should give great weight to strongly held views of a competent client regarding decisions of all kinds." AMERICAN BAR ASSOCIATION, STANDARDS FOR CRIMINAL JUSTICE MONITORS AND MONITORING, DEFENSE FUNCTION (4th ed. 2017), Standard 4-5.2(a), *Control and Direction of the Case*. "The decisions ultimately to be made by a competent client, after full consultation with defense counsel, include: ¶ (i) whether to proceed without counsel; ¶ (ii) what pleas to enter; ¶ (iii) whether to accept a plea offer; ¶ (iv) whether to cooperate with or provide substantial assistance to the government; ¶ (v) whether to waive jury trial; ¶ (vi) whether to testify in his or her own behalf; ¶ (vii) whether to speak at sentencing; ¶ (viii) whether to appeal; and ¶ (ix) any other decision that has been determined in the jurisdiction to belong to the client." *Id.*, Standard 4-5.2(b). *See also McCoy v. Louisiana*, 138 S. Ct. 1500, 1508 (2018) ("Trial management is the lawyer's province: Counsel provides his or her assistance by making decisions such as 'what arguments to pursue, what evidentiary objections to raise, and what agreements to conclude regarding the admission of evidence.' . . . Some decisions, however, are reserved for the client – notably, whether to plead guilty, waive the right to a jury trial, testify in one's own behalf, and forgo an appeal."); *Jones v. Barnes*, 463 U.S. 745, 751 (1983) ("[i]t is . . . recognized that the accused has the ultimate authority to make certain fundamental decisions regarding the case, as to whether to plead guilty, waive a jury, testify in his or her own behalf, or take an appeal"); *Florida v. Nixon*, 543 U.S. 175, 187 (2004); *Roe v. Flores-Ortega*, 528 U.S. 470, 477 (2000); *Garza v. Idaho*, 139 S. Ct. 738, 746, 748 (2019);

Cooke v. State, 977 A.2d 803, 809, 843 (Del. 2009) ("Here, defense counsel pursued a 'guilty but mentally ill' verdict over Cooke's vociferous and repeated protestations that he was completely innocent and not mentally ill. This strategy deprived Cooke of his constitutional right to make the fundamental decisions regarding his case."; "We conclude that defense counsel's strategy infringed upon the defendant's personal and fundamental constitutional rights to plead not guilty, to testify in his own defense, and to have the contested issue of guilt beyond a reasonable doubt decided by an impartial jury."); *United States v. Read*, 918 F.3d 712 (9th Cir. 2019) (although the defendant was not mentally competent to represent himself, his attorney could not present a defense of insanity over his objection consistently with *McCoy*); *People v. Bloom*, 12 Cal. 5th 1008, 1015, 508 P.3d 737, 745, 292 Cal. Rptr. 3d 769, 777-78 (2022) ("At trial, defense counsel conceded Bloom's responsibility for the deaths of all three victims in an effort to pursue a mental capacity defense to the murder charges. Bloom, however, was willing to accept responsibility only for the killing of his father and expressly objected to admitting responsibility for the deaths of the other two victims. In conceding responsibility for these victims against Bloom's wishes, defense counsel violated Bloom's Sixth Amendment right to choose the fundamental objectives of his defense under *McCoy* . . . ."); *State v. Tribble*, 193 Vt. 194, 204, 67 A.3d 210, 216 (2012) (counsel cannot raise a diminished-capacity defense over the defendant's objection, nor may counsel waive the defendant's right to confrontation by "stipulat[ing] to allow the State to take a preservation deposition of a critical witness for use in lieu of live testimony at trial"); *People v. Flores*, 34 Cal. App. 5th 270, 273, 246 Cal. Rptr. 3d 77, 79 (2019) (counsel improperly "overrode Flores's stated goal of maintaining his innocence of the alleged acts. Instead, in pursuit of the understandable objective of achieving an acquittal, . . . [counsel] conceded the actus reus of the charged crimes . . . . [in an attempted vehicular murder trial by "conced[ing] the act of driving and instead assert[ing] that Flores never formed the premeditated intent to kill necessary for first degree murder," and then, "at a subsequent trial on weapons possession charges, . . . conced[ing] that Flores possessed certain firearms, instead arguing that the possession was not 'knowing' because Flores did not understand the prohibited nature of the weapons"]. Although any reasonable lawyer might agree with counsel's judgment, *McCoy* instructs that this is a decision for the client to make."); *State v. Humphries*, 181 Wash. 2d 708, 714, 336 P.3d 1121, 1124 (2014) (a defense attorney may not "stipulate an element of the crime [at trial] . . . over the defendant's known and express objection"); *State v. Luby*, 904 N.W.2d 453, 455 (Minn. 2017) ("defense counsel provided ineffective assistance by conceding the only disputed elements of the charged offenses – premeditation and intent – without his consent"); *State v. Brown*, 2018-01999 (La. 9/30/21), 330 So.3d 199, 226 (La. 2021) (in a capital trial the defendant instructed his attorney not to call the defendant's mother as a witness in mitigation at the penalty stage; when the lawyer insisted that the mother be called, the defendant requested that he be permitted to discharge the lawyer and represent himself; the trial judge informed the defendant that he could not limit the lawyer's choice of witnesses if he continued to be represented by counsel: he was required to choose between allowing the lawyer to call his mother or waiving the right to counsel and proceeding *pro se* in the penalty trial; the defendant chose to proceed *pro se* and was sentenced to death; the Louisiana Supreme Court holds his *Faretta* waiver (see § 1.4 *infra*) invalid because the trial judge misinformed the defendant regarding his options: it joins "[o]ther jurisdictions [that] have similarly held that a capital defendant's right to instruct his counsel not to present mitigating evidence encompasses the right to limit the amount and/or type of mitigating evidence counsel may present."); *Figueroa-Sanabria v. State*, 2023 WL 4246244 (Fla. 2023) (same ruling where a capital defendant wanted no mitigation evidence presented at the penalty trial). Counsel should advise the client regarding all of these issues that are ultimately for the client to decide. *See McCoy v. Louisiana, supra*, 138 S. Ct. at 1509 ("Counsel . . . must . . . develop a trial strategy and discuss it with her client, . . . explaining why, in her view, conceding guilt [or other strategic courses] would be the best option."); counsel should thoroughly research and investigate all legal and factual matters bearing on available options and should advise the client of that information together with each option and its consequences; and counsel may also urge the client forcefully to choose the options that counsel believes to be in the client's best interests. However, particularly when it comes to defining those interests – determining the ultimate goals that should be pursued in the litigation – the client has the last word; Colin Miller, *The Real* McCoy*: Defining the Defendant's Right to Autonomy in the Wake of* McCoy v. Louisiana, 53 LOYOLA U. CHI. L. J. 405 (2022); Natalia Hamilton, Note, *The Right to Decide An Attorney is Wrong: The Extent of a Defendant's Right to Control the Objective of the Defense and Reject Counsel's Trial Strategy*, 74 BAYLOR L. REV. 285 (2022). For thoughtful reflections on the moral and ethical morass that counsel must navigate in cases of mentally disturbed clients who insist upon courses of action that counsel views as severely self-damaging, *see* Steve Zeidman, *Whose Case Is It Anyway? Florida v. Nixon and McCoy v. Louisiana: Pro-Defendant or Pro-Government?*, 37-SUM CRIMINAL JUSTICE 26 (2022).

In other matters (designing and implementing strategy, formulating the client's legal contentions, selecting evidence and shaping its presentation, and so forth), the bottom-line judgments are for counsel to make. "An attorney undoubtedly has a duty to consult with the client regarding 'important decisions,' including questions of overarching defense strategy. . . . That obligation, however, does not require counsel to obtain the defendant's consent to 'every tactical decision.' *Taylor v. Illinois*, 484 U.S. 400, 417-418 . . . (1988) (an attorney has authority to manage most aspects of the defense without obtaining his client's approval)." *Florida v. Nixon, supra*, 543 U.S. at 187. *See also United States v. Rosemond*, 958 F.3d 111, 122 (2d Cir. 2020) ("[c]onceding an element of a crime while contesting the other elements falls within the ambit of trial strategy"); *Christian v. Thomas*, 982 F.3d 1215 (9th Cir. 2020) (alternative ground) (counsel who followed his client's instructions to contest identity and argue that the client was not the perpetrator of a murder did not violate *McCoy* by arguing self-defense as an alternative theory for acquittal); *and see Nix v. Whiteside,* 475 U.S. 157, 166 (1986) ("counsel must take all reasonable lawful means to attain the objectives of the client" while remaining obedient to the applicable rules of professional conduct, such as the prohibition against knowingly presenting perjurious testimony).

"Immediately upon appointment or retention, defense counsel should work to establish a relationship of trust and confidence with each client." AMERICAN BAR ASSOCIATION, STANDARDS FOR CRIMINAL JUSTICE MONITORS AND MONITORING, DEFENSE FUNCTION (4th ed. 2017), Standard 4-3.1(a), *Establishing and Maintaining An Effective Client Relationship*. "Defense counsel should actively work to maintain an effective and regular relationship with all clients," and this "obligation . . . is not diminished by the fact that the client is in custody" (*id.*, Standard 4-3.1(f)). Even if a "client appears to have a mental impairment or other disability that could adversely affect the representation," "this does not diminish defense counsel's obligations to the client, including maintaining a normal attorney-client relationship in so far as possible" (*id.*, Standard 4-3.1(c)). The same is true if the client is a minor or elderly; these cases and cases involving clients with a mental impairment or other disability often require that defense counsel pay "special attention" to "us[ing] language and means that the client is able to understand" (*id.*, Standard 4-3.1(d)). *See also* ABA MODEL RULES OF PROFESSIONAL CONDUCT, Rule 1.14(a) ("When a client's capacity to make adequately considered decisions in connection with a representation is diminished, whether because of minority, mental impairment or for some other reason, the lawyer shall, as far as reasonably possible, maintain a normal client-lawyer relationship with the client."); Barry Kozak, *The Forgotten Rule of Professional Conduct – Representing a Client with Diminished Capacity*, 49 CREIGHTON L. REV. 827 (2016).

If counsel reasonably believes that factors such as mental illness or developmental disability so severely "diminish" the client's "capacity to make adequately considered decisions in connection with the representation . . . [that] a normal client-lawyer relationship with the client" cannot be maintained, and if counsel furthermore "reasonably believes" that the client "is at risk of substantial physical, financial or other harm unless action is taken and [that the client] cannot adequately act in the client's own interest," then counsel may take "reasonably necessary protective action, including consulting with individuals or entities that have the ability to take action to protect the client and, in appropriate cases, seeking the appointment of a guardian ad litem, conservator or guardian." *Id.*, Rule 1.14(a), (b). *See* Fredrick E. Vars, *The Value of a Guardian Ad Litem in a Sell Proceeding*, 43-MAR THE CHAMPION 16 (March 2019).

The preceding principles, honed by scholars and practitioners familiar with the intricacies of criminal defense work, provide an indispensable compass for defense attorneys as they try to navigate the complex world of criminal practice. Yet, even the most experienced, committed defense attorneys will admit to sometimes feeling baffled and frustrated by difficulties in dealing with particular clients. These include, for example, the client who seems hell-bent on doing something that is tactically dangerous; the client who is antagonistic to counsel for no apparent reason (or at least not one that is evident to counsel); and sometimes simply a client whom counsel personally dislikes. In such situations, it is useful for attorneys to remind themselves that criminal defendants usually are under extreme stress, not only because of the criminal charge that hangs over their heads but also because of a variety of difficult life circumstances that comprise the background for the charge. *See generally* STEPHEN ELLMANN, ROBERT D. DINERSTEIN, ISABELLE R. GUNNING, KATHERINE R. KRUSE & ANN C. SHALLECK, LAWYERS AND CLIENTS: CRITICAL ISSUES IN INTERVIEWING AND COUNSELING 34-47 (2009); *see also id.* at 6-7 (explaining the ideal of client-centeredness); Heather M. Harris, *Building Holistic Defense: The Design and Evaluation of a Social Work Centric Model of Public Defense*, 31 (No. 6) CRIMINAL JUSTICE POLICY REVIEW 800 (2020). Also, counsel needs to keep in mind that a client's decisions about the case, including decisions regarding such fundamental matters as whether or not to take a guilty plea, may be influenced by a host of complicated feelings about family and self that the client may not feel comfortable sharing with a stranger like counsel, however well-meaning counsel may be. *See, e.g.*, Binny Miller, *Give Them Back Their Lives: Recognizing Client Narrative in Case Theory*, 93 MICH. L. REV. 485, 570-75 (1994). Defense attorneys should approach this work with a humble recognition of the limits of their ability to understand the circumstances of their clients' lives and relationships, and should reconcile themselves to the sometimes painful reality that faithful adherence to the ethos of defense work requires providing the best possible defense even (and perhaps especially) to the most difficult clients. They should also be aware of the damaging effects that the stresses and painful exposures of their own lives may have on their ability to maintain a dispassionate perspective on their clients. *See, e.g.,* Amy F. Kimpel, *Violent Videos: Criminal Defense in a Digital Age*, 37 GA. ST. U. L. REV. 305 (2021).

1.4. *A Defendant's Right to Proceed Pro Se*

A mentally competent defendant has the federal constitutional right to waive counsel, including the right to dismiss court-appointed counsel, and to proceed *pro se. Faretta v. California*, 422 U.S. 806 (1975). *See, e.g., Tatum v. Foster*, 847 F.3d 459 (7th Cir. 2017); *Tennis v. State*, 997 So.2d 375 (Fla. 2008); *State v. Samuel*, 422 S.C. 596, 813 S.E.2d 487 (2018). The standard of competency for this purpose is the same as the standard for competency to stand trial under *Dusky v. United States*, 362 U.S. 402 (1960), and cognate cases discussed in § 16.7 *infra*: "whether the defendant has 'sufficient present ability to consult with his lawyer with a reasonable degree of rational understanding' and has 'a rational as well as factual understanding of the proceedings against him.'" *Godinez v. Moran*, 509 U.S. 389, 396 (1993). *See United States v. Taylor*, 21 F.4th 94, 101-02 (3d Cir. 2021) (reversing a trial judge's refusal to allow the defendant to waive counsel and proceed *pro se*) ("[T]he District Court appears to have misdirected its focus when evaluating Taylor's request to represent himself. In his *pro se* filings and at the suppression hearing, Taylor advanced 'sovereign citizen' arguments. . . . The District Court focused on these arguments, noting that Taylor's claims were 'not founded on any rational legal principles' and 'sen[t] up a red flag.' . . . The record further indicates that the District Court had the merits of Taylor's claims in mind rather than his appreciation for the consequences of representing himself when it denied his request . . . . ¶ . . . In [*United States v.*] *Peppers*, [302 F.3d 120 (3d Cir. 2002),] we held that the district court erred because it denied the defendant's request to represent himself after focusing its inquiry on the defendant's knowledge of the law and practical ability to mount a defense. . . . We determined that, instead, the court should have investigated whether the defendant appreciated 'the structural limitations or perils of representing himself.'"); *and see United States v. Jones*, 65 F.4th 926 (7th Cir. 2023) (upholding a trial court's decision granting a defendant the right to proceed *pro se* in a similar case, even though the defendant's trial performance was a shambles). However, defendants may be denied the right to proceed *pro se* if the court finds that their mental condition is such that, while "competent enough to stand trial under *Dusky* . . . [if represented by counsel, they] . . . still suffer from severe mental illness to the point . . . [of being] not competent to conduct trial proceedings by themselves." *Indiana v. Edwards*, 554 U.S. 164, 178 (2008). (Reconciling *Edwards* and *Godinez* is not easy. *See* Todd A. Berger, *The Aftermath of* Indiana v. Edwards*: Re-Evaluating the Standard of Competency Needed for Pro Se Representation*, 68 BAYLOR L. REV. 680 (2016); Christina L. Patton, E. Lea Johnston, Colleen M. Lillard, & Michael J. Vitacco, *Legal and Clinical Issues Regarding the Pro Se Defendant: Guidance for Practitioners and Policy Makers*, 25 (No. 3) PSYCHOLOGY, PUBLIC POLICY, AND LAW 196 (2019); Richard J. Bonnie, *Competence for Criminal Adjudication: Client Autonomy and the Significance of Decisional Competence* (forthcoming, OHIO STATE JOURNAL OF CRIMINAL LAW), *available at* https://ssrn.com/abstract=4365151.) Granting a defendant leave to proceed *pro se* without an adequate inquiry into his or her competence "deprive[s the defendant] . . . of two distinct protections . . . : (1) protection of . . . [the] constitutional right to counsel . . . [despite] a mental disorder that prevent[s] him [or her] from understanding the significance and consequences of waiving that right . . .; and (2) protection of . . . [the] right to a fair trial . . . [insofar as s/he might be] unable to present a defense because of . . . mental impairment . . . ." *People v. Waldron*, 14

Cal. 5th 288, 309-10, 522 P.3d 1059, 1073, 303 Cal. Rptr. 3d 652, 669 (2023). When the defendant wishes to waive the right to counsel and to exercise the *Faretta* right of self-representation, s/he must be competent both to confer with counsel regarding the consequences and advisability of the preliminary waiver and then to handle the trial (or plea) proceedings without counsel's aid. *See People v. Wycoff*, 12 Cal. 5th 58, 89, 493 P.3d 789, 809, 283 Cal. Rptr. 3d 1, 26 (2021) ("It might be argued that a defendant who intends to waive counsel does not need to be able to consult with counsel, and therefore the first prong of the *Dusky* standard does not apply when competence to waive counsel is at issue. The argument fails as a matter of logic because a defendant who is represented and is considering whether to waive counsel needs to consult with counsel in order to understand and weigh the pros and cons of that decision.").

"'It is undeniable that in most criminal prosecutions defendants could better defend with counsel's guidance than by their own unskilled efforts.' . . . Thus, a defendant must state his request to proceed pro se 'unambiguously to the court so that no reasonable person can say that the request was not made.'" *United States v. Williams*, 2023 WL 2945900, at *1 (3d Cir. 2023). *Compare Bolden v. Vandergriff*, 69 F.4th 479, 483 (8th Cir. 2023) (holding that a state trial judge was not obliged to allow a defendant to proceed *pro se* when the defendant's waiver of counsel was conditional: applying AEDPA's restricted standard of review (see § 49.2.3.2 *infra*), the Eighth Circuit finds that "Bolden conditioned his self-representation request on his speedy trial motions being denied, and wanted counsel to depose witnesses even after being informed counsel could not do so if he was *pro se*. From these facts, a court could reasonably conclude Bolden's waiver of the right to counsel was not unequivocal."). "[I]n situations where a defendant clearly, unequivocally, and timely invokes the right to self-representation, the trial court must inform the defendant 'of the dangers and disadvantages of self-representation,' . . . and conduct a "'searching or formal inquiry" to ensure that [the] waiver [of counsel] is knowing, intelligent, and voluntary . . . .'" *Cassano v. Shoop*, 1 F.4th 458, 466 (6th Cir. 2021); *United States v. Hakim*, 30 F.4th 1310, 1314-15 (11th Cir. 2022) ("Although Hakim was represented by counsel at trial, he lacked representation during the pretrial process. At his arraignment, Hakim expressed his desire to waive his right to counsel and to represent himself. The magistrate judge found that Hakim's waiver was knowing after misinforming him that the maximum sentence he could receive if convicted was 12 months of imprisonment. After trial, the district court sentenced Hakim to 21 months of imprisonment. Hakim now argues that his purported waiver of counsel was not knowing. Because the magistrate judge gave materially incorrect information about 'the possible punishment he faced, we hold that there was no knowing and intelligent waiver of [Hakim's] right to counsel.' . . . And because 'the defendant need not show prejudice to obtain a reversal,'. . . we vacate and remand."). This is the nearly ubiquitous practice in both state and federal courts. *See, e.g., Godinez v. Moran, supra*, 509 U.S. at 392-93; *United States v. Hamett*, 961 F.3d 1249, 1255 (10th Cir. 2020) ("'[a] proper *Faretta* hearing apprises the defendant of the following: 'the nature of the charges, the statutory offenses included within them, the range of allowable punishments thereunder, possible defenses to the charges and circumstances in mitigation thereof, and all other facts essential to a broad understanding of the whole matter'"); *United States v. Johnson*, 24 F.4th 590 (6th Cir. 2022); *United States v. Hansen*, 929 F.3d 1238 (10th Cir. 2019); *State v. Murray*, 469 S.W.3d 921 (Mo. App. 2015); *State v. Klessig*, 211 Wis. 2d 194, 207, 564 N.W.2d 716, 721 (Wis. 1997); *State v. Victor*, 13-888 (La.App. 5 Cir. 12/23/14), 167 So.3d 118 (La. App. 2014); *Cortez v. State*, 2014 WL 1423339 (Tex. App. 2014); *People v. Baines*, 39 N.Y.3d 1, 197 N.E.3d 1282, 176 N.Y.S.3d 843 (2022);

FLA. RULE CRIM. PRO. 3.111(d)(2); *cf. Ayers v. Hall*, 900 F.3d 829 (6th Cir. 2018); *but see Iowa v. Tovar*, 541 U.S. 77, 81 (2004) (holding that the federal Constitution does not *require* an admonition regarding the dangers and risks of self-representation but permits a defendant to waive counsel and plead guilty if "the trial court informs the accused of the nature of the charges against him, of his right to be counseled regarding his plea, and of the range of allowable punishments attendant upon the entry of a guilty plea"); *United States v. Schaefer*, 13 F.4th 875, 888 (9th Cir. 2021) (holding a waiver of counsel valid although the defendant was incorrectly advised regarding the length of the mandatory minimum sentence for the offenses charged; it was sufficient that the defendant be informed of the nature of the charges, the dangers and disadvantages of self-representation, and "the approximate range of his penal exposure," so that he could apprehend "the severity of his potential punishment"). The court may order the defendant to undergo a mental examination and/or may receive extrinsic evidence of relevant mental impairment. *See, e.g., People v. Shiga*, 6 Cal. App. 5th 22, 210 Cal. Rptr. 3d 611 (2016); *People v. Davis*, 2015 CO 36M, 352 P.3d 950 (Colo. 2015); *State v. Connor*, 292 Conn. 483, 528-30, 973 A.2d 627, 656-57 (2009); *State v. Bartlett*, 271 Mont. 429, 898 P.2d 98 (1995). If the court has reason to doubt the defendant's competence to be tried or to proceed *pro se*, it may not allow him or her to waive counsel until after the competency issue has been resolved. *State v. Bolden*, 558 S.W.3d 513 (Mo. App. 2016).

The position of a court-appointed lawyer whose client wishes to discharge counsel and proceed *pro se* is excruciatingly conflicted. On the one hand, the client's right to self-representation is one that counsel is obliged to respect. As *Faretta* explains, that right is grounded upon the client's interests in self-determination and autonomy; these are values that a client is entitled to have his or her lawyer uphold and advocate. So, for example, counsel is required to assist the client to make a record to support the claim that the client is competent to go it alone if that is what s/he wants. On the other hand, counsel owes it to the client to do everything within reason to save the client from the consequences – almost always disastrous – of an ill-advised decision to proceed *pro se*. So for example, counsel is required to insist upon a mental-health examination of a client whom counsel believes is probably *not* competent to make an advised decision to forgo counsel's services. There is no prescribed, easy course for navigating the narrow channel between the rock and the whirlpool here. Counsel can and must vigorously, repeatedly urge the client not to go it *pro se*; counsel can properly tell the client that the likely consequences of doing so are precisely as horrendous as counsel believes they are; but counsel should not exaggerate the client's risks or exposures or otherwise pressure the client to make a choice based on fear rather than reason. If counsel has a strong, factually solid basis for doubting the client's competency, counsel can and should request a court-ordered competency evaluation even over the client's objection (*see State v. Bartlett, supra*); but counsel should not lightly override the client's resistance to such an examination. Sometimes the difficulty of resolving counsel's conflicting obligations can be ameliorated by negotiating with the client and the court an arrangement in which the defendant does proceed *pro se* and personally conducts the defense, but counsel remains at the defendant's side in a "standby" or "advisory" capacity, available to consult with the defendant throughout all proceedings. (The role of standby counsel is the subject of *McKaskle v. Wiggins*, 465 U.S. 168 (1984), and its progeny. *See* Kelly Rondinelli, Note, *In Defense of Hybrid Representation: The Sword to Wield and the Shield to Protect*, 27 WILLIAM & MARY BILL OF RIGHTS J. 1313 (2019). *See also People v. Baines, supra*, 39 N.Y.2d at 8, 197 N.E.3d at 1286, 176 N.Y.S.3d at 847 ("when the court, in its discretion, permits standby counsel . . . , it should explain to the defendant the court's rules regarding the role of a legal advisor or standby counsel and how that role differs from representation by an attorney").) One practical advantage of the standby-counsel procedure is that quite often a defendant who accepts it at the outset will soon come to realize that s/he is floundering and hurting his or her case, and will agree to have counsel resume first-chair responsibilities. In this situation, judges are very likely to allow the switchback and even to give counsel considerable latitude to undo whatever damage the client has already incurred. *Cf. People v. Costan*, 169 A.D.3d 820, 822, 94 N.Y.S.3d 131, 134 (N.Y. App. Div., 2d Dep't 2019) (the trial court "improvidently exercised its discretion" and violated the right to effective assistance of counsel by denying a request for an adjournment of the suppression hearing by defense counsel, who had been "act[ing] in the limited capacity of advisor [prior to the suppression hearing] since the defendant wished to proceed pro se" but who then "agreed to represent the defendant at the suppression hearing"; counsel "expressed his concern that he had not had an adequate opportunity to review voluminous discovery materials," and the accused was entitled to "'assistance by an attorney who has taken the time to review and prepare both the law and the facts relevant to the defense'").

Clients who inform their lawyers that they want to proceed *pro se* frequently flip-flop from day to day, agreeing to counsel's representation one day, then changing their minds and insisting on self-representation when they next speak with counsel, and then reverting to willingness to be represented by counsel. Patient, tactful, low-keyed negotiation with the client, urging him or her to keep an open mind and to rethink any decision to appear *pro se*, is required in this situation. And counsel should advise the client not to communicate personally with the court or with the prosecution until counsel and the client have worked the matter through and reached a final understanding about how the client wishes to proceed. *Cf. United States v. Bauzó-Santiago*, 867 F.3d 13 (1st Cir. 2017).

"The trial judge may terminate self-representation by a defendant who deliberately engages in serious and obstructionist misconduct" (*Faretta v. California, supra*, 422 U.S. at 834 n. 46) or whose performance demonstrates that s/he is unable or unwilling "to abide by rules of procedure and courtroom protocol" (*McKaskle v. Wiggins, supra*, 465 U.S. at 173). But to justify termination, the defendant's conduct must be seriously disruptive; the mere asking of an objectionable question on cross-examination of a government witness, for example, is insufficient justification, even if the defendant should have known that the question was improper. *United States v. Engel*, 968 F.3d 1046 (9th Cir. 2020).

Chapter 2

Outline and Flow-Chart of a Criminal Case

2.1. *Different Procedures for Offenses of Differing Seriousness*

Most jurisdictions have two or more distinct sets of criminal procedures to govern charges of differing degrees of gravity. The jurisdictions vary regarding the number of sets of procedures employed (usually two or three), the charges governed by each set, and the particular courts, stages, and practices involved in each set. Local statutes, rules, and customs must be consulted. (In federal practice, for example, criminal prosecutions in the United States District Courts are governed by Rules 1-57 and 59-61 of the Federal Rules of Criminal Procedure; Rule 58 provides a somewhat different set of rules for proceedings in petty-offense and misdemeanor cases.)

The following sections of this chapter provide a brief description of the typical stages in each set of procedures in a three-set jurisdiction. In such a jurisdiction, *summary procedure* is used for petty state charges and for most municipal ordinance violations when ordinance violations are conceived as being criminal rather than civil matters. *Misdemeanor procedure* is used for charges of middling seriousness, and *felony procedure* for serious charges. (The terms *summary procedure*, *misdemeanor procedure*, and *felony procedure* are used as generic artifices here; the boundary between the second and third categories in some jurisdictions corresponds only roughly to the technical felony-misdemeanor line.) From *summary* through *misdemeanor* to *felony procedure*, the process becomes increasingly elaborate and increasingly protracted. A summary defendant may be tried, convicted, and sentenced within hours of arrest. A felony defendant is often not formally charged in the court having jurisdiction to try the charge (that is, s/he is not indicted) for months after arrest.

It is meaningless to generalize about the duration of "ordinary" cases of the three types; the variations within each type are extreme. Counsel principally familiar with civil litigation will notice, however, that the pace of criminal litigation is generally far more rapid. The early stages (through bind-over) are usually completed within days or weeks, and (except when the defendant is serving a sentence on another conviction) there is nothing like the years of pretrial delay common in civil cases.

2.2. *Summary Procedure*

2.2.1. *Complaint and Warrant or Summons*

Summary cases ordinarily begin with the filing of a complaint against the defendant before a member of the minor judiciary [hereafter called, generically, a magistrate]. The complainant, who may be a private citizen or a police officer, appears before the magistrate and signs and swears to a written (often printed-form) document, called the complaint, which describes what the defendant did (often in the conclusory language of the criminal statute) and characterizes it as an offense. If the magistrate is satisfied that an offense is legally stated, s/he issues a warrant authorizing the arrest of the defendant, or in many jurisdictions s/he may issue a summons or notice ordering the defendant to appear before the magistrate on a designated date. This procedure, in the jargon, is called the swearing out of a warrant by the complainant.

It should be noted that the complaint ordinarily has two discrete functions in summary procedure: (1) It constitutes the charging paper or initial pleading against the defendant in the court having jurisdiction to try the charge, and (2) it serves as the basis for the issuance of an arrest warrant. In the former aspect its technical sufficiency is governed by state law, but in the latter aspect it must also satisfy the Fourth Amendment to the Constitution of the United States (see § 25.2 *infra*), which requires that arrest warrants be supported by a sworn statement of facts in sufficient detail to permit the issuing magistrate to make an independent determination whether there is probable cause to believe that the defendant has committed the offense charged (see §§ 25.7.2, 25.7.4 *infra*). Conclusory forms of complaint that are commonly used may be sufficient as pleadings under state law, but they are assailable under the Fourth Amendment insofar as the validity of an arrest or detention subsequently comes into issue (*cf. In re Walters*, 15 Cal. 3d 738, 751, 543 P.2d 607, 616-17, 126 Cal. Rptr. 239, 248-49 (1975)) – for example, in connection with a motion to suppress illegally obtained evidence (see § 25.39 *infra*) or in connection with a motion to dismiss the prosecution in those few jurisdictions in which the magistrate's jurisdiction depends upon a valid arrest (*e.g., City of St. Paul v. Webb*, 256 Minn. 210, 97 N.W.2d 638 (1959); *State v. Duren*, 266 Minn. 335, 123 N.W.2d 624 (1963)) or when state law makes a valid arrest the precondition for some other exercise of authority (such as a requirement that a driver submit to breath or blood testing for intoxication (*e.g., Roseborough v. Commonwealth*, 281 Va. 233, 704 S.E.2d 414 (2011); *State v. Christon*, 160 Wis. 2d 50, 468 N.W.2d 33 (Table) (Wis. App. 1990))).

2.2.2. *Arrest*

In a limited number of cases (principally involving offenses that constitute breaches of the peace), police are authorized to make arrests for summary offenses without a warrant. When a defendant is arrested without a warrant, the officer brings him or her before a magistrate and immediately files the complaint or has a private complainant file it. Practice varies on whether in these cases the magistrate then issues a *pro forma* warrant. Even when they are authorized by law to arrest without a warrant, police will often refuse to do so in summary cases but will require the private complainant to swear out a warrant.

2.2.3. *Stationhouse Bail*

Police who have made an arrest for a summary offense with or without a warrant are ordinarily authorized to release the defendant on bail for his or her appearance before the magistrate on a designated date. The amount of this "stationhouse" bail is sometimes subject to police discretion and sometimes regulated by a bail schedule prescribed by a statute or court rule, setting the bail for specified offenses. When the amount is determined solely by the police, they often have their own more or less inflexible bail schedule.

2.2.4. *Trial*

When the defendant is brought before the magistrate or appears pursuant to a summons or a bail obligation, trial is often had on the spot. If a recently arrested defendant requests a continuance to obtain a lawyer, a continuance is usually granted for a few days. Brief continuances may also be granted the prosecution or the defense because of the unavailability of witnesses or the requirements of adequate preparation.

The complaint (or, in some jurisdictions, the warrant) constitutes the charging paper. The defendant is asked to plead to it. If s/he pleads guilty, the magistrate proceeds to sentence. If s/he pleads not guilty, an evidentiary trial is had.

In theory, the prosecution presents its evidence first at trial, and the charge should be dismissed if the prosecution's evidence is insufficient, without requiring the defendant to testify or to present defensive evidence. In practice, however, magistrates frequently begin the trial by simply reading the police report or asking the officer to state under oath that it is true and then asking the defendant to tell his or her side of the story. This shortcut procedure is neither authorized by law nor is it constitutional; but if the prosecution's case is relatively simple and easily provable or if the defendant has a good defensive story, the better course for the defense is usually to go along with the magistrate's chosen practice and not to rock the boat by raising legal or constitutional objections to the manner in which the magistrate wishes to proceed. Summary trials before magistrates are ordinarily very informal, and since the magistrate will sometimes acquit a technically guilty defendant on the basis of mitigating circumstances that appeal to his or her sense of fairness, it is helpful to keep on the magistrate's good side. Nevertheless, in appropriate cases – particularly (1) when the complainant or the arresting officer does not appear in court or (2) when there is doubt that the prosecution's evidence will establish the elements of any offense or (3) when the defendant does not wish to testify or has no believable exonerating story to tell or would be assisted in testifying by the prior testimony of prosecution witnesses or (4) when, on the whole, the defendant appears unlikely to attract the magistrate's sympathies – the defendant can, and should, insist upon a procedurally proper trial.

The constitutional presumption of innocence gives every criminal defendant a right to require that the prosecution prove the facts establishing guilt "by probative evidence and beyond a reasonable doubt" (*Estelle v. Williams*, 425 U.S. 501, 503 (1976) (dictum); see § 38.1 *infra*). This means that "one accused of a crime is entitled to have his guilt or innocence determined solely on the basis of the evidence introduced at trial, and not on grounds of official suspicion, indictment, continued custody, or other circumstances not adduced as proof at trial" (*Taylor v. Kentucky*, 436 U.S. 478, 485 (1978); *Holbrook v. Flynn*, 475 U.S. 560, 567-68 (1986) (dictum)). Thus the prosecution must produce legally admissible evidence, subject to cross-examination (*see Brookhart v. Janis*, 384 U.S. 1 (1966); *cf. Moore v. United States*, 429 U.S. 20 (1976) (per curiam)), that is sufficient "to convince a trier of fact beyond a reasonable doubt of the existence of every element of the offense" (*Jackson v. Virginia*, 443 U.S. 307, 316 (1979); *see also Pilon v. Bordenkircher*, 444 U.S. 1, 2 (1979) (per curiam)). This fundamental constitutional model of a criminal trial is not dispensable merely because the offense or the penalty is minor. *See, e.g., Thompson v. City of Louisville*, 362 U.S. 199 (1960); *Johnson v. Florida*, 391 U.S. 596, 598 (1968) (per curiam); *Vachon v. New Hampshire*, 414 U.S. 478, 480 (1974) (per curiam); *cf. Berkemer v. McCarty*, 468 U.S. 420 (1984).

In every criminal prosecution the Fifth Amendment privilege against self-incrimination gives the defendant a right not to testify if s/he chooses to remain silent. *Griffin v. California*, 380 U.S. 609 (1965); *Carter v. Kentucky*, 450 U.S. 288 (1981); *and see Baxter v. Palmigiano*, 425 U.S. 308, 317, 318-19 (1976) (dictum); *Jenkins v. Anderson*, 447 U.S. 231, 235 (1980) (dictum). S/he therefore cannot be called upon to make a defense before the prosecution has presented and proved its case in open court. *Cf. Brooks v. Tennessee*, 406 U.S. 605 (1972).

Defense counsel will usually have to take primary responsibility for reminding the magistrate (as tactfully as possible) of these basic principles and of other applicable rules of law in summary trials because such trials are customarily conducted informally as a matter of local practice. Except in some metropolitan areas, the state is frequently not represented by a law-trained prosecutor: The arresting police officer or a ranking police officer conducts the prosecution, and the district attorney's office is not involved. In many localities, indeed, the magistrate is not a lawyer: The Supreme Court of the United States has rejected the contention that law-trained judges are constitutionally required for the trial of minor offenses, at least if a trial *de novo* by a law-trained judge is available as a matter of right on appeal (see § 2.2.5 *infra*). *North v. Russell*, 427 U.S. 328 (1976).

Because of the casual, assembly-line atmosphere and carelessness or even ignorance of formal legal procedures that pervade summary trials, defense counsel who wants procedural regularity may have to demand it explicitly and tenaciously.

2.2.5. *Disposition and Review*

A magistrate has jurisdiction to make the final disposition in summary cases; that is, s/he may acquit the defendant or convict and sentence the defendant. Review of the conviction and sentence, usually by a trial court of record – the court of general jurisdiction of the locality – is frequently but not invariably allowed. This review may take the form of a technical "appeal" (available either as of right or on the discretionary allowance of an appeal by the court of record), or it may take the form of a prerogative writ proceeding, commonly *certiorari*. In some jurisdictions both appeal and *certiorari* may lie.

Counsel should be aware that the time for filing an appeal typically is short, sometimes only five days or so; periods for filing *certiorari* tend to be somewhat longer. Local statutes should be checked and often appeal papers prepared in anticipation of conviction.

Appeal commonly is for trial *de novo*. This means that, once an appeal is filed, the prosecution recommences from scratch and the defendant stands as a person newly accused in the court of record, which tries the case by hearing evidence exactly as though the proceeding had begun in that court. The prosecution (now, generally by a law-trained prosecutor) presents its evidence, the defendant may present evidence, the court acquits or convicts, and upon conviction the court sentences the defendant afresh. This means, of course, that when the magistrate has not imposed the statutory maximum sentence, a defendant who appeals for trial *de novo* risks a harsher sentence on the appeal. *See Colten v. Kentucky*, 407 U.S. 104 (1972); *Ludwig v. Massachusetts*, 427 U.S. 618, 627 (1976). S/he may be able to avoid this risk by using other forms of appeal proceedings or *certiorari* proceedings that involve more limited review, raising only questions of the jurisdiction of the magistrate, the constitutionality and construction of the underlying criminal statute, or other issues of "law" not requiring factual determination and not occasioning an entire trial *de novo* and resentencing. The defendant is constitutionally protected, to some extent, against the prosecutor's "upping the ante" by filing new and more serious charges in the court of record in retaliation for the defendant's appeal (*Blackledge v. Perry*, 417 U.S. 21, 28 (1974); *Thigpen v. Roberts*, 468 U.S. 27 (1984); *and see Bordenkircher v. Hayes*, 434 U.S. 357, 362-63 (1978) (dictum); *United States v. Goodwin*, 457 U.S. 368, 372-77 (1982) (dictum); *Wasman v. United States*, 468 U.S. 559, 565-66 (1984) (plurality opinion) (dictum)).

Appeal, and in some cases *certiorari*, may lie, even though the defendant has pleaded guilty in the magistrate's court. This plea is inadmissible against the defendant in a *de novo* trial on appeal, since it is rightly regarded simply as a procedural device for kicking the case upstairs. Methods of taking appeal or petitioning for a prerogative writ vary.

Ordinarily the defendant must file both an appearance (bail) bond and a cost bond (or a single bond covering both appearance and costs) as the condition of appeal. Part or all of this may be waived under state procedure (and the cost bond, at least, must be waived as a matter of federal constitutional law, see § 5.2 *infra*) for indigents.

After disposition in the court of record, appeal on questions of law (or on particular questions of law specified by statute) may lie to an appellate court.

2.3. *Misdemeanor Procedure*

2.3.1. *Complaint and Warrant or Summons*

Like summary cases, misdemeanor cases frequently begin with a complainant's filing a complaint (sometimes called a criminal arrest complaint or an affidavit for an arrest warrant) before a magistrate. Upon the magistrate's *ex parte* consideration of the complaint, s/he may issue an arrest warrant or, in some cases in some jurisdictions, a summons or notice to appear.

In some localities (principally large cities), there is an administrative practice of having an assistant district attorney examine the complaint before it is filed. Police present their complaints to that assistant as a matter of routine, and a private citizen who goes before a magistrate will be referred by the magistrate to the district attorney's office. Where this practice prevails, the assistant district attorney checks the complaint for substance and form and attaches a paper (sometimes called a buck slip) indicating that s/he has cleared the complaint.

2.3.2. *Arrest and Bail*

More frequently than in summary cases, arrests are made without a warrant. In most jurisdictions, police are authorized to make warrantless arrests on probable cause for misdemeanors involving a breach of the peace and for any misdemeanor committed in their presence (so-called *on view* or *sight* arrests).

Following an arrest with or without a warrant, the police bring the defendant in front of a magistrate. There, in the case of a warrantless arrest, a complaint is filed, and in some jurisdictions a *pro forma* warrant is issued.

Police are often authorized to admit arrested persons to bail in misdemeanor cases. A misdemeanor arrest warrant will frequently carry an endorsement by the issuing magistrate setting the amount of bail. If it does not or if arrest is made without a warrant, the police set stationhouse bail in an amount governed by their discretion or by bail schedules prescribed by legislation, court rule, or police administration; and the defendant may also apply to a magistrate or a court of record for bail.

2.3.3. *First Court Appearance: The Preliminary Hearing*

Soon after arrest the defendant is brought – or after the defendant's release on stationhouse bail or after service of a summons s/he appears – before a magistrate for a preliminary hearing. The term *preliminary hearing* is used confusingly to mean sometimes one, sometimes another, or sometimes both of two proceedings, more clearly differentiated by the names *preliminary arraignment* (see § 2.3.4 *infra*) and *preliminary examination* (or PX, for short) (see § 2.3.5 *infra*).

When a preliminary hearing includes both of these proceedings, the magistrate reads the complaint or charging paper to the defendant and advises the defendant of the rights to have or waive counsel and to have a preliminary examination. The magistrate appoints counsel if the defendant is entitled to counsel (see § 11.5.1 *infra*) and does not waive legal representation; the magistrate asks the defendant how s/he pleads, and – upon a plea of not guilty – hears prosecution evidence (usually presented by a law-trained prosecutor) to determine whether there is sufficient proof (described in technical language as "probable cause" or a "*prima facie* case") to justify detaining the defendant pending the filing of charges and a trial in a court of record. Upon a plea of guilty the magistrate simply commits the defendant (that is, orders the defendant detained for trial) without further examination. In either case, the magistrate sets the amount of bail upon which a defendant who has been ordered detained will be released pending appearance in the trial court; or if stationhouse bail has previously been set, s/he may continue the defendant on that same bail. (In some jurisdictions the defendant is not asked to plead to the complaint; s/he is simply informed that s/he has a right to a preliminary examination and asked whether s/he elects or waives the examination.)

The preliminary hearing in a misdemeanor case, unlike the magistrate's hearing in a summary case, is not a dispositive proceeding. The magistrate cannot convict the defendant; s/he can only commit the defendant ("bind the defendant over") for proceedings in the court of record, which alone has jurisdiction to try the prosecution on the merits. Similarly, the magistrate cannot acquit a defendant; s/he can only discharge the defendant from custody on the ground that a *prima facie* case has not been made out. Such a discharge does not bar the defendant's rearrest and subsequent bind-over by the same or another magistrate on a fresh record. In some jurisdictions discharge does – and in some it does not – preclude the prosecutor from proceeding without rearrest to charge the defendant in a court of record by filing an information (see § 2.3.6 *infra*) and thus requiring the defendant to go to trial on the merits of the offense for which s/he was discharged. When the prosecutor is permitted to proceed in this fashion following a magistrate's discharge, the sole effect of the discharge is to allow the defendant to remain at liberty prior to conviction.

In felony cases (see § 2.4.3 *infra*) and in misdemeanor cases in jurisdictions permitting grand jury indictments for misdemeanors, discharge by the magistrate usually does not preclude the grand jury from indicting the defendant and thereby forcing the defendant to trial. Practice varies with regard to whether defendants indicted after a magistrate's discharge will remain at large throughout the trial or may be arrested on a bench warrant issued by the criminal court upon the indictment (see § 2.4.4 *infra*).

2.3.4. *Preliminary Arraignment*

2.3.4.1. *Procedure in Jurisdictions That Do Not Afford a Full Preliminary Hearing*

In some jurisdictions misdemeanor defendants are not entitled to the full preliminary hearing described in § 2.3.3 *supra*; they receive only a preliminary arraignment. This means that they are brought or appear before a magistrate; the charges are read to them; they are advised of their rights to counsel, to bail, and to trial; counsel is appointed for them, if appropriate; they are sometimes asked to plead to the charges; bail is set by the magistrate; and unless bail has already been posted in a sufficient amount (see § 2.3.2 *supra*) or is posted forthwith, they are remanded into custody pending their first appearance in a court of record or until they post bail for that appearance.

Under *Gerstein v. Pugh*, 420 U.S. 103 (1975), discussed in § 11.2 *infra*, a defendant who has been arrested without a warrant is constitutionally entitled to some form of judicial determination of probable cause before s/he can be committed to jail or required to post bail for trial. As construed in *Gerstein*, "the Fourth Amendment requires the States to provide a fair and reliable determination of probable cause as a condition for any significant pretrial restraint of liberty" (*Baker v. McCollan*, 443 U.S. 137, 142 (1979) (dictum)). *See also Manuel v. City of Joliet, Ill.*, 580 U.S. 357, 364-68 (2017). Jurisdictions that do not provide a full preliminary hearing must, therefore, have a mechanism for making this determination as part of their preliminary arraignment procedure – for example, by having the magistrate review a sworn complaint or affidavits to assure that they disclose sufficiently incriminating facts, in sufficiently concrete detail, to establish probable cause. *See In re Walters*, 15 Cal. 3d 738, 543 P.2d 607, 126 Cal. Rptr. 239 (1975).

If the defendant pleads not guilty or if no plea is required at this kind of preliminary arraignment, the defendant may be given a date for his or her first appearance in the court of record (that is, for a formal arraignment), or the case may be referred to the calendaring officer of the court of record ("the trial court"). The prosecutor will thereafter file an information against the defendant in the trial court (see § 2.3.6 *infra*), and the defendant's next trip to court will be his or her formal arraignment in the trial court upon that information (see §§ 2.3.6, 14.1-14.12 *infra*).

If the defendant pleads guilty at the preliminary arraignment, the case is ordinarily calendared or referred to be calendared for a single appearance in the trial court, at which the defendant will be arraigned upon an information (which may be filed in open court on the date of this appearance), and the defendant will be expected to plead guilty before the trial judge, who will often impose sentence forthwith. (See § 11.7.1 *infra*.) The reason for requiring the defendant to plead at the preliminary arraignment in some jurisdictions that do not provide for a full preliminary hearing is to facilitate the setting of an early date for these proceedings at arraignment in the trial court in cases in which the defendant is not contesting guilt. See § 28.2 *infra*.

2.3.4.2. *Procedure in Jurisdictions That Afford a Full Preliminary Hearing*

In jurisdictions in which the defendant is entitled to a full preliminary hearing – both the preliminary arraignment described in § 2.3.4.1 *supra* and the preliminary examination described in § 2.3.5 *infra* – it is often the case that only the preliminary arraignment is held at the time of the defendant's first appearance before the magistrate. This may be the general practice in the jurisdiction or it may be the procedure used in a particular case because of practicability. Frequently the defendant has no lawyer at that time. So, after the charges have been read and the defendant has been advised of the rights to counsel, to bail, and to a preliminary examination, the proceeding is adjourned to a later date to permit the defendant to retain counsel. When the defendant is indigent and does not waive counsel, the magistrate may appoint counsel to appear for him or her at the delayed preliminary hearing date or, under the clumsy system in effect in some localities, may refer the case to the trial court for the appointment of counsel.

Appointment of trial counsel for indigent defendants is constitutionally required in all criminal prosecutions, whether classified as felony, misdemeanor, or summary prosecutions, in which any term of imprisonment is going to be imposed as a result of conviction (*Argersinger v. Hamlin*, 407 U.S. 25 (1972); *Scott v. Illinois*, 440 U.S. 367 (1979); *Baldasar v. Illinois*, 446 U.S. 222 (1980)), "'even for a brief period'" (*Alabama v. Shelton*, 535 U.S. 654, 657 (2002)), including cases in which the court imposes "a suspended sentence that may 'end up in the actual deprivation of a person's liberty'" (*id.* at 658) in the event of a violation of probation or some other condition of the suspended sentence. The Supreme Court has held this right to appointed counsel applicable at the preliminary arraignment and preliminary examination stages of felony prosecutions (*see White v. Maryland*, 373 U.S. 59 (1963) (per curiam); *Coleman v. Alabama*, 399 U.S. 1 (1970); *Moore v. Illinois*, 434 U.S. 220 (1977); *cf. Gerstein v. Pugh*, *supra*, 420 U.S. at 122-23), and it should apply at the parallel stages of misdemeanor prosecutions as well (*Harvey v. Mississippi*, 340 F.2d 263 (5th Cir. 1965), approved in *James v. Headley*, 410 F.2d 325, 327 (5th Cir. 1969) (dictum); *State v. Young*, 863 N.W.2d 249 (Iowa 2015)).

When the preliminary hearing is set over – either because the defendant is unrepresented or because local practice routinely requires a second separate appearance for preliminary examination after the preliminary arraignment – the magistrate may commit the defendant pending the preliminary examination and may set new bail for the defendant's appearance at that examination or may continue the defendant's release on whatever bail s/he has previously posted.

The preliminary examination can be waived by a defendant, and many magistrates accept or even coerce these waivers from uncounseled accuseds at their first appearance. Coercion, and perhaps even acceptance, of a waiver of preliminary examination by a defendant who is not represented by a lawyer is unconstitutional. (See § 11.5.1 *infra*.) Remedies for the deprivation of preliminary examination are discussed in §§ 11.4, 11.6 *infra*.

2.3.5. *Preliminary Examination*

At the preliminary examination, ordinarily the prosecution may amend the complaint or charging paper to charge additional or other offenses relating to the episode for which the defendant was arrested or summoned.

The prosecution presents its evidence; but since it is required to make only a *prima facie* case at this stage, it frequently discloses only a part of what it will ultimately present against the defendant at trial. In some jurisdictions or localities magistrates will receive, and base a bind-over upon, hearsay evidence. Where this is permitted, the prosecutor frequently calls only the investigating police officer. Cross-examination by defense counsel is permitted (although it is frequently unconscionably limited by the magistrate, again on the theory that only a *prima facie* showing, not guilt, is at issue); and the defendant may, although s/he usually does not, present exculpatory evidence.

At the conclusion of the hearing, the magistrate may discharge the defendant or may bind the defendant over for trial on specified charges. In many jurisdictions these may be any charges on which there is sufficient evidence in the magistrate's record to constitute probable cause; they need not be limited to the charges made in the complaint. (If, however, the complaint failed to give the defendant fair notice of the charges on which s/he is subsequently bound over, so that s/he was denied the opportunity to defend against those charges – or at least to decide advisedly whether to attempt to defend against them – at the preliminary examination, this practice is subject to serious constitutional challenge. See § 11.10 *infra*.) The magistrate now sets bail for the defendant who is bound over. Frequently, but not invariably, s/he will continue the amount of bail previously set.

2.3.6. *Information and Arraignment*

The misdemeanor defendant is tried in a court of record. Prosecution in that court begins with the filing of an information, which is a sworn statement by the prosecuting attorney describing what the defendant did (often in conclusory terms that track the statutory definition of the offense charged) and characterizing it as criminal. In some jurisdictions the prosecutor may charge in an information only offenses for which the defendant has been previously bound over; in others s/he may charge a bound-over defendant with any related offenses (or sometimes any offenses at all) of which there is evidence in the magistrate's transcript, whether or not the magistrate held the defendant for those offenses; in still others the prosecutor (sometimes as a matter of right, sometimes by leave of court) may charge a bound-over defendant with offenses that go beyond the magistrate's transcript and may also file an information against a defendant who has been entirely discharged by the magistrate or who has never been arrested and brought before a magistrate.

The defendant is arraigned on the information; that is, the information is read or handed to the defendant in open court, and s/he is required to plead to the charges in it. Ordinarily s/he has had advance notice of the arraignment date, and frequently the case proceeds to trial immediately following a plea of not guilty at arraignment or to sentence immediately following a plea of guilty or *nolo contendere*. If trial or sentencing is not immediate, a trial date or sentencing date is usually set following the entry of the defendant's plea.

Special pleas (for example, double jeopardy) and motions and objections attacking the information (for failure to charge an offense or on other grounds) or the propriety of the proceedings at the preliminary hearing or any other anterior stage are – depending upon local practice – required to be made by the defendant either before arraignment or before entering one of the general pleas (not guilty; guilty; *nolo contendere*) or before the start of trial.

In many localities, there are more or less formal procedures for "diversion" of criminal prosecutions: – that is, for suspension of the charges against the defendant so that more lenient dispositions are possible than would ordinarily follow a criminal trial and conviction. For example, the criminal charges may be dismissed if a defendant manifesting mental disorder agrees to voluntary civil commitment proceedings or if the prosecutor elects to undertake involuntary civil commitment proceedings in lieu of proceeding criminally. Or the criminal charges may be adjourned in contemplation of dismissal ("ACD'd") – a practice (also called "stetting" in some jurisdictions) under which the criminal charges are held in abeyance for a designated period of time on the understanding that, if the defendant shapes up and behaves (or completes certain restitutionary or corrective actions), the prosecution will then be dismissed. Arraignment is commonly the stage of proceedings at which diversion is on the table for discussion by counsel and the court. Defense counsel proposing a diversion plan is ordinarily advised to broach the subject with the prosecutor *before* arraignment unless the prosecutor is expected to be unsympathetic and the judge sympathetic. (In jurisdictions where diversion is a commonplace practice, it is usually available in summary prosecutions and in felony prosecutions as well as in misdemeanor prosecutions, but defense counsel will seldom want to resort to it in summary-prosecution cases because the consequences of the diversion are likely to be less favorable to the defendant than the relatively mild criminal sentence that can be anticipated upon conviction.)

If counsel is representing a client whose age falls within the concurrent jurisdiction of the juvenile court (which usually covers juveniles who were below the age of 18 – or, in some States, below the age of 17 – at the time of the crime), and if local law provides for the possibility of transfer of a juvenile's case from adult criminal court to juvenile court, counsel will need to consider whether to seek transfer of the case to juvenile court. See § 21.7 *infra*.

2.3.7. *Trial; Disposition; Review*

Most jurisdictions give the defendant a right to trial by jury for the majority of misdemeanor offenses; all are required by the federal Constitution to recognize the right to jury trial for "serious" misdemeanors – a category that includes, at the least, any misdemeanor for which a sentence of more than six months' imprisonment is authorized. See § 32.1 *infra*. Misdemeanor defendants, however, frequently waive a jury and elect a bench trial.

Evidentiary trial is had in the usual fashion: The prosecution presents its case in chief first. The defendant customarily moves for an acquittal on the prosecution's evidence (see Chapter 38 *infra*) or "demurs to the evidence," as the procedure is called in some jurisdictions. If acquittal is denied, the defendant may present defense evidence. The prosecution may then present rebuttal evidence, although this is far less common in misdemeanor than in felony cases. The defendant renews his or her motion for acquittal (see Chapter 41 *infra*). If it is denied, counsel make their closing arguments to the jury or the bench; then, in a jury-trial case, comes the judge's charge. The jury or judge returns a verdict or finding of acquittal or conviction; and, in the event of conviction, the judge often imposes sentence without more ado. In some jurisdictions the convicted defendant has a right to a postponement of several days before sentence is pronounced (called, in the jargon, "demanding his or her time"), but deferred sentencing hearings and presentence reports are not commonplace in misdemeanor cases.

Following the filing and disposition of any authorized post-trial motions (see § 2.4.5 *infra*) and the entry of a formal judgment of conviction and commitment (or sentence to a fine), the defendant may appeal for review of the ordinary sort by an appellate court. Bail pending appeal is usually allowed in the discretion of the trial judge, reviewable for abuse. In some jurisdictions bail pending appeal is allowed as a matter of right in misdemeanor cases; in others it is a right in any case in which the sentence does not include a term of imprisonment.

2.4. *Felony Procedure*

2.4.1. *Arrest and Bail*

Felony procedure is generally similar to misdemeanor procedure through the stage of the magistrate's bind-over. A few significant differences deserve note. Ordinarily police are authorized to arrest without a warrant when they have probable cause to believe that a suspect has committed a felony; most felony arrests are, in fact, made without warrants. Magistrates often have little or no power to issue summonses in lieu of arrest warrants in felony cases, and they sparingly exercise what little power they have. As a result, felony prosecutions almost invariably involve an arrest, and it is typical for the complaint to be filed after arrest. Stationhouse bail is also much less frequently authorized in felony than in misdemeanor cases, and in some jurisdictions magistrates themselves are powerless to admit an arrested person to bail on some or all serious but bailable felony charges. In these cases bail-setting must be sought by *habeas corpus* or by a motion or other statutorily prescribed procedure in a court of record. This means that most defendants get at least a short taste of jail at the beginning of a felony case.

2.4.2. *Preliminary Hearing; The Role of the Prosecutor*

A law-trained prosecutor is more frequently involved in the drafting of felony complaints than of misdemeanor complaints, and s/he sometimes participates with the police in postarrest interrogation of a defendant. Prosecutors therefore tend to know more about felony cases earlier in the process and to undertake early responsibility for deciding whether and what to charge.

They also tend to prepare more carefully for the preliminary examination, which in felony cases is almost never left solely to the police.

Magistrates are generally more willing in felony than in misdemeanor matters to grant the prosecution or the defense time to prepare for the examination, and prosecutors will often request a continuance for the purpose of defeating the defendant's right to a preliminary examination by the device described in §§ 2.4.4, 11.4 *infra*.

In any event, more in felony cases than in misdemeanor cases do preliminary arraignment and preliminary examination assume the aspect of two distinct procedural stages, often separated by a few days or longer unless, of course, the defendant at preliminary arraignment waives a preliminary examination and is immediately bound over.

2.4.3. *The Grand Jury*

The principal difference between misdemeanor and felony procedure involves the intervention of the grand jury in felony cases. In many jurisdictions felony defendants may be prosecuted only by indictment. An indictment is a charging paper (in content similar to an information) returned by a grand jury. A grand jury is a body of citizens, usually 15 to 23 in number, ordinarily chosen from the general venire of jurors for a term of court, who meet in secret to hear the prosecutor's presentation of evidence (or, in theory, any other witnesses that the grand jury may choose to subpoena) in support of written charges (called "bills of indictment") drafted by the prosecutor (or, in theory, any other charges that the grand jury may want to consider). Grand jury proceedings are not attended by a judge; the grand jury takes its legal instructions from the prosecutor; neither the defendant nor defense counsel is present during its evidentiary hearings; the defendant and defense witnesses may be called to testify by the grand jury in its discretion (subject to any valid claim of the privilege against self-incrimination).

If a majority of grand jurors is satisfied that there is probable clause to believe that the defendant named in a bill is guilty or that there is *prima facie* evidence of the defendant's guilt or that the evidence against the defendant would warrant conviction by a trial jury if unrebutted and believed (the standards are differently phrased in different jurisdictions but differ little in substance), the grand jury "returns" (that is, reports out to the court) the bill of indictment endorsed as a "true bill." This is the indictment that requires the defendant to go to trial. If a majority of the jurors is unwilling to return a true bill, the jurors "ignore" the bill ("no-bill" or "*ignoramus*" the case), a disposition that precludes the prosecutor from proceeding to trial at this juncture but does not bar the prosecutor from resubmitting the bill to the same or another grand jury at any time within the statute of limitations. (In some jurisdictions, a resubmission may be made only with leave of court.)

It should be noted that a felony defendant's right to prosecution only by indictment of a grand jury may be waived in most jurisdictions. On a written waiver of the right, the case is prosecuted by information (as in misdemeanor procedure), or in some jurisdictions the grand jury returns an indictment based solely upon the bill and written waiver, without hearing evidence.

A number of jurisdictions permit felony charges (or some subclass of less serious felony charges) to be prosecuted by information. In these jurisdictions the grand jury procedure is available but not required; the prosecutor has the option to proceed by indictment or by information.

2.4.4. *Relation of the Grand Jury to Preliminary Hearing*

In theory (and in most cases in actuality) the grand jury does not act on a defendant's case until after s/he has had a full preliminary hearing and been bound over (the style in felony cases is "bound over to the grand jury"). But the grand jury is legally empowered to indict any person without an antecedent bind-over, preliminary hearing, or even arrest; and once its indictment has been returned, a judge of the criminal court may, without further inquiry, issue a "bench warrant" authorizing the defendant's arrest and detention pending trial. Using these two legal authorities, a prosecutor who does not want to expose the prosecution's case at preliminary examination will frequently – often as a matter of routine practice in some types of cases, such as sex and narcotics cases – (a) request the magistrate at preliminary arraignment to continue the preliminary hearing of an arrested accused, (b) submit the case to the grand jury during the period of the continuance, (c) obtain an indictment and a bench warrant, and (d) by thus obviating the need for a bind-over to justify holding the defendant for trial, effectively circumvent the defendant's right to a preliminary examination. The possibilities for defeating this prosecutorial tactic are discussed in § 11.4 *infra*.

When a bench warrant is issued, the issuing judge will ordinarily set bail by endorsement on the warrant. If s/he does not, a motion for bail may be made to any judge of the court. If the bail endorsed on the warrant is too high, a motion to reduce it is appropriate.

2.4.5. *Arraignment; Trial; Disposition; Review*

The indictment, like an information, serves as the accusatory pleading on which the defendant is tried. S/he is arraigned by being read the indictment in open court and asked how s/he pleads to it. Ordinarily s/he will plead not guilty, guilty, or *nolo contendere* (for present purposes, the equivalent of a guilty plea) or request a continuance to permit adequate preparation before pleading. As in misdemeanor practice (see § 2.3.6 *supra*), special pleas, motions, and objections attacking the indictment, the grand jury proceedings, or other preliminary proceedings are required to be filed – depending on the jurisdiction – prior to arraignment, to the entry of the pleas of not guilty, guilty, or *nolo contendere*, or to trial. (See Chapter 20 *infra*.) In jurisdictions that allow felony prosecutions to be initiated by information, the arraignment procedure for information-based cases is typically identical to that for indictment-based cases. Valid challenges to the facial sufficiency of an information to charge an offense or other defects in the information require dismissal of the prosecution (see § 20.4 *infra*); well-taken motions aimed at deflecting or shaping the course of proceedings – such as motions for diversion (see §§ 21.1 - 21.6 *infra*), or for a change of venue (see §§ 13.9, 17.4, 22.1 - 22.3 *infra*), or for transfer of the case to juvenile court if the client is a minor and local law provides for such transfers (see § 21.7 *infra*) – call for appropriate relief before the case proceeds further.

On a guilty plea the defendant may be sentenced forthwith, following arguments by counsel or following a brief evidentiary hearing on the question of sentence. Ordinarily, a defendant who wishes to address the court personally is permitted to make an unsworn statement. (Practice differs as to whether, and to what extent, counsel is permitted to guide the defendant's statement by questioning.) Alternatively, sentencing may be deferred pending a presentence investigation by the probation officer of the court or a fuller evidentiary hearing or both. More frequently than in misdemeanor procedure, a convicted felony defendant has a right to "demand [his] [her] time" and thereby secure a delayed sentencing proceeding.

In murder cases (and, less often, in the case of other offenses divided into degrees), a defendant is sometimes permitted to plead guilty only to the offense generally, following which plea a judge or jury hears evidence to determine the degree of the offense and to set the sentence. Similarly, a jury may be impaneled to fix sentence on a plea of guilty to any felony for which the applicable statutes authorize or require jury sentencing.

After a plea of not guilty to a felony, the case seldom proceeds to trial immediately following arraignment. Rather, it is assigned a future trial date. The case is heard by a jury unless the defendant waives jury trial. Trial practice is similar to that in misdemeanor cases but with a host of minor differences: Rules governing joinder of offenses and defendants may be different, more time and greater *voir dire* questioning of prospective jurors is generally allowed in selecting a felony jury, more peremptory challenges to jurors are generally permitted in felony trials, and so forth. Following conviction, greater use is made of the practices of deferred sentencing, presentence investigation, and evidentiary hearings on sentence than in misdemeanor cases.

Post-trial motions by a convicted defendant seeking a new trial (on grounds including trial error, jury misconduct, and newly discovered evidence) or sentencing correction are authorized within specified time limits. These limits are ordinarily very short, so counsel will need to be alert to prepare and file post-trial motions promptly (or to request an extension of time ["EOT"] to file them [in courts where EOTs are allowable]). In many jurisdictions, post-trial motions must include all claims of error that the defense wishes to preserve for appeal.

Appeal lies from the final judgment to an appellate court for consideration of claims of trial-court error within the ordinary scope of appellate review. Time limits for filing a notice of appeal (or bill of errors, or whatever form of document a jurisdiction requires in order to perfect appellate jurisdiction) are also characteristically very short and may or may not (depending on the jurisdiction) be extendable by the trial court on motion. Bail pending appeal is allowed in the discretion of the trial court, subject to appellate revision for abuse.

2.5. *Flow-Chart of Summary, Misdemeanor, and Felony Procedures*

Set out below is a flow-chart of the three sorts of procedures described in the foregoing sections of this chapter:

OUTLINE AND FLOW-CHART OF A CRIMINAL CASE § 2.5

FELONY PROCEDURE

MAGISTRATE

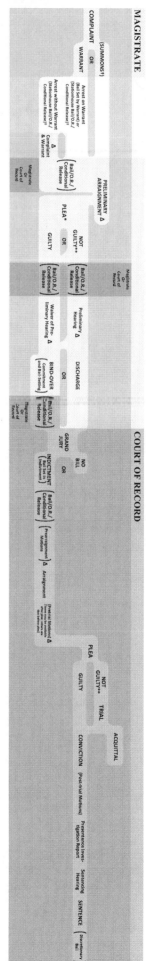

COURT OF RECORD

MISDEMEANOR PROCEDURE

MAGISTRATE

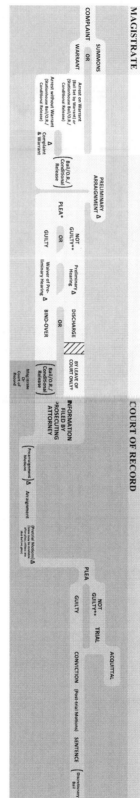

COURT OF RECORD

SUMMARY PROCEDURE

MAGISTRATE

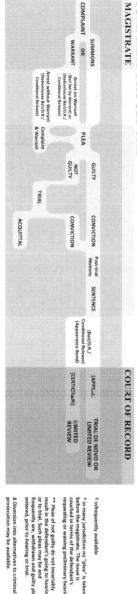

COURT OF RECORD

† Infrequently available

* In many jurisdiction no "plea" is taken before the magistrate. The issue is couched in terms of the defendant's requesting or waiving preliminary hearing.

** Pleas of not guilty do not invariably result in the defendant's going to hearing or to trial. Such pleas may be and frequently are, withdrawn and guilty pleas entered, prior to hearing or trial.

Δ Diversion into alternatives to criminal prosecution may be available.

A downloadable version of this chart is available at www.ali.org/trial-manual.

PART TWO: INITIAL STAGES OF THE CASE THROUGH ARRAIGNMENT

Chapter 3

The Lawyer's Entrance into the Case – First Steps

3.1. *Introduction: Stages at Which the Lawyer May Enter the Case; The Need to Move Quickly*

Defense counsel may have occasion to enter a criminal case at almost any of the stages described in Chapter 2. In the early stages, at least, the crucial first steps to be taken are essentially the same. They are, in essence: (1) to make contact with the client, obtain the client's authorization to represent him or her, warn the client against speaking with the police or others, and obtain information that counsel can use to seek the client's release; (2) to speak to the investigating officer, find out whatever counsel can about the charges and the availability of release on the client's own recognizance or stationhouse bail, and erect all possible protections against police interrogation, searches, and identification procedures; and (3) to try to arrange for the client's release.

The major differences in the tasks that confront counsel at the different stages of entry involve the order in which the various initial steps are required to be taken and the amount of time available to familiarize oneself with the situation and its demands and to make decisions. The lawyer who has some general knowledge of the interests of the client that need to be protected at a given stage can usually begin to function adequately notwithstanding both a lack of detailed information concerning the intricacies of local practice and a lack of opportunity to prepare completely on technical matters. S/he will have to learn the details and the relevant technical points of substantive criminal law and procedure rapidly as s/he proceeds about the work of providing representation.

In these situations, as in all later stages of the case, counsel's preparation and research should be as thorough as practicable. Knowledge of the individual case and client, of the applicable law, and of the local procedures and functionaries can spell the difference between wise choices of action and foolish ones. But at the outset of a criminal case particularly, a trade-off does exist between the virtues of time-consuming preparation and the importance of getting started quickly to prevent the client's interests from being irreparably damaged by fast-breaking events that will not wait for counsel to make a consummately prepared appearance.

A. *Representing Clients Who Have Been Arrested and Are Still at the Police Station*

3.2. *Police Practices Following Arrest*

Representation of a client in custody shortly after arrest requires at least some general knowledge of post-arrest practices. These practices are described in the four subsections that follow.

3.2.1. *Logging in*

Following an arrest, the arrested person (hereafter called "defendant") is usually taken to the police station (or divisional or precinct headquarters) in the precinct in which the arrest took place. The defendant's arrival at the station is ordinarily, but not invariably, noted in a police log. In some jurisdictions the police treat logging-in as part of the "booking" or "slating" process described in § 3.2.4 *infra.* The log normally contains a dozen or so defendants to the page, and it records not merely the name and the time of logging but also the time and the place of arrest, some identifying characteristics of the defendant (such as gender, race, and date of birth), and the arrest charge.

Some police departments conceive logging-in as a recording routine unrelated to "booking" and maintain two books – the log and the blotter. Under this latter practice all persons brought to the station may be logged in on arrival, and those against whom it is decided to lodge charges may later be noted in the arrest book or "blotter." Or persons against whom it is clear that charges will be lodged may be noted immediately on the blotter, whereas persons brought in "for investigation" or "on suspicion" may be noted in the log (sometimes called the "small book").

In any event, police generally feel no compelling obligation to make an immediate log or blotter entry when there are investigative reasons for not doing so. For example, the police may refrain from logging in a defendant whom they want to interrogate at length, free of any interference from a defendant's relatives or a defense lawyer. Such omissions or delays may violate published police procedures (and may, in some cases in some jurisdictions, violate requirements prescribed by statutes, court rules, or judicial criminal-procedure rulings), but officers dealing with a serious crime or an unappetizing defendant often take these requirements lightly.

In addition to recording the defendant's name in a logbook showing either arrests or arrivals at the station, the police in many jurisdictions will record the defendant's name and any personal property taken from the defendant in a property log. Unlike property seized as the proceeds or evidence of a crime (and held by the police or the prosecution until trial), this personal property can be retrieved at any time by the defendant or counsel (with proper authorization). Frequently, a defendant's personal property will include clothing, footwear, or other items that counsel will want to retrieve in order to substantiate a defense of misidentification. It may also include cell phones and other electronic appliances that counsel should retrieve promptly, before police investigation or processing of the case alerts officers to the possibility that these gadgets have potential evidentiary value and are subject to seizure and inspection with a search warrant.

3.2.2. *Interrogation and Other Investigative Procedures*

Whatever the logging-in practice, the police usually subject the defendant to some interrogation subsequent to arrival at the station and prior to the full "booking" process. If the arrest charge is at all serious, the case will be assigned from the outset to – and the interrogation will be conducted by – a rank officer, detective, special deputy, criminal investigator, or other specialized investigative agent (depending, of course, on the size and the organization of the police force). In a metropolitan police department, the interrogation is normally handled by detectives in their own headquarters in the precinct stationhouse. When officers from special squads, such as homicide, narcotics or vice, are involved, the defendant may be taken – either immediately from the place of arrest or from the station where s/he was initially brought by arresting officers – to the central headquarters of the special squad.

The interrogation is designed to secure the defendant's admission of the offense for which s/he was arrested, the defendant's implication of any other persons involved in the offense, and the defendant's admission of other "uncleared" or "open" offenses that s/he may have committed. In particular cases, such as those involving the arrest of persons known or believed to be gang members, the police may also seek, through interrogation, to learn general information about recent developments in the neighborhood or the gang or about its members, which information they believe to be useful for intelligence or crime control.

In addition to interrogation, a defendant may be subjected to other investigative procedures before or immediately after booking. S/he may be exhibited to witnesses in a lineup or show-up. S/he may be taken to the scene of the crime to "reenact" or demonstrate what happened. S/he may be taken home or elsewhere to assist the police in finding secreted or discarded weapons, loot, contraband, or evidence; and in this connection, s/he may be asked to give consent to warrantless police searches that, without this consent, would require a search warrant. Specimens of the defendant's hair or blood, swabs, washes, or body scrapings may be taken for laboratory analysis. Each of these police actions may develop incriminating evidence. Legally, a defendant may have rights not to be subjected to some of these procedures altogether and not to be subjected to others in the absence of his or her attorney or in the absence of a judicial warrant. But these rights can be waived – and they often will be waived unless counsel takes adequate steps to insure their protection.

3.2.3. *Defendant's Rights of Communication*

Theoretically, any arrested person has the right under *Miranda v. Arizona,* 384 U.S. 436 (1966), to make contact with the outside world, in order to obtain counsel prior to undergoing interrogation. *Minnick v. Mississippi,* 498 U.S. 146, 152-54 (1990). *Miranda* expressly requires that any in-custody interrogation be preceded by several warnings including the warning that the suspect has the right to the presence of counsel, and, if indigent, the right to court-appointed counsel, during interrogation. *Dickerson v. United States*, 530 U.S. 428, 435 (2000); *J.D.B. v. North Carolina*, 564 U.S. 261, 269 (2011); *Berghuis v. Thompkins*, 560 U.S. 370, 380 (2010) (dictum); see §§ 26.5, 26.7 *infra*. "[A] person taken into custody [must] be advised immediately" of these rights (*Doyle v. Ohio*, 426 U.S. 610, 617 (1976) (dictum); *see, e.g., Stansbury v. California*, 511 U.S. 318 (1994); *Berkemer v. McCarty*, 468 U.S. 420 (1984)), and "the police [must] respect the accused's decision to exercise the rights outlined in the warnings" (*Moran v. Burbine,* 475 U.S. 412, 420 (1986) (dictum); *see, e.g., Missouri v. Seibert*, 542 U.S. 600, 608, 611-12 (2004) (plurality opinion); *id.* at 620-22 (Justice Kennedy, concurring); *Smith v. Illinois,* 469 U.S. 91 (1984) (per curiam)). State statutes commonly give arrestees the right to make a phone call to an attorney and – less commonly – also to a bail bondsman and/or a relative. *See, e.g.,* WEST'S ALASKA STAT. ANN. § 12.25.150(b); CAL. PENAL CODE § 851.5; WEST'S GEN.

LAWS RHODE ISLAND ANN. § 12-7-20.

As a practical matter, however, police often proceed to interrogate defendants without offering them any opportunity to make a phone call prior to questioning. In some cases in which the police have failed to give the defendant an opportunity to contact counsel, it may be possible to argue that any resulting confession or identification testimony must be suppressed under federal or state constitutional doctrines (*see Haynes v. Washington*, 373 U.S. 503 (1963); and see generally Chapters 26, 27 *infra*) or under state statutes requiring that the police afford an arrestee an opportunity to make a telephone call (*see, e.g., Commonwealth v. Jones*, 362 Mass. 497, 502-04, 287 N.E.2d 599, 603-04 (1972) (explained in *Commonwealth v. Jackson*, 447 Mass. 603, 615, 855 N.E.2d 1097, 1106 (2006)) (intentional police denial of an arrestee's "statutory right to use a telephone" can result in suppression of "an incustody [sic] inculpatory statement or corporeal identification"); *State v. Moorehead*, 699 N.W.2d 667 (Iowa 2005); *State v. Beaupre*, 123 N.H. 155, 159, 459 A.2d 233, 236 (1983)); *and see State v. Hellstern*, 856 N.W.2d 355 (Iowa 2014) (requiring suppression of the results of a breath test to which the defendant submitted after the police had denied him the right to speak privately with counsel by phone); *Zsupnik v. State*, 789 P.2d 357 (Alaska 1990) (same); *State v. Matviyenko*, 212 Or. App. 125, 157 P.3d 268 (2007) (same); *State v. Carcieri*, 730 A.2d 11 (R.I. 1999) (the applicable statute "mandates that a police officer not only provide notice of a suspect's right to a confidential telephone call, but also a reasonable opportunity to speak privately with the recipient of the call, if the call was made for the purpose of securing an attorney or bail" (*id*. at 15); remedies for violation of these rights "must be considered on a case-by-case basis" (*id*. at 16), and "if 'the prosecution has improperly obtained incriminating information from the defendant in [violation of his constitutional or statutory rights] * * * the remedy characteristically imposed is . . . to suppress the evidence or to order a new trial if the evidence has been wrongfully admitted and the defendant convicted.' *United States v. Morrison*, 449 U.S. 361, 365 . . . (1981).'" (730 A.2d at 16.)); *cf. People v. Salamon*, 2022 IL 125722, 202 N.E.3d 283, 301, 460 Ill. Dec. 741, 759 (2022) ("violation of . . . [a former Illinois statute providing that "Persons who are arrested shall have the right to communicate with an attorney of their choice and a member of their family by making a reasonable number of telephone calls or in any other reasonable manner. Such communication shall be permitted within a reasonable time after arrival at the first place of custody."] must be considered in the determination of voluntariness because it effectively prevents a suspect from exercising his or her constitutional rights prior to and during custodial interrogation"); *State v. McQueen*, 248 N.J. 26, 31, 34, 50, 256 A.3d 966, 969-70, 980 (2021) (construing the state constitution to hold that the police violated the defendant's right to privacy by permitting the defendant, upon arrest and transportation to the police station, "to make a telephone call from one of the stationhouse's landlines" without "tell[ing] him his conversation would be recorded or accessible to law enforcement without his consent or a warrant"; the court accordingly suppresses the resulting recording of the defendant's telephone conversation with his girlfriend in which he gave her instructions for retrieving his handgun; "An arrestee transported to a police station, who is in custody and given the opportunity to make a telephone call, would naturally reach out to a family member or friend (if not an attorney) for advice, support, or comfort. The warrantless and surreptitious monitoring or recording of calls of an arrestee who is presumed innocent does not comport with the values of privacy that are prized in our free society."); *Application of Newbern*, 175 Cal. App. 2d 862, 1 Cal. Rptr. 80 (1959) (vacating a conviction because the police refused to allow the defendant, arrested for public drunkenness, to phone a physician for the purpose of retaining him to administer a blood alcohol test), followed in *In re Newbern*, 55 Cal.2d 508, 513, 360 P.2d 47, 50, 11 Cal. Rptr. 551, 554 (1961) ("[t]he denial of an opportunity to procure a blood test on a charge of intoxication prevents the accused from obtaining evidence necessary to his defense and is a denial of due process of law entitling him to his discharge").

3.2.4. *Booking or Slating; Fingerprinting; and Photographing*

Following the period of interrogation and the decision of the police to formally charge the defendant with an offense, the charges are noted in police records. This is the booking or slating process, which involves making a record of the name of the defendant and of some identifying data (usually gender, race, date of birth, address, phone), the time and place of the arrest, and the offenses charged. This information is recorded in summary form on a police blotter and, in more detail, on arrest cards, in arrest reports, in paper or electronic files, in computer data bases, or in more than one of these media.

The booking or slating process may also include the police officer's filling out extensive, specialized printed or electronic forms. The forms commonly include some type of arrest report, calling for the defendant's name, nickname, age, date of birth, identifying characteristics (gender, race, height, weight), address and phone number. They often require information concerning the time, date, and location of the offense; the time, date and location of the arrest; whether any other defendants were arrested for the same offense; whether any force was employed in effecting the arrest; whether the defendant confessed to the offense and possibly also what the defendant said. In addition to these arrest reports, the police frequently prepare a supplement to the original "event" or "incident" or "complaint" report that was filed at the time when the crime was first reported. This supplement usually recounts the details of the arrest, possibly the content of any confessions or admissions, the results of any identification procedures, and a statement of whether the arrest "closes" the case or whether there are still unarrested perpetrators being sought. Finally, in particular cases, the police may fill out additional forms. For example, firearms cases require special forms listing serial numbers and descriptions of guns and bullets; narcotics cases require detailed information about the nature and weight of the drugs and the property numbers assigned to the drugs, as well as a "buy report" by the undercover officer; eyewitness identifications may require special cards or forms listing the description originally given and the words spoken by the witness in identifying or failing to identify the defendant. The nature of the forms and the precise procedures followed by the police vary greatly among jurisdictions. It is important that counsel become familiar with both the types of forms used locally and the information contained upon those forms, in order to subpoena documents that can prove invaluable at trial. See §§ 9.17, 9.18, 9.20 *infra.*

The defendant's fingerprints and photograph are almost invariably taken as a part of the booking process. These may be used in various ways in the investigation of the charge for which the defendant has been arrested. In addition, they will usually be retained by the police or placed into a central data system for use in later investigations.

3.3. *Responding to a Phone Call from a Recently Arrested Client Who Is at the Police Station or from a Relative or Friend of the Client*

In some cases, counsel may receive a phone call from a client who is at the police station. In other cases, counsel may be called by a relative or friend on behalf of an arrested client. Subsection 3.3.1 explains the steps that counsel should take immediately in the first of these situations; subsection 3.3.2 does the same for the second. Both subsections provide cross-references to later sections that explain follow-up steps counsel should take in their respective settings.

3.3.1. *A Phone Call from a Client Who Is At the Police Station: Ascertaining the Client's Whereabouts; Assuring the Privacy of the Conversation*

An arrested person who calls the attorney while in police custody should be asked to identify his or her whereabouts by precinct or headquarters's name and street address or, if these are unknown, by general location and building description. S/he should be asked whether s/he has heard or seen anything suggesting that s/he might be taken by the police to any other location; if so, where and when. As a failsafe, s/he should also be asked the street location where s/he was arrested, the charge, and whatever s/he knows about the identity of the arresting and investigating officers.

Once counsel has obtained this information bearing on the client's location, counsel should move on to the steps set forth in sections 3.4 (describing the additional information counsel should obtain from the client and the advice that should be given to the client), 3.5 (discussing the telephone conversations that counsel should have with the police on the client's behalf), and 3.6 (recommending that counsel go to the police station and identifying steps s/he should take while there). Section 3.7 describes some precautions counsel can take if s/he is unable to go to the police station.

3.3.2. *A Phone Call from a Relative or Friend of a Client Who Is At the Police Station: Locating the Client and Gaining Access to the Client By Telephone*

3.3.2.1. *The Matters to Cover in the Phone Conversation with the Client's Relative or Friend*

If the call requesting the attorney to represent a defendant in police custody comes from a relative or friend of the client rather than the client himself or herself, counsel must move quickly to try to find the client and prevent him or her from making any incriminating statements to the police. The lawyer's success at that job can literally mean the difference between conviction and acquittal when the case gets to trial.

Because of the need for prompt action, counsel should keep the phone conversation with the client's relative or friend as brief as possible. (Counsel should be sure to explain the need for succinctness, in order to avoid seeming insensitive to the caller's fears and concerns.) At this point the only vital information is that which is needed to locate the defendant, gain access to him or her, and establish oneself in the eyes of the police as defendant's counsel. The attorney

31

should obtain the following from the caller:

1. The defendant's name (with spelling).

2. The caller's name (with spelling) and relationship to the defendant. The police may require that the attorney furnish this information in order to establish the attorney's right to visit the defendant for an initial interview.

3. The caller's telephone number(s) (cellphone, home landline, and phone number at work), so that counsel can call back for a follow-up conversation after locating and communicating with the client. If the caller does not have a cellphone, counsel should ask for the cellphone number of a family member or friend who can reach the caller easily.

4. Authorization from the caller to represent the defendant, at least at this stage.

5. Any information the caller may have about which police station the defendant was taken to. If the caller does not know, the attorney should ask: where the arrest was made; whether it was made by uniformed or plainclothes police officers; and whether the officers belonged to a special squad (such as homicide, robbery, burglary, narcotics, vice) or were otherwise identifiable by the caller.

6. The offense for which the defendant was arrested, if the caller knows. The nature of the offense may be important in attempting to locate the defendant, especially if a special squad is involved in the interrogation. But a lengthy description of the facts leading up to the arrest is not only unnecessary but counterproductive at this stage, in light of the need for quick action.

7. Any information the caller can provide about whether the defendant's family or friends can and will put up bail for the defendant, and how much they are likely to be able to raise for this purpose.

3.3.2.2. *Locating the Client*

The most effective way to locate the defendant is usually a series of trial-and-error telephone calls. The order of the calls depends in part upon the amount of time that has elapsed since the arrest, but the first call should ordinarily go to the desk officer of the police station for the precinct where the arrest occurred, and the second call should go to the detectives who are likely to be interrogating the defendant there. If counsel fails to obtain information about the defendant's whereabouts from the precinct-station desk or detectives, calls should next be made to the headquarters of any potentially relevant special squads.

If these phone calls prove fruitless, counsel should call the commanding officer on duty in the arrest precinct, explain that the client has disappeared following an arrest in the commander's precinct, and request that the commander locate the client immediately and inform counsel where s/he is being held. If the commander claims ignorance, counsel should ask for the name and phone number of the highest ranking official of the police department then on duty and should call this official to confront him or her with the client's disappearance and make the same requests. Counsel should next call a member of the prosecutor's staff and object to the incommunicado detention of the defendant. "'Holding incommunicado is objectionable because arbitrary – at the mere will and unregulated pleasure of a police officer,'" *Ashcraft v. Tennessee*, 322 U.S. 143, 152 n.8 (1944); it violates both Due Process (*Hamdi v. Rumsfeld*, 542 U.S. 507 (2004); *Jauch v. Choctaw County*, 874 F.3d 425 (5th Cir. 2017)) and the Fourth Amendment to the federal Constitution. "[T]he Fourth Amendment requires a judicial determination of probable cause as a prerequisite to extended restraint of liberty following arrest." *Gerstein v. Pugh*, 420 U.S. 103, 114 (1975). All else failing, counsel should call a judge of the court of record of the county and ask to appear before the judge at the earliest possible time to present a petition for a writ of *habeas corpus* directed to the chief of police, the prosecutor, or both, charging them with the illegal custody of the defendant. *See Rasul v. Bush*, 542 U.S. 466, 474 (2004): "'[a]t its historical core, the writ of habeas corpus has served as a means of reviewing the legality of Executive detention, and it is in that context that its protections have been strongest.' *INS v. St. Cyr*, 533 U.S. 289, 301, . . . (2001). *See also Brown v. Allen*, 344 U.S. 443, 533, . . . (1953) (Jackson, J., concurring in result) ('The historic purpose of the writ has been to relieve detention by executive authorities without judicial trial')."

3.3.2.3. *Keeping Records of Calls*

It is essential that counsel keep a record of the times at which s/he made telephone calls to locate the defendant and the names (correctly spelled), ranks, and badge numbers of all officers to whom s/he spoke. These may be needed in moving to suppress incriminating statements on the ground of unnecessary police delay (see § 26.11 *infra*) or on the theory that such delay was a factor in producing an involuntary statement (see § 26.3.2 *infra* and particularly *Haynes v. Washington*, 373 U.S. 503 (1963)). In more extreme cases of police delay, the information may be needed for petitions for a writ of *habeas corpus* to free the defendant from police custody.

3.3.2.4. *Persuading a Police Officer to Allow Counsel to Speak with a Recently Arrested Client on the Telephone*

If counsel is able to locate the client, counsel should try to gain access to the client by telephone as quickly as possible. Police officers taking counsel's call will often be strongly resistant to the notion of counsel's speaking with the client. In attempting to cut through police interference, it is usually wise to begin by seeming cooperative and congenial. Most police officers experience a surfeit of angry phone calls from citizens, victims, and lawyers, and they usually react to aggressive calls from defense lawyers truculently. By contrast, a cordial phone conversation that attempts to deal with the officer on a professional-to-professional basis may be disarming and eventually successful.

In dealing with the police, it is always useful to anticipate their interests and, if possible, offer counsel's assistance in achieving the officers' goals in exchange for counsel's access to the client. Thus, for example, counsel might say:

Officer, until I speak with my client, it's my duty, as [his] [her] lawyer, to tell you that [he] [she] does not wish to answer any questions until I get there. Now, if I can have a chance to talk with [him] [her] on the phone right now, so that I can get a better sense of what this case is all about, it may be that I'll end up advising [him] [her] to cooperate with you and possibly to cut a deal. But, I can't make any decision about that, and I certainly can't advise my client about that unless you let me talk with [him] [her] on the phone.

Although it is *very* rare that counsel will ever end up advising the client to cooperate with the police, the fact that this advice is prudent in even a small number of cases means that counsel should not feel reluctant to promise to *consider* advising the client in that manner.

In all such dealings with the police, counsel should take precautions against later being misquoted (for example, by an officer who testifies that s/he questioned the defendant only after both the client and the attorney waived counsel's presence during the interrogation). Counsel should make notes of the conversation immediately and, when time permits, write a memo to the file regarding the content of the conversation.

If an amiable approach fails to shake police refusals to allow counsel to speak with his or her client, more aggressive demands are in order. Insistence that the police respect the client's rights to communication (see § 3.2.3 *supra*) can be racheted up by threatening to hold the officers legally responsible if they continue to stonewall. Successful civil-rights actions against police for violating the rights of arrestees are not commonplace, but there have been enough of them to make many officers buckle in the face of defense counsel who appear determined to enforce those rights by litigation. *See, e.g., Thompson v. Clark*, 142 S. Ct. 1332 (2022); *Parada v. Anoka County*, 54 F.4th 1016 (8th Cir. 2022); *Haze v. Harrison*, 961 F.3d 654 (4th Cir. 2020); *Barnett v. MacArthur*, 956 F.3d 1291 (11th Cir. 2020); *Alcocer v. Mills*, 906 F.3d 944 (11th Cir. 2018), and 800 Fed. Appx. 860 (11th Cir. 2020); *Jauch v. Choctaw County*, 874 F.3d 425, 427 (5th Cir. 2017); *Crowe v. County of San Diego,* 608 F.3d 406 (9th Cir. 2010), and cases collected in § 6.10 concluding paragraph *infra*; *and see Stewardson v. Biggs*, 43 F.4th 732, 736 (7th Cir. 2022) (sustaining a claim for damages against a police officer who failed to intervene when he saw his subordinate use a leg sweep to knock a pretrial detainee to the floor of his cell, after having witnessed the same subordinate slam the detainee's face into a wall a minute before: "It is clearly established that '[a]n officer who is present and fails to intervene to prevent other law enforcement officers from infringing the constitutional rights of citizens is liable under [28 U.S.C.] § 1983 if that officer had reason to know . . . excessive force was being used,' and 'the officer had a realistic opportunity to intervene to prevent the harm from occurring.'"); *but see Vega v. Tekoh*, 142 S. Ct. 2095 (2022); *Egbert v. Boule*, 142 S. Ct. 1793 (2022).

If the officer allows counsel to speak to the client, counsel should cover the matters described in § 3.4 *infra*. Counsel should also talk further with the police to try to obtain additional information about the case, provide protections for the client from interrogation and other police investigative procedures, and explore the possibility of the police releasing the client on his or her own recognizance (O.R.) or on bail. See § 3.5 *infra*. Thereafter, counsel should go to the police station if at all possible and follow the steps recommended in § 3.6 *infra*. Section 3.7 presents some alternative precautions counsel can take if s/he is unable to go to the police station.

If the officer does not allow counsel to talk with the client on the telephone, counsel should record the officer's name and badge number and the name and phone number of his or her commanding officer and should then give the officer the precautionary instructions itemized in § 3.5 subdivision 2(e) *infra*. Counsel should immediately call the commanding officer and attempt to persuade him or her to order the arresting officer to permit counsel to speak with the client on the phone. If the commanding officer proves unbudging, counsel should deliver the same set of precautionary instructions and should inform the commanding officer that counsel is memorializing those requests and the time when counsel gave them to both the arresting officer and the commanding officer. Counsel should then go promptly to the police station where the defendant is being held (see § 3.6 *infra*). Frequently, counsel will obtain better results in person than s/he did on the phone.

3.4. *Matters to Cover in a Telephone Conversation With A Client Who is Presently in Police Custody*

3.4.1. *Preliminary Matters to Discuss with the Client*

The first thing to do is to obtain an explicit statement by the client that s/he wants counsel to represent him or her. (If counsel was initially contacted by a relative or friend of the client, counsel should explain that the caller asked counsel to represent the client and to give whatever help counsel can provide.) Counsel should ask the client whether s/he wants counsel to represent him or her and explain that counsel is willing to represent the client for the time being, at least until there is time to get together and talk about whether the client wants counsel to continue on the case. Assuming the client is willing to be represented by counsel, counsel should obtain an explicit statement to that effect from the client and then should tell the client that counsel is now formally the client's lawyer. In the event that counsel is able to follow the preferred course of personally traveling to the police station (see § 3.6 *infra*), counsel should also tell the client that s/he will be coming down to see the client immediately (or as soon as counsel anticipates s/he can get there), giving a specific time estimate.

The other preliminary matter to which counsel should attend in the phone conversation with the client is to ensure that the conversation will be private. Counsel should ask the client which room in the police station s/he is calling from (detectives' room? an interrogation room?) and whether any officers might be listening to the call. If there is any possibility that a police officer or other individual may be eavesdropping on the conversation, counsel should warn the client to use "yes" and "no" answers whenever possible. In serious felony cases, particularly those with some notoriety or those involving gang activity or major drug rings, counsel also must be alert to the possibility of wiretapping of the police phone or of police officers listening on an extension phone and must modify his or her own end of the phone conversation accordingly. Surreptitious eavesdropping on attorney-client conversations is impermissible (*see, e.g., Matter of Neary*, 84 N.E.3d 1194 (Ind. 2017)) but it does happen and is difficult to prove, so counsel is wise to avoid touching on any subjects that may reveal incriminating information or potential defense activity.

3.4.2. *Protecting the Client from Police Interrogation*

The first and most emphatic advice that the attorney should give in a telephone conversation with a client who is presently in custody is:

> Say nothing to the police. Tell them nothing at all. Do not answer any questions from the police until you and I have had a chance to talk privately.
>
> If the police try to question you or to talk to you at all – about *anything* – tell them your lawyer told you not to talk. If they say anything about having evidence against you or if they tell you what the evidence is or if they bring in someone else who says something against you, then they are just trying to get you to talk. Don't fall for it. If they promise to drop the charges after you confess or if they threaten to stick you with more charges if you don't talk, they're just trying to trick you. Don't fall for any of their tricks. Whatever they say, tell them your lawyer told you not to talk.
>
> Sometimes, the police tell arrested people that their lawyers don't know anything and that only the police know what's good for you. That's just another police trick. They're trying to get you to say something so that they can get the judge to lock you up for a long time.
>
> So, make sure you don't say anything to them. Just keep saying that your lawyer told you not to talk.

This phraseology is preferable to any of the other standard formulations used by lawyers in advising their clients not to confess. Telling the client not to say "anything" is better than telling him or her not to "make a statement," since many clients believe that a "statement" means a written, signed confession. It is also better than advising the client not to make any written or oral confessions, since often clients will not understand that "confessions" include what they believe to be exculpatory statements (for example: "I didn't break into the house, I just stood outside as a lookout"). Advising the client to say explicitly "My lawyer told me not to say anything" is better than advising the client to remain silent, because it is more concrete and therefore easier for the client to understand; it gives the client *something* to say instead of having to suffer the discomfort of standing mute in the face of questions or accusations, and so it may be easier for the client to do; and it avoids the risk that the client's total silence may later be used against him or her as a "tacit admission." See § 26.20 *infra*.

The advice not to talk to the police should be given in *all* cases. Concededly, there is sometimes a possibility that wholehearted cooperation on the client's part might result in the police exercising their discretion to drop the charges or at least to release the client pending preliminary arraignment. However, the possibility of obtaining those benefits is usually so slim and the consequences of confession so devastating in the long run that a cost-benefit analysis has to result in advising the client not to talk. In the few cases in which the client's alibi or explanation is so foolproof that it would have persuaded the police to drop the charges, that same result can usually be achieved through negotiations with the prosecutor involving none of the risks that talking to the police entails. Counsel can minimize even the comparatively negligible risk of adverse consequences flowing from a lack of cooperation with the authorities by telling the client to explain that s/he is refusing to speak with the police solely because of counsel's advice. By placing the onus on the attorney, the client can obtain whatever benefits might accrue from appearing to be cooperative while avoiding the overwhelmingly detrimental consequences of a confession.

3.4.3. *Cautioning the Client Against Speaking with Cellmates or Visitors*

In addition to telling the client not to speak with the police, counsel should caution the client against speaking with cellmates or codefendants. Cellmates may be snitches, and codefendants may become turncoats. Counsel should be aware that this is a lesson that most clients find hard to accept. Counsel may wish to mention that a large number of people who get busted end up snitching in order to save their own skins.

Counsel should also warn the client about the possibility that the police will eavesdrop on any visits or telephone conversations that s/he may have with family or friends while at the police station. To minimize this danger, it is wise to advise the client (i) to make and receive no visits or phone calls except from counsel or from close family members who need to be reassured that the client is all right, and (ii) during any family calls and visits, to say nothing unnecessary and certainly nothing about the client's actions or whereabouts before s/he was arrested or anything else that might have any connection with the case.

3.4.4. *Advising the Client About Lineups, Show-ups, and Other Police Investigative Procedures*

Once counsel has fully warned the client against speaking with the police and against speaking with cellmates, codefendants, and visitors, counsel will have established the most urgently needed protections of the client's interests. There is additional advice that counsel can give regarding other police investigative procedures, but this should be given if, and only if, counsel believes that the client is capable of assimilating the lengthy discourse involved and will not suffer such information overload that s/he ends up forgetting some of counsel's critical advice about talking to no one. That judgment by counsel needs to be based on the client's age, emotional state, and degree of physical exhaustion. Throughout the phone conversation, counsel should periodically ask the client questions that will force the client to repeat back the advice that counsel has just given (for example: "Okay, now what are you going to say when the police say that if you tell them what happened, they'll drop the charges and you can go home?"). Such questions will not only serve as a mechanism for double-checking the client's comprehension of the previously given advice, but they will also enable the attorney to gauge whether the client's current attention span warrants venturing into the realm of useful-but-not-indispensable additional advice.

If the client seems reasonably alert, counsel should next advise him or her how to deal with lineups and other identification procedures that may occur while s/he is at the police station. It is presently unclear to what extent the police can lawfully compel an unwilling accused to submit to identification confrontations in the absence of counsel. See § 27.6 *infra.* The client should accordingly be advised to object to any lineup, show-up, or confrontation for identification purposes that is held in counsel's absence, and to tell the police, if they say anything about showing the client to any witness for possible identification, that the client wants to have his or her lawyer present and that s/he is asking the police either to phone the lawyer (giving them the lawyer's number) or to let the client phone the lawyer, so that the lawyer can come down to the station and represent the client during any identification procedure. The client should also be instructed that in the event that the police do display the client to any person for identification, the client should not speak any words or answer any questions – including his or her name – during the procedure. S/he should not, however, physically resist being exhibited; and if the police insist on going ahead with the exhibition after s/he has told them that s/he objects to it, the client should follow whatever orders the police may give with regard to the client's going up onto a lineup stage or stepping forward or walking about or speaking words that everyone in the lineup is asked to speak. S/he should never attempt to hide his or her face or to make faces. These tactics, or a failure to obey instructions to step forward or to walk about or to say words that other persons in the lineup speak, will only focus attention on him or her and thereby increase the chances of being identified as the perpetrator; they may also be used against the client as evidence of guilt; and physical resistance to the officers may result in a beating or the lodging of assault-upon-an-officer charges or both. If the police tell the client that s/he is being taken to a lineup or identification room, s/he should orally object to the absence of counsel but should not sit down or physically refuse to go, since this action may result in the witnesses being brought back to view the client in the cell – a far more suggestive form of confrontation than the lineup itself. If the police tell the client that s/he is being taken anywhere to be shown to witnesses, s/he should insist, *first*, that s/he be given a chance to phone his or her lawyer and to have the lawyer present and, *second*, that s/he not be shown to witnesses except in a lineup with other people who resemble the client. Once in a lineup or identification confrontation, s/he should observe and remember everything about it that s/he can, particularly (a) how many other persons were in the lineup, how they were dressed, and what they looked like (getting their names, if possible without attracting attention to the client, or afterwards if the client sees these persons again while s/he is in custody); (b) how many witnesses were asked for identifications, what they said, what the officers said to them, their names, and what they looked like; (c) how many police officers were present and their names, badge numbers, and descriptions; and (d) the time and place of the lineup. The client should not attempt to take notes during the lineup or in any place where s/he may be observed by the witnesses to the lineup, but when s/he returns to the cell, s/he should request paper and a pen from the guards and immediately write down everything that s/he can remember.

The client should also be instructed that if anyone asks for permission to go to the client's house or to any other place in order to search for evidence or weapons or pieces of clothing or anything else, s/he should say, "My lawyer told me to say, 'No,'" whether or not s/he thinks that the things the police are looking for will be found or that the search will prove the client innocent. S/he should be instructed to give the same answer if the police ask the client to lead them to any place or thing or to act out or demonstrate any action; and to object to being taken from the cell area for any reason, saying that s/he wants to stay there and wait for an attorney who is coming. S/he should be instructed not to sign any forms or papers and not to write down anything for the police. Again, the proper answer is "My lawyer told me to say 'No' until s/he gets here." The client should be instructed that if anyone attempts to inspect or examine his or her body, to take swabs or washes or scrapings from it, to cut nails or take hair samples, the client should tell them "My attorney said to wait until s/he gets here"; but if they go ahead anyway, the client should not try to fight them off.

3.4.5. *Advising the Client How to Deal with News Reporters*

Counsel should advise the client not to talk to reporters or other media representatives and, if asked questions by them, to tell them that counsel has insisted that s/he say nothing at all to anyone until counsel gets there. If media representatives start taking photographs with cameras or cellphones, the client should not attempt to duck or dodge, cover his or her face, or make faces, but should remain calm and follow any police directives about whether to stand in a certain place or move to some other location. If the client has the opportunity to ask the police to prevent the taking of photographs before a camera or cellphone is aimed, s/he should do so; but s/he should not attempt to call out or signal an officer after a camera or cellphone has been positioned for a photograph. Photographs of a defendant dodging or shouting or behaving in any other manner that could seem furtive or menacing can be exceedingly prejudicial.

3.4.6. *Concluding the Telephone Conversation with the Client in Police Custody*

At the conclusion of the phone conversation, counsel should try to reduce the client's anxiety by letting the client know when counsel will be back in touch with the client and what counsel will be doing to try to secure the client's release:

1. If counsel intends to adopt the preferred course of action of going to the police station (see § 3.6 *infra*), counsel should tell that to the client, and give the client a reasonable time estimate of how long it will take for counsel to get to the station. Counsel should tell the client not to worry if the client is moved before counsel arrives, since counsel will try to track the client down and visit the client wherever s/he has been taken. Counsel should add, however, that there is a possibility that the police will not allow counsel to see the client and that if the client does not see counsel, it is because of police interference and not due to any lack of effort on counsel's part.

2. If counsel is not going to go to the station or if counsel is not planning to leave for the station immediately, counsel should give the client a telephone number at which counsel can be reached.

3. Whether counsel intends to go to the police station or not, counsel should:

   a. Offer to phone someone on the client's behalf (*e.g.*, a spouse or domestic partner or parent or other family member to reassure them that the client is all right; and/or an employer or fellow employee to explain that the client may not be able to show up for work);

   b. Explain that counsel will take all of the steps that might help to secure the client's immediate release (which, depending on local practice, might include talking with the police about releasing the client on his or her own recognizance or on stationhouse bail, see §§ 3.5, 3.8 *infra*);

    c.   Explain that if the client is not released, then the client will be taken to court, and the judge will decide whether to release the client or set bail; counsel will be in court with the client, and counsel will try to convince the judge in court to release the client or, if bail is set, to make it as low as possible.

Before ending the conversation, counsel should instruct the client to get the attention of a police officer and tell the officer, while counsel listens on the phone, that the client does not wish to talk further with the police in the absence of counsel and that the client wants all further dealings with the police to be conducted by counsel on the client's behalf. Once the client has made a statement of this sort, with counsel in a position to testify that s/he heard it made, the client has obtained the fullest possible protection against police interrogation while in custody, short of counsel's physical presence. For, under the rule of *Edwards v. Arizona,* 451 U.S. 477 (1981), the police may not thereafter question the client, even with full *Miranda* warnings and waivers, "unless the [client] . . . himself [or herself] initiates further communication, exchanges or conversations with the police" (*id.* at 485). *See also Minnick v. Mississippi,* 498 U.S. 146, 150-56 (1990); *Smith v. Illinois,* 469 U.S. 91, 95 (1984) (per curiam); *Shea v. Louisiana,* 470 U.S. 51, 54-55 (1985); *Montejo v. Louisiana,* 556 U.S. 778, 794-95 (2009) (dictum). The procedure advised in this paragraph is important; without it, counsel's own admonitions to the police not to interrogate the client may be ignored, and any promises made by the police that they will not interrogate the client may be broken. *See Moran v. Burbine,* 475 U.S. 412 (1986). *But cf. People v. Grice,* 100 N.Y.2d 318, 321-22, 324, 794 N.E.2d 9, 10-12, 13, 763 N.Y.S.2d 227, 229-30, 232 (2003) (state constitutional right to counsel attaches, and "interrogation is prohibited unless the right is waived in the presence of counsel," if an attorney or "the attorney's professional associate" informs the police "'of the fact that the defendant is represented by counsel or that an attorney has communicated with the police for the purpose of representing the defendant'").

3.5. *Telephone Conversations with the Police on Behalf of a Client Who Is Presently in Police Custody*

In dealing with the police on behalf of a recently arrested client who is still in police custody, counsel should pursue three major goals: (i) to prevent the police from interrogating the client or conducting other investigative procedures; (ii) to secure the immediate release of the client; and (iii) to obtain as much information as possible about the facts of the offense for which the client has been arrested.

The prevention of interrogation should be counsel's primary objective, since a confession will severely limit counsel's chances of winning the case at trial and preventing long-term incarceration. However, in structuring conversations with the police, the topic of interrogation should normally be left for last, since counsel's efforts to prevent interrogation will be seen by the police as marking the beginning of an adversarial relationship between them and counsel;

from that point onward, counsel can expect that the officer(s) will cease being cooperative and providing information.

Thus counsel should ordinarily structure conversations with the police in the following manner:

1.   Ask to speak to whatever officer happens to be with the client at the moment, whether that is the arresting officer, the investigating officer, the booking officer, or a detective. (This will be the officer most likely to be on the verge of – or in the course of – interrogating the client. Imminent interrogation should be the attorney's immediate concern; later phone calls or a trip to the police station can deal with officers who might be planning to interrogate the client later on; as for interrogations that have already taken place, there is very little counsel can do about those until the time comes to start preparing motions to suppress.)

2.   In the conversation with the officer, counsel should:

    a.   Begin by explaining that counsel is representing the client.

    b.   "Confide" in the officer that counsel has no information about the case whatsoever, and therefore would appreciate some idea of why the client was arrested. (As a practical matter, this approach is much more likely to elicit information about the case than an aggressive demand for information or a series of lawyer-like questions.) Follow up with questions about the facts of the crime and the grounds for the arrest as the officer sees them (couching the questions, to the extent plausible, as requests for clarification of things that the officer has already said). In the course of any ensuing conversation about the arrest, counsel should ask the officer what specific charges are now placed against the client (being sure to ask "Is that all the charges?"); whether other charges are being considered; and if so, what they are.

    c.   If the police have authority to release a defendant on bail or without bail (usually called "own recognizance" or "O.R.") – which may be the case only in summary and misdemeanor cases, see § 3.8 *infra* – counsel should talk with the officer about whether O.R. is possible and, if not, whether stationhouse bail is available (and, if so, what the bail amount is) for the charges on which the client was arrested and any other additional charges that may be placed against the client.

    d.   Ask the officer where the client is now, including the precise location within the building; whether there are any plans to move the client elsewhere and, if so, where and when; whether the officer will be handling all of the remaining booking of the client or whether that will be handled by other officers, and, if so, who.

e.   Having obtained all possible information concerning the charges, facts of the offense, and possibilities for release, deliver the following instructions, advice, and requests regarding police interrogation and other investigative procedures:

(i)   Tell the officer that counsel is requesting the officer not to interrogate the client or to ask the client any questions; tell the officer that counsel has instructed the client to say nothing, to answer no questions, and to waive no rights; tell the officer that, as attorney for the defendant, counsel is informing the officer that the client is hereby asserting his or her right to refuse to answer questions and his or her right to refuse to answer questions without the presence of counsel; if counsel intends to go to the police station, add that counsel is requesting that no interrogation take place until counsel arrives at the station (expressing the hope that counsel will be able to cooperate with the officer as soon as s/he arrives but saying that s/he must really ask the officer not to deal any further with the client at this time, until counsel has had a chance to confer with the client and to find out what the matter is all about).

(ii)   Tell the officer not to ask for the client's consent to conduct any searches or investigations; tell the officer that counsel has instructed the client to give no consents; and tell the officer that counsel, on behalf of the client, is informing the officer that the defendant refuses to consent to any search or other investigation.

(iii)   Tell the officer not to place the client in a lineup or exhibit the client for identification or make any physical or mental examination, body inspection, or test of any sort on the client in the absence of counsel; tell the officer that counsel has instructed the client to give no consents and to participate in no investigative procedures in the absence of counsel; state that, as counsel for the defendant, counsel is asserting the defendant's right to have counsel present during any identification or other investigative procedure.

(iv)   Say to the officer that counsel is formally requesting that the officer relay the foregoing instructions and requests for the handling of the defendant to any other officers who may become involved in the booking or interrogation of the defendant or who may come into contact with the defendant while s/he is at the police station.

f.   Conclude the phone conversation with the officer as follows:

(i)   If the client has indicated that s/he needs medical treatment, tell the officer to take the client to the hospital (see § 6.10, third paragraph *infra*), and then ask what hospital the client will be taken to [adding, if appropriate, that counsel will meet them at the hospital].

(ii)   If counsel intends to go to the police station, tell the officer that counsel will be at the station as soon as s/he possibly can, and request that the officer not move the client from the station for any purpose (except for medical treatment if the client has indicated that s/he needs medical treatment).

(iii)   Take the officer's name (with spelling), rank, and badge number, and ask the officer where s/he will be and how counsel can contact him or her during the next few hours.

3.   Having completed the phone conversation with the officer who currently has custody of the client, counsel then should repeat that conversation: (a) with any officers that the first officer indicated would later be involved in the booking of the defendant or investigation of the case; and (b) with any other officers who will likely take part in the booking or investigation or in interrogating the defendant, notwithstanding the first officer's failure to mention them.

3.6. *Counsel's Activities on the Client's Behalf at the Police Station*

After speaking by telephone with the client (if possible) and the police, counsel should go as quickly as possible to the police station. The following discussion canvasses the matters that counsel should attend to at the station. If counsel is unable to go to the station personally or to send someone (like a law partner or law clerk), then counsel should make the additional phone calls described in § 3.7 *infra*.

Upon arriving at the police station, counsel should show the desk officer some identification (like a Bar I.D. card) or other document confirming that counsel is an attorney. S/he should say that s/he is representing the defendant (or has been asked to represent the defendant) and that s/he wishes to see the defendant immediately. If a delay of more than a few minutes occurs, s/he should repeat this request and ask, alternatively, to see the commanding officer. If the commanding officer proves obstructive, counsel may be able to obtain assistance from the prosecutor's office. In some urban areas, a deputy prosecutor is assigned to be on call for after-hours emergencies and can be reached by phone through the prosecutor's office or perhaps by e-mail. In extreme situations, counsel should contact a judge of the local court of record and arrange to present a prompt petition for a writ of *habeas corpus* directed to the chief of police, the prosecutor, or both. Again, in some areas, there is an emergency judge available for after-hours crises. If the desk officer or the commanding officer tells counsel that s/he can see the client but only after the completion of interrogation (or lineup procedures, or other investigative procedures, or booking), counsel should insist that the procedures stop until counsel has had a chance to confer with the client.

Once counsel reaches the client, s/he should request the use of a room in which the two can consult privately. As soon as counsel and the client are out of earshot of the police and other persons, counsel should immediately instruct the client that: (a) s/he should respond to any questions from the police or anyone else by saying "my lawyer told me not to talk"; (b) s/he should respond to any requests for permission to search for evidence or weapons or anything else by saying "my lawyer told me to say, 'no'"; (c) s/he should not sign or write any papers for the police or anyone else; (d) s/he should not agree to leave the cell area or go with the police to any other place except to court or another holding facility (but s/he should not forcibly resist a police officer's attempt to take him or her to another location); and (e) if the police say that they intend to exhibit the client to any witnesses or subject him or her to any sort of bodily or mental examination, s/he should ask to phone counsel so that s/he can confer with counsel and have counsel present during the proceeding, and she should say that s/he does not want the exhibition or examination to be held in the absence of counsel. Once these crucial instructions have been given, counsel can move on and ask the client for information about the client's background (home life, employment, etc.) that counsel can use in trying to persuade the police to release the client (see § 3.8 *infra*). Thereafter, to the extent that time permits, counsel can question the client about the information that counsel will need at the preliminary arraignment (see § 3.21 *infra*) and in seeking to have the client released on bail if prearraignment bail-setting procedures are available (see §§ 3.8.3, 4.4-4.5 *infra*).

After the interview with the client has been completed, there are several matters that counsel will need to discuss with the police. The first matter that should be covered (before the conversation with the police takes a confrontational turn, leading to the drawing of battle lines) is the subject of the client's release. If the police have authority to release a defendant on his or her recognizance, counsel should do whatever s/he can to persuade the officer to exercise that authority favorably. See § 3.8.1 *infra*. If the police have authority to release defendants on stationhouse bail, counsel should ask whether bail is available for the charge on which the client has been arrested and, if so, what the bail amount is.

After the subject of the client's release has been resolved to whatever extent it can be at this point, counsel should ask the investigating officer whether the client has made any written or oral statements. If s/he has, counsel should request to see them or, in the case of oral statements, to be told of their contents immediately. Counsel should ask whether the client has been exhibited to any possible witnesses for identification purposes and whether any tests or examinations have been conducted on the client. If so, counsel should ask the nature of the identification proceedings or tests, who conducted them, what results they produced, and the names of all persons present during the identification or testing procedures. Counsel should ask whether any future identification or testing procedures are anticipated, what procedures and when; and s/he should ask and arrange to be present when they are conducted. Counsel should tell the investigating officer that s/he has instructed the client not to talk to anyone and not to give any consents or waivers in counsel's absence; and s/he should ask the officer not to question or talk with the client unless counsel is present and not to take any consents or waivers from the client without counsel's prior approval.

Before leaving a client in custody, counsel should have the client inform an officer, in counsel's presence, that the client does not wish thereafter to talk or deal with the police or prosecuting authorities without counsel but wants to communicate with them only through counsel. See § 3.4.6 *supra*. Counsel should give the officer counsel's professional card and should also give one to the desk officer on the way out.

Counsel who obtains permission to attend identification or examination procedures should ordinarily act as unobtrusively as possible. S/he should not attempt to interfere with them in any way or to play any part in them while any potential identifying witness is present. Prior to the exhibition of the client and *out of sight and earshot of any potential identifying witness*, counsel should (a) inform the police that s/he objects to the identification proceeding altogether, if she does (for example, if s/he contends that the client has been illegally arrested or is being illegally detained, see § 27.7 *infra*), and (b) object to any feature of the proposed exhibition procedure that she believes will impair its reliability (see §§ 27.2-27.4 *infra*). Counsel should couple the latter objection with affirmative suggestions for modification of the procedure only if s/he is reasonably confident that (i) the police will adopt those suggestions and (ii) the result will be that the client is not identified. (If the client *is* identified through a procedure endorsed by counsel, counsel's role in shaping the proceeding can only hamstring subsequent defense challenges to the propriety or reliability of the identification; if the police reject counsel's suggestions, a prosecutor will later be able to contend that those suggestions limit the aspects of the identification proceeding about which the defense can complain in a suppression motion.) During the proceeding itself – while potential identifying witnesses are present – counsel's role is strictly that of an observer. S/he should watch and take notes on everything that happens, be sure to get the names of all persons present, and ask questions both before and afterwards about anything s/he does not understand.

Before the proceeding begins, counsel should ask whether it will involve the defendant's performing any kind of action – for example, speaking (to provide a voice exemplar) or turning or walking about on a lineup stage. If so, counsel should request the opportunity to confer privately with the defendant in advance of the exhibition procedures, so that s/he will not have to interrupt them for the purpose of giving the defendant advice. Counsel may or may not have suggestions to offer the client about how s/he should behave in performing the actions s/he will be called upon to take. But even if counsel does not, it is ordinarily helpful for counsel to forewarn the client specifically what those actions will be, because foreknowledge may reduce the danger that the client will exhibit guilty-looking signals as a result of nervousness or surprise.

At a lineup or show-up, counsel should ask to speak to the possible identifying witnesses *before* the defendant is exhibited to them. It will be the rare case in which the police will permit such interviews. But at the earliest time when counsel can obtain access to the witnesses, counsel should ask them (i) to think back to their original observation of the person whom they saw in connection with the offense and to describe that person as s/he then appeared; (ii) to describe the circumstances under which they observed that person; (iii) how sure they are that they could recognize the person if they saw the person again; (iv) by what characteristics they could recognize the person; (v) what descriptions of the person they gave to the police prior to the present identification proceeding; (vi) whether they have been asked by the police to attempt to identify any persons other than those exhibited in the current proceeding, either in the flesh or by photograph or video, and whether they made any identifications on these occasions; and (vii) what they were told by the officers who brought them or asked them to come to the station today.

When there is more than one identifying witness, counsel should, if possible, speak separately with each. Interviewing identifying witnesses as a group will result in the loss of important information unique to each of them and will probably cause them to homogenize their impressions, to the client's ultimate detriment.

Whenever counsel is permitted to attend a show-up, counsel should object to the show-up procedure and request that the police conduct a lineup instead. Counsel should point out the likelihood that any show-up results will be suppressed in court because there are no exigencies requiring a show-up instead of a lineup. See § 27.3.1 *infra.*

Counsel should urge the officers conducting the lineup to follow procedures which assure against unreliable identifications. In localities where statutes, court rules or law-enforcement guidelines prescribe protective practices (such as those modeled by the Louisiana statute summarized in § 27.3 *infra*), counsel should insist that they be followed. Elsewhere, s/he should try to persuade the officers to adopt as many of these "best practices" (LA. CODE CRIM. PRO. art. 251 (A)) as s/he can. At the least, s/he should attempt to ensure that any lineup is composed of at least six persons who resemble the defendant in general characteristics – age, skin color, height, weight, body type, hair style, clothing, and accessories; and counsel should ask that all subjects be exhibited in street clothes, not jail garb or, in the case of police officer "fillers" in the line, articles of clothing that are identifiable as parts of a police uniform. If more than one witness is to view the lineup, the witnesses should not be present during one another's viewings; the positions of all subjects in the lineup should be changed between witnesses; and the witnesses should not be assembled where they can talk together either before or after the conclusion of the proceedings. At the lineup, counsel should record the names, descriptions, and means of later contacting all witnesses who are present to view the lineup (whether or not they attempt to make any identifications), what is said to them, and what they say. Counsel should also record the names, descriptions, and contact information for all persons in the lineup array. Counsel should record the manner in which the lineup is conducted, including distances, lighting, any directions to the subjects to walk, motion, or speak; what they do; and when in the course of these proceedings any identification is made. S/he should also note the names, ranks, and badge numbers of all officers present and of those who brought witnesses to the lineup. Similar interviews, observations, and notes should be made at show-ups.

Police detectives and officers usually record their own observations of lineups and show-ups in handwritten notes and typed reports. It is commonplace for the array of persons on a lineup stage to be photographed in a composite still, and in some jurisdictions the entire lineup proceeding is videotaped by the police. Counsel should note whether any of these records are being made, so that s/he can later subpoena them or request their production through pretrial discovery proceedings. See §§ 9.18, 9.20 *infra.*

In the case of other testing procedures, counsel should record the names of all technicians and officers present and the means of contacting them and should ask them to describe for counsel what procedures, materials, substances, chemicals, and so forth, they are using, as they proceed. If possible, counsel should get them to describe, *before* any testing is done, what indicators or results they believe will demonstrate positive and negative findings. Counsel should also ask them whether their testing procedures will affect the substances being tested and, if so, request that they leave a sufficient amount of the substances untouched for subsequent defense testing. Any refusals of the technicians or officers to cooperate in these regards or to explain what they are doing should be noted.

3.7. *Actions That Can Be Taken to Protect the Client's Rights in Lieu of a Trip to the Police Station*

There is no fully adequate substitute for a trip by counsel to the police station. However, if for some reason counsel cannot go to the station, there are phone calls s/he can make that will further some of the same objectives.

After counsel's preliminary phone conversations with the police (§§ 3.3.2.4 and 3.5 *supra*) and after speaking with the client by telephone (§ 3.4 *supra*), attorneys who cannot go to the stationhouse should phone the police again, ask for the officer who is currently responsible for handling the client's case, and:

1. If the police have the authority to release the defendant on his or her own recognizance (O.R.), try to persuade the officer to do so. See § 3.8.1 *infra*.

2. If O.R. is not an option but stationhouse bail is, elicit all information necessary for obtaining stationhouse bail. See § 3.8.2 *infra*.

3. Reiterate and reinforce all advice, instructions, and requests that counsel gave in the earlier phone conversation with this officer or other officers regarding police interrogation of the client, identification procedures, and other investigative procedures. See § 3.5 *supra*.

3.8. *Securing the Client's Release on Bail or Own Recognizance or By Habeas Corpus*

The most effective protection against stationhouse investigative procedures is, of course, for counsel to secure the client's release as rapidly as possible. As long as a defendant remains in the hands of the police, they can conveniently conduct any number of investigative procedures that may produce incriminating evidence. Ordinarily, too, getting out of custody is what the client most wants at this stage.

3.8.1. *Release on the Client's Own Recognizance ("O.R.")*

In some jurisdictions, the police have authority (most commonly in summary and misdemeanor cases) to release a defendant immediately after booking, without bail, pending the defendant's first court appearance on the charge. This practice is usually called "own recognizance" ("O.R.") or "release on the defendant's own recognizance" ("R.O.R.").

Often, eligibility for stationhouse release on O.R. is defined categorically, in terms of the type or degree of offense charged and sometimes also whether the defendant has a prior record and/or pending charges; the police are not expected to exercise discretion in releasing defendants on the basis of their individual characteristics or situation. But in some localities the police do have such discretion, either in all summary/misdemeanor cases or in those where specified eligibility criteria are met. Counsel may be able to influence the exercise of that discretion by telling the decision-making officer favorable information about the client's life circumstances (*e.g.*, that continued custody could cost the client his or her job, or would cause profound hardship for the client's family). Even if the police are not formally recognized as having discretion to allow or refuse a defendant release on O.R. – where entitlement to O.R. depends solely on the nature of the charge and the defendant's record – the arresting officer (or the booking or investigating officers) may be able to effectuate a client's release by choosing the offense with which the defendant is charged so that it is one for which O.R. is authorized. In these situations too, counsel may be able to invoke the sympathy of an officer who is making the initial charging decision or an officer who has authority to reduce the initial charge.

3.8.2. *Stationhouse Bail*

The police may have authority (again, most commonly in summary and misdemeanor cases) to release defendants on bail immediately after booking. This is usually called "stationhouse bail." The amount of bail is ordinarily set according to a fixed schedule and depends on the offense charged. In some localities, however, the police exercise a limited discretion in setting the amount. The police also may exercise *de facto* discretion by their determination of what offense to charge the defendant with. *Cf.* § 3.8.1 *supra*.

3.8.3. *Seeking O.R. or a Lower Bail From a Magistrate or Court*

If O.R. and stationhouse bail are not available or are refused, or if bail is fixed in an amount that the client cannot make or deems excessive, local practice may provide for an application to a magistrate or judge for release on the client's own recognizance or bail at a manageable level. In the absence of any provision for some other procedure, a petition for *habeas corpus* is the customary, time-honored forum for seeking O.R. or bail. *United States v. Hamilton*, 3 U.S. (3 Dall.) 17 (1795); *Ex parte Bollman*, 8 U.S. (4 Cranch) 75, 99-100 (1807); *State v. Brown*, 2014-NMSC-038, 338 P.3d 1276, 1284 (N.M. 2014) ("In 1679, Parliament adopted the Habeas Corpus Act to ensure that an accused could obtain a timely bail hearing . . . ."); *State v. Bevacqua*, 147 Ohio St. 20, 23, 67 N.E.2d 786, 788 (1946) ("The accused may, upon refusal of the court to reduce the bail fixed, sue out a writ of habeas corpus in a court of competent jurisdiction where bail may immediately be given pending hearing and a final adjudication made as to whether the bail required in the court, in which the charge pends, is excessive. Upon this question the authorities are practically unanimous."); *accord, DuBose v. McGuffey*, 2022-Ohio-8, 168 Ohio St.3d 1, 4, 195 N.E.3d 951, 955 (2022) ("habeas corpus is the proper vehicle by which to raise a claim of excessive bail in pretrial-release cases"); *State ex rel. Gerstein v. Schulz*, 180 So.2d 367, 369 (Fla. App. 1965) ("The jurisdiction of the circuit court, in habeas corpus, to grant bail when it has been refused by a trial court is well recognized, without regard to whether the circuit court so acting has appellate jurisdiction of the court involved. The authority of the circuit court to so proceed stems from the guarantee of bail by the Declaration of Rights, coupled with the power granted to that court by the Constitution to issue writs of habeas corpus."); II MATTHEW HALE, PLEAS OF THE CROWN 143 (1st Amer. ed. 1847); *see, e.g., Ex parte Bynum*, 294 Ala. 78, 312 So.2d 52 (1975); *People ex rel. Tseitlin ex rel. Robinson v. Ponte*, 133 A.D.3d 694, 19 N.Y.S.3d 173 (mem.) (N.Y. App. Div., 2d Dep't 2015); *Ex parte Bentley*,

2015 WL 9592456 (Tex. App. 2015). Procedures for securing the client's release on recognizance, for getting bail set by a magistrate or judge, and for posting bail are considered in §§ 4.7-4.14 *infra*.

If counsel is unsuccessful in obtaining the client's release by proceedings in the designated court of first instance, counsel can seek relief in a higher court (by appeal, in some jurisdictions; by an original *habeas corpus* petition or bail application, in other juridictions). *See, e.g., Commonwealth v. Madden*, 458 Mass. 607, 939 N.E.2d 778 (2010). Procedures for obtaining pretrial release on O.R. or bail are ordinarily cumulative; that is, a lawyer whose client is refused O.R. or bail, or reasonable bail, by the police can go next to a magistrate, then to a judge of a court of record, then to an appellate court or judge. Similarly, if one bail-setting authority is unavailable, the lawyer may proceed up the ladder to the next level, informing the higher-level authority (by affidavit or other documentation) of counsel's unsuccessful efforts to reach the lower-level authority. In most jurisdictions, a defendant who is denied relief by one judge may also seek the same relief from another judge of coordinate jurisdiction; the governing procedural doctrine is that *habeas corpus* proceedings are not subject to *res judicata*. *Sanders v. United States*, 373 U.S. 1, 7-8 (1963); *Schlup v. Delo*, 513 U.S. 298, 317 (1995).

The basic doctrinal rules relating to bail – conferring a right to bail and prohibiting excessive bail – are described in §§ 4.2-4.4 and 4.6 *infra*. Notwithstanding these rules, the usual approach of lower courts in setting bail is to pay attention first to the nature of the offense charged and then to the prior criminal record of the defendant. Prosecutors customarily rely exclusively on these two factors in arguing against favorable bail settings; both the categorization of the criminal charge as a serious one in the abstract and any particularly ugly or aggravating facts in the circumstances of the individual case can be counted upon to increase the amount of bail required. Conversely, defense counsel wants to concentrate on mitigating elements in the offense and in the defendant's record. As counsel moves up the line of courts to those in which legal doctrine is likely to be important, however, s/he will also want increasingly to take account of the statutory and constitutional principles of bail discussed in §§ 4.2-4.4 and 4.6. These focus on the amount of security required to assure the defendant's appearance at trial; they therefore require consideration of the question whether the defendant has sufficient stability of residence, employment, and family contacts to indicate that s/he is a good risk for release without financial security or for release on a smaller amount of bail than would ordinarily be demanded of one charged with the offense for which the defendant is held. In attempting to show this to a court, counsel should not rely merely upon the client's account of his or her background or even the client's sworn statement (see § 4.5 *infra*) but should verify the client's account independently and obtain supporting affidavits if time permits. A Bail Project or R.O.R. Project should be brought in immediately if one exists in the area. See § 4.6 *infra*.

Documentation of all of the facts likely to weigh in the defendant's favor in an appellate court should be presented to the court of first instance, even though counsel expects the first-instance judge to disregard them. Technically, appellate courts review lower-court bail and O.R. decisions under an abuse-of-discretion standard, so appellate judges will want to assure themselves that any information on which they rely was before the court below. If the time required to document facts that will favor the defendant in a higher court would unduly delay counsel's filing of a request for bail or O.R. in the court of first instance, counsel should file the initial request without that documentation but, in anticipation of the probable denial of the original request, s/he should prepare a successor request *with* the documentation for filing in the court of first instance before proceeding upstairs. Repeated applications to the same court are permissible because, as mentioned above, "[t]he inapplicability of res judicata to habeas . . . is inherent in the very role and function of the writ" (*Sanders v. United States, supra*, 373 U.S. at 8).

3.8.4. *Habeas Corpus*

If the client has been arrested illegally (that is, arrested without probable cause or otherwise in violation of constitutional or statutory restrictions on the arrest power, see § 25.7 *infra*) or is being detained too long without a preliminary arraignment or without a judicial determination of probable cause (see § 11.2 *infra*), then the client's confinement is illegal and should be challenged immediately by a petition for a writ of *habeas corpus* directed to the chief of police and the prosecutor. *Habeas* is the appropriate remedy for any kind of illegal detention. *Braden v. 30th Judicial Circuit Court of Kentucky*, 410 U.S. 484 (1973); *Boumediene v. Bush*, 553 U.S. 723, 739 (2008) ("The Framers viewed freedom from unlawful restraint as a fundamental precept of liberty, and they understood the writ of habeas corpus as a vital instrument to secure that freedom."); *see, e.g., People ex rel. Chakwin on Behalf of Ford v. Warden, New York Correctional Facility, Rikers Island*, 63 N.Y.2d 120, 470 N.E.2d 146, 480 N.Y.S.2d 719 (1984); §§ 4.11.1-4.11.2 *infra*; and see § 4.13 *infra* with regard to *habeas corpus* in a federal district court.

Habeas corpus may also be available if the client is being subjected to illegal or abusive methods of investigation while in custody, although in such a case the writ would not order the client's outright release but would order only that the client be released unless the improper investigative techniques are discontinued. In *Bell v. Wolfish*, 441 U.S. 520, 527 n.6 (1979), the Supreme Court raised and reserved "the question of the propriety of using a writ of habeas corpus to obtain review of the conditions of confinement, as distinct from the fact or length of the confinement itself." This means that insofar as *federal* judicial relief may be required, counsel would do best to caption the initial federal pleading in the alternative, as a petition for a writ of *habeas corpus* under 28 U.S.C. § 2241(c)(3) and as a civil complaint for injunctive relief under 28 U.S.C. § 1343(3) and 42 U.S.C. § 1983. *See Ziglar v. Abbasi*, 582 U.S. 120, 144-45 (2017); *Winston v. Lee*, 470 U.S. 753 (1986); *Nelson v. Campbell*, 541 U.S. 637 (2004); *Hill v. McDonough*, 547 U.S. 573 (2006); and *cf. Hutto v. Finney*, 437 U.S. 678 (1978); *County of Riverside v. McLaughlin*, 500 U.S. 44, 56-57 (1991); *cf. Atencio v. Arpaio*, 674 Fed. Appx. 623 (9th Cir. 2017). State law, of course, determines whether the appropriate *state*-court remedy would be an injunction or a conditional writ of *habeas corpus* or both.

In a few jurisdictions, *habeas corpus* may also be available to a pretrial detainee to challenge the substantive constitutionality of the statute under which s/he is held (*see, e.g., Ex parte Jones*, 2018 WL 2228888 (Tex. App. May 16, 2018)), although in most jurisdictions the earliest proceeding in which such a challenge can be made is a motion to dismiss the charging paper after one has been filed in a criminal prosecution (see § 13.1 subdivision (D)(7) *infra*).

B. *The "Wanted" Client: Representing Clients Who Have Not Yet Been Arrested But Who Are Being Sought by the Police*

3.9. *The Initial Phone Call from the "Wanted" Client or from Someone Concerned about the Client*

An attorney may receive a call from a client who is "wanted" by the authorities in either of two basic situations: when a potential client contacts the attorney for the first time because of his or her suspicion (or knowledge) that s/he is being sought by the police; or when an already-existing client suspects (or knows) that s/he is being sought by the police for crimes other than the one(s) on which s/he is already being represented by the attorney. If the attorney is contacted by the client himself or herself (rather than by a relative or friend on behalf of the client), the contact usually takes the form of a phone call: Few clients trust an unknown (or even partially known) attorney enough to appear in the attorney's office and face what the client believes to be a significant risk of betrayal to authorities.

Sometimes counsel may receive a call or visit from the family member or the friend of a potentially "wanted" client, acting at the client's instance or because the caller is independently worried about the prospect of an arrest. If this person appears to be genuinely concerned with protecting the client and promoting the client's best interests, counsel should have him or her put counsel directly in touch with the client, and counsel should then proceed as described in the following paragraphs and sections through § 3.13. If the person appears to be motivated by his or her own interests without regard to the client's, counsel will ordinarily want to decline any involvement in the matter. Representation of anyone in this situation is all too likely to embroil counsel in ethical and personal conflicts s/he would be wise to avoid.

In all dealings with "wanted" clients, the attorney must be sensitive to the paranoia that develops when an individual leads the life of a fugitive. At the beginning of any phone conversation with a "wanted" client, counsel should explain that the attorney-client privilege covers anything that the client may say about his or her situation and current whereabouts. It is clear under the code of ethics that such conversations do, indeed, fall within the attorney-client privilege. If any attorney labors under the delusion that lawyers are obliged to surrender their clients or facilitate their clients' arrests by telling the authorities where the client can be found, ethical considerations militate that the attorney either refuse to speak with the "wanted" client at all or, at the very least, begin the conversation by warning the client that the attorney may relay to the police any or all of the information that the client divulges. If an attorney, albeit aware of the attorney-client shield, nevertheless feels personally uncomfortable with knowing the client's location, that attorney certainly has the prerogative of asking the client not to reveal his or her whereabouts to the attorney. (Indeed, that type of request may have the fringe benefit of noticeably reducing the client's suspicions about the attorney.)

In any event, after settling the issue of attorney-client privilege, counsel should elicit precisely why the client believes that s/he is wanted by the authorities. A client ordinarily becomes aware that s/he is wanted for arrest because of police efforts to locate the client, because of news reports, or because s/he learns of the arrest of companions. S/he may be wrong in believing that s/he is wanted, and counsel acting on behalf of a supposedly wanted client should be careful when making inquiries of the authorities not to give them any ideas or information that they do not already have. Before calling them, the attorney should question the client thoroughly about why the client believes that s/he is wanted, in order to assure that his or her belief is well-founded. If its source is a family member or acquaintance whom the client trusts but whose information seems to counsel to be vague or dubious, counsel is advised to speak to that source directly before making any contact with law enforcement.

Other matters to cover in an initial interview of a client in this situation are discussed in § 3.22 *infra*.

3.10. *Making Inquiries of the Police and Prosecutor*

After obtaining the client's permission to contact the authorities, counsel needs to consider how much information can be revealed to them without suggesting that the client feels or is guilty of some offense and ought to be wanted by the police if s/he is not already. Forearmed with a plausible, non-incriminating reason for the inquiry, counsel should phone the police officer who would logically handle the client's arrest (either those officers who are said to be looking for the client or the desk officer in the precinct station for the district of the client's residence, or a "warrants squad" officer if the department has a separate section responsible for serving arrest warrants and if a warrant may have been issued) or the prosecutor's office (if, in this locality, the prosecutor's office customarily gets involved in prearrest investigations and charging decisions) or, in some jurisdictions, the division of the court clerk's office that is responsible for maintaining records of all judicially approved arrest warrants. Counsel should identify himself or herself as an attorney, say that s/he has been informed that the police may be looking for the client, and ask whether this is so. If it is, s/he should ask whether an arrest warrant for the client has been issued, what the charges are, and whether the warrant specifies a bail figure. If there is no warrant or if the warrant does not specify a bail figure, counsel should ask whether the police are authorized to release arrestees on O.R. or to set bail on the charges for which the client is sought, and what the amount of any bail required will be.

Particularly in cases in which the police are seeking the client for a warrantless arrest, the precinct desk officer may have little information to give counsel and may refer counsel to the investigating officers. In any event, on the basis of the information counsel receives from the desk officer (or prosecutor or court clerk), counsel should consider whether s/he wants to speak directly with the investigating officers in order to ask them about the nature of the charges, the circumstances of the supposed offense or offenses, and the likelihood of police release after arrest on the client's own recognizance or stationhouse bail. This will depend on whether counsel believes that s/he can get more information than s/he will be giving out in such a conversation. It also will depend on counsel's assessment of the likelihood that an offer to arrange the surrender of the wanted client can be used as leverage to bargain for concessions from the police on the issue of post-arrest release of the client. As indicated in §§ 3.8.1 and 3.8.2 *supra*, the police may have (or may claim that they have) little discretion in granting release on a client's own recognizance or stationhouse bail. Nevertheless, in some jurisdictions they do have a range of *de jure* discretion and they – or the prosecutor – can always exercise *de facto* discretion either by (1) changing the offense charged (unless a warrant has been issued) or (2) agreeing to go jointly with counsel to a magistrate or judge (who is not bound by the bail schedule) and to recommend that bail be set in an amount different from the bail-schedule figure.

In some cases, the police will refuse to make any concessions on release or bail in return for the client's surrender, because they feel that they do not have discretion to make them, or because they are confident that they can soon and easily arrest the client anyway, or because they want to have the client detained following his or her apprehension in order to further their in-custody investigations or to keep the client "off the street." If the police stonewall, counsel should phone the prosecutor's office and attempt to negotiate a surrender and the setting of reasonable release terms (O.R. or manageable bail) directly with a prosecuting attorney. If the prosecutor is willing, the arrest of the defendant can take place in the courthouse itself, and the arresting officer can take the defendant directly to the court detention area to await the prosecutor's completion of the charging documents preliminary to the client's immediate release. If the prosecutor is unwilling, counsel often can arrange with a courtroom clerk to have the case called so that the client can surrender in open court.

Even though these alternative procedures for arranging surrender are available, counsel should ordinarily begin by attempting to negotiate with the police. Generally, police officers are more interested than prosecutors in "closing" open police cases by arrest, since the officers will thereby generate self-serving statistics. Accordingly, police officers have the greatest incentive to agree to bargains proposed by defense counsel, such as the trade-off of surrender for post-arrest release.

3.11. *The Follow-up Conversation with the Client*

After talking with the authorities, counsel will want to confer again with the client, to discuss the client's feelings about surrendering and to advise the client concerning the wisdom of that course in general as well as the specifics of any agreements that counsel thinks s/he can negotiate with the authorities and the mechanics of surrender if one is arranged.

3.11.1. *Counseling the Client on the Advisability of Surrender*

There are several potential benefits to surrendering: (a) The most significant from the client's perspective will be the possibility of post-arrest release by the police, pursuant to any agreements that counsel can negotiate. (b) A less immediate but equally tangible benefit will be the enhanced likelihood of release on O.R. or a low bail at arraignment, since counsel will be able to argue to the judge that the client's decision to surrender voluntarily demonstrates both that flight is unlikely and that the defendant is a responsible individual. (c) By surrendering at a prearranged time with counsel present, the client can avoid the embarrassment and inconvenience of being dragged out of his or her home or place of employment by the police and can preclude the risk of physical injury from a violent confrontation with the arresting officer. (d) By surrendering in the presence of counsel, the client ensures that there will be no post-arrest custodial interrogation.

The alternative course of not surrendering and of attempting to evade the police entails significant risks (of inconvenience, embarrassment, possible physical injury, and greater likelihood of pretrial detention) and usually provides very little benefit unless the offenses charged are not serious ones and the client is able to leave the jurisdiction permanently. Although evasion may buy the client a little extra time "on the street," the police are fairly assiduous about executing arrest warrants for felonies and other major crimes. Long delays are characteristic only in congested metropolitan precincts and when the charges are for minor offenses.

Counsel will need to advise the client concerning all of these factors so that the client can make an informed decision whether to surrender. Although counsel can (and often should) advise the client to surrender, the final decision must be left to the client.

3.11.2. *Other Matters to Discuss with the Client*

If time permits, counsel should conduct a further, full-scale interview of the client (see Chapter 6) or as much of one as is practicable. Here, counsel should focus upon exploring with the client factual information and tactical considerations that will enable counsel and the client to decide whether before, at, or immediately after, the client's surrender, (a) the client should make an oral or written statement to the police, propose a lineup, or otherwise cooperate with police investigative procedures (see § 6.12 *infra*); (b) counsel should begin discussing the facts of the case with the police or prosecutor in an effort to persuade them to drop the charges (see Chapter 8 *infra*); or (c) counsel should begin to engage in plea bargaining with the prosecutor (see §§ 15.8-15.13 *infra*), including in the bargaining package an agreement for the client's release on O.R. or the setting of a reasonable bail amount.

3.12. *Arranging the Surrender*

If the client decides to surrender, then the attorney can finalize the negotiations with the police and arrange the mechanics of the surrender. Counsel should insist upon securing assurances from the police that the client will not be interrogated, exhibited to witnesses for identification, or subjected to searches or examinations while in custody prior to being released. A time and place for surrender should be agreed upon, and counsel should accompany the client to assure that the arrangements which s/he has made with the police or prosecutor are carried out. Before the surrender, counsel should make a detailed file memorandum recording the agreed-upon surrender terms, identifying the officer or official with whom they were arranged, and noting the time and manner (*e.g.*, a phone conversation between specified phone numbers) in which the officer or official agreed to the terms.

If the police and prosecutor are both unwilling to make satisfactory arrangements or if counsel suspects that the agreements which they have made against interrogation and other post-arrest investigative procedures or their agreements to release the client immediately on O.R. or a specified amount of bail will not be honored faithfully, s/he should phone a magistrate, explain the problem, and request a time when s/he can surrender the client in open court, make bail, and have the client released forthwith. When bail in a reasonable amount has not been previously set by an arrest warrant or by a stationhouse bail schedule or through counsel's negotiations with the authorities, counsel should appear before a magistrate or judge to have bail set, in the manner indicated in § 3.8.3 *supra* and in §§ 4.7-4.14 *infra*, or to have an arrest warrant setting bail issued *before* the surrender of the client.

Arrangements should also be made in advance, either with a professional bail bondsman or by getting the requisite cash, securities, or property deed in hand, to have the necessary security for posting bail available at the time of surrender.

An attorney seeking to avoid harmful publicity arising from the surrender of a client of notoriety should consider picking a time and place inconvenient or inaccessible to the media. Once reporters have obtained facts about a case or photographs of the defendant, it is virtually impossible to restrain their subsequent dissemination, notwithstanding its prejudicial impact on the defendant and his or her ability to get a fair trial. *See Oklahoma Publishing Co. v. District Court*, 430 U.S. 308 (1977); *Smith v. Daily Mail Publishing Co.*, 443 U.S. 97, 103 (1979). Conversely, if there are strategic reasons for memorializing the client's arrest (such as concern that arresting officers may mistreat the client), the surrender should be made in open court or in some location, such as the courthouse steps (*compare Glik v. Cunnliffe*, 655 F.3d 78 (1st Cir. 2011), *and ACLU of Illinois v. Alvarez*, 679 F.3d 583 (7th Cir. 2012), *with Enoch v. Hamilton County Sheriff's Office*, 818 Fed. Appx. 398 (6th Cir. 2020)) where counsel can videorecord it. *See Project Veritas Action Fund v. Rollins*, 982 F.3d 813, 817 (1st Cir. 2020) (affirming "the District Court's . . . ruling that . . . [a Massachusetts statute] violates the First Amendment by prohibiting the secret, nonconsensual audio recording of police officers discharging their official duties in public spaces"); *Irizarry v. Yehia*, 38 F.4th 1282, 1289 (10th Cir. 2022) ("well-established First Amendment principles show that filming the police performing their duties in public is protected activity"); *Sharpe v. Winterville Police Department*, 59 F.4th 674 (4th Cir. 2023); *Collins v. Barela*, 2023 WL 2973784, at *6 (D. Colo. 2023) ("The Tenth Circuit has held that an individual is engaged in constitutionally protected activity when they film police activity . . . . Nor does the Court find constitutional significance in the fact that Plaintiff asked his acquaintance to record the incident, as opposed to recording the incident himself.").

3.13. *The Surrender*

If in the course of the actual surrender of the client, a police officer begins to renege on his or her agreements with counsel, counsel should inform the officer that unless s/he adheres to the agreed-upon surrender terms, counsel will inform the local defense bar that that particular officer cannot be trusted in negotiations on surrender or any other matters. Since many officers are very concerned with closing cases and amassing arrest statistics, the threat to their credibility as honest traders may cause (or at least encourage) the officer to adhere to the original terms of the agreement. Should the officer persist in violating the terms of a surrender agreement, counsel should make a file memorandum detailing the incident, for potential use in (a) seeking immediate corrective action from superior officers, a prosecutor, or a judge (in a *habeas corpus* or injunctive proceeding (see § 3.8.4 *supra*)) and (b) later litigating motions to suppress any evidence obtained by the police during the client's detention (see Chapters 25-27 *infra*).

C. *Appointment or Retainer at Preliminary Arraignment*

3.14. *Preliminary Arraignment*

The preliminary arraignment is usually the first proceeding following arrest at which the defendant is taken before a judicial officer (ordinarily a magistrate, justice of the peace, or judge of some other minor court). In many instances it is also the first time that the defendant has an opportunity to see a lawyer. Counsel is often appointed, particularly in felony cases, at the preliminary arraignment. In some instances just about the only function performed at the preliminary arraignment is the appointment of counsel. But in some jurisdictions the defendant may be called upon to plead to the charges, and frequently s/he is required to decide whether to insist upon, or waive the right to, a preliminary examination – that is, a hearing before the magistrate at which the prosecution will have to establish probable cause to hold the defendant for trial. See §§ 2.3.3-2.3.5 *supra*; §§ 11.1, 11.7 *infra*. In jurisdictions that permit transfer of a case from adult criminal court to juvenile court if the accused comes within the concurrent jurisdiction of the juvenile court (see § 21.7 *infra*), local law may require that defense counsel seek such a transfer at the preliminary arraignment.

3.15. *Insistence on Adequate Time*

It is essential that a newly appointed or newly retained attorney not act precipitously in making decisions at the preliminary arraignment. Often the magistrate, anxious to push cases along, pressures defense counsel to make immediate elections. Elections made in haste at the preliminary arraignment – to enter or not to enter a plea, to waive or to demand a preliminary examination, to insist upon or to waive the time limits for preliminary examination – may prejudice the defendant's rights or preclude the raising of vital defenses at a later stage. Counsel must, therefore, insist upon a reasonable opportunity to interview the client and to weigh alternative courses of action. Allowance of five or ten minutes to do these things, as magistrates will suggest in some instances, seldom provides sufficient time to make critical decisions. Counsel who is forced to proceed in this situation ought (a) to object strenuously, asserting that s/he is not prepared to go ahead, stating the circumstances of counsel's recent entry into the case, and invoking the client's Sixth Amendment right to effective representation by counsel, see § 3.23.3 *infra*; (b) to enter no plea; and (c) to waive no subsequent procedures, such as preliminary examination or indictment. Counsel should be sure that his or her objections, requests for adequate preparation time, and declaration of inability to represent a previously unknown client on such short notice are recorded by the court reporter.

3.16. *Preliminary Examination*

When a defendant at preliminary arraignment is offered an opportunity to ask for a preliminary examination, s/he should ordinarily request the examination. This is frequently an important opportunity, perhaps the only one, to get discovery of the prosecution's case. Waiver of preliminary examination ought to be the exception rather than the rule. There are, however, some cases in which waiver would be well advised. See §§ 11.7.3, 28.2 *infra*. For this reason, counsel should insist on *time to decide one way or the other* whether s/he wants a preliminary examination and should resist the magistrate's blandishments to "go on with the examination now, since you won't lose anything that way." If the magistrate insists on going forward, counsel should formally ask for a continuance, again citing the Sixth Amendment. (See § 3.23.3 *infra*.) If this is denied, it is usually wise to let the examination proceed over counsel's recorded objection rather than to waive it. See generally Chapter 11 *infra*.

3.17. *Pleas*

When a defendant is asked to enter a plea to the charges, counsel should consider entering a guilty plea only if some very distinct advantage accrues to the defendant from doing so. Sometimes the prosecutor will agree to accept a plea to a less serious charge than that for which the defendant is being held or will agree to a favorable fine or sentencing disposition at this stage. The final choice of alternatives, between accepting a prosecution offer to dispose of the case at the preliminary arraignment and going on to the criminal court, should be left to the client, for s/he must live with the outcome. When in doubt, counsel should advise against a guilty plea, since a not guilty plea can ordinarily be switched later to a guilty plea with greater freedom and with fewer possible adverse consequences than attend attempts to switch the other way. In all events, counsel should exercise care before recommending disposition of a case at preliminary arraignment. Although in most instances a favorable offer from the prosecutor is motivated by the desire to avoid cluttering up the criminal trial dockets with cases that the prosecutor does not consider important, sometimes it reflects the prosecutor's doubts that s/he can prove any charge against the defendant. See generally Chapter 15 *infra*.

3.18. *Bail*

The preliminary arraignment provides an opportunity to have bail set or reduced, or O.R. allowed, for a client who has not previously been released on bail. Counsel will need to be prepared with facts concerning the defendant's background to support requests for O.R. or for a favorable bail setting or for a bail reduction. When it appears likely that the difference in the amount of bail set will justify the inconvenience of the intervening detention to the defendant, it may be better for counsel who first comes into a case at preliminary arraignment to ask that the case be passed for a few hours or even for a day in order to obtain verified information about a client rather than to proceed with only the information that the client can provide on the spur of the moment without supporting investigation. See generally Chapter 4. Clients left in custody for this purpose should be given the warnings and protections set out in §§ 3.4.2-3.4.6, 3.6 *supra*, and their custodians should be given the admonitions advised in §§ 3.4.6, 3.5, 3.6 *supra*.

D. *Representing Clients Who Are at Large Prior to Preliminary Arraignment: Clients Who Have Been Served with a Summons or Notice to Appear; Clients Who Have Been Released on Stationhouse Bail or O.R.'d at the Police Station*

3.19. *Counsel's Expanded Opportunities and Responsibilities if the Client is At Large Prior to Preliminary Arraignment*

If a client is at large prior to preliminary arraignment – because the client was served with a summons or notice to appear (see §§ 2.2.1, 2.3.1 *supra*) or because an arrested client was released on stationhouse bail or on the client's own recognizance at the police station (see § 3.8

supra) – counsel will need to prepare for the preliminary arraignment just as s/he would in other scenarios discussed in this chapter and in Chapters 10-11 *infra*.

Even if the client was O.R.'d by the police or released after posting stationhouse bond, counsel cannot assume that there is no risk of pretrial detention following preliminary arraignment. In many jurisdictions, it is a common practice for magistrates and judges at preliminary arraignment to set a bond for a previously O.R.'d defendant or to increase the amount of bail for a defendant who posted stationhouse bail. Counsel certainly has a strong argument that the defendant's appearing for court after having been previously released is a compelling reason for maintaining the same conditions of release, but counsel cannot count on persuading the magistrate or judge. Accordingly, counsel needs to prepare for a bail determination at preliminary arraignment just as s/he would in other cases. (See Chapter 4.) Counsel also must advise the client of the risk of detention so that the client has realistic expectations of what may happen in court and can make arrangements for raising additional bail money if needed and for protecting his or her job and fulfilling family obligations in the event of detention.

Cases in which the client is at large prior to arraignment do, however, provide counsel with opportunities that are unavailable in other scenarios discussed in this chapter. Counsel will usually have much more time to prepare for the preliminary arraignment. Accordingly, counsel can conduct a full-scale interview of the client (as discussed in Chapter 6) rather than the more abbreviated initial interviews discussed in §§ 3.21-3.23 *infra*. Ideally, counsel will have the time to begin investigating the case and thereby gather information s/he can use to argue for O.R. or low bail at preliminary arraignment and to inform counsel's witness examinations and arguments at a preliminary examination. Such early investigation also may yield information that counsel can use to try to persuade the prosecutor who will appear at the preliminary arraignment that the prosecution should forego bringing a charge, or should file a lesser charge than s/he might otherwise file, or should agree to some diversion procedure (see § 2.3.6 *supra*). As a result of such investigation, counsel may even be in a position to consider – and to counsel the client about – the advisability of a guilty plea at the preliminary arraignment, which would rarely be the case in other scenarios discussed in this chapter. See § 3.17 *supra*. Counsel needs to move as quickly as possible to take advantage of all of these opportunities because they may be critical to securing the client's release at the preliminary arraignment and a favorable outcome to the case.

E. *Considerations Relating to the First Interview with the Client*

3.20. *Pressures on the First Interview*

In most of the scenarios discussed in this chapter, counsel will not be able to conduct the type of full-scale initial interview of the client that is described in Chapter 6. A lengthy, thorough interview of this sort will often be impossible if counsel first makes contact with the client while s/he is in police custody (section A of this chapter) or while s/he is wanted for arrest (section B) or when s/he is already before the court at preliminary arraignment (section C). Usually the only scenario in which a full-scale interview can be conducted prior to preliminary arraignment is when the client was served with a summons or notice to appear or was released on stationhouse bail or on the client's own recognizance (O.R.) at the police station (section D).

In the scenarios in which counsel is operating under great time pressure, the concerns of thorough preparation will sometimes have to be sacrificed to a need for speed in seeing the client and obtaining from the client some limited information required for an immediate purpose, such as getting bail set. But although it is frequently essential that counsel act quickly, the value of quick action may well be negated if counsel proceeds in ignorance. The first interview with the client is psychologically critical, quite out of proportion to its other functions in the case. The defendant who senses ignorance or disorganization as the characteristic of a previously unknown lawyer, particularly a court-appointed lawyer, is going to have enormous difficulties in ever establishing a satisfactory attorney-client relationship. It is therefore essential for counsel to plan in advance – even if necessarily hurriedly – to deal with the significant questions and decisions s/he is going to be faced with when s/he meets the client for the first time.

3.21. *The Client in Custody*

3.21.1. *Preparing to Address the Client's Concerns and Questions*

A major concern of the client who is in custody shortly after arrest will ordinarily be to obtain release on O.R. or bail quickly. S/he is likely to ask counsel whether and how arrangements can be made to get the client released. Counsel should know as much as possible about the answers to these questions before the initial interview. If counsel is not already familiar with the law and practices of O.R. and bail in the jurisdiction (see Chapter 4), s/he should quickly do the necessary research and make inquiries of an experienced local criminal attorney, a reliable bail bondsman, or a staffer of an available R.O.R. Project. If possible, counsel should already have taken the first steps toward securing the client's release on O.R. or bail (see §§ 3.8.1-3.82 *supra*), except in cases in which these forms of pretrial release are legally unavailable or obviously ill-advised (see § 4.18 *infra*).

A second question that the client will almost invariably ask counsel at the initial interview is what are the penalties for the offense[s] with which the client is charged. If counsel knows the charges, s/he should research the potential penalties in preparation for the interview. If s/he does not know the charges before leaving for the stationhouse, it is a good idea to take copies of the criminal code along so that s/he can look up the penalties when s/he learns the charges from the investigating officer or the desk officer. Recidivist sentencing provisions and enhancement provisions (for "armed" offenses and the like) are complex in many jurisdictions; they are applicable to a wide range of offenses. It is useful for counsel to have a photocopy of these provisions at hand or else ready access to them on a tablet or phone or laptop. What counsel *does* know about the case before meeting with the client – the circumstances surrounding the arrest as these have been reported to counsel by the client or another caller on the client's behalf (see §§ 3.3.1, 3.3.2.1 *supra*) – will often inform counsel what other sections of the code are likely to be relevant.

Finally, counsel should prepare for the initial interview by obtaining at least a preliminary notion of the elements of the offense with which the client is charged, so as to be able to take the client's story from the outset with an eye to the relevant issues. And if – without wasting time en route to the stationhouse – counsel can pick up some gum or candy and a pack of cigarettes to leave with the client, that is the kind of thoughtfulness that may pave the way toward a good attorney-client relationship.

3.21.2. *Matters to Cover in the Interview*

Counsel will have a lot of questions to ask the client in their first interview. Particularly important are matters that, if not identified and pursued by defense investigation within a few hours after arrest, may later be undiscoverable or discoverable only at inordinate cost. Seeing a client in custody provides a unique opportunity to explore the circumstances surrounding the client's arrest, any attendant search, and the post-arrest handling of the client by the police, including interrogation, lineups or other identification confrontations, and tests or examinations conducted in the stationhouse. The police personnel involved may still be on the scene where the client can point them out to counsel, or at least the client's memory of their appearance will be fairly fresh. Another high priority is the identification of possible witnesses to the charged offense who can still be located at this time but who may be difficult or impossible to track down later. Inquiry into these and similar urgent matters must be made of the client immediately.

Nevertheless, the interview at this stage had best be kept relatively abbreviated for many reasons, including the client's impatience, counsel's lack of opportunity to prepare, and the absence of guaranteed privacy. An abbreviated initial interview would be directed at the following goals: (a) obtaining a summary description of the facts relating to the offense with which the defendant is charged, particularly its location and any physical characteristics of the place or of objects that should be seen or preserved quickly; (b) discussion of the circumstances surrounding the arrest – whether it was made pursuant to a warrant, whether an accompanying search was made, and the results of any search (see Chapter 25 *infra*); (c) some discussion of defenses that may be available to the client, particularly factual ones, and an identification of possible witnesses, with attention to factors that may require immediate steps to locate them while the trail is relatively fresh; (d) a review of what police activities the client has encountered or observed since the client's arrest, including any abuse, interrogation, viewing by eyewitnesses, physical examinations and tests, and attempts to discuss or implicate the defendant in other crimes (see §§ 3.2 *supra*; Chapters 25-27 *infra*); and (e) thorough exploration of facts that counsel will need in seeking the client's release on O.R. or manageable bail (see §§ 4.4, 4.5, 4.12.3 *infra*).

Before counsel leaves a client in custody, s/he should give the client (or repeat, if s/he has previously given by telephone) all the instructions described in §§ 3.4.2-3.4.5 *supra* for dealing with the police (see § 6.12 *infra*). S/he should have the client inform the police, in counsel's presence, that the client wishes thereafter to communicate with the police and prosecuting authorities only through the medium of counsel. See §§ 3.4.6, 3.6 *supra*. Counsel should then give (or repeat) instructions to the investigating officer not to interrogate the client, seek consents or waivers from the client, conduct any tests or examinations on the client, or exhibit the client for identification in counsel's absence. See §§ 3.4.6, 3.5, 3.6 *supra*. The name, rank, and number of the officer to whom counsel gives these instructions should be noted.

Counsel should also inquire of the client whether s/he has any complaints about his or her present treatment in custody. Major abuses should be investigated immediately (see § 6.10

infra); minor grievances can often be resolved quickly through counsel's mediation with the desk officer, the investigating officer, or the commanding officer at the station. The importance of apparently small matters (for example, securing the return of the client's eyeglasses or medications that were taken away at the time of arrest; arranging the release of cash from the client's property envelope) cannot be overstated: These provide opportunities for counsel to do something visibly positive for the client and thereby win the client's confidence. See §§ 6.3-6.5 *infra*.

3.21.3. *"Rights Card" to Give to a Client in Custody*

It is a wise practice for counsel to make and carry a supply of cards or forms that s/he can give to clients in custody for their use in preserving their rights during police investigation. Such a card may read, for example:

> My lawyer has instructed me not to talk to anyone about my case or anything else and not to answer questions or reply to accusations. On advice of counsel and on the grounds of my rights under the Fifth and Sixth Amendments, I shall talk to no one in the absence of counsel. I shall not give any consents or make any waivers of my legal rights. Any requests for information or for consent to conduct searches or seizures or investigations affecting my person, papers, property, or effects should be addressed to my lawyer, whose name, address, and phone number are _____. I want all communications with the authorities henceforth to be made only through my lawyer. I request that my lawyer be notified and allowed to be present if any identification confrontations, tests, examinations, or investigations of any sort are conducted in my case, and I do not consent to any such confrontations, tests, examinations, or investigations.

The client should be instructed to show this card to any officer or other person who asks the client questions, accuses the client of anything, talks to the client in any way about the case, or starts to examine or exhibit the client while in custody.

Cards of this sort serve four important purposes. First, they enable the client to assert his or her rights even if s/he is unable to remember what they are or what to say in order to claim them. Many clients who are simply given the oral advice suggested in § 6.12 *infra* will forget most of it. Second, they allow the client to make an *express* claim of his or her rights. In some situations, the mere silence of the client may not be sufficient to protect the client's interests fully. See §§ 26.8, 26.20, 39.10 subdivision (I) *infra*. Also, as a practical matter, it may be difficult for the client psychologically to maintain silence in situations that seem to call for some response; the response of flashing the card gives the client something to *do* to relieve this tension. Third, the card makes it easier for the defense to prove in court that the client claimed his or her rights and waived none of them. Any lawyer who has seen a police witness flash a "*Miranda* card" in the courtroom appreciates the probative force of a written record in the inevitable disputes about what was said between officers and arrestees behind the closed doors of a stationhouse. Defense counsel should attempt to give the client something of an even break in this swearing contest. Fourth, the card gives the client a sense of reassurance in his or her capacity to handle the often frightening experience of confronting police investigators in confinement, and it also gives the client an added ground for confidence in counsel's professional ability and concern.

3.22. *The Wanted Client*

In the case of a client who is wanted but unapprehended (discussed in section B of this chapter), there may be time and opportunity for a thorough initial interview, covering all of the matters mentioned in §§ 6.1-6.6, 6.8-6.10, 6.12, and the relevant portions of the interview checklist in § 6.15 *infra*. But often the likelihood of the client's imminent arrest will make it impractical to conduct such an extensive interview.

If a more rushed interview is necessary, counsel should concentrate upon (1) the facts surrounding the offense for which the client is wanted, including both the facts that would support a charge against the client and the facts relevant to possible defenses against that charge; (2) the client's attitude toward surrendering voluntarily (see §§ 3.11-3.11.1 *supra*); (3) the specific arrangements that can be made for a voluntary surrender and for the client's prompt release on bail or recognizance thereafter or for the client's protection while in custody if prompt release appears unlikely (see §§ 3.10-3.12 *supra*); (4) advice to the client regarding his or her rights in custody following either a voluntary surrender or arrest and how the client should behave in custody in order to assert and preserve those rights (see §§ 3.4.2-3.4.6 *supra*; § 6.12 *infra*); and (5) the client's attitude toward contesting guilt, on the one hand, or acknowledging guilt and either beginning plea negotiations or attempting to obtain the dropping or reduction of charges by an appeal to police or prosecutorial discretion, on the other hand (see §§ 15.8-15.13 and §§ 8.1-8.6 *infra*, respectively).

Whether the interview is thorough or has to be abbreviated, a primary emphasis should be placed upon the facts and considerations relevant to those decisions immediately facing counsel and the client, identified in §§ 3.11-3.11.2 *supra*. Before the interview counsel should have obtained from the police as much information as possible about the nature of the charges and the police version of the facts underlying them. These should be discussed with the client for the purpose of determining whether there are any factual defenses or equitable considerations that might persuade the police or a prosecutor not to proceed with the client's arrest but to drop charges. If that outcome appears unlikely, the next questions on the agenda are whether, when, and under what conditions to arrange a voluntary surrender. Next come the questions whether, following surrender, the client ought to make a statement to the police or otherwise cooperate with their investigation and whether, before or immediately after the client's surrender (or arrest), counsel should commence plea bargaining with the prosecutor.

Obviously, in an interview that explores these subjects, counsel will need to know and to tell the client the specific penalties for the offense[s] with which the client is, or is likely to be, charged. Even more in the case of the wanted client than in the case of the just-arrested client (see § 3.21.1 *supra*), counsel will be expected to come into the interview with this information in hand. Counsel will also need to be conversant with the legal elements of the offense[s]. S/he will need to know the procedures for setting and posting bail, the amounts of bail customarily required, and the availability of O.R. and other forms of conditional release, for the offense[s] in question. See Chapter 4. Finally, counsel should be prepared to advise the client what to expect concerning police procedures following surrender or arrest and how to respond to those procedures. Under no circumstances should a client be permitted to surrender without first being given detailed advice with regard to how s/he should act in custody. See §§ 3.4.2-3.4.5, 3.6 *supra*; § 6.12 *infra*.

3.23. *The Client at Preliminary Arraignment*

3.23.1. *Ensuring That There Is Sufficient Time for An Adequate Interview*

Counsel entering the case at the time of the defendant's first appearance in court (usually at the preliminary arraignment) is particularly likely to be confronted with a drastic curtailment of the opportunity for an initial client interview. Counsel's first task will often be to impress upon the court the necessity for allowing him or her sufficient time to discuss essential matters with the new client. In addition to whatever rights to a continuance and to legal representation at preliminary arraignment may be provided by state law, counsel should invoke the client's federal Sixth and Fourteenth Amendment rights to counsel (see § 3.23.3 *infra*), which guarantee the opportunity for lawyer-client consultation in the course of judicial proceedings when there are "tactical decisions to be made and strategies to be reviewed" (*Geders v. United States*, 425 U.S. 80, 88 (1976)). If counsel is denied ample time for an adequate interview, s/he should object and should resist as strongly as possible being pressed to proceed with the preliminary arraignment.

3.23.2. *Essential Information to Obtain*

Some information relating to the nature of the charge and to the date of the offense will be available from court records (principally the complaint) at the arraignment. Armed with this information, counsel should interview the client to determine what the client knows about the facts of the case; whether s/he thinks that s/he has any available defense and what that might be; whether the client has a history of mental illness or shows any signs of mental unbalance or incomprehension of the court proceedings; and whether the client has a prior criminal record or has other charges presently pending or outstanding. Counsel should also determine from the court record, from the prosecuting officer, or from the client whether bail has been set and in what amount; s/he should ascertain from the client how much bail the client can make; and if bail has not been set or if it is unreasonably or unmanageably high, s/he should obtain from the client all the facts relevant to the setting or reduction of bail. See §§ 4.4, 4.5, 4.11.3 *infra*. These facets of the case are generally most critical to the decisions confronting counsel at the preliminary arraignment. See §§ 3.14-3.18 *supra*; §§ 4.7, 11.1, 11.7, 16.1 *infra*. Their importance varies, however, depending upon the jurisdiction in which counsel is practicing. In many jurisdictions rights not asserted and motions not made prior to or at the preliminary arraignment may be irrevocably forgone. In the absence of firm knowledge about matters that must be handled prior to this arraignment, counsel should seek a continuance pending further research.

3.23.3. *Request for a Continuance*

Requests for a continuance for time to interview, investigate, research, prepare, and subpoena relevant evidence should be predicated upon the defendant's Sixth and Fourteenth Amendment rights to adequate representation by counsel and should be supported by (a) an explicit statement of the circumstances of counsel's belated entry into the case and (b) an explicit representation that counsel is unprepared to protect the client's interests at arraignment at this time. *See, e.g., Routhier v. Sheriff, Clark County*, 93 Nev. 149, 151-52, 560 P.2d 1371, 1372 (1977) ("During the preliminary examination the magistrate, upon defense counsel's demand, directed a prosecution witness to divulge the name of the police informant who allegedly set up and witnessed the transaction which led to the felony charge. However, the magistrate refused to order disclosure of the informant's address. He also refused to continue the examination to permit Routhier to call and interrogate the 'newly discovered' witness. The refusal to grant the continuance is the central issue on appeal. ¶ It is undisputed that the informant was a material witness and, since that name was not disclosed until the preliminary examination was in progress, we hold that the magistrate's failure to grant the continuance was error; the district judge should have so ruled" (citing, *inter alia, Coleman v. Alabama*, 399 U.S. 1 (1970))).

The Sixth and Fourteenth Amendments guarantee the right to counsel at preliminary arraignment (*Rothgery v. Gillespie County*, 554 U.S. 191, 198, 213 (2008); *White v. Maryland*, 373 U.S. 59 (1963) (per curiam); *Arsenault v. Massachusetts*, 393 U.S. 5 (1968) (per curiam); *Coleman v. Alabama, supra; Gerstein v. Pugh*, 420 U.S. 103, 122-23 (1975) (dictum); see § 11.5.1 *infra*); and the right to counsel in any judicial proceeding ordinarily comports the right to have adequate time to enable counsel to prepare to conduct the proceeding (*e.g., Powell v. Alabama*, 287 U.S. 45 (1932); *Hawk v. Olson*, 326 U.S. 271 (1945); *Megantz v. Ash*, 412 F.2d 804 (1st Cir. 1969); *Rastrom v. Robbins*, 440 F.2d 1251 (1st Cir. 1971); *Moore v. United States*, 432 F.2d 730, 735 (3d Cir. 1970) (en banc); *Twiford v. Peyton*, 372 F.2d 670 (4th Cir. 1967); *Garland v. Cox*, 472 F.2d 875 (4th Cir. 1973); *MacKenna v. Ellis*, 263 F.2d 35, 41-44 (5th Cir. 1959); *Gandy v. Alabama*, 569 F.2d 1318 (5th Cir. 1978); *Davis v. Johnson*, 354 F.2d 689 (6th Cir. 1966), *aff'd after remand*, 376 F.2d 840 (6th Cir. 1967); *Linton v. Perini*, 656 F.2d 207 (6th Cir. 1981); *Wolfs v. Britton*, 509 F.2d 304 (8th Cir. 1975); *United States v. King*, 664 F.2d 1171 (10th Cir. 1981)); *United States v. Nguyen*, 262 F.3d 998 (9th Cir. 2001); *Randolph v. Secretary Pennsylvania Department of Corrections*, 5 F.4th 362 (3d Cir. 2021); *State v. Maher*, 305 N.C. 544, 290 S.E.2d 694 (1982); *People v. Suchy*, 143 Mich. App. 136, 371 N.W.2d 502 (1985); *State v. Johnson*, 2021-NCSC-165, 379 N.C. 629, 634, 866 S.E.2d 725, 729 (2021) ("As defendant's request for a continuance before the trial court raised a constitutional issue, we review de novo the constitutional issue. The constitutional guarantees of assistance of counsel and confrontation of one's accusers and adverse witnesses implicitly provide that 'an accused and his counsel shall have a reasonable time to investigate, prepare[,] and present his defense.' . . . 'To establish a constitutional violation, a defendant must show that he did not have [adequate] time to confer with counsel and to investigate, prepare[,] and present his defense.'"); *State v. Tanner*, 2021-00698 (La. 5/23/21), 316 So.3d 826 (Mem), 2021 WL 2201222, at *1 (La. 2021) ("The State should also be mindful that, while the Sixth Amendment primarily guarantees the right to effective counsel, it also includes the right to an attorney who has been given adequate time to prepare for trial."); *Akau v. State*, 144 Hawai'i 159, 439 P.3d 111 (2019); *Commonwealth v. Mackrides*, 255 A.3d 1269 (Table), 2021 WL 2029820 (Pa. Super. 2021); *People v. Cache*, 2021 WL 5371017 (Cal. App. 2021); *People v. Gilbert*, 2022 CO 23, 510 P.3d 538 (Colo. App. 2022); *People v. Costan*, 169 A.D.3d 820, 94 N.Y.S.3d 131 (N.Y. App. Div., 2d Dep't 2019) (suppression hearing); *cf. People v. Williams*, 61 Cal. App. 5th 627, 657, 275 Cal. Rptr. 3d 848, 871 (2021); *Conic v. State,* 2021 Ark. App. 185, 624 S.W.3d 322 (2021). "[T]he denial of opportunity for appointed counsel to confer, to consult with the accused and to prepare his defense, could convert the appointment of counsel into a sham and nothing more than a formal compliance with the Constitution's requirement that an accused be given the assistance of counsel. The Constitution's guarantee of assistance of counsel cannot be satisfied by mere formal appointment." *Avery v. Alabama*, 308 U.S. 444, 446 (1940) (dictum). "We have many times repeated that not only does due process require that a defendant, on trial in a state court upon a serious criminal charge and unable to defend himself, shall have the benefit of counsel, . . . but that it is a denial of the accused's constitutional right to a fair trial to force him to trial with such expedition as to deprive him of the effective aid and assistance of counsel." *White v. Ragen*, 324 U.S. 760, 763-64 (1945).

Despite the useful rhetoric of *Avery* and the authorities just cited, which may be invoked in support of a motion for a continuance, counsel should keep in mind that appellate courts review denials of continuances only under an "abuse of discretion" standard and are slow to find abuse. "Not every restriction on counsel's time or opportunity to investigate or to consult with his client or otherwise to prepare for trial violates a defendant's Sixth Amendment right to counsel. . . . [B]road discretion [is] . . . granted trial courts on matters of continuances; only an unreasoning and arbitrary 'insistence upon expeditiousness in the face of a justifiable request for delay' violates the right to the assistance of counsel." *Morris v. Slappy*, 461 U.S. 1, 11-12 (1983). *See also United States v. Cronic*, 466 U.S. 648, 659-62 (1984); *but see Winston v. Lee*, 470 U.S. 753, 758 n.3 (1985); *Lee v. Kemna*, 534 U.S. 362 (2002), *relief granted on remand*, 2004 WL 1575555 and 2004 WL 1719449 (W.D. Mo. 2004). It is, therefore, imperative to make a detailed factual record both of counsel's unpreparedness and of the justifications for it when requesting a continuance.

Chapter 4

Bail

4.1. *Introduction*

As indicated in § 3.8 *supra*, one of defense counsel's first tasks is to arrange for the arrested client's release from custody as quickly as possible. Immediate steps to free the client on bail or another form of conditional release are outlined in that section. This chapter examines forms of conditional release and their problems in greater detail.

4.2. *Arrest and Conditional Release*

Anglo-American criminal procedure typically calls for an arrest at the outset of prosecution. The purpose of the arrest is to secure the defendant's presence for trial and for punishment in the event of conviction. The assumption underlying arrest is that pretrial detention may be necessary to secure a defendant's presence and that, if necessary, it is authorized.

A qualifying assumption, which evolved early in the history of English criminal procedure and became one of the great rallying points in the long English struggle for individual liberty, is that a defendant *should not* be detained prior to trial if some other less oppressive means of securing the defendant's presence is practicable. *See* I JAMES FITZJAMES STEPHEN, A HISTORY OF THE CRIMINAL LAW OF ENGLAND 233-43 (1883); II FREDERIC POLLOCK & FREDERIC WILLIAM MAITLAND, THE HISTORY OF ENGLISH LAW 584-90 (2d ed., 1968 re-issue of the 1898 edition); IX WILLIAM SEARLE HOLDSWORTH, A HISTORY OF ENGLISH LAW 115-19 (1st ed. 1926); ZECHARIAH CHAFEE, HOW HUMAN RIGHTS GOT INTO THE CONSTITUTION 51-64 (1952). In early English practice an accused was released in the custody of kinsmen, who obliged themselves to assure the accused's presence for trial. As bailees of the accused's body, they were called bails, and when the custom grew of requiring them to post some valuable security for their obligation, the security posted – and the general practice of releasing a defendant on security or bond conditioned upon appearance at trial – came to be called bail. The right of a criminal accused to pretrial release on bail was protected by the celebrated English Habeas Corpus Act of 1679, whose legacy is the Habeas Corpus Clause of the federal Constitution and of many state constitutions. It was reconfirmed by the Bill of Rights of 1689, whose prohibition of excessive bail remains enshrined in the Eighth Amendment and similar state constitutional provisions. Today the bail right is, to some degree, guaranteed by the constitutions and statutes of every American jurisdiction. See § 4.3 *infra*.

Although the constitutions speak only of "bail," their purpose is to approve, if not to require, the defendant's release pending trial on the least onerous conditions likely to assure appearance for trial. *See Holland v. Rosen,* 895 F.3d 272, 291 (3d Cir. 2018). Several different forms of conditional release are currently in use. *Bail* involves the defendant's secured promise to appear. S/he signs a bail bond, in which s/he undertakes to be present for trial (or for some other stage in the criminal proceeding), and s/he posts cash or negotiable securities, or pledges personal or real property, to guarantee the performance of that undertaking. It may be required that another person (a "surety") execute the bond, as a joint obligor, and post or pledge negotiables or personal or real property for the defendant's appearance. Surety companies or bonding companies today perform this service in consideration of a premium (usually about 10 per cent of the face of the bond) regulated by law (and often on condition of the defendant's pledging additional collateral to protect the surety). A defendant may also be released on an unsecured promise to pay a designated sum in default of appearance. This is frequently called *release on his or her own bond*. Or s/he may be released on a simple promise to appear, a practice ordinarily called *release on his or her own recognizance ("R.O.R")* or just *own recognizance ("O.R.")*. Occasionally defendants today are still *released into the custody of some other person*, on the informal assurance of that person (sometimes an attorney) that they will appear. This latter practice is used principally in petty cases and cases involving defendants who are minors. (In the latter type of case, counsel may need to arrange for the parent or other family member to appear at the police station or at court to take custody of the child. Whenever representing a minor, counsel should also be alert to the possibility that local law may allow for transfer of the case to juvenile court. See § 21.7 *infra*.) Other forms of conditional release are noted in §§ 4.3.1, 4.8 *infra*.

The past several decades have seen a progressive evolution away from money bail as the primary form of pretrial release. This movement began as a response to criticisms that jailing indigents who could not afford bail was unfair, counterproductive, and a potential violation of federal and state Equal Protection guarantees. See § 4.6 *infra*. It later broadened into a more general shift from bail to other forms of conditional release, even in the case of defendants who have the wherewithal to post bond or at least to pay a bond premium. Release on recognizance, often coupled with various restrictions on a releasee's behavior (see § 4.10 *infra*) has become widespread, as a matter of routine practice in some localities and on a case-by-case basis in others. More recently, federal and New Jersey statutory reforms have pioneered regimes in which money bail can be demanded only as a last resort, when other forms of pretrial release are found inadequate to guarantee a defendant's appearance for trial and to protect the safety of the public and other individuals. *See* 18 U.S.C. § 3142; N.J. STAT. ANN. § 2A:162-17; *Holland v. Rosen, supra*. In 2021, Illinois became the first jurisdiction to abolish money bail entirely (effective January 1, 2023), replacing it with a system in which (1) all arrested persons are "presumed . . . entitled to release on personal recognizance" pending trial, subject to prescribed conditions only to the extent "necessary to assure the defendant's appearance in court, assure that the defendant does not commit any criminal offense, and complies with all [other] conditions of pretrial release," and (2) "[d]etention only shall be imposed when it is determined that the defendant poses a specific, real and present threat to a person, or has a high likelihood of willful flight." [2020 Amendment to HB 3653, § 110-1.5(a), (b), (c).]

4.3. *The Right to Bail*

4.3.1. *State Constitutional and Statutory Guarantees of Bail*

Most jurisdictions give arrested persons an absolute right to have bail set for their release on any noncapital charge. This right may be conferred by the state constitution, a state statute, or both.

State constitutions usually guarantee the right to bail expressly, although many of these have an exception for capital cases (see § 4.3.3 *infra*) and some have one or more additional exceptions – *e.g.*, for enumerated crimes such as murder and treason; or for enumerated crimes when combined with a finding of a need for preventive detention due to a risk of danger to others, or when combined with a finding that the defendant was already on bail for another specified offense or was on probation or parole or had previously been convicted of a specified offense.

In many jurisdictions, the state constitution contains both this kind of explicit guarantee of a right to bail and also a prohibition against "excessive bail." Other state constitutions contain only a prohibition against "excessive bail," with no explicit recognition of the underlying right to have bail set. The Eighth Amendment to the Constitution of the United States contains a provision of this latter sort. It may be strongly argued that these "excessive bail" clauses assume and thus compel an underlying right to bail. The historical evidence supports this view (*see* Caleb Foote, *The Coming Constitutional Crisis in Bail*, 113 U. PA. L. REV. 959, 965-89, 1125 (1965)), as does the logic classically expressed by Justice Butler in *United States v. Motlow*, 10 F.2d 657, 659 (Butler, Circuit Justice, 1926): "The provision forbidding excessive bail would be futile if magistrates were left free to deny bail." *See also Hunt v. Roth*, 648 F.2d 1148, 1156-62 (8th Cir. 1981), *vacated as moot sub nom. Murphy v. Hunt*, 455 U.S. 478 (1982) (per curiam); *United States ex rel. Goodman v. Kehl*, 456 F.2d 863, 868 (2d Cir. 1972) (dictum); *Trimble v. Stone*, 187 F. Supp. 483, 484-85 (D. D.C. 1960). Nevertheless, the Supreme Court of the United States has hinted at a contrary conclusion (*United States v. Salerno*, 481 U.S. 739, 752, 753-55 (1987), citing *Carlson v. Landon*, 342 U.S. 524, 544-46 (1952)) and has pointedly reserved the question "whether the Excessive Bail Clause speaks at all to Congress' power to define [that is, to limit] the classes of criminal arrestees who shall be admitted to bail" (*United States v. Salerno, supra*, 481 U.S. at 754). The *Salerno* case upheld the facial constitutionality of federal preventive detention legislation enacted in 1984, providing that "[i]f, after a hearing . . . , [a] . . . judicial officer finds that no condition or combination of conditions [of pretrial release] will reasonably assure . . . the safety of any other person and the community, he shall order the detention of [an arrested] . . . person [charged with a crime of violence, an offense punishable by life imprisonment or death, or an enumerated major drug offense or recidivist felony offense] prior to trial," 18 U.S.C. § 3142(e). The legislation also allows detention without bail upon a finding, under similar procedures, that no condition or combination of conditions of pretrial release "will reasonably assure the appearance of the person" for trial, but this latter provision was not at issue in *Salerno*, which raised only the question whether the Eighth Amendment or the Due Process Clause of the Fifth Amendment "limits permissible government considerations [in the regulation of pretrial release] solely to [preventing the accused's possible] . . . flight." 481 U.S. at 754. The Court held that neither constitutional provision had this effect: that although "[i]n our society liberty is the norm, and detention prior to trial or without trial is the carefully limited exception," *id.* at 755, the exception includes the power to deny pretrial release "when the government musters convincing proof that the arrestee, already indicted or held to answer for a serious crime, presents a demonstrable danger to the community," *id.* at 750. In reaching this result, the Court emphasized that the statute:

(i) "operates only on individuals who have been arrested for a specific category of extremely serious offenses," *id.*;

(ii)   permits pretrial detention only when a judicial officer has found both (a) "probable cause to believe that the charged crime has been committed by the arrestee," *id.*, and (b) "that no conditions of release can reasonably assure the safety of the community or any person," *id.*;

(iii)   requires the latter finding to be made (a) "by clear and convincing evidence," *id.*, and (b) after "a full-blown adversary hearing," *id.*, which (c) must be "prompt," *id.* at 747, and (d) is attended by "numerous procedural safeguards," *id.* at 755 (that is, the arrestee "may request the presence of counsel . . . , may testify and present witnesses in his behalf, as well as proffer evidence, and . . . may cross-examine other witnesses," *id.* at 742);

(iv)   denies the presiding judge "unbridled discretion in making the detention determination," but rather specifies "the considerations relevant to that decision," which "include the nature and seriousness of the charges, the substantiality of the government's evidence against the arrestee, the arrestee's background and characteristics, and the nature and seriousness of the danger posed by the suspect's release," *id.* at 742-43;

(v)   provides that a decision to detain (a) must be supported by "written findings of fact and a written statement of reasons for [the] . . . decision," *id.* at 752, and (b) is subject to "expedited appellate review," *id.* at 743;

(vi)   restricts "the maximum length of pretrial detention . . . by . . . stringent time limitations," *id.* at 747; and

(vii)   meanwhile "requires that detainees be housed in a 'facility separate, to the extent practicable, from persons awaiting or serving sentences or being held in custody pending appeal,'" *id.* at 748.

See also Hilton v. Braunskill, 481 U.S. 770, 778-79 (1987) (endorsing *Salerno*); *Foucha v. Louisiana*, 504 U.S. 71, 80-82 (1992) (discussing *Salerno* at length); *Zadvydas v. Davis*, 533 U.S. 678, 691 (2001) (*Salerno* "not[es] that 'maximum length of pretrial detention is limited' by 'stringent' requirements"); *Jennings v. Rodriguez*, 138 S. Ct. 830 (2018) (declining to address the question whether aliens detained pending deportation proceedings have a constitutional right to bail; Justice Breyer's dissent for three Justices argues at length that "[t]he Due Process Clause foresees eligibility for bail as part of 'due process.' . . . Bail is 'basic to our system of law.' . . . ¶ The Eighth Amendment reinforces the view that the Fifth Amendment's Due Process Clause does apply. The Eighth Amendment forbids '[e]xcessive bail.' It does so in order to prevent bail being set so high that the level itself (rather than the reasons that might properly forbid release on bail) prevents provisional release. . . . That rationale applies *a fortiori* to a refusal to hold any bail hearing at all. Thus, it is not surprising that this Court has held that both the Fifth Amendment's Due Process Clause and the Eighth Amendment's Excessive Bail Clause apply in cases challenging bail procedures.") (138 S. Ct. at 862). Even at this, the Court in *Salerno* appeared to concede the possibility that the statute "might operate unconstitutionally under some conceivable set of circumstances" (*id.* at 745) and upheld it only against a "facial challenge" (481 U.S. at

748). *Compare Schall v. Martin*, 467 U.S. 253 (1984) (rejecting a Due Process challenge to a somewhat less protective New York statute authorizing "brief pretrial detention" of juveniles charged with delinquency (*id.* at 263), upon "a finding of a 'serious risk' that [the] . . . juvenile may commit a crime before [the trial] . . . date" (*id.*)), *with State v. Wein*, 244 Ariz. 22, 24, 417 P.3d 787, 789 (2018) (reading *Salerno's* authorization of pretrial detention narrowly and striking down state statutory and state constitutional provisions that "prohibit bail for all persons charged with sexual assault if 'the proof is evident or the presumption great' that the person committed the crime, without considering other facts that may justify bail in an individual case. We hold that these provisions, on their face, violate the Fourteenth Amendment's Due Process Clause. Unless the defendant is accused of committing sexual assault while already admitted to bail on a separate felony charge, the trial court must make an individualized bail determination before ordering pretrial detention."), *and Lopez-Valenzuela v. Arpaio*, 770 F.3d 772, 780-92 (9th Cir. 2014) (en banc) (holding that the Due Process Clause invalidates an Arizona constitutional amendment making illegal immigrants ineligible for bail when charged with serious felony offenses), *and Brangan v. Commonwealth*, 477 Mass. 691, 80 N.E.3d 949 (2017) ("[W]here a judge sets bail in an amount so far beyond a defendant's ability to pay that it is likely to result in long-term pretrial detention, it is the functional equivalent of an order for pretrial detention, and the judge's decision must be evaluated in light of the same due process requirements applicable to such a deprivation of liberty." *Id.* at 705, 80 N.E.3d at 963. A "judge may not consider a defendant's alleged dangerousness in setting the amount of bail, although a defendant's dangerousness may be considered as a factor in setting other conditions of release. Using unattainable bail to detain a defendant because he is dangerous is improper." *Id.* at 706, 80 N.E.3d at 963-64.). *Salerno* is a poorly reasoned decision that deserves little respect from state courts called upon to construe state constitutional "excessive bail" and "due process" clauses; and its reasoning in support of preventive detention has no application at all, of course, to state constitutions that contain the common form of clause making all noncapital offenses bailable. *See, e.g., Ex Parte Colbert*, 805 So.2d 687, 688-89 (Ala. 2001) (denial of bail based on the defendant's history of violence and the consequent danger to the community violated the state constitution's guarantee of "an absolute right to bail in all noncapital cases"); *In re Underwood*, 9 Cal. 3d 345, 348, 350, 508 P.2d 721, 722, 724, 107 Cal. Rptr. 401, 402, 404 (1973) (then-existing state constitutional guarantee of bail [later modified] was not subject to "a 'public safety' exception" for "persons dangerous to themselves or others"); *State v. Sutherland*, 329 Or. 359, 364, 369, 987 P.2d 501, 503, 505 (1999) (state statute authorizing pretrial detention for enumerated crimes violated the state constitutional provision "*requir[ing]* courts to set bail for defendants accused of crimes other than murder or treason"); *Simms v. Oedekoven*, 839 P.2d 381, 383, 385 (Wyo. 1992) (state statute "which permits detention without bail for an accused who is found to be a flight risk" violates the state constitutional provision that "provides without equivocation that 'all persons shall be bailable'").

State statutes also generally allow a right to bail in all noncapital cases. Most of these statutes give discretion to magistrates and courts of record to set the amount of bail in individual cases, but some contain schedules listing the amounts of bail for specified offenses or authorize courts to promulgate such schedules. A number of jurisdictions have statutes that permit the police to release arrested persons on "stationhouse bail" in specified classes of cases, usually summary offenses and misdemeanors. See § 3.8.2 *supra*. These statutes also may leave the amount of bail to be determined by police discretion or may contain – or authorize the judicial promulgation of – bail schedules. (Even in the absence of express statutory authorization, some courts formally or informally promulgate bail schedules to which they conform as a matter of routine in fixing bail, although they will make exceptions in unusual circumstances. Police also frequently operate pursuant to administratively promulgated schedules, and they are less willing than courts to vary the bail-setting in individual cases.) Statutes ordinarily regulate procedures relating to bail in more detail than do constitutional provisions: They identify the authorities who are empowered to set and to receive bail; prescribe proceedings for the setting and posting of bail; describe the allowable forms of bonds; limit charges for commercial bonds and otherwise regulate commercial bail bondsmen; and define the conditions and procedures for forfeiture. Some statutes authorize release on the defendant's own recognizance (see §§ 3.8.1, 4.2 *supra*) or upon the defendant's deposit of the bail-premium amount with the clerk of court (see § 4.8 *infra*). For example, the Federal Bail Reform Act, 18 U.S.C. §§ 3141-3142(d), governing federal criminal cases outside the District of Columbia, provides for a scheme of pretrial release in which money bail is not to be demanded unless other forms of conditional release (R.O.R., release in the custody of a responsible person, travel or residence restrictions, a bail-premium deposit) are not reasonably likely to secure the defendant's appearance at trial (*see, e.g., United States v. Mobley*, 720 Fed. Appx. 441 (10th Cir. 2017); *Bell v. Wolfish*, 441 U.S. 520, 536 n.18 (1979) (dictum)). *Cf.* D.C. CODE § 23-1321.

Even in jurisdictions where statutes provide a broad right to bail (and where legislatures do not follow the lead of Congress by enacting "preventive detention" legislation), the fact that the state constitution also guarantees the bail right may be significant for several reasons. First, it is invariably in the constitutions, not the statutes, that the prohibition of "excessive bail" is found. These constitutional "excessive bail" clauses are the defendant's essential protection both against exorbitant judicial bail-setting in individual cases and against exorbitant amounts prescribed by legislative bail schedules. Second, the statutes regulating bail may be unconstitutional in other respects than exorbitance. For example, the Supreme Court of the United States has construed the Eighth Amendment's Excessive Bail Clause to require that the amount of bail be set in each individual case, in view of the circumstances of each individual defendant, in an amount no greater than is necessary to assure the defendant's appearance for trial. *Stack v. Boyle*, 342 U.S. 1 (1951). (This aspect of *Stack* was reaffirmed in *United States v. Salerno*, 481 U.S. at 754 (dictum) ("when the government has admitted that its only interest is in preventing flight, bail must be set by a court at a sum designed to ensure that goal, and no more").) Under this construction, uniform bail schedules for offenses, although widely used, appear to be *per se* unconstitutional. *See Ackies v. Purdy*, 322 F. Supp. 38 (S.D. Fla. 1970). Or a statute prohibiting defendants' release on bail in specified categories of cases (such as "where the proof is evident or the presumption great") may be invalid because it conflicts with a constitutional provision which only authorizes and does not require the denial of bail in such cases. *See People v. Davis*, 337 Mich. App. 67, 972 N.W.2d 304 (2021). Third, where state laws define the jurisdiction of some appellate courts in terms of the presence of a constitutional question, the constitutional status of the bail right permits a resort to those courts that would be unavailable if the right were merely statutory.

4.3.2. *Federal Constitutional Rights to Bail in State Criminal Cases*

For several reasons it would be significant if the federal Constitution guaranteed a right to bail (or a right against excessive bail, see § 4.3.1 *supra*) in state criminal cases. First, the substance of such a right would be determined by federal case law, including decisions such as *Stack v. Boyle*, 342 U.S. 1 (1951), which may be more liberal than state-law bail decisions. Second, a defendant's federal constitutional rights to bail could be enforced not merely in the state courts but (after exhaustion of state-court remedies) by *habeas corpus* in the federal courts. See § 4.14 *infra*.

It has not yet been authoritatively decided whether a state criminal defendant does have any federal constitutional rights in connection with bail. *See Simon v. Woodson*, 454 F.2d 161, 164-65 (5th Cir. 1972). But strong arguments are available to support such rights:

Beginning with *Mapp v. Ohio*, 367 U.S. 643 (1961), the Supreme Court has followed a course of decisions that has "incorporated" into the Due Process Clause of the Fourteenth Amendment – and thus made binding upon the state courts – virtually all of the other major criminal procedure guarantees of the Bill of Rights. *See Gideon v. Wainwright*, 372 U.S. 335 (1963) (Sixth Amendment right to counsel): *Mincey v. Arizona*, 437 U.S. 385 (1978) (Fourth Amendment right against unreasonable search and seizure); *Malloy v. Hogan*, 378 U.S. 1 (1964) (Fifth Amendment privilege against self-incrimination); *Pointer v. Texas*, 380 U.S. 400 (1965) (Sixth Amendment right of confrontation): *Klopfer v. North Carolina*, 386 U.S. 213 (1967) (Sixth Amendment right to speedy trial); *Washington v. Texas*, 388 U.S. 14 (1967) (Sixth Amendment right to compulsory process); *Duncan v. Louisiana*, 391 U.S. 145 (1968) (Sixth Amendment right to jury trial); *Benton v. Maryland*, 395 U.S. 784 (1969) (Fifth Amendment right against double jeopardy); *Coolidge v. New Hampshire*, 403 U.S. 443 (1971) (Fourth Amendment right against unreasonable searches and seizures; under *Mapp*, the same doctrinal rules that govern federal cases apply to state criminal cases); *McDonald v. City of Chicago*, 561 U.S. 742 (2010) (Second Amendment right to keep and bear arms); *Timbs v. Indiana*, 139 S. Ct. 682 (2019) (Eighth Amendment right against excessive fines); *see generally Faretta v. California*, 422 U.S. 806, 818 (1975); *Herring v. New York*, 422 U.S. 853, 856-57 (1975); *McDonald v. City of Chicago, supra*, 561 U.S. at 759-66. The guarantee of the Eighth Amendment against excessive bail eminently qualifies for similar incorporation for several reasons:

(a) Historically, the struggle to establish the right to bail was central in the evolution of the English conception of the liberty of the citizen. *See* Caleb Foote, *The Coming Constitutional Crisis in Bail*, 113 U. PA. L. REV. 959, 965-68 (1965). See also § 4.2 *supra*. Thus the right fairly falls within even the most conservative test for incorporation: It is a "'principle of justice so rooted in the traditions and conscience of our people as to be ranked as fundamental,'" *Palko v. Connecticut*, 302 U.S. 319, 325 (1937).

(b) The bail right is universally recognized in American state constitutions. *See* Comment, *Determination of Accused's Right to Bail in Capital Cases*, 70 YALE L.J. 966, 977 (1961); *Comment*, 7 VILL. L. REV. 438, 450 (1962). This, too, is evidence of its fundamental quality. *Cf. Ferguson v. Georgia*, 365 U.S. 570, 574-83 (1961); *Baldwin v. New York*, 399 U.S. 66, 72-73 (1970).

(c) The Supreme Court has recognized that "[u]nless this right to bail before trial is preserved, the presumption of innocence, secured only after centuries of struggle, would lose its meaning." *Stack v. Boyle*, 342 U.S. 1, 4 (1951). And the Court has already held that the other principal reflection of the presumption of innocence – the right against conviction except on proof beyond a reasonable doubt (*see Taylor v. Kentucky*, 436 U.S. 478, 483-86 (1978)) – is embodied in the Fourteenth Amendment (*e.g.*, *In re Winship*, 397 U.S. 358 (1970); *Ivan V. v. City of New York*, 407 U.S. 203 (1972); *Mullaney v. Wilbur*, 421 U.S. 684 (1975); *Sandstrom v. Montana*, 442 U.S. 510 (1979); *Francis v. Franklin*, 471 U.S. 307 (1985); *Jackson v. Virginia*, 443 U.S. 307 (1979) (dictum); *cf. Cool v. United States*, 409 U.S. 100, 104 (1972); *County Court of Ulster County v. Allen*, 442 U.S. 140, 156 (1979) (dictum); *and see Estelle v. Williams*, 425 U.S. 501, 503 (1976) (dictum). *But see Bell v. Wolfish*, 441 U.S. 520, 532-33 (1979)).

(d) The Supreme Court has incorporated the Eighth Amendment's prohibition of cruel and unusual punishments (*Robinson v. California*, 370 U.S. 660 (1962); *Furman v. Georgia*, 408 U.S. 238 (1972); *Woodson v. North Carolina*, 428 U.S. 280 (1976)) and the Eighth Amendment's prohibition of excessive fines (*Timbs v. Indiana*, 139 S. Ct. 682 (2019)). The reasoning of *Washington v. Texas*, 388 U.S. 14, 17-18 (1967), suggests that this circumstance favors the incorporation of the balance of the amendment as well. *And see Timbs v. Indiana, supra,* 139 S. Ct. at 687: "Under the Eighth Amendment, '[e]xcessive bail shall not be required, nor excessive fines imposed, nor cruel and unusual punishments inflicted.' Taken together, these Clauses place 'parallel limitations' on 'the power of those entrusted with the criminal-law function of government.'"

(e) Several federal decisions have concluded, albeit usually in dictum, that the Fourteenth Amendment does incorporate the Excessive Bail Clause of the Eighth. *Hunt v. Roth*, 648 F.2d 1148, 1155-56 (8th Cir. 1981), *vacated as moot sub nom. Murphy v. Hunt*, 455 U.S. 478 (1982) (per curiam); *Meechaicum v. Fountain*, 696 F.2d 790 (10th Cir. 1983); *United States ex rel. Keating v. Bensinger*, 322 F. Supp. 784, 786 (N.D. Ill. 1971); *Sistrunk v. Lyons*, 646 F.2d 64, 66-71 (3d Cir. 1981) (dictum); *Henderson v. Dutton*, 397 F.2d 375, 377 n.3 (5th Cir. 1968) (dictum); *Pilkinton v. Circuit Court*, 324 F.2d 45, 46 (8th Cir. 1963) (dictum); *Goodine v. Griffin*, 309 F. Supp. 590, 591 (S.D. Ga. 1970) (dictum); *Hernandez v. Heyd*, 307 F. Supp. 826, 828 (E.D. La. 1970) (dictum), and cases cited. And the Supreme Court has cited the *Pilkinton* case, with apparent approval, for the proposition that "the Eighth Amendment's proscription of excessive bail has been assumed to have application to the States through the Fourteenth Amendment" (*Schilb v. Kuebel*, 404 U.S. 357, 365 (1971) (dictum)). *See also McDonald v. City of Chicago*, 561 U.S. 742, 764 & n.12 (2010) (dictum) (including the Eighth Amendment's "prohibition against excessive bail" among "the provisions of the Bill of Rights" that the Court has recognized as incorporated in the Fourteenth Amendment, and citing *Schilb v. Kuebel*, 404 U.S. 357 (1971) for this proposition); *Baker v. McCollan*, 443 U.S. 137, 144 n.3 (1979) (dictum); *Simpson v. Miller*, 241 Ariz. 341, 387 P.3d 1270 (2017) ("Arizona's Constitution and laws forbid bail for defendants accused of sexual conduct with a minor under age fifteen when the proof is evident or the presumption great that the defendant committed the crime. Because that prohibition is not narrowly focused to protect public safety, we hold that it violates the Fourteenth Amendment's due process guarantee." *Id*. at 344, 387 P.3d at 1273. "The right to bail in non-capital cases is rooted in American and Arizona law." *Id*. at 345, 387 P.3d at 1274. "The bail provisions enacted through Proposition 103 are similar in some respects to those upheld in [*United States v.*] *Salerno*[, 481 U.S. 739 (1987), discussed in § 4.3.1 *supra*]. Like the Bail Reform Act, they are limited to specific serious crimes, they are intended to protect public safety by preventing defendants from committing future crimes, and they require a full-blown adversarial hearing. But unlike the hearing in *Salerno* to determine that a defendant posed a danger to specific individuals or the community at large, the hearing at issue here determines only 'if the proof is evident or the presumption great' that the person committed the offense charged. It does not consider whether the defendant poses a danger to others."); *State v. Wein*, 244 Ariz. 22, 417 P.3d 787 (2018), summarized in § 4.3.1 *supra*.

Even if the Eighth Amendment bail right were not incorporated, the Due Process Clause of the Fourteenth Amendment would require the allowance of some form of conditional release in cases in which pretrial incarceration adversely affected the defendant's right to a fair trial – for example, when it impeded his or her ability to locate witnesses important to the defense. *See Kinney v. Lenon*, 425 F.2d 209 (9th Cir. 1970); *Jennings v. Rodriguez*, 138 S. Ct. 830, 862 (2018) (Justice Breyer, dissenting) ("[b]ail . . . 'permits the unhampered preparation of a defense'"). Pretrial incarceration can be shown to prejudice a defendant's defense in a broad range of ways and situations covering many criminal cases. *See* Foote, *supra* at 1137-51. And protracted pretrial detention itself "raises a constitutional [due process] issue at some point" (*United States v. Gonzales Claudio*, 806 F.2d 334, 339 (2d Cir. 1986)). *See, e.g., United States v. Cardona*, 2020 WL 1905308 (D. Mass. 2020); *United States v. Omar*, 157 F. Supp. 3d 707 (M.D. Tenn. 2016); *United States v. Ailemen*, 165 F.R.D. 571 (N.D. Cal. 1996) (a magistrate's report that includes a thorough canvass of the federal caselaw).

Whether or not any underlying substantive federal constitutional right to bail exists, it seems plain that "[a]s to . . . offenses . . . for which a state has provided a right of bail it may not, any more than as to other substantive or procedural benefits under its criminal law system, engage in such administration as arbitrarily or discriminatorily to effect denial or deprivation of the right to a particular accused" (*Mastrian v. Hedman*, 326 F.2d 708, 711 (8th Cir. 1964) (dictum)). *Accord, Atkins v. Michigan*, 644 F.2d 543, 549-50 (6th Cir. 1981); *cf. Connecticut Board of Pardons v. Dumschat*, 452 U.S. 458, 463 (1981) (dictum) ("[a] state-created right can, in some circumstances, beget yet other rights to procedures essential to the realization of the parent right"); *Board of Pardons v. Allen*, 482 U.S. 369 (1987). This is so because the Due Process and Equal Protection Clauses of the Fourteenth Amendment require that all state-law rules be fairly and even-handedly applied (*e.g., Schware v. Board of Bar Examiners*, 353 U.S. 232 (1957)), particularly when liberty is at stake in their application (*e.g., Papachristou v. City of Jacksonville*, 405 U.S. 156, 170-71 (1972); *Humphrey v. Cady*, 405 U.S. 504, 512 (1972)). "Even in applying permissible standards, officers of a State cannot [adversely affect a citizen's interests] . . . when there is no basis for their finding that he fails to meet these standards, or when their action is invidiously discriminatory." *Schware v. Board of Bar Examiners*, *supra*, 353 U.S. at 239. *See, e.g., Frederickson v. Landeros*, 943 F.3d 1054 (7th Cir. 2019). These concepts forbid the deprivation of liberty by factually baseless or legally arbitrary applications of any legal rules. *See, e.g., Thompson v. City of Louisville*, 362 U.S. 199 (1960); *Shuttlesworth v. City of Birmingham*, 382 U.S. 87, 93-95 (1965); *Wolff v. McDonnell*, 418 U.S. 239, 556-67 (1974); *Goss v. Lopez*, 419 U.S. 565, 574- 76 (1975); *Vitek v. Jones*, 445 U.S. 480, 488-89 (1980); *Hicks v. Oklahoma*, 447 U.S. 343, 346-47 (1980); *Logan v. Zimmerman Brush Co.*, 455 U.S. 422, 428-36 (1982). As applied to the question of bail, they entitle a state criminal defendant to have his or her "motion for bail . . . handled without 'arbitrariness' and 'discriminatoriness'" (*United States ex rel. Keating v. Bensinger*, *supra*, 322 F. Supp. at 787) and require federal constitutional relief if "[w]hat the state court did [in administering its local bail rules can be shown to] . . . be beyond the range within which judgments could rationally differ in relation to the apparent elements of the situation" (*Mastrian v. Hedman*, *supra*, 326 F.2d at 711 (dictum)).

The implications of the Equal Protection Clause of the Fourteenth Amendment for pretrial incarceration of indigents who cannot afford to post bail are considered in § 4.6 *infra*.

4.3.3. *Capital Cases*

In many jurisdictions some or all capital cases are excepted from the right to bail. A common constitutional and statutory formulation provides that all offenses are bailable except capital offenses where the proof is evident or the presumption great. Some courts read this archaic language to mean capital cases in which the death penalty is likely to be imposed. *See, e.g., Application of Peters*, 351 P.2d 1020 (Okla. Crim. App. 1960); *Ex parte Sierra*, 514 S.W.2d 760, 761 (Tex. Crim. App. 1974); *Trammell v. State*, 284 Ala. 31, 32, 221 So.2d 390, at 390 (1969). Others read it more literally to mean capital cases in which the prosecution has strong evidence. *See In re Verden*, 291 Mo. 552, 563, 237 S.W. 734, 737 (Mo. 1922) ("the proper test is whether the evidence before the judge on the hearing for bail tends strongly to show guilt of a capital offence"). Some jurisdictions require the prosecution to demonstrate the defendant's guilt of a capital charge by a preponderance of the evidence in order to justify the denial of bail. *See Fry v. State*, 990 N.E.2d 429 (Ind. 2013) (collecting the authorities from numerous jurisdictions) The least demanding standard is that of jurisdictions which require only that the prosecution establish "probable cause. *Harnish v. State*, 531 A.2d 1264 (Maine 1987). *But see Commonwealth v. Talley*, 265 A.3d 485, 522-26 (Pa. 2021) and cases cited ("[U]nder Article I, Section 14 [of the Pennsylvania Constitution] 'proof is evident or presumption great' constitutes its own unique standard, one that lies in the interstice between probable cause and proof beyond a reasonable doubt. Unlike the *prima facie* standard, it requires both a qualitative and quantitative assessment of the evidence adduced at the bail hearing. This dual inquiry finds ample support in extra-jurisdictional caselaw. Following Pennsylvania's lead, thirty-five other States adopted a constitutional provision providing for a right to bail conditioned upon a showing that the 'proof is evident or presumption great.' Of the twenty-two jurisdictions in which courts have interpreted the phrase, appellate courts in twenty States have held that the government's burden is more stringent than probable cause but less demanding than proof beyond a reasonable doubt, and that the inquiry includes a qualitative assessment of the evidence. . . . ¶ 'Proof is evident or presumption great' calls for a substantial quantity of legally competent evidence, meaning evidence that is admissible under either the evidentiary rules, or that is encompassed in the criminal rules addressing release criteria. . . . The Commonwealth's 'feel[ings]' about evidence that it 'may be able to introduce' are not relevant considerations. . . . And, because a court must be able to evaluate the quality of the evidence, it also cannot rely upon a cold record or untested assertions alone. . . . ¶ When the Commonwealth seeks to deny bail, the quality of its evidence must be such that it persuades the bail court that it is substantially more likely than not that the accused is nonbailable, which is just to say that the proof is evident or the presumption great. In making its case, the Commonwealth cannot satisfy its burden of persuasion solely 'by stacking inference upon inference.' . . . Nor can 'the connection between the evidence' and what it seeks to prove be 'conjectural.' . . . Rather, the combination of the evidence and inferences must be 'reasonable, credible, and of solid value.' . . . ¶ If the balance of the evidence is rife with uncertainty, legally is incompetent, requires excessive inferential leaps, or lacks any indicia of credibility, it simply is not evident proof, nor can it give rise to a great presumption, that the accused is not entitled to bail."). Under any of these constructions, defense counsel should be alert to the potential of an application for bail as a discovery device for learning what the prosecution's evidence is.

The invalidation of some forms of the death penalty as cruel and unusual punishments in *Furman v. Georgia*, 408 U.S. 238 (1972), spawned considerable litigation over the meaning of the term *capital* in state laws making "capital" offenses non-bailable. Several courts held that offenses punishable by a constitutionally unenforceable death penalty are no longer "capital"; hence they are bailable. Other courts held that offenses remain "capital" and non-bailable if they are statutorily punishable by death, even though the death penalty may no longer be constitutionally imposed. The confusion was compounded when most pre-*Furman* death-penalty States reenacted the death penalty after *Furman* in various forms thought to escape the prohibition of that decision. Some of these States added laws providing capital punishment for restricted classes of offenses without repealing the old, broader death penalty statutes struck down by *Furman*. Decisions of the Supreme Court of the United States in 1976 and 1978 sustained various forms of the new statutes and invalidated others. See §§ 48.14-48.15 *infra*. These decisions have engendered still a third wave of death penalty laws in some States. Since 1984, capital-punishment statutes have been repealed in a handful of jurisdictions and declared unconstitutional under state constitutions in another handful. What offenses are now "capital" in States in these various postures is questionable, particularly where older statutes were not technically repealed by the newer ones or where the newer statutes authorize capital punishment only upon a finding of enumerated "aggravating circumstances" in addition to the elements of the offense. *Compare, e.g., State v. Johnson*, 61 N.J. 351, 294 A.2d 245 (1972), and cases cited *and Commonwealth v. Truesdale*, 449 Pa. 325, 296 A.2d 829 (1972), and cases cited *with Hudson v. McAdory*, 268 So.2d 916 (Miss. 1972), *and People ex rel. Dunbar v. District Court of the Eighteenth Judicial District*, 179 Colo. 304, 500 P.2d 358 (1972); *and Ex parte Bynum*, 294 Ala. 78, 312 So.2d 52 (1975), and cases cited; *and see State v. Ameer*, 2018-NMSC-030, 458 P.3d 390 (N.M. 2018) and cases cited ("There being no death penalty statutorily authorized for any crimes committed on or after July 1, 2009, following legislative repeal of the last vestiges of capital punishment for offenses committed on or after that date, and Defendant having been charged with committing his offense after that date, the detention order based on the capital offenses exception must be reversed." (*Id.* at 405.) "Our research reveals that no case in any jurisdiction . . . has held that a constitutional provision guaranteeing bail in all but "capital offenses" will permit bail to be denied after a *legislative* abolition of capital punishment for an offense, as has occurred in New Mexico." *Id.* at 395.).

There are few reported cases addressing the question whether a defendant is eligible for bail when s/he is charged with an offense that is capitally punishable under a State's current law but the prosecutor has indicated that the death penalty will not be sought. These cases answer the question in the negative (*State v. Moyers*, 214 So.3d 1147 (Ala. 2014); *Maniscalco v. Superior Court*, 19 Cal. App. 4th 60, 23 Cal. Rptr. 2d 322 (1993); *compare State v. Clark*, 2011 WL 2163544 (Del. Super. Ct. 2011) (granting bail in such a case with the acquiescence of the prosecution)), but that result is questionable in jurisdictions where the courts have held that constitutional invalidation of the death penalty makes a formerly capital offense non-capital for bail purposes. The logic of the latter cases is that the reason for the preclusion of bail in "capital" cases is that the prospect of the death penalty creates a special incentive for flight. *See State v. Johnson, supra*, 61 N.J. at 360, 294 A.2d at 250 ("The underlying motive for denying bail in capital cases was to secure the accused's presence at the trial. In a choice between hazarding his life before a jury and forfeiting his or his sureties' property, the framers of the many State Constitutions felt that an accused would probably prefer the latter. But when life was not at stake and consequently the strong flight-urge was not present, the framers obviously regarded the right to bail as imperatively present."). That logic is equally applicable when the prosecutor has taken the death penalty off the table.

It is important to note that constitutional and statutory provisions excepting designated capital offenses from the general right to bail are often construed as merely denying an absolute right to bail, not as disallowing release on bail. In the designated cases magistrates and judges may still admit a defendant to bail in their discretion. *E.g., In re Losasso*, 15 Colo. 163, 24 P. 1080 (1890); *State v. Arthur*, 390 So.2d 717 (Fla. 1980); *State v. Pichon*, 148 La. 348, 86 So. 893 (1921); *Ex parte Bridewell*, 57 Miss. 39 (1879); *In re Corbo*, 54 N.J. Super. 575, 149 A.2d 828 (1959) (dictum), *cert. denied*, 29 N.J. 465, 149 A.2d 859 (1959); *In re West*, 10 N.D. 464, 88 N.W. 88 (1901); *Ex parte Dexter*, 93 Vt. 304, 107 A. 134 (1919).

4.4. *Amount of Bail*

If not set by a master bail schedule, the amount of bail is determined by the bail-setting authority (police officer, magistrate, judge, or court clerk by designation of the judge) in light of a number of factors. Most important are (1) the nature of the offense (seriousness of the possible penalty, aggravating circumstances that indicate the defendant's dangerousness if released, and so forth), (2) the defendant's character and reputation (and particularly criminal record), (3) the defendant's financial assets (how much money has to be tied up in bail to keep the defendant in place), (4) the defendant's employment status and record (as an indication of reliability and of the defendant's dependence on staying where s/he is; it is also significant that the defendant may lose his or her job if jailed for a period), (5) the defendant's family status and roots in the community (length of time the defendant has resided in the location, presence of family there, other factors indicating inconvenience of flight, such as residence in public housing, receipt of social security or public assistance payments, and so forth).

The Supreme Court of the United States has said, construing the Eighth Amendment, that "when the government['s] . . . only [asserted] interest is in preventing flight, bail must be set by a court at a sum designed to ensure that goal, and no more" (*United States v. Salerno*, 481 U.S. 739, 754 (1987) (dictum)), and that an individualized inquiry into the circumstances of each defendant is required in setting the amount (*Stack v. Boyle*, 342 U.S. 1 (1951)). *See also, e.g., DuBose v. McGuffey*, 2022-Ohio-8, 168 Ohio St.3d 1, 3, 195 N.E.3d 951, 955 (2022) ("[a] bail amount that is 'higher than an amount reasonably calculated to' ensure the accused's presence in court is 'excessive'"; the Ohio Supreme Court affirms an order of an intermediate appellate court from $1,500,000 to $500,000 the bail set for a defendant charged with robbery-murder); *Reeves v. State*, 923 N.E.2d 418, 421-22 (Ind. App. 2010) (under the excessive bail clause of the Indiana Constitution, "'[b]ail is excessive where the amount set represents a figure higher than that reasonably calculated to assure the accused party's presence at trial"; the trial court must "set

Reeves' bail in an amount that takes into account the statutory factors identified in . . . [the relevant bail statute] and . . . explain its rationale for the bail imposed in relation to those standards"); *Robinson v. State*, 95 So.3d 437, 438-39 (Fla App. 2012) ("Evidence of Robinson's financial status, attendance at court proceedings, family ties, long-term residence in the community and employment history was sufficient to show that bail in the amount of $500,000 [set on two charges of aggravated child abuse, a first-degree felony] was excessive. While Robinson has some financial resources, the record demonstrates that $500,000 is well beyond his financial abilities. Because '[b]ail should not be fixed in so excessive an amount as to preclude the probability of the accused's being able to furnish it,' . . . we conclude that the bail is excessive, particularly given his ties to the community and employment."); *Ex parte Martinez-Velasco*, 666 S.W.2d 613 (Tex. App. 1984) ("[a]lthough bail should be set sufficiently high to give reasonable assurance that the accused will comply with the undertaking, the amount of bail should not be set so high as to amount to an instrument of oppression" (*id.* at 615); in a prosecution for delivery of cocaine having a street value of between two and three million dollars, the Court of Appeals finds in an uncontested order that bail set at $750,000 is excessive: "Although the appellant is a citizen of Ecuador, he has resided and conducted his business in the United States for the past thirteen years, and has apparently established strong friendship ties in the United States, even if he has no family here. The evidence shows that he has no prior criminal record and that no threats, force, or violence were involved in his apprehension and arrest. *Id.* at 617.). Bail set according to substantive standards (for example – as is common – by reference solely to the heinousness of the offense) or by procedures (such as use of a bail schedule or refusal of a hearing to consider the defendant's background) that are inconsistent with these canons is unconstitutional (*see Ackies v. Purdy*, 322 F. Supp. 38 (S.D. Fla. 1970)) and can be challenged by *habeas corpus* or any other method of review prescribed by local law. The use of pretrial risk assessment instruments to predict a defendant's likelihood of flight or arrest on new charges is usefully criticized in PRETRIAL JUSTICE INSTITUTE, THE CASE AGAINST PRETRIAL RISK ASSESSMENT INSTRUMENTS (November 2020), *available at:* https://university.pretrial.org/HigherLogic/System/DownloadDocumentFile.ashx?DocumentFile Key=7a99ffae-f435-4645-5748-4dab1cc56653&forceDialog=0.

As a general matter, the police, magistrates, and many trial-court judges wholly disregard the constitutional conception of bail expressed in *Stack v. Boyle*. Instead of determining the amount of bail in the light of particularized factors relevant to the likelihood of flight and the "function of bail" as an "assurance of the presence of an accused" at trial (342 U.S. at 5), they consider only the seriousness of the offense charged and the defendant's prior criminal record in setting the bail figure. Appellate courts are far more likely to make bail determinations under the proper *Stack v. Boyle* standards. See § 3.8.3 *supra*. This means that defense counsel must gather factual information pertinent to both the standards that will likely be used at the lower levels (circumstances of the charged offense; defendant's criminal history) and the standards that will likely be used on any appeals (defendant's stability in the community, general reliability, and financial situation). Counsel should be prepared to vary the emphasis on these several factors as s/he moves from court to court.

The next section consists of a form for use in obtaining a sworn statement from a defendant detailing the factors pertinent to setting the amount of bail. It may be used in affidavit form to support a motion for bail, for reduction of bail, or for release on recognizance. Counsel should also attempt to support its assertions by proof from sources other than the defendant, since many judges distrust the interested statements of an accused in these matters. Compare §§ 48.11-48.12 *infra*.

4.5. *Questionnaire for Obtaining Information Pertinent to Bail from Criminal Defendants*

The following questionnaire is designed principally for counsel's use in obtaining from a client information pertinent to the amount of bail that should be set. Counsel can, however, easily convert the questionnaire into a form that can be notarized and submitted to a magistrate or judge in support of an application for bail in a manageable amount or for reduction of bail or for release on nominal bail or on recognizance, as is appropriate. Of course, caution must be observed not to use the form in this fashion if a client's answers may supply incriminating information or investigative leads that are not already known to the police and the prosecution. The same caution suggests that ordinarily the details of the charged offense should be obtained from the arresting or prosecuting officer, not from the defendant. See § 8.3.1 *infra*.

Questionnaire for Bail Information

Name: _____   Age: _____

Address: _____
        Number   Street

_____
       City   State   Zip Code

Phone number: _____

Email address: _____

E-text / website contact information: _____

How long have you lived at your current address? _____

Do you own your home?   ☐ Yes   ☐No

Do you have a home mortgage? ☐ Yes   ☐No

How much is the mortgage? _____

What's the value of the home? _____

[Check ☐ if this value is from tax assessment]

[if not, what's the source of the estimated value? _____]

Is any other person a co-owner?   ☐ Yes ☐ No

If so, who? _____

Do you rent your home?   ☐ Yes   ☐No

How much is your rent? _____

Is any past due rent now unpaid? ☐ Yes   ☐No

How much? _____

Is this public housing?   ☐ Yes   ☐No

Do you receive any kind of rent assistance or subsidy? ☐ Yes ☐No

Source and amount: _____

Address immediately before present address:

_____

Number   Street

_____

City   State   Zip Code

How long did you live at that address? _____

Are you currently employed?   ☐ Yes   ☐No

Job: _____

Kind of work

Employer's name: _____

Employer's Phone number: _____

Employer's Email address: _____

Employer's E-text / website contact information: _____

Name of supervisor if other than employer: _____

Supervisor's Phone number: _____

Supervisor's Email address: _____

Supervisor's E-text / website contact information: _____

Address of workplace:

_____

Number   Street

_____

City   State   Zip Code

Employer's address if other than workplace:

_____

Number   Street

_____

City   State   Zip Code

How long have you been employed by this employer? _____

   Amount now earned per week: _____ (In stating the amount earned per
   week, use the take-home pay *after* all deductions from gross wages, including automatic
   deductions for child support and debts as well as for taxes, FICA, and medical insurance
   premiums.)

   Is your job waiting for you if you are released at this time? ☐ Yes ☐ No

Job immediately before present job:

_____

   Kind of work

Employer's name: _____

   Employer's Phone number: _____

   Employer's Email address: _____

   Employer's E-text / website contact information: _____

Name of supervisor if other than employer: _____

   Supervisor's Phone number: _____

   Supervisor's Email address: _____

   Supervisor's E-text / website contact information: _____

   Between what dates were you employed by this employer?

_____ to _____
        Month   Year   Month   Year

Reason for leaving that employment: _____

If you are currently unemployed: Since when have you been unemployed? _____

   Are you receiving unemployment compensation? ☐ Yes ☐ No

   Amount: _____

Describe any efforts you've been making to get work: _____

Are you enrolled as a student in any school? ☐ Yes ☐ No

Name of school: _____

Address of school:

_____
   Number   Street

_____
      City   State   Zip Code

Contact person at school (teacher, principal, dean, or other):

    Name: _____

    Title: _____

    Phone number: _____

    Email address: _____

    E-text / website contact information: _____

If you are a student and have a part-time job, please fill out all of the employment information requested at pages Q-2 and Q-3 above; and write "PART-TIME" in the space between "Are you currently employed?" and the "Yes" check box in line 5 on page Q-2.

Assets: Do you own:

    ◊ any land/buildings/property other than your home?   ☐ Yes   ☐ No

    Describe the property: _____

    Value: _____

    Is any other person a co-owner?   ☐ Yes ☐ No

    If so, who? _____

If you have a mortgage or mortgages, please fill out the information under "Debts" on page Q-6.

[Assets – continued]   Do you own:

◊ an automobile or other vehicle?   ☐ Yes ☐ No

Value: _____

Is any other person a co-owner?   ☐ Yes ☐ No

If so, who? _____

If you have a mortgage or installment payment arrangement, please fill out the information under "Debts" on page Q-6.

◊ a bank account?   ☐ Yes ☐ No   Amount: _____

Is any other person a co-owner?   ☐ Yes ☐ No

If so, who? _____

◊ other property?   ☐ Yes ☐ No

Describe the property: _____

Value: _____

Is any other person a co-owner?   ☐ Yes ☐ No

If so, who? _____

Do you have any other source of income than your job?
(include social security, if any)   ☐ Yes   ☐ No

_____
Nature of source   Amount

_____
Nature of source   Amount

Debts and Liabilities: Do you have

◊ home mortgage(s)? ☐ Yes ☐ No

    Creditor: _____   Amount: _____

    Any unpaid past due amount? ☐ No ☐ Yes: _____

◊ debt(s) on vehicle mortgage or installment purchase of a vehicle? ☐ Yes ☐ No

    Creditor: _____   Amount: _____

    Any unpaid past due amount? ☐ No ☐ Yes: _____

◊ debt(s) on installment purchase of other property? ☐ Yes ☐ No

    Item: _____ Creditor: _____ Amount: _____

      Any unpaid past due amount? ☐ No   ☐ Yes: _____

    Item: _____ Creditor: _____ Amount: _____

      Any unpaid past due amount? ☐ No   ☐ Yes: _____

◊ other debt(s)? ☐ Yes ☐ No

    Creditor: _____   Amount: _____

      Any unpaid past due amount? ☐ No   ☐ Yes: _____

    Creditor: _____   Amount: _____

      Any unpaid past due amount? ☐ No   ☐ Yes: _____

◊ other unpaid account(s)?

    Creditor: _____   Amount: _____

      Nature of account or obligation: _____

    Creditor: _____   Amount: _____

      Nature of account or obligation: _____

Do you have court-ordered obligations to support any person? ☐ Yes ☐ No

_____
Name of person   Relationship   Amount ordered

    Any unpaid past due amount? ☐ No ☐ Yes: _____

_____
Name of person   Relationship   Amount ordered

    Any unpaid past due amount? ☐ No ☐ Yes: _____

Do you have any other dependents? ☐ Yes ☐ No

_____
Name of person   Relationship   Indicate any fixed obligation

_____
Name of person   Relationship   Indicate any fixed obligation

Does your family receive public assistance or welfare payments? ☐ Yes ☐ No

    Agency from which payments received: _____

    Amount: _____

Do you have any medical or health condition requiring medication or treatment? ☐ Yes ☐ No

    Nature of condition: _____

    Nature and frequency of treatment: _____

    Cost of treatment: _____

    Source of funds relied on to pay costs: _____

    Medical personnel to contact for confirmation:

        Name: _____
        Title: _____
        Phone number: _____
        Email address: _____
        E-text / website contact information: _____

Does any member of your family have any medical or health condition requiring medication or treatment?   ☐ Yes ☐ No

Nature of condition: _____

Nature and frequency of treatment: _____

Cost of treatment: _____

Source of funds relied on to pay costs: _____

Medical personnel to contact for confirmation:

      Name: _____
      Title: _____
      Phone number: _____
      Email address: _____
      E-text / website contact information: _____

Do you have any illness or physical disability that makes it difficult to get around? ☐ Yes ☐ No

    If yes, describe it:

_____

_____

    Medical personnel to contact for confirmation:

      Name: _____
      Title: _____
      Phone number: _____
      Email address: _____
      E-text / website contact information: _____

Does anyone in your immediate family have any such illness or disability? ☐ Yes ☐ No

    If yes, describe it:

_____

_____

Medical personnel to contact for confirmation:

Name: _____

Title: _____

Phone number: _____

Email address: _____

E-text / website contact information: _____

With what members of your family – and/or other individuals – do you now live?

Name	Age	Relationship

Name	Age	Relationship

Do you have any other family in this city/town? ☐ Yes ☐ No

county? ☐ Yes ☐ No

State? ☐ Yes ☐ No

Name	Age	Relationship

Address: Number	Street	City	State

Name	Age	Relationship

Address: Number	Street	City	State

Present criminal charge(s): _____

_____

Criminal record (all *arrests*, from latest to earliest, *including juvenile arrests*, in all jurisdictions):

For each episode that is not currently pending:

Date of arrest: _____

Jurisdiction (city and State): _____

Charge(s): _____

Disposition if not by court: _____

Plea (guilty or not guilty or *nolo* or insanity; if guilty or *nolo*, of what charges):_____

Court disposition (conviction or acquittal or other: if conviction, of what charges):_____

Sentence:_____

Date sentence imposed: _____

   If sentence was incarceration:

      Length of time served: _____

Institution[s] in which time was served: _____

Client's prison number: _____

If released on parole:
      Release date: _____
      Has parole term ended? □ Yes □ No – time remaining: _____
      Parole officer:
            Name: _____
            Phone number: _____
            Email address: _____
            E-text / website contact information: _____

Were any charges of parole violation ever made?   □ Yes □ No
            Date of charge: _____
            Nature of violation charged: _____
            Disposition: _____
            Current Status:_____

If sentence was probation:

    Date probation began: _____

    Length of probationary term: _____

    Probationary conditions: _____

    Has probation period ended? □ Yes □ No – time remaining: _____

    Probation officer:

        Name: _____

        Phone number: _____

        Email address: _____

        E-text / website contact information: _____

    Were any charges of probation violation ever made?   □ Yes   □ No

    Date of charge: _____

    Nature of violation charged: _____

    Disposition: _____

    Current Status:_____

Are there any outstanding warrants for you on any criminal charge or for any violation of parole or probation?   □ Yes   □ No

    Details: _____

               _____

Pending criminal matters (all *arrests*, from latest to earliest, *including juvenile arrests*, in all jurisdictions):

For each episode that is currently pending:

Date of arrest: _____

Jurisdiction (city and State): _____

Charge(s): _____

    Name of Court: _____

    Docket Number:_____

    Current status:_____

    Released on own recognizance or bond?   □ Yes   □ No

    Released on bail?   □ Yes   □ No

        Amount of bail posted: _____

        Form of bail posted: _____

        If commercial bonding company:

            Bonding company name: _____

            Contact person's name: _____

            Phone number: _____

Email address: _____

E-text / website contact information: _____

Is a lawyer representing you on this charge?

Name of attorney: _____

Street address of attorney: _____

Phone number of attorney: _____

Email address of attorney: _____

E-text / website contact information for attorney: _____

_____

Your Signature

4.6. *Bail and the Indigent*

The anomaly and injustice of jailing people simply because they are too poor to make bail have been abundantly argued in the literature since the mid-1960's. *See, e.g.*, DANIEL J. FREED & PATRICIA M. WALD, BAIL IN THE UNITED STATES: 1964 (A Report to the National Conference on Bail and Criminal Justice, Washington, D.C., May 27-29, 1964) (1964); JOHN S. GOLDKAMP, TWO CLASSES OF ACCUSED – A STUDY OF BAIL AND DETENTION IN AMERICAN JUSTICE (1979); PAUL B. WICE, FREEDOM FOR SALE – A NATIONAL STUDY OF PRETRIAL RELEASE (1974); Richard A. Cohen, *Wealth, Bail, and the Equal Protection of the Laws*, 23 VILL. L. REV. 977 (1978); Caleb Foote, *The Coming Constitutional Crisis in Bail*, 113 U. PA. L. REV. 959, 1125 (1965), reprinted in CALEB FOOTE, ed., STUDIES ON BAIL 181-283 (1966); Lee Silverstein, *Bail in the State Courts – A Field Study and Report*, 50 MINN. L. REV. 621 (1966). Cognizant of the economic discrimination worked by the requirement of money bail as a condition of pretrial release, courts are increasingly tending to relax the necessity for posting "good" bail if an accused has a stable background in the community. *See, e.g.*, *In re Humphrey*, 11 Cal. 5th 135, 143, 482 P.3d 1008, 1012-13, 276 Cal. Rptr. 3d 232, 237-38 (2021) (recognizing "a 'clear and growing movement' that is reexamining the use of money bail as a means of pretrial detention" and holding that the "common practice of conditioning freedom solely on whether an arrestee can afford bail is unconstitutional. Other conditions of release – such as electronic monitoring, regular check-ins with a pretrial case manager, community housing or shelter, and drug and alcohol treatment – can in many cases protect public and victim safety as well as assure the arrestee's appearance at trial. What we hold is that where a financial condition is nonetheless necessary, the court must consider the arrestee's ability to pay the stated amount of bail – and may not effectively detain the arrestee 'solely because' the arrestee 'lacked the resources' to post bail. . . . ¶ . . . In order to detain an arrestee [on the theory that "no option other than refusing pretrial release can reasonably vindicate the state's compelling interests"] a court must first find by clear and convincing evidence that no condition short of detention could suffice and then ensure the detention otherwise complies with statutory and constitutional requirements."); *see also In re Humphrey*, 19 Cal. App.5th 1006, 1041-45, 228 Cal. Rptr. 3d 513, 538-42 (Cal. App. 2018), *aff'd and ordered precedential in relevant part by In re Humphrey*, 472 P.3d 435, 268 Cal. Rptr. 3d 119 (Mem.) (Cal. 2020); *Brangan v. Commonwealth*, 477 Mass. 691, 707, 80 N.E.3d 949, 964-65 (2017) ("[W]here. . . it appears that the defendant lacks the financial resources to post the amount of bail set by the judge, such that it will likely result in the defendant's long-term pretrial detention, the judge must provide findings of fact and a statement of reasons for the bail decision, either in writing or orally on the record. The statement must confirm the judge's consideration of the defendant's financial resources, explain how the bail amount was calculated, and state why, notwithstanding the fact that the bail amount will likely result in the defendant's detention, the defendant's risk of flight is so great that no alternative, less restrictive financial or nonfinancial conditions will suffice to assure his or her presence at future court proceedings."); *State v. Pan*, 345 Conn. 922, 291 A.3d 82 (2022), quoted in § 4.15.1 *infra*; *Lee v. Lawson*, 375 So.2d 1019 (Miss. 1979); *State v. Blake*, 642 So.2d 959 (Ala. 1994).

In a number of jurisdictions, the traditional money bail system has been modified by legislation or court rule to require consideration of less onerous conditions of pretrial release where those are found sufficient, on a case-by-case basis, to assure the defendant's appearance for trial. *See, e.g.*, SMITH-HURD ILL. COMP. STAT. ANN. ch.725, § 5/110-2 (effective January 25, 2023) ("When from all the circumstances the court is of the opinion that the defendant will appear as required either before or after conviction and the defendant will not pose a danger to any person or the community and that the defendant will comply with all conditions of bond . . ., the defendant may be released on his or her own recognizance. . . . A failure to appear as required by such recognizance shall constitute an offense . . . . ¶ This Section shall be liberally construed to effectuate the purpose of relying upon contempt of court proceedings or criminal sanctions instead of financial loss to assure the appearance of the defendant, and that the defendant will not pose a danger to any person or the community and that the defendant will comply with all conditions of bond. Monetary bail should be set only when it is determined that no other conditions of release will reasonably assure the defendant's appearance in court, that the defendant does not present a danger to any person or the community and that the defendant will comply with all conditions of bond."); ME. REV. STAT. ANN. title 15, § 1026 (dictating a similar preference for R.O.R. over monetary bail); CONN. SUPER. CT. RULE [PRACTICE BOOK 1998] § 38-4 [implementing CONN. GEN. STAT. § 54-64a] ("(a) Except as provided in subsection (c) of this section, when any defendant is presented before a judicial authority, such authority shall, in bailable offenses, promptly order the release of such defendant upon the first of the following conditions of release found sufficient to reasonably ensure the defendant's appearance in court: ¶ (1) The defendant's execution of a written promise to appear without special conditions, ¶ (2) The defendant's execution of a written promise to appear with nonfinancial conditions; ¶ (3) The defendant's execution of a bond without surety in no greater amount than necessary; ¶ (4) The defendant's deposit with the clerk of the court of an amount of cash equal to 10 percent of the amount of the surety bond set . . . ¶ (5) The defendant's execution of a bond with surety in no greater amount than necessary. . . ." Subsection (c) governs cases of "a serious felony or a family violence crime" and provides a similar list of alternatives and a similar directive to set the least onerous alternative but adds that this alternative must "reasonably ensure" both "the defendant's appearance in court and that the safety of any other person will not be endangered. . . ."); 18 U.S.C. § 3142 (providing a similar roster of alternative release conditions and directing the use of the least restrictive alternative); TEX. CODE CRIM. PRO. art. 17.028, amendment effective January 1, 2022 ("(a) Without unnecessary delay but not later than 48 hours after a defendant is arrested, a magistrate shall order, after individualized consideration of all circumstances and of the factors required by Article 17.15(a), that the defendant be: ¶ (1) granted personal bond with or without conditions; ¶ (2) granted surety or cash bond with or without conditions; or ¶ (3) denied bail in accordance with the Texas Constitution and other law. ¶ (b) In setting bail under this article, the magistrate shall impose the least restrictive conditions, if any, and the personal bond or cash or surety bond necessary to reasonably ensure the defendant's appearance in court as required and the safety of the community, law enforcement, and the victim of the alleged offense.").

In major metropolitan areas there are agencies (generally called R.O.R. Projects or Bail Projects) that interview defendants shortly after arrest and investigate their backgrounds to determine whether they are eligible under the agency's standards of stability for a recommendation to the court that they be released on recognizance. The courts generally follow these recommendations. Counsel representing an indigent defendant should contact such an agency, if one exists, for help in getting the client released. Concerning the need for caution against the use of pretrial risk assessment instruments to predict a defendant's likelihood of flight or arrest on new charges, *see* THE CASE AGAINST PRETRIAL RISK ASSESSMENT INSTRUMENTS cited in § 4.4 *supra*.

On the level of legal right, an argument for the proposition that detention of an indigent in default of bail which s/he cannot make violates the Habeas Corpus Clause, the Eighth Amendment, the Due Process and Equal Protection Clauses of the Fourteenth Amendment, and cognate state constitutional guarantees is fully developed in the Foote article cited above, and may be pressed on *habeas corpus* in state and federal courts. Professor Foote's Equal Protection arguments, in particular, draw strong support from subsequent decisions condemning the incarceration of indigents in default of payment of fines imposed upon conviction (*Williams v. Illinois*, 399 U.S. 235 (1970); *Tate v. Short*, 401 U.S. 395 (1971); *In re Antazo*, 3 Cal. 3d 100, 473 P.2d 999, 89 Cal. Rptr. 255 (1970); *Robertson v. Goldman*, 179 W. Va. 453, 455-56, 457, 369 S.E.2d 888, 890-91, 892 (1988)). *Cf. Bearden v. Georgia*, 461 U.S. 660 (1983); *Estelle v. Williams*, 425 U.S. 501, 505-06 (1976) (dictum). In 1977, those arguments prevailed in a path-breaking decision, *Pugh v. Rainwater*, 557 F.2d 1189 (5th Cir. 1977), *rev'd en banc*, 572 F.2d 1053 (5th Cir. 1978). Although the Former Fifth Circuit *en banc* disapproved on narrow grounds the original panel decision in *Pugh* holding Florida's pretrial release system facially unconstitutional, a majority of the court endorsed the panel's essential conclusion that "[t]he incarceration of those who cannot [afford to post money bail], without meaningful consideration of other possible alternatives [that is, other forms of pretrial release], infringes on both due process and equal protection requirements" (572 F.2d at 1057). "We have no doubt that in the case of an indigent, whose appearance at trial could reasonably be assured by one of the alternate forms of release, pretrial confinement for inability to post money bail would constitute imposition of an excessive restraint" and hence violate the Constitution (*id.* at 1058). A new Florida pretrial release rule, promulgated while the *Pugh* case was pending on appeal, was adjudged "subject to constitutional interpretation and application" (*id.*) because it did not appear to the *en banc* majority that "the automatic setting of money bails [which had been Florida's prior practice] will continue [under the new rule] and that the unnecessary and therefore constitutionally interdicted pretrial detention of indigents will be the inevitable result" (*id.*). The majority pointed to a drafting committee note on the new Florida rule which said that the rule "'leaves it to the sound discretion of the judge to determine *the least onerous form of release* which will still insure the defendant's appearance'" (*id.* at 1058 n.8 (emphasis added by the court)) and expressed confidence that the Florida courts would follow this interpretation of the rule in view of "the absence of a constitutional alternative" (*id.*). In a civil rights suit challenging the constitutionality of bail practices in Harris County, Texas, a federal district court judge ruled that the county's "consistent and systematic policy and practice of imposing secured money bail as de facto orders of pretrial detention in misdemeanor cases" violates the Equal Protection and Due Process Clauses, and the court granted a preliminary injunction enjoining county judges and officials from "detaining misdemeanor defendants who are otherwise eligible for release but cannot pay a secured financial condition of release." *ODonnell v. Harris County*, 251 F. Supp. 3d 1052, 1059-60 (S.D. Tex. 2017). The Court of Appeals affirmed the district "court's rulings that the County's bail system violates both due process and equal protection" (*ODonnell v. Harris County*, 892 F.3d 147, 157 (5th Cir. 2018), *overruled on another issue in Daves v. Dallas County, Texas*, 22 F.4th 522 (5th Cir. 2022) (en banc)). The Circuit's due process analysis proceeded from the premise that "[l]iberty interests protected by the due process clause can arise from two sources, 'the Due Process Clause itself and the laws of the States.' . . . ¶ . . . Texas state law creates a right to bail that appropriately weighs the detainees' interest in pretrial release and the court's interest in securing the detainee's attendance[:] . . . . state law forbids the setting of bail as an 'instrument of oppression.' Thus, magistrates may not impose a secured bail solely for the purpose of detaining the accused. And, when the accused is indigent, setting a secured bail will, in most cases, have the same effect as a detention order." (*Id.* at 157-58.) Under "the current [Harris County] procedures[,] . . . secured bail orders are imposed almost automatically on indigent arrestees. Far from demonstrating sensitivity to the indigent misdemeanor defendants' ability to pay, Hearing Officers and County Judges almost always set a bail amount that detains the indigent. . . . [This] procedure does not sufficiently protect detainees from magistrates imposing bail as an 'instrument of oppression.'" (*Id.* at 159.) Turning to the issue of equal protection, the Circuit observed that "the Supreme Court has found that heightened scrutiny is required when criminal laws detain poor defendants *because of* their indigence" (*id.* at 161). Under *San Antonio Independent School District v. Rodriguez*, 411 U.S. 1, 20 (1973), "indigents receive a heightened scrutiny where two conditions are met: (1) 'because of their impecunity they were completely unable to pay for some desired benefit,' and (2) 'as a consequence, they sustained an absolute deprivation of a meaningful opportunity to enjoy that benefit'" (*id.* at 162). "Both aspects of the *Rodriguez* analysis apply here: indigent misdemeanor arrestees are unable to pay secured bail, and, as a result, sustain an absolute deprivation of their most basic liberty interests— freedom from incarceration. Moreover, this case presents the same basic injustice: poor arrestees in Harris County are incarcerated where similarly situated wealthy arrestees are not, solely because the indigent cannot afford to pay a secured bond. Heightened scrutiny of the County's policy is appropriate." *Id.* "The [district] court's thorough review of empirical data and studies found that the County had failed to establish any 'link between financial conditions of release and appearance at trial or law-abiding behavior before trial.'" *Id.*

> "In sum, the essence of the district court's equal protection analysis can be boiled down to the following: take two misdemeanor arrestees who are identical in every way – same charge, same criminal backgrounds, same circumstances, etc. – except that one is wealthy and one is indigent. Applying the County's current custom and practice, with their lack of individualized assessment and mechanical application of the secured bail schedule, both arrestees would almost certainly receive identical secured bail amounts. One arrestee is able to post bond, and the other is not. As a result, the wealthy arrestee is less likely to plead guilty, more likely to receive a shorter sentence or be acquitted, and less likely to bear the social costs of incarceration. The poor arrestee, by contrast, must bear the brunt of all of these, simply because he has less money than his wealthy counterpart. The district court held that this state of affairs violates the equal protection clause, and we agree." (*Id.* at 163.)

See also ODonnell v. Salgado, 913 F.3d 479, 481-82 (5th Cir. 2019) (per curiam) (explaining that after the district court's issuance of a new injunction and denial of a stay (321 F. Supp. 3d 763 (S.D. Tex. 2018), and 328 F. Supp. 3d 643 (S.D. Tex. 2018)), and the circuit court's subsequent granting of the State's motion for a stay pending appeal (900 F.3d 220 (5th Cir. 2018)), "[t]he original appellants were defeated in the November 2018 elections and, by operation of law, were replaced by the current appellants, who, on January 7, 2019, moved for voluntary dismissal of the appeal," and the appeal was "'dismissed as of January 07, 2019, pursuant to appellants' motion'"; but the circuit court denies the appellees' motion to vacate the court's prior opinion on the stay pending appeal, even though "there is not, and never will be, a merits panel," because "[t]his panel took great strides to decide the motion for stay correctly" and "published the opinion after making certain it was a correct rendition of the law and the facts," and, "[a]s a result of the dismissal, the published opinion granting the stay is this court's last statement on the matter and, like all published opinions, binds the district courts in this circuit"). *See also McNeil v. Community Probation Services*, LLC, 2019 WL 633012, at *13-*15 (M.D. Tenn. 2019), *ruling on an unrelated issue aff'd*, 945 F.3d 991 (6th Cir. 2019) (in a case challenging the practice of detaining indigents who are unable to pay the bail amount pre-printed on violation-of-probation arrest warrants for misdemeanor probationers, and in which the bail amounts are determined prior to arrest and "without an opportunity for the arrestee to be heard or present evidence regarding ability to pay or alternative conditions of release," the district court conducts a thorough review of the federal caselaw and concludes that: "to survive an equal protection challenge, the distinction created by the current bail system . . . between indigent misdemeanor probation arrestees and other arrestees must be narrowly tailored to meet a compelling governmental interest. ¶ . . . Defendants have not shown that arrestees who are able to pay the secured bail amount are more likely to appear for their revocation hearing and less likely to commit crime. . . . ¶ Given the complete absence of evidence supporting the bail system in Giles County for indigent misdemeanor probation arrestees, the Court concludes that, even if it applied the rational basis standard, Defendants have failed to show the current bail system rationally furthers a legitimate governmental interest. . . . ¶ As to Plaintiffs' due process claim, the Court is persuaded . . . that the system of setting secured bail as described in the stipulated facts is constitutionally deficient in failing to provide notice and an opportunity for the arrestee to be heard, and for failing to provide oral or written findings regarding the arrestee's ability to pay, alternative conditions of release, and the need for pre-revocation detention"; it therefore issues a preliminary injunction against "detaining any person on misdemeanor probation . . . based on a secured financial condition of release (*i.e.,* secured bail amount) on a violation of probation warrant if the warrant is not accompanied by a record showing that the condition (*i.e.,* secured bail amount) was imposed after: (1) notice to the arrestee and an opportunity to be heard by an appropriate judicial officer; and (2) findings by that judicial officer concerning the arrestee's ability to pay, alternatives to secured bail, and whether pre-revocation detention is necessary to meet a compelling governmental interest."); *Jones v. City of Clanton*, 2015 WL 5387219, at *4 (M.D. Ala. 2015) ("The use of a secured bail schedule to detain a person after arrest, without a hearing on the merits that meets the requirements of the Fourteenth Amendment regarding the person's indigence and the sufficiency of the bail setting, is unconstitutional as applied to the indigent. Without such a hearing, no person may, consistent with the Fourteenth Amendment, continue to be held in custody after an arrest because the person is too poor to deposit a monetary sum set by a bail schedule. If the government offers release from custody after an arrest upon the deposit of money pursuant to a bail schedule, it cannot deny release from custody to a person, without a hearing regarding the person's indigence and the sufficiency of the bail setting, because the person is unable to deposit the amount specified by the schedule."). *But see Schultz v. Alabama*, 42 F.4th 1298 (11th Cir. 2022) (a 2-1 decision finding no facial violation of equal protection or due process in a bail scheme under which arrested persons who post bail are released immediately – usually within about 90 minutes – but indigents must remain in custody for up to 72 hours pending a release hearing).

4.7. *Procedures for Setting Bail*

When an arrest warrant is issued for a person, the issuing authority usually sets the amount of bail under which the arrestee is to be held. This amount is endorsed on the arrest warrant. If there is no such endorsement or if an arrest is made without a warrant, the police, a magistrate, a judge of the criminal court of record, the court clerk, or more than one of these agencies (depending upon the nature of the offense) may set bail following the arrest, on request of the arrestee or counsel. The amount of bail is inscribed on a charging instrument (often called "a copy of the charge") and recorded in whatever paper or electronic records the bail-setting authority maintains. If an arrest is made in a county other than that in which the offense is charged, the police officer, magistrate, or court at the place of arrest usually has authority to set bail. In any case in which bail has not been set prior to the preliminary arraignment, it is ordinarily set by the magistrate at that arraignment (except for serious offenses that, in some jurisdictions, are not bailable by magistrates but only by courts of record in *habeas corpus* proceedings). See §§ 2.2.3, 2.3.2-2.4.1, 3.18 *supra.*

Procedures for getting bail set before and after the preliminary arraignment are governed by statute, court rule, and local custom, and they vary widely. See § 4.3.1 *supra*. Sometimes counsel is required to obtain a "copy of the charge" from the arresting officers and to present it to a magistrate or judge *ex parte*. Sometimes *habeas corpus* is employed (see § 3.8.3 *supra, and, e.g., DuBose v. McGuffey*, 2022-Ohio-8, 168 Ohio St.3d 1, 4, 195 N.E.3d 951, 955 (2022) ("habeas corpus is the proper vehicle by which to raise a claim of excessive bail in pretrial-release cases")); sometimes, a simple motion for bail with supporting affidavits. Statutory regulation (including applicable bail schedules) should be checked in counsel's jurisdiction to determine the persons who have the authority to set bail and the limitations of authority of each.

4.8. *Types of Bail Allowable*

Three types of bail are ordinarily acceptable: cash or negotiable securities, a surety bond posted by a licensed bonding company, and a real property bond (usually in the form of a deed to property). Whereas cash, securities, and a property deed are returned when the defendant has fulfilled the bail obligation by appearing, the premium paid to a bonding company for the posting of a surety bond is not recoverable. This premium is the surety company's compensation for the risk it incurs in posting its security.

Premiums that companies may charge for bail bonds are usually regulated by statute (about 10 per cent of the face of the bond, or a little more or less depending on the face amount), but the companies are free to agree or refuse to serve any individual and are usually free to impose conditions when they insure a client, such as a pledge of collateral security to hold the company harmless in the event of default.

By statute, in some jurisdictions, a defendant may make bond by depositing the premium amount directly with the clerk of court, recoverable upon appearance. Some premium-deposit statutes authorize or require the clerk to retain a small portion of the deposit as an "administration fee." The Supreme Court of the United States has found such a practice constitutionally unobjectionable. *Schilb v. Kuebel*, 404 U.S. 357 (1971).

4.9. *Choice Among the Types of Bail*

If cash, securities, or a property bond can be posted by the client without hardship, these will be the least costly forms of bail in the long run. However, counsel will want to consider the impact on the disposition of the case which might result from the disclosure that the defendant has the means to make bond in these forms. Particularly in gambling, drug-dealing, prostitution, counterfeiting, and automobile theft cases – and in others involving the lurking suspicion of organized crime – a defendant who posts a sizable cash bond may find that that fact has leaked to the trial judge or jury, with expectable prejudice. Still worse, the fact will likely be considered by the judge at sentencing. In any event, if there is any chance that the defendant will want to dispose of his or her real property in the near future, a property bond should not be used. And if the defendant is one who cannot be easily contacted about appearing or if the chance of the defendant's failure to appear is more than slight, a bonding company is probably the best choice.

Bail bondsmen are located near most police stations and are usually available around the clock. Before undertaking to secure the appearance of a client, they will want to know about the client's employment, permanence of residence, criminal record, family status, and the nature of the charge. Of course, they want some immediate cash, but they frequently accept part payment of their premium at the outset. Because of their continuous contact with the police and their familiarity with local court practices and personnel – as well as their knowledge of institutions and people in the neighborhood surrounding the precinct – bondsmen are often a good source of information, especially on procedures relating to the quick release of an accused. However, they differ widely in their helpfulness, trustworthiness, and crucial matters such as demands for collateral security (see the preceding paragraph). So, when practicable, counsel not familiar with the local bondsmen should inquire of some reputable attorney who knows them.

Counsel should consult local practice concerning the availability of procedures for court deposit of a "premium" amount or fractional portion of the bond, as described in § 4.8 *supra*. If the client is indigent, counsel should inquire whether there is a local R.O.R. Project of the sort described in § 4.6 *supra*. In any event, the release of arrested persons without security, either on their own bond or on their own recognizance (see § 4.2 *supra*), is a growing practice (see §§ 4.3.1, 4.6 *supra*), and these forms of release should always be urged on the bail-setting authority. One or the other form is most likely obtainable by a person with strong roots in the community and a stable employment and family situation. The defendant's bail questionnaire set out in § 4.5 *supra* is useful to document the justifications for a client's release without security; but counsel should support the facts asserted in the statement with proof from sources other than the client if this is practicable.

4.10. *Additional Conditions Imposed Upon Defendants Released on Bail or O.R.*

Court orders (and sometimes police forms) releasing defendants on bail or O.R. often impose restrictions and regulations on the releasee's behavior. *See, e.g., Fischer v. Superintendent, Strafford County House of Corrections*, 163 N.H. 515, 44 A.3d 493 (2012). They may prohibit the releasee from contacting specified individuals (*e.g.*, the complainant or victim, potential witnesses, codefendants) or consorting with specified classes of persons (*e.g.*, people on probation or parole, ex-convicts, "gang" members). They may impose travel restrictions (or even "house arrest") or curfews. *See, e.g., People ex rel. Spivack v. Schiraldi*, 200 A.D.3d 938, 155 N.Y.S.3d 546 (Mem) (N.Y. App. Div., 2d Dep't 2021). They may forbid the possession or use of drugs or alcohol or firearms or vehicles or even cell phones. *See, e.g.*, ARIZ. REV. STAT. § 13-3967(D); PA. RULE CRIM. PRO. 527; N.M. Rule Crim. Pro. Forms 9-302, 9-303. They may limit the releasee's use of the internet. *But see Packingham v. North Carolina*, 582 U.S. 98, 101, 108 (2017) (striking down, on First Amendment grounds, a state statute that made "it a felony for a registered sex offender to gain access to a number of websites, including commonplace social media websites like Facebook and Twitter"; the Court explains that "to foreclose access to social media altogether is to prevent the user from engaging in the legitimate exercise of First Amendment rights," and "[e]ven convicted criminals . . . might receive legitimate benefits from these means for access to the world of ideas, in particular if they seek to reform and to pursue lawful and rewarding lives"); *People v. Morger*, 2019 IL 123643, 160 N.E.3d 53, 57, 61, 442 Ill. Dec. 480, 484, 488 (2019) (relying on *Packingham, supra*, to strike down, as "unconstitutionally overbroad," a state statute mandating that a sentencing order of probation for "a sex offense, as defined in the SORA [Sex Offender Registration Act]," include a probationary condition "ban[ning] . . . the [probationer's] use of social media . . . , whether or not a minor was involved [in the sex offense] and whether or not the use of social media was a factor in the commission of the offense"). They frequently prescribe that the defendant must refrain from any criminal behavior. (The latter restriction is not rendered unimportant by its obvious redundancy. It means that if the defendant is arrested for a subsequent offense, s/he can be summarily incarcerated for violation of this release condition without the procedural protections that would be a precondition for confinement on the new charge.)

Subjection to electronic monitoring – most commonly in the form of GPS tracking devices employing non-removeable bracelets and anklets – is increasingly in vogue. *See, e.g.*, CAL. PENAL CODE § 1203.018; 725 SMITH-HURD ILL.COMP. STAT. ANN. § 5/110-5(f); BALDWIN'S KY. REV. STAT. ANN. §§ 431.067, 431.517; WEST'S VA. CODE ANN. § 53.1-131.2(B); *In re Anunobi*, 278 S.W.3d 425 (Tex. App. 2008); *State v. Clark*, 2011 WL 2163544 (Del. Super. Ct. 2011); *but see Commonwealth v. Norman*, 484 Mass. 330, 142 N.E.3d 1 (2020) (holding that the requirement of submission to GPS tracking as a condition of pretrial release violates the state constitution). This development is a mixed blessing for defendants. On the one hand, it enables counsel to urge that bail (or high bail) is unnecessary to assure against flight because the client can be safely O.R.'d (or released on lower bail) with a tracker. *See, e.g.*, WASH. SUPER. CT. CRIM. RULE 3.2(b); *State v. Guillen*, 2001-NMCA-079, 130 N.M. 803, 32 P.3d 812 (N.M. App. 2001); *Palmer-Tesema v. Pinkney*, 2018-Ohio-1852, 2018 WL 2149209 (Ohio App. 2018). On the other hand, some judges will *add* GPS tracking (and the costs of the GPS equipment and monitoring, see *e.g.*, MICH. COMP. LAWS ANN. § 765.6b) to the same oppressive roster of release conditions – including high bail – that they would have ordered in the absence of the tracking. Counsel should discuss with the client both the benefits and the risks of a GPS surveillance arrangement. (When the client is an addict or a predictable recidivist – because, for example, s/he is an habitual shoplifter, spouse abuser, or street fighter – neither s/he nor counsel would be well advised to provide the law enforcement community with a persuasive means to prove the client's contemporaneous proximity to the site of all future criminal occurrences. *See, e.g., People v. Hill*, 2017 WL 410178, at *4 (Cal. App. 2017).)

If electronic surveillance or any other oppressive requirement is included among the conditions for a client's release on bail or O.R., counsel should be alert to the possibility of having the condition rescinded later on grounds of changed circumstances. *See, e.g., Commonwealth v. Madden*, 458 Mass. 607, 939 N.E.2d 778 (2010). Courts ordinarily have discretion to modify the conditions initially imposed on defendants released before trial if the defendant's subsequent behavior or other supervening circumstances call for increased or decreased restrictions. *See, e.g., State v. Paul*, 465 N.J. Super. 290, 293, 242 A.3d 897, 899 (2020) ("Rule 3:26-2(c)(2) governs a defendant's motion to relax conditions of his or her pre-trial release under the Criminal Justice Reform Act, N.J.S.A. 2A:162-15 to -26. The Rule empowers the trial court to recalibrate a releasee's conditions upon a showing of 'a material change in circumstance.' We hold that pre-trial discovery that has reduced the 'weight of the evidence' against the defendant may constitute such changed circumstances. So may a defendant's compliance with restrictive conditions over an extended period, if such compliance coincides with another material change demonstrating that the defendant's pre-trial behavior may be adequately managed by less restrictive means than initially imposed. As the trial court here did not review defendant's motion to relax his release conditions under Rule 3:26-2(c)(2), we grant defendant's motion for leave to appeal, reverse the trial court's order denying relief, and remand for reconsideration.").

4.11. *Procedures for Posting Bail*

After the amount of bail has been set and the means to make up that amount are in hand, the bail is "posted" with the appropriate authority, who orders the defendant's release or issues a receipt or form authorizing the defendant's release. Posting bail involves depositing with the authority the defendant's signed bond (ordinarily a form document), the surety's bond, if any (also a form), and whatever cash, securities, or deeds are put up for bail, and obtaining a receipt and any additional form required to authorize release. If the authority with whom bail is posted is not the same authority that set the bail, the order or endorsement setting the amount of bail must also be presented.

The identity and procedure of the bail-setting official ordinarily governs the identity of the authority with whom the bail must be posted. When bail is set by the police, it is usually posted with the police; inquiry of the desk officer will locate the proper recipient. Bail set by a magistrate on an arrest warrant or on a copy of the charge or similar procedure (see § 4.7 *supra*) is ordinarily also posted with the police, whereas bail set by a magistrate at a hearing may have to be posted with the magistrate's clerk. Bail set by a court of record is ordinarily posted with the clerk of the court, but in some localities it may have to be posted with a marshal's office, sheriff's office, or other bureau at the detention facility.

In any case in which bail is not posted with the police, counsel or someone acting for the client must deliver the bail receipt or release order or both to the police. It is usually wise for counsel or a trusted paralegal to do this and to wait at the stationhouse until the defendant is physically ushered out of custody, because the investigating officers may delay release in order to conduct additional interrogation or to perform identification or forensic testing procedures. When a professional bondsman is used, the bondsman will usually offer to take the release papers to the station and get the client out of custody. But, particularly in the case of a vulnerable client, counsel is best advised to do these tasks personally or assign them to a reliable associate. Even the most trustworthy and competent professional bondsmen are less likely than counsel to put a high priority on protecting the defendant's interests by moving quickly.

4.12. *Problems in Getting Bail Set or Posting Bond*

4.12.1. *Problems in Locating the Defendant or Identifying the Charges*

Counsel will often encounter considerable difficulty in locating an arrested client for the purpose of getting information needed to arrange the setting of bail, or of having the client sign an affidavit or other document for use in arranging bail, or of having the client sign the bail bond, or of having the client released promptly once the bond is posted. Especially in urban areas, arrestees may be shuttled through several police quarters before they come to rest in one or another jail or detention facility to await a judicial hearing.

A related problem is the difficulty of identifying the exact charges, and all the charges, against the defendant. Often these are not determined by the police until after their investigation of their prisoner is well advanced. Counsel can obviate some of the frustration in these areas by getting as much information as possible about the client's status from the police when s/he first talks with them about the case. See § 3.5 *supra*. S/he should ask the desk officer and the investigating officer (a) exactly where the client is now; (b) whether the client is going to be taken anywhere else; (c) if so, where; (d) what are the present charges (repeating them to the officer and asking, "Have I got them *all*, now?"); (e) whether other charges are being considered or investigated; and (f) what the other charges are. It is also useful to ask each officer tactfully where *s/he* will be during the next several hours and how *s/he* can be reached so that counsel can locate the officer and ask for an accounting if the officer's information proves wrong (for example, if the client is removed from the station where the officer said that s/he would be held). Frequently it makes sense to leave a client in custody for several hours or even overnight until the specific charges are firmed up. Otherwise, counsel may have bail set and a bond posted only to find that the defendant has been held on additional charges or to learn that a released defendant has been rearrested on additional charges. See § 4.16 *infra*. Of course, on the other side, the desirability of getting the client out of the hands of the police quickly weighs heavily.

Counsel should consider contacting the prosecutor's office for assistance if obstructions or problems arise in securing the client's release or admission to bail – if, for example, the police appear uninformative or hostile; or if a client cannot be located after reasonable inquiry of them; or if the police fail to lodge charges against a client who is detained; or if stationhouse bail authorized by law is not quickly set or if it is set in an excessive amount; or if the client is being moved around rapidly; or if interrogation or improper investigation of a client in custody appears to be going on. Usually in urban areas a deputy prosecutor is assigned to be on call for after-hours emergencies and can be reached through the prosecutor's office; but if there is no such arrangement, a prosecutor may be reachable on his or her cellphone or a home landline or perhaps by e-mail. If insufficient assistance is obtained from the prosecutor, an application to a court of record is next in order. Traditionally, *habeas corpus* is available to secure relief in these situations. See §§ 3.8.3-3.8.4 *supra*; §§ 4.12.2, 4.13 *infra*. If counsel is dissatisfied with the relief s/he gets, s/he may appeal the adverse disposition of the *habeas* petition to an appellate court and seek an expedited hearing, or in most jurisdictions s/he may apply for an original writ of *habeas corpus* from the appellate court or one of its judges. Following unsuccessful exhaustion of state-court remedies, a federal *habeas corpus* proceeding can be filed. (See § 4.14 *infra*.)

4.12.2. *Problems in Locating Officials to Set or Receive Bond*

Counsel may also have trouble identifying or locating the person designated to set bail or to approve a bond and authorize the prisoner's release. Police can be very helpful in these regards when they want to cooperate, and inquiry of the desk officer or of the arresting or investigating officers is often fruitful. If they appear to be acting obstructively, a call to the commanding officer may be advised. Bondsmen in the area are likely to have helpful tips.

If all else fails, an application to a judge for a writ of *habeas corpus* may be required. This should invoke the judge's jurisdiction to entertain *habeas corpus* for the purpose of admitting a detained accused to bail. *See, e.g., People ex rel. Chakwin on Behalf of Ford v. Warden, New York Correctional Facility, Rikers Island*, 63 N.Y.2d 120, 470 N.E.2d 146, 480 N.Y.S.2d 719 (1984); and see § 3.8.3 *supra*; § 4.13 *infra*. It should assert that other attempts to secure the prisoner's admission to bail have failed, and it should be supported by an affidavit of counsel reciting counsel's futile efforts and any obstruction of them by the authorities. In a serious case arising after court hours, the judge may be contacted by e-mail or cellphone or a home landline with an inquiry whether s/he will receive a petition by e-mail or fax or by delivery of a hard copy to his or her home. This frequently results in the judge's telephoning the police and informally arranging to clear up the problem. Obviously, a lawyer who contacts a judge after court hours should be prepared to show that s/he has made every practicable effort to get relief elsewhere first.

4.12.3. *"Hold" Orders*

Even when an arrested person is charged with a bailable offense, s/he may be refused release on bail if a "hold" or "detainer" is lodged against him or her by authorities from other localities where s/he is wanted on outstanding arrest warrants for additional offenses or by local, out-of-county, or out-of-state probation or parole authorities responsible for supervising him or her at the time of the present arrest. (From the standpoint of the latter authorities, the new charges constitute potential probation or parole violations, which may justify the initiation of revocation proceedings.) These detainer practices require close attention and often quick footwork by counsel. In counsel's first discussion with an arrested client, s/he must ask (a) whether the client is on probation or parole; (b) whether there are any warrants out for the client or whether the client is wanted anywhere on any other charges; and (c) whether there is anything the client might be wanted for in any other county or State. Once counsel is aware that s/he is representing a probationer, parolee, or fugitive, s/he may decide to defer attempts to secure bail until the various "detainers" have been lodged and s/he has had a chance to contact the issuing authorities to try to clear them up. In any event, s/he will avoid paying a bond premium for a defendant who cannot be released by reason of the detainers. On the other hand, some probation or parole authorities may not have a defendant arrested if s/he has posted bail on a new offense, whereas they automatically place a "hold" on a probationer or parolee in custody. In this situation counsel may want to hustle to post bail before the "hold" order is lodged with the defendant's custodian. *Cf. Alcocer v. Mills*, 906 F.3d 944 (11th Cir. 2018), and 800 Fed. Appx. 860 (11th Cir. 2020) (an arrestee stated a Fourth Amendment claim by alleging that she was detained overnight when sheriff's officers, suspecting without probable cause that she was an illegal alien and the subject of an Immigration and Customs Enforcement "hold," refused to release her despite her posting of bail on the arrest charge; she was released only after the supposed "hold" was cleared by a fax from an ICE agent); *Barnett v. MacArthur*, 956 F.3d 1291 (11th Cir. 2020) (an arrestee stated a Fourth Amendment claim by alleging that, pursuant to a Sheriff's policy of routinely holding persons arrested for DUI for eight hours, she was detained despite passing two breathalyzer tests and after posting bail).

Probation and parole officers can frequently be persuaded informally to lift detainers (or not to lodge them) by (a) describing the new offense to them in terms which persuade them that the defendant's guilt is dubious or that the offense is trifling even if the defendant is guilty; (b) pointing out, if this is true, that the judge who set bail on the new offense set relatively low bail, thus expressing the belief that the defendant was not likely to flee; (c) pointing out that the new offense is much less serious than the old one, if this is so, and urging that it would be inappropriate to institute heavy back-time revocation proceedings on the basis of a criminal charge for which the defendant will be amply punished (assuming his or her guilt) by the far lighter penalties applicable to the new offense; or (d) persuading them that the new offense is a minor lapse from grace on the part of a probationer or parolee who is otherwise making a good adjustment and that if s/he is jailed for even a short period of time because of the detainer, s/he will lose his or her job, will be dropped from a rehabilitation program in which s/he is enrolled, or will otherwise suffer consequences harmful to the prospect of successfully "making it" on probation or parole. If, notwithstanding these points, the probation or parole officer is adamant about enforcing a detainer, counsel may want to insist that an immediate preliminary revocation hearing conformable to the requirements of *Morrissey v. Brewer*, 408 U.S. 471 (1972), and *Gagnon v. Scarpelli*, 411 U.S. 778 (1973), be held or, if it is not held, that the detainer be lifted. (In federal cases, *see also* FED. RULE CRIM. PRO. 32.1(b).) Unless this constitutionally required preliminary hearing is held, the lodging of a detainer resulting in the defendant's non-bailability on a new charge ought to be as assailable as is detention upon a violator's warrant for the old charge alone (*compare Moody v. Daggett*, 429 U.S. 78, 88 (1976)); therefore, the detainer may be challenged in *habeas corpus* proceedings (see §§ 4.13, 4.14 *infra*) if the probation or parole authorities decline either to lift it or to provide a prompt *Morrissey-Scarpelli* hearing (*cf. Braden v. 30th Judicial Circuit Court*, 410 U.S. 484 (1973)). Counsel should also be aware of the cases suggesting that revocation decisions by probation and parole officials are no longer as immune from substantive judicial review as they were once thought to be. *See Arciniega v. Freeman*, 404 U.S. 4 (1971); *Douglas v. Buder*, 412 U.S. 430 (1973); *Bearden v. Georgia*, 461 U.S. 660, 666 n.7 (1983); *cf. Superintendent v. Hill*, 472 U.S. 445, 455 (1985) (dictum); *but see Black v. Romano*, 471 U.S. 606 (1985).

If the detainer is based upon an out-of-state warrant, little can be done about it locally (*see Michigan v. Doran*, 439 U.S. 282 (1978); *California v. Superior Court (Smolin)*, 482 U.S. 400 (1987)); efforts will have to be focused upon getting the underlying charges dismissed or upon posting bail for appearance on those charges in the courts of the jurisdiction that issued the warrant. The same may be true in the case of out-of-county but in-state arrest warrants, or it may be possible to post bail locally on both the local and out-of-county charges. Formal procedures permit this in some States; elsewhere, it can be arranged informally through the judges of both courts involved. In federal practice, bail can be set and posted in the district of arrest for appearance in another district, under FED. RULE CRIM. PRO. 5(c)(3)(E) and 40. If pretrial delay is protracted, the speedy-trial rights and remedies discussed in §§ 28.5.3-28.5.4 *infra* come into play; those sections should be consulted in the light of § 28.5.1 *infra*.

Counsel representing a client who is not a United States citizen should be aware that the courts are permitting Immigration and Customs Enforcement to detain foreign nationals to await deportation proceedings even when they have been bailed on criminal charges. *See United States v. Vasquez-Benitez*, 919 F.3d 546 (D.C. Cir. 2019); *United States v. Lett*, 944 F.3d 467 (2d Cir. 2019). This is another situation in which it may be wise to delay efforts to have monetary bail set for the client, lest s/he end up paying the premium for a useless bond.

4.13. *Review and Renewal of Efforts to Have Bail Set*

Statutory provisions authorizing stationhouse bail, bail-setting by a magistrate, and bail-setting by a court of record are usually cumulative: that is, they give the police, magistrates, and judges concurrent jurisdiction to set bail. In the absence of, or in addition to, any statutory procedures for bail-setting by the court of record, that court almost invariably has jurisdiction to issue writs of *habeas corpus*. By immemorial tradition, *habeas corpus* lies for the admission to bail of persons detained under criminal process; hence the grant of *habeas corpus* power without more ordinarily carries with it the power to set bail for a criminal accused. See § 3.8.3 *supra*.

As a result of the cumulative or concurrent character of the bail-setting authorizations, counsel for a client who is denied bail or whose bail is set in an excessive or unobtainable amount may proceed to apply *seriatim* for relief to each authorized official. Dissatisfied with the setting of stationhouse bail, s/he may apply first to a magistrate, then to a court of record pursuant to a statutory bail-setting procedure, then to the same court or to a judge of that court by *habeas corpus* (*e.g., State v. Thornton*, 84 Md. App. 312 578 A.2d 1212 (1990)), then to other judges of the same court or other courts of record having *habeas corpus* jurisdiction (*e.g., People ex rel. Klein v. Krueger*, 25 N.Y.2d 497, 255 N.E.2d 552, 307 N.Y.S.2d 207(1969); and see § 3.8.3 *supra* regarding the inapplicability of *res judicata* in *habeas* proceedings). Denial of relief under the statutory bail-setting procedures may or may not be reviewable by appeal or mandamus; denial of *habeas corpus* relief generally is appealable (*see, e.g., Ex parte Ramirez-Hernandez*, 642 S.W.3d 907 (Tex. App. 2022)); and, in addition, in most States appellate courts and their judges also have original *habeas* jurisdiction (*see, e.g., Bryan v. Slaughter*, 2021 WL 5833042, at *2 (Mont. 2021) ("[h]abeas corpus is available to review a decision of a district court on a motion to set bail"); *Mohamed v. Eckelberry*, 162 Ohio St. 3d 583, 584-85, 166 N.E.3d 1132, 1133 (2020) ("in an original action, an appellate court may permit a habeas petitioner to introduce evidence to prove his claim and then exercise its own discretion in imposing an appropriate bail amount"); *In re Humphrey*, 19 Cal. App. 5th 1006, 228 Cal. Rptr. 3d 513 (2018), *ruling on the merits aff'd, In re Humphrey*, cited and quoted in § 4.6 *supra*; *In re Scott*, 2018 WL 6717025, at *8 (Cal. App. 2018); *Blackwood v. McPhaul*, 134 Ohio App.3d 138, 730 N.E.2d 452 (1999)). Furthermore, the denial of relief, whether under the statutory procedures or by *habeas corpus*, generally presents no technical bar to second or subsequent applications to the same official, court, or judge; renewed motions for the reduction of bail and successive petitions for a writ are frequently entertained.

The restrictions upon how repeatedly and how far up the chain of authority counsel may press attempts to get the client admitted to bail are, therefore, practical rather than doctrinal. As a matter of common sense and courtesy to the courts, counsel is advised (a) to go first to the lowest official authorized to set bail and then to proceed up the chain of dignity, passing to a higher court only when a lower one has denied relief or is demonstrably unavailable to receive an application for relief; (b) to avoid repeater applications to the same authority unless a convincing showing of some new and significant fact, not previously discoverable, or some changed circumstance can be made; and (c) to quit wasting time and credit with the courts when s/he thinks s/he has obtained as good a deal as s/he is realistically likely to get in a case. (Judges, too, can count, and they recognize that a $100 difference in the bond set is a $10 difference in the premium.)

Some lower-court judges are prone to set bail in amounts that are manifestly beyond the defendants' means, in order to assure their continued incarceration. If counsel can convince an appellate court that this is the case, s/he is likely to obtain a significant reduction. *See, e.g., Ex parte Melartin*, 464 S.W.3d 789, 796 (Tex. App. 2015): "When bail is set so high that a person cannot realistically pay it – and an aggregate amount of $7.2 million would certainly qualify under that standard – the trial court essentially 'displaces the presumption of innocence and replaces it with a guaranteed trial appearance.' . . . That is clearly not the function of bail."); *Norton-Nugin v. State*, 179 So.3d 557, 559 (Fla. App. 2015) ("the amount of bail cannot be used to punish an accused").

4.14. *Federal Habeas Corpus to Secure Release on Bail*

Sections 4.3.2 and 4.6 *supra* summarize the arguments that a state criminal defendant has federal constitutional rights to bail. To the extent that the arguments prevail, those rights are not left for their vindication exclusively to the state courts. The federal district courts, in the exercise of the *habeas corpus* jurisdiction given by 28 U.S.C. § 2241(c)(3), are authorized to discharge from custody persons confined in violation of the Constitution; thus they may order the release on bail of state criminal defendants whom the Constitution requires to be bailed. *See Rivera v. Concepcion*, 469 F.2d 17 (1st Cir. 1972); *Dawkins v. Crevasse*, 391 F.2d 921 (5th Cir. 1968); *Sheldon v. Nebraska*, 401 F.2d 343, 346 (8th Cir. 1968) (dictum); *United States ex rel. Keating v. Bensinger*, 322 F. Supp. 784 (N.D. Ill. 1971); *cf. Schall v. Martin*, 467 U.S. 253 (1984) (by implication); *Kinney v. Lenon*, 425 F.2d 209 (9th Cir. 1970).

Federal courts will not grant relief to a state prisoner who has not exhausted available remedies in the state courts. But exhaustion is made out whenever either (a) the state courts have denied relief on the merits (*Braden v. 30th Judicial Circuit Court*, 410 U.S. 484, 489-92 (1973) (speedy trial); *Rivera v. Concepcion, supra* (bail)); or (b) state court relief is delayed to such an extent that it becomes ineffective in light of the grievance sought to be remedied (*Phillips v. Vasquez*, 56 F.3d 1030, 1033-38 (9th Cir. 1995) (postconviction relief); *Dixon v. Florida*, 388 F.2d 424 (5th Cir. 1968) (same); *St. Jules v. Beto*, 462 F.2d 1365 (5th Cir. 1972) (same); *Dozie v. Cady*, 430 F.2d 637 (7th Cir. 1970) (same); *United States ex rel. Goodman v. Kehl*, 456 F.2d 863, 869 (2d Cir. 1972) (dictum) (bail)). Under the latter theory even relatively short delays by the state courts in acting upon bail matters may constitute exhaustion, since "[r]elief in this type of case must be speedy if it is to be effective." *Stack v. Boyle*, 342 U.S. 1, 4 (1951).

Counsel may, therefore, be advised to file a federal petition for *habeas corpus* simultaneously with, or shortly after, an application for bail to the state courts; to bring the federal proceeding to a hearing within not more than eight days in strict conformity to 28 U.S.C. § 2243; to file at the hearing a supplemental petition or affidavits reciting that the state courts have denied or delayed release on bail during the preceding eight days or more; and to argue that on this showing the federal court is authorized to entertain on the merits the petitioner's federal claims to pretrial release. *Cf. In re Shuttlesworth*, 369 U.S. 35 (1962). The simultaneous-filing procedure is technically permissible because satisfaction of the exhaustion doctrine is not a prerequisite of federal *habeas corpus* jurisdiction but merely a condition precedent to the federal court's ordering relief on the merits. Exhaustion of state remedies after the filing of the federal *habeas* petition, but before the time when the federal court is asked to act upon it, is quite sufficient. *Sharpe v. Buchanan*, 317 U.S. 238 (1942); *Davis v. Jackson*, 246 F.2d 268 (2d Cir. 1957).

4.15. *Judicial Modification of the Amount of Bail or Conditions of Release; Revocation of Bail*

4.15.1. *Reduction of the Amount of Bail; Substitution of O.R. for Bail Initially Set*

Apart from the procedures discussed in the preceding paragraphs, a court of record in which a criminal case is pending ordinarily has statutory or inherent authority and discretion to entertain an application for reduction of the defendant's bail or for the defendant's release on his or her own bond or recognizance at any time. *See, e.g., State v. Brown*, 2014-NMSC-038, 338 P.3d 1276 (N.M. 2014) (reversing a trial court's decision denying a motion for modification of a $250,000 bail setting and ordering the defendant's release on nonmonetary conditions); *Rawls v. State*, 540 So.2d 946, at 946 (Fla. App. 1989) (finding an abuse of discretion in a trial court's rigid adherence to a county bond schedule, the Court of Appeals orders that a $20,000 bond setting on charges of possessing cocaine and cannabis be reduced to $5,000, explaining that the defendant "has been adjudicated indigent[,] . . . has substantial ties to the community[,] . . . had no prior arrests, . . . lived with his parents until his arrest and confinement[,] . . . [and] could not post bond in the amount set by the court. There was no showing that . . . [he] would likely flee the court's jurisdiction."); *People v. Watson*, 71 Misc. 3d 642, 142 N.Y.S.3d 919 (N.Y. Sup. Ct., N.Y. Cty. 2021) (finding that the judge at preliminary arraignment failed to consider all of the defendant's individual financial and nonfinancial circumstances relevant to a proper setting of the percentage of a partially secured bond, the trial court reduces the percentage from ten percent to two percent in order to make it possible for the defendant to post the bond); *cf. United States v. Taylor*, 289 F. Supp. 3d 55 (D. D.C. 2018) (revoking a magistrate judge's detention order and releasing the defendant to detention in his sister's home); *and see State v. Pan*, 345 Conn. 922, 291 A.3d 82 (2022) ("[P]retrial detention may carry very serious consequences in addition to, and as a result of, the defendant's loss of liberty. Pretrial detention can affect employment situations, housing arrangements and family relationships, and also increases the likelihood of a criminal conviction, either by interfering with the defendant's ability to assist in his own defense or by increasing the possibility of a guilty plea." *Id.* at 952-53, 291 A.3d at 103. With these considerations in mind, the court institutes a series of bail-setting practices which recognize that "the 'heavy flow of judicial business . . . during arraignment sessions' . . . along with the fact that it may be difficult at the time of a defendant's arraignment for the parties to marshal the evidence necessary to hold a meaningful hearing in a relatively complex case involving high bonds" (*id.* at 952, 291 A.3d at 103) make it "critical that a defendant have a meaningful opportunity to seek review of his initial bond through a more extensive hearing process than was initially held at arraignment,": "[S]hould a defendant be unable to make the initial bond set at arraignment, and counsel has a good faith basis to believe modification is warranted, the defendant may file a motion for modification of bond . . . . [W]ith . . . 'reasonable promptness' . . . the trial court shall then schedule the matter on an expedited basis for a more extensive hearing than is feasible at arraignment, at which financial and nonfinancial conditions may be considered without prejudice to the defendant." *Id.* at 953, 291 A.3d at 103-04. "Following the modification hearing, the trial court must make a de novo determination regarding whether the bond initially set is reasonable. If the court determines that the initial bond is unreasonable, it must set a new, reasonable bond. In making this determination, we agree with the Massachusetts Supreme Judicial Court that, when 'it appears that the defendant lacks the financial resources to post the amount of bail set by the judge, such that it will likely result in the defendant's long-term pretrial detention, the judge must provide findings of fact and a statement of reasons for the bail decision, either in writing or orally on the record,' including the 'consideration of the defendant's financial resources . . . [,] how the bail amount was [determined], and . . . why . . . no alternative, less restrictive financial or nonfinancial conditions will suffice to [en]sure his or her presence at future court proceedings.'" *Id.* at 957, 291 A.3d at 106.). A motion to reduce the bail amount or for R.O.R. would ordinarily be filed on behalf of a defendant who is jailed in default of posting the amount of bail previously set and who seeks reduction as a means of obtaining release on some lesser amount that s/he can make. But a defendant who has posted bond and obtained release may also ask the court to reduce that bond, upon a showing that bail in the amount posted is unnecessary to assure his or her presence for trial. Such a motion will be useless to the defendant who has posted bond with a professional bonding company, since s/he has paid his or her premium already and cannot recover it. But the motion should be considered when cash, securities, or property has been put up as security and the client is in need of funds.

4.15.2. *Increase in the Amount of Bail; Revocation of Bail*

Most jurisdictions authorize a judge who has set bail or a judge of the criminal court to increase the amount of the bond upon a showing that the bond previously set is insufficient to assure the defendant's presence at trial or when the defendant has failed to appear for a scheduled court proceeding or has violated a condition of provisional release (see § 4.10 *supra*). When this is done, the defendant who has been released on the old bond is rearrested on a bench warrant and held until s/he posts the new bond.

Sometimes trial judges will assert or assume a power to revoke a defendant's bond entirely when s/he has skipped bail, failed to appear for a court date, violated a release condition, or otherwise misbehaved (by, for example, threatening witnesses, engaging in disruptive courtroom behavior, or committing a new criminal offense). Revocation orders are authorized by statute or court rule in some jurisdictions. *See, e.g., Commonwealth v. Morales*, 473 Mass. 1019, 44 N.E.3d 843 (2016); 18 U.S.C. § 3148(a), (b); *United States v. Gennaco*, 834 F. Supp. 2d

38 (D. Mass. 2011). Outright revocation is difficult to justify in the absence of explicit statutory authority; and, even under this authority, it is arguably unconstitutional in jurisdictions in which the state constitution guaranties an absolute right to bail (see § 4.3.1 *supra*). Consistently with this guarantee, a defendant's bad history of bail-jumping or other misconduct when released on a previous charge could not support denial of bail on a new charge, and the result should be the same when the issue is revocation of release on the current, initial charge. To the extent that the defendant's violation of a bail obligation or other misconduct demonstrates a greater likelihood of future flight, that likelihood should justify only an increase in the amount of bail, not the outright denial of bail. *But see State v. Ayala*, 222 Conn. 331, 610 A.2d 1162 (1992).

In jurisdictions whose constitutions have been interpreted as conferring a less than absolute right to bail and in which statutes or court rules authorize revocation of bail or conditional release under specified circumstances, the defendant is entitled to a hearing on the prosecution's motion for revocation; the prosecutor ordinarily bears the burden of proof in showing that those circumstances exist; and the court has discretion to deny revocation even if the circumstances are shown. This is the rule in federal practice under the Excessive Bail Clause of the federal Constitution as currently construed (*see United States v. Salerno*, 481 U.S. 739 (1987), discussed in § 4.3.1 *supra*). Revocation of bail as a purely *punitive* measure, without regard to the likelihood of future flight or future misbehavior, is impermissible (*see Bitter v. United States*, 389 U.S. 15 (1967) (per curiam); *cf. United States v. Salerno, supra*, 481 U.S. at 746-47 (dictum); *Bell v. Wolfish*, 441 U.S. 520, 535-37 (1979) (dictum)), but revocation is permitted under the circumstances spelled out in 18 U.S.C. § 3148 (b) – that is, when a judge, after a hearing:

> (1) finds that there is –
> (A) probable cause to believe that the person has committed a Federal, State, or local crime while on release; or
> (B) clear and convincing evidence that the person has violated any other condition of release; and
> (2) finds that—
> (A) based on the factors set forth in . . . [18 U.S.C. § 3142(g)], there is no condition or combination of conditions of release that will assure that the person will not flee or pose a danger to the safety of any other person or the community; or
> (B) the person is unlikely to abide by any condition or combination of conditions of release.

See, e.g., *United States v. Wilks*, 15 F.4th 842, 848 (7th Cir. 2021) (reversing a bail revocation order where "First, the judge did not find by clear and convincing evidence that Wilks violated a condition of release . . . [and] ¶ Second, the judge did not explain why detention was necessary according to the criteria of § 3148 (b)(2)(A) or (B)"). *Compare State v. Blair*, 39 So.3d 1190, 1194 (Fla. 2010) (recognizing a trial court's power to revoke a defendant's bail if s/he fails to appear for a court date and to order him or her to be detained pending trial if, but only if, (1) the failure to appear is found to have been willful, and (2) the court at a revocation hearing also finds "'that "no conditions of release can reasonably protect the community from risk of physical harm to persons, assure the presence of the accused at trial, or assure the integrity of the judicial process."' Art. I, § 14, Fla. Const.").

4.16. *Duration of Bail; Effect of Additional or Superseding Charges*

In many jurisdictions, new bail can be demanded for a defendant's appearance at each of the several stages of a criminal prosecution. In a felony case, for example, bond is technically reset at every stage: by a magistrate initially, for appearance at preliminary hearing; by the magistrate again, following bind-over, for the grand jury; by the grand jury, in its indictment, for appearance at the trial. As a practical matter, most bond is set, and bail bonds are written, at whatever pretrial stage, to assure the defendant's appearance at the trial. Interim resettings simply copy or "continue" the amount previously set. (In summary proceedings, however, as noted in § 2.2.5 *supra*, new bail is set and actually demanded, sometimes in an increased amount, for appeal from a magistrate's conviction for trial *de novo* in a court of record.)

Bail set and a bond written for appearance on one charge may not, however, carry over to other charges growing out of the same incident: A defendant who is bound over and bonded out for assault with a deadly weapon may be rearrested and required to post new bail if the grand jury indicts him or her for assault with intent to kill. Local law and the terms of any bonding contract should be carefully studied in consideration of this problem, which could prove costly for a defendant or even land the defendant in jail despite payment of an irrecoverable bond premium on a superseded charge. Frequently, practical resolutions of the problem can be arranged, by persuading the police, prosecutor, magistrate, or judge to (a) keep the original charge pending in lieu of dismissing it and (b) release the defendant on nominal bail on the second charge, in view of his or her secured obligation to appear on the first.

4.17. *Legal Obligations and Consequences of the Bond Contract and Bail Status*

Complex contractual and noncontractual rights and obligations are created by the transactions involved in a defendant's release on an appearance bond, particularly a bond in which a third party joins as surety. The defendant promises, and the surety guarantees the court, that the defendant will appear; in the event of nonappearance, the posted security is forfeit.

Common law – and sometimes statute – gives the surety the right to arrest the defendant at any time without process or cause (and to return the defendant to the State without extradition if s/he is arrested abroad), whether or not the defendant is in default on his or her obligation to appear. By thus seizing and producing the defendant in court, the surety is discharged of its obligation on the bond. (It should be noted that there is a practice in some localities to insist invariably upon the posting of at least a nominal surety bond, even in cases in which release on recognizance is plainly warranted. The purpose of the practice is to create a surety having broad common-law powers to pursue the defendant out of the State and to return him or her without extradition. Its consistency with the constitutional Extradition Clause and with the protective procedural provisions of the widely adopted Uniform Criminal Extradition Act [*see Cuyler v. Adams*, 449 U.S. 433 (1981)] is dubious at best.) However, in a case in which a commercial bond is used, the surety agrees by contract with the defendant to post a bond for the defendant's appearance in consideration of the statutorily regulated premium, and this contractual obligation may explicitly or implicitly qualify the surety's arbitrary common-law power to surrender the non-defaulting defendant. In any event, so long as defendants are not in default, the courts are ordinarily willing to protect them against any attempt by a bonding company to get out of its bail obligation by returning them to custody without some extremely cogent reason. These attempts – or any abuse or overreaching of a defendant by a bondsman – should be promptly reported by counsel to the presiding judge of the criminal court, who will ordinarily deal with it informally but effectively by sending a clear signal to the bondsman to stop.

On the other hand, a defendant who *is* in default of his or her obligation to appear for scheduled proceedings thereby is exposed to substantial liabilities in addition to the prospect of arrest on a bench warrant (see § 4.18 *infra*). The defendant's promise to appear runs in favor of the surety as well as the court; and if, having posted collateral with the surety to secure that promise (see § 4.8 *supra*), the defendant defaults, the surety contract ordinarily allows the bonding company to forfeit this collateral, to withdraw its own security (to the extent that this is not forfeited by the court), and – as at common law – to arrest the defendant anywhere at any time and return him or her to the jurisdiction without process or extradition. The defaulting defendant also becomes liable to the court for the amount of the bond; in addition, s/he may incur criminal liability in some jurisdictions under statutes that make bail-jumping an offense.

4.18. *Forfeiture*

If a defendant defaults on the obligation to appear, the presiding judge normally issues a bench warrant for the defendant's arrest. When the defendant is brought before the court on this warrant, s/he is given the opportunity to explain his or her nonappearance in a summary (and ordinarily feisty) proceeding. Depending upon the merit of the defendant's excuse, the judge may "sue out" (that is, forfeit) the defendant's bail bond or may allow the defendant to be re-released on the bond – or on a higher bond – usually with a strict admonition to keep his or her judicial appointments in the future. (Ordinarily, a court also has the power to forfeit bail when the defendant first fails to appear. In such a case it would have to reinstate the bail if it later chose to re-release the defendant on the same bail.) In some jurisdictions if the defendant voluntarily appears within a statutorily specified period of time and before being arrested for failure to appear, s/he will also have the opportunity to plead his or her excuse to the court and thus to avert forfeiture in the court's discretion.

4.19. *To Bail or Not to Bail*

In most cases clients want to be enlarged on bail or recognizance before trial, and this enlargement is in their best interests. Apart from the obvious point that life is sweeter on the streets than in jail, pretrial detention may be seriously harmful to a defendant in many ways. It may disrupt the defendant's family relations and cause the defendant to lose his or her job. It will certainly interfere, to some extent, with the defendant's ability to assist counsel in preparing his or her defense, particularly in cases in which factual investigation is required among persons or in neighborhoods with which counsel is unfamiliar or where counsel will be seen as an unwelcome stranger (see § 9.4 *infra*) and in cases in which a site visit is critical to preparation of the defendant's testimony or to counsel's understanding of the facts (see § 9.5 *infra*). Interviewing clients in jail usually is more troublesome, time-consuming, and unsatisfactory from the point of view of good lawyer-client rapport than interviewing them in counsel's office. While in jail, the client is accessible to such police investigative techniques as renewed interrogation and lineups; s/he is prey to snitches (fellow inmates who will subsequently testify, truly or falsely, that the defendant made incriminatory statements to them in jail); and s/he is exposed to the influence of jail-house lawyers, whose advice can make counsel's job very difficult. Jail conditions are, of course, frequently deplorable; medical care is seldom adequate; and the jailed client is in jeopardy of sexual assault and other forms of abuse from fellow inmates. The client who spends the pretrial period in jail often comes to trial looking and feeling like a loser, with the result that s/he is likely to be treated as one by the jury and the judge. Finally, the jailed client cannot – as the bailed client can – be placed in a community situation (a job, job-training program, counseling program, and so forth) in which a good adjustment record can be made that will reap dividends at the time of sentencing. See § 12.18 *infra*. For all these reasons, it is generally advisable for counsel to secure the client's release before trial, if at all possible. Moreover, the best way for a lawyer to gain a client's confidence usually is by *doing* something for the client; and one of the earliest and most appreciated things that the lawyer can do for a criminal defendant is to get the defendant out of jail.

There are, however, some instances in which it is better for the client to remain in jail prior to trial. This may be so when (a) it is clear from the outset that the client is going to plead guilty and will almost certainly receive a sentence including some jail time; (b) it is preferable for the client to do the jail time sooner rather than later; *and* (c) state law or local practice requires that the full period of pretrial incarceration be credited against sentence under computation formulas that compare favorably with the formulas for computing postsentencing time. (Before reaching the conclusion that these latter conditions are met, counsel must usually conduct a thorough study of the intricacies of the sentencing and correctional laws of the jurisdiction. *Cf. McGinnis v. Royster*, 410 U.S. 263 (1973).) A still stronger argument for leaving the defendant in jail before trial appears when the defendant is charged with an offense for which it is the local practice to give a "time served" sentence (that is, a sentence equivalent to the period of pretrial incarceration, with full credit for the pretrial incarceration) when the defendant has served any considerable period of time in jail before trial, whereas a bailed defendant is likely to draw a *longer* sentence. It is common, for example, for judges to want to give defendants convicted of certain offenses some significant "taste of jail" without caring exactly how much. As a rule of thumb, therefore, they may habitually give a time-served sentence to any defendant who has spent, say, a month or more in jail before trial. When the same judge comes to sentence a bailed defendant for the same offense, the judge's habitual practice – or the structure of the State's sentencing law or the processing procedures of the local correctional facility – may require that the shortest jail-time sentence imposed be, say, three months. In this situation a defendant obviously stands to shorten his or her sentence by forgoing bail. Once again, in order to make advised decisions in these matters, counsel must be thoroughly familiar with the details of the jurisdiction's sentencing and corrections law; also, s/he must usually inquire among knowledgeable local criminal lawyers concerning the local judges' sentencing habits.

Chapter 5

State-Paid Assistance for the Defense: Obtaining
State Funding for Counsel's Time and for Defense Services

5.1. *Availability of State Funding Under Local Practice*

5.1.1. *Funding for Counsel's Time*

As explained in § 2.3.4.2 *supra*, indigent defendants have a Sixth Amendment right to court-appointed counsel in all felony cases (*Gideon v. Wainwright*, 372 U.S. 335 (1963); *Johnson v. Zerbst*, 304 U.S. 458 (1938)) and on any charges of misdemeanors or petty offenses for which a term of imprisonment is going to be imposed as a result of conviction, "'even for a brief period'" (*Alabama v. Shelton*, 535 U.S. 654, 657 (2002)), including cases in which the court imposes "a suspended sentence that may 'end up in the actual deprivation of a person's liberty'" (*id.* at 658) in the event of a violation of probation or some other condition of the suspended sentence. This constitutional mandate of counsel applies not only to the trial stage of a criminal case but also to all pretrial proceedings "at or after the time that adversary judicial proceedings have been initiated against [a defendant] . . . 'whether by way of formal charge, preliminary hearing, indictment, information, or arraignment'" (*Brewer v. Williams*, 430 U.S. 387, 398 (1977)). *See Missouri v. Frye*, 566 U.S. 133, 140 (2012) ("It is well settled that the right to the effective assistance of counsel applies to certain steps before trial. The 'Sixth Amendment guarantees a defendant the right to have counsel present at all "critical" stages of the criminal proceedings.' . . . Critical stages include arraignments, postindictment interrogations, postindictment lineups, and the entry of a guilty plea."); *Padilla v. Kentucky*, 559 U.S. 356, 364 (2010) ("Before deciding whether to plead guilty, a defendant is entitled to "the effective assistance of competent counsel."); *Rothgery v. Gillespie County*, 554 U.S. 191, 213 (2008) ("[A] criminal defendant's initial appearance before a judicial officer, where he learns the charge against him and his liberty is subject to restriction, marks the start of adversary judicial proceedings that trigger attachment of the Sixth Amendment right to counsel."); *Shabazz v. State*, 2018 Ark. App. 399, 557 S.W.3d 274, 280 (2018) ("the Sixth Amendment right to counsel applies to suppression hearings"); *People v. Smith*, 30 N.Y.3d 626, 92 N.E.3d 789, 69 N.Y.S.3d 566 (2017) (the defendant had a right to representation by counsel on the prosecution's pretrial motion to compel him to submit to a buccal swab). It extends though sentencing (*Mempa v. Rhay*, 389 U.S. 128 (1967); *Lafler v. Cooper*, 566 U.S. 156, 165 (2012); *United States v. Freeman*, 24 F.4th 320 (4th Cir. 2022) (en banc); *Lewis v. Zatecky*, 993 F.3d 994 (7th Cir. 2021)), post-sentencing proceedings (*Richardson v. Superintendent Coal Township SCI*, 905 F.3d 750 (3d Cir. 2018); *Parker v. State*, 604 S.W.3d 555 (Tex. App. 2020)), and at least the first appeal as of right from conviction and sentence (*Douglas v. California*, 372 U.S. 353 (1963); *Swenson v. Bosler*, 386 U.S. 258 (1967); *Halbert v. Michigan*, 545 U.S. 605 (2005)); *cf. Belknap v. State*, 426 P.3d 1156 (Alaska App. 2018) (the right to counsel extends to motions for the sentencing credit authorized by a statute providing such credit to defendants who were on court-ordered electronic monitoring programs during their bail release); *and compare Martinez v. Ryan*, 566 U.S. 1 (2012), *and Trevino* v. *Thaler*, 569 U. S. 413 (2013), *and Commonwealth v. Bradley*, 261 A.3d 381 (Pa. 2021), *with Coleman v. Thompson*, 501 U.S. 722 (1991), *and Davila v. Davis*, 582 U.S. 521 (2017), and *Shinn v. Ramirez*, 142 S. Ct. 1718 (2022).

In a number of jurisdictions, a statute or local rule establishes an even broader guarantee of court appointment of counsel for indigent defendants in misdemeanor and petty-offense prosecutions, requiring court-appointed counsel whenever a term of imprisonment is *authorized* – or, in some States, whenever a term in excess of a specified length is authorized – whether or not such a sentence is actually imposed. *See Scott v. Illinois*, 440 U.S. 367, 385–88 & nn.18-22 (1979) (Brennan, J., dissenting) (collecting the relevant authorities).

If counsel is appointed to represent an indigent defendant and if counsel is not already familiar with the local rules, practices, and procedures for compensation of court-appointed counsel, s/he should check with the clerk of court and with lawyers in the jurisdiction who have experience in representing indigent clients in criminal cases. Payment will usually require detailed record-keeping of counsel's time and expenses, and it is therefore essential that counsel know in advance what types of expenses are covered and what types of documentation will be required.

5.1.2. *Funding for Defense Services*

In capital cases, most jurisdictions authorize the provision of expert consultants and investigative assistance to indigent defendants at public expense. (*See, e.g.*, 18 U.S.C. § 3599(f), providing indigents in federal capital cases with "investigative, expert, or other services [that] are reasonably necessary for the representation of the defendant," a standard elaborated in *Ayestas v. Davis*, 138 S. Ct. 1080, 1093, 1094 (2018), as asking "whether a reasonable attorney would regard the services as sufficiently important," considering "the potential merit of the claims that the . . . [defendant] wants to pursue, the likelihood that the services will generate useful and admissible evidence, and the prospect that the . . . [defendant] will be able to clear any procedural hurdles standing in the way.") In noncapital cases there is great variation from State to State and sometimes from locality to locality, with some courts furnishing little or no aid to indigents beyond the appointment of counsel. (Federal practice is governed by the Criminal Justice Act of 1964, 18 U.S.C. § 3006A(e).) Even where state or county payment for defense support services is authorized, it is frequently limited by statutorily specified ceilings that render it inadequate or is doled out by budget-conscious judges in amounts that are insufficient to meet the real needs of defense. Procedures for drawing down whatever funds are available may also be unsatisfactory. In some localities the court must approve each specific defense expenditure in advance, upon a showing of need in a form that discloses the nature of defense trial preparation to the prosecutor. See § 5.4 *infra*. In other localities defense counsel is reimbursed, after a *post facto* audit, for expenditures that the judge finds were reasonable. The latter system puts the defendant in the unconscionable posture of having to rely on the ability and willingness of the defense attorney to advance sums that may not be repaid. *Cf. State v. Robinson*, 123 N.H. 665, 465 A.2d 1214 (1983).

If counsel is appointed to represent an indigent client and if counsel is not already familiar with the local rules and practices for obtaining funding for defense services, s/he should ascertain from the clerk of court what expenses and services, if any, will be provided out of public funds and how to apply for them. Whether counsel is appointed or retained, if the client cannot afford fees and costs for court process, expert witnesses, consultative services, or investigative aids that counsel believes are legitimately needed, counsel should ascertain the local practice for requesting funds and should comply with it insofar as possible. *See Hinton v. Alabama*, 571 U.S. 263, 264, 267, 273-74 (2014) (per curiam). Pretrial orders denying funds to defendants who have made an adequate showing of indigency and of need can be challenged by appeal in some jurisdictions and by prerogative writ in others. *See, e.g., Duke v. State*, 311 Ga. 135, 856 S.E.2d 250 (2021); *State v. Brouillette*, 166 N.H. 487, 98 A.3d 1131 (2014); *Kimminau v. Avilez*, 2014 WL 5507295 (Ariz. App. 2014); *Johnny S. v. Superior Court*, 90 Cal. App. 3d 826, 153 Cal.Rptr. 550 (1979); § 31.1 *infra*. To the extent that local practice fails to authorize public payment for services that counsel needs or when it unreasonably restricts them – either by limiting the amounts available or by imposing crippling procedural preconditions – counsel may have to challenge the practice as unconstitutional. In this situation counsel should move the court to authorize the necessary expenditures without requiring the defendant to comply with the objectionable preconditions or else dismiss the prosecution, on the ground that failure to provide an impecunious defendant with adequate financial resources for a fair defense denies the defendant the Equal Protection of the Laws and the Due Process of Law guaranteed by the Fourteenth Amendment. See §§ 5.2-5.4 *infra*.

Reasonable recoupment provisions (that is, requirements that an indigent defendant who has been provided state-paid defensive assets repay the state if and when s/he becomes financially able to do so) are not *per se* unconstitutional (*Fuller v. Oregon*, 417 U.S. 40 (1974)), but the terms of any recoupment statute should be carefully reviewed in the light of *Rinaldi v. Yeager*, 384 U.S. 305 (1966), and *James v. Strange*, 407 U.S. 128 (1972).

5.2. *Rights Under the Equal Protection Clause*

In *Griffin v. Illinois*, 351 U.S. 12 (1956), the Supreme Court held that the Equal Protection Clause compelled a state to furnish a free transcript of a criminal trial to a convicted defendant who needed the transcript for presentation of an appeal and who could not afford to pay for it. Noting that a nonindigent defendant could purchase a transcript and that under Illinois practice convicted defendants "needed a transcript in order to get adequate appellate review of their alleged trial errors" (*id.* at 16), the Court decided the case on the broad ground that "[t]here can be no equal justice where the kind of trial a man gets depends on the amount of money he has" (*id.* at 19). *See also Williams v. Illinois*, 399 U.S. 235, 241 (1970); *Bearden v. Georgia*, 461 U.S. 660, 664 (1983); *Estelle v. Williams*, 425 U.S. 501, 505-6 (1976) (dictum); *Black v. Romano*, 471 U.S. 606, 614-15 (1985) (dictum).

Following *Griffin*, the Court has required the provision of free transcripts to indigents on both direct and collateral criminal appeals (*e.g., Draper v. Washington*, 372 U.S. 487 (1963); *Long v. District Court*, 385 U.S. 192 (1966); *Gardner v. California*, 393 U.S. 367 (1969); *Williams v. Oklahoma City*, 395 U.S. 458 (1969); *Mayer v. City of Chicago*, 404 U.S. 189 (1971); *see also M.L.B. v. S.L.J.*, 519 U.S. 102, 107, 110-12 (1996) [discussing the *Griffin-Mayer* line of precedent]; *compare United States v. MacCollom*, 426 U.S. 317 (1976)); the waiver of filing fees for both appeals and collateral-attack proceedings (*Burns v. Ohio*, 360 U.S. 252 (1959); *Smith v. Bennett*, 365 U.S. 708 (1961); *see also M.L.B. v. S.L.J., supra*, 519 U.S. at 111 & n.4 [discussing *Burns v. Ohio* and *Smith v. Bennett*]); and the provision of appointed counsel on at least a criminal defendant's first appeal as of right from conviction (*Douglas v. California*,

372 U.S. 353 (1963); *Swenson v. Bosler*, 386 U.S. 258 (1967); *Halbert v. Michigan*, 545 U.S. 605 (2005); *see also Coleman v. Thompson*, 501 U.S. 722, 755-56 (1991) (dictum); *Martinez v. Ryan*, 566 U.S. 1, 8-9 (2012) (dictum); *compare Ross v. Moffitt*, 417 U.S. 600 (1974); *Wainwright v. Torna*, 455 U.S. 586 (1982) (per curiam); *Pennsylvania v. Finley*, 481 U.S. 551 (1987); *Murray v. Giarratano*, 492 U.S. 1 (1989) (plurality opinion)). The full purport of the *Griffin* line of cases remains to be developed. But it is possible to state its principle comprehensively as a command that the state which prosecutes an indigent defendant must furnish him or her with every defensive resource which is necessary "to assure . . . an adequate opportunity to present his [or her] claims fairly in the context of the State's [criminal] . . . process" (*Ross v. Moffitt, supra*, 417 U.S. at 616 (dictum)) if a nonindigent defendant could purchase that resource.

Cases such as *Roberts v. LaVallee*, 389 U.S. 40 (1967), establish that this command extends to matters needed for trial preparation. *See, e.g., United States ex rel. Wilson v. McMann*, 408 F.2d 896 (2d Cir. 1969); *Peterson v. United States*, 351 F.2d 606 (9th Cir. 1965). *Britt v. North Carolina*, 404 U.S. 226 (1971), in particular, describes the command as a requirement "that the State . . . provide indigent prisoners with the basic tools of an adequate defense or appeal, when those tools are available for a price to other prisoners" (*id.* at 227); and although a free transcript was not required "in the narrow circumstances of [the *Britt*] . . . case" itself (*Id.*), the Court detailed those circumstances in a manner which leaves no doubt that generally an indigent defendant must be given free transcription of all relevant prior judicial proceedings "as a discovery device in preparation for trial, and as a tool at the trial itself for the impeachment of prosecution witnesses" (*id.* at 228; *see id.* at 229-30).

In *Mayer v. City of Chicago*, 404 U.S. 189 (1971), the Court phrased the Equal Protection requirement in terms of assuring "the indigent as effective [a trial] . . . as would be available to the defendant with resources to pay his own way." 404 U.S. at 195. In addition, *Mayer* firmly resists the notion that an indigent defendant's needs are to be "balanced" against the cost to the state of providing them or denied if they are too expensive. "*Griffin* does not represent a balance between the needs of the accused and the interests of society; its principle is a flat prohibition against pricing indigent defendants out of as effective [a defense] . . . as would be available to others able to pay their own way. . . . The State's fiscal interest is, therefore, irrelevant." 404 U.S. at 196-97. *See also Bounds v. Smith*, 430 U.S. 817, 825 (1977) ("the cost of protecting a constitutional right cannot justify its total denial").

Certainly, the most immediate implications of the *Griffin-Roberts-Britt-Mayer* line of decisions require that the state record all court proceedings in an indigent case at public expense, and that prior to trial a defendant who moves for free transcripts of earlier proceedings – at least in the same case, and perhaps in related cases – must be provided with them in adequate time to use them for trial preparation. See §§ 11.5.3, 11.8.7 *infra*.

An indigent defendant's right to compulsory process *in forma pauperis* to secure the attendance of material defense witnesses (see §§ 11.5.3, 29.4.4 *infra*) also seems obvious. *See Greenwell v. United States*, 317 F.2d 108 (D.C. Cir. 1963); *Welsh v. United States*, 404 F.2d 414, 417 (5th Cir. 1968); *compare United States v. Pitts*, 569 F.2d 343, 348-49 & n.10 (5th Cir. 1978); *United States v. Valenzuela-Bernal*, 458 U.S. 858, 867 n.7 (1982) (dictum).

Under *Ake v. Oklahoma*, 470 U.S. 68 (1985), an indigent defendant who "demonstrates to the trial judge that his [or her] sanity at the time of the offense is to be a significant factor at trial . . . must [be given free] . . . access to a competent psychiatrist who will conduct an appropriate examination and assist in evaluation, preparation, and presentation of the defense" (*id.* at 83). *Accord, McWilliams v. Dunn*, 582 U.S. 183 (2017) ("Our decision in *Ake v. Oklahoma* . . . clearly established that, when certain threshold criteria are met, the State must provide an indigent defendant with access to a mental health expert who is sufficiently available to the defense and independent from the prosecution to effectively 'assist in evaluation, preparation, and presentation of the defense.'" (*id.* at 186); "Unless a defendant is 'assure[d]' the assistance of someone who can effectively perform these functions, he has not received the 'minimum' to which *Ake* entitles him." (*id.* at 187-88)); *Conley v. Commonwealth*, 599 S.W.3d 756 (Ky. 2019); *Beshears v. State*, 254 So.3d 1133 (Fla. App. 2018) (applying *Ake* to require the appointment of an expert to assist an indigent defendant in investigating a potential defense of temporary insanity caused by his prescription medication). Although *Ake* ultimately framed its result as a due-process holding, the opinion unmistakably draws heavily on equal-protection precedents (*see* 470 U.S. at 76-77) and equal-protection concerns. "This Court has long recognized that when a State brings its judicial power to bear on an indigent defendant in a criminal proceeding, it must take steps to assure that the defendant has a fair opportunity to present his defense. This elementary principle, grounded in significant part on the Fourteenth Amendment's due process guarantee of fundamental fairness, derives from the belief that justice cannot be equal where, simply as a result of his poverty, a defendant is denied the opportunity to participate meaningfully in a judicial proceeding in which his liberty is at stake." *Id.* So, when rising *Ake* claims, counsel does well to couch them under both the Due Process and Equal Protection Clauses and to invoke *Britt*'s formulation that "the State must, as a matter of equal protection, provide indigent prisoners with the basic tools of an adequate defense . . . when those tools are available for a price to other prisoners." *Britt, supra*, 404 U.S. at 227. This framing of the issue provides the runup for asking judges the persuasive rhetorical question: "If you were representing a defendant with adequate financial resources, would you take this case to trial without retaining an expert in the field of [whatever specialty counsel is seeking]?"). *See, e.g., Cowley v. Stricklin*, 929 F.2d 640 (11th Cir. 1991); *Bush v. McCollum*, 231 F. Supp. 560 (N.D. Tex. 1964), *aff'd*, 344 F.2d 672 (5th Cir. 1965); *In re Allen R.*, 127 N.H. 718, 721-22, 506 A.2d 329, 331-32 (1986) (respondent in a delinquency case had federal and state constitutional rights to a state-paid psychologist to testify on *Miranda* issues at a confession suppression hearing). Although *Ake* itself dealt only with psychiatric experts, the Court's reasoning applies to other kinds of expert assistance as well. The *Ake* decision is grounded upon the state's obligation to afford an indigent defendant "access to the raw material integral to the building of an effective defense," 470 U.S. at 77. The same obligation exists whether the necessary "raw material" is a psychiatrist or some other type of expert. "'Criminal cases will arise where the only reasonable and available defense strategy requires consultation with experts or introduction of expert evidence.'" *Hinton v. Alabama*, 571 U.S. 263, 273 (2014) (per curiam). In these cases, the state must furnish the necessary funds. *See, e.g., Little v. Armontrout*, 835 F.2d 1240, 1241, 1244-45 (8th Cir. 1987) (en banc) (the trial court violated Due Process by denying the defense's motion for appointment of an "expert in hypnosis" to assist the defense at a pretrial suppression hearing and at trial in challenging the hypnotically enhanced identification of the defendant by the complainant); *Williams v. Martin*, 618 F.2d 1021 (4th Cir. 1980) (requiring the provision of a state-paid independent pathologist to an indigent defendant charged with homicide when the cause of death is debatable and medically complicated); *Cherry v. Estelle*, 507 F.2d 242, 243 (5th Cir. 1975), *subsequent history in* 424 F. Supp. 548 (N.D. Tex. 1976) (impliedly recognizing the right to provision of a state-paid independent ballistics expert under certain circumstances (*see Hoback v. Alabama*, 607 F.2d 680, 682 n.1 (5th Cir. 1979))); *Bowen v. Eyman*, 324 F. Supp. 339 (D. Ariz. 1970) (requiring provision of a state-paid defense expert when the prosecution has failed to conduct potentially exonerating chemical tests); *English v. Missildine*, 311 N.W.2d 292 (Iowa 1980) (requiring funding for a defense handwriting expert and for deposition expenses); *People v. Djurdjulov*, 2017 IL App (1st) 142258, 86 N.E.3d 1139, 416 Ill. Dec. 854 (2017) (reversing a conviction on the ground that the trial court erred under *Ake* by denying the defendant's request for funding to retain an expert to review cell phone data); *People v. Propp*, 508 Mich. 374, 383, 976 N.W.2d 1, 5 (2021) (in a murder case in which the defense requested but was denied funds to retain an expert in erotic asphyxiation to support the defense theory that the victim's death was accidental, the intermediate appellate court erred in affirming the defendant's conviction without evaluating his *Ake* claim under the proper standard: "whether there was a reasonable probability that the expert would have been helpful to the defense and whether the denial of expert assistance rendered the trial fundamentally unfair"); *Brown v. Eighth Judicial District Court in and for County of Clark*, 133 Nev. 916, 921, 415 P.3d 7, 11 (2017) (holding that an indigent defendant facing charges of lewdness with a minor is entitled to funding for an expert "regarding psychological issues involving child testimony, parental influence on that testimony, children's motivations regarding false allegations, and the influences upon a child's accusations in a sexual prosecution" and to "the services of an investigator to serve subpoenas on and obtain statements from witnesses and to investigate the circumstances of the allegations"); *People v. Williams*, 328 Mich. App. 408, 412, 938 N.W.2d 42, 45 (2019) (holding that a defendant at a *Miller v. Alabama* resentencing hearing is entitled to funding for mitigation experts "to analyze the *Miller* factors, including experts with specialized knowledge in adolescent development"); *People v. Orozco*, 210 P.3d 472, 474 (Colo. App. 2009) (reversing a conviction for sexual assault on a minor because the trial judge erred "in denying . . . [the defendant's] motion for funds to hire an expert who would have testified about the likelihood of physical evidence [which was absent] being present if . . . [the minor] was sexually assaulted as he said he was"; the defendant was represented by private counsel retained by his sister, but the sister had become unable to pay counsel, and the defendant himself was indigent); *Jones v. Sterling*, 210 Ariz. 308, 314-15, 110 P.3d 1271, 1277-78 (2005) (requiring provision of an expert to assist in the development of a selective-prosecution defense when the defendant has presented a credible preliminary showing of discrimination); *Jacobson v. Anderson*, 203 Ariz. 543, 57 P.3d 733 (Ariz. App. 2002) (a defendant in a prosecution for vehicular manslaughter and reckless endangerment is entitled to necessary funding for an accident reconstructionist and a criminalist); *People v. Lawson*, 163 Ill. 2d 187, 206, 218-230, 644 N.E.2d 1172, 1181, 1187-92, 206 Ill. Dec. 119, 134-39 (1994) ("trial court abused its discretion by denying defendant's motion for expert assistance" of a shoeprint expert "to testify at trial and assist in the preparation of his defense"); *People v. Watson*, 36 Ill. 2d 228, 221 N.E.2d 645 (1966) (requiring provision of a state-paid examiner of questioned documents); *People v. Kennedy*, 502 Mich. 206, 917 N.W.2d 355 (2018), *enforced by granting a new trial, People v. Kennedy*, 2020 WL 7089842 (Mich. App. 2020), summarized in § 5.4 *infra* (applying *Ake* to a defendant's request for appointment of a state-paid DNA expert); *State v. Moore*, 321 N.C. 327, 328, 331, 343-46, 364 S.E.2d 648, 649-50, 656-58 (1988) (trial judge erred in denying the defendant's request for appointment of an independent psychiatrist to assist in challenging the voluntariness of his confession, and also erred in denying the defense's request for a fingerprint expert to challenge the "state expert's conclusion that defendant's palm print was found at the scene of the attack"); *Rey v. State*, 897 S.W.2d 333, 335, 346 (Tex. Crim. App. 1995) (trial judge violated Due Process by denying the defense's motion for the appointment of "an independent forensic pathologist" to "assist in the evaluation, preparation and presentation of his defense"), and cases collected in *id.* at 338 n.4; *Stephen A. Saltzburg, The Duty to Investigate and the Availability of Expert Witnesses*, 86 FORDHAM L. REV. 1709 (2018). From these authorities and Due Process principles sketched in § 5.3 *infra*, the argument for state-paid investigative services, when reasonably needed, seems plain. *See State v. Wang*, 312 Conn. 222, 245, 92 A.3d 220, 235 (2014) ("we hold that due process, as guaranteed under the fourteenth amendment to the United States constitution, requires the state to provide an indigent self-represented criminal defendant with expert or investigative assistance when he makes a threshold showing that such assistance is reasonably necessary for the preparation and presentation of his defense"); *Corenevsky v. Superior Court*, 36 Cal. 3d 307, 682 P.2d 360, 204 Cal. Rptr. 165 (1984); *Staten v. Superior Court*, 2003 WL 21419614 (Cal. App. 2003); *State v. Second Judicial District Court*, 85 Nev. 241, 453 P.2d 421 (1969); *Mason v. Arizona*, 504 F.2d 1345, 1351-52 (9th Cir. 1974) (dictum); *Smith v. Enomoto*, 615 F.2d 1251, 1252 (9th Cir. 1980) (dictum). *But see Bergman v. Howard*, 54 F.4th 950 (6th Cir. 2022) (A defendant charged with multiple homicide counts based on a fatal vehicle collision requested state funding for a toxicologist "for two reasons. Counsel could not understand the results of Bergman's blood tests. A toxicologist could explain in plain English whether problems existed with the state's testing and whether the drugs found in Bergman's system would have impaired her driving. Alternatively, counsel asked for a toxicologist to confirm the state's test results by retesting the preserved blood samples from Bergman's driving incidents." *Id.* at 955. The trial court "categorically rejected the request for an expert to retest the samples. As the court saw things, Bergman's speculation that the state scientists might have conducted invalid tests did not warrant a new round of testing. Yet the court did not 'rul[e] out [a] consultant-type expert' if defense counsel followed up with a clear explanation of what he needed the expert for. . . . Counsel apparently never offered additional briefing on this topic." *Id.* at 955-56. The defendant was convicted; the Michigan Court of Appeals upheld the convictions; and a Sixth Circuit panel applies AEDPA's stringent limitation of federal habeas review (see § 49.2.3.2 *infra*) to deny relief: "[T]he Michigan appellate court's logic – that Bergman failed to make an adequate showing to obtain a toxicologist – fits comfortably within the 'leeway' given to the state courts as a result of the lack of clarity on how to apply *Ake*." *Id.* at 959. "*Ake*'s precise holding – that a state must provide an expert psychiatrist to an indigent defendant who makes a substantial showing of an insanity defense – does not directly control here. Bergman did not claim to be insane when she got behind the wheel of her . . . [vehicle]. She sought a toxicologist, not a psychiatrist. She wanted this expert to review the testing methods and results of the state's forensic scientists and to rebut . . . [a state expert's] opinions about the effects of the drugs in her system on her driving. Did the Michigan court's refusal to provide this different type of state-funded expert qualify as an 'unreasonable application' of *Ake*'s clearly established holding? ¶ We think not. The Supreme Court has left open how *Ake* should extend to experts other than psychiatrists . . . ." *Id.* at 958.).

The right to state funding under *Ake* applies not only to defendants represented by a public defender but to those who are proceeding *pro se* (*see State v. Wang, supra*) and those with *pro bono* volunteer counsel (*see, e.g., State v. Brown*, 139 N.M. 466, 472, 134 P.3d 753, 759 (2006) ("Brown, an indigent defendant represented by *pro bono* counsel, is entitled both to the constitutional right to counsel and the constitutional right to be provided with the basic tools of an adequate defense. Although Brown was initially appointed a Department attorney, we do not believe that alone is enough to ensure that his constitutional rights are protected. Brown is also constitutionally entitled to be provided with the basic tools of an adequate defense. That right is not contingent upon the appointment of Department counsel; it is inherent under the state and federal Constitutions. . . . Thus, we conclude that since Brown's constitutional rights are compromised by his having been denied public funding for expert witness fees, there is a strong constitutional basis for us to reverse the Court of Appeals. We conclude that the more persuasive and reasoned approach in this case is that argued by Brown. That is, indigent defendants represented by *pro bono*, contract, or Department counsel should have equal access to expert witness funding *provided that* the expert witness meets all of the standards promulgated by the Department. ¶ We find additional, albeit secondary, support for our decision from the cases of our sister states. It appears that the majority of state courts that have examined this issue have concluded that under the U.S. Constitution and their respective state statutes, indigent defendants represented by *pro bono* or retained counsel are entitled to state funding for various defense costs, including expert witness fees."); *Duke v. State*, 311 Ga. 135 856 S.E.2d 250 (2021); *State v. Garvins*, 65 Conn. L. Rptr. 596, 2017 WL 6884033 (Conn. Super. 2017)), provided that an adequate showing of indigency – *i.e.*, inability to afford the necessary services – is made. Similarly, when friends or relatives pay for counsel to represent an indigent defendant, their indigency need not be shown in order to bring *Ake* rights into play. *See People v. Djurdjulov, supra*, 2017 IL App (1st) 142258, 86 N.E.3d at 1150, 416 Ill. Dec. at 865 ("A defendant needs to establish only his own indigence as part of the proof needed to show a right to fees. . . . He need not show the indigence of relatives or other persons he knows. Friends, relatives, or others who help with some of the costs of defense have not thereby committed themselves to paying all costs necessary for the defense."); *State v. Burns*, 398 Utah Adv. Rep. 32, 4 P.3d 795 (Utah 2000); *Brown v. Eighth Judicial District Court in and for County of Clark, supra*, 133 Nev. at 919-20, 415 P.3d at 10-12; *English v. Missildine, supra*; *Clarke v. Superior Court*, 2010 WL 553586, at *3 (Cal. App. 2010) ("It is undisputed that Clarke has no money of his own. The only question is whether he does not qualify as an indigent because his parents have paid a fee to counsel. On this record, the answer is no: the record is devoid of any evidence that the sum of $35,000 is sufficient to cover the fee of counsel (after over three years of representation) and ancillary experts or that Clarke's parents have promised to continue to pay counsel or costs and expenses."); *cf. People v. Greer*, 2022 CO 5, 502 P.3d 1012, 1019 (Colo. 2022) (holding, in the context of an application for state-funded counsel by a defendant who lives rent-free with his parents and whose parents pay all household expenses, that "income from members of a defendant's household who contribute monetarily to the household should be excluded from an indigency determination when such income is unavailable to the defendant" for his defense needs); *but see State Public Defender v. Amaya*, 977 N.W.2d 22, 32-38 (Iowa 2022) (reviewing the authorities and observing that "courts facing constitutional challenges to their state's rules about ancillary services have been divided over the issue of whether limiting the ancillary services to only state-provided counsel violates an indigent defendant's constitutional rights. The divide turns on the court's determination of whether the constitutional right to ancillary services is tethered to, or severable from, the right to counsel. Courts that conclude the constitutional rights are tethered hold a state may limit access to state funding for ancillary services to indigent defendants represented by state-provided counsel. . . . ¶ Other courts hold a state's funding mechanism that limits ancillary services to court-appointed attorneys is unconstitutional because the rights are related but distinct under *Ake*, so bundling the ancillary services with court-appointed counsel did not satisfy the separate constitutional right." *Id.* at 34.).

5.3. *Rights Under the Due Process Clause*

Despite its equal-protection flavor, *Ake v. Oklahoma* is conventionally read as a due process case. *See* 470 U.S. at 86-87 & n.13; *and e.g.*, *People v. Kennedy*, 502 Mich. 206, 218, 917 N.W.2d 355, 361-62 (2018) ("*Ake* . . . sets forth the due process analysis that a court must use when an indigent criminal defendant claims he or she has not been provided 'the basic tools of an adequate defense' and therefore did not have 'an adequate opportunity to present [his or her] claims fairly within the adversarial system.'); *Moore v. Kemp*, 809 F.2d 702, 710 (11th Cir. 1987) (en banc) ("In *Ake,* the Court concluded that the due process clause's guarantee of fundamental fairness is implicated 'when [an indigent] defendant demonstrates to the trial judge that his sanity at the time of the offense is to be a significant factor at trial' and that 'the State must, at a minimum, assure the defendant access to a competent psychiatrist who will conduct an appropriate examination and assist in evaluation, preparation, and presentation of the defense.'"). *Cf. Evitts v. Lucey*, 469 U.S. 387, 404-05 (1985). A criminal defendant's inability to marshal the information necessary to present his or her version of the facts, in the context of a litigation process that is quintessentially adversary, smacks of fundamental unfairness. It was just this consideration that led the Supreme Court in *Gideon v. Wainwright*, 372 U.S. 335 (1963), to hold that the right to counsel is a component of Due Process (*see Argersinger v. Hamlin*, 407 U.S. 25, 31-33 (1972); *Ross v. Moffitt*, 417 U.S. 600, 610 (1974) (dictum); *Middendorf v. Henry*, 425 U.S. 25, 41 (1976) (dictum); *McCoy v. Court of Appeals*, 486 U.S. 429, 435 (1988) (dictum)); and counsel unaided in a case in which counsel needs aid to provide an adequate defense hardly satisfies the *Gideon* command (*Williams v. Martin*, 618 F.2d 1021, 1025, 1027 (4th Cir. 1980)). In *McCoy v. Court of Appeals*, the Supreme Court considered the obligations of court-appointed counsel on appeal and concluded that the constitutional "principle of substantial equality [between defendants who can and those who cannot afford to retain counsel] . . . require[s] that appointed counsel make the same diligent and thorough evaluation of the case as a retained lawyer. . . ." (486 U.S. at 438). Appointed counsel at the trial level have obligations that are at least as demanding (*see id.* at 435); and "thorough evaluation of the case" cannot be performed without adequate investigative resources. "Because the right to counsel [announced in *Gideon*] is so fundamental to a fair trial, the Constitution cannot tolerate trials in which counsel, though present in name, is unable to assist the defendant to obtain a fair decision on the merits." *Evitts v. Lucey, supra,* 469 U.S. at 395; *see also Rogers v. Israel,* 746 F.2d 1288 (7th Cir. 1984). The federal caselaw cited in §§ 3.23.3 *supra* and § 18.9.2.1 *infra* to the effect that defense counsel must be given adequate time to prepare, also suggests that s/he must be given adequate resources with which to prepare. A like command may be implicit in the Sixth and Fourteenth Amendment rights to compulsory process, see §§ 18.9.2.4, 29.4.4 *infra,* and in the Due Process requirement of a fair adversarial balance in criminal procedures, see § 18.9.2.7 *infra.*

Perhaps timely disclosure to the defense of the prosecutor's case and such exculpatory or mitigating materials as diligent police investigation has unearthed may fulfill these Due Process requirements. That, however, is subject to considerable doubt, since the police are not likely to be as vigorous in their researches for a defendant as in those against the defendant. In any event, the denial to an indigent defendant both of disclosure of the products of the state's investigation (see §§ 18.1-18.10 *infra*) and of resources to conduct his or her own investigation clearly invites attack under the Due Process Clause. For this reason counsel is advised to couple a full range of discovery requests with applications for state-paid investigative and expert assistance. See § 18.7.3 *infra.*

5.4. *Procedures*

Whatever local procedures are available for requesting state-paid assistance should be employed unless their use is unduly burdensome. *See, e.g., McWilliams v. Dunn,* 582 U.S. 183, 196 (2017) (rejecting, as unsupported by the record, the state's argument that defense counsel failed to adequately request additional expert assistance; the Court explains that the record shows that "[w]hen defense counsel requested a continuance at the sentencing hearing, he repeatedly told the court that he needed 'to have someone else review' the Goff [neuropsychological] report and medical records," and "[c]ounsel also explicitly asked the trial court what else he was supposed to ask for to obtain an expert: 'Would Your Honor have wanted me to file a Motion for Extraordinary Expenses to get someone?'"). If the local procedures are too restrictive to satisfy counsel's needs, counsel should file a motion requesting state funding and challenging the relevant aspects of local practice. *See, e.g., People v. Lawson,* 163 Ill. 2d 187, 222, 224, 230, 644 N.E.2d 1172, 1189, 1192 , 206 Ill. Dec. 119, 136, 139 (1994) (rejecting the state's argument that "an accused is not entitled to funds for expert assistance unless he identifies the specific expert and provides an estimate of the costs involved"; "a denial of expert assistance funding to a criminal accused, who has not yet identified the particular individual he wishes to hire and given an estimate of costs, but who has otherwise demonstrated his constitutional entitlement to such assistance, represents the elevation of form over substance"); *State v. Moore,* 321 N.C. 327, 345-47, 364 S.E.2d 648, 657-58 (1988) (rejecting the state's argument that a defense motion for appointment of an expert must "present a specific basis for questioning the accuracy of the state[] [expert's] determination"; "The state's proposed test would demand that the defendant possess already the expertise of the witness sought."). *Cf. Hinton v. Alabama,* 571 U.S. 263, 264,

267, 273-74 (2014) (per curiam) ("Hinton's trial attorney rendered constitutionally deficient performance" by presenting a toolmark "expert he knew to be inadequate" when counsel "could not find a better expert willing to work for $1,000" and counsel mistakenly "believed that he was unable [under state law] to obtain more than $1,000 to cover expert fees"; the trial judge who granted counsel's request for funding for an expert cited a $1,000 statutory maximum, but counsel should "have corrected the trial judge's mistaken belief that a $1,000 limit applied" and sought additional funding); *Yun Hseng Liao v. Junious*, 817 F.3d 678, 682-83, 695 (9th Cir. 2016) (the defendant was deprived of effective assistance of counsel because his lawyer relied on a court clerk's erroneous statement that a motion for funds for an additional expert evaluation of the defendant had been denied when in fact it had been granted; counsel's "failure to verify what the court clerk" said, and counsel's failure to conduct "any further inquiry into the status of his motion," and his decision to instead proceed "to trial without the benefit of the [additional] medical examination" were prejudicial because they "eviscerated a viable defense"); *People v. Kennedy*, 502 Mich. 206, 226-27, 917 N.W.2d 355, 366-67 (2018), *enforced by granting a new trial, People v. Kennedy*, 2020 WL 7089842 (Mich. App. 2020) (holding that *Ake* supersedes the state statutory provision regulating appointment of defense experts for an indigent, and adopting a "reasonable probability" standard for applying *Ake*: "Until an expert is consulted, a defendant might often be unaware of how, *precisely*, the expert would aid the defense. If, in such cases, the defendant were required to prove in detail with a high degree of certainty that an expert would benefit the defense, the defendant would essentially be tasked with the impossible: to get an expert, the defendant would need to already know what the expert would say. At the same time, the defendant's bare assertion that an expert would be beneficial cannot, without more, entitle him or her to an expert; otherwise, every defendant would receive funds for experts upon request. ¶ A majority of states confronting this problem have adopted a reasonable probability standard. In *Moore v Kemp*, [809 F.2d 702, 712 (11th Cir. 1987)], the United States Court of Appeals for the Eleventh Circuit discussed this standard as follows:

> [A] . . . defendant must show the trial court that there exists a reasonable probability both that an expert would be of assistance to the defense and that denial of expert assistance would result in a fundamentally unfair trial. Thus, if a defendant wants an expert to assist his attorney in confronting the prosecution's proof – by preparing counsel to cross-examine the prosecution's experts or by providing rebuttal testimony – he must inform the court of the nature of the prosecution's case and how the requested expert would be useful. At the very least, he must inform the trial court about the nature of the crime and the evidence linking him to the crime. By the same token, if the defendant desires the appointment of an expert so that he can present an affirmative defense, such as insanity, he must demonstrate a substantial basis for the defense, as the defendant did in *Ake*. In each instance, the defendant's showing must also include a specific description of the expert or experts desired . . . [and] should inform the court why the particular expert is necessary. We recognize that defense counsel may be unfamiliar with the specific scientific theories implicated in a case and therefore cannot be expected to provide the court with a detailed analysis of the assistance an appointed expert might provide. We do believe, however, that defense counsel is obligated to inform himself about the specific

scientific area in question and to provide the court with as much information as possible concerning the usefulness of the requested expert to the defense's case.").

If the local rules require that expenditures be approved in advance by the court, on the filing of an affidavit or motion describing the services for which each expenditure is required and/or justifying the need for those services, counsel should request leave to make the required filing *ex parte* under seal. Counsel should insist that the defendant is not required to disclose the theory and strategy of the defense to the prosecutor – and certainly cannot be compelled to disclose potentially self-incriminating information (see §§ 12.6.4.3, 16.6.1, 18.12 *infra*) – as the precondition of state financial assistance. *Cf. Simmons v. United States*, 390 U.S. 377, 384-94 (1968), and cases cited following *Simmons* in § 16.6.1 *infra*. The double-bind problem is recognized in *United States v. Branker*, 418 F.2d 378, 380-81 (2d Cir. 1969) (dictum); *cf. United States v. Kahan*, 415 U.S. 239 (1974) (per curiam); but *Branker*'s proposed solution to it – precluding prosecutorial use at trial of any evidence disclosed by the defendant in proceedings seeking *forma pauperis* assistance – is probably insufficiently protective to justify compelling the disclosure in the first place, at least in the absence of a formal grant of use and derivative-use immunity (*see Maness v. Meyers*, 419 U.S. 449, 461-63, 468-70 (1975); *Pillsbury Co. v. Conboy*, 459 U.S. 248, 256-57 & n.13 (1983)). In any event, Congress has now resolved the issue in federal practice by providing that indigents' requests for funding for support services should be considered by district courts *ex parte. See* 18 U.S.C. § 3006A(e)(1). Notably, *Ake v. Oklahoma*, 470 U.S. 68, 82-83 (1985), explicitly states that the federal constitutional right to state-paid expert assistance which *Ake* recognizes is triggered when "the defendant is able to make an *ex parte* threshold showing to the trial court" of the facts which support that right. *See, e.g., Andrews v. State*, 243 So.3d 899, 901-02 (Fla. 2018) ("In making a showing of particularized need [for funding to retain a defense expert], a defendant may be required to expose privileged information or attorney work product, depending on the type of expert assistance requested. Requiring a defendant to reveal to the prosecutor the name of an expert witness whom the defendant may wish to consider calling, along with the reasons why this witness may be of value to the defense, is 'contrary to the work-product doctrine because it would serve to highlight the thought processes and legal analysis of the attorneys involved.' . . . Even if the defendant is only required to disclose the expert's name and area of expertise, that is information that the State would otherwise not be entitled to know at that stage. In fact, the State's presence at the hearing puts the defendant in the difficult situation of having to choose between fully supporting the motion for the appointment of an expert and not revealing information to the State that it would not otherwise be privy to. . . . ¶ Additionally, depending on the reason for the expert requested, it is possible that a defendant may be forced to disclose self-incriminating information, in violation of the defendant's Fifth Amendment rights. . . . ¶ Accordingly, ex parte hearings are necessary in this context to protect indigent defendants' rights. Federal law and other states also require ex parte hearings in this context."); *Brooks v. State*, 259 Ga. 562, 565, 385 S.E.2d 81, 84 (1989) ("While exercising . . . ["the right of the indigent defendant to obtain the expert assistance necessary to assist in preparing his defense"], the defendant also has the right to obtain that assistance without losing the opportunity to prepare the defense in secret. Otherwise, the defendant's 'fair opportunity to present his defense,' acknowledged in *Ake,* will be impaired.");

accord, Putnal v. State, 303 Ga. 569, 579-82, 814 S.E.2d 307, 315-17 (Ga. 2018) (detailing in a useful exposition many of the ways in which a refusal to allow an indigent to proceed *ex parte* and under seal when applying for state funding can prejudice the defense); *State v. Touchet*, 642 So.2d 1213, 1214 (La. 1994) ("[A]n indigent defendant's request for funding may be filed **ex parte** and that such request is to be considered **in camera** by the trial court. The state is to be notified of the **ex parte** hearing, and, while not to be present or participate initially in the hearing itself, is to be allowed to file an opposition to the motion. The trial court is then to determine, **in camera,** whether the defendant has made a showing that the proceedings should continue **in camera** so as to protect the defendant from disclosure of his defense. If the defendant fails to show a need for secrecy, the state is to be allowed to participate in the hearing; if the defendant makes the required showing, then the hearing is to continue **in camera.** We further hold that, in this hearing, the defendant must show his need for the expert assistance and the amount of funds necessary to secure such assistance. Once this showing is made, the trial court is empowered to order the state to provide the needed funds."); *State v. Ballard*, 333 N.C. 515, 516 , 428 S.E.2d 178, at 178 (1993) ("[w]e hold that an indigent defendant who requests that evidence supporting his motion for expert psychiatric assistance be presented in an *ex parte* hearing is constitutionally entitled to have such a hearing, and that the trial court erred in denying defendant's request to be heard on this matter *ex parte*."); *State v. Dahl*, 874 N.W.2d 348, 353-54 (Iowa 2016) ("If the trial court requires defense counsel to make a record of the facts supporting a defendant's reasonable need for investigative services in the presence of the prosecutor, the State could deduce defense counsel's trial strategy from those disclosures. Disclosure of the defense counsel's trial strategy to the State impairs an indigent defendant's right to effective assistance of counsel. . . . ¶ 'The right to counsel is the right to the effective assistance of counsel.'. . . However, we need not decide whether the trial court's failure to provide an ex parte hearing on Dahl's application for appointment of a private investigator violated any of Dahl's constitutional rights because we agree with Congress [citing 18 U.S.C. § 3006A(e)(1)] that an open hearing may possibly cause a defendant to reveal his defense. ¶ Accordingly, we exercise our supervisory powers . . . to articulate a protocol to balance the statutory right of an indigent defendant to the appointment of a private investigator . . . against his or her burden to present sufficient information to the trial court to support the granting of an application for appointment of a private investigator at state expense. . . . ¶ When a trial court deems an indigent defendant's application for appointment of a private investigator may have some merit but does not contain adequate information for the court to determine whether it should grant the application, the court should hold an ex parte hearing before ruling on the merits of the application. At that hearing, the court should require the defendant to provide additional information that will allow it to rule on the merits. If the court holds an ex parte hearing, the court must report the ex parte hearing. The court must also seal any transcript or order that would disclose defense strategy or work product and file a separate order announcing its decision to grant or deny the application."); *People v. Quitugua*, 2021 Guam 20, 2021 WL 5918910, at *2 (Guam 2021) ("Quitugua argues he is entitled to an *ex parte hearing* for his expert funding request because seeking expert assistance and explaining to the court the need for expert consultation are protected from the People by the work product doctrine. . . . Quitugua reasons that seeking an expert, and any details about the nature and need for the expert, are protected because these details would reveal potential defense strategy. . . . We agree. While there is no explicit statutory requirement to provide *ex parte* hearings, we find that, in the interest of due process and fairness, our trial courts must grant an indigent defendant's request to hold a hearing for expert funding *ex parte*, and the substantive reasons for this request should be made under seal. ¶ *Ex parte* hearings protect indigent defendants' privilege against self-incrimination, prevent the premature disclosure of a defense strategy, and preserve the right to effective assistance of counsel.); *cf. Morrison v. State*, 575 S.W.3d 1, 7 (Tex. App. 2019) ("'[T]he Sixth Amendment . . . imposes on the State an affirmative obligation to respect and preserve the accused's choice to seek assistance,' which means, 'at the very least, the prosecutor . . . [has] an affirmative obligation not to act in a manner that circumvents and thereby dilutes the protection afforded by the right to counsel." . . . Because billing records exist to secure an indigent defendant's right to the appointment of counsel, the prosecutor's 'affirmative obligation' requires a prosecuting attorney to refrain from reviewing indigent defense billing records during the case against the defendant, regardless of how the prosecutor may acquire that information and regardless of whether any privilege attendant to those records was waived by public disclosure. ¶ If the prosecutor nevertheless reviews those records, he purposefully intrudes into the defendant's attorney-client relationship. If, at trial, (1) any of 'the State's evidence originated in the [intrusion],' (2) the information obtained from the records was 'used in any other way to the substantial detriment of [the defendant],' or (3) the State learned details about the defendant's trial preparations from the records, then the intrusion prejudiced the defendant. . . . Error of this type is fundamental and may be raised on appeal even in the absence of a trial objection."); *United States v. Sellers*, 275 F.R.D. 620, 624-25 (D. Nev. 2011) (Federal Criminal "Rule 17(b) allows an *ex parte* application by a defendant unable to pay for an order compelling a witness to appear. Rule 17(c) [dealing with subpoenas duces tecum], however, does not contain any language allowing an *ex parte* application for pretrial production by a defendant without financial means. Courts are split as to whether a party may make an *ex parte* application for a pretrial subpoena *duces tecum* . . .¶ This court agrees with those courts which have found that an indigent defendant should be permitted to make an *ex parte* application for pretrial production of documents under limited circumstances, such as where identification of the source of evidence potentially imperils the source or integrity of evidence; or where notice of a subpoena *duces tecum* would compromise defense counsel's trial strategy; or where a constitutional interest of a defendant is implicated. . . . ¶ . . . The court also finds Seller's [sic] application and supporting affidavit were appropriately filed *ex parte* and should remain sealed to protect the mental impressions and trial strategy of defense counsel."); Donna H. Lee, Note, *In the Wake of* Ake v. Oklahoma*: An Indigent Criminal Defendant's Lack of Ex Parte Access to Expert Services*, 67 N.Y.U. L. REV. 154, 170-71 n.122 (1992).

In assessing the sufficiency an indigent defendant's "threshold showing" of a need for any particular sort of expert or investigative assistance, *Ake* adopts the analytic framework of *Mathews v. Eldridge*, 424 U.S. 319, 335 (1976). *See Ake v. Oklahoma, supra*, 470 U.S. at 77. Although the *Mathews* analysis formally requires consideration of three factors ("the private interest that will be affected by the action of the State"; "the governmental interest that will be affected if the safeguard is to be provided"; and "the probable value of the additional or substitute procedural safeguards that are sought, and the risk of an erroneous deprivation of the affected interest if those safeguards are not provided" (*id.*), the first two factors generically favor the defendant in most criminal prosecutions – and certainly in all prosecutions for crimes that entail the possibility of a severe sentence. (The "private interest" against undergoing heavy criminal punishment is obvious; the only relevant "governmental interest" is in minimizing fiscal expenditures, and this interest can ordinarily be taken into account by adjusting the *amount* allocated for defense services.) So the key to showing that the specific circumstances of the defendant's case generate an entitlement to any given type and amount of assistance will ordinarily be to satisfy *Mathews*'s third consideration by making an adequate factual demonstration of "the probable value . . . [to the defense case of the kind of expert or investigative assistance] sought, and the risk of an erroneous deprivation of the . . . [defendant's "fundamental [right] . . . to present witnesses in his own defense" (*Chambers v. Mississippi*, 410 U.S. 284, 302 (1973); see § 39.1 *infra*) if those . . . [particular defense services] are not provided" (*Ake v. Oklahoma, supra*, 470 U.S. at 77). Counsel will need to show that the services which the requested expert or investigator can perform are "likely to be a significant factor in [the defendant's] . . . defense [and that] with such assistance, the defendant might have a reasonable chance of success" (*id.* at 82-83). *See, e.g., McWilliams v. Dunn, supra*, 582 U.S. at 195 ("[N]o one denies that the conditions that trigger application of *Ake* are present [in this case]. McWilliams is and was an 'indigent defendant,' . . . . His 'mental condition' was 'relevant to . . . the punishment he might suffer,' . . . . And, that 'mental condition,' *i.e.*, his 'sanity at the time of the offense,' was 'seriously in question,' . . . . Consequently, the Constitution, as interpreted in *Ake*, required the State to provide McWilliams with 'access to a competent psychiatrist who will conduct an appropriate examination and assist in evaluation, preparation, and presentation of the defense.'"). *Compare Caldwell v. Mississippi*, 472 U.S. 320, 323 n.1 (1985) (finding no violation of Due Process in the denial of funds for defense experts where an indigent defendant "offered little more than undeveloped assertions that the requested assistance would be beneficial").

McWilliams v. Dunn, supra, raised the question whether "a State must provide an indigent defendant with a qualified mental health expert retained specifically for the defense team, not a neutral expert available to both parties" (582 U.S. at 197), but the Court left that question unresolved (*id.* at 197-98). It upheld McWilliams' right to a state-paid mental health expert on the narrower ground that "*Ake* clearly established that a defendant must receive the assistance of a mental health expert who is sufficiently available to the defense and independent from the prosecution to effectively 'assist in evaluation, preparation, and presentation of the defense'" (*id.* at 197) and that the trial court's order requiring "Dr. John Goff, a neuropsychologist employed by the State's Department of Mental Health" to examine McWilliams "'in order to have the test results available for his sentencing hearing'" (*id.* at 190) did not provide the requisite assistance.

"We are willing to assume that Alabama met the *examination* portion of this requirement by providing for Dr. Goff's examination of McWilliams. . . . But what about the other three parts? Neither Dr. Goff nor any other expert helped the defense evaluate Goff's report or McWilliams' extensive medical records and translate these data into a legal strategy. Neither Dr. Goff nor any other expert helped the defense prepare and present arguments that might, for example, have explained that McWilliams' purported malingering was not necessarily inconsistent with mental illness (as an expert later testified in postconviction proceedings . . .). Neither Dr. Goff nor any other expert helped the defense prepare direct or cross-examination of any witnesses, or testified at the judicial sentencing hearing himself." (*Id.* at 198-99.)

Despite the Court's "unwillingness to resolve the broader question whether *Ake* clearly established a right to an expert independent from the prosecution" (*id.* at 197), defense counsel should feel comfortable in arguing that the answer to that question is, yes. Two aspects of *McWilliams* support this answer. First, the Court notes that McWilliams' brief "points to language in *Ake* that seems to foresee that consequence. See, *e.g.*, 470 U.S., at 81, 105 S. Ct. 1087 ('By organizing a defendant's mental history, examination results and behavior, and other information, interpreting it in light of their expertise, and then laying out their investigative and analytic process to the jury, *the psychiatrists for each party* enable the jury to make its most accurate determination of the truth on the issue before them' (emphasis added))" (*id.*). Second, *McWilliams* came to the Court in a federal habeas corpus posture, so the issue presented was not whether *Ake* requires the appointment of an independent defense expert but, rather, whether *Ake* so "clearly established" that requirement as to make it enforceable in collateral-attack proceedings governed by 28 U.S.C. § 2254(d) [see § 49.2.3.2 *infra*]. Under the Supreme Court's § 2254(d) jurisprudence, a finding that a right is "clearly established" by any given precedent requires a significantly stronger showing than that the right flows logically from the precedent. *See, e.g., Virginia v. LeBlanc*, 582 U.S. 91, 94-96 (2017). So the defense answer to a prosecutor's predictable argument that *McWilliams* leaves room for the denial of an independent defense expert under *Ake* is "not much room." In any event, counsel should urge trial courts that the appointment of an independent defense expert is the only way in which the federal constitutional requirements of *Ake* and *McWilliams* can be safely or efficiently implemented. The *McWilliams* opinion itself observes that "As a practical matter, the simplest way for a State to meet this [*Ake*] standard may be to provide a qualified expert retained specifically for the defense team. This appears to be the approach that the overwhelming majority of jurisdictions have adopted. See Brief for National Association of Criminal Defense Lawyers et al. as *Amici Curiae* 8-35 (describing practice in capital-active jurisdictions)." *McWilliams*, 582 U.S. at 197. And "as a practical matter," any trial court that seeks to satisfy *Ake* and *McWilliams* by appointing a neutral expert rather than a defense-team expert is engaging in a risky crapshoot. In the ordinary case, the first point in time at which the facts necessary to adjudicate a defense contention that a neutral expert provided less-than-adequate assistance under a *post hoc* record-specific audit of the expert's performance will be the conclusion of the presentation of evidence. In many cases, as in *McWilliams*, such an adjudication will be impossible until after trial, appeals, and initial postconviction proceedings have become past history. (Note the *McWilliams* Court's partial reliance on what "an expert later testified in postconviction proceedings" (*id.* at 199).) At these late stages, the finding of an *Ake-McWilliams* violation will require that the trial be aborted (or the conviction set aside) and a retrial ordered. Trial judges should be responsive to the argument that jeopardizing the finality of the trial they are conducting by failing to take the "simplest," safest step for implementing *Ake* – "to provide a qualified expert retained specifically for the defense team" (*McWilliams*, 582 U.S. at 197) – would be altogether improvident.

Confronted with a state-law or local requirement that a defendant document specific defense needs or proposed expenditures as the precondition of receiving funds for expert or investigative assistance, counsel who believes that such documentation will result in improvident disclosure of defense planning to the prosecutor should submit an affidavit or declaration

— asserting the needs or proposed expenditures of the defense in unrevealing, conclusory form (see § 29.4.4 *infra*);

— averring that a more particularized description would reveal counsel's "litigating strategies" (*United States v. Valenzuela-Bernal*, 458 U.S. 858, 862 n.3 (1982), § 18.13 *infra*) or would reveal leads to potentially incriminating matter (see § 18.12 *infra*) or both, and would thus unconstitutionally subject the defendant to a burden to which defendants with money are not subjected;

— citing *Ake*; and

— offering to make the detailed showing *ex parte*, in chambers.

Cf. Greenwell v. United States, 317 F.2d 108 (D.C. Cir. 1963).

When no state procedure is applicable, a simple motion to the court for provision of state-paid assistance or, in the alternative, for dismissal of the prosecution by reason of deprivation of the opportunity to prepare a defense, is probably most appropriate. The motion may be supported by counsel's affidavit (1) describing defense investigative and preparatory needs insofar as they can be described without making any harmful disclosures, and (2) offering to make a fuller showing *in camera* or by sealed affidavits to be considered by the court *ex parte*. The motion should also be supported, of course, by the defendant's detailed affidavit of poverty. The latter affidavit can be prepared from the information furnished by the client in response to the questions in the bail-information questionnaire set out in § 4.5 *supra*.

Chapter 6

Interviewing the Client

6.1. *Establishing the Lawyer-Client Relationship*

The first interview with a criminal client is probably the most important exchange that counsel will have with the client. It largely shapes the client's judgment of the lawyer. Any initial impressions counsel makes may be indelible. At the least, this interview will strongly affect all future dealings between the two. The lawyer's primary objective in the initial interview is to establish an attorney-client relationship grounded on mutual confidence, trust, and respect.

To gain the client's confidence, counsel must convey a sincere interest in helping the client as well as project the image of a competent, knowledgeable lawyer. The client must be given an adequate opportunity to explain his or her problems, and counsel must be able to respond to them with reasonable assurances and to answer any questions needing immediate attention or preoccupying the client.

6.2. *Preparing for the Interview*

Proper preparation for an interview is indispensable if counsel hopes to gain the client's confidence and trust. Counsel needs to be acquainted with the specific charges against the client and the elements of the charged offenses in order to avoid floundering when taking the client's story. Knowledge of the applicable penalty provisions is indispensable in order to answer the question – which the client will almost certainly ask – what kind of a sentence the client is facing.

In the course of locating a client in custody or of checking out the status of a "wanted" client, counsel will ordinarily have spoken to the desk officer in the arrest precinct or in the defendant's home precinct and to the investigating officer. In these conversations, counsel should be sure to learn the specific charges against the defendant as well as any other charges being considered. See §§ 3.5, 3.10 *supra*. If counsel can review the relevant statutes quickly, s/he should take the time, before the initial interview, to look up the elements of the crime *and particularly the penalty*, including any applicable probation provisions, parole provisions, and recidivist sentencing provisions. See § 3.21.1 *supra*.

Counsel should undertake to be as well informed as time permits about the prospects and procedures for getting the client conditionally released from custody. See § 3.21.1 *supra*. If counsel has the chance, without significantly delaying the initial interview, s/he should also try to learn from the investigating officer the sort of factual case the police have against the defendant. But if the defendant is in custody, it is usually better to get in to see the defendant quickly than to tarry very long in talking to the police about the case.

6.3. *Putting the Client at Ease and Establishing a Relationship of Trust*

An understanding of the client's mindset is essential in striking up an attorney-client relationship. Counsel must remember that the client is a person in trouble and that the last thing s/he needs is more trouble from counsel. Counsel should therefore make the beginning of the initial interview with the client as undemanding as possible. Questions should be kept very simple until the client's abilities to understand questions, to think, and to articulate answers have been evaluated. Thereafter, counsel should keep well within the limits of the client's vocabulary and comprehension skills. (Counsel who is dealing with a mentally impaired client should be attentive at the outset to determine as well as s/he can the areas and dimensions of the impairment. *See generally* Christopher Slobogin, *The American Bar Association's Criminal Justice Mental Health Standards: Revisions for the Twenty-First Century*, 44 HASTINGS CONST. L. Q. 1, 4, 8, 19-20 (2016). See also § 16.1.1 *infra*. Careful observation may lay the foundation for a later decision to have the client mentally examined (see §§ 16.1.2, 16.3 *infra*) and may provide facts to support an application to the court, if that proves advisable, for court-ordered or state-paid examination (see § 16.3 *infra*). The nature and degree of the client's disability may also prove significant in later attacking confessions s/he has made to the police, purported consents to police searches and seizures, and other purported waivers of rights. In any event, the way in which counsel gives the client precautionary advice (see §§ 3.4.2 - 3.4.6, 3.6, 3.21.2 *supra*) and information will need to be tailored to the client's comprehension level.) If the client's primary language is not English, and if counsel is not sufficiently fluent in that language, counsel should ordinarily try to obtain a disinterested interpreter rather than a member of the client's family who may intrude his or her own biases into the interview and before whom the client may be ashamed to tell the truth. Regarding professional interpreters, *see* Marcia Resler, *You Had Me at 'No hablo English': The Best Practices of Working with Interpreters*, 43-AUG THE CHAMPION 36 (2019).

Counsel should avoid displaying any indication that the client is making a bad impression or is at fault for failing to answer counsel's questions relevantly. Conversely, counsel wants to convey the sense that the client is doing well and is giving counsel helpful information. The client usually enters upon this meeting with certain preconceptions about lawyers that are far from favorable. These include the notions that lawyers are self-interested, uncaring, grasping, and untrustworthy. If the client is street-wise, s/he is also likely to hold the more specific belief that criminal defense lawyers only want to talk their clients into pleading guilty to save themselves the trouble of trying cases. Counsel should attempt to rectify, or at least alleviate, these preconceptions by showing genuine concern for the client as an individual human being – not just another faceless defendant in a parade of stereotyped defendants – and by showing a willingness to work on the client's behalf.

To build rapport with the client, counsel should make use of any available personalizing touches. Offering to do concrete things for the client (for example, if the client is in lock-up, offering to contact the client's spouse or domestic partner or other family members; or, if the client evidences particular concern over the police officers' seizure of the client's cash or other personal property, promising to look into the situation and do whatever can be done to retrieve the property) is a more credible demonstration of counsel's willingness to work for the client than general self-touting professions of industriousness in the future.

Perhaps the single most important impression to convey is that counsel views his or her own job as being exclusively to serve and help the client to the best of counsel's abilities. S/he should avoid giving the client any grounds for suspicion or confusion about the lawyer's role or loyalties or motives – doubts which may arise if the lawyer begins to ask for information without saying why s/he wants it. The client should be told that the lawyer's only purpose and only interest are to represent the client and that, in order to make sure that nothing is overlooked which could help the client, counsel needs certain information. If the relevance of counsel's questioning to the client's needs and interests is not perfectly obvious – obvious, that is, to a layperson, not a lawyer – counsel should explain why s/he is asking this or that.

The client should be made to feel comfortable and secure in the presence of counsel. When explaining something to the client, it is usually better to ask "okay?" than "Do you understand that?" Whatever the client tells counsel should be received with interest and an attempt to understand, even if it does not appear relevant to the immediate tasks at hand as counsel conceives them. Patience in hearing the client out is crucial. Under stress s/he may be rambling and inarticulate. S/he should not be shut off without explanation – or at all, unless time is pressing; and, when s/he must be turned from one subject to another, counsel should explain the need to change the subject in a way that does not make the client feel like a fool.

6.4. *Giving the Client a Business Card*

As a means for establishing rapport and putting the client at ease, it is often useful to give the client a business card and to use the card as a prop to reinforce certain messages. Pointing out the lines on the card containing counsel's phone numbers, counsel should explain that s/he is giving the client the numbers so that the client can call whenever the client has questions or has information to impart to counsel. Counsel can say explicitly that it will be necessary for counsel and the client to keep in touch and to work together closely in fighting against the charges. This reinforces the message that counsel is there to help the client, and it also conveys the crucial idea that the client should inform counsel about any and all case-related information s/he can think of. Finally, it implicitly tells the client that the client will also need to make an effort to get along with counsel and to assist in finding witnesses and preparing the case.

6.5. *Explaining the Attorney-Client Relationship*

A useful way to emphasize that counsel's sole interest lies in serving the client, without sounding like this is a sales pitch learned on a used car lot, is to find some obviously relevant, operational reason for describing counsel's role. Often the best occasion comes in connection with an explanation of the attorney-client privilege – an explanation that is independently necessary, in any event, in order to assure the client that s/he can tell his or her story to counsel in complete confidence. Counsel may say something like this, for example:

> Now, I'm going to ask you to tell me some things about yourself and also about this charge they have against you. Before I do, I want you to know that everything you tell me is strictly private, just between you and me. Nothing you tell me goes to the police or the prosecutor or the judge or your family or anybody else. Nobody can make me tell them what you said to me, and I won't.

> Maybe you've heard about this thing that they call the attorney-client privilege.

The law says that when a person is talking to [his] [her] lawyer, whatever [he] [she] tells the lawyer is confidential and secret between the two of them. This is because the law recognizes that the lawyer's obligation is to [his] [her] client and to nobody else; that the lawyer is supposed to be 100 per cent on the client's side; that the lawyer is only supposed to help [his] [her] client and never do anything – or tell anybody anything – that might hurt the client in any way. The prosecutor is the one who is supposed to represent the government in prosecuting cases; and the judge's job is to judge the cases. But the law wants to make sure that – even if everybody else is lined up against an accused – there is one person who is not supposed to look out for the government but to be completely for the person who's accused of the crime. That is the person's lawyer.

As your lawyer, I am completely for you. And I couldn't be completely for you if I could be forced to tell anybody else the things that you say to me in private. So you can trust me and tell me anything you want without worrying that I will ever pass it along to anyone else because I won't. I can't be questioned or forced to talk about what you tell me, even by a court, and I am not allowed to tell it to anyone else without your permission because I am 100 per cent on your side, and my job is to work for you and only for you; so everything we talk about stays just between us. Okay?

6.6. *Settling the Roles of Attorney and Client and Explaining the Need for a Truthful Rendition of the Facts*

Counsel can further allay the client's suspicions by explaining that all of the fundamental decisions about the objectives of representation will be made by the client and not by counsel. Counsel should indicate that every major decision about how the defense will proceed – such as whether to go to trial or to offer a guilty plea – will be the client's to make: Counsel will keep the client advised of any developments in the case and, when decisions of any consequence have to be made, counsel will discuss all of the options with the client, so that the client can make well-informed choices. Counsel should explain that s/he will raise any defense that the law permits and will take any action necessary to protect the client's rights. But counsel should also mention that it will be counsel's role to make strategic judgments about how to investigate the case, how to formulate the defense in legal terms, and what evidence to present if the case goes to trial. Counsel should promise to talk with the client about issues of this sort, and to get the client's thinking about the best possible strategies to adopt, before counsel makes decisions that will necessarily depend, in the final analysis, upon counsel's legal training and experience.

The explanation of roles also provides a convenient opportunity for impressing on the client that counsel will need to get from the client a complete, truthful account of all of the facts relating to the case, in order to investigate and prepare for trial effectively. If counsel delays making this point until counsel begins asking questions about the circumstances of the crime and the client's involvement or non-involvement, the client may get the impression that counsel expects the client to lie and is warning the client not to. It's better to use counsel's preliminary explanations of attorney-client role relationships, near the beginning of the interview, to introduce the point that counsel's ability to defend the client effectively depends on the client giving counsel a complete, accurate, honest picture of the facts.

Having covered the roles of attorney and client, counsel can easily turn to the need for a full and accurate account of the facts that the client knows, believes, or can foresee that other people will believe concerning the crime, the client's whereabouts and behavior at the time of the crime, and the client's interactions with other persons (complainants and victims, potential codefendants, potential witnesses, police and other law-enforcement personnel) who may be involved in the case. Counsel should explain that some clients think an attorney wants to hear only favorable information, but that that is incorrect and harmful to the client's defense. Unless counsel is told about every unfavorable fact that the police and the prosecution could try to show, counsel will be unprepared to challenge those facts, and counsel may develop a defense strategy that will fall apart instead of one that will work. Counsel can also mention that many people accused of a crime have gotten convicted precisely because they did not tell their lawyers about damaging facts that the prosecutor came up with at trial, catching defense counsel by surprise. Counsel should reassure the client that it is not counsel's job to judge the client, but rather to represent the client whether s/he is guilty or innocent, and that that is precisely what counsel intends to do. In addition to saying these words, counsel has to incorporate their message in counsel's own conduct and questioning style: Counsel must avoid giving any sign of moral condemnation of the client's conduct.

6.7. *Note-taking During the Interview: Explaining the Need for Taking Notes; Techniques for Taking Notes in the Least Disruptive Manner*

It is advisable to explain to the client early in the interview counsel's need to take notes. Naive clients will often be apprehensive about counsel's recording things they say which are incriminating or even merely embarrassing. They may fear that counsel will turn these notes over to the prosecutor or the judge or will disclose them to the client's family or acquaintances. System-savvy clients will often fear that a record of what they told counsel in an initial interview will box them in against subsequent changes in their story.

An effective way of alleviating these concerns is by linking the explanation of note-taking with counsel's preceding explanation of the attorney-client privilege. Counsel should begin by saying: "I hope you won't mind if I take notes of some of the things you tell me" and then explain that these notes are only for counsel's own use, to help counsel remember details of what the client says. Counsel should tell the client that counsel will never show the notes to anyone else, and that no one – not even a court – can force counsel to show them the notes, because whatever counsel writes down is legally protected by the rule of attorney-client privilege. In this manner, counsel simultaneously reinforces his or her earlier explanation of attorney-client privilege by giving the client a concrete demonstration of how the privilege works in practice. It is also useful to tell the client that counsel understands that the client may later remember or learn information which differs from the client's present recollections, and that counsel's notes are only intended to record the client's best efforts to recall relevant facts at the time of this preliminary discussion.

When the client begins to relate relevant facts about his or her background or the circumstances of the offense, counsel will have a natural tendency to start taking notes immediately. This is a temptation to be resisted. Counsel does better to postpone writing or typing anything for a while after the client starts providing pertinent information, because looking the client in the eye and appearing interested in the client's words – not immediately falling into the role of indifferent stenographer – are the most effective techniques for establishing rapport and encouraging recollection and disclosure. After engaging the client in a conversational run-through of the gist of the information counsel is seeking (or hearing the client out if s/he is one who has a story s/he is anxious to tell), counsel can move on into note-taking mode by (a) asking "would it be okay now if I took some notes about what we've been discussing?"; (b) summarizing aloud the essential material that the client has thus far related, while counsel writes it down and asks, item by item, "have I got that right?"; and then (c) continuing with alternating periods of conversational interchange and this kind of note-taking.

In summarizing things the client has said and requesting his or her ratification of them while counsel takes notes, counsel should not preface this procedure with language like "let's go back over what's important" or "I want to get down the key points in what you've said." These throat-clearing overtures imply that everything the client has said but counsel omits from the summary is *un*important, *not* "key." The result of these inadvertently judgmental pronouncements is likely to be to leave the client miffed by counsel's apparent dismissal of some matters that the client cares about, or to telegraph to the client, prematurely, that there is a particular version of the story that counsel wants the client to tell, or both. Deadpan formulas like "let me make sure I'm understanding what you said about [event *A*] or [topic *B*]" work best. As counsel summarizes and writes, s/he can ask clarifying or amplifying questions.

Long periods of writing in silence should be avoided. If an extended note has to be written, counsel should vocalize it as s/he writes and then ask the client, "Is that correct?" (At later stages of the relationship with a client, writing or reading notes silently for a protracted period may occasionally be useful for particular purposes – for example, to give the client a chance to absorb or think over a point without feeling pressured to respond quickly, or to unnerve a client who counsel believes is lying – but these are exceptions to the general rule that the client should not ordinarily be left hanging while counsel concentrates on counsel's notes.) Once the client gets into the swing of his or her story, it is usually wise for counsel to take notes of every significant point while the client is talking. Excessive writing is ill-advised, however, because it impedes counsel's ability to observe the client's nonverbal expressions and also suggests that counsel is more interested in the facts than in the client as a person.

Perhaps the best way to take sufficiently detailed notes without excessive writing is to develop the knack of writing down key words and key phrases, using the client's own language rather than translating it or summarizing it in counsel's terms. *After the interview,* when counsel is alone, s/he can go over the notes while memory of the interview itself is fresh and can write out or dictate a lengthier, more detailed and coherent version of what the client said, together with counsel's observations, interpretations, and impressions. Using the client's exact words in the original notes will stimulate counsel's recall of the things that were said before and after the noted words. Counsel should review the notes and prepare the refined interview report as soon as possible after the interview. When counsel has enough control over his or her schedule, s/he will find it useful to leave a half-hour or so free immediately following interviews for the latter purpose. This may appear profligate, but experience shows that it is more efficient than either trying to write out copious notes during an interview or trying to reconstruct the details of information obtained in an interview by going over terse notes half a day or more after they were taken.

Detailed records of client interviews, particularly of interviews conducted shortly after the time of the offense with which the client is charged, are invaluable tools in defense work. They serve subsequently to refresh both counsel's and the client's memories. They can be used for a wide range of practical purposes: *e.g.*, to support counsel's representations of fact during efforts to convince the prosecutor to drop or reduce the charges or during plea bargaining; to support counsel's representations to the court in support of requests for continuances, state-paid investigative or consultative assistance, or *forma pauperis* subpoenas to gather defensive evidence; to support counsel's representations to the court in support of motions; to assist in preparing the defendant to testify. They will also be admissible at trial in the client's behalf if the prosecution seeks to create the impression that the client's trial testimony is a recent fabrication. In addition, notes will shield counsel from unwarranted attacks (such as inadequate representation and suppression of facts favorable to the defense) should the defendant ultimately be convicted.

In some jurisdictions, however, interview notes or reports may be discoverable by the prosecution and usable to impeach the client if s/he testifies at trial. See §§ 9.11, 18.11, 27.12(b), 33.03 *infra*. When this is the case, counsel may be able to insulate these materials against disclosure by (1) including within counsel's written notes of the client's oral statements sufficient analytic and evaluative commentary to imbue the whole writing with "work product" protection (*see Upjohn Co. v. United States,* 449 U.S. 383, 397-402 (1981)); and (2) not reading or submitting the notes to the client for approval after counsel has put them into final form (*cf. Goldberg v. United States,* 425 U.S. 94, 105-07 (1976)). For discussion, see §§ 9.11, 18.13 *infra*. Counsel can develop and employ a set of covert codes through which s/he – but not a judge who may later inspect the notes on a prosecutor's motion for discovery – can distinguish counsel's summaries and commentaries from phrases that are direct quotations of the client's words. (As simple a gimmick as consistently using "S/he states" and "S/he believes" to signal direct quotation, while using "S/he says" and "S/he feels" to signal other matter, will usually do the trick.) But, even with these precautions, "work product" protection is not completely guaranteed, particularly if the client testifies at trial (*see United States v. Nobles,* 422 U.S. 225, 236-40 (1975), discussed in §§ 18.10.2, 18.12, 18.13, 39.4 *infra*). Where disclosure to the prosecution is a possibility under local practice, counsel must weigh its risks against the advantages of preserving retrievable, contemporaneous documentation of client-interview material.

6.8. *Interviewing the Client About the Facts of the Offense*

In situations other than a rushed interview at the police station or on the day of preliminary arraignment (see §§ 3.20-3.21.3, 3.23 *supra*), counsel is advised to begin the substantive portion of the initial interview by asking about the facts of the offense charged. A client expects his or her attorney to be interested in the client's innocence or justification and in hearing about defense witnesses. Counsel's avoiding or even delaying these subjects may be viewed by the client as incompetent lawyering or as a manifestation that the lawyer doubts the client's innocence.

While homing in on the facts of the offense, counsel's opening questions should avoid appearing to assume that the client knows anything about the crime itself, since the obvious corollary is that counsel thinks the client is guilty (or at least involved). A neutral way of beginning is by asking the client what the police say s/he did. A question like "Let's start with anything you know about what the police are saying happened" will usually prompt a narrative by the client, in which s/he will relate both the nature of the charges and the degree to which s/he has personal knowledge of the facts of the crime or, conversely, claims to know nothing about it. If s/he responds initially with nothing more than an abstract statement of the charges, counsel can follow up with "What led the police to think [that you're involved] *or* [that you did that], do you suppose?"

An effective way of conducting a fact interview is to employ a three-stage interviewing process:

1. Counsel should begin by inviting the client to tell the story in his or her own words, with few, if any, interruptions by the lawyer. This puts the client most at ease and gives the lawyer insight into what the client thinks is more and less important. It provides a collection of unsolicited details on which to cross-examine the client later if the lawyer suspects untruth. And it tells the lawyer something about how the client's mind works, how the client conceptualizes his or her situation, the client's concerns and attitudes, his or her intelligence and verbal ability. There is no sense in starting to ask questions that may be beyond the client's comprehension level or entirely at odds with what s/he thinks and feels the case is all about.

2. Once the client's narrative rendition of the facts is completed, counsel should go over the story again, aiding the client to remember and recount everything s/he can about the relevant events, conditions, things, and people. An effective way to tease out detail is to take up delimited blocks or parts of the client's story (bounded by a time period or event ["what happened that night before you left the house?" *or* "what was going on while you were with Sam?" *or whatever*] or by coherent topic lines ["how you and Sam came to be together that night" *or* "everything you remember about what the person you saw there looked like" *or whatever*]) and go through each block, one after another, using the journalistic "who, what, why, when, where, and how" approach to fill in specific, concrete observations omitted by the client when s/he related that block of information. A technique that works well with some clients is to cast all questions and answers in the present tense (for example: "and what do you do next?"), thereby stimulating the client's reliving of the experience.

3. In the third round of the interview, counsel should fill in additional details and elicit explanations. Counsel should pick up on words used by the client in rounds one and two, asking the client to explain any terms that are unfamiliar to counsel. Counsel should elicit the names, street addresses, phone numbers, email and e-text addresses of any and all witnesses to the crime or related events that happened prior to or subsequent to the crime. If the client is unable to provide a full name, counsel should seek out any identifying information, such as the

witness's nickname, social-media logo, place of employment, vehicle s/he uses, relatives, and friends. If the client is unable to provide a street address or phone number, counsel should ask the client where the witness hangs out or goes on particular recurring occasions ("goes bowling" *or* "shops for food," *or whatever*) so that counsel can arrange for the client or a relative or friend of the client to accompany counsel or a defense investigator to the spot and try to point out the witness. Counsel should also fill in any omissions or unclarities in the client's rendition of the events. Counsel can spot the less obvious omissions by putting himself or herself in the client's situation and deducing what the client would be likely to have seen, heard, and felt, as well as by imagining the natural consequences of the events described by the client.

In interviewing the client about the facts of the offense, counsel should refrain from overtly cross-examining the client unless the client is obviously lying and discovery of the truth appears immediately necessary for effective defense investigation. Blatant manifestations of distrust can irreparably injure the attorney-client relationship. Counsel will have ample opportunities later to put tough questions to the client, after the attorney-client relationship has solidified. See § 6.14 *infra*.

6.9. *Interviewing the Client About Facts Needed for Suppression Motions*

To gather the facts needed for drafting and litigating suppression motions, counsel will need to elicit all of the information that the client knows about the police investigation of the case as well as the circumstances of the client's arrest, booking, and interrogation. Counsel should begin with any contact that the client had with the police in connection with the case prior to arrest – for example, investigative interviews that did not lead to arrest at that point in time, police searches of the client's house prior to the arrest, and police interviews with relatives or friends of the client prior to the arrest. Counsel then should take the client step-by-step through the sequence of events beginning with the police accosting of the client to arrest him or her, teasing out a detailed account of the arrest, police searches and seizures, administration of *Miranda* warnings, and interrogation. Thereafter, counsel should use the same sort of chronological approach to cover all of the details of the booking process and any interrogation that took place in the police car on the way to the station or at the stationhouse.

If the client was arrested on the scene rather than some days or months later, and if s/he has been in custody since the time of arrest, counsel also will want to record the articles of clothing that the client is wearing and their colors. These could be highly significant in showing that the client's attire at the time of arrest did not match the complainant's and/or eyewitnesses' description of the perpetrator. If the client was not arrested on the scene, or if the client was released after arrest and thus has had an opportunity to change clothes prior to seeing counsel, counsel will need to ask the client to describe what s/he was wearing on the day of arrest (if s/he remembers) and to identify any witnesses who can corroborate the client's description.

6.10. *Complaints of Brutality or Mistreatment; Other Custodial Complaints*

If the client reports that s/he has been abused by the police, custodial personnel, or other inmates, counsel should promptly investigate these allegations. The client should be questioned in detail respecting the time, place, and nature of any official misconduct (including any failure by officers to prevent or stop or record abuse of the client by other inmates), its background, and the identity or description of all persons involved or present at the time. Observable contusions and lacerations on the client should be photographed in color. A private physician should be summoned to examine major injuries if possible; the county medical society or a civil liberties group, like the American Civil Liberties Union, can help find a physician for this purpose. Witnesses should be interviewed who last saw the client prior to arrest and who can testify concerning his or her physical condition at that time. Counsel should also investigate whether any police officers or facility guards who were involved in the incident sustained injuries of their own, since the justification most commonly given for injuries to a client is that the officer or guard had to use force to effectuate the arrest or subdue an unruly prisoner.

As long as counsel takes these steps to avert the risk of further abuse and to gather evanescent evidence before bruises and memories fade, counsel can delay until later any decisions about what should be done to rectify injuries already inflicted upon the client. If there appears to be merit in an action for damages in a state court or in the federal courts under the Civil Rights Act, 42 U.S.C. § 1983 (*see Monroe v. Pape*, 365 U.S. 167 (1961); *Lombardo v. City of St. Louis, Missouri*, 141 S. Ct. 2239 (2021); and see § 3.3.2.4 *supra*); *but see Pearson v. Callahan*, 555 U.S. 223 (2009); *Richmond v. Badia*, 47 F.4th 1172 (11th Cir. 2022); and cases cited in the last paragraph of § 25.7.4 *infra*, regarding law enforcement officers' qualified immunity from § 1983 liability) or under *Bivens v. Six Unknown Named Agents of Federal Bureau of Narcotics*, 403 U.S. 488 (1971) (*see Snowden v. Henning*, 2023 WL 4195838 (7th Cir. 2023); *but see Egbert v. Boule*, 142 S. Ct. 1793 (2022); *Dyer v. Smith*, 56 F.4th 271 (4th Cir. 2022); *Pettibone v. Russell*, 59 F.4th 449 (9th Cir. 2023), regarding the precept against extending *Bivens* liability to "new contexts"), counsel can subsequently speak with the client about the desirability of filing such an action, through counsel or some other attorney whom the client selects. *See, e.g., Kingsley v. Hendrickson*, 576 U.S. 389 (2015); *Atencio v. Arpaio*, 674 Fed. Appx. 623 (9th Cir. 2017). Sometimes the prospect of a civil-rights action can provide valuable leverage in plea-bargaining in the criminal case; sometimes threats to bring such an action will arouse resentment and sour the bargaining atmosphere. Some clients will view the mention of a possible civil-rights action as a sign that counsel cares for their welfare and knows how to protect them; but there is a risk that by adverting to that possibility, counsel will raise unrealistic expectations on the part of the client or the client's family members about the likelihood of success in § 1983 actions or about counsel's subsequent availability to file one. All told, counsel does best to restrict discussion during early client interviews to gathering detailed factual information regarding any abuse and any means for documenting it; s/he should not affirmatively broach the subject of civil litigation and – if the client brings up that subject – s/he should tell the client that the time is not yet ripe to talk about it.

Frequently, clients who are in custody complain about lack of medical treatment, exercise, food, and numerous other things. Most of these problems can be corrected administratively by informing the authorities in charge about them. Counsel should see the commanding officer on duty if the client is in a police station or the ranking jail official if s/he is in a jail. State-court relief may be available if the conditions of the client's confinement are substantially out of line with civilized standards. *See, e.g., Michaud v. Sheriff of Essex County*,

390 Mass. 523, 458 N.E.2d 702 (1983); *Wayne County Jail Inmates v. Lucas*, 391 Mich. 359, 216 N.W.2d 910 (1974), *subsequent history in Wayne County Jail Inmates v. Wayne County Chief Executive Officer*, 178 Mich. App. 634, 444 N.W.2d 549 (1989); *Facility Review Panel v. Holden*, 177 W. Va. 703, 356 S.E.2d 457 (1987); *Rokita v. Pennsylvania Department of Corrections*, 273 A.3d 1260 (Pa. Commonwealth Ct. 2022) (sustaining claims for relief under the federal Eighth Amendment and Americans With Disabilities Act in a case in which a prisoner seeks medical treatment for opioid addiction: "Rokita's Eighth Amendment claim is stated simply. By Rokita's averment, his opioid use problem has resulted in a medical diagnosis. Rokita's substance use disorder might fall into any number of 'serious' categories: being diagnosed by a physician; being obvious to a lay person as requiring medical attention; affecting his daily activities; or causing unnecessary or chronic pain, etc. . . . Indeed, it is well understood that opioid addiction can result in extreme and potentially dangerous withdrawal symptoms. But even greater risks can follow. Absent effective treatment during incarceration, relapses and overdoses upon release from incarceration are sadly common occurrences – such overdoses are the leading cause of death among inmates after their release. . . . It is thus conceivable that, should his claim be permitted to proceed, Rokita may be able to establish that he has a 'serious medical need' within the meaning of the Eighth Amendment." *Id.* at 1269. "[T]he Department's policy deprives Rokita of the benefit of a health service that could potentially be beneficial in treating his disability. . . . Under these circumstances, it is conceivable that Rokita could establish that he has been denied the benefit of a health service by a public entity, by reason of his disability, and that a claim is viable under Title II of the ADA." *Id.* at 1275). Federal-court relief is available if:

(A)   those conditions expose him or her to a substantial risk of serious physical harm (*see, e.g., Presson v. Reed*, 65 F.4th 357 (8th Cir. 2023) (allegations that jail officials denied a pretrial detainee access to his prescription medication, with the result that he suffered severe pain, depression, and vomiting, state a Fourteenth Amendment Due Process claim); *Pastora by and through Toghraie v. County of San Bernardino*, 2023 WL 3734264, at *3 (9th Cir. 2023) ("'[T]he elements of a pretrial detainee's medical care claim against an individual defendant under the due process clause of the Fourteenth Amendment are: (i) the defendant made an intentional decision with respect to the conditions under which the plaintiff was confined; (ii) those conditions put the plaintiff at substantial risk of suffering serious harm; (iii) the defendant did not take reasonable available measures to abate that risk, even though a reasonable official in the circumstances would have appreciated the high degree of risk involved – making the consequences of the defendant's conduct obvious; and (iv) by not taking such measures, the defendant caused the plaintiff's injuries.' . . . '[R]efusing to provide' Pastora 'with necessary medical care when she cried, screamed, and yelled for immediate help after injuring herself,' after which Pastora died, states a claim under this standard."); *Mendiola-Martinez v. Arpaio*, 836 F.3d 1239 (9th Cir. 2016) (applying *Hope v. Pelzer,* 536 U.S. 730 (2002), to sustain the section 1983 claim of a pretrial detainee who was shackled and restrained during labor and postpartum recovery); *Fairchild v. Coryell County, Texas*, 40 F.4th 359 (5th Cir. 2022) (sustaining excessive force claims on behalf of the parents of a 5' 6", 220-pound female pretrial detainee who died after two jailers, in attempting to subdue her after she refused their commands to stop tapping her hairbrush on her cell door, got her face-down on the floor and held her there, handcuffed, for more than two minutes with one 230-pound jailer kneeling on her lower back and the other 390-pound jailer pressing his forearm against her neck); *Sebastian v. Ortiz*, 918 F.3d 1301 (11th Cir. 2019) (sustaining the section 1983 claim of an arrestee who alleged that the arresting officer caused serious, permanent nerve injuries to his wrists and hands by applying unnecessarily tight handcuffs to him, with intent to punish him, after he refused the officer's request to search the interior of his car following a routine traffic stop; the court emphasizes that he was "neither resisting arrest nor attempting to flee" (*id.* at 1305) and that his claim involved "serious and substantial injury intentionally and gratuitously inflicted on an individual of ordinary vulnerability" (*id.* at 1309)); *Knighten v. Ramsey*, 2023 WL 2998424, at *2 (10th Cir. 2023) ("Dumping someone out of a wheelchair and onto the ground is entirely gratuitous. Deputy Ramsey did not temper the amount of force he used, nor was there an apparent 'security problem' or threat 'reasonably perceived by the officer,' as the complaint does not allege that Mr. Knighten was "actively resisting." *Id.* While the nature of Mr. Knighten's exacerbated injury is admittedly unclear, that does not bar him from adequately alleging an excessive force claim."); *Clark v. Coupe*, 55 F.4th 167, 183 (3d Cir. 2022) ("By alleging prison officials imposed solitary confinement for months, knowing the isolation carried a substantial risk of exacerbating his mental illnesses but keeping him there until he suffered serious harm, Clark alleged conduct that no reasonable corrections officer could conclude was constitutionally permissible . . . " consistently with the Eighth Amendment); *Castro v. County of Los Angeles*, 833 F.3d 1060, 1064, 1069-73 (9th Cir. 2016) (en banc) (parsing *Bell v. Wolfish*, 441 U.S. 520 (1979), and *Kingsley v. Hendrickson, supra*, to uphold the grant of section 1983 relief to a pretrial detainee for violation of his "due process right . . . to be protected from harm at the hands of other inmates"); *LaBrec v. Walker*, 948 F.3d 836, 841 (7th Cir. 2020) ("[i]t is well established that prison officials face a duty to protect prisoners from violence at the hands of other prisoners," citing *Farmer v. Brennan*, 511 U.S. 825 (1994)); *Westmoreland v. Butler County, Kentucky*, 29 F.4th 721 (6th Cir. 2022) (allegations that jail personnel failed to protect a pretrial detainee after he informed them that he was worried about violence from other inmates who had been told he was a snitch sufficed to state a claim of violation of due process); *Fierro v. Smith*, 39 F.4th 640 (9th Cir. 2022) (the Court of Appeals reverses a judgment in favor of defendant prison officials in a civil rights trial for damages by an inmate who was assaulted by members of a prison gang after his repeated requests to be placed in protective custody, based on fears that he had been targeted for violence by the gang, were denied; its opinion clarifies the rules governing jury instructions regarding deference to prison authorities' decisions); *Pittman v. County of Madison, Ill.*, 746 F.3d 766, 778 (7th Cir. 2014) ("When an inmate presents an officer with a request to see a crisis intervention person and the officer also is aware that the reason for the request well may be a serious psychological condition that is beyond the officer's capacity to assess definitively, the officer has an obligation to refer that individual to the person who, under existing prison procedures, is charged with making that definitive assessment. The danger of serious consequences, including death, is obvious."); *accord, Burke v. Regalado*, 935 F.3d 960 (10th Cir. 2019); *Sandoval v. County of San Diego*, 985 F.3d 657, 661-62, 667 (9th Cir. 2021) (allegations that jail medical staff left a pretrial detainee "unmonitored for eight hours, despite signs that he was under the influence of drugs, and then failed to promptly summon paramedics when they discovered him unresponsive and having a seizure" stated a Due Process claim in a civil rights action: "Individuals in state custody have a constitutional right to adequate medical treatment."); *Howell v. NaphCare, Inc*, 67 F.4th 302, 311 (6th Cir. 2023) ("While Farmer's criminal-law recklessness standard still governs a prisoner's Eighth Amendment deliberate indifference claim, . . . [the Sixth Circuit has held that *Kingsley v. Hendrickson, supra*] changed the standard for pretrial detainees under the Fourteenth Amendment, adopting a civil-law recklessness standard that 'calls a person reckless who acts or . . . fails to act in the face of an unjustifiably high risk of harm that is either known or so obvious that it should be known.'"; under this standard, a Fourteenth Amendment claim was sufficiently pleaded by allegations that a pretrial detainee who had fallen to the ground, was complaining of pain and told a NaphCare nurse who examined him that he could not feel his legs was restrained in the jail's psychiatric unit for observation instead of being sent to a hospital   although the nurse had seen medical records showing that he suffered from sickle cell anemia – and a second NaphCare nurse thereafter failed to make appropriate periodic checks on his condition); *Sanchez v. Young County, Texas*, 956 F.3d 785, 791 (5th Cir. 2020) ("[f]or pretrial detainees, . . . [the] rights [protected by the Fourteenth Amendment] include the right to medical care . . . and the right to be protected from known suicidal tendencies"); *De Veloz v. Miami-Dade County*, 756 Fed. Appx. 869, 877 (11th Cir. 2018) ("In this particular case, no party disputes that placing a female in the general population of a male detention facility created an extreme condition and posed an unreasonable risk of serious harm to the female's future health or safety. Nor should they dispute this. It is abundantly clear to us that housing a biological female alongside 40 male inmates poses an outrageous risk that she will be harassed, assaulted, raped, or even murdered."); *Byrd v. Hobart*, 761 Fed. Appx. 621, 623-24 (7th Cir. 2019) (sustaining a claim for redress of unsanitary prison kitchen conditions: "contemporary standards require that officials 'provide inmates with "nutritionally adequate food that is prepared and served under conditions [that] do not present an immediate danger to the health and well-being of the inmates who consume it."' . . . ¶ . . . [W]here inmates have observed mice droppings, mice, and cockroaches literally in and on the food, a reasonable jury could conclude that the risk of harm to Byrd (who eats this food daily) is both substantial and obvious."); *Coston v. Nangalama*, 13 F.4th 729 (9th Cir. 2021) (in a case in which prison authorities required an inmate to go cold turkey after he was found to have been hoarding and conveying to another inmate morphine pills prescribed to treat his degenerative joint disease, the inmate is entitled to a new trial because the district court erred in instructing the jury that deference should be given to the security-based concerns of prison officials); *Hardeman v. Curran*, 933 F.3d 816, 821-23 (7th Cir. 2019) (sustaining a claim that jail authorities violated Due Process by failing to provide inmates with adequate water for drinking and sanitation during a period when a water booster pump was being replaced: "Pretrial detainees may assert a conditions-of-confinement claim under the Fourteenth Amendment's Due Process Clause. . . . ¶ For many years, we analyzed pre-conviction Fourteenth Amendment and post-conviction Eighth Amendment conditions-of-confinement claims under the same standard . . . . The Supreme Court put a halt to that equation, however, when it indicated that the interests of pretrial detainees and prisoners derive from separate sources and must be assessed differently. See *Kingsley* . . . . It is true that *Kingsley* directly addressed only claims of excessive force, and so some circuits have understood its holding to be confined to those facts. . . . We, however, have not taken that approach. Recognizing 'that the Supreme Court has been signaling that courts must pay careful attention to the different status of pretrial detainees,' we have held that a pretrial detainee's claims of inadequate medical care 'are subject only to the objective unreasonableness inquiry identified in *Kingsley*.'. . . ¶ The plaintiffs in this case suggest that we should extend *Kingsley* further from the medical context to the general conditions-of-confinement problem we have here. We see no principled reason not to do so. . . . ¶ . . . We therefore hold that *Kingsley*'s objective inquiry applies to all Fourteenth Amendment conditions-of-confinement claims brought by pretrial detainees."); *but see Geddes v. Weber County*, 2022 WL 3371010 (10th Cir. 2022) (a confusing unreported decision holding that only the Fourth Amendment, not the Fourteenth, applies to excessive-force claims based on jailers' abuse of a detainee prior to a probable-cause hearing); *Thomas v. Tice*, 948 F.3d 133 (3d Cir. 2020) (sustaining a claim that prison authorities violated the Eighth Amendment by unduly protracted detention of an inmate in a "dry cell" – a cell without access to any water, used for observation when it is suspected that an inmate has ingested contraband); *McClure v. Haste*, 820 Fed. Appx. 125, 128 (3d Cir. 2020) (a detainee placed in an excessively cold disciplinary segregation cell ripped the stuffing out of his mattress and crawled inside to keep warm; when returned to his regular cell, guards required him to sleep on the unstuffed mattress on a cement slab for more than 200 days; finding that these facts stated a claim for an Eighth Amendment violation, the circuit court notes that the Amendment forbids conditions of confinement that result in """"the denial of the minimal civilized measure of life's necessities"""" [citing cases that quote *Farmer v. Brennan*, 511 U.S. 825, 834 (1994)] and that "'[s]leep is critical to human existence, and conditions that prevent sleep have been held to violate the Eighth Amendment.'[ ]"); *Taylor v. Riojas*, 141 S. Ct. 52, 53 (2020) (per curiam) (finding an Eighth Amendment violation where correctional officers confined an inmate "for six full days . . . in a pair of shockingly unsanitary cells. The first cell was covered, nearly floor to ceiling, in '"massive amounts" of feces': all over the floor, the ceiling, the window, the walls, and even '"packed inside the water faucet."' . . . . Correctional officers then moved Taylor to a second, frigidly cold cell, which was equipped with only a clogged drain in the floor to dispose of bodily wastes. . . . Because the cell lacked a bunk, and because Taylor was confined without clothing, he was left to sleep naked in sewage.")); or

(B)   the conditions are arbitrarily intrusive (*e.g.*, *Mulvania v. Sheriff of Rock Island County*, 850 F.3d 849 (7th Cir. 2017); *Ware v. Louisiana Department of Corrections*, 866 F.3d 263 (5th Cir. 2017); *Bearchild v. Cobban*, 947 F.3d 1130 (9th Cir. 2020); *Henry v. Hulett*, 969 F.3d 769 (7th Cir. 2020) (en banc) (holding that the Fourth Amendment protects prison inmates against particularly degrading and abusive strip searches: "Strip searches are 'demeaning, dehumanizing, undignified, humiliating, terrifying, unpleasant, embarrassing, repulsive, signifying degradation and submission.'" *Id.* at 778. "We conclude that a diminished right to privacy in one's body, unlike a right to privacy in one's property and surroundings, is not fundamentally incompatible with imprisonment and is an expectation of privacy that society would recognize as reasonable. We therefore join every other circuit to have addressed the question and hold that the Fourth Amendment protects (in a severely limited way) an inmate's right to bodily privacy during visual inspections, subject to reasonable intrusions that the realities of incarceration often demand." *Id.* at 779. "We highlight that our holding today – that inmates maintain a privacy interest, although diminished, in their bodies – pertains to pretrial detainees and convicted prisoners alike." *Id.*)); *West v. Radtke*, 48 F.4th 836, 853 (7th Cir. 2022) (allegations that a male inmate was subjected to strip searches by a transgender guard state a Fourth Amendment claim: "highly invasive cross-sex privacy intrusions like strip searches are unreasonable under certain circumstances (namely, absent exigent circumstances)"; and, in the case of a Muslim inmate, constitute a violation of the Religious Land Use and Institutionalized Persons Act [42 U.S.C. § 20000cc-1]); or

(C)   the conditions punish constitutionally protected conduct such as the exercise of First Amendment rights (*Martin v. Duffy*, 977 F.3d 294 (4th Cir. 2020) (a complaint that a prison guard captain placed an inmate in administrative segregation in retaliation for his complaint of sexual abuse by another guard states a First Amendment claim); *Williams v. Radford*, 64 F.4th 1185 (11th Cir. 2023) (allegations that a prisoner was placed in disciplinary confinement and that his cell was searched and trashed in retaliation for his complaints about a guard state a First Amendment claim); *cf. Burns v. Martuscello*, 890 F.3d 77 (2d Cir. 2018) (holding that a prison inmate may not constitutionally be placed in restrictive custody for refusing to serve as a snitch or to provide false information regarding a purported assault); *Fuqua v. Ryan*, 890 F.3d 838, 848-49 (9th Cir. 2018) (holding that the Religious Land Use and Institutionalized Persons Act [42 U.S.C. § 20000cc-1] requires a federal court to hear an administratively exhausted claim that a state prisoner was disciplined for refusing to work on a religious holiday); *Jones v. Van Lanen*, 27 F.4th 1280 (7th Cir. 2022) (allegations that prison officials retaliated against an inmate because the numerous grievances he had filed alerted them that he was planning to file a civil rights action complaining about his conditions of confinement state a claim of violation of the First Amendment); or

(D)   the conditions directly abridge constitutional or statutory rights (*e.g., Turner v.*

Safley, 482 U.S. 78 (1987) (establishing the general rule that "when a prison regulation impinges on inmates' constitutional rights, the regulation is valid if it is reasonably related to legitimate penological interests" and identifying "several factors [that] are relevant in determining the reasonableness of . . . [a] regulation at issue" (*id.* at 89): "First, there must be a 'valid, rational connection' between the prison regulation and the legitimate governmental interest put forward to justify it. . . . Thus, a regulation cannot be sustained where the logical connection between the regulation and the asserted goal is so remote as to render the policy arbitrary or irrational. Moreover, the governmental objective must be a legitimate and neutral one. We have found it important to inquire whether prison regulations restricting inmates' First Amendment rights operated in a neutral fashion, without regard to the content of the expression. . . . ¶ A second factor relevant in determining the reasonableness of a prison restriction . . . is whether there are alternative means of exercising the right that remain open to prison inmates. . . . ¶ A third consideration is the impact accommodation of the asserted constitutional right will have on guards and other inmates, and on the allocation of prison resources generally. . . . ¶ Finally, the absence of ready alternatives is evidence of the reasonableness of a prison regulation." (*Id.* at 89-90.)); *accord, Thornburgh v. Abbott,* 490 U.S. 401 (1989); *and see Human Rights Defense Center v. Baxter County Arkansas,* 999 F.3d 1160 (8th Cir. 2021) (a jail's postcard-only policy for nonlegal mail would violate the First Amendment rights of a publisher of legal self-help publications if it constituted a total ban against sending inmates those publications); *Whitehead v. Marcantel,* 766 Fed. Appx. 691 (10th Cir. 2019) (a complaint that prison authorities refused to allow an inmate to receive hardback books, books from non-approved vendors, information from the internet, and newspaper articles sent by mail states a First Amendment claim that requires the authorities to justify these restrictions by showing that they are reasonably related to a legitimate penological interest); *Jones v. Slade,* 23 F.4th 1124 (9th Cir. 2022) (although a prison regulation banning receipt of materials containing depictions of drugs, violence, sex and gang activity is found to be reasonably related to the legitimate penological interest of averting the encouragement of inmate misbehavior, the application of the regulation to forbid rap music while admitting other forms of media containing such depictions is not content-neutral under *Turner* and may therefore violate the First Amendment; also, the confiscation from an inmate of two religious texts by Elijah Muhammad is *prima facie* actionable as a possible violation of a right under RLUIPA to read Nation of Islam religious works during Ramadan); *Richardson v. Clarke,* 52 F.4th 614 (4th Cir. 2022) (a prison warden's policy requiring the removal of head coverings in certain areas of the prison, including the dining hall, visiting room and administrative buildings, violates RLUIPA as applied to a Muslim inmate's *kufi*); *Mack v. Yost,* 63 F.4th 211, 228 (3d Cir. 2023) (sustaining a claim for violation of the Religious Freedom Restoration Act of 1993 where "Mack plausibly alleged that . . . [two prison guards] had placed 'indirect pressure . . . on [him]' 'to stop praying at work' by creating a 'hostile work environment' that drove him to 'betray [his] religious beliefs'"); *Haze v. Harrison,* 961 F.3d 654, 658 (4th Cir. 2020) (recognizing a First Amendment claim when jail personnel opened mail between an inmate and his lawyer and forwarded some of it to a prosecutor's office: "[o]pening an incarcerated person's legal mail outside of his presence can chill protected speech."); *Mitchell v. Peoples*, 10 F.4th 1226, 1228 (11th Cir. 2021) ("A simple rule has governed prison mail procedures in our Circuit for nearly 50 years: a prison official may not open an inmate's properly marked legal mail outside of his presence. . . . According to Mitchell, Detective Eileen Simpson ordered jail staff to confiscate and review all his incoming and outgoing mail. Following that order, J.M. Perkins, a jail officer and mail clerk, opened and read Mitchell's legal mail outside his presence. Mitchell complained, but the mailroom supervisor turned a blind eye, allowing the policy to proceed unchecked; he even threatened Mitchell to keep him from filing more grievances. Mitchell argues that all this conduct violated his First Amendment right to free speech and that it was clearly established that the officials' conduct was unlawful. We agree."); *Vogt v. Wetzel*, 8 F.4th 182, 184 (3d Cir. 2021) ("we join several of our sister courts and hold that, under the Supreme Court's decision in *Procunier v. Martinez*, 416 U.S. 396 (1974), prisons must notify inmates when their incoming mail is rejected"); *Benning v. Commissioner, Georgia Department of Corrections*, 2023 WL 4140765 (11th Cir. 2023) (an inmate has a First Amendment and due process right to be notified and given an opportunity for departmental appeal when his outgoing emails are intercepted and their transmission blocked under prison policies that forbid inmates to send emails which request that they be forwarded to others or which contain information for or about another inmate); *Leek v. Androski*, 2022 WL 1134967, at *3-*5 (10th Cir. April 18, 2022) ("Leek argues that he has sufficiently alleged access-to-courts claims. Prisoners do not have a 'freestanding right to a law library or legal assistance.'. . . Thus, to state an access-to-courts claim, the plaintiff must satisfy a 'threshold determination' that he or she has 'standing to assert' such a claim by alleging actual injury. . . . To establish actual injury, the plaintiff 'must show that any denial or delay of access to the court prejudiced him [or her] in pursuing litigation.' . . . ¶ Leek alleged that when he arrived at Lansing, he was immediately placed in segregation in the restrictive-housing unit where there is no law library. Leek was informed that to obtain cases, he had to submit forms 'requesting specific cases by cit[ation]' and that 'no law books would be delivered' to the restrictive-housing unit. When Leek submitted forms requesting cases from the library, he received some cases but was informed that he could only request 'three cases at a time' and had to return them within one week. Some forms Leek submitted went unprocessed. And when Leek requested additional cases, prison officials would not provide any until he returned the ones he had previously requested. Consequently, Leek was consigned to respond to the district court's show-cause order in *Scoggin* 'with only the few cases, notes, and books he had in his personal property.' Since then, the district court in that case (the same district judge who presided over this one) has dismissed the case for failure to state a claim. ¶ We conclude that the district court should not have dismissed Leek's access-to-courts claim stemming from the impediments he faced in litigating *Scoggin* while at Lansing."); *Johnson v. Baker*, 23 F.4th 1209 (9th Cir. 2022) (RLUIPA requires that prison officials allow a Muslim inmate to possess scented oil for ablutions before each of his five daily prayers); *Jones v. Carter*, 915 F.3d 1147 (7th Cir. 2019) (applying RLUIPA to require prison officials to provide a Muslim inmate with halal meals that include meat); *Maye v. Klee*, 915 F.3d 1076 (6th Cir. 2019) (holding prison chaplains liable for violations of the First Amendment and equal protection when they refused to permit a Muslim inmate to participate in Eid al-Fitr, the end-of-Ramadan feast); *cf. Robbins v. Robertson*, 782 Fed. Appx. 794 (11th Cir. 2019) (sustaining a claim that prison authorities violated the First Amendment by failing to provide a Muslim inmate a nutritionally adequate vegan diet, causing him to become seriously ill; the court declines to elaborate the standards applicable to the inmate's parallel Eighth Amendment claim); *Greenhill v. Clarke*, 944 F.3d 243 (4th Cir. 2019) (sustaining a claim that prison authorities violated the First Amendment and RLUIPA by refusing to allow a Muslim inmate to participate in televised prayer services and to maintain a beard of four inch length); *Byrd v. Haas*, 17 F.4th 692 (6th Cir. 2021) (recognizing that an Ifa prisoner may have claims under the First Amendment, Equal Protection Clause, and RLUIPA based upon the failure of prison authorities to permit group worship by members of his faith and their refusal to allow him to possess consecrated beads and other religious articles); *Emad v. Dodge County*, 2023 WL 4188509, at *5 (7th Cir. 2023) ("If free exercise in jail means anything, it means that jailers, absent some extraordinary justifications, cannot treat inmates differently based on religion."); *Fox v. Washington*, 949 F.3d 270 (6th Cir. 2020) (requiring prison authorities to justify their refusal to allow members of Christian Identity, a white separatist religion, to conduct communal worship and baptism; under RLUIPA, justification would require a showing that the prohibition of these religious practices is the least restrictive means available to further a compelling governmental interest.); *Ackerman v. Washington*, 16 F.4th 170 (6th Cir. 2021) (Corrections Department policies requiring Jewish Prisoners to eat vegan meals on certain Jewish holidays violate RLUIPA); *Ashaheed v. Currington*, 7 F.4th 1236 (10th Cir. 2021) (sustaining a claim that a Muslim prison inmate's First Amendment free-exercise rights were violated when a prison guard, motivated by anti-Muslim animus, required him to shave his beard); *Williams v. Hansen*, 5 F.4th 1129 (10th Cir. 2021) (sustaining a claim that prison authorities violated the First Amendment by banning Native American religious services for a period of at least nine days and possibly up to 30 days and by banning the use of tobacco in such services for 30 days after concluding that tobacco intended for religious services had been diverted for personal use by another prisoner); *Richey v. Dahne*, 733 Fed. Appx. 881 (9th Cir. 2018) (a complaint that prison authorities refused to process a prisoner's grievance complaint against a guard because it contained the unflattering comment that the guard was "extremely obese" states a First Amendment claim).

Any physical abuse of an inmate that amounts to excessive force violates the Fourth Amendment even if the resulting harm is minimal. *Johnson v. City of Miami Beach*, 18 F.4th 1267, 1271 (11th Cir. 2021) (sustaining the section 1983 claim of an inmate who was deliberately elbowed in the face by an officer; the inmate had been verbally belligerent and initially refused to enter a jail cell but did not physically resist when pushed into the cell; an officer followed him into the cell and struck him in the face; the inmate "was later treated for a small laceration to his mouth.") The potential for harm is a factor that enters into the determination of whether force is excessive. *E.g.*, *Young v. Kent County Sheriff's Department*, 2022 WL 94990, at *4 (6th Cir. January 10, 2022) (courts employ a "totality-of-the-circumstances test [that] balances . . . [the inmate's] interest in bodily integrity against the . . . [jail officer's] interest in safety, taking into account such factors as whether the . . . [officer's] force was commensurate with the threat that . . . [the inmate] posed"); *Myrick v. Fulton County, Georgia*, 69 F.4th 1277, 1300-01 (11th Cir. 2023) ("Claims alleging excessive force by pretrial detainees are governed by the Fourteenth Amendment's Due Process Clause. . . . A detainee must show 'that the force purposely or knowingly used against him was objectively unreasonable.' . . . ¶ Objective reasonableness turns on the 'facts and circumstances of each particular case.' . . . A court 'must make this determination from the perspective of a reasonable officer on the scene, including what the officer knew at the time, not with the 20/20 vision of hindsight.' . . . The following non-exhaustive list of factors bears on the reasonableness of the force used: ¶ the relationship between the need for the use of force and the amount of force used; the extent of the . . . [inmate's] injury; any effort made by the officer to temper or to limit the amount of force; the severity of the security problem at issue; the threat reasonably perceived by the officer; and whether the   [inmate] was actively resisting. ¶ . . . A court also needs to consider the 'legitimate interests that stem from the government's need to manage the facility in which the individual is detained, appropriately deferring to policies and practices that in the judgment of jail officials are needed to preserve internal order and discipline and to maintain institutional security.'"). See § 25.7.4 last paragraph *infra* regarding police use of excessive force against arrestees.

Recourse to the courts is appropriate if requests for necessary medical attention are not promptly honored. In addition to state statutes and regulations that impose responsibility on custodial officers for the well-being of prisoners, the Due Process Clause of the Fourteenth Amendment requires that a prisoner's serious medical needs be met by his or her custodians. *Estate of Perry v. Wenzel*, 872 F.3d 439, 453 (7th Cir. 2017) (under the Fourth and Fourteenth Amendment standards applicable to arrestees detained prior to a probable-cause determination, when "'the State takes a person into its custody and holds him there against his will, the Constitution imposes upon it a corresponding duty to assume some responsibility for his safety and general well-being'"); *Estate of Clark v. Walker*, 865 F.3d 544, 553 (7th Cir. 2017) (recognizing, in the context of arrestees detained following a probable-cause determination, that "[t]he Supreme Court has long held that prisoners have an Eighth Amendment right to treatment for their 'serious medical needs'"); *Sims v. Griffin*, 35 F.4th 945, 949 (5th Cir. 2022) ("[u]nder our caselaw, '[a] serious medical need is one for which treatment has been recommended or for which the need is so apparent that even laymen would recognize that care is required'"); *Christmas v. Corizon Health Services*, 2022 WL 5337649 (11th Cir. 2022) (same); *Lancaster v. Monroe County, Ala.*, 116 F.3d 1419, 1425 (11th Cir. 1997) ("the case law ha[s] made it clear that an official acts with deliberate indifference when he knows that an inmate is in serious need of medical care, but he fails or refuses to obtain medical treatment for the inmate"); *accord, Barton v. Taber*, 908 F.3d 1119, 1124 (8th Cir. 2018) ("In light of the evidence of Barton's recent car accident, his severe intoxication, and his drug ingestion, we conclude that a jury could find that Barton was experiencing a medical need so obvious that a layperson would recognize that he needed prompt medical attention"); *Dyer v. Houston*, 964 F.3d 374 (5th Cir. 2020) (sustaining a Due Process claim against police officers who, knowing that an arrested teen while strung out on LSD had banged his head some 46 times against the metal cage, windows, and rear seat of the patrol car *en route* to jail, failed to inform the jail authorities that he needed medical attention); *Adkins v. Morgan County, Tennessee*, 798 Fed. Appx. 858 (6th Cir. 2020) ("Based on the testimony that . . . [Adkins' cellmate] informed . . . [a jail guard] of Adkins's condition, a jury could find that . . . [the guard] was made aware of Adkins's severe back and stomach pain, inability to walk, and incontinence [but responded that Adkins was "faking it"] and declined to take action until Adkins awoke completely unable to move his legs." *Id.* at 862. "Adkins's constitutional right to receive adequate medical care given the symptoms he exhibited was clearly established." *Id.* at 864-65.); *Estate of Jensen v. Clyde*, 989 F.3d 848, 859 (10th Cir. 2021) (allegations that a jail nurse ignored the medical needs of an inmate stated an actionable claim: "Ms. Clyde was aware that: Ms. Jensen had opiates in her system; she looked sick and was 'walking like a skeleton'; she had been soiling her sheets and had diarrhea; she had been vomiting for four days straight; and that she was unable to keep food or water down. We believe that these circumstances – particularly her self-report that she had been vomiting for four days and could not keep down water – present a risk of harm that would be obvious to a reasonable person."); *Brawner v. Scott County, Tennessee*, 14 F.4th 585 (6th Cir. 2021) (reversing a judgment granted as a matter of law against a plaintiff claiming that she suffered permanent injuries as a result of prolonged epileptic seizure activity during pretrial detention because a jail nurse who knew that she had suffered seizures and had been taking seizure-suppression prescription medication before her arrest ignored her need for continuing medication); *Foster v. Maloney*, 785 Fed. Appx. 810 (11th Cir. 2019) (jail officials were obliged to provide medical attention for an inmate suffering visible signs of methadone withdrawal including elevated blood pressure, slurred speech and loss of body control); *Greene v. Crawford County, Michigan*, 22 F.4th 593, 607 (6th Cir. 2022) (allegations that jail officials failed to provide medical care to a pretrial detainee who displayed hallucinations and other symptoms of delirium tremens over a two-day period stated an actionable due process claim; "'delirium tremens is a severe form of alcohol withdrawal and is unquestionably a serious medical condition within the meaning of the Fourteenth Amendment'"); *Colson v. City of Alcoa, Tennessee*, 2021 WL 3913040 (6th Cir. September 1, 2021) (allegations that a pretrial detainee complained of an injury to her knee by the arresting officer and that in the station house she fell down at one point, yelling "ow, ow my fucking knee" stated a claim of a sufficiently serious medical need, sufficiently obvious to a layperson as requiring a doctor's attention, to support a due process claim of violation of the right to medical treatment, although the detainee was intoxicated and the jail personnel attributed her fall and her unsteadiness on her feet to inebriation); *Gordon v. County of Orange*, 888 F.3d 1118 (9th Cir. 2018); *Kindl v. City of Berkley*, 798 F.3d 391 (6th Cir. 2015); *Lance v. Morris*, 985 F.3d 787 (10th Cir. 2021); *Rife v. Oklahoma Department of Public Safety*, 854 F.3d 637 (10th Cir. 2017); *see City of Revere v. Massachusetts General Hospital*, 463 U.S. 239, 244-45 (1983) (dictum) ("The Due Process Clause . . . does require the responsible government or governmental agency to provide medical care to persons . . . who have been injured while being apprehended by the police."); *accord, Perry v. Bone*, 2021 WL 816939 (M.D. Ala. 2021); *Youngberg v. Romeo*, 457 U.S. 307, 315 (1982) (dictum) ("The mere fact that Romeo has been committed under proper procedures does not deprive him of all substantive liberty interests under the Fourteenth Amendment. . . . Indeed, the state concedes that respondent has a right to adequate food, shelter, clothing, and medical care. ¶ . . . [T]he right to personal security

constitutes a 'historic liberty interest' protected substantively by the Due Process Clause
. . . [and] not extinguished by lawful confinement, even for penal purposes."); *Collins v. City of Harker Heights, Texas*, 503 U.S. 115, 127-28 (1992) (dictum) ("The 'process' that the Constitution guarantees in connection with any deprivation of liberty . . . includes a continuing obligation to satisfy certain minimal custodial standards."); *Mitchell v. Kallas*, 895 F.3d 492, 499 (7th Cir. 2018) (recognizing an Eighth Amendment claim against a DOC mental health director for failure to provide hormone therapy for a transgender inmate: "Prison officials have been on notice for years that leaving serious medical conditions, including gender dysphoria, untreated can amount to unconstitutional deliberate indifference."); *Stevens v. Beard*, 2022 WL 17748110, at *2 (9th Cir. 2022) ("gender dysphoria can be a serious medical need"); *Williams v. York*, 891 F.3d 701, 707 (8th Cir. 2018) ("[an] inmate's right to treatment for serious and painful dental conditions has been clearly-established for more than three decades"); *cf. City of Canton, Ohio v. Harris*, 489 U.S. 378 (1989). And "[i]t would be odd to deny an injunction to inmates who plainly proved an unsafe, life-threatening condition in their prison on the ground that nothing yet had happened to them. The Courts of Appeals have plainly recognized that a remedy for unsafe conditions need not await a tragic event." (*Helling v. McKinney*, 509 U.S. 25, 33 (1993)). (*Helling* is a prison case, but the law is clear that "[p]retrial detainees are entitled to the same, if not greater, medical care as are convicted inmates" (*Anderson v. City of Atlanta*, 778 F.2d 678, 686 n.12 (11th Cir. 1985)). *See, e.g., Shorter v. Baca*, 895 F.3d 1176, 1183 (9th Cir. 2018) (noting that a pretrial detainee's "constitutional claims [of ill treatment in a jail facility] 'arise[ ] from the due process clause of the fourteenth amendment and not from the eighth amendment prohibition against cruel and unusual punishment.'. . . ('[T]he more protective fourteenth amendment standard applies to conditions of confinement when detainees . . . have not been convicted [of a crime.]')"); *accord, Hopper v. Plummer*, 887 F.3d 744, 751-54 (6th Cir. 2018).).

When an inmate has a disabling medical condition, officials' failure to accommodate the disability may also give rise to a claim under Title II of the Americans with Disabilities Act (42 U.S.C. § 12132). *See, e.g., Gorman v. Bartch*, 152 F.3d 907 (8th Cir. 1998); *Robertson v. Las Animas County Sheriff's Department*, 500 F.3d 1185 (10th Cir. 2007); *Cadena v. El Paso County*, 946 F.3d 717 (5th Cir. 2020); *Douglas v. Muzzin*, 2022 WL 3088240 (6th Cir. 2022); *cf. Pennsylvania Department of Corrections v. Yeskey*, 524 U.S. 206 (1998); *Brooks v. Colorado Department of Corrections*, 12 F.4th 1160 (10th Cir. 2021); *Williams v. Kincaid*, 45 F.4th 759 (4th Cir. 2022).

When counsel represents a vulnerable client who is at risk of assault by jailmates – sexual predators, violent aggressors, codefendants with a grudge or an interest in coercing the client to corroborate their version of the facts – counsel should insist on having the client housed in quarters inaccessible to these dangers and protected from them when in common-use facilities. In addition to the case law in the preceding paragraph, there is a developing doctrine of "state-created danger" which has now been recognized by a significant majority of federal courts and which can be invoked in urging jail authorities to adopt adequate protections for such clients. *See, e.g., Irish v. Fowler*, 979 F.3d 65 (1st Cir. 2020) collecting the circuit precedents.

6.11. *Fee-setting*

If counsel is going to handle the case on a fee basis rather than as court-appointed counsel for an indigent client or as a *pro bono* matter, counsel also will need to discuss fees with the client. Misunderstandings about fees are a vexatious and unnecessary irritant, and it behooves counsel to come to an early and very clear fee agreement. After determining the nature of the case and the evidentiary and investigatory problems likely to be involved, counsel should calculate a fair fee and agree upon it with the client. Fee-setting in a criminal case is typically based on an advance estimate of the amount of time that will be necessary to handle the case and not on a post-audit hourly basis. What expenses are to be paid by whom and what exact stages of the process (that is, through to, but not including, trial; *or* through trial; *or* through a first appeal; *or* whatever) are to be covered by the fee should be explicitly stated and the agreement reduced to writing and signed. It is wise for counsel to advise the client that failure to pay the full fee before trial will result in counsel's withdrawal from the case. Experience indicates that fees in criminal cases are hard to collect after trial, no matter what its outcome.

6.12. *Advice to the Client at the Conclusion of the Interview*

At the conclusion of the initial interview, counsel should give the client the warnings set out below. These warnings should be given, whether or not the client is in custody and whether or not s/he has previously been given the same warnings.

Counsel should advise the client to:

1. Say nothing at all to the police, tell them nothing under any circumstances, and reply to all police questions or approaches by saying that the client's lawyer has told the client not to answer questions or to talk with anyone unless the lawyer is present.

2. Tell police officers who start any conversation with the client or who make any requests of the client that they need to talk to counsel about whatever they want; show the officers counsel's business card (see § 6.4 *supra*) and tell them to phone or email counsel; and (if counsel has given the client a rights card (§ 3.21.3 *supra*)) show that to the officers as well.

3. Handle approaches by prosecuting attorneys in the same way, and under no circumstances discuss any offer or deal with the police or prosecuting attorneys in counsel's absence.

4. Discuss the case with no one, including cellmates, codefendants, codefendants' lawyers, reporters, or any persons who may have been involved in events relating to the case or who may have information about those events; and tell anyone who wants to discuss the case or who has information about it to contact counsel.

5. Neither write nor sign any papers or forms requested by the police or prosecuting attorneys or relating to the case in any way.

6. Refuse (if the client is at liberty) to go anywhere with the police or with prosecuting attorneys who may ask the client to accompany them, unless they

have an arrest warrant; and tell them that if they want the client to go anywhere or to do anything, they should contact counsel first.

7. Refuse (if the client is in custody) to participate in any lineup or to appear before any person for possible identification in counsel's absence; refuse to accompany the police or prosecuting attorneys to any place outside of the regular cell and recreation areas of the detention facility, except to court, in counsel's absence; object to any inspection of the client's body, physical examination, or test of any sort in counsel's absence; request permission to telephone counsel immediately in the event that the police begin any lineup or identification procedure, inspection, examination or test; and, if put in a lineup or exhibited for identification over his or her objection, observe and remember all of the circumstances (see § 3.4.4 *supra*).

8. Refuse consent to anyone who may ask the client's permission to search the client's home or automobile or any place or thing belonging to the client (including items in the possession of the police), or who may request access to the client's cell phone, computer, camera, or other communications or recording device.

9. Respond to all accusations and to anyone who gives any evidence against the client or says anything against the client by stating that the client's lawyer has told the client not to talk to anybody unless the lawyer is present.

10. Do not try to duck or dodge if media photographers have trained a camera on the client, and do not try to shield his or her face, but – if any police officers or custodial personnel are present – tell them to stop the photographer from taking pictures. See § 3.4.5 *supra*.

11. Telephone counsel as soon as possible if anything at all comes up relating to the case – if anyone whom the client does not know tries to talk to him or her about it; if the client hears that a codefendant or other person involved in events relating to the case has snitched on the client; or if the client gets any new information or receives any communication from the court about the case.

12. If the client goes or is taken to court and counsel is not present when the client's case is called, tell the judge that counsel is supposed to be present and request that the judge wait for counsel to arrive (if the client knows that counsel is aware of this court date) or that the judge telephone counsel or permit the client to telephone counsel and inform counsel that the client is in court (if the client suspects that counsel does not know about the proceedings).

In some situations, counsel may decide that it is in the client's interest to make a statement to the police or to the prosecutor or otherwise to cooperate in their investigations. This is most common in cases in which counsel believes that the authorities can be persuaded to drop charges (see §§ 9.15, 18.6 *infra*) or in cases in which a favorable plea bargain appears to be negotiable (see §§ 15.10, 15.13 *infra*), particularly when the authorities and the client are considering the client's turning state's evidence and testifying against accomplices. Even if the client is contesting guilt and a trial appears likely, there are instances (rare, to be sure) in which the defense stands to gain by cooperating with the prosecution's evidence-gathering efforts. For example, defense counsel who has interviewed an eyewitness to the offense and is confident that the witness will not identify the defendant in a lineup may want to have a lineup held. Or if the defendant's story includes an admission of some incriminating facts (for example, presence at the scene of the offense, or commission of the *actus reus*) but denies others (for example, taking any part in the *actus*, or having the requisite *mens rea*) or asserts facts supporting some affirmative defense (for example, self-defense, or mistake of fact), a written or oral statement to the police may be advised as the best means of putting the defendant's version of the facts before a judge or jury without the defendant's being subject to impeachment. (Prosecutors tend to present these incriminating admissions in their case-in-chief, even when they have ample independent proof of the facts admitted. And if the prosecution offers only a portion of the defendant's statement, the defense is entitled to put the whole of it into evidence.) Thus adduced at trial – whether by the prosecution or the defense – the statement does not open the defendant up to either cross-examination or the sorts of impeaching evidence (see §§ 39.10, 39.13.1 *infra*) to which the defendant would be exposed if s/he told the same story on the stand in court.

Counsel's decisions to cooperate in the staging of a lineup, to permit the client to make a statement, or to provide other evidence to the prosecution in these situations will, of course, qualify the general advice to the client described earlier. In all of these cases, however, counsel should be present during any face-to-face dealings between the client and the police or prosecutors, and counsel should examine any writing or physical evidence before it is turned over to them. The client should never be allowed to communicate with the authorities in counsel's absence. Hence it is best always to give the client the full roster of advice in this section without modification; then if circumstances justify exceptions to the general rules stated here, counsel can subsequently work with the client to decide upon these exceptions and to implement them.

If the client is in police custody at the time of the interview, counsel should not leave without first having the client personally tell a police officer, with counsel listening (and coaching if necessary), that the client does not wish to speak to the police or prosecuting authorities at any time in the future in the absence of counsel but wants to conduct all communications with the authorities from now on solely through the medium of counsel. See § 3.4.6 *supra*.

6.13. *Offering to Contact the Client's Family*

Counsel will ordinarily want to be in touch with the client's family very early in the case. See § 9.6 *infra*. The family will often be worrying about the client, particularly if s/he has been arrested and retained in custody; and the client will often be worrying about the family's fears and concerns. It is therefore a good idea, if at all possible, for counsel to telephone or visit – or at least to send a message to – the client's family shortly after an initial interview of a client in custody, to (a) give them whatever reassurances counsel can about the client's current situation and the prospects of release, (b) inform them when and how counsel will subsequently contact them and how they can contact counsel, and (c) inform them when, where, and how they can visit the client.

At the close of the initial interview with the client, counsel should offer to get in touch with the client's family in this way. Counsel should ask the client whether s/he would like counsel to do this and, if so, whom to call. It is important for counsel to keep in mind that the client is undergoing a frightening experience and that any help that counsel can give him or her on a human level is well worth the effort.

6.14. *Subsequent Interviews with the Client*

Usually the client must be interviewed on more than one occasion. In counsel's preparation for trial, facts will be discovered that were untouched in earlier interviews, and these must be reviewed and analyzed with the client. Increasingly, the client should be cross-examined in a fashion that may range from counsel's mild expression of surprise at a contradiction to open incredulity and grilling, depending upon counsel's best judgment of what is necessary at once to preserve the lawyer-client relationship and to get the truth. Clients may lie to their lawyer for a variety of reasons (*e.g.*, fear of alienating the lawyer by revealing that the client actually committed the crime or some other act the lawyer might dislike; an attempt to cover up a family member's or friend's involvement; bad advice from cellmates or others about the need to withhold unfavorable information from counsel). If a client is to be saved from himself or herself, s/he must be made to tell counsel the truth. And whether or not s/he is lying, s/he must be confronted with any inconsistencies among the pieces of the story s/he is telling or between the client's story and other information obtained by counsel, since these inconsistencies may be exposed at trial.

One way to cross-question the client vigorously without creating the impression that counsel disbelieves or distrusts the client is to engage in an explicit exercise of role-playing, in which counsel first prepares and rehearses the testimony that the client might give in his or her own defense at trial and then plays prosecutor for purposes of cross-examining the client. This kind of dry run of cross-examination, as well as direct examination, will be necessary later, in any event, in any case in which the client is considering testifying at trial. (See §§ 29.5.3, 29.5.4, 29.6 *infra*). During the case-planning and investigative stages (see Chapters 7 and 9 *infra*) and before undertaking plea bargaining or deciding on a plea (see Chapters 8 and 14 *infra*), the same technique can be used to confront the client with any embarrassing holes or contradictions in the client's story while maintaining an attitude of complete confidence in the client's truthfulness, although "the prosecutor" will have some pretty tough questions to throw at the client. At some point during these interviews with the client, preferably near the time of trial when counsel has all the information that s/he will have at trial, the client should be given an objective appraisal of the case, with counsel avoiding unfounded optimism or pessimism.

6.15 *Interview Checklist*

The following checklist covers most of what the lawyer will have to learn from a client in order to develop an effective defense at all stages of a criminal case from first contact through trial. It models a thorough interviewing process; more than a single interview will ordinarily be needed to gather all of the information it includes. When the charge is relatively minor, less extensive fact-gathering may be adequate. But counsel will do well to assume at the outset that all of the subjects flagged by this checklist need to be on the agenda; decisions to curtail coverage should be made deliberately only after counsel has enough of a sense of the case to be sure that it is safe to omit the matters listed in any specific area.

Attorney's file no.: _____

Criminal case no.: _____

Client's name: _____

Charges: _____

_____

Date and hour of interview: _____

Place of interview: _____

_____

Name of interviewer: _____

INTERVIEW SHEET

Name (have the client spell even common names):

All aliases and nicknames:

Street address (if apartment or room, include number):

Phones, land and cell (and name of person whose phone it is, if not the client's own):

Email, e-text, and website addresses:

Date of birth:

Place of birth:

Place of residence at time of arrest:

Prior places of residence (from latest to earliest):

Residence: From (date):   To (date):

Education:

<table>
<tr><td></td><td>Name/location of school</td><td>Current Grade</td><td>Date last attended</td></tr>
</table>

Elementary:

High School:

Vocational School:

College:

Other:

Armed Forces:

Branch of service:

Date of beginning of active duty:

Date of discharge:

Type of discharge:

Rank at time of discharge:

Any honors or medals:

Combat service:

Time overseas:

Court martial charges, if any (including: finding; date of finding; sentence, if any; portion of sentence remitted; and portion of sentence served, facilit[y][ies] in which the client was held, and the dates when the client was in each facility):

Present employment:

For each employer if more than one:

Name of employer:

Street address:

Phone:

Email, e-text, and website addresses:

Type of business:

Client's immediate supervisor:

Client's job designation:

Narrative description of what the client does in the usual course of his or her work:

Pay (starting):   (ending):

Employed since (date):

Indicate season if seasonal:

If presently unemployed, check ☐

Since (date):

Receiving unemployment compensation?   ☐ Yes ☐ No

Amount:

Other means of support:

Prior employment:

For each employer if more than one:

Name of employer:

Street address:

Phone:

Email, e-text, and website addresses:

Type of business:

Client's immediate supervisor:

Client's job designation:

Narrative description of what the client did in the usual course of his or her work:

Pay (starting):   (present):

Employed from (date):   to (date):

Indicate season if seasonal:

Reason for leaving:

Social security number:

Marital status:

    □ Single

    □ Divorced

    □ Married

        □ Ceremonial

        □ Common-law

        □ Cohabiting ("domestic partnership")

Current spouse or domestic partner:

Name:

Street address:

Phone:

Email, e-text, and website addresses:

Dates of beginning of relationship [and of marriage]:

Employed: □ Yes □ No

Employer's name:

Employer's street address:

Employer's phone:

Employer's email, e-text, and website addresses:

Narrative description of what the spouse or partner does in the usual course of his or her work:

Previous marriages or domestic relationships:

For each spouse or domestic partner:

Name:

Street address:

Phone:

Email, e-text, and website addresses:

Dates of beginning and end of relationship [and of marriage]:

Street address[es] where client lived with spouse or domestic partner:

Employed: □ Yes □ No

Employer's name:

Employer's street address:

Employer's phone:

Employer's email, e-text, and website addresses:

Narrative description of what the spouse or partner did in the usual course of his or her work:

Children (list all children, whether they live with the client or not):

For each child:

Name:

Age:

Street address:

Phone:

Email, e-text, and website addresses:

Employed: □ Yes □ No

Employer's name:

Employer's street address:

Employer's phone:

Employer's email, e-text, and website addresses:

Narrative description of what s/he does in the usual course of his or her work:

Client's father:

Name:

Living □   Deceased □

If living:

Age:

Street address:

Phone:

Email, e-text, and website addresses:

Employed: □ Yes □ No

Employer's name:

Employer's street address:

Employer's phone:

Employer's email, e-text, and website addresses:

Narrative description of what father does in the usual course of his work:

Client's mother:

Name:

Living ☐   Deceased ☐

If living:

Age:

Street address:

Phone:

Email, e-text, and website addresses:

Employed: ☐ Yes ☐ No

Employer's name:

Employer's street address:

Employer's phone:

Employer's email, e-text, and website addresses:

Narrative description of what mother does in the usual course of her work:

Siblings:

For each sibling:

Name:

Age:

Street address:

Phone:

Email, e-text, and website addresses:

Employed: □ Yes □ No

Employer's name:

Employer's street address:

Employer's phone:

Employer's email, e-text, and website addresses:

Narrative description of what sibling does in the usual course of his or her work:

By whom was the client raised? Indicate if parents were separated during any period of the client's childhood. If the client was raised by persons other than a parent, get data for those persons as for parents, *supra.*

Is the client a non-citizen? If so, what is his or her immigration status? (Even legal immigrants may be at risk of immigration consequences following an arrest or charge, either as a result of the unfavorable outcome of the criminal case or merely because government officials learn of the client's non-citizen status. For discussion of potential immigration issues, see §§ 15.3, 15.6.1 *infra.*) What is the client's nationality if not U.S.? Is a spouse or domestic partner or family member a non-citizen? If so, what is his or her immigration status? What is his or her nationality? Has s/he ever expressed concern about immigration problems if government officials learn of his or her non-citizenship status or whereabouts?

Has the client or a family member ever had contact with immigration authorities? If so, what is the name of any individual immigration agent known by the client to be involved, and what is that agent's title, office or department, street address, phone, email, e-text, and website addresses? If the names of individual agents are unknown, what is the name of the agency or department involved, and its street address, phone, email, and website addresses? Does the client or a family member or acquaintance have paper or electronic documents that would contain this contact information?

Does (or did) client use drugs?   □ Yes   □ No

Type(s):

Since (date):

Present frequency of use:

Has the client received treatment for a drug problem or participated in any form of detoxification or rehabilitation program (including peer-group programs)?   □ Yes   □ No

For each occasion:

Describe treatment or regimen:

Dates of beginning and end of treatment or regimen:

Name of agency:

Address:

Phone:

Email and website addresses:

Name(s) of counselor(s) or professional personnel:

Street address:

Phone:

Email, e-text, and website addresses:

Does the client or a family member or acquaintance have paper or electronic documents that would contain this contact information or information about the client's treatment or performance?

Does (or did) client use alcohol?   □Yes   □No

Volume and frequency of use:

If heavy drinker, since (date):

Has the client received treatment for an alcohol problem or participated in any detoxification or rehabilitation program (including AA or other peer-group programs)??   □ Yes □ No

For each occasion:

Describe treatment or regimen:

Dates of beginning and end of treatment or regimen:

Name of agency:

Street address:

Phone:

Email and website addresses:

Name(s) of counselor(s) or professional personnel:

Street address:

Phone:

Email, e-text, and website addresses:

Does the client or a family member or acquaintance have paper or electronic documents that would contain this contact information or information about the client's treatment or performance?

Client's physical and mental condition:

Present physical disabilities:

Present physical illnesses:

Is client presently under medical care?   □ Yes   □ No

   Doctor's name:

   Street address:

   Phone:

   Email, e-text, and website addresses:

Serious physical injuries (and all head injuries):

   For each injury:

      Type:

      Cause:

      Date:

      If hospitalized, name, street address, and city of hospital, and dates of hospitalization:

      Name[s] of physician[s] and other individual professional personnel:

         For each individual known:

         Phone:

         Email, e-text, and website addresses:

      Does the client or a family member or acquaintance have paper or electronic documents that would contain identifying or contact information for this hospital or information about the client's treatment or performance?

Has the client ever been in a mental hospital or institution?   □ Yes □ No

   For each hospital or institution:

   Name, street address, and city of hospital:

   Admission date: Discharge date:

Event[s] leading to hospitalization:

Diagnosis:

Name[s] of physician[s] and other individual professional personnel:

> For each individual known:

> > Phone:

> > Email, e-text, and website addresses:

> > Does the client or a family member or acquaintance have paper or electronic documents that would contain identifying or contact information for this hospital or institution or information about the client's treatment or performance?

Has the client ever been found mentally incompetent by a court?   □ Yes □ No

> For each occasion:

> > Name and location of court:

> > Name of judge:

> > Name[s] of attorney[s]:

> > Date of adjudication:

> > Nature of proceeding:

> > Event[s] leading up to proceeding:

> > Does the client or a family member or acquaintance have paper or electronic documents that would contain this contact information or information about the client's treatment or performance?

Has the client ever been treated by a psychiatrist or psychologist? □ Yes □ No

> For each treating professional:

> > Name:

Street address:

Phone:

Email, e-text, and website addresses:

Date treatment began: Date treatment ended:

Circumstances leading to treatment:

Diagnosis:

Nature of treatment:

Does the client or a family member or acquaintance have paper or electronic documents that would contain this contact information or information about the client's treatment or performance?

Has the client ever undergone a psychiatric or psychological evaluation?   □ Yes □ No

For each evaluator:

Name:

Street address:

Phone:

Email, e-text, and website addresses:

Circumstances leading to evaluation:

Diagnosis or result of evaluation:

Does the client or a family member or acquaintance have paper or electronic documents that would contain this contact information or information about the client's treatment or performance?

Prior criminal record (all *arrests*, from latest to earliest, *including pending charges, and including juvenile adjudications and arrests*, and in all jurisdiction):

For each episode:

Date of arrest:

Jurisdiction (city and State):

Charge(s):

Disposition if not by court:

Plea (guilty or not guilty or *nolo* or insanity; if guilty or *nolo*, of what charges):

Trial by judge or jury:

Name of judge:

Court disposition (conviction or acquittal or other: if conviction, of what charges):

Sentence:

Date sentence imposed:

Name of attorney:

Street address of attorney:

Phone number of attorney:

Email, e-text, and website addresses of attorney:

Sentence of incarceration:

     Length of time served:

     Institution[s] in which client was incarcerated:

     Client's prison number:

Sentence of probation or parole:

     From (date):   To (date):

     Names of all probation and parole officers:

          Street address of each officer:

Phone number of each officer:

Email, e-text, and website addresses of each officer:

Was client ever charged with violation of probation or parole conditions?

□ Yes □ No

Date of violation and nature of violation charged:

Disposition of violation charge:

Does the client or a family member or acquaintance have paper or electronic documents that would contain identifying or contact information for the courts, judges, cases, prosecutors, defense attorneys, probation and parole officers involved or information about the proceedings and dispositions?

Was Client on Probation or Parole at the Time of this Arrest? □ Yes □ No

On which of the above prior charges? (indicate by number):

Check whether probation □   or parole □

Amount of back time owed:

Was Client Under any Pending Charges at the Time of this Arrest?   □ Yes □ No

Which of the above prior charges was pending (indicate by number):

Form of conditional release on that charge:

If the client was on bail for that charge, get the data specified under **Present custodial status** / Bail, *infra*

Does the client or a family member or acquaintance have paper or electronic documents that would contain identifying or contact information for the courts, judges, cases, prosecutors, defense attorneys, probation and parole officers involved or information about the proceedings and dispositions?

Was the Client Wanted for Arrest on Other Charges in any Jurisdiction at the Time of this Arrest?   □ Yes □ No

For each charge:

Jurisdiction:

Charge(s):

Nature of incident:

How client knows s/he is wanted:

Name of law enforcement agency involved, if known:

Street address:

Phone number:

Email and website addresses:

Officers involved, if known:

Street addresses:

Phone numbers:

Email, e-text, and website addresses:

Does the client or a family member or acquaintance have paper or electronic documents (such as a warrant or notice) that would contain identifying or contact information for the agencies and agents involved or information about the nature of the charges and status of proceedings?

Has the client consulted an attorney about these charges?   ☐ Yes ☐ No

Name of attorney:

Street address of attorney:

Phone number of attorney:

Email, e-text, and website addresses of attorney:

Present custodial status:

Jail (name and address):

Prison (name and address):

Jail or prison number:

Bail:

    Where posted:

    When posted:

    Amount:

    Form (cash, property, professional surety):

    If bonding company:

        Street address:

        Phone number:

        Contact person:

        Email, e-text, and website addresses:

    Who paid for the bail:

    Has collateral security been put up? ☐ Yes ☐ No

        If so:

        Nature of collateral: _____

        Amount secured: _____

        Who put up the collateral: _____

    Does the client or a family member or acquaintance have paper or electronic documents that would contain identifying or contact information for the bondsman and terms of the bond?

Other form of conditional release (describe):

Facts relating to the offense charged and the client's connection with it or whereabouts and activities at the time of the offense; facts relating to the client's arrest and subsequent interactions with law enforcement agents.

The client should be asked to tell everything s/he knows about the present charge, in chronological order: what s/he did, what happened to him or her, who was involved, when and how the client was arrested, and everything that the police have done with the client since arrest. At the conclusion of the client's story, counsel should ask questions – who, what, why, when, where, and how – for clarification. Before terminating the interview, counsel should be sure s/he knows at least the following:

The client's version of the events on which the charge is based or, if the client denies involvement, where the client was and what s/he was doing at the time of the events on which the charge is based.

Witnesses (indicate if immediate contact is advised for any reason):

> Witnesses to the events on which the charge is based (including the complainant and persons who may be prosecution witnesses):

> Alibi witnesses:

> Background and character witnesses:

For each witness:

> Name (get spelling and all aliases and nicknames):

> Street address:

> Phone:

> Email, e-text, and website addresses:

> Physical characteristics useful for identifying the individual:

> Other information helpful in locating the witness (where does s/he work, where does s/he hang out, is s/he on public assistance, and so forth, as appropriate):

Arrest:

Who, what, why, when, where, and how?

For all officers involved in the event, everything the client knows about the officer's:

Name:

Badge number:

Rank or title:

Agency or Department:

Street address:

Phone number:

Email and website addresses:

Physical characteristics useful for identifying the individual:

Does the client or a family member or acquaintance have paper or electronic documents (such as a warrant or notice) that would contain identifying or contact information for the agencies and officers involved or information about the nature of the charges and status of proceedings?

Who was with the client when s/he was arrested? Were they also arrested? Get information as for witnesses, *supra.*

Was the client under the influence of drugs when arrested or had s/he taken drugs recently?　　□ Yes □ No

Was client drunk when arrested or had s/he taken alcohol recently? □ Yes □ No

Was client ill when arrested? □ Yes □ No　If so, describe illness:

Was client struck or roughly handled during arrest or thereafter?　□ Yes　□ No

If so, describe injuries:

Date and time of arrest:

Exact location of arrest:

Did the arresting officers have a warrant?　□ Yes　□ No

What did they say the charge was?

What questions did they ask the client?

What did the client tell them?

Did police at the time of the arrest or any other time take anything from the client's person, home, place of work, automobile, place where the client was, or from the premises or property of any other person?　□ Yes　□ No

Things taken:

Did police have a search warrant?　□ Yes　□ No

Describe circumstances under which the things were taken:

For all officers involved, everything the client knows about the officer's:

Name:

Badge number:

Rank or title:

Agency or Department:

Street address:

Phone number:

Email and website addresses:

Physical characteristics useful for identifying the individual:

For all other persons present, get information as for witnesses, *supra:*

Did police make any other search of the client's person or possessions, or enter the home, place of work, automobile, or place where the client was, or search the property or enter the premises of any other person? □ Yes □ No

Did police have a search warrant?   □ Yes □ No

For all officers involved, everything the client knows about the officer's:

    Name:

    Badge number:

    Rank or title:

    Agency or Department:

    Street address:

    Phone number:

    Email and website addresses:

    Physical characteristics useful for identifying the individual:

    For all other persons present, get information as for witnesses, *supra:*

After arrest:

    Every location to which client was taken by police:

    Exact times of confinement in each place:

    Number of officers present in each place:

    For all officers involved, everything the client knows about the officer's:

        Name:

        Badge number:

        Rank or title:

        Agency or Department:

        Street address:

Phone number:

Email and website addresses:

Physical characteristics useful for identifying the individual:

Was the client interrogated? □ Yes □ No

Where did the interrogation take place?

When and how long?

For all officers involved, everything the client knows about the officer's:

Name:

Badge number:

Rank or title:

Agency or Department:

Street address:

Phone number:

Email and website addresses:

Physical characteristics useful for identifying the individual:

For all other persons present, get information as for witnesses, *supra.*

Was a lie detector test given? □ Yes □ No

What specific questions did the officers ask? (This is often a good means of learning something about the prosecution's case.)

Did the police confront the client with any evidence against the client? If so, what:

Did the police tell the client that any person had incriminated the client or that any codefendant or purported co-perpetrator had confessed? If so, who:

Did the client tell the police anything? □ Yes □ No

Did the client make a written statement?　　□ Yes　□ No

Did s/he sign it?　　　□ Yes　□ No

Did the client fill out or sign any forms?　　□ Yes　□ No

   Describe the forms:

What did the client say in any written or signed statement or in filling out any form? (The client should be asked to tell counsel everything s/he remembers, in detail.)

Did the client make an oral statement?　　□ Yes　□ No

   Was it tape-recorded or video-recorded?　　□ Yes　□ No

   Was it stenographically transcribed?　　□ Yes　□ No

   Did anybody write it out or take notes on it?　　□ Yes　□ No

   Other circumstances at the time of the client's statement, in detail:

   What did the client say in any oral statement? (The client should be asked to tell counsel everything s/he remembers, in detail.)

For each written or oral statement or form filled out:

Was the client previously warned:

   That s/he had a right to remain silent?　　□ Yes　□ No

   That anything s/he said could be used against him or her?　　□ Yes　□ No

   That s/he had a right to a lawyer before making a statement?　　□ Yes　□ No

   That if s/he could not afford a lawyer, one would be appointed before any questioning?
                □ Yes　□ No

What did the client say in response to these warnings?

Was the client asked whether s/he understood each warning?　　□ Yes　□ No

How did s/he respond?

Was s/he asked whether s/he was willing to make a statement after having been given these warnings?　　□ Yes　□ No

How did s/he respond?

Was s/he asked to sign a form or card with these warnings on it?　　□ Yes　□ No

How did s/he respond to each warning, waiver, or question on the form or card?

Did any codefendant or purported co-perpetrator confess or incriminate the client? If so, everything the client knows about the person's:

> Name (get spelling and all aliases and nicknames):
>
> Street address:
>
> Phone:
>
> Email, e-text, and website addresses:
>
> Physical characteristics useful for identifying the individual:
>
> Other information helpful in locating the person (where does s/he work, where
>
> does s/he hang out, is s/he on public assistance, and so forth, as appropriate):

Was the client given any physical examination; was a DNA or blood sample taken; was hair taken or combed; was a drug or alcohol test administered or body inspection of any sort made; was the client examined by a doctor or mental health professional?

> Where:
>
> When:
>
> Describe the examination, test, or inspection:
>
> For all persons present, everything the client knows about the person's:
>
> > Name:
> >
> > Badge number:
> >
> > Rank or title:

Agency or Department:

Street address:

Phone number:

Email and website addresses:

Physical characteristics useful for identifying the individual:

Did anyone say anything about what the examination, test, or inspection showed?
□ Yes □ No

Was the client asked for permission to make the examination, test, or inspection?
□ Yes □ No

How did s/he respond?

Was s/he told that s/he had a right to refuse or to have an attorney present?
□ Yes □ No

How did s/he respond?

Was the client exhibited in a lineup or brought, under any circumstances, before any person for identification?   □ Yes □ No

Where:

When:

Describe the situation:

All persons present (including police, identifying witnesses, other persons in lineup, codefendants): everything the client knows about the person's:

Name:

Badge number:

Rank or title:

Agency or Department:

Street address:

Phone number:

Email and website addresses:

Physical characteristics useful for identifying the individual:

What did the police say to the identifying witness:

What did the identifying witness say:

Was the client asked for permission to put him or her in the lineup or to exhibit him or her for identification?　　　　　□ Yes □ No

How did s/he respond?

Was s/he told that s/he had a right to refuse or to have an attorney present?
　　　　　□ Yes □ No

　　　If so, how did s/he respond?

Was s/he asked to do anything during the identification procedure (walk around, turn to one side, gesture, speak)?　　　　　□ Yes □ No

　　　If so, what did s/he do or say?

Was s/he told that s/he had a right not to do these things?　　□ Yes □ No

　　　If so, how did s/he respond?

Was the client asked to reenact anything?　　　□ Yes □ No

　　　　　If so, get the same information as for lineup and identification procedures, *supra*):

Was client asked to give permission for the search of any place or thing? □ Yes　　　□ No

　　Where:

　　When:

　　By whom was the request made?

For all persons present, everything the client knows about the person's:

        Name:

        Badge number:

        Rank or title:

        Agency or Department:

        Street address:

        Phone number:

        Email and website addresses:

        Physical characteristics useful for identifying the individual:

For what place or thing was permission to search requested?

What was the search supposed to be looking for?

What was said to the client by the person requesting permission?

What did the client say?

Was the client told that s/he had a right to refuse permission?   □ Yes □ No

How did s/he respond?

Was anything said about a search warrant?   □ Yes □ No

What was the client told about the warrant?

Prior judicial proceedings on the present charges:

        Has the client already appeared in court on the present charges?   □ Yes □ No

        For each prior court appearance:

                When:

                What court:

Name, street address or location, department and room number of court:

Nature of proceedings:

Who was present (names or descriptions of judge, prosecutor, police):

For all persons present (judge, court reporter, prosecutor, police, codefendants, witnesses), everything the client knows about the person's:

Name:

Badge number:

Rank or title:

Agency or Department:

Street address:

Phone number:

Email and website addresses:

Physical characteristics useful for identifying the individual:

Were charges read or shown to the client?   □ Yes □ No

What were they:

Was the client asked to plead?   □ Yes □ No

What did s/he plead:

Who testified:

What did they testify:

Did the client testify?

What did s/he testify?

Was the client represented by a lawyer?   □ Yes □ No

Name of attorney:

Street address of attorney:

Phone number of attorney:

Email, e-text, and website addresses of attorney:

Physical characteristics useful for identifying the individual:

Does the client or a family member or acquaintance have the attorney's card or any paper or electronic documents that would contain identifying or contact information for the attorney or information about the nature of the charges and proceedings?

What else happened in court:

Was the client given a slip of paper or a form of any sort?   □ Yes □ No

If so, where is it? (Counsel wants to obtain this form as soon as s/he can get it from the client or the client's family, since it will state the charges and next court appearance date more accurately than the client can remember them and will contain the court's case number.)

Are there any codefendants or uncharged, purported co-perpetrators? □ Yes □ No

For each one, everything the client knows about the person's:

Name:

Street address:

Phone number:

Email and website addresses:

Physical characteristics useful for identifying the individual:

If the person is in custody, where:

If at liberty, get information as for witnesses, *supra.*

What role did the codefendant or uncharged, purported co-perpetrator play in connection with the offense charged, according to (1) the police; (2) the prosecutor; (3) the codefendant or uncharged, purported co-perpetrator himself or herself; (4) any witnesses who spoke to the issue?

For each attorney who represented a codefendant, everything the client knows about:

Name of attorney:

Street address of attorney:

Phone number of attorney:

Email, e-text, and website addresses of attorney:

Physical characteristics useful for identifying the individual:

When relevant, counsel should obtain:

1.   Information relating to bail (see § 4.5 *supra*).

2.   The client's signed release giving counsel the right to inspect all hospital, prison, court, and juvenile court records relating to the client (releases for each on separate sheets).

3.   A signed retainer and fee agreement (see § 6.11 *supra*).

Chapter 7

Case Planning

7.1. *Evolving a General Strategy for Defending the Case: Reaching and Refining a Set of Aims and Objectives*

Effective defense work requires counsel to attend to an extensive roster of tasks simultaneously during the period prior to trial. In addition to court appearances at arraignments and hearings (see Chapters 2-4 *supra*; Chapters 11, 14 *infra*), defense counsel must seek out and take statements from prosecution witnesses, conduct discovery and field investigation, draft and litigate motions, interview defense witnesses and prepare them to testify, engage in plea negotiations with the prosecutor, subpoena police reports and other documents, consult defense experts, and confer with the client. See Chapter 10 *infra*.

This complex set of tasks is complicated further by time pressures. Various factors affect how quickly a case progresses: the seriousness of the charges; the speedy-trial rules of the jurisdiction; prosecutors' workload and court congestion; whether the defendant is at liberty or incarcerated pending trial, and so forth. Depending upon these factors and the stage of the case at which counsel enters it, counsel may have only a short period within which to perform the multitude of tasks that need to be completed before trial. And some of the tasks may involve long delays beyond counsel's control. For example, if counsel subpoenas reports from a police department, hospital or public agency, s/he should anticipate that the records division of that institution will be slow in responding; or if counsel plans to retain an expert witness, s/he should expect that it will take some time to locate an appropriate expert and for the expert to schedule and perform the examinations or tests that counsel needs.

The only possible solution to this problem – albeit an imperfect solution – is to begin performing the tasks as soon as counsel has a skeletal understanding of the facts of the case, and thereafter to revise counsel's plans and strategies progressively as additional information becomes known. The first substantial interview of the client will tell counsel the most important foundational facts: the circumstances surrounding the offense from the client's perspective, or the client's account of his or her whereabouts and activities elsewhere if s/he denies involvement in the offense. Counsel needs to form a tentative plan of action immediately after this interview. That plan had best take the form of a provisional "theory of the case" (see § 7.2.1 *infra*) which will shape counsel's next moves, at least until such time as new information warrants a revision of counsel's working strategy.

This chapter is designed to assist counsel in forming a plan of action and implementing it. Every case is unique in its facts and in the series of tasks that must be performed to prepare it for trial. But some generalizations are possible regarding techniques and considerations that can usefully guide counsel's strategic planning. Section 7.2 describes a process for developing a theory of the case and explains the ways in which counsel can use the defense theory to guide the vital fact-gathering process (§ 7.2.2 *infra*), the selection and drafting of motions (§ 7.2.3 *infra*), and the actions that counsel should take early in the case to begin preparing for sentencing in the event of a conviction at trial or a guilty plea (§ 7.2.4 *infra*). Section 7.3 discusses ways in which counsel can use narrative thinking in case planning.

Planning techniques of this sort can help counsel to make efficient use of whatever time is available to work on a case. But they will be of little avail if counsel's overall caseload is so high that s/he does not have sufficient time to devote to the case at each point at which actions or judgments are demanded. Accordingly, counsel is obliged – both by the Sixth Amendment's guarantee of effective assistance of counsel and by the canons of ethics requiring thorough and competent preparation – to limit counsel's caseload and other responsibilities so as to ensure adequate time for providing each client with the high quality of representation to which s/he is entitled. *See* AMERICAN BAR ASSOCIATION, MODEL RULES OF PROFESSIONAL CONDUCT, Rule 1.1 (2015); AMERICAN BAR ASSOCIATION, CODE OF PROFESSIONAL RESPONSIBILITY EC 6-4 (1980); American Bar Association, Formal Op. 06-441 (May 13, 2006) ("Ethical Obligations of Lawyers Who Represent Indigent Criminal Defendants When Excessive Caseloads Interfere with Competent and Diligent Representation"); *Wilbur v. City of Mount Vernon*, 989 F. Supp. 2d 1122 (W.D. Wash. 2013); *Public Defender, Eleventh Judicial Circuit of Florida v. State*, 115 So.3d 261, 270, 274, 279, 282 (Fla. 2013); *State ex rel. Missouri Public Defender v. Waters*, 370 S.W.3d 592, 597, 605-08, 612 (Mo. 2012); *Carrasquillo v. Hampden County District Courts*, 484 Mass. 367, 142 N.E.3d 28 (2020) ("The government of the Commonwealth . . . has a constitutional obligation to ensure that there is an adequate supply of publicly funded defense attorneys available to represent eligible indigent criminal defendants." *Id.* at 368, 142 N.E.3d at 34: "Ordering assignment of additional cases to public defenders who are already carrying maximum caseloads risks making them ineffective, by hindering them from, among other responsibilities, giving adequate attention to contesting pretrial detention if necessary, investigating their cases, making strategic decisions, filing pretrial motions, and preparing for trial, thereby defeating the very purpose of the right to counsel." *Id.* at 388-89, 142 N.E.3d at 49.); *Tucker v. State*, 162 Idaho 11, 19-20, 394 P.3d 54, 62-63 (2017) ("Appellants alleged systemic, statewide deficiencies plaguing Idaho's public defense system. Appellants seek to vindicate their fundamental right to constitutionally adequate public defense at the State's expense, as required under the Sixth Amendment to the U.S. Constitution, and Article I, Section 13 of the Idaho Constitution. They have not asked for any relief in their individual criminal cases. Rather, they seek to effect systemic reform. Their allegations find support in both *Gideon v. Wainwright,* 372 U.S. 335, 342 (1963), and *State v. Montroy*, 37 Idaho 684, 690, 217 P. 611, 614 (1923), which make clear that it is the State's obligation to provide constitutionally adequate public defense at critical stages of the prosecution. Alleging systemic inadequacies in a public defense system results in actual or constructive denials of counsel at critical stages of the prosecution suffices to show an injury in fact to establish standing in a suit for deprivation of constitutional rights."); *Kuren v. Luzerne County*, 637 Pa. 33, 79-80, 146 A.3d 715, 743 (2016), and cases cited (holding that "there is a cognizable cause of action whereby a class of indigent defendants may seek relief for a widespread, systematic and constructive denial of counsel when alleged deficiencies in funding and resources provided by the county deny indigent defendants their constitutional right to counsel. The consequences of holding otherwise would be untenable, and would be fundamentally irreconcilable with the United States Supreme Court's pronouncements on the role of the right to counsel in our system of justice."); *State v. Peart*, 621 So.2d 780, 789, 791 (La. 1993) ("We take reasonably effective assistance of counsel to mean that the lawyer not only possesses adequate skill and knowledge, but also that he has the time and resources to apply his skill and knowledge to the task of defending each of his individual clients. ¶ . . . [T]he Louisiana indigent defender system . . . has resulted in wide variations in levels of funding, both between different . . . [Indigent Defender Boards] and within the same IDB over time. The general pattern has been one of chronic underfunding of indigent defense programs in most areas of the state. . . . ¶ [H]aving found that evidence in the record before us shows that the provision of indigent defense services in Section E of Orleans Criminal District Court is in many respects so lacking that defendants who must depend on it are not likely to be receiving the reasonably effective assistance of counsel the constitution guarantees, we find that a rebuttable presumption arises that indigents in Section E are receiving assistance of counsel not sufficiently effective to meet constitutionally required standards. . . . This presumption . . . is to apply prospectively only; . . . it will be applicable to all indigent defendants in Section E who have . . . [Orleans Indigent Defender Program] attorneys appointed to represent them hereafter, so long as there are no changes in the workload and other conditions under which OIDP assigned defense counsel provide legal services in Section E."); Jay C. Hauser, Note, *Funding the Unfunded Non-Mandate: An Equal Justice Case for Adequate Funding of Public Defense*, 25 U. PA. J. L. & SOC. CHANGE 287 (2022). As the ABA Standards for Criminal Justice explain:

> "Defense counsel should not carry a workload that, by reason of its excessive size or complexity, interferes with providing quality representation, endangers a client's interest in independent, thorough, or speedy representation, or has a significant potential to lead to the breach of professional obligations. A defense counsel whose workload prevents competent representation should not accept additional matters until the workload is reduced, and should work to ensure competent representation in counsel's existing matters. Defense counsel within a supervisory structure should notify supervisors when counsel's workload is approaching or exceeds professionally appropriate levels."

AMERICAN BAR ASSOCIATION, STANDARDS FOR CRIMINAL JUSTICE MONITORS AND MONITORING, DEFENSE FUNCTION (4th ed. 2017), Standard 4-1.8(a), *Appropriate Workload*.

7.2. *Developing a Theory of the Case and Using It to Guide Case Planning*

7.2.1. *Developing the Defense Theory of the Case*

On the basis of the first full-scale client interview (see Chapter 6) and whatever other information counsel obtains when entering a case (see §§ 3.5, 3.10, 6.2 *supra*), counsel should formulate a preliminary defense "theory of the case." The "theory of the case" is a detailed summary of the defense that counsel will mount at trial; it weaves together the version of the facts and an articulation of the legal rules or normative precepts on which counsel will rely to secure a favorable verdict. The theory of the case that counsel develops at this stage must be tentative and flexible enough to change as new information is gathered. Counsel does not yet have a complete picture of what the prosecution witnesses and defense witnesses will say and what pertinent scientific, tangible, or documentary evidence exists or can be produced to prove or disprove guilt. So counsel's initial theory of the case should always be considered a work-in-progress. As new facts are learned, counsel should continually update the theory of the case, interpolating the new information and reassessing previous judgments about options and alternative courses of action.

In order for the prosecution to establish guilt at trial, it will have to prove both (i) that a crime was committed, and (ii) that the defendant was the person who committed it. A defense theory of the case will usually involve attacks upon either one or both of these two components. Counsel should be alert to the recognized, recurring causes of erroneous convictions and to the literature documenting them (*see, e.g.*, Clanitra Stewart Nejdl, & Karl Pettitt, *Wrongful Convictions and Their Causes: An Annotated Bibliography*, 37 (No. 3) NORTHERN ILL. U. L. REV. 1 (2017); Rebecca Brown & Peter Neufeld, *Chimes of Freedom Flashing: For Each Unharmful Gentle Soul Misplaced Inside a Jail*, 76 N.Y.U. ANNUAL SURVEY AMER. L. 235 (2021); §§ 37.7, third paragraph; 37.14 *infra*) but needs to keep in mind that the range of potential prosecutorial miscues and concomitant defense theories is wide and that each individual criminal case requires a thorough-going, unique canvass of possible strategies for defeating the prosecution's case.

7.2.1.1. *Defense Theories That Refute the Prosecution's Assertion That a Crime Was Committed*

There are essentially three ways of precluding the prosecution from proving that a crime was committed.

First, the defense can show that, even accepting the prosecution's basic version of events, there is insufficient proof of one or more of the legal elements of the crime charged. For example, if the crime (or the degree of crime) requires proof of a certain monetary value (such as Grand Larceny or certain degrees of Destruction of Property), counsel can refute the existence of that particular crime either by contending that the prosecution has failed to prove the requisite value or by presenting defense evidence that the object in question was not worth as much as the prosecution asserts. Or, if the crime involves a mental element, the defense can refute it either by contending that the prosecution's evidence is not sufficient to warrant the inference that the defendant entertained the requisite *mens rea* or by presenting defense evidence (through the defendant, other defense witnesses, or both) that controverts the existence of the guilty mental state.

Second, the defense can show that, even accepting the prosecution's basic version of events, some affirmative defense renders the defendant's actions noncriminal. For example, in a murder case, the prosecution witnesses may be truthfully recounting their observations of the defendant's stabbing of the victim; but when their testimony is meticulously parsed and/or supplemented with defense evidence (consisting of testimony by the defendant, other defense witnesses, physical evidence, and so forth), the defense will ask the fact-finder to conclude that the victim provoked the attack by actions which induced the defendant to have a reasonable fear of imminent bodily harm, within the applicable doctrine of self-defense.

Third, the defense can show that the prosecution's witnesses are not telling the truth, either because they are fabricating (*i.e.,* lying or fantasizing) or because they are honestly mistaken. For an illustration of a strategy for challenging the prosecution's theory of the case as the product of honest but premature tunnel vision and confirmation bias on the part of the police, see § 37.7, third paragraph *infra*. As a general matter, it is easier to prove mistake than outright fabrication because the fact-finder (judge or jury) will ordinarily be reluctant to believe that a prosecution witness is lying under oath. However, a theory of fabrication may prevail if the defense can show that the witness has a compelling motive to lie. A theory that the complaining witness is fabricating the existence of a crime can be supported with evidence that:

(i)   The witness has a motive to accuse the defendant falsely in order to get him or her into trouble because of past incidents that have caused the witness to be angry at or jealous of the defendant or the defendant's family or friends;

(ii)   The witness has some other motive for fabricating a crime, such as: to collect insurance money; to cover up some other criminal behavior of the witness or the complainant; or to win a reward from law enforcement authorities for snitching (for example, dismissal of pending charges against the complainant; a financial reward; admission into a witness protection program); or

(iii)   (In cases in which the complaining witness is a police officer) the officer fabricated the crime in order to inflate his or her arrest figures and thereby gain credit with superiors (by, for example, planting drugs on the defendant in a drug case) or in order to cover up an ill-founded arrest that would have made the officer look bad or exposed the officer to a civil suit for false arrest (and, when violence was involved in the arrest, for assault and battery).

A theory that the complaining witness is mistaken in thinking a crime took place can be supported by showing that some innocent set of events occurred which the complainant misinterpreted as a crime. For example: the defendant merely asked the complainant for a hand-out, and the complainant thought the defendant was shaking him or her down in a robbery; the police encountered the defendant running away from the vicinity of a closed shop with a burglar alarm ringing and therefore assumed the defendant had attempted to break in, when, in fact, the alarm went off because of a short circuit and the defendant was running to find and alert the shop owner; a store security guard observed the defendant taking merchandise past a cash register and arrested the defendant for shoplifting, when the defendant was merely looking for a register that was less crowded. Of course, in addition to explaining away the complainant's testimony as a fabrication or a mistake, counsel will have to explain away the testimony of any eyewitnesses. The theory may be the same for the eyewitnesses as for the complainant, or it may be different (as, for example, when the defense asserts that the complainant is mistaken and that an eyewitness is lying in a desire to support the complainant, who is a relative or co-worker).

7.2.1.2.   *Defense Theories That Refute the Prosecution's Assertion That the Defendant Was the Perpetrator*

The prosecutorial evidence linking the defendant to the crime will usually take the form of one or more of the following: (i) an identification of the defendant by the complainant, an eyewitness, or both; (ii) an incriminating statement by the defendant, confessing to the offense, admitting conduct or exhibiting knowledge that implicitly implicates the defendant, or reciting an alibi that the police have shown to be false; (iii) testimony or statements by a codefendant or uncharged snitch identifying the defendant as the perpetrator; and/or (iv) scientific evidence, such as DNA analysis, serology evidence in sex offenses, fingerprint analysis, hair analysis, fiber analysis identifying threads found at the crime scene as stemming from an article of the defendant's clothing, or a swab of the defendant's hand showing that s/he recently fired a gun.

Several of these forms of prosecutorial evidence are subject to suppression or exclusion on pretrial motions. Motions to suppress identification testimony are covered in Chapter 27, and motions to suppress confessions, admissions, and other statements are covered in Chapter 26. Motions to sever a codefendant's case from the defendant's on the ground that the codefendant made a statement incriminating the defendant, and back-up arguments that the statement should, at the very least, be redacted to remove all references to the defendant, are described in § 23.9.1 *infra*. Challenges to the admissibility of scientific evidence are discussed in § 39.15.

Assuming that the defense does not succeed in suppressing or excluding the incriminating evidence of the defendant's identity as the perpetrator, there are several ways of refuting the evidence at trial.

Identification testimony by the complainant or an eyewitness can be challenged by asserting that the witness, although honest, is mistaken in identifying the defendant for one or more of the following reasons:

(i)   The defendant bears some resemblance to the actual perpetrator and was selected because s/he was the only one among the suspects viewed (in a show-up, lineup or photo array) who fit the perpetrator's description.

(ii)   The police caused (or helped to cause) the identification by something they said to the witness or by their employment of a suggestive identification procedure that conveyed to the witness who it was that the police wished the witness to identify.

(iii)   Some event occurred that caused the witness to superimpose the defendant's face, which s/he saw after the offense (or, less usually, on an unrelated occasion before the offense), on top of the memory of the perpetrator's face, and the witness now honestly but mistakenly believes that defendant's face was the perp's. This theory can be used when, for example: the witness saw the defendant in police custody or at the police station and deduced that the police naturally would have caught the right person; the witness saw the defendant in the vicinity of the crime or heard the defendant saying something similar to the words spoken by the perpetrator or saw the defendant wearing clothes similar to those worn by the perpetrator; or the witness and the defendant had an encounter that suggested to the witness that the defendant was the perpetrator.

(iv)   The witness is identifying a person of another race or ethnicity, and thus the identification process is subject to the weaknesses and vagaries of cross-racial or cross-ethnic identification.

Material useful in challenging the accuracy and reliability of eyewitness identification testimony will be found in §§ 27.3, 30.1 subdivision 13, and 37.10 *infra* and in *Dennis v. Secretary, Pennsylvania Department of Corrections*, 834 F.3d 263, 314-45 (3d Cir. 2016) (en banc)

(McKee, C.J., concurring).

Identification testimony by the complainant or an eyewitness also can be refuted by asserting that the witness is lying. To make this theory persuasive, the defense might urge, for example, that:

(i)   The witness bears a grudge against the defendant.

(ii)   The witness needs to pin the crime on somebody in order to escape prosecution for his or her own complicity in it or in order to gain some benefit, such as the dismissal of pending charges against the witness or cash compensation as an informer, and the defendant happens to be an available scapegoat (because the defendant fits the description of the perpetrator or was at the scene of the crime or possesses a criminal record that would make the defendant's guilt believable).

(iii)   Although there is no clear motive to which the defense can point, the defense does not bear the burden of proving why the eyewitness is lying but merely has to raise a reasonable doubt of his or her veracity; and the untrustworthy demeanor of the witness is sufficient to raise a reasonable doubt.

These same theories can be used to discredit a codefendant or snitch who identifies the defendant as the perpetrator.

A confession or incriminating statement by the defendant, which the defense was unable to suppress on constitutional grounds in a pretrial hearing, may nevertheless be assailable at trial under state-law doctrines of involuntariness. See § 26.12 *infra*. Even when such challenges are unavailable or unlikely to prevail, counsel can argue to the fact-finder at trial that the circumstances under which the statement was made render it untrustworthy. See § 26.3.4 penultimate paragraph and § 26.18 *infra*. Typical circumstances that may persuade a judge or jury to discredit a defendant's confession in whole or in part are overbearing police interrogation; police promises of leniency if the defendant confesses; a defendant's drug or alcohol intoxication, physical injuries, depression or lack of sleep; a defendant's suggestibility (resulting from, *e.g.*, mental impairment or a desire to please the authorities) or limited competence in the language in which s/he confessed; fear of recrimination by a third party if the defendant does not take the rap; and motivation to protect a family member or loved one by taking the rap. When details in a purportedly incriminating statement make the difference between guilt and innocence, counsel can contest the prosecution's interpretation of the statement by pointing out ambiguities in the defendant's words or in the questions to which s/he was responding. Finally, the facts may support a thesis that the police fabricated the statement in an attempt to bolster their case. (Judges sitting as the fact-finder in a bench trial are often loth to conclude that police officers are lying; juries may be more receptive to claims of police perjury, particularly if jurors or their relatives or friends have had bad experiences with cops or come from communities where cops are in bad odor at the time of the trial.)

In challenging a prosecution case based on scientific evidence, counsel can employ any one or more of three approaches. (i) S/he can present a defense expert who reached a conclusion contrary to that of the prosecution expert, and can assert that the defense expert's conclusion is the correct one, or at least that a reasonable doubt has been raised. (ii) S/he can use a defense expert, or cross-examination of the prosecution expert, to show that even if the prosecution expert's conclusions are correct, they are not very damning. For example, the impact of a scientific finding that the defendant has the same blood type as the perpetrator can be minimized by showing that one-quarter of the human race shares that blood type. (iii) S/he can use a defense expert, or cross-examination of the prosecution expert, to show that there are potential inaccuracies or uncertainties in the scientific method employed (in general, or under the circumstances of this particular case) that raise legitimate doubts about the correctness of the prosecution expert's results. Most genuine experts are sufficiently cautious that they will freely admit the potential for inaccuracy that plagues many scientific tests. Material useful in challenging the accuracy and reliability of forensic-science evidence presented by the prosecution will be found in § 37.14 *infra*.

In any case in which the prosecution is likely to use scientific evidence at trial, counsel should consider retaining a defense expert to consult with counsel about these possible approaches and to testify at trial if appropriate. When the client is indigent, counsel can request court funds to retain the expert. See Chapter 5 *supra*. Often, it will be worthwhile to test the waters by talking with the prosecution's expert prior to retaining a defense expert. Many forensic experts on the police force, unlike line police officers, are willing to talk with defense attorneys. By questioning the prosecution's expert about the nature, bases, and degree of certainty of his or her conclusions, and particularly by inquiring whether there is anything unusual or difficult about the analysis of the data being interpreted in this case, counsel can make a preliminary assessment of the utility of challenging the expert testimony with a rival witness. If, for example, the prosecution's scientific evidence is based upon a simple, straightforward test, the test is normally highly accurate, its application in the present case was routine, and the tester seems unshakeable, it may be wise to stick to factual defenses rather than retaining a rival expert, especially if the defendant is a paying client who can ill afford the expert's fee. Additional factors to consider in assessing the likelihood of successfully challenging the prosecution's forensic-science evidence are discussed in § 37.14 *infra*.

In a case in which the prosecution seeks to identify the defendant through a chain of circumstantial evidence linking him or her to the criminal episode, defense counsel can challenge the chain as a whole – instead of, or in addition to, attacking particularly vulnerable links – on a theory that the police investigation went astray at the outset, latched onto the wrong person as a suspect, and then locked into this mistake as a result of tunnel vision. See § 37.7, third paragraph *infra*; *and see Kyles v. Whitley*, 514 U.S. 419, 446 (1995); *Lindsey v. King*, 769 F.2d 1034, 1042 (5th Cir. 1985); *United States v. Crosby*, 75 F.3d 1343, 1347-48 (9th Cir. 1996); *Mendez v. Artuz*, 303 F3d. 411, 416 (2d Cir. 2002).

7.2.1.3. *The Building Blocks for Constructing a Defense Theory of the Case*

Ultimately, counsel's selection of a theory of the case will depend on an evaluation of the relative strengths of the prosecution's evidence and the evidence available to the defense. The defendant is often a vital source of ideas and information pointing to potential defense evidence, because s/he is positioned at the center of events from the defense perspective and can give counsel both a general framework for constructing a favorable version of what happened and specific leads to possible defense witnesses. S/he may also be able to provide some insights into provable biases of prosecution witnesses. S/he is substantially less likely, however, to be able to assist counsel in identifying other areas of weakness in the prosecution's evidence. So constructing a successful theory of the defense will usually require counsel to take the initiative in identifying, investigating, and developing exploitable flaws in the prosecution's case. And counsel will almost always have to bear primary responsibility for canvassing the full range of potential challenges to the prosecution's theory of the case, for determining whether these can be combined or are mutually incompatible (or incompatible with theories based upon potential defense evidence) and for assessing what combination or election of defenses has the greatest likelihood of success.

In looking for potential weaknesses in the prosecution's case, counsel should obtain all pretrial statements made by each prosecution witness – whether to police or other persons – and should minutely compare the texts of what the witness said at different times. If a version of events that a witness gave soon after the crime is more favorable to the defense than the witness's present version, the defense theory of the case may be that the witness's memory has faded over time and that the witness's present inability to remember significant details casts doubt on anything s/he now says that was not in his or her original statement. Or the theory may be that the witness's self-inconsistencies demonstrate that s/he is fabricating his or her entire tale (or at least its incriminating parts) in order to procure the defendant's conviction (because that will benefit the witness in some way, or because of personal animosity arising from jealousy, anger, revenge-seeking, or other bias); the witness has never been able to tell a straight story; so none of his or her conflicting versions of the tale are worthy of belief. Inconsistencies between the statements of different prosecution witnesses can be used to support similar defense theories. When those witnesses have had opportunities to talk with one another before trial, defense counsel will often be able to demonstrate that their successive statements are increasingly compatible and to argue that this homogenization discloses the factual vacuum at the core of the prosecution's case. The homogenizing process may be demonstrable even when prosecution witnesses have interacted little during the pretrial period; it is a natural consequence of the prosecutor's rehearsing witnesses to present a unified version of what happened; and defense counsel can argue that it has critically impaired the fact-finder's ability to reach any confident, reliable conclusions about facts that the prosecution is required to prove beyond a reasonable doubt.

Another technique for pinpointing exploitable weaknesses in the prosecution's case is to consider whether there are aspects of the prosecution witnesses' conduct that fail to comport with normal human behavior. For example, if the complainant or eyewitness has known the defendant for years, it stands to reason that s/he would give the police the defendant's name as soon as s/he is interviewed by them. If s/he failed to give the defendant's name to the authorities until some time later, counsel can use this quirk to support a theory that the witness has decided to pin the crime on the defendant falsely as a result of a grudge that began after the date of the crime (or a longstanding grudge that the witness was not quick enough to act upon at the time of the police interview). In order to detect anomalies of this sort, counsel will often find it productive to trace through, from beginning to end, an imaginary "normal" scenario for a crime like the one charged. By comparing that scenario with the provable events in the defendant's own case, counsel can identify actions and statements on the part of prosecution witnesses that are out of whack with behavior that a trier of fact would expect from people in the witnesses' purported circumstances.

A similar fact-modeling process, mentally tracing step-by-step the normal sequence of police procedures in a case such as the defendant's, will enable counsel to pinpoint exploitable flaws in the police officers' versions of searches, seizures, confessions, and identification procedures. For example, in a case in which counsel is challenging a police officer's *Terry* frisk of the defendant (see § 25.10 *infra*) and the officer claims that s/he believed the bulge in the defendant's pocket was a gun, counsel can develop the officer's failure to take the normal steps for protecting himself or herself from an armed suspect, such as radioing for backup, drawing his or her own service revolver, and immobilizing the defendant by having him or her "assume the position" with hands up against a wall or against a car, well away from coat or pants pockets.

7.2.1.4. *Implications of the Choice of Defense Theory for Trial Preparation*

There are several ways in which the defense theory of the case will shape counsel's trial preparation.

First of all, the theory of the case will inform the way in which counsel assigns priorities to the tasks to be performed in the defense investigation of the case. As a practical matter, even though counsel may wish to arrange an investigative interview of every possible prosecution and defense witness, often that will not be feasible. In many jurisdictions, the prosecution is not obligated to inform the defense of the identity of all of its witnesses (see § 18.7.2 *infra*), and the investigator will have to spend considerable time searching for unknown prosecutorial witnesses. Even defense witnesses may not be easy to find, since often the client has no idea of the names or addresses of people who were standing on the street, observing the events. In an imperfect world, in which each aspect of the defense investigation consumes time and limited investigative resources, counsel will have to determine the relative importance and temporal urgency of tasks, looking first – or directing an investigator to look first – for certain witnesses, documents, and exhibits. Thus, for example, in an assault case in which the defendant's self-defense claim does not dispute the occurrence of the assault or even the manner in which the assault was committed but instead depends upon an incident earlier the same day in which the complainant threatened to kill the defendant the next time they met, counsel will assign priority to finding any witnesses to the earlier threat and witnesses who can recount a history of threats and violence by the complainant against the defendant or attest to the complainant's reputation for violence. Of course, counsel's initial assignment of priorities will have to be progressively revised in accordance with new information that is learned. For example, if the prosecution reveals in discovery that prosecution witnesses will recount the defendant's making statements during the assault that are inconsistent with a theory of self-defense, counsel then will have to assign top priority to finding defense witnesses who describe the sound track of the assault differently.

Once counsel has identified the most important witnesses, the defense theory of the case determines what questions should be asked of those witnesses. In essence, counsel is working backwards from a goal defined by the theory of the case. Having identified what ultimate picture of events and people the defense will want to ask the fact-finder to accept at the end of the trial, counsel can specify what defensive facts need to be elicited during the trial, and thence counsel can deduce the questions that need to be asked of witnesses to learn those facts. This focusing function of the defense theory of the case also plays an important role in deciding, for example, which expert witnesses to retain and what to ask them to evaluate; what legal research has to be conducted in preparation for drafting jury instructions or making bench arguments on the merits at trial; and what additional legal research and planning have to be undertaken in anticipation of evidentiary issues that are likely to come up at trial.

Third, the defense theory of the case will shape counsel's decisions about what motions to file. For example, if the defendant made a statement to the police telling a wholly exculpatory story of self-defense and if the defense theory at trial will mirror that statement, counsel may decide to refrain from filing a motion to suppress the statement. Or if the defense's theory at trial depends upon testimony by a codefendant and if a severance of the codefendant's case from the defendant's will probably have the practical result of rendering the codefendant unavailable as a defense witness, counsel may opt in favor of abandoning a legally viable severance motion. See § 23.7 *infra.*

Fourth, the defense theory of the case will shape the way in which counsel conducts the preliminary hearing and any suppression hearings. As explained in §§ 11.4, 11.8.2, 24.2 *Infra,* evidentiary hearings of this sort can be used for the purpose of laying a foundation for later impeachment of prosecution witnesses at trial. If, at the time of the preliminary hearing or suppression hearing, counsel has a vision of what the defense theory will be at trial, counsel can design his or her cross-examination at the hearing to serve this purpose most effectively, creating the best possible transcript material for use at trial even if this requires the curtailment or sacrifice of some lines of cross-examination that might have increased the defense's relatively marginal chance of winning the hearing itself. See § 24.4 *infra.*

These are only some of the more significant ways in which the defense theory of the case can shape trial preparation. It would not be an overstatement to say that the theory of the case should inform every single act of counsel's. For example, counsel's decision whether to seek a continuance or whether to assert a speedy trial demand when the prosecution seeks a continuance will depend upon the availability of defense witnesses needed to prove the defense theory of the case. Counsel's advice to the client about whether to take the witness stand at trial will depend upon the theory of the case, as well as additional considerations such as whether the judge is likely to penalize the defendant at sentencing for what the judge may view as perjurious testimony.

7.2.2. *Gathering the Facts Needed to Support the Defense Theory of the Case*

There are four institutionally recognized methods for gathering factual information bearing on a case:

(i)   Client interviews (see Chapter 6).

(ii)   Defense investigation, including interviewing potential prosecution and defense witnesses, collecting and examining police reports and other documents (whether onsite or by subpoenaing them), and inspecting physical scenes and objects (see Chapter 9).

(iii)   Informal and formal procedures for discovery of materials from the prosecution (see Chapter 18).

(iv)   Retention of expert witnesses who can perform scientific tests, such as ballistics, serology, or fingerprint examinations, that will shed light on the pertinent facts (see Chapter 30).

In addition to these methods, there are three informal means of gleaning facts: filing motions that will require the prosecutor to respond with pleadings that reveal aspects of the prosecution's case; conducting hearings, such as the preliminary hearing and suppression hearings, in such a way as to gain disclosure of the prosecution's case at trial (see §§ 11.4, 11.8.2, 22.2, 24.4.2 *infra*); and informal conversations with the prosecutor about the case during plea negotiations, other meetings, or casual conversations while waiting for a court hearing to begin (see § 15.10 *infra*).

Counsel should take advantage of all of these means of obtaining factual information. Because some of them involve more lag time than others, the former procedures should be set in motion first so that they will be completed in time for trial. Generally, the following steps should be taken at the earliest practicable time:

(i)   Counsel should prepare subpoenas for documents. These will not take counsel long to prepare and must be prepared early because it may take a long while for the relevant agencies to comply with the subpoenas.

(ii)   Counsel should direct an investigator to start tracking down and interviewing prosecution and defense witnesses and gathering necessary documents and exhibits. Counsel should use the theory of the case to assign priorities to these investigative tasks, explaining to the investigator the order in which s/he should perform the various necessary tasks. If counsel does not have an investigator and the client is indigent, counsel should promptly file a motion for court funds to retain an investigator (see Chapter 5 *supra*; § 9.4 *infra*).

(iii)   Counsel should identify and contact any expert consultants and expert witnesses who may be needed (see §§ 16.2-16.3, 30.1-30.5 *infra*), or, if counsel is representing an indigent client, file a motion for court funds to retain the experts (see Chapter 5 *supra*; §§ 16.3, 30.3 *infra*).

(iv)   Counsel should conduct an immediate informal discovery session with the prosecutor or, if the prosecutor is unable to meet that day, schedule an appointment as early as possible.

By taking these steps expeditiously, counsel will gather the information needed to shape further investigation of the case, the information needed to prepare suppression motions and other substantive motions (see Chapter 17), and the information needed to conduct plea negotiations effectively (see §§ 15.3-15.7 *infra*). The motions proceedings and plea negotiations, in turn, will provide counsel with more facts, which can be used in conducting suppression hearings and the trial.

7.2.3. *Filing Motions That Are Consistent with the Theory of the Case*

The motions that counsel should ordinarily consider filing – in addition to motions for state-paid defense resources that the defendant cannot afford (see Chapter 5) – are:

(i)   Motions for dismissal of the charging paper on grounds of its facial insufficiency, the court's lack of jurisdiction, legal bars to prosecution (such as claims of double jeopardy; of an applicable statute of limitations; or of the unconstitutionality of the criminal statute underlying the charge), or fatal defects in required pre-charge procedures (see Chapters 12, 13, 20).

(ii)   Motions for a change of venue (see §§ 22.1-22.3 *infra*) or recusal of a judge (see §§ 22.4-22.7 *infra*).

(iii)   Motions for various forms of diversion (see Chapter 21 *infra*).

(iv)   Motions to expedite or delay the pace of proceedings (see Chapter 28 *infra*).

(v)   Motions for discovery (see § 18.7 *infra*).

(vi)   Motions for protective orders to forestall potentially damaging prosecutorial activities (see §§ 9.14, 17.4, 18.7.4, 18.9.2.6-18.9.2.7 *infra*).

(vii)   Motions to suppress tangible evidence, confessions and incriminating statements, and identification testimony (see Chapters 24-27).

(viii) Motions for severance of counts or defendants (see Chapter 23).

This is not, of course, an exclusive list: counsel may have to develop motions to deal with case-specific problems, such as, for example, prosecutorial interference with defense access to witnesses (see § 9.14 *infra*). Counsel should familiarize himself or herself with local rules setting deadlines for the filing of motions. See § 17.7 *infra*.

7.2.4. *Setting in Motion the Process Needed to Prepare for Sentencing in the Event of Conviction*

Effective representation of a client at sentencing often requires that counsel begin preparing for the possibility of conviction and sentencing very early in the case. *See, e.g.,* AMERICAN BAR ASSOCIATION, STANDARDS FOR CRIMINAL JUSTICE MONITORS AND MONITORING, DEFENSE FUNCTION (4th ed. 2017), Standard 4-8.3(a), *Sentencing* ("Early in the representation, and throughout the pendency of the case, defense counsel should consider potential issues that might affect sentencing."); *Jones v. Ryan*, 52 F.4th 1104, 1118 (9th Cir. 2022) (in a capital case, "'[t]he timing of this investigation [of mental health factors bearing on sentencing] is critical.' . . . '[L]egal experts agree that preparation for the sentencing phase of a capital case should begin early and even inform preparation for a trial's guilt phase[.]' . . . Moreover, the 1989 ABA Guidelines state that '[c]ounsel should conduct independent investigations relating to the guilt/innocence phase and to the penalty phase of a capital trial[,]' and '[b]oth investigations should begin *immediately upon counsel's entry into the case and should be pursued expeditiously.*' ABA Guidelines for the Appointment and Performance of Counsel in Death Penalty Cases, Guideline 11.4.1(A), p. 13 (1989) (emphasis added); *see also id.* at Guideline 11.8.3, p. 23 ('[P]reparation for the sentencing phase, in the form of investigation, should begin immediately upon counsel's entry into the case.').")."). Mitigating information about a client's background may take a long time to gather, especially if it is necessary to obtain prior institutional records of various sorts. In a case in which counsel may ultimately argue at sentencing for probation with a condition of participation in a community-based program (*e.g.*, an alcohol- or drug-treatment program), it will often be useful for the client to voluntarily enroll in the program (or one like it) well before trial, so that, in the event of conviction, counsel will be able to show the sentencing judge documentation of the client's faithful participation in the program and of beneficial effects already apparent.

Accordingly, counsel's theory of the case should dictate not only a detailed plan for trial preparation but also a blueprint of plans for sentencing in the event of conviction, the steps that should be taken in advance to prepare for sentencing, and when each of those steps should be taken. To develop this blueprint, counsel will need to "become familiar with the client's background, applicable sentencing laws and rules, . . . what options might be available as well as what consequences might arise if the client is convicted . . ., available sentencing alternatives and . . . community and other resources which may be of assistance in formulating a plan for meeting the client's needs." *Id.* As counsel works on the case, s/he must "continually evaluate the impact that each decision or action may have at later stages, including . . . sentencing. . . ." AMERICAN BAR ASSOCIATION, STANDARDS FOR CRIMINAL JUSTICE MONITORS AND MONITORING, DEFENSE FUNCTION (4th ed. 2017), Standard 4-1.3(f), *Continuing Duties of Defense Counsel.*

"Defense counsel should also consider whether consultation with an expert specializing in sentencing options or other sentencing issues is appropriate." AMERICAN BAR ASSOCIATION, STANDARDS FOR CRIMINAL JUSTICE MONITORS AND MONITORING, DEFENSE FUNCTION (4th ed. 2017), Standard 4-8.3(a), *Sentencing.* At some point in the case, it may be appropriate for counsel to seek court funds to retain a mitigation expert. See Chapter 5. But it will often be possible – and advisable – for counsel to consult with a mitigation expert informally before that point.

7.3. *The Role of Narrative Theory in Case Planning*[1]

---

[1] This section is a shortened version of the *Introduction* in Ty Alper, Anthony G. Amsterdam, Todd Edelman, Randy Hertz, Rachel Shapiro Janger, Jennifer McAllister-Nevins, Sonya Rudenstine & Robin Walker-Sterling, *Stories Told and Untold: Lawyering Theory Analyses of the First Rodney King Assault Trial*, 12 CLINICAL L. REV. 1 (2005). Elaboration of the points presented here and additional authorities can be found at pages 4-32 of that article.

7.3.1. *The Nature of Narrative and Its Importance in Litigation*

"Narrative," as we use the term, means constructing and telling stories and includes the rhetorical creation of an imaginative world in which the story can happen – a world that gives the story its point. *See* JEROME BRUNER, ACTS OF MEANING 86 (1990); Jerome Bruner, *The Narrative Construction of Reality*, 18 CRIT. INQUIRY 1, 13-14 (1991). There are several reasons why this narrative process is crucial in litigation.

First, narrative is "a primary and irreducible form of human comprehension" (Louis O. Mink, *Narrative Form as a Cognitive Instrument*, in ROBERT H. CANARY & HENRY KOZICKI (eds.), THE WRITING OF HISTORY: LITERARY FORM AND HISTORICAL UNDERSTANDING 129, 132 (1978)) – humankind's basic tool for giving meaning to experience or observation – for understanding what is going on. It is the way most people make sense of the world most of the time. "[N]arrative . . . gives shape to things in the real world and often bestows on them a title to reality." JEROME BRUNER, MAKING STORIES: LAW, LITERATURE, LIFE 8 (2002). We link perceptions into happenings, happenings into events, events into stories; and our narrative expectations tell us how each story hangs together and how it will end. Jurors bring this everyday sense-making process to their work and use it to descry the "facts" from the evidence. *See, e.g.,* REID HASTIE, STEVEN D. PENROD & NANCY PENNINGTON, INSIDE THE JURY (1983); Nancy Pennington & Reid Hastie, *A Cognitive Theory of Juror Decision Making: The Story Model,* 13 CARDOZO L. REV. 519 (1991). Trial lawyers seeking to persuade jurors of a particular version of the facts need to tap into the process. *See, e.g.,* Anthony G. Amsterdam & Randy Hertz, *An Analysis of Closing Arguments to a Jury,* 37 N.Y.L. SCH. L. REV. 55 (1992).

Second, the narrative process also tells us how a story *should* end. "[N]arrative is necessarily normative" (Bruner, *Narrative Construction of Reality, supra* at 15), providing the interface between facts and values. "Stories fly like arrows toward their morals." WILLIAM H. GASS, TESTS OF TIME 4 (2002). They embody a society's manifest of moral imperatives. *See* BRUNER, ACTS OF MEANING, *supra* at 47. So, effective story-telling by a lawyer can help to make the lawyer's case to jurors who want to reach the *right* result.

Third (an elaboration of the preceding point), the narrative process is specialized for reconciling our expectations about the normal, proper course of life with deviations from it. "Deviance is the very condition for life to be 'narratable.'" PETER BROOKS, READING FOR THE PLOT: DESIGN AND INTENTION IN NARRATIVE 139 (1992). The launching pad of narrative is *breach*, a violation of expectations, disequilibrium. *See* BRUNER, MAKING STORIES, *supra* at 15-20. The landing pad of narrative is *balance*, the reestablishment of equilibrium. *See* ANTHONY G. AMSTERDAM & JEROME BRUNER, MINDING THE LAW 45-47, 121-24 (2000). Narrative has always done for the human mind what juries are called upon to do for the body politic in every trial, and particularly in criminal trials – to deal with deviance by restoring order. Small wonder, then, if jurors resort to narrative to do much of the work.

Fourth, jurors come to their task equipped not only with the narrative process as a mode of thought but with a store of specific narratives channeling that process. Stock scripts and stock stories accreted from exposure to the accountings and recountings that continually bombard us –

through television, movies, newspapers, books, the internet, and word of mouth from our earliest childhood (*see* BRUNER, ACTS OF MEANING, *supra* at 82-84) – provide all of us with walk-through models of how life is lived, how crimes are committed, how reality unfolds. When a juror perceives the familiar lineaments of one or another of these narratives emerging from the evidence, s/he "recognizes" what is afoot and s/he is cued to interpret other pieces of evidence and eventually the whole of it consistently with the familiar story line. "This means that in order to perform effectively, many lawyers, particularly litigators, may be obliged to keep abreast of (in order to tap into) the popular storytelling forms and images that people commonly carry around in their heads." Richard Sherwin, *The Narrative Construction of Legal Reality*, 18 VT. L. REV. 681, 692 (1994).

Fifth, evidentiary trials in which facts are contested are not conducted on the premise of Kurosawa's *Rashomon* – that multiple inconsistent versions of reality are all equally true – nor do most jurors operate on this premise. The uncompromising ontological first principle of every trial is that *something real really happened out there*. Jurors are permitted to vote that they cannot tell what happened, but this verdict is conceptualized as a failure of persuasion on the part of whichever party bears the burden of proof. And every trial lawyer knows that it is very dangerous – a desperation tactic of last resort – to stake his or her case on the argument that the truth is so recondite that the opposing party has failed to meet its burden on that account alone. Even if the lawyer's aim is simply to cast enough doubt on the opponent's case to prevent the jury from agreeing that an applicable burden of proof has been met, s/he will almost always want to suggest some alternative thing or things that could plausibly have *really happened out there*, instead of the thing that the opponent needs to prove. Under these circumstances trials of "the facts" tend to turn into story-telling contests. There is a hard core of material that the contestants must incorporate and account for in their stories – for example, the jury in a homicide trial may know from seemingly incontrovertible ballistics and fingerprint evidence that at some point in time the defendant handled the gun that fired the fatal shots – and the story-teller is required to encompass these mandatory materials in his or her plot. But where they cease to "tell the whole story," the story-telling competition begins; and the story-teller whose tale best interprets the mandatory materials consistently with the audience's understanding of the human scene can hope to carry off the prize.

Sixth, story-telling offers the litigator a vital means to expand or change the audience's understanding of the human scene. And it equips the litigator to explore in his or her own head, as a necessary prelude, a range of *possibilities* for expanding or changing the audience's perception of that scene. For, in addition to its other functions, narrative serves as the mind's primary way of surveying alternative possible worlds. It is imagination's instrument for getting beyond the familiar and the obvious, for playing out never-experienced scenarios and projecting the consequences of counterintuitive conceptions. It enables us to travel paths we have not walked before and to see where they lead, to create realms of *what if* where we can experiment with new varieties of thinking and believing, of doing and being. *See* AMSTERDAM & BRUNER, MINDING THE LAW, *supra* at 235-39; JEROME BRUNER, ACTUAL MINDS, POSSIBLE WORLDS (1986).

So, what follows from all this? Our reason for rehearsing the functions that the narrative process serves in litigation is not to encourage litigators to make greater use of narrative. That would be as superfluous as exhorting fish to make greater use of water. Litigators are inextricably immersed in narrative; they cannot survive without it. *See* AMSTERDAM & BRUNER, MINDING THE LAW, *supra* at 110. Our aim is rather to suggest that litigators will navigate the medium more effectively to the extent that they *focus consciously* on narrative construction as an integral part of their work, *survey systematically and creatively* the range of options available to them in constructing narratives, and make *strategic choices* among the options with an understanding of the basic elements of narrative construction and how those elements fit together.

7.3.2. *The Specific Uses that a Litigator Can Make of Narrative*

The following inventory enumerates potential uses of narrative in jury-trial litigation. Some involve the litigator's own thinking (categories 1 and 2 immediately below). (We include in the term "litigator" all members of a litigation team.) Some have to do with gauging the thinking of other people in the litigation process (category 3). Some involve making explicit references or implicit allusions to stock scripts in communications aimed at the jury (categories 4, 5 and 6). In subpart 7, we catalog the range of techniques by which a litigator communicates to the jury; and in subpart 8, we briefly discuss the choice between explicit and implicit invocations of stock scripts.

1. *Using narrative to generate hypotheses that guide investigation and to avoid shutting down investigation by making premature judgments.* To be efficient, factual investigation must be directed by working hypotheses about what happened and why. See § 7.2.1.4 *supra*. Hypotheses fleshed out in narrative form – with a scene, characters, actions, instruments, and motives (see § 7.3.3 *infra*) – serve this function particularly well, because their projection requires the litigator to construct in his or her imagination a world containing all of the details that are necessary for the plot to unfold. These details in turn suggest others that would probably exist in conjunction with the necessary details, or that could *not* coexist with the necessary details, providing specific focuses for investigation.

Projecting alternative possible causal or explanatory stories that could fit around information already in hand enables a litigator to multiply hypotheses. And having multiple hypotheses in mind throughout a litigation can be crucial to success. Litigators tend too often to zero in on the first plausible version of events that emerges from available information, or at most the first couple of plausible scenarios. They tend to confine their investigations to attempting to confirm the most immediately obvious favorable scenario (or two) or to refute the most immediately obvious unfavorable scenario (or two). They forget that the fundamental tenet of effective investigation is: *The world is a mysterious, surprising place, where strange things happen.* Narrative provides the best safeguard against these tendencies. Narrative restores the mystery of the world. Insisting upon telling oneself alternative possible stories even after it has become "obvious" what happened is an invaluable check against premature closure.

2. *Using narrative to develop a theory of the case.* As explained in § 7.2.1 *supra*, a defense lawyer's *theory of the case* is a detailed summary of the factual propositions that counsel plans to assert as the basis for a favorable verdict or decision, with the facts organized in such a way that they invoke the application of the normative dictates (substantive rules of law;

procedural rules, such as those relating to burdens of proof and presumptions; considerations of fairness, propriety, and other moral values; empathy or sympathy) that counsel will rely on. The defense theory of the case should inform every aspect of counsel's preparation and presentation. See § 7.2 *supra*. Because of the efficacy of narrative in mediating facts and norms, the theory of the case usually takes the form of a story. When it does, counsel will often benefit from modeling it on one or more of the stock stories current in the culture, and s/he will almost always benefit by considering alternative possible versions of the story and assessing their relative believability by drawing on the culture's current register of accepted stories as examples of what is plausible and coherent, what makes a tale hang together sufficiently to be convincing.

Even when counsel's theory of the case cannot be encompassed by a single story, it is likely to depend in part upon the persuasiveness of key facts. Jurors' probable reactions to evidence of those facts can sometimes be usefully gauged by reference to the prevalence of similar factual elements in the scenes, plots, and characters of currently accepted story types. Conversely, if a theory of the case calls for discrediting the opposing party's story or components of it, popular narratives featuring an appearance/reality dichotomy – as many popular detective stories, courtroom dramas and other suspense "thrillers" do – can suggest useful litigation strategies for reducing the opponent's evidence to the status of deceiving appearances.

3. *Using narrative to fathom or affect the thinking of witnesses and other sources of information, jurors and other trial participants.* Litigators must constantly make strategic decisions on the basis of predictions about how people are thinking or how they will react to something that the lawyer does. In investigative interviewing and in interviews preparing witnesses to testify at trial, the litigator frames questions in ways that are designed both to elicit information and to shape it by structuring the framework within which the witness understands the information and its significance. Because memories are commonly stored and recounted in narrative form and the information remembered is affected by the stories the witness has in mind or can be gotten to think about as giving the information meaning (*see* BRUNER, ACTS OF MEANING, *supra* at 55-58), counsel needs to be alert to detect those stories and the possibilities for rewriting them. This is equally true in cross-examining the prosecution's witnesses. Witnesses who have had little or no prior experience with the law are frequently playing out in their heads scripts for appropriate witness responses that they have picked up from TV or the movies; this is a setting in which life tends to imitate art almost slavishly. And even witnesses who have had considerable prior experience in a witness role (such as police officers) often have organized aspects of that experience (such as cross-examination by defense lawyers) – together with the courtroom stories they have heard (*e.g.*, at the precinct station) – into scripts that can be put to good use by a cross-examiner who discerns them.

Voir dire examination of prospective jurors calls for much of the same sensitivity to narrative processes and stock scripts as witness interviewing and examination. So, often, does predicting how the prosecutor will interpret and react to what defense counsel does. And whether or not counsel makes deliberate use of narrative strategies, techniques and allusions in his or her own presentation of the case, the jurors are likely to be perceiving and interpreting the evidence they hear as the unfolding of a story that they recognize from familiar models. Counsel has to anticipate the stories jurors will see in the evidence, in order either to deconstruct them or to turn them to advantage.

4. *Using narrative to attune the jury to lines of thinking that advance the litigator's case or set back the opposing party's case.* Narrative involves a special way of thinking, of processing information, of proceeding from premises to conclusions. If a litigator can get jurors into a narrative mindset early in a trial – by, for example, stressing in *voir dire* interchanges with prospective jurors, in an opening statement, and/or in the way s/he talks about the trial process when making and arguing objections in the hearing of the jury – that the jury's job is to [reconstruct the story] [figure out the real story] [get to the bottom of the story] of what happened, s/he can tap into this mode of thinking and use it to shape the jurors' understanding of the case.

One important characteristic of narrative thinking, for example, is that it is inescapably hermeneutic. In a story, the meaning of the whole is derived from the parts at the same time that the meaning of the parts is derived from the whole. *See* Bruner, *Narrative Construction of Reality, supra* at 7-11. In a deductive evidence-marshaling jury argument, this process can be derided as "circular" or as "bootstrapping," but a litigator can make it acceptable, even necessary, to a jury despite this derision if s/he can persuade the jurors that the process is the best way to see how the story hangs together.

Another important characteristic of narrative thinking is that it generates expectations through a presumption of relevancy. This is why a reader knows that if s/he is told in Chapter One there is a gun hanging on the wall, s/he can expect a gunshot and a dead body or at least a near miss by the end of Chapter Three. *See* ANTON TCHEKHOV, LITERARY AND THEATRICAL REMINISCENCES 23 (Samuel S. Koteliansky trans. 1927). A related structural feature of stories is that they translate Time into a sequence of events that must be "of relatively equal importance (or value), and . . . of approximately similar 'kinds'" (GASS, *supra* at 11). These aspects of narrative thinking can be used to imbue small items or events with large significance. And narrative thinking not only intensifies people's ordinary tendency to regard the actions of other people as a product of will – indeed, of character – rather than of external circumstances. It also gives this tendency the twist of focusing attention on "'reasons' for things happening, rather than strictly [on] . . . their 'causes'" (Bruner, *Narrative Construction of Reality, supra* at 7). By working with these and other distinctive qualities of narrative thinking, a litigator can cue the jurors to process what they see and hear at trial in ways that bolster his or her case, undermine the opposition's, or both.

5. *Using particular narratives to accredit, discredit, configure or code pieces of evidence or information.* A jury is likely to find evidence persuasive to the extent that the "facts" it portrays conform to the jurors' understanding of The Way the World Works. Jurors enter a trial with strong views, based on personal experience and on the second-hand information prevalent in their cultural milieu, about The Way the World Works. But these views are neither monolithic nor immutable. We all carry around in our heads an inharmonious assortment of notions, sometimes even flatly inconsistent notions, about what is usual, plausible, probable, possible, right, in human affairs. These notions usually take story form. *See* AMSTERDAM & BRUNER, MINDING THE LAW, *supra* at 39-47. Depending on which stories are salient when we are trying to make sense of things, we can come to different conclusions about what happened and why. By reminding the jury of apt stories to be thinking about as it receives and evaluates the evidence at

a trial, a litigator can prompt the jurors to be more trusting or more skeptical regarding particular kinds of evidence or the facts the evidence is offered to prove.

The stories can be drawn from "news" or fiction. For example, when objecting in open court to the admission of crime-lab evidence on grounds of unreliability (see § 33.11 *infra*), counsel might refer to media exposés of ineptitude at forensic laboratories (see § 37.14 *infra*). Additionally or alternatively, counsel could make disparaging comparisons between the crime-scene investigators in the present case and those in well-known TV entertainment series like *CSI*, where the forensic science techniques are invariably sophisticated and flawless.

Stories are also useful in coding items of evidence or other pieces of a case. Coding is the process by which words, images, objects, and ideas become associatively linked with others, so that the former bring the latter to mind. *See* AMSTERDAM & BRUNER, MINDING THE LAW, *supra*, at 187-92. Narrative construction involves considerable coding, which contributes heavily to the verisimilitude of good stories. And the conceptual, emotional, even sensory "baggage" packed into an item by narrative coding travels with the item beyond the story where the packing was done.

6. *Using particular narratives to cue the jury's interpretation of the case as a whole or to free the jury from sets that dispose it to fit the case into a harmful mold.* The ultimate task of the jurors in any jury trial is not only to decide what happened in terms of physical bodies moving in space and time, or even bodies moved by minds possessing specified mental states. It is also to *interpret and categorize the actions and mental states as understandable human behavior* susceptible to legal and moral judgment."Placing things, events, and people in these categories is very much a matter of *what stock script one recognizes* as being in play or *what story one chooses to tell.*" *Id.* at 47. A litigator who taps into stock narratives familiar to jurors – either the conventional story lines of prevalent news and entertainment *genres* or specific books, films, or TV shows that are recognizable by name, by leading characters, or by other signature features – can put those narratives to work as a cognitive framework for the jury's interpretation of the evidence that will shape an understanding of "what really happened" and what it means.

7. *Techniques for communicating narratives to the jury.* One virtue of grounding a litigator's case in stock stories is that s/he can begin to evoke the scripts and trappings of the story during pretrial proceedings or at the very outset of the trial. This makes it possible to use the *voir dire* examination of prospective jurors to sound out the jury's likely reactions to a story before the litigator commits to it by presenting evidence or even taking an overt position regarding the facts of the case in opening argument.

If story-based images have attached to a case in pretrial publicity, that makes it easier for the litigator to advert to them in connection with *voir dire* examination of prospective jurors. But if they have not, it may still be possible to use language evocative of stock narratives in talking with the jurors on *voir dire* or in framing written *voir dire* questions in courts where the judge conducts the oral questioning. These evocations have the dual purpose of priming the jury early to think in terms of the narratives that a litigator expects to tap into later and of giving the litigator an opportunity to observe any reactions of prospective jurors to the narrative. Their reactions may suggest that s/he will be wise to play it down – or, conversely, to play it up – or to strike particular jurors.

Means for suggesting narratives to the jury at later points in the trial abound. During opening and closing argument, counsel may or may not be permitted to make explicit references to stories current in public discourse, but s/he will usually be able to trigger recognition of widespread and recurrent stock narratives – and even of the better-known books or films or TV series that exemplify them – by implicit allusions. She can usually find occasions for similar allusions in questioning witnesses and in making and arguing objections. Witnesses can be prepared to testify in ways that make the narratives come to mind. The litigator's style of witness examination and even his or her physical activity in the courtroom can be designed to summon up the narratives s/he wants the jurors to recognize in the evidence. For example, it is advisable for counsel to consult the client extensively at the defense table in cases where the prosecution is seeking to depict the client as impulsive and lacking in self-control but not in cases where the prosecution's theory is that the defendant was a criminal mastermind.

8. *Choosing between explicit and implicit invocation of stock stories.* When a litigator has the option of making more or less explicit references to the stock stories that s/he wants jurors to have in mind, s/he needs to balance the values of clarity and dramatic emphasis against their risks. One risk is related to the risk of premature commitment. The more unequivocally a litigator has announced his or her reliance on a particular narrative, the more difficult it will be to back off it if subsequent developments weaken that theory of the case or reveal a better one. Overt or overly clear identification of a particular stock story as the theme of a litigator's case invites opposing counsel to argue that the case is built around a fable or that the facts don't fit the fable. More oblique reference to the stock story would confront opposing counsel with a hard choice between ignoring it or reinforcing it by recognizing it and undertaking to refute it. And if a refutation seemed sufficiently persuasive, the litigator could always reply, "That isn't what I meant at all." Similarly, the clarity of a reference increases the extent to which it offers traction for resistance. A juror may be roused to quarrel with the story who would not have reacted to a more ambiguous reference that was nonetheless sufficient to engage the imaginations of jurors more in tune with the tale.

7.3.3. *The Basic Structure and Process of Narrative*

Journalists learn and teach that the recipe for making stories is the Five W's: *Where? Who? What? When? Why?* There is a conspicuous resemblance between this formula and literary theorist Kenneth Burke's Pentad or "Five Key Terms of Dramatism":

1. Scene: the situation, the setting, the where and when;
2. Agent: the actors, the cast of characters;
3. Act: the action, the plot;
4. Agency: the means, the instruments of action;
5. Purpose: the motivations, goals, aims of the characters.

KENNETH BURKE, A GRAMMAR OF MOTIVES xv (1945). Either roster will serve as a handy checklist of the elements that need attention in constructing stories for the uses identified in the preceding subsection. "Elements" as in *elemental*. For each element represents a whole

163

dimension in which choices are possible and arrays of variables should be canvassed before making the final choices.

The five dimensions are, of course, interconnected. They need to be in tune. *See id.* at 3. Choices made in one dimension affect each of the others. (For example, adding characters to a story may require an expansion of the scene to encompass a longer period of time or a wider stage. It may also, by increasing the complexity of the interpersonal dynamics, change the motivations of the characters previously onstage.) Intensifying the focus upon one dimension may diminish the significance of another. *See id.* at 17. And transmutations from one dimension to another can be accomplished by the narrative alchemy that Kenneth Burke describes as re-forging distinctions in the "great central moltenness" where all of the dimensions have a common ground (*see id.* at xix). (Capital defense attorneys, for example, transmute Scene into Agent when they construct mitigation stories in which the defendant's childhood environment becomes the Villain of the plot.)

The interdependence and partial interchangeability of Scene, Agent, Act, Agency, and Purpose make narrative a highly variable and flexible medium. Still, there is a certain constancy in the way in which agents act to pursue their purposes within the temporal framework of the scene. This constancy resides in what is usually called "plot" – the "principle of interconnectedness and intention [necessary] . . . in moving through the discrete elements – incidents, episodes, actions – of a narrative" (BROOKS, *supra* at 5). It reflects "a 'mental model' whose defining property is its unique pattern of events over time" (Bruner, *Narrative Construction of Reality*, *supra* at 6). Most stories have a common plot structure. The unfolding of the plot requires (implicitly or explicitly):

(1)   an initial *steady state* grounded in the legitimate ordinariness of things

(2)   that gets disrupted by a *Trouble* consisting of circumstances attributable to human agency or susceptible to change by human intervention,

(3)   in turn evoking *efforts* at *redress* or *transformation*, which lead to a *struggle*, in which the efforts succeed or fail,

(4)   so that the old steady state is *restored* or a new (*transformed*) steady state is created,

[(5)   and the story often concludes with some *point* or *coda* – say, for example, Aesop's characteristic *moral of the story*: "Bird of a feather flock together," or "One lie will lead to another and ultimately seal one's doom" – a/k/a *This is the Way the World Works.*"]

See AMSTERDAM & BRUNER, MINDING THE LAW, *supra* at 113-14. For illustrations of the structure in appellate opinions, see *id.* at 77-99, 143-64.

7.3.4. *The Special Features of Narrative in a Jury-Trial Setting*

Although stories have a core of common elements and a common basic structure, they differ widely depending upon the purposes for which they are told, the setting in which they are told, and the conventions and constraints of that setting. Fictional stories told for didactic purposes (in the tradition of Aesop's Fables) have different conventions and constraints than do cautionary tales, or novels and dramas aimed at exploring the human condition, or novels and movies and TV shows aimed at entertainment. Purportedly nonfiction stories told by historians have different conventions and constraints than those told by ethnographers and anthropologists or by propagandists. The following conventions and constraints bind the stories that litigators can tell in jury trials:

First, the stories that litigators ask the jury to believe as constituting "the facts" of the case (although not necessarily the stories to which they refer for analogies or illustrations) *must appear to be true.* Jurors view their job as getting at the truth of what happened. A litigator's version of events must appear to be true not only from the standpoint of verisimilitude (lifelikeness) but from the standpoint of external referentiality (conformity to any information that jurors will take to be objective "fact"). And a trial litigator's resources for creating facts are limited. S/he cannot, like a novelist or playwright, conjure physical props out of thin air or put into the mouths of witnesses any words that s/he cannot convince them to utter under oath. If admissible evidence of fact X just isn't out there (or if bad luck or a client's inability to pay for thoroughgoing investigation prevents the litigator from obtaining evidence of fact X), then the litigator's story at trial has either got to jibe with the nonexistence of fact X or contain a sub-story that explains why fact X is unprovable though true.

Further, some jurors have an unshakeable belief that truth is a matter of objective fact to be discerned exclusively by logical deduction from physical evidence and the accurate testimony of reliable witnesses. These jurors will resent and resist any suggestion by a trial attorney that the jury needs to *interpret* the evidence. They will be positively outraged at the idea that *stories* have anything to do with truth-finding. Such jurors are not immune to the influence of narrative. Indeed, their denial of the need for interpretation in fact-finding may make them peculiarly prone to reach uncritical conclusions on the basis of stories that they do not realize they have in their heads – like the very story that the only way to get at truth is Sherlock Holmes'. But a litigator facing jurors of this sort needs to tell his or her stories in the manner advised by the classic rhetors, using art to conceal his or her art.

Second, a litigator's story to a jury usually needs to accommodate the opposition's story (because it needs to trump it) *and always needs to be made as immune as possible against challenge.* Trial stories are stories told in contemplation of contest. Except on the rare occasions when a story can be unveiled for the first time in rebuttal closing argument, the opposition will get a chance to refute it or coopt it. This means that, to the extent possible, stories should be built in such a way that an assault on any piece will not bring down the whole; vulnerable pieces should be eliminated; loose ends are usually better left hanging than tucked in, if the opposition is likely to pull them out again. And, the litigator always needs to consider whether something s/he is thinking of putting into his or her story can be spun by the opposition to support a competing story.

Third, a litigator's story to a jury will invariably be an incomplete story, a story without a last chapter. It has to point to a concluding chapter that the jury's verdict will write. It has to have a role for jury to play, and that role has to be made an attractive one – sleuth, quester-after-Truth, avenger, righter-of-otherwise-irremediable-wrongs.

And, fourth, of course, *the last chapter that the jury is called upon to write must be a verdict in favor of the litigator's client.* Q.E.D.

Chapter 8

Dealings with the Police and Prosecutor

8.1. *General Considerations in Dealing with the Police and Prosecutor*

8.1.1. *Counsel's Goals in Contacts with the Police and Prosecutor*

Counsel should usually establish contact with the investigating officers as early as possible in the course of a case. Thereafter, s/he should speak to them whenever the needs of the client dictate. Similarly, counsel should establish contact with the prosecuting attorney as soon as one is assigned to the case and should communicate with him or her periodically thereafter.

The purposes of these contacts are (a) to learn as much as possible about the charges against the defendant (those already lodged and others that may later be lodged) and potential prosecution evidence; about the temperament of the prosecutor and of any officer who may play a role in the charging process or who may testify at a trial; about the prosecutor's and officers' attitudes regarding the crime and the defendant as a person; and about their other concerns, their motivations, objectives, and plans; (b) to protect the defendant during police and prosecutorial investigative activity; (c) to persuade the police or the prosecutor to drop or reduce charges or to agree to some form of diversion (see § 2.3.6 *supra*); and (d) if appropriate – with the client's approval – to negotiate a mutually agreeable disposition or settlement of the case.

8.1.2. *The Importance of Amiability and Honesty*

Contact with the police and prosecutor is likely to be productive only if it is amiable. Even when dealing with hostile or offensive adversaries, counsel should play the diplomat's role. It is wise to establish two distinct levels of discourse with the police and the prosecuting attorney: (a) things said that counsel is free to disclose and to use in presenting the case at trial and (b) things said "off the record" or in confidence. Counsel should always make clear the level on which s/he is talking with the police and prosecution. If police officers or the prosecutor get the feeling that they have been "double-crossed" – that counsel has revealed information communicated in confidence – *all* communications to counsel in this and future cases are likely to be terminated abruptly.

8.1.3. *Discussions With the Police Generally*

Except in cases in which there are particular reasons to keep a low profile (for example, when counsel's independent researches disclose that the police conducted a slipshod initial investigation and are doing no further investigating, so that counsel prefers to let sleeping hounds lie), the more frequently counsel speaks with the police, the better. Every conversation with an officer gives counsel a little additional information about how the officer views the case, what the officer will testify, what the officer knows concerning other prosecution evidence, and how eager the officer is to see the client convicted. Details that the officer tells counsel may be useful in impeaching the officer if the case goes to trial. (These statements may be used in questioning the officer on cross; and if s/he denies making them or professes not to remember making them, they may be proved extrinsically to the extent that they are "noncollateral." See § 37.4 *infra*.)

Equally important, the more frequent the conversations between an officer and counsel, the more difficult it is for the officer to recall what s/he has said to counsel, and the more cautious s/he will be not to embroider the facts when testifying.

Discussions with the police are usually most fruitful before a prosecuting attorney is assigned to the matter because until that stage the officers regard it as "their case," are freer to talk about it, and have more influence in relevant decisions (see §§ 8.2, 8.3, 8.6 *infra*).

8.1.4. *Discussions With the Prosecutor Generally*

Once a prosecutor has been assigned to the case, frequent conversation with him or her is useful both as a means for acquiring factual information and as a means for learning and influencing the prosecutor's attitude. "Defense counsel should always urge the prosecutor to disclose facts even though defense counsel must then proceed to verify them. Overtures to the prosecution are not an indication of weakness, and experienced defense counsel routinely approach the prosecutor at an early stage of their own investigation." Commentary to AMERICAN BAR ASSOCIATION, STANDARDS FOR CRIMINAL JUSTICE, Standard 4-4.1, *Duty to Investigate* (2d ed. 1986).

The more the prosecutor sees that counsel is involved with the case, the more s/he is likely to conclude that counsel is working hard at it. The value of this is twofold. First, if the prosecutor thinks that defense counsel is going all out, the prosecutor's estimate of the time and trouble involved in trying the case will increase and so may the prosecutor's willingness to offer concessions in order to settle the case before trial. Second, counsel's visible dedication to a client often tends to make the prosecutor's own attitude toward the client more sympathetic, because the prosecutor figures that the client must have something on the ball to inspire all that zeal.

Both of these impressions can, of course, backfire in some cases, causing the prosecutor to prepare more thoroughly or to develop a more competitive turn of mind. Counsel should seek to learn as much as possible about this particular prosecutor's practices and psychology by asking other informed defense practitioners. Particularly when a prosecutor is carrying a heavy caseload, counsel may be wise to keep contact with him or her down to a minimum, in order to decrease the visibility of the case or to avoid arousing the prosecutor's combativeness.

8.2. *Navigating a Criminal Justice System in Which the Police and Prosecutor Typically Exercise Discretion on Many Important Issues*

8.2.1. *The Exercise of Discretion by the Police*

The criminal process, particularly in its early stages, is honey-combed with police discretion.

Not all persons who are known by the police to have committed a crime are arrested. Many minor infractions are handled by a warning from the officer.

When a person is arrested, the arresting officer initially decides what the charge should be, arrests the person on that charge, and takes the person to the precinct. Here the desk officer reviews the available facts, including the arresting officer's story, the arrestee's story, information about the arrestee and the crime that is disclosed by an initial records search, and information received in connection with the apprehension and processing of codefendants or other suspects. S/he may then book the arrestee on the same charge that the arresting officer selected or on a different charge; or, again, if the offense is not serious, s/he may send the arrestee home without lodging any charges.

If the offense is serious, an arrestee will be taken (either routinely or after the exercise of similar discretion by the desk officer) to an investigating officer or detective. See § 3.2.2 *supra*. Now it is the investigating officer's job to determine whether the arrestee has committed a crime and, if so, what crime. The investigating officer, too, may decide that the arrestee is not guilty, or that the case is weak, or that for some reason it should not be prosecuted – or should be diverted (see § 2.3.6 *supra*) – and may send the arrestee home. Or the officer may decide to charge the arrestee with one or more offenses, which may or may not be those for which s/he was arrested.

After further investigation the officer may, once again, drop or reduce or divert or increase or add to the charges that s/he originally lodged. The fact that the arrestee has been booked initially on one charge does not guarantee that s/he will not subsequently be charged with other offenses growing out of the same set of facts or with other crimes growing out of other facts that s/he has admitted or to which s/he has been connected.

8.2.2. *The Exercise of Discretion by the Prosecutor*

The prosecutor reviews the charges lodged by the police. On the basis of the police report, discussion with the investigating officers and, sometimes, an independent investigation, the prosecutor may decide to drop or divert the charges, or to proceed on the charges made by the police, or to charge more serious or less serious or different offenses. S/he thus determines the charges to be presented at the preliminary hearing.

Thereafter it is the function of the magistrate or judge at the preliminary hearing to determine the charges on which the defendant is to be held for trial or for the grand jury. However, in a case that can be prosecuted by information (see §§ 2.3.6, 2.4.3 *supra*), the prosecutor is often permitted to charge additional offenses for which the defendant was not bound over. And in indictable cases, the prosecutor is usually free to present to the grand jury whatever charges s/he pleases. See §§ 2.3.6, 2.4.4 *supra*.

After the bind-over and after an information or indictment has been filed, ordinarily the prosecutor remains free to drop the prosecution (a) formally, by entering a *nolle prosequi* (usually called *nol pros*) – for which leave of court is sometimes required but ordinarily given routinely when requested (*cf. Rinaldi v. United States*, 434 U.S. 22, 29-30 n.15 (1977) (per curiam), discussing federal practice) – or (b) informally, by an indefinite continuance (often called *stetting*). In most jurisdictions, neither of these forms of disposition precludes the prosecutor from later reactivating the charges. Therefore, if counsel's discussions with the prosecutor have produced an understanding that the prosecutor intends to discontinue the prosecution entirely – and if that understanding is sufficiently firm so that there is little risk of jeopardizing it by asking that it be recorded – counsel should request that the prosecutor state on the record that s/he intends to take no further action against the defendant on the *nol-prossed/stetted* charges. If the defendant then relies upon this assurance in any significant way, counsel will have obtained the maximum possible insurance against a prosecutorial about-face. *See Commonwealth v. Cosby*, 252 A.3d 1092 (Pa. 2021).

The prosecutor also retains discretion – again, sometimes subject to leave of court or to the requirement that the prosecutor file a statement of reasons with the court – to accept a plea of guilty to a lesser offense than that charged in the information or the indictment. S/he continues to have discretion to shunt the case into some of the diversion programs described in § 2.3.6 *supra*; judicial approval of the diversion is usually required after bind-over; but many judges are content to rubber-stamp any diversion arrangement that a prosecutor recommends.

If the defendant is convicted, either by pleading guilty or by going to trial, the prosecutor may recommend a sentence to the court or may inform the court that the defendant is cooperating. The court has complete discretion to accept or reject the prosecutor's sentencing recommendation, and practice varies locally in this regard; but it is fair to say that there are few places where the position taken by the prosecutor on sentence is wholly unimportant. Additionally, when the defendant is a recidivist, the prosecutor generally exercises considerable discretion to "charge the priors": that is, to invoke the stiffer penalties allowed by law for second or successive convictions.

8.2.3. *Factors Influencing Discretion*

The factors that may influence the police or the prosecutor not to press charges – or to press less serious charges – or to divert a prosecution – or to exercise their discretion in favor of the accused in other ways – are innumerable. *See* Megan S. Wright, Shima Baradaran Baughman & Christopher Robertson, *Inside the Black Box of Prosecutor Discretion, available at* https://ssrn.com/abstract=3893820. A few important ones, however, deserve mention.

Many prosecutors will not charge an individual whom they personally believe to be innocent, no matter how strong the evidence appears. Personal belief in an arrestee's innocence is usually less important to the police, but not unimportant.

The likelihood of conviction – the strength of the prosecution's case – is also more important to the prosecutor than to the police. (It is the prosecutor who stands to look like a fool in court; police efficiency is judged in terms of clearance by arrest.) In assessing the strength of the prosecution's case, the prosecutor must consider the weight of the evidence, the likely availability of the evidence at the time of trial, and the habits, attitudes, and sympathies of judges and juries in the locality. *See* Anna Offit, *Prosecuting in the Shadow of the Jury,* 113 Nw. U. L. REV. 1071 (2019).

Docket congestion and his or her own workload tell with the prosecutor. Particularly if a case is relatively unimportant (in terms of the egregiousness of the crime and the probable future dangerousness of the accused) and if preparing and presenting it in court are going to involve much time and work, the prosecutor will tend to favor a non-court disposition. This is particularly so if s/he is confident that the disposition will leave pertinent parties – principally the police, the complainant, and the news media – satisfied.

Both the police and the prosecutor are concerned with the accused's past record, which they view as indicative of whether the defendant is a likely source of future trouble to them or of danger to the community. A defendant with a good record is likely to get a break, especially if the offense charged is one that carries a penalty that seems unduly harsh. If an available diversion program offers means for keeping tabs on the defendant, or resources for dealing with problems that appear to have been factors in the defendant's criminal behavior (like alcohol or drug abuse, homelessness, or domestic strife), it may provide a satisfactory alternative to continued criminal prosecution.

Both police and prosecutor are also concerned with the question whether, if a case goes to trial, the evidence will disclose serious police misconduct or ineptitude.

Finally, both police and prosecutor are likely to view favorably the accused's willingness to cooperate in apprehending or in convicting other offenders or in solving other crimes.

8.2.4. *The Role of Defense Counsel in Navigating the Discretion-Riddled System*

The implications of the large discretion exercised by police and prosecutors, of its exercise at numerous points in the criminal proceeding, and of the variety of factors that affect it should be obvious. Counsel must begin early and work continuously to project to these officials the best possible image of the client and of the facts surrounding the charge.

At the same time, hard practicality – as well as the compulsions of professional and personal integrity – precludes the projection of an image that subsequently is likely to be found inaccurate. Counsel also has to worry about his or her own image. If s/he is not trusted, s/he either will not be dealt with or s/he will not be dealt with fairly. If s/he appears lazy, careless, or weak, s/he is likely to be taken advantage of, and the police or the prosecutor may bear down heavily in the hope that s/he will capitulate. The stronger counsel appears to be, the more trouble the case will appear to be to prosecute. On the other hand, if s/he is too combative, s/he may raise the spirit of combat in the police or the prosecutor.

Usually, counsel's most effective posture is one of complete sincerity, of unquestioning commitment to protect every right that the law gives the client, of unflagging willingness to work as hard as necessary in the client's behalf, yet of infinite reasonableness in seeking some fair accommodation that will dispose of the case in the most efficient and just manner. When counsel takes a hard line on a point, it must appear to be because the facts of the case are strong, not because s/he is an inventive, tricky, or obstructive lawyer. Counsel is merely doing the right thing and knows how to do it well. If the alternative to a reduced charge is a long trial, this is not because counsel wants to make trouble for the prosecutor but because the greater charge requires the finding of a certain state of mind; counsel's client certainly did not have the state of mind; the stories of a dozen witnesses make this clear; counsel has statements from them all; and s/he is going to have to call them all. If the complainant is unconvincing, the police and the prosecutor should not believe the complainant's version of the story; and it is a matter of some, but secondary, importance that a jury also is not likely to believe the complainant or to convict the defendant. In any event, the important thing is that the criminal process not bear so harshly on the defendant that it will defeat its own aims and leave everybody concerned with a mess of troubles.

8.3. *Early Dealings with the Police*

8.3.1. *Initial Discussions with the Arresting and Investigating Officers*

Before (or, if that is impracticable, then immediately after) the initial interview with the client, counsel should speak to the investigating officer and ask what are the charges against the defendant and the facts of the case as the officer understands them. Counsel should ask whether any other or additional charges are being considered and, if so, what charges. S/he should ask the names of all witnesses. S/he should ask to see the police report, which the officer may or may not be willing to disclose. Counsel should also speak to the arresting officer to ask what s/he observed, what s/he was told, whether s/he knows of other witnesses, and what their names and addresses are.

Counsel should tell both officers that s/he will probably speak with them again and should ask what times and places are convenient to see or call them. Counsel should not attempt to bargain or argue with the officers. Rather, s/he should seek to learn as much as possible about the evidence the police have against the client, what they think of the client as a person (or as a problem), and whether they are hostile, sympathetic, or indifferent to the client. If they appear sympathetic, counsel can then raise the question whether they are amenable to dropping or reducing the original charges or agreeing to some form of diversion.

If counsel is unacquainted with the officers involved, it is useful to check out their reputations with an experienced local criminal lawyer, reliable bondsman, or R.O.R. Project staffer who would know whether information given by these particular officers can be trusted. Even when the officers appear trustworthy, however, it is generally not prudent to tell the police of counsel's plans, the facts counsel knows, or the client's reaction to the charge. The only *quid pro quo* that counsel can offer for their information at this early stage is friendliness, courtesy, and sincere appreciation for their willingness to be helpful.

8.3.2. *Protecting the Client from Police Investigative Activity*

Before concluding counsel's initial discussions with an arresting or investigating officer, counsel should tell the officer in the most amiable and inoffensive manner possible (1) that the police and other law enforcement personnel are not to interrogate or speak to the client or to confront the client with any evidence or witness except in counsel's presence; (2) that they are not to ask the client for any permissions, consents, or waivers but should address these requests to counsel; (3) that the client (if detained) is not to be taken or removed from the present place of detention for any purpose without notice to counsel; (4) that the client is not to be put in a lineup or exhibited for identification in the absence of counsel; and (5) that the client is not to be subjected to any physical or mental examination, personal inspection, or scientific test in counsel's absence. See §§ 3.5, 3.6, 3.21.2 *supra*. Counsel can temper the appearance of obstructionism that is inescapably latent in these admonitions by saying that counsel has to err on the side of caution in preserving all of the client's legal rights until such time as counsel has learned enough about the case to determine whether any of those rights should be waived in the interest of cooperation with the authorities. See § 3.3.2.4 *supra*.

To demonstrate counsel's willingness to be as accommodating as possible, counsel should offer to be available on reasonable notice to attend any lineups, identification viewings, examinations, or tests or to discuss the case or its investigation with the police. Counsel should ask whether the police intend to conduct any of these proceedings. If they do, s/he should try to arrange with the investigating officer to have them all done at a mutually convenient time. If they do not, or if they have not yet decided, counsel should give the officer his or her phone number and email address and request that the officer contact counsel in the event that they subsequently do decide to conduct any of these sorts of investigations, so that counsel can be present.

If the client is in custody, counsel should also have the client personally advise the investigating officer or one of the custodial officers, in counsel's presence, that the client henceforth does not want to converse with the police or prosecuting authorities without counsel's assistance but wants to deal with them only through counsel. See §§ 3.4.6, 3.6, 3.21.2 *supra*. (To guard against the possibility that the police do not notify counsel or will not wait for counsel to appear, the client must also be advised to make appropriate objections and to look for and remember the things which counsel would have wanted to observe. See §§ 3.4.2, 3.4.4, 3.6, 3.21.3, 6.12 and the relevant items in the checklist, § 6.15 *supra*.)

Police may well disregard counsel's requests or harass counsel by scheduling lineups, identification viewings, examinations, or tests at inconvenient hours or scheduling them one a day over a period of time. If counsel concludes that the police are conducting improper investigative proceedings or are scheduling investigative proceedings abusively or without adequate notice to counsel, s/he should call the prosecutor and ask the prosecutor to mediate a reasonable agreement with the police regarding the methods and timing of subsequent investigation.

If the prosecutor declines to intervene or cannot solve the problem, counsel should consider whether there are grounds to move the court to enjoin further police investigations, suppress the results of those already conducted, or both. See §§ 3.4.6, 3.8.4 *supra*; § 18.9.2.7 *infra*; Chapters 25-27 *infra*. In this connection, particular attention should be paid to the potential interaction of the constitutional doctrine of *Gerstein v. Pugh*, 420 U.S. 103 (1975), discussed in § 11.2 *infra*, and of *Kirby v. Illinois*, 406 U.S. 682 (1972):

- *Gerstein* requires that any person arrested without a warrant be given a prompt postarrest determination of probable cause by a judicial officer unless (perhaps) s/he is equally promptly indicted by a grand jury. *Powell v. Nevada*, 511 U.S. 79, 80 (1994); *County of Riverside v. McLaughlin*, 500 U.S. 44, 47, 52-53 (1991); *Atwater v. City of Lago Vista*, 532 U.S. 318, 352 (2001) (dictum); *Baker v. McCollan*, 443 U.S. 137, 142-43 (1979) (dictum); *Albright v. Oliver*, 510 U.S. 266, 274 (1994) (plurality opinion) (dictum); and see § 2.3.4.1 *supra*; §§ 11.2, 11.3 *infra*. Failing either a prompt probable-cause determination or a prompt indictment, his or her detention becomes unconstitutional (*see Manuel v. City of Joliet, Ill.*, 580 U.S. 357, 364-69 (2017)), and s/he is entitled to release on *habeas corpus*. See § 3.8.4 *supra*. Although the Supreme Court has not yet ruled on the question whether "a suppression remedy applies" to a *Gerstein* violation through "failure to obtain authorization from a magistrate for a significant period of pretrial detention" (*Powell v. Nevada, supra*, 511 U.S. at 85 n.*), the rationale of the Fourth Amendment exclusionary rule should require suppression. *See, e.g., Anderson v. Calderon*, 232 F.3d 1053, 1071 (9th Cir. 2000) (dictum) ("we conclude that the appropriate remedy for a *McLaughlin* violation is the exclusion of the evidence in question – if it was "fruit of the poisonous tree"); *Norris v. Lester*, 545 Fed. Appx. 320, 321, 327 (6th Cir. 2013) ("appellate counsel was ineffective for failing to argue [under *County of Riverside v. McLaughlin, supra*] that [Norris'] confession was obtained after the violation of his constitutional right to a prompt probable-cause determination"). *But see Lawhorn v. Allen*, 519 F.3d 1272, 1290-92 (11th Cir. 2008); *People v. Willis*, 215 Ill. 2d 517, 831 N.E.2d 531, 294 Ill. Dec. 581 (2005); *and compare State v. Huddleston*, 924 S.W.2d 666, 673 (Tenn. 1996) ("we conclude that the exclusionary rule should apply when a police officer fails to bring an arrestee before a magistrate within the time allowed by *McLaughlin*"), *with State v. Carter*, 16 S.W.3d 762, 766-68 (Tenn. 2000) ("In *State v. Huddleston*, this Court determined that when a person confesses after having been detained for more than 48 hours following an arrest without a warrant and without a judicial determination of probable cause, the confession should be excluded unless the prosecution establishes that the confession '"was sufficiently an act of free will to purge the primary taint of the unlawful invasion."' . . . The burden is on the State to prove by a preponderance of the evidence the admissibility of a confession obtained under the circumstances here presented. . . .¶ . . . *Huddleston* . . . focused on the reason for the continued detention of the arrestee; that is, whether the individual was being held without probable cause 'for the purpose of gathering additional evidence to justify the arrest. . . .' . . . ¶ Here . . . there is no evidence that Carter was held for the purpose of gathering additional evidence or for other investigatory purposes"; this consideration and others support a finding that the prosecution met its burden showing dissipation of the taint of a *Gerstein* violation.).

- The judicial probable-cause determination required by *Gerstein* marks the initiation of "adversary judicial proceedings" – the "first formal charging proceeding" (*Moran v. Burbine*, 475 U.S. 412, 428 (1986); *see also id.* at 429-32) – that, according to *Kirby*, triggers the defendant's Sixth Amendment right to counsel (*see* §§ 2.3.4.2, 3.23.3 *supra*; §§ 26.10.1, 27.6 *infra*). And "once the adversary judicial process has been initiated, the Sixth Amendment guarantees a defendant the right to have counsel present at all 'critical' stages of the criminal proceedings" (*Montejo v. Louisiana*, 556 U.S. 778, 786 (2009) (dictum); *see, e.g., United States v. Wade*, 388 U.S. 218 (1967); *Rothgery v. Gillespie County, Texas*, 554 U.S. 191, 198, 213 (2008); *Moore v. Illinois*, 434 U.S. 220, 227-29 (1977)). (An indictment equally triggers this Sixth Amendment right. *E.g., Estelle v. Smith*, 451 U.S. 454, 469-70 (1981).)

- The police should not be permitted to delay the point at which an arrestee acquires his or her Sixth Amendment rights under *Kirby* simply by failing to comply with the *Gerstein-McLaughlin* Fourth-Amendment timetable for making a probable-cause determination. So, whether or not a judicial probable-cause proceeding is actually made in the case of any particular defendant, that defendant's full roster of Sixth Amendment rights attaches at the expiration of the *Gerstein-McLaughlin* deadline; and no police investigative proceeding after that point in time is permissible in the absence of counsel.

8.3.3. *Lobbying the Police to Drop or Reduce the Charges or to Agree to a Diversion Arrangement*

Counsel should ordinarily not bargain or negotiate with the police. The costs in disclosure are too great, the dispositive power of the police is too limited, and counsel's later opportunities to negotiate with the prosecutor are ample. But in cases in which the facts already known to the police will support an argument that no charges are warranted or that the charges should be less severe than those the police have made or are contemplating, counsel should urge the police to drop or reduce the charges.

For this purpose, counsel may want to discuss the legal elements of the offense the police have in mind, and to demonstrate that some required element is missing. When it is clear that the police are not about to let the case go without lodging *some* charge against the client, counsel can suggest a specific lesser charge. Discussion of legal and factual weaknesses in the evidence against the client is recommended, however, only if that discussion is not likely to teach the police how they can fill gaps in their case by further investigation or fabrication.

Generally counsel does better to try to persuade the investigating officers that facts discovered since the arrest or ambiguities in the facts cleared up since the arrest exonerate the client than to argue that there was no basis for the arrest in the first place. Police feel called upon to defend their arrests and may reject any notion that the arrest was unfounded.

References to the client's good record and to the severity of the damage that a serious criminal charge could do to someone in the client's circumstances – causing the client to be fired from a good job or suspended from school or to lose custody of his or her children, for example – may persuade the officers to drop or reduce the charges or to agree to a diversion arrangement. If the client is a minor and could be prosecuted in either juvenile or adult court (either by being initially prosecuted in juvenile court and then transferred to adult court, or by being initially prosecuted in adult court and then transferred to juvenile court), and if counsel has concluded that the client is likely to fare better in juvenile court (see § 21.7 *infra*), counsel might try to persuade the officers to speak to the prosecutor about the appropriateness of proceeding in juvenile court. Portraying the client sympathetically or explaining apparently unfavorable traits ("That kid is not being tough, officer; he's scared stiff in this police station.") may also be helpful.

Police (or prosecutors later in the pretrial process) may condition their willingness to drop charges upon the defendant's agreement to waive claims of civil liability for illegal arrest, mistreatment following arrest, wrongful prosecution, and so forth, against the officers and governmental agencies involved. Counsel should evaluate the costs and benefits of entering into any such agreement and should be prepared to negotiate for favorable terms. Counsel's leverage in negotiating is enhanced by state and federal rules limiting the conditions that may be exacted as the price for dismissing charges, and limiting officials' power to coerce defendants to accept oppressive conditions. *See, e.g., Marshall v. City of Farmington Hills*, 578 Fed. Appx. 516, 520 (6th Cir. 2014) ("A release-dismissal is enforceable only if a court 'specifically determine[s]' that: (1) it was entered into voluntarily; (2) there is no evidence of prosecutorial misconduct; and (3) enforcing the agreement 'will not adversely affect relevant public interests.'"). *Compare Town of Newton v. Rumery*, 480 U.S. 386, 398 & n.10 (1987) (establishing the three-part test applied in *Marshall* for the validity of release dismissal agreements), *with Cowles v. Brownell*, 73 N.Y.2d 382, 538 N.E.2d 325, 540 N.Y.S.2d 973 (1989) (strongly disapproving release dismissal agreements in general, although reserving the possibility that some might be enforceable), *and compare Cain v. Darby Borough,* 7 F.3d 377 (3d Cir. 1993) (en banc), *and Coughlen v. Coots*, 5 F.3d 970 (6th Cir. 1993), *and Lynch v. City of Alhambra*, 880 F.2d 1122 (9th Cir. 1989), *with Woods v. Rhodes*, 994 F.2d 494 (8th Cir. 1993), *and Gonzalez v. Kokot*, 314 F.3d 311 (7th Cir. 2002), regarding the case-by-case application of *Rumery* by the federal courts of appeals.

8.4. *Early Dealings with the Prosecutor*

Counsel's early dealings with the prosecutor are principally aimed at learning the prosecutor's evidence and the prosecutor's attitude toward the seriousness of the offense and the character of the defendant. Counsel should ask the prosecutor what the prosecution's proof consists of and what the prosecutor thinks is an appropriate and reasonable disposition of the case. Counsel should ask to see specific items in the prosecution's case file, such as the police report or an incriminating statement by the defendant or a codefendant.

If counsel can honestly and convincingly urge the client's innocence or the unfounded nature of a given charge, s/he may attempt to convince the prosecutor at this stage to drop charges or to present lesser ones. Counsel should remember that the prosecutor's personal view of guilt or innocence is important and that it is based on information – both favorable and unfavorable to the defendant – that may not be admissible as evidence in court. A complainant's shabby character or prior unfounded complaints may do counsel no good when the case goes to trial; it is with the prosecutor that they can be put to good effect. If the client is a minor and if the prosecutor has the power to send the case to juvenile court (either informally by referring the case to the office that prosecutes delinquency cases or by supporting a defense motion to transfer the case to juvenile court), and if juvenile court is likely to be a more favorable forum for the case (see § 21.7 *infra*), counsel might tell the prosecutor about aspects of the client's life and family that are likely to cause the prosecutor to feel that the state's interest is also best served by proceeding in juvenile court (*e.g.*, that the client regularly attends school, has mostly stayed out of trouble, seems to have a promising future, has a supportive family, and/or will benefit from supervision by juvenile probation officers).

In rare cases, when counsel is very sure of the client, s/he may consider suggesting a lie detector test. This suggestion should never be made without the client's prior consent and only in a case in which counsel, after a thorough factual investigation and a skeptical cross-examination of the client in the light of that investigation, is completely persuaded of the client's innocence.

Almost never should the suggestion of a lie detector test include a stipulation of its admissibility in evidence. Polygraphs are fairly reliable, but when they err, it is usually on the side of false positives (incorrect indications that a truthful answer is a lie). In the more typical case, counsel's greatest effectiveness will be in urging reduced charges based on factual weaknesses in the prosecution's evidence, the defendant's good record or sympathetic character, the excessive harshness of the penalty for the greater charge, and/or the availability of a lesser charge with a more fitting penalty. Or counsel may be able to convince the prosecutor that a diversion arrangement will satisfy the state's interests in the case more efficiently, or more economically, or more humanely than continuing to press for a criminal conviction and sentence.

Occasionally, a prosecutor who is indisposed to exercise discretion favorably will profess to have none. Defense counsel faced with an unbudging protestation that the prosecutor's "hands are tied" may find it useful to write a short letter or memorandum to the prosecutor demonstrating that they are not (*see, e.g.*, *Bond v. United States*, 572 U.S. 844, 864-65 (2014); *United States v. Lovasco*, 431 U.S. 783, 794-95 & n.15 (1977); *Bordenkircher v. Hayes*, 434 U.S. 357, 364-65 (1978); *United States v. Batchelder*, 442 U.S. 114, 123-25 (1979); *Rummel v. Estelle*, 445 U.S. 263, 281 (1980); *United States v. Goodwin*, 457 U.S. 368, 380 & n.11 (1982); *Wayte v. United States*, 470 U.S. 598, 607-08 (1985); *Ball v. United States*, 470 U.S. 856, 859 (1985); *McCleskey v. Kemp*, 481 U.S. 279, 311-12 (1987); *Young v. United States ex rel. Vuitton et Fils*, 481 U.S. 787, 807 (1987); *Town of Newton v. Rumery*, 480 U.S. 386, 396-97 (1987) (plurality opinion); *cf. Marshall v. Jerrico, Inc.*, 446 U.S. 238, 248 (1980); *Heckler v. Chaney*, 470 U.S. 821, 831-32 (1985)), before calling the prosecutor to resume discussions. (This tells the prosecutor nothing that s/he does not already know, but it is a nicer way of pointing out that you also know it than by calling the prosecutor a liar.)

In dealing with the prosecutor, counsel should always have a thorough grip of all the possible lesser charges on the books. Counsel will often find that it is most effective to urge the prosecutor to drop or reduce charges prior to preliminary hearing, since, once the magistrate has bound a defendant over on a charge, there is considerable inertial pressure on the prosecutor to take it to trial. This is especially so when the prosecutor and magistrate are of different political parties and the prosecutor is required to project a public image of being no less tough on crime than is the magistrate.

Plea negotiation, which may follow unsuccessful attempts to persuade the prosecutor to drop or reduce charges without a guilty plea or other *quid pro quo*, is discussed in §§ 15.8-15.13 *infra*.

8.5. *Talking with a Complainant About Dropping the Charges*

By law, by police or prosecutorial routine, or by judicial practice, some minor charges are pressed only on private complaint. In these cases particularly, efforts to persuade the complainant to drop charges are important. But they may also be important in cases in which the offense is prosecuted or the prosecution is continued past the stage of the complaint without formal concern for the complainant's wishes. As a practical matter the complainant's attitude, even in the latter cases, is likely to affect the exercise of prosecutorial discretion.

There is nothing wrong with defense counsel's talking to a complainant about dropping the charges, so long as counsel is honest and not overbearing. *See, e.g.*, N.Y. County Lawyers' Ethics Opinion 711, N.Y. LAW J., August 21, 1996, at 2, col. 3, *available at* https://www.nycla.org/siteFiles/Publications/Publications486_0.pdf (a defense attorney may "ask[ ] the complaining witness to request the prosecution to drop the charges," as long as counsel does not "bully" or lie to the witness or "seek to advise the complaining witness as to whether the benefits of dropping the charges outweigh the benefits of going forward"). It is usually a good idea to have a reliable witness present during the discussion, or unfounded charges against counsel may later be made.

In cases in which the complainant appears sympathetic, the damaging effect of the prosecution on the defendant's record or the harshness of the possible penalty may be mentioned. When guilt is clear, offers of restitution will frequently satisfy complainants who have suffered property loss as a result of minor offenses. With the client's consent these offers may properly be made.

8.6. *Offers to Cooperate with the Police or Prosecution*

The police or the prosecution will sometimes offer a client the opportunity to "cooperate" by testifying against accomplices in exchange for dismissal or reduction of charges or in exchange for a recommendation of leniency to the trial judge. Such an arrangement should rarely be made with the police. Unless the prosecutor is brought in, counsel should decline to discuss it.

In evaluating an offer to which the prosecutor is a party, counsel must be sure to learn the nature of the evidence that the prosecution has against the client or else s/he may buy a bad bargain. Some prosecutors use cooperation offers to "break" multi-defendant cases that they cannot prove against *any* of the defendants; therefore, counsel should ask to see the police reports or the witnesses' statements establishing the client's guilt before counsel discusses "cooperation."

There are basically three kinds of promises that the prosecution can make:

(a)   An immunity grant under an applicable immunity statute or "state's evidence" statute is legally binding and can be relied upon to protect the client.

(b)   An informal promise by the prosecutor not to prosecute or not to press certain charges is only as good as the prosecutor's word.

(c)   The promise of a favorable sentencing recommendation by the prosecutor is not even that good, since judges in most jurisdictions are free to ignore the recommendation.

The third kind of promise should never be accepted without inquiry of experienced criminal lawyers in the area who know the judge or judges (and, often, then only if the prosecutor can assure counsel that the case will be brought on for sentencing before a particular judge). Neither the second nor the third kind of promise should be accepted without a basis for trust in the prosecutor. Local statutes should be studied to see whether the bargain can be cast in a mold that brings it within the scope of a legally enforceable immunity provision. (In rare cases, a court may enforce an explicit agreement by a prosecutor to grant a defendant specified accommodations in return for cooperation even without such a formal grant of immunity, but this prospect is too chancy – too dependent upon unpredictable contingencies – to be a safe course of action under ordinary circumstances. *See Johnson v. State*, 238 So.3d 726 (Fla. 2018).) The prosecutor should also be asked what s/he can do to assure the client against retaliation by codefendants: for example, an arrangement that they be committed to an institution other than the client's; or an arrangement for the client's formal admission into a witness protection program.

After counsel has learned exactly what is expected of the client and what the client will receive, and after counsel has decided how good the bargain is, s/he should explain it to the client. The contingencies in the promised benefits (particularly those relating to sentencing recommendations) should be very carefully pointed out. Counsel should also warn the client of the possibility of recrimination by other prisoners if the client testifies against a codefendant, even though the client and codefendant are sent to different institutions. Ultimately, the decision must be the client's. Advising the client in the matter involves many of the same considerations involved in advising a client whether to accept a negotiated plea. *See* §§ 15.14-15.17 *infra*.

The final agreement with the prosecutor should specify precisely the proceedings in which the client is required to testify and should not leave unclear the scope of the client's obligations in the event that proceedings against the codefendant later take varying twists (for example, prosecution of the codefendant on multiple charges involving separate trials; reprosecution of the codefendant following reversal of an initial conviction). *See Ricketts v. Adamson*, 483 U.S. 1 (1987).

Chapter 9

Defense Investigation

A. *General Aspects of Defense Investigation*

9.1. *Introduction: Scope of the Chapter*

Hang out for long with experienced defense attorneys and you will hear this story about the seventy-year-old indigent drunk-and-disorderly recidivist appearing for arraignment in front of a judge who had sent him to jail half-a-dozen times in the past. "As you know, Sam," the judge tells him, "if you can't afford to hire yourself a good defense lawyer, I can assign you one cost-free." "Thanks," says Sam, "but if it's all the same to Your Honor, this time I'd rather you assign me one or two good defense witnesses."

Believable facts are the fuel that drives criminal defense work. Factual information is always counsel's most vital resource, not only in litigating the case at trial but in performing every other crucial defense function: – urging the police or prosecutor to drop or reduce charges, negotiating a plea bargain with the prosecutor, advocating a favorable sentencing disposition to a probation officer or a judge.

Investigation is counsel's principal means for obtaining and vetting the information s/he needs. Although there are other fact-gathering tools – formal discovery proceedings (see Chapter 18); motions practice (see Chapter 19); plea-bargaining discussions (see Chapter 15); informal interchanges with a prosecutor (see § 7.2.2 *supra*) – they tend to be less reliable and comprehensive than independent defense spadework: meticulously searching the streets, paper and electronic files and records, and the internet.

One key component of defense investigation, the interview with the client, is discussed in Chapter 6. The following aspects of investigation are discussed in the present chapter: locating and interviewing defense witnesses (§§ 9.7-9.11 *infra*); interviewing and taking statements from prosecution witnesses (§§ 9.12-9.16 *infra*); observing the scene of the crime and other relevant sites (§ 9.5 *infra*); and gathering documents and exhibits (§§ 9.17-9.20 *infra*). An additional form of investigation – the retention of expert consultants to look into aspects of a case that may have forensic-science angles – is discussed in Chapter 30.

9.2. *Using the Defense Theory of the Case to Guide the Investigation*

Section § 7.2 *supra* describes a process for counsel's developing a defense theory of the case and using it to guide investigation. Because counsel's time and resources are not unlimited, the investigation must be selective – often painfully so. A well-considered theory of the case provides the basis for efficient selectivity and thoughtful assignment of priorities. *See State v. Petric*, 2020 WL 4726485, at *8 (Ala. Crim. App. 2020) ("'Defense counsel must, "at a minimum, *conduct a reasonable investigation* enabling [counsel] to make informed decisions about how best to represent [the] client."[ ] This includes investigating all reasonable lines of defense, especially "the defendant's 'most important defense.'" Counsel's "failure to consider alternate defenses constitutes deficient performance when the attorney 'neither conduct[s] a reasonable investigation nor ma[kes] a showing of strategic reasons for failing to do so.'"'").

In most cases, one single issue or a very few issues should stand out as having paramount importance. The prosecution must prove all of the elements of the crime it has charged, but the defense needs to do nothing more than defeat one of those elements. It is seldom profitable to take on more than one or, at most, a couple. The defense should aim at the few weakest points in the prosecution's case or at the few strongest points in the defendant's defense. *See In re Gay*, 8 Cal. 5th 1059, 1083, 457 P.3d 502, 519, 258 Cal. Rptr. 3d 363, 384 (2020) (in a prosecution for the murder of a police officer in which defense counsel's theory of the case was that a codefendant, not the defendant, was the shooter, counsel performed ineffectively in failing to conduct an adequate investigation: "Gay was charged with the murder of a police officer. In such a case, peace officers would have had every incentive to ensure that those responsible were convicted. Exculpatory testimony from a peace officer would have been some of the most persuasive evidence a defense attorney could present. Through discovery, . . . [defense counsel] was aware of evidence that . . . [the codefendant] freely confessed to the shooting. The professionally appropriate response to this information would have been to contact each peace officer mentioned as having had contact with . . . [the codefendant] to ask about any confessions they had witnessed or knew of and to solicit evidence that . . . [the codefendant], alone, killed [the] Officer . . . .").

As § 7.2 also suggests, however, counsel must avoid premature fixation on his or her initial defense theory. While searching for facts to support that theory, counsel must be alert to those that do not and to facts that suggest a preferable theory. *See State v. Petric, supra,* 2020 WL 4726485, at *8 (Ala. Crim. App. 2020) (""Constitutionally effective counsel must develop trial strategy in the true sense – not what bears a false label of 'strategy' – based on what investigation reveals witnesses will actually testify to, not based on what counsel guesses they might say in the absence of a full investigation.""). Counsel's best investigative strategy will be to go first to the sources that are most likely to contain information relevant to his or her preliminary, working theory of the case; but in exploring those sources, s/he should collect all other information potentially germane to the case that can be gathered from the same or nearby sources with relatively little additional time and effort. Counsel must constantly re-evaluate the information s/he has thus far gathered and determine whether to stay on the same track or switch to a new one. By keeping his or her eyes open and plans flexible as s/he excavates the locations of most likely paydirt, s/he may find unexpected nuggets that call for digging in new directions. Counsel must always have priorities but be willing to change them.

9.3. *Starting Promptly and Preserving Perishable Evidence*

Counsel's first priority should be to establish a rational order of priorities. To do this, counsel must get a quick picture of the case in broad outline. In addition to interviewing the client to obtain his or her version of events, counsel will need to learn the essence of the prosecution's version. Because the discovery process described in Chapter 18 may take some time to launch, and because most police officers are reluctant to talk with a defense attorney or investigator, the most effective technique for rapidly uncovering the prosecution's basic version of events is usually to go to the police station and obtain a copy of the incident report filled out by the police at the time the complainant first called in about the crime (see § 9.20 subdivision one *infra*) and/or the arrest report filled out when the defendant was apprehended (see § 9.20 subdivision two).

A quick start is essential in investigation. *See, e.g.*, *United States v. Scott*, 24 M.J. 186, 192 (U.S. Ct. Military Appeals 1987) (holding trial counsel ineffective for failure to perform a prompt investigation of a potential alibi defense: "A defense counsel has 'the duty . . . to conduct a prompt investigation of the circumstances of the case and to explore all avenues leading to facts relevant to the merits of the case and the penalty in the event of conviction.' . . . [AMERICAN BAR ASSOCIATION, STANDARDS FOR CRIMINAL JUSTICE], The Defense Function, Standard 4–4.1 (2d ed. 1979)." [carried forward as AMERICAN BAR ASSOCIATION, STANDARDS FOR CRIMINAL JUSTICE MONITORS AND MONITORING, DEFENSE FUNCTION (4th ed. 2017), Standard 4-4.1(c), *Duty to Investigate and Engage Investigators* ("[d]efense counsel's investigative efforts should commence promptly and should explore appropriate avenues that reasonably might lead to information relevant to the merits of the matter, consequences of the criminal proceedings, and potential dispositions and penalties")]; *Hughes v. Vannoy*, 7 F.4th 380, 388 (5th Cir. 2021) (quoting the extant ABA Standard with approval); *People v. Jones*, 186 Cal. App. 4th 216, 237-38, 111 Cal. Rptr. 3d 745, 761 (2010) (same); *Nelson v. State*, 2021 WL 2982927, at *8-*9 (Md. Ct. Special App. 2021) (same); *State v. Tetu*, 139 Hawai'i 207, 215-16, 386 P.3d 844, 852-53 (2016) ("A review of several jurisdictions' codes and performance standards for defense attorneys indicates that in order to assure competent representation, defense counsel should investigate the crime scene and consider seeking access as early as possible, unless circumstances suggest it would be unnecessary in a given case. The American Bar Association's ABA Standards for Criminal Justice: Prosecution and Defense Function (ABA Standards) states, 'Many important rights of a criminal client can be protected and preserved only by prompt legal action.' *Id.* § 4–3.7(a) (4th ed. 2015). Thus, '[d]efense counsel should promptly seek to obtain and review all information relevant to the criminal matter, including but not limited to requesting materials from the prosecution.' *Id.* § 4–3.7(b). In addition to seeking information from other sources aside from law enforcement, see also *id.* § 4-4.1(c), counsel for a defendant has a specific duty with regard to investigating a case. 'Defense counsel's investigative efforts should commence promptly and should explore appropriate avenues that reasonably might lead to information relevant to the merits of the matter . . . .' *Id.* ¶ The commentary to the ABA Standards emphasizes that 'without adequate investigation[,] the lawyer is not in a position to make the best use of such mechanisms as cross-examination or impeachment of adverse witnesses at trial.'15 Am. Bar Ass'n, ABA Standards for Criminal Justice: Prosecution Function and Defense Function § 4-4.1 Commentary, at 183 (3d ed. 1993). The commentary further states that if there were eyewitnesses to the alleged crime, then 'the lawyer needs to know conditions at the scene that may have affected their opportunity as well as their capacity for observation.' *Id.*"); *Wilson v. Sirmons*, 536 F.3d 1064, 1085 (10th Cir. 2008) ("Under the American Bar Association Guidelines, 'preparation for the sentencing phase, in the form of investigation, should begin immediately upon counsel's entry into the case.' ABA Guidelines 11.8.3 (1989). The reason for the ABA's direction is obvious – there must be sufficient time for interviews, research, and adequate testing before strategic planning can even begin. Additionally, if counsel waits until immediately before trial, it is too late to correct any invalid tests or to pursue leads discovered during the testing process, a requirement for counsel to be effective. . . . The rush to prepare will invariably lead to unnoticed and untapped resources.");

Jones v. Ryan, 52 F.4th 1104 (9th Cir. 2022) ("'[L]egal experts agree that preparation for the sentencing phase of a capital case should begin early and even inform preparation for a trial's guilt phase[.]' . . . 'Counsel's obligation to discover and appropriately present all potentially beneficial mitigating evidence at the penalty phase should influence everything the attorney does before and during trial[.]'" *Id.* at 1118. "'The timing of this investigation is critical.' . . . The Supreme Court has found constitutional error 'where counsel waited until one week before trial to prepare for the penalty phase, thus failing to adequately investigate and put on mitigating evidence.' . . . 'If the life investigation awaits the guilt verdict, it will be too late.'" *Id.*); *Bond v. Beard*, 539 F.3d 256, 288-89 (3d Cir. 2008); *In re Gay, supra,* 8 Cal. 5th at 1077-78, 457 P.3d at 516, 258 Cal. Rptr. 3d at 379-80. Physical evidence and human memory deteriorate rapidly. An object of importance may be discarded or carried off by persons unknown. Witnesses may disappear or forget. Particularly in urban areas, individuals are highly mobile. They may go away suddenly and leave no trace. Or if they remain in the area, they may soon blend into the neighborhood, becoming impossible to locate as their principal identifying characteristic – proximity to the offense or arrest – dissolves. If and when they are ever found again, they may be useless as witnesses because they have forgotten crucial details.

It is especially important to move quickly in tracking down and speaking with alibi witnesses. Alibis depend critically upon the witness's having a detailed recollection of what s/he and the defendant were doing at a precise point in time. Since often those activities will be quite ordinary, such as hanging out on a street corner, even the slightest delay on counsel's part can cause uncertainties to creep in. After a couple of days, and certainly after a couple of weeks, the witness will no longer be certain whether a street-corner conversation with the defendant took place at, for example, 9 p.m. or 9:10. And the entire alibi could depend on that ten minute difference if the distance between the scene of the crime and the location of the conversation could be traversed in ten minutes. There are certain techniques the defense can use in jogging alibi witnesses' memories and preserving alibi evidence, see § 39.26 *infra,* but the best technique is to get to the witness while his or her memory is fresh.

Before presenting an alibi theory at trial, defense counsel will have to make a rigorously critical review of the credibility of the testimony supporting that theory. Alibis are often difficult to sell to a judge or jury. *See* Lisa J. Steele, *Alibi Defenses: Millstone or Key to the Jailhouse Door?*, 45-FEB THE CHAMPION 20 (2021). But counsel should not allow initial skepticism regarding a client's claim of alibi to dampen or delay thoroughgoing investigation of potential alibi witnesses. *See State v. Syed*, 463 Md. 60, 83, 204 A.3d 139, 152 (2019) (dictum) ("Where a defendant provides his or her counsel with information about an alibi witness, the attorney has an affirmative duty to make reasonable efforts to investigate the information that was provided."); *Skakel v. Commissioner of Corrections*, 329 Conn. 1, 35-36, 188 A.3d 1, 23 (2018) ("counsel is obligated to make all reasonable efforts to identify and interview potential alibi witnesses"); *Lichau v. Baldwin*, 333 Or. 350, 39 P.3d 851 (2002) (finding defense counsel ineffective for withdrawing an alibi notice without having subpoenaed available military and other records and interviewed witnesses supporting the defendant's claim that he was not in Oregon at the time of the offense); *Code v. Montgomery*, 799 F.2d 1481 (11th Cir. 1986) (finding defense counsel ineffective for failing to investigate an alibi defense when the defendant asserted that he had never been in the vicinity of the crime); *Wade v. Armontrout*, 798 F.2d 304 (8th Cir. 1986) (finding that defense counsel performed ineffectively in failing to investigate an alibi defense when the defendant asserted that he was at home with his mother at the time of the crime and that she would testify in his defense); *Stitts v. Wilson*, 713 F.3d 887, 893 (7th Cir. 2013) ("When a defendant's alibi is that he was at a nightclub at the time of the shooting, where there are presumably many people, we cannot fathom a reason consistent with Supreme Court precedent that would justify a trial counsel's decision to interview only a single alibi witness without exploring whether there might be others at the venue who could provide credible alibi testimony. There is simply no evidence in the record to suggest that exploring the possibility of other alibi witnesses 'would have been fruitless' under these circumstances."). *See also, e.g., Rivas v. Fischer*, 780 F.3d 529, 531, 532-33, 550 (2d Cir. 2015) (when the chief medical examiner "changed his estimate as to the time of death six years after the fact, seemingly on the basis of no new evidence," to a time when the defendant "had an incomplete alibi," "any reasonable attorney . . . [would have] conclude[d] that investigating the basis of [the medical examiner's] new findings was essential," and therefore defense counsel's failure to investigate further violated his "'duty to make reasonable investigations or to make a reasonable decision that makes particular investigations unnecessary'"). *Cf. Hewitt-El v. Burgess*, 53 F.4th 969 (6th Cir. 2022).

Counsel's other top priorities when starting the investigation should be to locate and preserve contact with items or information sources that are perishable: – physical objects that are mobile or changeable; witnesses who are mobile or imprecisely identified but related to some specific location at a recent point in time; witnesses whose involvement is such that they may forget if not questioned quickly. Counsel should move on these items as rapidly as s/he can. This is so not only because of the risk of irreparable losses but also because early investigation makes the most efficient use of counsel's limited resources: an hour's search while the track is warm may be worth days later. Once a reasonable effort has been made to find the known perishable items, counsel should evaluate everything s/he has, estimate the points of strength, and proceed with further investigation to consolidate them.

9.4. *Use of an Investigator*

Whether counsel should hire an investigator or conduct the investigation personally will depend in part upon the financial resources available to the defense. If the defendant is indigent, counsel can request state funding for investigative services. State statutes and rules commonly provide for such funding. *See, e.g., Kimminau v. Avilez*, 2014 WL 5507295 (Ariz. App. 2014); *Johnny S. v. Superior Court*, 90 Cal. App. 3d 826, 153 Cal. Rptr. 550 (1979). Insofar as they do not, or to the extent that they fall short of providing the amount of funding needed by the defense, counsel can invoke the constitutional doctrines surveyed in §§ 5.2-5.3 *supra*, as the basis for requesting adequate investigative support. *See, e.g., State v. Wang*, 312 Conn. 222, 245, 92 A.3d 220, 235 (2014); *State v. Second Judicial District Court*, 85 Nev. 241, 453 P.2d 421 (1969); *Staten v. Superior Court*, 2003 WL 21419614 (Cal. App. 2003); *Mason v. Arizona*, 504 F.2d 1345, 1351-52 (9th Cir. 1974) (dictum); and *cf. Hinton v. Alabama*, 571 U.S. 263, 264, 267, 273-74 (2014) (per curiam); *Stubbs v. Thomas*, 590 F. Supp. 94, 99-102 (S.D. N.Y. 1984). Procedures for seeking state funding are discussed in § 5.4 *supra*.

An investigator is recommended, when practicable, for several reasons. Money spent to hire an investigator is usually economically spent, since an investigator's time is less costly than counsel's. Counsel does, or will, have other things to do in the case that can be done only by a lawyer, which may occupy counsel at times when investigative needs are critical. A good investigator also has sources of information unavailable to all but the most experienced defense lawyers in a locality – community contacts, official contacts (acquaintances in the police department, prison records department, probation department, and so forth), and contacts with other professional fact gatherers (news reporters, social workers, bail bondsmen, local politicians and their staffers). An investigator can be called to testify if any conflicts arise between the stories given by witnesses at trial and the stories they previously gave in an investigative interview, whereas judges usually have discretion to refuse to allow a lawyer to take the witness stand in a case in which s/he is appearing as counsel. And, if counsel decides that photographs or recordings are necessary for the defense, a person other than counsel will have to take them and be available to testify to lay a foundation for their admission into evidence, should the prosecutor not stipulate to their authenticity and accuracy.

Intelligent use of an investigator, however, requires thoughtful attention by counsel. *See State v. Petric*, 2020 WL 4726485, at *18 (Ala. Crim. App. 2020) ("'[A]lthough lawyers are not prohibited from employing the services of non-lawyer assistants and delegating functions to them, the lawyer is required to supervise the delegated work and retains complete responsibility therefor.' . . . '[A]n attorney must supervise work done by lay personnel and a lawyer stands ultimately responsible for work done by his non-lawyer employees '") Counsel must explain the case and the initial theories of the defense fully to the investigator at the outset and must inform the investigator periodically of counsel's current thinking in order to avoid squandering defense resources in the collection of useless information. Frequent, regularly scheduled check-ins by phone ordinarily serve this purpose best; most of the time, they can be kept brief.

If counsel is practicing in a jurisdiction that permits the prosecutor to obtain notes of interviews of witnesses who testify at trial for the defense, counsel will need to explain to the investigator the reasons for refraining from taking notes when interviewing defense witnesses and for reporting orally to counsel about the content of the interviews. See § 9.11 *infra*.

9.5. *The Importance of Personally Observing the Scene of the Crime and Other Relevant Sites*

Whether or not counsel uses an investigator, it is usually wise for counsel personally to inspect the site of any important event in the case: – the offense, the arrest, a search and seizure. Although counsel will be principally looking for specific items, s/he will often perceive others that put a whole new complexion on the case – items having a significance that would escape anyone but counsel. Frequently, for example, at the time of trial, when a prosecution witness is testifying about events in detail not previously known to the defense, it becomes apparent to counsel who has been at the scene – and only because s/he has been at the scene – that the witness is mistaken or confused on matters of spatial relations. (A witness who, on direct examination, has carefully drawn a diagram of an unobstructed street corner can be quite visibly flustered by the question on cross-examination whether there is not, in fact, a substantial construction barrier on that corner.) Where necessary, counsel should seek a court order for access to a crime scene that is not otherwise available to counsel. *See, e.g., State in the Interest of A.B.*, 219 N.J. 542, 547, 554, 561, 99 A.3d 782, 785, 789, 793 (2014) (the trial court did not "abuse[ ] its discretion by entering a discovery order allowing the accused, his attorney, and his investigator to inspect and photograph specified areas of the alleged victim's home for no more than thirty minutes in the presence of a prosecutor's investigator"; "The right to the effective assistance of counsel in a criminal proceeding includes the right to conduct a reasonable investigation to prepare a defense."; "a defense attorney's visit to the scene of the crime is a rather ordinary undertaking, and in some circumstances, such an inspection might constitute a professional obligation. . . . The State generally will have thoroughly investigated a crime scene, securing evidence and taking photographs. Familiarity with a crime scene may be essential for an effective direct or cross-examination of a witness – and even for presenting exculpatory evidence."; "The [trial] court issued the inspection order only after carefully weighing the . . . [juvenile defendant's] fair-trial rights and [complainant] N.A.'s privacy interests and imposing reasonable time and manner restrictions.").

It is also helpful in many cases for counsel to participate in a re-enactment of pertinent events, such as a search-and-seizure episode in which the client claims that the police barged through an apartment doorway without knocking, whereas the police will expectably claim that they knocked and saw illicit activities inside when the door was opened. By playing the role of a police officer in this situation, counsel can become dramatically aware of physical restrictions on the witness's field of vision that may break the officer's testimony wide open on a motion to suppress. Of course, counsel should be sure that the scene has not undergone changes between the time of the critical events and that of counsel's visit. And re-enactments should not be undertaken, if avoidable, in places where the public or the police can watch the replay.

9.6. *Enlisting the Aid of the Client's Family*

Counsel should consider whether the client's domestic partner, parents, siblings, or members of the client's extended family can play a useful role in finding witnesses or leads. In talking to such family members, counsel should explain the importance and difficulty of thorough investigation and the help the family can render in this regard.

Additionally, if the defendant is in custody, the family should be encouraged to visit the client in order to keep up his or her morale as s/he awaits trial. Counsel also may want to have the family make efforts to persuade the client's employer not to fire the client or, if the client has already lost that job as a result of arrest, to find the client a new job in anticipation of the possibility that his or her prospective employment status will become a significant sentencing factor in the event of a conviction. (Counsel discussing these matters with family should take care not to convey the impression that s/he expects the client to be convicted. S/he can avert that impression by adopting a tone along the lines of *we don't know at this point how the case may turn out, but it's always a good idea to prepare for all possible outcomes including a worst-case scenario.*)

B. *Locating and Interviewing Defense Witnesses*

9.7. *The Need to Interview Any Witnesses Whom the Defendant Wishes to Call*

As explained in § 9.2 *supra,* counsel will ordinarily determine the order and scope of the defense investigation, and which witness interviews have priority, in accordance with counsel's theory of the case. The one exception to this rule is that counsel must talk with any witnesses whom the client requests be interviewed, however tangential they may appear to counsel. Notwithstanding counsel's belief that these witnesses are unimportant, counsel may be wrong. Moreover, every client is entitled at least to the small comfort that his or her lawyer does not disbelieve the client without fair inquiry. *See Lee v. Kink*, 922 F.3d 772, 774 (7th Cir. 2019) (defense counsel's failure to contact potential witnesses after receiving affidavits indicating that they might have exculpatory information would constitute ineffective assistance); *cf. Moore v. Secretary Pennsylvania Department of Corrections,* 640 Fed. Appx. 159, 163 (3d Cir. 2016) ("counsel is deficient where . . . they did not fully investigate a witness that they knew may be exculpatory"); *Cook v. Foster*, 948 F.3d 896 (7th Cir. 2020). Finally, failure to look for witnesses named by the client is, perhaps, the most frequent ground of post-conviction attacks against the competence of trial counsel. *See, e.g., Cannedy v. Adams*, 706 F.3d 1148, 1159-62 (9th Cir. 2013). *See also Mosley v. Butler*, 762 F.3d 579, 587-88 (7th Cir. 2014). Accordingly, counsel should make efforts to find the witnesses and, if the witnesses cannot be located, inform the client of that fact and also make notes of counsel's efforts to find them and of the conversation with the client. If counsel succeeds in finding the witnesses but decides, after talking with them, that they have nothing useful to say or are unconvincing, counsel should discuss these matters with the client and make a file note both of the reasons for counsel's conclusions and of the discussion of them with the client. See §§ 1.3, 6.6 *supra*.

9.8. *Locating Witnesses*

Primary sources for identifying and locating witnesses include the defendant, his or her family and friends (and their phones and handhelds), the police, the prosecutor, news media and their reporters, social media, and various websites. If these provide inadequate leads, counsel must resort to visiting the scene as quickly as possible and contacting any person who might be connected with the incident to inquire who knows or saw anything relevant. Counsel should seek out and interview all persons known to have been present at the scene and approximate time of the crime. *See Johnson v. Premo*, 315 Or. App. 1, 9, 499 P.3d 814, 819 (2021) ("[a]dequate trial counsel would have recognized the importance in a capital murder case of contacting the people nearby who were likely to have information about the victim, people associated with the residence, and the events of the night in question, when a violent murder occurred in a nearby home in the early morning hours when many residents would likely have been at home"). This aspect of defense investigation is time-consuming and often frustrating. Its importance, however, cannot be emphasized enough.

Counsel should always ask any person interviewed whether other witnesses were present and then get the fullest possible description of them. When identification is by name, the spelling of the name and its phonetic spelling should be taken, if possible. The more kinds of contact information counsel can obtain for each witness – street addresses, phone numbers, email and e-text addresses, website and social media logos – the better. Counsel should ask whether the witness has any aliases or nicknames; where the witness lives or lived; where s/he works or worked; whether s/he is on public assistance and, if so, where s/he collects checks, food stamps, or any other regular source of income; whether s/he belongs to a union or frequents a hiring hall and, if so, which one; where s/he "hangs out" and with whom; whether s/he has a girlfriend or boyfriend, and where that person lives; whether the witness plays the numbers or gambles in some other manner and where; whether s/he has ever been in prison, been arrested, or been in the military.

In trying to locate a witness when only the witness's name is known, checks should be made of on-line resources, electric and gas companies, voting registrations, tax assessment records, traffic courts, the Department of Motor Vehicles, credit card companies, credit-rating bureaus, hospital and department store billing records, probation and parole departments, the Veteran's Administration, the Department of Public Welfare, and the Social Security Office. If the neighborhood is known as well, counsel should also check local social work agencies, settlement houses, churches, finance companies, debt-collection agencies, employment agencies, labor union offices and hiring halls, political ward leaders, liquor stores, bars, and the precinct station.

If the crime took place in a public area (on the street or in the lobby or the hallway of a building), it is often productive to go door-to-door to every store front, house, and apartment or room that abuts or overlooks the scene of the crime. This canvassing technique will usually produce witnesses who were in a position to see the crime or events immediately preceding or following it. Counsel also should check whether any CCTV or other electronic surveillance equipment covers the location. If so, counsel should take steps to examine the recordings as soon as possible and, if they look helpful, to obtain copies. Here again, time is of the essence: Many surveillance devices do not retain recordings for more than 24 or 48 hours.

If the scene of the investigation is a low-income or working-class neighborhood, counsel and/or the investigator should dress in casual clothes. Dressing in a suit may make the attorney or investigator look like a plain-clothes police detective or probation officer, thereby ensuring that no one on the street will talk to him or her. It is often very effective to have the defendant or one of his or her relatives or friends accompany counsel or the investigator, to demonstrate that counsel or the investigator has benign intentions and to introduce counsel or the investigator to contacts on the street.

9.9. *Keeping Track of Witnesses*

Having located and interviewed defense witnesses, counsel should be sure to gather the information necessary to keep track of them in the event that they change their residence address and/or telephone number prior to the trial date. Although counsel may have decided provisionally that particular individuals will not be called as witnesses (because their information is not helpful or because their appearances, backgrounds, or uncertainty of recollection leaves them too susceptible to discrediting cross-examination), it is rare that counsel can predict all the future contingencies that may make it necessary to call any individual as a witness after all. It is wise to keep tabs on every witness interviewed who knows anything about the case.

In interviewing the witness, counsel should ask for not only (a) the witness's current contact information – street address, land and cell phone numbers, email and e-text addresses, website and social media logos, place of employment – but also (b) any plans the witness may have to move, and when and where, and (c) in any event, the full range of contact information for other persons through whom s/he can be reached when needed. The rapport-building preliminary conversation described in § 9.10 *infra* lends itself naturally to a discussion of the witness's interests, hobbies, work and leisure activities; if counsel makes notes of these, it may be possible to use the information to track the witness down in the event that s/he changes his or her address and phone number.

9.10. *Interviewing Defense Witnesses*

Witness interviews should be conducted in person if at all practicable. *See* Sean O'Brien & Quinn O'Brien, *Put Down the Phone! The Standard for Witness Interviews Is In-Person, Face-to-Face, One-on-One*, 50 HOFSTRA L. REV. 339 (2022).

Counsel (or the defense investigator) should ordinarily begin any interview of a witness by identifying himself or herself as the attorney (or attorney's investigator) for the defendant. Counsel (or the investigator) should show the witness some form of identification.

Then it is usually advisable to engage the witness briefly in some topic of casual conversation to put the witness at ease and establish rapport. The choice of topic will depend upon the witness and upon counsel's (or the investigator's) own style. If the defendant is in custody, and the witness is a relative or friend of the defendant, the witness will usually be eager to hear about the defendant's health and emotional state, and this topic can serve as an effective ice-breaker. If the witness is a stranger to the defendant, counsel will need to come up with some topic that the witness and counsel have in common: photographs, trophies, and posters on the witness's wall may suggest hobbies or interests about which counsel can speak knowledgeably. Of course, if counsel is ignorant of the subject matter or if such casual conversation is not consistent with counsel's personal style, s/he should skip these rapport-building devices. Visibly artificial attempts at striking up a conversation are often worse than jumping immediately into the business at hand.

Frequently, counsel will need to overcome a witness's reluctance to talk. The witness may be unwilling to "get involved" because s/he is queasy about what s/he will have to do as a witness or because s/he is worried about the degree of inconvenience it will entail. Counsel will need to overcome this reticence by an effective pitch of some sort. One argument that sometimes works is to stress the importance of the witness's giving information, since s/he is the only one who has it and the client's liberty is at stake. Counsel can also say that the right thing for the witness to do as [a member of defendant's family] [a friend of the defendant] [a neighbor of the defendant] [a citizen] [*or* whatever], is to step up and tell counsel whatever s/he knows; and that if the witness were, unfortunately, placed in the predicament of counsel's client, s/he would expect others to come forward. If all else fails and counsel believes the witness has important information, counsel can subpoena the witness and hope that the witness will talk to counsel prior to trial. However, this should not be done – except in an otherwise altogether hopeless case – if the prosecutor is probably unaware of the witness and if there is a substantial chance that the witness's story will be damning.

The basic three-stage interviewing process sketched in § 6.8 *supra* is usually effective in taking a witness's story. In addition, counsel should ask every witness whether the witness has discussed the case with anyone else, with whom, and what was said. Particular care should be taken to have the witness describe in detail what s/he has told the police and any prosecution agents to whom s/he has spoken, what they said, and what specific questions they asked. The line of questioning pursued by these investigators often gives counsel valuable insights into the opposition's theory of the case, as well as leads to areas and sources of information that the defense would not otherwise hit upon.

Just as counsel must cross-examine his or her client, when interviewing the client, so s/he must cross-examine other witnesses. This has several purposes: to dig out the truth – and in detail – as an aid to counsel's further investigation; to evaluate the witness's potential contribution to the defense if called to testify at a trial; and to educate and prepare the witness for cross-examination by the prosecutor. The latter two purposes can generally be served at a subsequent interview; therefore, unless the first purpose is compelling, counsel may be advised to forego too vigorous cross-examination in an initial witness interview. Counsel stands to gain considerably by being in the witness's good graces, and it makes no sense to anger the witness unnecessarily by pressing the witness hard before favorable relations are established. If a witness finds it an uncomfortable or unpleasant experience to be interviewed by counsel, the witness will not be readily available for subsequent interviewing and may even shade his or her story so as to discourage counsel from calling him or her at trial. The approach to cross-examining one's client suggested in § 6.14 *supra* – describing the questioning as a role play or dry run of the cross-examination that the prosecutor might conduct at a trial – is also a useful device for asking other potential defense witnesses the probing questions that are necessary to test the durability of their stories without implying that counsel personally has any doubts about their truthfulness.

If cross-questioning shakes a witness (or may leave the witness feeling shaken) but counsel concludes that the witness's story is nevertheless sufficiently solid to be potentially useful to the defense, counsel should follow up with some supportive questioning that will assist the witness to regain a warranted measure of confidence and should end by reassuring the witness that the witness is doing just fine. Counsel should never let a witness leave an interview feeling that his or her story has been demolished or disbelieved unless, in fact, counsel is convinced that the story is a fabrication. Minor inconsistencies and errors that counsel realizes are unimportant because they are perfectly natural and will not seriously impair the witness's credibility may nevertheless cause a legally unsophisticated witness to experience painful self-doubts. Unless those doubts are assuaged by some comfort from counsel at the end of the interview, the witness is likely to dwell on them following the interview, and the witness's story is likely to become weaker, more hesitant, and more heavily qualified than it needs to be or should be.

9.11.   *Refraining from Taking Written Statements of Defense Witnesses or Taking Verbatim Interview Notes in Jurisdictions Where They Are Discoverable by the Prosecution*

In some jurisdictions, the prosecution can obtain court-ordered discovery of written statements that defense counsel or a defense investigator obtains from defense witnesses and (less frequently) even the attorney's or investigator's notes of oral statements taken from defense witnesses. See §§ 18.11, 34.7.2, 39.4 *infra. But see Martin v. Office of Special Counsel, Merit Systems Protection Board*, 819 F.2d 1181, 1187 (D.C. Cir. 1987) ("In *Hickman* [*v. Taylor*, 329 U.S. 497 (1947),] the Supreme Court held that witness statements prepared at the request of an attorney are privileged work product and not subject to discovery unless the discovering party can show the statements are 'essential' to her case. . . . The Court also held that attorney *notes* taken during witness interviews are, for all practical purposes, *always* privileged."). Where such statements and notes are discoverable, they can be used by the prosecutor both to impeach the witnesses' testimony at trial and more generally to guide prosecution investigation aimed at refuting the defense case. Accordingly, defense attorneys in these jurisdictions should ordinarily refrain (and instruct investigators to refrain) from taking written statements of defense witnesses or taking notes during the interview of a defense witness.

Section 18.13 *infra* suggests that the information given by the witness can usually be preserved (to assist counsel to remember it and possibly for the purpose of refreshing the witness's recollection later), with minimum risk of prosecutorial discovery, by recording the information in a "strategy memorandum." Particularly if this is done by counsel rather than by counsel's investigator, the contents of the memo are likely to be insulated from discovery as "attorney work product." Whenever counsel conducts an interview personally, s/he should record the information in such a strategy memorandum, interweaving legal theories and strategic considerations with the information obtained from the witness. If a defense investigator conducts the interview, s/he should be instructed to report the content of the interview orally to counsel so that counsel can record the information in a strategy memorandum. The concluding paragraph of § 6.7 *supra* suggests a technique for writing the memo so that counsel can later identify the passages in it that are verbatim transcriptions of the witness's own words – the passages that are simultaneously most useful for defense trial preparation and most susceptible to prosecutorial discovery – but a judge examining the memo on the prosecutor's motion will probably not be able to segregate and disclose those passages.

C. *Interviewing and Taking Statements from Adverse Witnesses*

9.12. *The Unique Aspects of Interviewing Adverse Witnesses*

Counsel should undertake to identify all potential prosecution witnesses and should interview each of them except in the very rare case in which there are compelling reasons not to. *See, e.g., United States v. Tucker*, 716 F.2d 576 (9th Cir. 1983) (finding defense counsel ineffective for, *inter alia*, failing to interview prosecution witnesses before trial: counsel's "ability to cross-examine the government's witnesses effectively was seriously compromised by his failure to interview them, since he would have little idea as to the specific areas of testimony which could be challenged" (*id.* at 583); "[t]he cases repeatedly stress the importance of interviewing witnesses to the preparation of a defense" (*id.* at 583 n.17); "'[e]ffective investigation by the lawyer has an important bearing on competent representation at trial, for without adequate investigation the lawyer is not in a position to make the best use of such mechanisms as cross-examination or impeachment of adverse witnesses at trial'" (*id.* at 583 n.18, quoting Commentary to AMERICAN BAR ASSOCIATION, STANDARDS FOR CRIMINAL JUSTICE, Standard 4-4.1, *Duty to Investigate*); *Larsen v. Adams*, 718 F. Supp. 2d 1201 (C.D. Cal. 2010) (same). Many of the investigative techniques that have been described in connection with defense witnesses will also prove effective in dealing with adverse witnesses. The methods described in § 9.8 *supra* for tracking down witnesses, in § 9.9 for keeping tabs on witnesses, and in § 9.10 for interviewing witnesses will ordinarily be useful, whether the interviewee is a potential defense witness or a potential prosecution witness.

The primary difference in dealing with potential prosecution witnesses is that counsel will usually want to take a written or recorded statement from all such witnesses, or, if the witness refuses to write out or to record a statement, counsel will want to take verbatim notes of what the witness says. Techniques for taking these statements and notes are described in §§ 9.13 - 9.14 *infra*. (Unlike defense-friendly witnesses, potential prosecution witnesses are not likely to be willing to write out a statement in longhand.) There are additional considerations when the adverse witness is a police officer (see § 9.15 *infra*) or a codefendant or uncharged co-perpetrator (see § 9.16 *infra*). Finally, there are special steps that counsel will need to take and possibly motions to file when an adverse witness reports that s/he has been instructed by police or prosecutors to refuse to talk with the defense. See § 9.14 *infra*.

9.13. *Taking Statements from Adverse Witnesses*

9.13.1. *The Reasons for Taking Statements*

In interviewing prosecution witnesses, the defense has two central goals: (i) to learn facts about the prosecution's case that will enable counsel to pinpoint weaknesses and develop rebuttal evidence; and (ii) to elicit statements from the witness, at a time when s/he has probably not yet been coached by the prosecutor (or at least has not been extensively coached), which can be used to impeach the witness at trial.

The best way of nailing down the witness's statements for use as impeachment material is to record what s/he says in a written document signed by the witness. S/he will have a hard time credibly disowning the making or the details of statements s/he has signed, and an even harder time if s/he has handwritten the statements. Local practice may prescribe a form that gives written statements the effect of sworn affidavits (*see, e.g.,* 28 U.S.C. § 1746); counsel should have this form in an electronic file for instant retrieval when interviewing adverse witnesses, so that it can be inserted into the witnesses' statements without fanfare or delay which may cause a witness to think twice about signing anything.

Section § 9.11 *supra* advises counsel ordinarily not to take written statements from potential defense witnesses because they are susceptible to court-ordered discovery by the prosecution. Taking written statements from a prosecution witness usually presents no such risk because most jurisdictions' pretrial discovery rules provide that the prosecutor can obtain statements only of those witnesses whom defense counsel intends to call to testify in the defense case-in-chief at trial. There are a few jurisdictions that extend the prosecution's discovery rights to include statements taken by defense counsel from prosecution witnesses. *See, e.g., Commonwealth v. Durham*, 446 Mass. 212, 843 N.E.2d 1035 (2006). But even in these jurisdictions, it is usually advisable for counsel to take written statements from adverse witnesses because the statement will seldom tell the prosecutor anything that s/he cannot learn directly from the witness, and the impeachment value of a statement made in writing is particularly high.

If counsel is not sure whether a particular individual will turn out to be a likely defense witness or a likely prosecution witness, the safest course of action is to interview the witness initially without taking notes. If it then appears that the witness's story is more damaging than helpful to the defense, counsel can take a written statement.

9.13.2. *Arranging To Be Accompanied to Interviews of Adverse Witnesses*

Whenever counsel conducts an interview of an adverse witness, counsel will want to bring along an observer (either counsel's investigator or a law partner or some other employee). This "shotgun rider" serves two principal functions. First, s/he will be available to testify concerning what the adverse witness said, should occasion arise for the defense to impeach that witness with a prior inconsistent statement. Second, the "shotgun rider" can protect counsel against possible charges of berating, overbearing, or attempting to corrupt the witness.

9.13.3. *Techniques for Taking a Written Statement; Contents of the Statement*

The preliminary procedures for identifying oneself and attempting to build rapport, described in § 9.10 *supra,* should be used in interviewing potential prosecution witnesses. The identification of counsel (or counsel's investigator) is essential to ward off a witness's claiming at trial that the interviewer misrepresented himself or herself as working for the police or the prosecutor's office. Establishing some degree of rapport – some human connection between interviewer and witness – is important, if at all possible, in order to break through the witness's reluctance to talk with someone "from the other side" and the witness's almost inevitable disinclination to sign a document proffered by a stranger.

Once counsel (or the investigator) has established as much rapport as seems likely on a first contact, s/he should go through the witness's version of the facts once without taking a statement or even mentioning the possibility of a written statement. Having heard the story once through, counsel should then ask the witness to go through the story once more, and while s/he does so, counsel or the investigator should write up the witness's account in narrative form in a multi-page statement. The three-round format for fact-interviewing, described in § 6.8 *supra,* lends itself nicely to the interviewing of an adverse witness. The first round, in which the witness tells the story in his or her own words, is conducted without anything being written down. The second round, in which counsel goes through the witness's statement in detail, is the stage at which counsel (or the investigator) will simultaneously write down what the witness is saying. And, during the third round, as counsel asks the witness for additional details and clarification, counsel (or the investigator) can make corrections and additions to the written statement.

The statement should begin with a formal heading containing wording such as the following:

> This is the statement of [name of witness], date of birth _____, given to [names of counsel or investigator and of any other individual who accompanies the interviewer], on [date and time of statement] at [location where the statement is given, such as "the living room of my apartment, 250 Main Street, apartment 4W"].

> I have been told by [name of counsel or investigator] that [he or she] is working for the defense of defendant, [name of defendant], who has been charged with

committing an offense on [date of offense] at [location of offense].

The body of the statement should be written in the first person singular, since it will be signed by the witness himself or herself. It should be written in the witness's own vernacular: Counsel (or the investigator) should faithfully record any grammatical errors or slang terms rather than damaging the statement's accuracy by correcting the witness's speech.

The statement should be written out in narrative form, in full sentences and paragraphs. Every other line should be skipped so that there is room for corrections by the witness. The pages of the statement should be consecutively numbered so that it will be impossible for the witness to claim later that counsel or the investigator added or deleted pages.

When counsel (or the investigator) has finished writing the statement, s/he should read the statement aloud to the witness, sitting next to him or her and allowing him or her to read along as counsel (or the investigator) reads aloud. The witness should be invited to make any additions, deletions, or corrections that s/he wishes, and every alteration of this type should be initialed by the witness. As each page is completed, the witness should be asked to initial the bottom of the page.

When the entire statement has been read aloud, the witness should be asked whether s/he has anything to add or correct, and any such additions or corrections should be made. Then counsel (or the investigator) should write a concluding paragraph with wording such as the following:

> I have read this [number of pages in the statement]-page statement and have had it read to me by [name of counsel or investigator]. I have also had the opportunity to make all of the additions, deletions, and corrections I desired. To the best of my knowledge, this statement is accurate, correct, and complete.

The witness then should be asked to sign the statement on the line immediately below the concluding paragraph and to record the date of the signature. Procedures for preserving and authenticating hard-copy witness statements are discussed in §§ 9.19 and 29.10.3 *infra*.

9.13.4. *Alternatives to a Signed Statement When the Witness Is Unwilling To Sign a Statement; Taking a Recorded Statement*

As persuasive as defense counsel or the investigator may be, some witnesses will never consent to sign a statement. However, there are some alternatives to a signed statement that are almost as effective for impeaching a witness at trial who strays from the account s/he gave counsel or the investigator.

Even if the witness is unwilling to sign the statement, s/he may be willing to initial each of the pages of the statement as well as all of the corrections. This initialing is, for counsel's purpose, tantamount to a signature, since it evidences the witness's adoption of the statement. Alternatively, the witness who is unwilling to sign or initial anything may be willing to write out in longhand on the statement any corrections that s/he wishes to make to counsel's (or the investigator's) original written version. This too can later be said persuasively to manifest an implied adoption of the whole document as corrected. Counsel can sometimes trigger written corrections by omitting some insignificant details when s/he (or the investigator) first writes out the statement; then, when reading the statement to the witness, recalling those details orally and asking the witness to pen them in briefly.

If the witness is unwilling to sign, initial, or even hand-correct the statement, counsel nevertheless should review the statement with the witness in its entirety and elicit the witness's oral ratification of its accuracy. If the witness is unwilling to orally ratify the statement, s/he should be asked to orally ratify counsel's (or the investigator's) notes. A casual-sounding question (like "Okay, so [what I've shown you here] *or* [what I've read to you] is what you remember, right?"), followed by an affirmative answer from the witness will suffice for impeachment purposes, allowing the defense investigator (or other shotgun rider) to testify that the witness orally ratified counsel's written statement or notes. *Cf. Goldberg v. United States,* 425 U.S. 94, 105, 107-08 n.12, 110-11 & n.19 (1976).

Electronic recording of an adverse witness's statement is an alternative to be considered. An audio recording is usually less effective for impeachment than a written statement taken as advised in § 9.13.3 because the imprecision of spoken language almost invariably produces a narrative that fails to commit the witness to the kind of specific, unambiguous admissions or assertions that can be nailed down in writing. When an adverse witness refuses to give counsel a written statement but is willing to make an audio recording, counsel should prepare the witness for the recording by going through the steps set out in the first two paragraphs of § 9.13.3. Until the witness's statement has been rehearsed to counsel's satisfaction in unrecorded form, it is unwise to make a record of it. An unrehearsed recording made by a witness of doubtful allegiance is a formula for disaster. Even after a satisfactory rehearsal, witnesses will often omit or blur important details, and counsel will have to follow up with pinpoint questions before ending the recording. Procedures for preserving the recording and authenticating it at a trial or hearing are discussed in §§ 9.19, 29.9 - 29.10.3 *infra.* Some jurisdictions have communications-security legislation that counsel will need to consult before opting for electronic recording of witness statements. *See, e.g., McDonough v. Fernandez-Rundle,* 862 F.3d 1314 (11th Cir. 2017).

9.14.   *Overcoming Prosecution Witnesses' Unwillingness to Talk with an Adversary; Steps to Take If the Witness Says That S/he Has Been Advised by the Prosecutor to Refuse to Talk with the Defense*

With some prosecution witnesses it will be necessary to overcome not only the natural reluctance to speak with a stranger (see § 9.10 *supra*) and whatever animosity the witness may be feeling toward counsel's client, but also a notion that witnesses are forbidden to speak with "the other side." Counsel will need to explain to these individuals that witnesses do not "belong" to one side or the other; that the witness has as much obligation as a citizen to talk to defense counsel as to the prosecution; and that if the witness does not do so, the trial will be unfair. Of course, an unsubpoenaed witness has no *legal* obligation to talk to either the prosecution or the defense *(e.g., United States v. White,* 454 F.2d 435, 438-39 (7th Cir. 1971)), and counsel must not suggest that s/he has. But the witness's *moral* obligation to tell what s/he knows to the defense, as well as to the police or prosecutor, should be emphasized.

If a prospective prosecution witness continues to refuse to talk to counsel, counsel should ask whether the prosecutor (or a police officer) has told the witness not to talk to the defense. If the answer is yes or if counsel is not satisfied with the truth of a no answer, counsel should call the prosecutor and ask whether any instructions have been given to any witness. If they have, counsel should point out to the prosecutor that the courts have repeatedly held that such instructions violate an accused's due process right to investigate the case. *See, e.g., Gregory v. United States,* 369 F.2d 185 (D.C. Cir. 1966); *United States v. Munsey,* 457 F. Supp. 1, 4-5 (E.D. Tenn. 1978); *Davis v. State,* 110 Nev. 1107, 881 P.2d 657 (1994); *State v. Blazas,* 432 N.J. Super. 326, 74 A.3d 991 (2013); *Kines v. Butterworth,* 669 F.2d 6, 8-9 (1st Cir. 1981) (dictum), and cases cited; *State v. Simmons,* 57 Wis. 2d 285, 203 N.W.2d 887, 892-93 (Wis. 1973) (dictum), and cases cited; *see also Soo Park v. Thompson,* 851 F.3d 910 (9th Cir. 2017); *United States v. Gonzales,* 164 F.3d 1285, 1292 (10th Cir. 1999); *United States v. Carrigan,* 804 F.2d 599, 603-04 (10th Cir. 1986); *Johnston v. National Broadcasting Company, Inc.,* 356 F. Supp. 904, 910 (E.D. N.Y. 1973); *Coppolino v. Helpern,* 266 F. Supp. 930 (S.D. N.Y. 1967); *People v. Eanes,* 43 A.D.2d 744, 350 N.Y.S.2d 718 (N.Y. App. Div., 2d Dep't 1973); *State v. Hofstetter,* 75 Wash. App. 390, 395-403, 878 P.2d 474, 478-82 (1994), and cases cited; *cf. State v. Murtagh,* 169 P.3d 602 (Alaska 2007) (finding that the due process clause of the Alaska Constitution was violated by each of the following provisions of a victim's rights statute which, in sexual offense cases, (1) required that criminal defense representatives (a) before interviewing a victim, tell the victim that the victim need not talk with the defense representative and that the victim can have a prosecuting attorney present during the interview; (b) before taking an unrecorded statement, obtain written authorization from the victim or witness reciting that s/he is aware that s/he has no legal obligation to talk to the defense representative; (c) before taking an electronically recorded statement, additionally tell the victim or witness that the interview will be electronically recorded and then obtain written authorization from him or her reciting that s/he is aware of the rights not to talk to the defense representative and to have a prosecuting attorney present; and (2) barred defense representatives from contacting a victim or a witness who had informed the defendant or defendant's counsel in writing that the victim or witness did not wish to be contacted by defense representatives: "Numerous cases hold that a prosecutor may not suggest, directly or indirectly, that witnesses not speak with defense representatives." *Id.* at 611. "We believe that requiring defense representatives to give unsolicited advice to victims and witnesses that they are not required to talk to the representative and may have a prosecutor present if they do conveys an implied suggestion to prospective interviewees that it would be best if no interview were given. This none-too-subtle warning, in turn, substantially interferes with defense efforts to obtain evidence. The added requirement in sexual offense prosecutions of written consent to an interview serves to strengthen the message of noncooperation." *Id.* at 612.); *and see Arizona Attorneys for Criminal Justice v. Ducey,* 2022 WL 16631088 (D. Ariz. 2022) (invalidating on First Amendment grounds an Arizona victims' rights statute that prohibited defense attorneys and investigators from initiating contact with a crime victim – defined as including the family of a homicide victim or incapacitated victim and the parent or guardian of a child victim – except through the prosecutor's office); *United States v. Ebrahimi,* 137 F. Supp. 3d 886 (E.D. Va. 2015) ("After a significant number of witnesses stated that they either did not wish to speak to the defense or would only speak to the defense in the presence of a government agent, the defense asked the Government whether it had instructed witnesses to only speak to the defense in the presence of a Government agent. The Government acknowledged that it began interviewing potential witnesses in preparation for trial . . . and at these meetings made several 'requests' of the witnesses. Specifically, the Government explained that it asked the witnesses to notify the Government if they were contacted by another party and asked to make a statement about the case. The Government also requested that if such a notification took place, the Government would request an agent to be present during the interview to memorialize any statement the witness provided. The Government stresses, and the Court does not doubt, that the Government informed the witnesses that all interviews, including those with the Government, were optional and voluntary." *Id.* at 887. "[T]he Government's conduct impermissibly interferes with the right to equal access to witnesses for two reasons. First, such requests necessarily obstruct Defendant's legitimate need for unhindered access to information in preparation for trial. Second, the Government's communication with potential witnesses could reasonably have been interpreted by the witnesses as an instruction by the Government or could have otherwise impermissibly influenced the witnesses." *Id.* at 888. "Accordingly, it is hereby ¶ **ORDERED** that a letter from the judge shall be distributed to potential witnesses with whom the Government has communicated, on Court letterhead, stating that 'the Court understands that in this case counsel for the Government "requested" that you notify the Government of interview requests by the defense and "requested" that you allow the presence of a Government agent at a defense interview. These requests are not in keeping with the Court's judgment here that as a witness, you are equally available to lawyers for the defense and the Government at your own discretion.' The letter shall further instruct the witnesses, 'As a witness who may testify in court, you have the option to consent to an interview by counsel for the defendant and counsel for the Government. You have the option to decline such an interview if you are inclined. An interview outside of court is a way the lawyers can learn more about your proposed testimony in preparation for trial. You are not required to notify the Government of contact with defense counsel. You are also not required to have a Government agent present at your interview, if you decide to consent to an interview.'" *Id.* at 889-90.); *United States v. Goldfarb*, 2008 WL 4531694 (D. Ariz. 2008), *as modified on rehearing*, 2009 WL 856326 (D. Ariz. 2009) (in written plea agreements with the defendant's codefendants, the Government included a provision that "[Cooperating defendant] agrees to notify the United States Attorney's Office of any contacts with any co-defendants or subjects or targets of the investigation, or their counsel, and agrees to provide prior notice of, and an opportunity for the government to be present at, any interviews between the [cooperating] defendant and any individual not employed by the government regarding any matters related to this case or any other investigation" (*id* at 1). "For the reasons set forth in *Gregory* [*supra*], the Court concludes that [this] paragraph . . . [is "improper and unenforceable" (2009 WL 856326, at *2)]. The prosecutor may not 'deny[ ] defense counsel access to the witness except in his presence.' . . . Such a requirement clearly discourages cooperating defendants from candidly discussing the litigation with co-defendants or their counsel." 2008 WL 4531694 at *2. "Counsel for the Government shall . . .fax to counsel for all cooperating witnesses a letter which states that (1) . . . [the quoted provisions] of the plea agreements, pursuant to the Court's order, will not be deemed binding upon the cooperating defendants, (2) the cooperating defendants are free to communicate with or be interviewed by co-defendants or their counsel without counsel for the Government being present, (3) any such communications will not be viewed unfavorably by the Government in evaluating the defendant's cooperation or in deciding what sentence should be recommended to the Court, and (4) the prosecutor's letter is being written pursuant to an order of the Court. The letter shall attach a copy of this order. The Court will also continue the trial in this case for one week to enable Defendant to approach cooperating defendants for interviews." *Id.* at *4.). *See generally* Brad Rubin & Betsy Hutchings, *Blockading Witnesses: Ethical Pitfalls for Prosecutors*, N.Y. LAW J., Dec. 6, 2006, at 4, col. 4. Counsel should add that such instructions clearly violate canons of professional ethics. *See* AMERICAN BAR ASSOCIATION, MODEL RULES OF PROFESSIONAL CONDUCT, Rule 3.4(f) (2015) (except in certain designated special circumstances, "[a] lawyer shall not . . . request a person other than a client to refrain from voluntarily giving relevant information to another party"); AMERICAN BAR ASSOCIATION, CANONS OF PROFESSIONAL ETHICS, Canon 39 (1937) ("[a] lawyer may properly interview any witness or prospective witness for the opposing side in any civil or criminal action without the consent of opposing counsel or party"); AMERICAN BAR ASSOCIATION, STANDARDS FOR CRIMINAL JUSTICE MONITORS AND MONITORING, PROSECUTION FUNCTION (4th ed. 2017), Standard 3-3.4(h), *Relationship With Victims and Witnesses* ("The prosecutor should not discourage or obstruct communication between witnesses and the defense counsel, other than the government's employees or agents if consistent with applicable ethical rules. The prosecutor should not advise any person, or cause any person to be advised, to decline to provide defense counsel with information which such person has a right to give. The prosecutor may, however, fairly and accurately advise witnesses as to the likely consequences of their providing information, but only if done in a manner that does not discourage communication."). *Cf. In re: Eric G. Zahnd*, Mo., No. DHP-17-023, disciplinary panel decision, December 7, 2017, summarized in 86 U.S.L.Week, No. 23, p. 850, *finding of ethical violation approved and reprimand ordered, In re: Eric G. Zahnd*, MBE # 47196, Supreme Court of Missouri Case No. SC96939 (May 22, 2018) (finding that a prosecutor violated the rules of professional conduct by issuing a press release naming and castigating individuals who had submitted letters of support at the sentencing of a convicted child abuser: "The threat of a public shaming of a non-suspect, non-criminal citizen should not be a tool of the Prosecutor's Office, used to force citizens to obey its will."). Counsel investigating possible violations of a client's rights in support of a suppression motion (see Chapters 24-27 *infra*) should be alert to the developing doctrine that "the right of access to the courts . . . is . . . denied when law enforcement officers conspire to cover up constitutional violations" (*Jutrowski v. Township of Riverdale*, 904 F.3d 280, 294 (3d Cir. 2018)).

Counsel then should ask the prosecutor to call the witness immediately and tell him or her that s/he can talk to the defense. Counsel should request that the prosecutor's phone conversation with the witness take place with defense counsel on the phone. If the prosecutor is resistant to this notion, counsel should explain that counsel's inability to independently verify the prosecutor's removal of the taint of the earlier instructions will necessitate counsel's filing a motion for sanctions in order to safeguard the defendant's constitutional right to unimpeded access to witnesses.

Unless the prosecutor gives complete satisfaction, counsel should file a motion with the court of record having jurisdiction of the case. Depending upon local practice, such a motion may be styled like ordinary motions or in the form of an Order to Show Cause. The motion should seek the following alternative forms of relief: (a) dismissal of the charging paper on the ground that the prosecutor's misconduct has so severely interfered with the preparation of the defense that there is no way either of knowing how much harm has been done or of setting it right at this stage (*see, e.g., United States v. Linder*, 2013 WL 812382 (N.D. Ill. 2013); *Davis v. State, supra*); (b) a court-ordered deposition of each of the witnesses with whom the prosecutor or any police officer has discussed the case, so that counsel can ask the questions that s/he would have asked in an investigative interview if not for the prosecutor's interference (*see, e.g., United States v. Carrigan,* 804 F.2d 599, 604 (10th Cir. 1986) (upholding a trial court's order of a deposition: "[a]n order merely to cease . . . [prosecutorial] interference, after the fact, might be insufficient because the witnesses' free choice might have been already perverted and the witnesses likely to refuse voluntary interviews")); or, at least (c) a hearing in which each of the witnesses who has spoken with the prosecutor or any police officer is brought before the court and instructed by the judge that s/he is free to speak to the defense. *Cf.* the procedure approved in *United States v. Mirenda,* 443 F.2d 1351, 1355 n.3, 1356 (9th Cir. 1971); *and see United States v. Vole,* 435 F.2d 774, 778 (7th Cir. 1970) ("[w]itnesses are the special property of neither party and in the absence of compelling reasons, the . . . court should facilitate access to them before trial whenever it is requested").

Of course, counsel may decide that the trouble and friction involved in this procedure are not justified by its likely yield or that at least this course of action should be delayed until counsel sees whether more ordinary discovery procedures (see Chapter 18) reveal what counsel wants.

9.15. *Interviewing Police Officers*

As explained in earlier sections, it is usually in the defendant's interest for counsel to talk with the police officers on the case as often as practicable. See §§ 8.1.1, 8.1.3, 8.2.4, 8.3.1, 8.3.3 *supra.* These conversations may reveal information that will be useful in preparing for a suppression hearing or trial and may also produce statements that can be used to impeach an officer at a suppression hearing or trial. See § 8.1.3 *supra.* Conversations with officers also may afford opportunities for counsel to persuade them to exercise whatever discretion they may have in the defendant's favor. See §§ 8.21, 8.24, 8.3.3 *supra. But cf.* §§ 8.3.3, 8.6 *supra* (explaining that counsel ordinarily should bargain or negotiate only with the prosecutor, not the police).

If a police officer refuses to speak with counsel, counsel should ask why. If the officer indicates that s/he has been instructed not to talk by the prosecutor or by a superior officer or that s/he is following a departmental policy, counsel should file the type of motion described in § 9.14 *supra,* challenging the prosecutor's or police department's interference with the defendant's due process right to investigate the case. Even if the officer's refusal to talk is not the product of prosecutorial or departmental interference and is merely an individual choice, counsel nevertheless may want to seek a judicial order compelling him or her to tell counsel what s/he knows, on the theory that police officers are not mere private witnesses but are state officials with criminal law enforcement duties and due process obligations (*Curran v. Delaware,* 259 F.2d 707 (3d Cir. 1958)), and hence may no more instruct themselves than they may instruct one another to refuse information to the defense (*cf. Coppolino v. Helpern,* 266 F. Supp. 930 (S.D. N.Y. 1967)).

Even when counsel succeeds in getting a police officer to talk, it is unlikely that counsel will persuade the officer to sign a written statement or even to permit counsel to write out a statement. However, as long as counsel conducts the interview with an investigator or other employee of counsel's present, that individual can serve as an impeachment witness if, at trial, the officer denies the information s/he related to counsel. See § 9.13.2 *supra.* Some officers may also be willing to ratify counsel's notes orally if counsel reads them aloud and asks "have I got that right?" See § 9.13.4 *supra.*

9.16. *Interviewing Codefendants and Uncharged Co-perpetrators*

It is essential that counsel try to speak with all codefendants of the client and all uncharged co-perpetrators. Although their version of the events may parallel and support the client's, it is equally likely that codefendants and uncharged co-perpetrators have turned state's evidence, or may do so in the future, and will end up testifying for the prosecution against the client. In addition, even when codefendants don't turn state's evidence, they may present a defense at trial that denies their own guilt by placing all of the blame on counsel's client.

Before questioning codefendants or co-perpetrators, counsel should ascertain whether they are represented by an attorney. If they are, a local rule or ethics opinion may require that counsel obtain consent from that attorney before interviewing his or her client. Even in jurisdictions that have no such rule, counsel should ordinarily follow this procedure as a matter of professional courtesy.

An interview with a codefendant or co-perpetrator should cover everything s/he knows about the criminal episode and charges and should get a detailed account of everything s/he has said or given to the authorities. Counsel should ask whether s/he has been approached about possibly testifying for the prosecution, and, if so, what s/he has discussed with whom and when. Counsel should take a written statement from each codefendant and co-perpetrator if s/he will give it. If not, counsel should attempt to get his or her oral confirmation of the accuracy of counsel's write-up or notes of what the codefendant or co-perpetrator has said. If s/he later testifies against the defendant, s/he can be impeached with a written statement or counsel's memorialization of what s/he said orally. See § 37.4 *infra.* If s/he does not testify, and if counsel wishes to call him or her as a defense witness but is stymied by a claim of the Fifth Amendment privilege, a written or memorialized oral statement may be admissible as an admission against penal interest, provided that counsel has followed the procedures required by local rules or caselaw for taking a statement against penal interest. (These usually include the requirement that the witness know at the time of the statement that it is against his or her penal interest. Accordingly, counsel or the investigator may need to advise the witness of that fact just before finalizing the statement.)

D. *Gathering Police Reports, Other Documents, and Physical Evidence That May Be Needed as Defense Exhibits at a Motions Hearing or at Trial*

9.17. *The Need to Gather the Materials, and the Timetable*

Counsel's prospects of prevailing at an evidentiary motions hearing or at trial will usually depend upon the thoroughness with which s/he has sought out and obtained police reports, other pertinent documents, electronically stored materials, and physical evidence relevant to the case. Police reports containing witnesses' prior statements are often the only way of learning what the prosecution witnesses will say at trial (since many will refuse to talk to counsel), so as to plan an effective cross-examination. These police reports are also indispensable for impeachment purposes. Official documents such as hospital records, Weather Bureau records, and the medical examiner's report in a homicide case are similarly invaluable in planning the defense theory of the case and in cross-examining prosecution witnesses whose stories are at odds with the official reports. Social media communications data – posts, comments, messages, bulletin boards, photos, logs and subscriber information stored by providers such as Facebook, Twitter, and Instagram – can provide crucial information: leads to locating witnesses; materials usable to refresh the recollections of the defendant and potential defense witnesses; materials usable for impeachment of complainants and alleged crime victims, codefendants who may flip, and other possible prosecution witnesses; similar materials in the accounts of the defendant and potential defense witnesses that counsel needs to know about because they may be available to the prosecutor as substantive evidence or for impeachment. Counsel is advised to track down these materials early in the defense-investigative process: they provide a relatively easy and inexpensive means of information gathering; they can open avenues, guide directions, and establish priorities for follow-up investigation that involves more difficult and expensive methods; and they are susceptible to being deleted at any time at an originator's instance. After they have been taken offline, they may still be reachable by defense subpoenas *duces tecum* directed to the social media service provider (*see Facebook, Inc. v. Superior Court*, 4 Cal. 5th 1245, 417 P.3d 725, 233 Cal. Rptr. 3d 77 (2018); *Facebook, Inc. v. Superior Court*, 10 Cal. 5th 329, 471 P.3d 383, 267 Cal. Rptr. 3d 267 (2020)), and counsel may want to seek such subpoenas as his or her investigation progresses. But getting hold of the social media communications data before they are deleted is a major trouble-saver. Conversely, if there are materials open for public viewing in the social-media accounts of the defendant, the defendant's family, or potential defense witnesses, counsel wants to learn about them early. They may include unflattering items that can be used by the prosecution for impeachment or that may be seized upon by news reporters and go viral, poisoning the atmosphere and making it difficult for the defendant to get a fair trial. Counsel will want to consider whether matters of this sort should be promptly deleted. Deletion may be ill-advised when the prosecutor is one who, in a case of the present kind, can be expected to conduct a comprehensive background investigation of electronic resources: if s/he is assiduous enough to obtain the deleted posting, s/he can do even more with the fact of deletion – as an indication that the defendant or witness is attempting to conceal embarrassing information – than s/he could have done with the contents of the posting itself. But in the case of prosecutors whose research is less thorough-going, deletion can put potentially damaging appearances completely out of play.

Counsel will need to begin gathering the documents and other materials as quickly as possible. Certain real evidence such as objects dropped at the scene of the crime – or the layout of the crime scene as it was at the time of the crime – is highly perishable and will disappear if counsel does not retrieve it or photograph it quickly. Even less obviously perishable objects may be lost through delay: In some jurisdictions, tape recordings of police radio communications are routinely erased after a certain number of months and the tapes re-used by the police department; private CCTV recordings tend to be destroyed by recycling much sooner, often after only after 24 or 48 hours. Finally, many documents (like police reports, hospital records, school reports, and even court transcripts) may take weeks to acquire; the acquisition process must be started early so that it can be completed in time for trial.

9.18. *Methods for Gathering the Materials*

Some of the materials that counsel will wish to gather are public documents, available for the asking. For example, in many jurisdictions, the initial police report (usually called a "complaint report" or "incident report") is a public document that can be obtained by simply going to the police station in the precinct in which the crime occurred and paying a nominal fee for photocopying the document.

Most of the documents and exhibits that counsel will wish to gather, however, will need to be subpoenaed. The constitutional and statutory law governing subpoena practice are described in § 29.4 *infra;* the procedures for obtaining subpoenas, in § 29.4.3; and the procedures for serving and enforcing them, in §§ 29.4.5-29.4.7.

Subpoenas for documents, called subpoenas *duces tecum*, are addressed to the custodian of records of whatever agency or entity is in possession of the documents, directing the custodian to appear in court with the original documents on the date of the motions hearing or trial. These subpoenas are ordinarily required to specify with considerable particularity the documents or records sought. In theory the subpoenas *duces tecum* are not to be employed for discovery but only to procure evidentiary matter for use at trial. As a practical matter, however, counsel can often persuade the custodian to permit counsel to inspect the subpoenaed document prior to the beginning of the court proceedings, or counsel may persuade the judge to order the custodian to show counsel the document before court, during preliminary proceedings, or during a recess, in the interest of saving time at trial. *See, e.g.. Teal v. Superior Court*, 117 Cal. App. 4th 488, 11 Cal. Rptr. 3d 784 (2004), summarized in § 18.13 *infra*. In federal practice, numerous cases recognize that the district courts have discretion to order that documents covered by a subpoena *duces tecum* be produced before trial (*see United States v. Sellers*, 275 F.R.D. 620, 623 (D. Nev. 2011), and cases cited), upon a showing that: "(1) the documents are evidentiary and relevant; ¶ (2) . . . they are not otherwise procurable by the defendant reasonably in advance of trial by exercise of due diligence; ¶ (3) . . . the defendant cannot properly prepare for trial without such production and inspection in advance of trial and the failure to obtain such inspection may tend unreasonably to delay the trial; ¶ [and] (4) . . . the application is made in good faith and is not intended as a general fishing expedition." *United States v. Iozia,* 13 F.R.D. 335, 338 (S.D. N.Y. 1952), *cited with approval in United States v. Nixon*, 418 U.S. 683, 702 (1974).

Physical objects and artifacts (including recordings) that are in the possession of law enforcement agencies or officers, government officials, or third parties can also be reached by subpoenas *duces tecum*. If counsel wishes to inspect them or to have them tested by defense experts before trial, a motion for production and inspection should be made. See § 18.7.3 subdivision 1 *infra*.

9.19. *Preserving Real Evidence*

When counsel obtains a physical object that has evidentiary value in the case, counsel will need to take certain steps to preserve it in its original form and to guard against allegations at trial that the object has been altered.

The object should be retained in the custody of some credible person (an investigator or counsel's administrative assistant will do) under lock and key. The custodian should bag the object and tag it with the name and number of the case to which it relates, and the date and time when the custodian received it and locked it down. S/he can then be called at trial to identify it and to testify that there has been no change in its condition since the time it was first received. Defense lawyers who maintain a strict, routine procedure of this sort for handling evidence will usually find that their reputation for doing so – or a pretrial representation to the prosecutor of counsel's proposed chain-of-custody testimony in the case at hand – will elicit a prosecution stipulation of authenticity and unchanged condition, rendering unnecessary any actual in-court appearance of defense chain-of-custody witnesses.

If the physical condition of any object is important and is subject to change, counsel should have the custodian inspect the object, photograph it, and make a written, signed description of its relevant characteristics at the time of its receipt. One copy of the photograph and of the description should be retained with the object, additional copies in counsel's case file.

At trial, counsel will either have to get an authenticity-and-unchanged-condition stipulation from the prosecutor or present witnesses who trace the chain of custody of the object between the time and place of its acquisition by counsel (or counsel's investigator) and the time and place of its deposit in counsel's locked evidence facility. These witnesses will have to identify the object in the courtroom as the one they handled; they will have to recount when, where, how, and from whom they received it, and when, where and how they subsequently deposited it in the secure facility or turned it over to the next person in the chain *en route* to the facility; and they will have to attest that the object was not altered while in their possession. For this reason, counsel should, if possible, have the object picked up in the first instance by counsel's investigator or administrative assistant rather than by counsel personally, since it is undesirable – and, in some courts, forbidden – for counsel to testify. The fewer people who handle the object on its way to the secure facility, the better. In most cases, counsel will also have to present the same kind of chain-of-custody testimony covering the period between the object's connection to relevant events (the crime scene, or whatever episode the object is offered to document) and the object's acquisition by counsel. It is wise to have written, signed statements made by all witnesses who will be called to provide this testimony. These statements, too, should be duplicated, and copies kept both with the object in lock-down and in counsel's file.

If counsel wishes to have tests made of the object or to show it to anyone, counsel should have the custodian deliver the object manually to the tester or person in question, and the custodian should then recover it manually when the test or inspection has been completed. The custodian should make notes of the date, time, place, and recipient of delivery and a similarly detailed record of the object's return, all to be locked in with the object. This simplifies problems of proving the identity of the object and the lack of change in its condition at the time of trial. If the object is to be left with the tester or person, even briefly, s/he should be instructed (1) not to allow it out of his or her possession until it is recovered by the custodian; (2) to keep it in a secure place, under lock-down, whenever s/he is not actually working with it; and (3) that s/he will very likely be required to testify in court (a) that s/he complied with the preceding two instructions, and (b) that s/he did nothing to impair the object's probative value while handling it.

When an object is to be tested, counsel should also instruct the tester to bag-and-tag it or to make some mark on the object that, while not affecting its probative quality, will allow the tester to identify it at trial as the same object that s/he tested. The expert's written report to counsel should describe the object and indicate what tag or mark the expert made.

9.20. *Types of Materials to Gather or Generate*

There are as many sources of information as there are different factual situations. Among the most useful to keep in mind are:

Complaint Reports

The complaint report (sometimes called "event report" or "incident report") is filled out by an investigating officer when the complainant first reports the crime. This document usually contains: identifying information about the complainant (name, street address, phone number, email); a record of the time and location of the crime; the complainant's description of the crime; the complainant's or eyewitnesses' descriptions of the perpetrator(s); and a list of any injuries suffered by the complainant. The complaint report is extremely useful at suppression hearings and at trial. The complainant's account of the events can be used to impeach the complainant if s/he diverges from this account in his or her testimony. The description of the perpetrator's appearance and attire is usually the only written record of the complainant's and eyewitnesses' descriptions prior to their observing the defendant in a show-up or lineup, and it can be used to impeach these witnesses if they subsequently mold their descriptions of the perpetrator to fit the defendant. Often the description of the injuries suffered by the complainant will contain the name of the hospital that treated those injuries, thereby identifying the hospital to which counsel should direct a subpoena for the complainant's medical records.

Arrest Reports

The arrest report is filled out by the officer who arrested (or assisted in the arrest of) the defendant. This document will identify the defendant by name and physical description (including supposed ethnicity and sometimes apparel) and may also contain some information about the defendant's background (including supposed gang affiliation). The report will be useful in suppression hearings because it often lists: incriminating statements allegedly made by the defendant; property allegedly seized from the defendant; and the precise time of arrest (which serves as a baseline for calculating the length of any interrogations before, during, and after the booking process). If arrest reports in the jurisdiction also contain a factual account of the offense, then counsel should obtain the arrest reports for all codefendants, since the accounts in those reports will often be inconsistent with the accounts in the defendant's arrest report, and such inconsistencies can be used to impeach the witnesses who gave the accounts to the officers, the officers who prepared the reports, or both.

Recordings of 911 Telephone Calls and Police Radio Communications

If a crime is reported by an emergency phone call to the police (usually called a "911 call"), many police departments record and temporarily store the recording of the telephone conversation between the caller and the police operator. Similarly, if the investigating officers engage in radio communications with the police dispatcher or with each other during the investigation of a case, many jurisdictions record and store recordings of the transmissions. These various recordings can be crucial, since they may contain descriptions of the perpetrator given by the complainant prior to viewing the defendant in a show-up or lineup, or they may demonstrate a sequence of events at odds with the complainant's or police officers' versions of the crime or the police investigation or both. In many jurisdictions these recordings are routinely erased after a designated period of time (in some jurisdictions, three months) and the tapes re-used; accordingly, defense counsel must subpoena them immediately after starting work on the case. *Cf. Freeman v. State*, 121 So.3d 888, 895-97 (Miss. 2013).

Arrest Photographs

When arrest photographs were taken, these will often be relevant and should be subpoenaed. When length of hair or facial hair is relevant to the description of the perpetrator, a mug shot will often be the best available evidence of the defendant's appearance at the time of the offense. In some jurisdictions the police take full-color photographs; if the defendant was arrested shortly after the offense, these will show the clothing s/he was wearing and can be used at a suppression hearing (to demonstrate inconsistencies with the complainant's description of the perpetrator – and thereby that the police lacked probable cause to arrest – or that the identification procedures were unreliable) and at trial (to argue that discrepancies between the appearance of the perpetrator and the appearance of the defendant on the day of the offense raise a reasonable doubt).

Eyewitness Identification Reports and Recordings

In some jurisdictions the police prepare special forms whenever an identification procedure is employed, to record the result of the procedure and the precise words used by the eyewitness in identifying (or failing to identify) the defendant. These forms are obviously important in connection with any identification suppression claim and also can be used to impeach the witness at trial if s/he claims a greater degree of certainty or a different basis for recognizing the defendant than is reflected in the witness's words at the time of the pretrial identification. It is increasingly common for police and prosecutors to video-record lineup proceedings (see § 27.3.2 *infra*) routinely. Show-ups (see § 27.3.1 *infra*) are less commonly recorded as a matter of routine but may be captured on police body vidcams. Counsel should subpoena these recordings or move for their disclosure in formal discovery after first requesting them from the prosecutor (see § 18.3 *infra*). If the prosecutor stonewalls and declines to acknowledge whether or not such recordings exist, counsel should include in the battery of defense discovery motions a set of interrogatories asking whether or not recordings of this sort were made.

Forms and Reports for Confessions; Recordings of Police and Prosecutors' Interrogations and Interviews and of Statements Made by the Defendant, Any Alleged Accomplices, and Witnesses

If the defendant gave a written statement, it will often be handwritten onto a police form which contains not only the content of the statement but the date and time when it was completed and signed by the defendant, and sometimes also the date and time of the beginning of the interrogation session that produced the statement. The form may also indicate the names and badge numbers of the officers who took the statement. This form – or whatever paper or electronic document the police use to record the statement if not a standard form – is ordinarily invaluable in providing information that counsel needs in order to calculate the duration and circumstances of interrogation as the basis for a suppression motion (see Chapters 24 and 26 *infra*) or for arguing at trial that the statement was made under conditions that render it unreliable. However, counsel should be aware that the times noted on a defendant's written statement may not be accurate: unscrupulous police officers may jiggle them to improve the prosecution case. Some police departments video-record or audio-record statements made by suspects and all or parts of the preceding interrogation (see § 26.14 *infra*) and/or interviews of potential witnesses; prosecutors and their investigators may do so as well. Counsel must obtain these recordings by subpoena or discovery (see the preceding paragraph); but, once again, s/he will want to be alert to the possibility that the police have been self-servingly selective in recording only portions of their interchanges with the defendant, other suspects, or witnesses, or that they have doctored the recording *ex post*. If a defendant's incriminating statement was oral and was never put into writing, there will often be notes about its making and contents in the arrest report or in supplementary investigation reports.

Additional Police Reports That Are Filled Out When the Crime Is of a Certain Type

Depending upon the nature of the case, any one or more of the following reports may also exist. These reports frequently contain a factual narrative of the crime that will prove useful at a suppression hearing or trial.

1. In drug possession or sale cases there will frequently be a "buy report" describing the transaction in detail if it was conducted by an undercover officer. There will always be a chemist's report documenting the nature and weight of the drug and possibly containing a police officer's description of the circumstances under which the drug came into the officer's possession.

2. In cases in which the police recover a firearm, there will usually be a weapons report describing the gun and its serial number and also describing any slugs and shell casings that were recovered. There will also usually be a ballistics report describing the results of a test-firing of the gun, reporting whether the gun is operable, and possibly also reporting the results of any tests to match the gun with expended bullets recovered in connection with this case or other cases.

3. In cases in which scientific evidence of the perpetrator's identity was recovered from the scene of the crime or the putative crime weapon – fingerprints, footprints, body fluids, hairs, clothing or fabric fragments, and so forth – there will usually be (a) reports by evidence technicians describing their collection of the evidence and (b) reports by the relevant police or lab experts describing the degree to which the recovered materials match the defendant's prints, secretions, hair, clothing, or whatever.

4. In cases of sex offenses there will usually be (a) reports of a physical examination of the complainant, describing physiological indications of forcible intercourse and noting the blood type and/or DNA of any foreign body fluids found on the complainant or the complainant's clothes, or at the scene of the offense, and (b) serology or DNA reports detailing test procedures used to identify the individual who is the source of these body fluids.

5. If the crime involved a shooting and the defendant is arrested shortly after the commission of the crime, there may be a report of an examination of the defendant's body or clothing to determine whether s/he recently fired a gun (a "gunshot residue" or "GSR" test).

6. If a complainant was injured, some jurisdictions require that the police fill out a specialized report describing the nature and extent of the injury and of any treatment administered before the complainant was turned over to hospital or other medical personnel.

7. In homicide cases there will usually be an autopsy report available from the medical examiner's or coroner's office.

Property Reports

These are of two kinds: (a) In many jurisdictions the investigating officers are required to fill out property reports whenever any tangible evidence is recovered from the suspect or from the scene of a crime. If the crime was a serious felony, some police departments dispatch a special "crime scene squad" which will produce its own reports on property recovered from the scene. (b) Whenever a defendant is incarcerated, personal property in his or her possession that is *not* viewed by the police as having evidentiary value is vouchered and stored in the lockup. Listed items on the voucher may have relevance for defense purposes overlooked by the officers.

Police Photographs and Diagrams

The police may have photographs and diagrams of the crime scene and possibly also a police artist's sketch or composite of the suspect. These materials are usually available to the defense only through the discovery procedures described in Chapter 18.

Police body camera and vehicle camera recordings

In many localities police officers wear body vidcams and/or police vehicles are equipped with vidcams. In some localities the officers are required to keep their vidcams running while they are engaged in arrests, car chases and other interactions with civilians. The recordings made by these vidcams are an invaluable source in any case in which the legality of police activity may be made the basis for a suppression motion (see Chapters 24-27 *infra*) or in which police officers may be called by the prosecution to testify to observations which support the prosecution's version of events that constitute elements of a criminal offense (see § 37.7 *infra*). Counsel can seek the recordings through informal and formal discovery proceedings (see the paragraph in this section titled *Eyewitness Identification Reports and Recordings*; and see Chapter 18 *infra*) or by subpoena (see § 9.18 *supra*).

Supplemental Investigation Reports

In addition to the complaint report and the arrest report, one or more supplemental investigation reports may be written up by the detectives or other officers who are interviewing potential witnesses, conducting searches for physical evidence, and/or seeking various sorts of incriminating information. In heavy felony cases, a series of supplementary reports (sometimes called "evidence supplements") will often track the progressive stages of an extended evidence-gathering process.

Police Regulations and Policy Statements

In many localities the police department has regulations or policy statements governing procedures for making arrests and *Terry* stops, conducting on-the-street pat-downs, taking confessions, and conducting identification viewings. Copies of these regulations and policy statements should be obtained, either informally from the police department or via subpoena. An officer's violation of his or her own department's internal regulations can be a weighty factor in a judge's determination of the validity of the police actions that produced evidence against counsel's client.

Reports and Other Materials Generated by the Booking Process

Various reports and materials are generated during the booking process described in §§ 3.2.1 and 3.2.4 *supra*. Those most often useful at a suppression hearing or at trial include:

1. The arrest photographs of the defendant mentioned earlier in this section;

2. Notations on the police blotter indicating the time when the defendant was received at the police station (often useful at a hearing on a motion to suppress incriminating statements, as a means for establishing the length of interrogation); and

3. Notations in the property book at the precinct station showing:

    (a) property that was seized from the defendant as evidence and

    (b) other personal property that was in the defendant's possession at the time of arrest.

Preliminary Hearing Transcripts

If a preliminary hearing has already been held in the case, counsel should obtain a copy of the transcript. Frequently, that transcript will prove useful in impeaching the police officers and other witnesses who testified. If a separate preliminary hearing was held for a codefendant or a co-perpetrator who is being charged in a different case number, transcripts of those hearings should also be obtained.

Search Warrants and Arrest Warrants and their Supporting Affidavits

If a search was conducted by the police pursuant to a search warrant or if the defendant was arrested pursuant to an arrest warrant, counsel should obtain the warrant and any affidavits the police filed in order to obtain the warrant. These items will usually be turned over by the prosecutor in informal discovery (see Chapter 18). Alternatively, counsel can obtain them from the office of the clerk of the court that issued the warrant. In addition to their obvious utility in litigating suppression motions, they ordinarily contain informational details that can be used at trial to undermine the prosecution's latter-day version of the criminal episode or the prosecution's retrospectively embroidered testimony identifying the defendant as a perpetrator.

Photographs

Although police photographs of the crime scene are often available through discovery (see Chapter 18), these will seldom be adequate to fulfill all defense needs, and counsel will have to commission the taking of additional photographs. Defense photographs should be taken from several angles and at several distances, so that all spatial relations involved are fully depicted. Counsel should remember that photographs are not admissible until a foundation has been laid by a person who testifies that they are an accurate reproduction of the scene that s/he observed. A photographer should therefore be selected who will be available at the time of the trial and who will make a good and personable witness. S/he should be informed that s/he will be asked at trial, as a basis for testifying that the photographs are accurate, whether s/he has a present recollection of the scene that s/he photographed. Counsel should ordinarily obtain:

1. Photographs of the scene of the crime (to show matters that are not apparent in the police photographs, such as the absence of street lights, in support of a contention that the scene was too dark for the complainant and eyewitnesses to get a good look at the perpetrator; or the presence of CCTV cameras in cases where the police appear to be claiming that no electronic surveillance records exist).

2. In cases involving motions to suppress tangible evidence, photographs of the scene of a challenged arrest or *Terry* stop (to help illustrate the precise course of events) or of the scene of a challenged search (to show, for example, that items which the police will testify were in "plain view" could not in fact have been seen from the officers' vantage point (*cf. United States v. Loines*, 56 F.4th 1099 (6th Cir. 2023)).

3. In cases involving a motion to suppress identification testimony or a misidentification defense at trial, photographs of the scene of a show-up identification (to illustrate, for example, how far the witness actually stood from the defendant during the show-up, or the dim lighting in the location where the show-up took place at the relevant time of day).

4.   In cases in which the defendant was injured, and that injury is relevant to the theory of the defense (for example, as evidence of physical abuse by the police in a hearing on a motion to suppress a confession or as evidence of an assault by the complainant in a self-defense case), photographs of the defendant's injuries. These should be taken as quickly as possible before the bruises fade or the injuries heal.

5.   In cases in which the defendant's hair length or facial hair at the time of the incident will be relevant to an identification suppression motion, motion to suppress tangible evidence (to show lack of probable cause to arrest), or misidentification defense at trial, photographs of the defendant.

Diagrams and Maps

Diagrams of the scene of the crime, the scene of the arrest, or the scene of a search will frequently prove useful in suppression hearings and at trial. In jurisdictions that have or can arrange the technology in the courtroom for projecting computerized images onto a screen for the fact-finder, such diagrams can be prepared in digital form. Otherwise, diagrams can be displayed on poster board or on large sheets of graph paper. Diagrams and maps should be drawn to scale whenever possible. In some cities it may be possible to obtain a large area map from the city planner's office. Street maps available online will suffice only if the characteristics of an area covering several square blocks is in issue and if precise measurements are unimportant. When a crime site is indoors and precise measurements *are* important, the architect's plans for the building may be available from the office of the building owner, construction company, or a government agency responsible for approving construction plans or conducting periodic inspections.

Records of Lighting and Weather Conditions

In hearings on identification suppression motions and in presenting a defense of misidentification at trial, it will frequently be important to show that an eyewitness's or complainant's ability to observe was limited because of poor lighting or weather conditions. Records showing weather conditions and the time of sunrise and sunset can usually be obtained from the United States Weather Bureau.

Medical Records of the Defendant

If a motion to suppress a defendant's incriminating statements involves a claim that the defendant was physically abused by the police, or that the defendant was ill or suffering some physical injury at the time of the statement, it will be essential to obtain hospital and other medical records pertaining to any examination or treatment that the defendant received more or less contemporaneously with the statement. Similarly, in assault prosecutions in which counsel is considering a self-defense theory, hospital and medical records bearing on any injuries the defendant received at the time of the episode underlying the charge are invaluable.

Medical Records of the Complainant

If one of the offenses charged is an assault or battery count that depends upon the prosecution's proving a certain kind or degree of injury, the medical records of the complainant will provide crucial information. Even when the nature of the complainant's injuries is not technically an element of the charge, his or her medical records may be useful to show that s/he is exaggerating the harm or the suffering s/he claims to have experienced, and counsel can then argue that the rest of the complainant's testimony is no more credible than his or her inflated account of injuries. Also, medical records frequently record the complainant's version of how s/he was injured, and this account may be useful in impeaching a complainant who testifies at a trial, preliminary examination, or motions hearing.

Records To Support an Alibi Defense

Various kinds of records can support an alibi defense. Depending upon the facts, counsel may find it useful to obtain: time-clock entries to demonstrate that the defendant was at work at the time of the crime; electronic records corroborating that the defendant's credit card or subway- fare card or highway-toll "e-z pass" or some other sort of transportation card or pass was used at a particular location at a particular time; phone or social-media records or electronic surveillance recordings placing the defendant elsewhere than at the crime scene at a relevant time; and network or local TV station logs documenting that the television program which the defendant claims s/he was watching (and the precise activity s/he describes seeing on the show) was, in fact, being aired at the time s/he says s/he viewed them.

News Media Files and Photographs

If the crime involved a certain amount of notoriety, it may have been reported in the local newspapers or other media. If so, news items may quote statements by the complainant or other witnesses that will be useful in impeaching them. In addition, newspapers may possess still photographs and TV stations may possess footage of relevant scenes, events, or people.

Other Possible Sources of Video Recordings of the Crime or Arrest or Other Relevant Events

Video footage of a crime or an arrest or some other episode relevant to a criminal case may be obtainable from a wide array of other sources than the news media. There are often CCTV cameras recording events inside and directly outside stores, malls, places of entertainment, parking garages, apartment houses and private homes, public housing projects, police stations, hospitals, other public buildings, parks, playgrounds and street areas. Counsel will need to move quickly to find and view any such recording and to have it copied if it appears useful, because many private and public establishments obliterate their recordings (by destroying them or by re-using the storage material) after a relatively short period of time. Videos recorded by passersby on their cellphones may be posted on YouTube, Facebook, or some other social media site, and searchable through the site. Witnesses to an event may have recorded some or all of the event on their cellphones; whenever counsel interviews a witness, counsel should ask whether the witness made such a recording and still has it.

Chapter 10

Summary of Things to Do Before First Court Appearance

10.1. ***Checklist of Things to Do for an Arrested Client Between the Time of Arrest and the Client's First Court Appearance***

I.   *Locate the client. See §§ 3.3.2.1 - 3.3.2.2 supra.*

II.   *Telephone the precinct or place of detention. See §§ 3.3.2.4, 3.4, 3.5 supra.*

A.   Obtain information about the charges and the amount of bail from the desk officer and the investigating officer.

B.   Tell the investigating officer not to speak with the client until counsel arrives, not to request consents or waivers from the client, and not to exhibit the client for identification or to make any examinations or tests on the client in counsel's absence.

C.   Speak to the client, tell the client that counsel is coming to see client immediately, and advise the client:

1.   To speak to no one about the case;
2.   To decline to answer any questions by the police or to give consents or waivers to the police, on advice of counsel;
3.   Not to write or sign any papers or forms;
4.   To decline to consent to any lineups, identifications, examinations, or tests in counsel's absence;
5.   Not to offer physical resistance if placed in a lineup or subjected to any examinations or tests, but to remember the circumstances of all lineups, identifications, examinations, and tests in counsel's absence, and to write out a description of them for counsel as soon as they are over;
6.   Not to dodge news photographers or cover his or her face.

D.   Have the client inform a police officer, with counsel listening on the phone, that the client wishes all future dealings and communications with the authorities to be conducted solely through counsel.

III. *Telephone the client's family or a bondsman or both and arrange to have bail money or security and a bail bond brought to the place of detention. See §§ 3.8, 4.7-4.12 supra.*

IV.   *Review the elements of the charge and penalty. See §§ 3.21.1, 6.2 supra.*

V.   *With proper identification, immediately go to the place of detention and*:

A.   Interview the client. See §§ 3.6, 3.20-3.21 *supra* and Chapter 6.

1.   Establish rapport. See §§ 6.1, 6.3-6.5 *supra*.
2.   Obtain the client's version of events leading to and following arrest. See §§ 3.21.2, 6.8-6.10, 6.15 *supra*.
3.   Obtain names of all potential witnesses. See §§ 3.21.1, 9.3, 9.7-9.8 *supra*.
4.   Obtain biographical information usable to persuade the police to release the client or drop charges. See § 3.6 third paragraph; § 3.8 *supra*.
5.   Obtain a statement or affidavit containing the information needed for bail-setting. See §§ 4.4-4.5 *supra*.
6.   Establish the roles of lawyer and client. See § 6.6 *supra*.
7.   Set the fee and state clearly what it covers. See § 6.11 *supra*.
8.   Repeat warnings and advice relating to the client's conduct in custody and in response to police investigative procedures, and have the client tell a police officer, in counsel's presence, that all subsequent communications between the client and the authorities are to be conducted through counsel. See §§ 3.4.2-3.4.5, 3.6, 3.21.2, 6.12 *supra*.
9.   Give the client counsel's professional card (see § 6.4 *supra*) and a "rights card" (see § 3.21.3 *supra*).
10.   Offer to talk to the client's family. See § 6.13 *supra*

B.   Speak to the investigating officer and:

1.   Verify the charges. See §§ 3.5, 4.12.1, 8.3.1 *supra*.
2.   Find out the police version of the offense and arrest. See §§ 3.5, 8.1.1, 8.1.3, 8.3.1, 9.3 *supra*.
3.   Obtain the names and contact information of all potential witnesses. See §§ 9.3, 9.8 *supra*.
4.   Urge the officer to consider dismissing or reducing the charges or agreeing to a diversion arrangement in cases where these options are realistic. See §§ 2.3.6, 8.1.1, 8.2.1, 8.2.3, 8.3.1, 8.3.3 *supra*.
5.   Repeat the requests not to question the client, exhibit or examine the client in counsel's absence, and so forth. See §§ 3.4, 3.5, 3.6, 3.21.2, 8.3.2 *supra*.
6.   Ask whether there are any plans to move the client elsewhere, exhibit the client, and so forth. See §§ 3.5, 3.6, 4.12.1, 8.3.2 *supra*.
7.   Ask how counsel can contact officer again. See §§ 4.12.1, 8.3.1 *supra*.

C.   Accompany and represent the client at any identification confrontations or testing procedures. See § 3.6 *supra*.

VI.   *Complete any arrangements necessary to secure the client's release on bail or recognizance, including resort to court, if necessary.* See §§ 3.8 and Chapter 4 *supra*.

VII.   *Begin the field investigation.*

A.   Locate objects and witnesses that may be lost if the search is delayed. See §§ 9.3, 9.8, 9.17 *supra*.

B.   Retain an investigator or photographer, if desired. See §§ 9.4, 9.20 subdivision twenty *supra*.

C.   Interview:

    1.   The police. See §§ 8.1.1, 8.1.3, 8.3.1-8.3.3, 9.15 *supra*.
    2.   The prosecutor. See §§ 8.1.1, 8.1.4, 8.4 *supra*.
    3.   The complainant. See §§ 8.5, 9.13-9.14 *supra*.
    4.   Witnesses. See §§ 9.7-9.14 *supra*.
    5.   Codefendants and uncharged co-perpetrators. See § 9.16 *supra*.
    6.   The client's family. See § 3.4.6 subdivision 3a and §§ 6.13, 9.6 *supra*.

D.   Visit the scene of the crime and any other relevant sites. See § 9.5 *supra*.

E.   Consider other possible other sources of information and pursue those that appear pertinent. See § 9.20 *supra*.

F.   Consider seeking a psychiatric examination of the client. See §§ 16.1.2, 16.2-16.6 *infra*.

VIII.   *Maintain contacts with the police and the prosecutor to explore whether they can be persuaded to drop or reduce charges or to arrange diversion of the prosecution (see §§ 2.3.6, 8.1.1, 8.2, 8.3.1, 8.3.3, 8.4, 8.6 supra), or, in cases in which the client is a minor who could be prosecuted in either juvenile or adult court and in which the juvenile court forum would be more advantageous to the client (see § 21.7 infra), whether the police or prosecutor can be persuaded to support transfer of the case to juvenile court (see §§ 8.2.1, 8.2.2 supra).*

10.2.   *A Note on the Coroner's Inquest and Similar Institutions*

In many jurisdictions a coroner or a coroner's jury or a medical examiner or an examining magistrate is required to investigate all cases of possible homicidal death to determine whether a criminal homicide has been committed. The statutes governing these investigations vary widely. They may or may not require a formal hearing as a part of the investigation, and they may or may not require a finding of homicidal death as the precondition of filing of a complaint (or an indictment or information) charging a particular person with the offense of homicide.

Whether or not it is a statutory prerequisite to a homicide prosecution, this sort of investigation will have important implications for the course of an ensuing prosecution because (a) it memorializes, often in the form of sworn testimony, both medical and nonmedical evidence bearing on the cause and circumstances of death that may be favorable to the defense; (b) it constitutes a source of discovery by defense counsel of similar evidence that may be favorable to the prosecution (see § 5.2 *supra*; § 18.9.2.8 *infra*); (c) it commits witnesses to their stories in a fashion that may shape or explain their later trial testimony and in a form that can be used for impeachment at trial (see § 37.4 *infra*); and (d) it frequently generates pretrial publicity that may be helpful or harmful to the defense.

The same consequences may attach to fire marshal's investigations in arson cases, when these are authorized by statute in a particular jurisdiction. They may also attach to legislative committee hearings or administrative "crime commission" investigations, as these are conducted in a number of States for the purpose of uncovering criminal activity and referring it to the prosecuting authorities.

Since, theoretically, none of these proceedings is directed against specific individuals, the statutes and resolutions authorizing them ordinarily make no allowance for any sort of participation by defense attorneys. However, when the proceedings are, in fact, aimed at particular persons or when they necessarily implicate identifiable persons (as in a homicide case in which the identity of the killer is clear and undisputed and the only question is whether the killing was justifiable), the federal Constitution may give these persons a right to appear by counsel, to cross-examine witnesses, and to present defensive evidence. The Supreme Court held in *Jenkins v. McKeithen*, 395 U.S. 411 (1969), that persons under investigation by one form of "crime commission" were entitled to these rights; and the logic of the *Jenkins* opinion appears to extend not only to most of the other common forms of "crime commissions" and legislative crime-investigating committees but also to the older and more pervasive institutions of the coroner (or equivalent) and the fire marshal. *But see Securities and Exchange Commission v. Jerry T. O'Brien, Inc.*, 467 U.S. 735 (1984).

Chapter 11

Preliminary Hearing

11.1. *Nature and Functions of the Preliminary Hearing*

The first judicial appearance of the defendant is called the preliminary hearing (or, in some States, the commitment hearing or the examining trial). This is the proceeding described in §§ 2.3.3-2.3.5, 2.4.2 *supra*. A magistrate (or a justice of the peace, municipal court judge, or other member of the minor judiciary) usually presides, although in most jurisdictions judges of courts of record also have statutory authority to sit as committing magistrates (see § 11.6.2 *infra*). Arrested defendants are brought before the magistrate for a preliminary hearing shortly after arrest. See §§ 11.1.1, 11.1.2, 11.2 *infra*. Summoned defendants are required by the summons to appear before the magistrate.

11.1.1. *The Formal Functions of the Preliminary Hearing*

The traditional function of the preliminary hearing is to provide an early postarrest safeguard against improvident detention. The magistrate hears the prosecution's evidence against an arrested person (or as much of it as the prosecution chooses to present at this stage) for the purpose of determining whether that person should be released from custody or whether s/he should be "bound over" or "held over" or "committed" – that is to say, incarcerated or required to post bail for his or her appearance – pending subsequent stages of a criminal prosecution. The standard used for this determination is "probable cause" (*see, e.g., State v. Berby*, 81 Wis. 2d 677, 683, 260 N.W.2d 798, 801-02 (1978) ("A defendant may be bound over for trial when the evidence at the preliminary hearing is sufficient to establish probable cause that a crime has been committed and that the defendant probably committed it. ¶ The probable cause that is required for a bindover is greater than that required for the issuance of an arrest warrant, but guilt beyond a reasonable doubt need not be proven. ¶ A defendant may not be bound over for trial unless it appears to a reasonable probability that a crime has been committed and that the defendant committed it."); compare § 25.7.4 *infra*) or, in some States, a *prima facie* case (see § 12.1.2 *infra*). If the prosecution's evidence establishes probable cause to believe that an offense was committed and that the arrested person committed it, the arrestee is bound over to await the filing of an information in the criminal court of record (see §§ 2.3.3, 2.3.4.2-2.3.6 *supra*) or to await the action of the grand jury upon a bill or bills of indictment (see §§ 2.4.3, 2.4.4 *supra*; § 12.1 *infra*). If the magistrate fails to find probable cause, the arrestee is discharged from custody. S/he may nevertheless be indicted (or, in some jurisdictions, prosecuted by information) and required to stand trial; but if s/he has been discharged by the magistrate at the preliminary hearing, s/he remains at liberty throughout the trial (unless either (1) s/he is rearrested, given a second preliminary hearing, and bound over (see § 11.11 *infra*) or (2) s/he is indicted and thereafter arrested and committed on a bench warrant supported by the indictment (see § 2.4.4 *supra*; § 12.17 *infra*)).

In many jurisdictions, the preliminary hearing has a second function: to weed out and foreclose prosecutions on groundless charges, so as to spare the accused the expense and degradation of a full-scale criminal trial. In these jurisdictions the prosecutor may not file an information (or may file an information only with leave of court) against a defendant who has not been bound over at a preliminary hearing. Some of the jurisdictions, in addition, limit the offenses that may be charged in an information to those specific charges upon which the magistrate bound the defendant over. *See, e.g., State v. Rodriguez*, 2009-NMCA-090, 146 N.M. 824, 826-28, 215 P.3d 762, 764-66 (2009). Other jurisdictions permit an information to charge any offense (or at least any offense "related" to the charges upon which the defendant was bound over) that is supported by probable cause appearing in the transcript of the evidence presented at the preliminary hearing, whether or not the magistrate bound the defendant over upon those specific charges. *See, e.g., State v. White*, 312 Wis. 2d 799, 754 N.W.2d 214 (2008); and see § 2.3.6 *supra*. These various restrictions upon prosecutions by information assign to the preliminary hearing a pretrial screening function that is complementary to the grand jury's (see § 2.4.3 *supra*; § 12.1 *infra*): A defendant may be charged in a criminal court only after the prosecutor has first made a showing of probable cause (or a *prima facie* case) either at a preliminary hearing or before the grand jury.

In addition to the two functions just described, the preliminary hearing has gradually accreted others that have received formal or theoretical recognition in varying degrees. Obviously, any procedure requiring the production of arrested individuals before a magistrate or judge shortly following arrest potentially protects citizens against police mistreatment and assures the early implementation of several procedural rights given to accused persons by the federal and state constitutions and laws. A postarrest judicial proceeding will realize this potential insofar as (1) a notation is made in court records that an arrested person is in custody and where s/he is in custody, thereby preventing secret imprisonments and enabling the arrestee's friends or attorney to locate the arrestee and to secure his or her release by *habeas corpus* if the confinement is unlawful (see §§ 3.3.2.2, 3.8.4, 4.12.1, 4.14, 8.3.2 *supra*); (2) the police are required to justify the arrest by showing probable cause (see §§ 2.3.4.1, 8.3.2 *supra*; §§ 11.2, 25.7.4 *infra*); (3) the arrested person is informed of his or her rights (see §§ 2.3.3 2.3.4.1 *supra*), principally the privilege against self-incrimination (see §§ 12.6.1, 18.12 *infra*), the right to bail (see Chapter 4), the right to counsel (see §§ 2.3.4.1, 2.3.4.2 *supra*; § 11.5.1, 26.10 *infra*), and the right to a preliminary examination (see § 2.3.4.2 *supra*; §§ 11.2-11.3 *infra*); (4) some of those rights are immediately implemented, for example, through the setting of bail and the appointment of counsel by the magistrate (see § 2.3.4.1 *supra*); and (5) custody of the accused is transferred from the arresting and investigating officers to other authorities – jailers responsible to the court for the arrested person's safekeeping and not charged with prosecutive duties. Increasingly, these various protective steps have been recognized as components of the preliminary hearing and as rights of the accused. Most of them, though not all, are given by statute, judicial decision, or practice in the large majority of jurisdictions. To assure their timely effectuation, almost every jurisdiction requires by statute or court rule that an arrested person be brought before a judicial officer "promptly" or "forthwith" or "without unnecessary delay" following arrest. *E.g.*, FED. RULE CRIM. PRO.5(a)(1)(A); MINN. RULE CRIM. PRO. 4.02, subd. 5(1); TENN. RULE CRIM. PRO. 5(a)(1).

11.1.2. *The Trend Toward Bifurcation of the Preliminary Hearing*

With the emergence of these additional functions, the preliminary hearing has tended to evolve from a single proceeding into two distinct procedural stages: the preliminary arraignment (sometimes called the preliminary appearance) and the preliminary examination (often nicknamed the PX or the "prelim"). As long as the hearing was concerned almost exclusively with the justifiability of pretrial detention, the important thing was the examination by the magistrate of the evidence against the arrestee. To the extent that a preliminary arraignment of any sort was held, it was either (as at common law) an inquisition of the prisoner (that is, a part of the taking of the evidence) or else a mere reading of the charges against the prisoner as a prelude to taking evidence. But as various procedural rights came to be afforded to an accused, the preliminary arraignment began to assume an independent significance: It became the stage of the proceedings at which the accused was informed of those rights and afforded an opportunity to exercise them. And once the right to counsel at the preliminary examination was given (see § 11.5.1 *infra*), a strong pressure was generated to split the originally unitary preliminary hearing into two separate court appearances. The defendant seldom had a lawyer when s/he first appeared in court; it was necessary either to adjourn the hearing for appointment or retainer of counsel or else to appoint counsel at the preliminary arraignment itself. Particularly where the preliminary examination had the screening function described in § 11.1.1 *supra*, lawyers appointed at the preliminary arraignment were prone to seek continuances of the examination in order to get the time necessary to prepare for it.

This development has proceeded at differing speeds and produced different practices in different localities. In some courts it is still customary to hold a single preliminary hearing shortly following arrest, at which (1) a complaint is filed against the defendant and is given or read to the defendant; (2) s/he is advised of his or her rights (the privilege against self-incrimination, the right to counsel, the right to bail, if any, and the right to have a preliminary examination at which the prosecution will have to show probable cause or a *prima facie* case to justify the defendant's detention); (3) counsel is appointed to represent the defendant (or if s/he has sufficient funds to retain counsel, s/he is given a brief recess for that purpose); (4) s/he is asked either to plead to the complaint or to elect or waive preliminary examination; and (5) unless s/he pleads guilty or waives examination or asks for a continuance of the examination, the court proceeds immediately to hear the prosecution's evidence. When the defense does seek a continuance of the preliminary examination, some of these courts may set it for a date several days or weeks later; others may adjourn for only an hour or two, with the admonition to counsel to "take a couple of hours to talk to your client and get prepared, if you want, but the prosecution has its witnesses here and we are going to proceed with the preliminary hearing today." At the other end of the spectrum, there are many localities that maintain entirely separate preliminary-arraignment and preliminary-hearing calendars. The arraignment, comprising steps (1) through (4) *supra* and the setting of bail (see §§ 2.3.3, 2.3.4.1, 3.18, 4.7 *supra*), is held soon after arrest, but the prosecution is not then expected to have its witnesses in court. The examination (unless the defendant waives examination) is set (either by the magistrate at the preliminary arraignment or routinely by an administrative judge or calendar clerk) for a date a week or two following the preliminary arraignment.

11.2. *The Federal Constitutional Rights to a Prompt Post-arrest Determination of Probable Cause and to a Prompt Preliminary Appearance*

In *Gerstein v. Pugh,* 420 U.S. 103 (1975), the Supreme Court of the United States held that the Fourth Amendment to the federal Constitution, which has long been construed as forbidding arrests without probable cause (see § 25.7 *infra*), entitles every arrested person to "a judicial determination of probable cause as a prerequisite to extended restraint of liberty following arrest" (420 U.S. at 114). Consequently, persons arrested without an arrest warrant (and hence without a prearrest judicial finding of probable cause) may not be confined pending trial unless they are given the opportunity for a probable cause determination "by a judicial officer . . . promptly after arrest" (*id.* at 125). *Accord, Powell v. Nevada*, 511 U.S. 79, 80 (1994); *County of Riverside v. McLaughlin*, 500 U.S. 44, 47, 52-53 (1991); *Atwater v. City of Lago Vista*, 532 U.S. 318, 352 (2001) (dictum); *Albright v. Oliver*, 510 U.S. 266, 274 (1994) (plurality opinion) (dictum); *Baker v. McCollan,* 443 U.S. 137, 142-43 (1979) (dictum).

Although the Court has been "hesitant to announce that the Constitution compels a specific limit" on *how* "promptly" after arrest the constitutional probable cause determination must be afforded, the Court has announced guiding principles "to provide some degree of certainty so that States and counties may establish procedures with confidence that they fall within constitutional bounds" (*County of Riverside v. McLaughlin, supra*, 500 U.S. at 56). "[A] jurisdiction that provides judicial determinations of probable cause within 48 hours of arrest will, as a general matter, comply with the promptness requirement of *Gerstein*." *Id.* But even a hearing provided within 48 hours "may nonetheless violate *Gerstein* if the arrested individual can prove that his or her probable cause determination was delayed unreasonably" (*id.*). "Examples of unreasonable delay are delays for the purpose of gathering additional evidence to justify the arrest, a delay motivated by ill will against the arrested individual, or delay for delay's sake." *Id.* In cases in which "an arrested individual does not receive a probable cause determination within 48 hours," the government bears the "burden . . . to demonstrate the existence of a bona fide emergency or other extraordinary circumstance" to justify the delay (*id.* at 57). *Accord, Powell v. Nevada, supra,* 511 U.S. at 80. "The fact that in a particular case it may take longer than 48 hours to consolidate [the probable cause determination with other] pretrial proceedings[, such as arraignment,] does not qualify as an extraordinary circumstance. Nor, for that matter, do intervening weekends." *County of Riverside v. McLaughlin, supra,* 500 U.S. at 57. *Cf. Alcocer v. Mills,* 906 F.3d 944 (11th Cir. 2018) (an arrestee stated a Fourth Amendment claim by alleging that she was detained overnight after posting bail because sheriff's officers suspected without probable that she was an illegal alien); *Williams v. Dart,* 967 F.3d 625, 632 (7th Cir. 2020) ("by conducting independent reviews of the courts' bail orders and on that basis continuing to hold persons already admitted to bail without purpose or plan for their release, the Sheriff arrogated to himself a decision that was not his to make. These allegations stated a claim under the Fourth Amendment.").

Gerstein is a very narrow decision in several regards. First, it fails, by its terms, to protect persons arrested under arrest warrants (*see Michigan v. Doran*, 439 U.S. 282, 285 n.3 (1978)) – unless the warrant itself is assailable because the procedures for issuing it failed to provide the requisite probable-cause determination (*cf. Manuel v. City of Joliet, Ill.*, 580 U.S. 357 (2017)) – and may also be inapplicable to persons indicted by a grand jury (see § 2.4.4 *supra*; § 11.4 *infra*). *Gerstein v. Pugh, supra*, 420 U.S. at 117 n.19. (*But see In re Walters,* 15 Cal. 3d 738, 543 P.2d 607, 126 Cal. Rptr. 239 (1975), extending *Gerstein* to require a postarrest probable cause determination in cases of arrests made under a warrant.)

Second, *Gerstein* does not require that the probable cause determination be "accompanied by the full panoply of adversary safeguards – counsel, confrontation, cross-examination, and compulsory process for witnesses" (*Gerstein v. Pugh, supra*, 420 U.S. at 119). To the contrary, it sanctions "[t]he use of an informal procedure" (*id.* at 121), in which there is no constitutional right to the appointment of counsel (*id.* at 122-23); no "confrontation and cross-examination" needs be allowed (*id.* at 121-22); and the determination of probable cause may presumably be made "on hearsay and written testimony" (*id.* at 120). All that is constitutionally required is "a fair and reliable determination of probable cause" (*id.* at 125; *see also Baker v. McCollan, supra*, 443 U.S. at 143 & n.2; *Hewitt v. Helms*, 459 U.S. 460, 475 (1983)). *But see Manuel v. City of Joliet, Ill., supra,* which opens the door to challenging a probable-cause determination based upon perjury or fabrication of evidence by investigative or prosecutorial agents; *Sanchez v. Hartley*, 810 F.3d 750, 754 (10th Cir. 2016) ("According to Mr. Sanchez, the detectives and investigator sought legal process based on the confession even though they either knew the confession was untrue or recklessly ignored that possibility. If Mr. Sanchez's allegation is credited, it would involve a constitutional violation, for we have held that the Fourth Amendment prohibits officers from knowingly or recklessly relying on false information to institute legal process when that process results in an unreasonable seizure."); *accord, Miller v. Maddox*, 866 F.3d 386 (6th Cir. 2017); *Black v. Montgomery County*, 835 F.3d 358 (3d Cir. 2016); and see § 25.17.3 *infra* for elaboration of this principle in the context of challenges to search warrants.

Third, *Gerstein* is not read by the lower courts as requiring a bail hearing on the 48-hour timetable set by *County of Riverside v. McLaughlin. See Mitchell v. Doherty*, 37 F.4th 1277 (7th Cir. 2022).

Finally, failure to give an accused a prompt probable cause determination does not foreclose subsequent prosecution or provide grounds for its dismissal; it merely renders the accused's pretrial confinement unconstitutional. *Gerstein v. Pugh, supra*, 420 U.S. at 119; *see Bell v. Wolfish*, 441 U.S. 520, 534 n.15 (1979).

Notwithstanding all of these limitations – which cumulatively render *Gerstein*'s "probable cause determination" a pale shadow of the preliminary examination already allowed by state law in most jurisdictions – *Gerstein* does have significant implications for state preliminary examination practice. In some States, *Gerstein*'s requirement of "prompt" probable cause determinations has the salutary effect of "acceleration of existing [state procedures]" (*Gerstein, supra*, 420 U.S. at 124). As noted above, the United States Supreme Court has established as a rule of thumb that promptness for *Gerstein* purposes ordinarily means within 48 hours, and it has said explicitly both that delays beyond 48 hours must be justified by a showing of extraordinary circumstances and that the practice of consolidating *Gerstein* determinations with other preliminary proceedings (such as an adversarial hearing on probable cause) "does not qualify as an extraordinary circumstance" (*County of Riverside v. McLaughlin, supra*, 500 U.S. at 57). Moreover, when the *Gerstein* requirement is violated, any confessions or other statements taken from the defendant during the period of excessive delay are arguably inadmissible in evidence as the fruits of an unconstitutional detention. See § 8.3.2 *supra*. In this respect, *Gerstein* provides the constitutional predicate for an updated version of what used to be known as the "*McNabb-Mallory*" exclusionary rule. See § 26.11 *infra*.

In addition to the Fourth Amendment *Gerstein* rule, there are Due Process protections against protracted detention of a suspect without fair and reliable procedures for determining his or her probable guilt. *See Oviatt By and Through Waugh v. Pearce*, 954 F.2d 1470, 1474 (9th Cir. 1992) (recognizing "a liberty interest in being free from extended incarceration without any arraignment or pretrial procedure"); *Harris v. Clay County*, 40 F.4th 266 (5th Cir. 2022) (the six-year jail detention of a defendant who had been found incompetent to stand trial and whose civil commitment proceeding had been dismissed violated due process); *Barnes v. District of Columbia*, 793 F. Supp. 2d 260 (D. D.C. 2011) (recognizing a due process claim in cases of "overdetention", which "generally means that once a prisoner was entitled to release—because of a court order, the expiration of a sentence, or otherwise—the authority having custody over that person held them too long." *Id.* at 266. "Overdetentions potentially violate the substantive component of the Due Process Clause by infringing upon an individual's basic liberty interest in being free from incarceration absent a criminal conviction." *Id.* at 274-275.); *accord, Traweek v. Gusman*, 414 F. Supp. 3d 847 (E.D. La. 2019); *Tatum v. Moody*, 768 F.3d 806 (9th Cir. 2014) (holding that "[w]here . . . investigating officers, acting with deliberate indifference or reckless disregard for a suspect's right to freedom from unjustified loss of liberty, fail to disclose potentially dispositive exculpatory evidence to the prosecutors, leading to the lengthy detention of an innocent man, they violate the due process guarantees of the Fourteenth Amendment" (*id.* at 816)); *Lopez-Valenzuela v. Arpaio*, 770 F.3d 772 (9th Cir. 2014) (en banc) (holding that the blanket preclusion of bail or pretrial release for undocumented aliens arrested on any of a broad range of felony charges, without regard to whether the individual alien's release would involve a risk of flight or other danger, violates due process); *Jauch v. Choctaw County*, 874 F.3d 425, 427 (5th Cir. 2017) ("Jessica Jauch was indicted by a grand jury, arrested, and put in jail – where she waited for 96 days to be brought before a judge and was effectively denied bail. The district court found this constitutionally permissible. It is not. A pre-trial detainee denied access to the judicial system for a prolonged period has been denied basic procedural due process . . . ."); *Hoffman v. Knoebel*, 894 F.3d 836, 840-41 (7th Cir. 2018) (dictum) ("We have said in the past that prolonged detention before receiving a hearing violates the Due Process Clause's substantive component. . . . But this case is simpler. The plaintiffs were not being held pending a hearing because the ostensible hearing already occurred. The problem was that the hearing itself was constitutionally deficient. . . . ¶ . . . [T]his is enough to show that the plaintiffs were deprived of a liberty interest without due process of law."); *Geness v. Cox*, 902 F.3d 344, 363-64 (3d Cir. 2018); *Crittindon v. LeBlanc*, 37 F.4th 177, 188 (5th Cir. 2022) ("it is without question that holding without legal notice a prisoner for a month beyond the expiration of his sentence constitutes a denial of due process"), and cases cited; *cf. Matzell v. Annucci*, 64 F.4th 425, 437 (2d Cir. 2023) (allegations that prison official denied an inmate entry into an early-release program in violation of the terms of his sentence stated a due process claim: "'[t]he general liberty interest in freedom from detention is perhaps the most fundamental interest that the Due Process Clause protects'"); *Armstrong v. Daily*, 786 F.3d 529, 551-52 (7th Cir. 2015) ("The constitutional violation that Armstrong asserts is the deprivation of his liberty without due process of law, as the result of the destruction of evidence by a state actor. . . . ¶ Armstrong's claim therefore has two essential elements: (1) the defendant destroyed exculpatory evidence in bad faith or engaged in other misconduct (2) that caused a deprivation of the plaintiff's liberty. . . . Taking Armstrong's allegations as true, and giving him the benefit of favorable inferences, we must assume that Daily and Campbell's actions caused Armstrong to suffer a loss of liberty as he languished in prison for three more years after Daily said he was excluded by the earlier DNA tests and after the last sample had been destroyed in the Y–STR test of the newly discovered stain."); *Parada v. Anoka County*, 54 F.4th 1016, 1020 (8th Cir. 2022) (holding that Parada's four-hour detention constituted discrimination on the basis of national origin and violated the Equal Protection Clause when based upon a county's "'unwritten policy requiring its employees to contact ICE [Immigration and Customs Enforcement] every time a foreign-born individual is detained, *irrespective* of whether the person is a U.S. citizen.' . . . The way it works is simple: 'If the individual [says] they were born abroad, the jail will send ICE a notification' and 'attempt[ ] to wait to start release procedures . . . until [it] hear[s] back,' which 'could take between 20 minutes and 6 hours.'"); *Kong v. United States*, 62 F.4th 608 (1st Cir. 2023).

11.3. *The State-Law Right to a Full Preliminary Examination*

Gerstein v. Pugh, 420 U.S. 103 (1975), does not support a federal constitutional right to a full-scale adversary preliminary examination. (An argument can be made for such a right, but it would stretch current Fourth Amendment doctrine. *See* Anthony G. Amsterdam, *Perspectives on the Fourth Amendment*, 58 MINN. L. REV. 349, 390-92 (1974).) Rather, by a 5-4 vote, *Gerstein* holds that the requisite determination of "probable cause to believe the suspect has committed a crime . . . [can be] decided by a magistrate in a nonadversary proceeding on hearsay and written testimony" (420 U.S. at 120; see *id.* at 119-25). *See also, e.g., Schall v. Martin*, 467 U.S. 253, 274-75 (1984). Most States, however, do provide by statute for the kind of adversarial evidentiary hearing described in § 11.5.2 *infra* (*see, e.g., Waugh v. State*, 564 S.W.2d 654 (Tenn. 1978)); and many state courts will enforce the state-law hearing requirement by reversing a conviction obtained at a trial following an inadequate preliminary examination, even though the trial itself was otherwise error-free. *E.g., State v. Essman*, 98 Ariz. 228, 403 P.2d 540 (1965); *State v. Howland*, 153 Kan. 352, 110 P.2d 801 (1941); *Green v. State*, 286 Md. 692, 410 A.2d 234 (1980); *Blandshaw v. State*, 245 S.C. 385, 140 S.E.2d 784 (1965). *See also, e.g., State v. Rodriguez*, 12009-NMCA-090, 46 N.M. 824, 826-28, 831, 215 P.3d 762, 764-66, 769 (2009) (vacating a conviction because the state charged the defendant "by information with an offense not considered or included in the bind-over order" and thereby deprived him "of his due process rights by subjecting him to criminal prosecution without probable cause"). In other jurisdictions, challenges to defects in the preliminary examination can be raised only by pretrial motion or writ and interlocutory appeal (which, in some jurisdictions, must be pursued before an indictment or information is filed); they are forfeited if superseded by error-free proceedings that suffice to justify the defendant's detention. *See, e.g., State v. Smith*, 344 P.3d 573 (Utah 2014); *compare People v. Wilson*, 469 Mich. 1018, 677 N.W.2d 29 (Table) (2004) ("[i]f a defendant is fairly convicted at trial, no appeal lies regarding whether the evidence at the preliminary examination was sufficient to warrant a bindover"), *with People v. Dodge-Doak*, 2022 WL 16858783 (Mich. App. 2022) ("Following the bindover, defendant filed a motion to remand in the circuit court, arguing that procedural irregularities in the preliminary examination warranted further proceedings in the district court. The prosecution filed a response, agreeing that a remand to the district court for further preliminary-examination proceedings was warranted because defendant was not allowed an opportunity to call witnesses. At the hearing on the motion to remand, the circuit court sua sponte dismissed the case because it found that the many errors committed during the preliminary examination made remand impracticable. . . . ¶ On appeal, the prosecution argues that the circuit court abused its discretion by dismissing the case instead of remanding to the district court for further proceedings. We disagree." *Id.* at *1. "Although defendant filed a motion to remand, we review the circuit court's actions under the standard applicable to motions to dismiss since the circuit court dismissed the case. The standard of review for a ruling on a motion to dismiss is abuse of discretion. . . ." *Id.* "[T]he circuit court chose one of the two permissible remedies for the district court's error, [and sufficient] . . . ¶ . . . reasons support the circuit court's decision to dismiss the case in lieu of remanding it to the district court for further proceedings. Although the circuit court may have reasonably decided to the contrary, its decision in this case was within the range of principled outcomes." *Id.* at *2.); *State v. Webb*, 160 Wis. 2d 622, 636, 467 N.W.2d 108, 114 (1991) ("Our holding [refusing to permit post-trial claims of defects in a preliminary hearing] applies only when the defendant fails to seek relief prior to trial. A defendant is not without remedy prior to trial. If the defendant is dissatisfied with what occurred at the preliminary hearing, he can seek relief before trial in a motion to dismiss brought before the trial court based on errors or insufficiencies of the preliminary hearing. He may challenge his bindover by way of a permissive interlocutory appeal from the non-final order binding him over for trial. . . . Further, he may challenge the bindover by supervisory writ if he can show that there was in fact a defect in subject matter or personal jurisdiction.").

11.4. *Challenging the Prosecutor's Use of a Supervening Indictment to Foreclose a Preliminary Examination*

In some jurisdictions, prosecutors commonly do an end run around the defendant's right to a preliminary examination by obtaining a continuance of the examination from the magistrate and then rushing to the Grand Jury to obtain a supervening indictment. Because the return of the indictment is alone sufficient to sustain the defendant's detention (see § 2.4.4 *supra*), it has traditionally been thought that indictment renders the preliminary examination unnecessary. *See, e.g., State ex rel. Rowe v. Ferguson*, 165 W. Va. 183, 268 S.E.2d 45 (1980); *People v. Moore*, 28 Ill. App. 3d 1085, 329 N.E.2d 893 (1975); *Lataille v. District Court of Eastern Hampden*, 366 Mass. 525, 320 N.E.2d 877 (1974); *and cf. State v. D'Anna*, 506 S.W.2d 200 (Tenn. Crim. App. 1973); 18 U.S.C. § 3060(e) (in federal criminal cases, "[n]o preliminary examination . . . shall be required to be accorded an arrested person . . . if at any time subsequent to the initial appearance of such person [at preliminary arraignment] . . . and prior to the date fixed for the preliminary examination . . . , an indictment is returned or . . . an information is filed . . . ."); FED. RULE CRIM. PRO. 5.1(a)(2).

This tactical ploy by the prosecution to prevent a preliminary examination may be fought at the time of the first appearance by defense counsel's objecting to any prosecution request for a continuance. See § 11.9 *infra*. But frequently defense counsel is in no position to oppose a continuance because s/he is not prepared to go forward with the hearing, particularly if s/he has just been appointed.

When an indictment is thereafter returned, it is technically true that the two formal functions of the preliminary examination (see § 11.1.1 *supra*) are mooted. Arguably, however, an indictment does not moot the need for the judicial determination of probable cause which was recognized as a Fourth Amendment imperative in *Gerstein v. Pugh*, 420 U.S. 103 (1975). *Gerstein* left unsettled the question whether an indictment by a grand jury satisfies its requirement of a probable cause determination by a "judicial officer" (*see* 420 U.S. at 125; *compare id.* at 117 n.19). Counsel can argue that grand juries lack the neutrality implicit in the "judicial officer" prescription because, as a practical matter, they are invariably dominated by the prosecutor (*see, e.g., Hawkins v. Superior Court*, 22 Cal.3d 584, 589-92, 586 P.2d 916, 919-21, 150 Cal. Rptr. 435, 438-40 (1978), and authorities cited; Abraham S. Goldstein, *The State and the Accused: Balance of Advantage in Criminal Procedure*, 69 YALE L.J. 1149, 1171 (1960), and authorities cited), and that the only procedural forum which state law provides for an unbiased *Gerstein* determination is a preliminary examination. Or if this broad contention fails, counsel may be able to point to deficiencies in the grand jury's proceedings in the particular case at bar which render its determination of probable cause unreliable (*cf.* §§ 12.1.3, 20.3 *infra*) and therefore inadequate to support the defendant's detention beyond the ordinary *Gerstein* time limits unless s/he is given a preliminary hearing. The latter argument finds strong analogical support in *Manuel v. City of Joliet, Ill.*, 580 U.S. 357 (2017):

> " . . . [P]retrial detention can violate the Fourth Amendment not only when it precedes, but also when it follows, the start of legal process in a criminal case. The Fourth Amendment prohibits government officials from detaining a person in the absence of probable cause. . . . That can happen when the police hold someone without any reason before the formal onset of a criminal proceeding. But it also can occur when legal process itself goes wrong – when, for example, a judge's probable-cause determination is predicated solely on a police officer's false statements. Then, too, a person is confined without constitutionally adequate justification. Legal process has gone forward, but it has done nothing to satisfy the Fourth Amendment's probable-cause requirement. And for that reason, it cannot extinguish the detainee's Fourth Amendment claim . . . .

> " . . . The judge's order holding Manuel for trial . . . lacked any proper basis. And that means Manuel's ensuing pretrial detention, no less than his original arrest, violated his Fourth Amendment rights. Or put just a bit differently: Legal process did not expunge Manuel's Fourth Amendment claim because the process he received failed to establish what that Amendment makes essential for pretrial detention – probable cause to believe he committed a crime." (*Id.* at 366-69.)

See also Kuri v. City of Chicago, Illinois, 990 F.3d 573 (7th Cir. 2021); *Williams v. Dart*, 967 F.3d 625, 632-33 (7th Cir. 2020), quoted in § 11.2 second paragraph *supra*; *Sanders v. Jones*, 728 Fed. Appx. 563, 565 (6th Cir. 2018) ("Applying *Manuel*, this court held in *King v. Harwood*, 852 F.3d 568 (6th Cir. 2017), . . . that the presumption of probable cause created by a grand jury indictment is rebuttable 'where (1) a law-enforcement officer, in the course of setting a prosecution in motion, either knowingly or recklessly makes false statements (such as in affidavits or investigative reports) or falsifies or fabricates evidence; (2) the false statements and evidence, together with any concomitant misleading omissions, are material to the ultimate prosecution of the plaintiff; and (3) the false statements, evidence, and omissions do not consist solely of grand-jury testimony or preparation for that testimony (where preparation has a meaning broad enough to encompass conspiring to commit perjury before the grand jury).'"); *accord, Miller v. Maddox*, 866 F.3d 386, 391 (6th Cir. 2017); *Jackson v. City of Cleveland*, 925 F.3d 793 (6th Cir. 2019). *Cf. Hoffman v. Knoebel*, 894 F.3d 836 (7th Cir. 2018), quoted in § 11.2 concluding paragraph *supra*.

In some States, the sections of the criminal code relating to preliminary hearing and to the grand jury can be construed together as making a magistrate's bind-over the jurisdictional prerequisite for grand jury consideration of any criminal charge that is initiated by arrest rather than by indictment. Here, denial of a full preliminary hearing renders an indictment invalid, and the prosecutor's end-run tactic can be thwarted by a motion to dismiss the indictment for lack of jurisdiction. *See, e.g., Moore v. State*, 578 S.W.2d 78 (Tenn. 1979); *State v. Funderburk*, 259 S.C. 256, 191 S.E.2d 520 (1972). In other States, the statutory scheme does not speak unambiguously concerning the relationship between preliminary hearings and the grand jury process. But counsel can argue that whenever the defendant has a right to a preliminary examination under a statute that makes no express provision for the termination of this right by indictment (*compare* 18 U.S.C. § 3060(e), *supra*), the right survives indictment (*see Commonwealth v. Brabham*, 225 Pa. Super. 331, 309 A.2d 824 (1973)), and that its denial prejudices the defense in ways that require the trial court, on a defendant's timely motion, to either (a) dismiss the indictment without prejudice to the prosecutor's seeking a new indictment if and after a preliminary examination has been held, or (b) stay proceedings on the indictment and refer the case to a magistrate to conduct a preliminary hearing before the defendant is required to plead to the indictment, or (c) conduct a preliminary hearing itself, with the arraignment judge or another judge of the trial court sitting as a committing magistrate (see § 11.1 *supra*; § 11.6.2. *infra*).

In support of the prejudice argument, counsel can point to the preliminary examination's informal function of providing discovery to the defense in a criminal justice system that eliminates or curtails most of the discovery mechanisms available in civil cases. A plurality of the Supreme Court of the United States adverted to the discovery function of the preliminary examination as a legitimate defense interest in *Coleman v. Alabama*, 399 U.S. 1, 9 (1970), in reasoning that the examination was a "critical stage" requiring the appointment of counsel. *Accord, Green v. State*, 286 Md. 692, 695-96, 410 A.2d 234, 236 (1980). Another plurality of the Court recognized that interest in *Adams v. Illinois*, 405 U.S. 278, 282 (1972), although holding it insufficient to warrant the retroactive application of *Coleman* in the absence of a showing of "actual prejudice" (405 U.S. at 285), at least in a jurisdiction that provided "alternative [discovery] procedures" (*id.* at 282). See § 11.8.3 *infra*. And the Oklahoma Court of Criminal Appeals has acknowledged that one of the purposes of the preliminary examination is that "it is a procedure whereby defendant may discover what testimony is to be used against him at the trial, as he may examine witnesses in detail and be prepared to cope with their testimony at the time of trial in case defendant is bound over" (*Beaird v. Ramey,* 456 P.2d 587, 589 (Okla. Crim. App. 1969)). Recognition of the defendant's discovery interest also appears in a significant line of District of Columbia federal criminal cases, which, prior to the enactment in 1968 of a statute deeming the return of a supervening indictment to be a valid basis for foregoing preliminary examination (18 U.S.C. § 3060(e)), held that denial of certain preliminary hearing rights are not cured by a supervening indictment. *Blue v. United States*, 342 F.2d 894 (D.C. Cir. 1964); *Dancy v. United States*, 361 F.2d 75 (D.C. Cir. 1966); *Ross v. Sirica*, 380 F.2d 557 (D.C. Cir. 1967). (In federal prosecutions, these cases have been overturned by the statute, of course (*see Coleman v. Burnett*, 477 F.2d 1187, 1198-1200 (D.C. Cir. 1973); *United States v. Anderson*, 481 F.2d 685, 691-92 (4th Cir. 1973), *aff'd*, 417 U.S. 211 (1974), and cases cited), but the reasoning of the *Blue-Dancy-Ross* line should remain persuasive in state jurisdictions where no statute expressly dictates a contrary result.) The same recognition of "the important discovery function served by an adversarial preliminary hearing" figures prominently in the decision of the California Supreme Court in *Hawkins v. Superior Court*, 22 Cal.3d 584, 588, 586 P.2d 916, 918-19, 150

Cal. Rptr. 435, 437-38 (1978), holding that a defendant who is denied a preliminary examination by the prosecutor's discretionary decision to proceed by indictment instead of by information is thereby denied the equal protection of the laws under the California Constitution. As the New York Court of Appeals has put it:

> "[S]ince the prosecutor must present proof of every element of the crime claimed to have been committed, no matter how skeletally, the preliminary hearing conceptually and pragmatically may serve as a virtual minitrial of the prima facie case. . . . In its presentation, the identity of witnesses, to greater or lesser degree, testimonial details and exhibits, perforce will be disclosed. Especially because discovery and deposition, by and large, are not available in criminal cases, this may not only be an unexampled, but a vital opportunity to obtain the equivalent. It has even been suggested that 'in practice [it] may provide the defense with the most valuable discovery technique available to him.' . . .

> ". . . Most important, early resort to that time-tested tool for testing truth, cross-examination, in the end may make the difference between conviction and exoneration." (*People v. Hodge*, 53 N.Y.2d 313, 318-19, 423 N.E.2d 1060, 1063, 441 N.Y.S.2d 231, 234 (1981) (*but see id.* at 319-20, 423 N.E.2d at 1063, 441 N.Y.S.2d at 234-35: "True, the State, by presenting the case to a Grand Jury in the first instance, may bypass the preliminary hearing stage entirely . . . . But, though in. . . [this situation] the People will have obviated the preliminary hearing process . . , once it pursues the path of the preliminary hearing, the defendant becomes entitled to have it conducted with full respect for his right to counsel.").)

See also State v. Graves, 126 S.W.3d 873, 877, 878 (Tenn. 2003) (state rule requiring preservation of "an electronic recording or its equivalent of a preliminary hearing," and mandating "dismissal of the indictment and a remand for a new preliminary hearing unless the State establishes (1) that all material and substantial evidence that was introduced at the preliminary hearing was made available to the defendant and (2) that the testimony made available to the defendant was subject to cross-examination" reflects "the importance of the preliminary hearing in general," including "its importance to the defense as a discovery tool" and the opportunity it affords the defense "to confront and cross-examine witnesses under oath"). These cases lay the foundation for an argument that would invalidate the use of the grand jury by the prosecutor to end-run preliminary examinations. The argument is that the supervening return of an indictment does not avoid the defendant's right to a preliminary examination, which accrues as an incident of his or her arrest prior to indictment, because the indictment – even if it justifies the defendant's detention for trial – leaves the defendant prejudiced by denial of a major benefit of the examination: discovery adequate to "provide the defense with valuable information about the case against the accused, enhancing its ability to evaluate the desirability of entering a plea or to prepare for trial" (*Hawkins v. Superior Court, supra*, 22 Cal.3d at 588, 586 P.2d at 919, 150 Cal. Rptr. at 438), together with the opportunity for "skilled interrogation of witnesses by [the defense] . . . lawyer [that] can fashion a vital impeachment tool for use in cross-examination of the State's witnesses at the trial, or preserve testimony favorable to the accused of a witness who does not appear at the trial" (*Coleman v. Alabama, supra*, 399 U.S. at 9). The prosecution cannot fairly be permitted to proceed in a fashion that gives it the advantages of two differing procedures – arrest without prescreening of the grand jury; indictment without discovery at the preliminary examination – and the disadvantages of neither. *Cf. People v. Hodge, supra*, 53 N.Y.2d at 318-20, 423 N.E.2d at 1063-64, 441 N.Y.S.2d at 234-35; *Coleman v. Burnett, supra*, 477 F.2d at 1207-12; *and see United States v. Milano*, 443 F.2d 1022, 1025 (10th Cir. 1971) (holding that under 18 U.S.C. § 3060(e) a preliminary examination is not required after indictment but reserving the question whether the same result would obtain in a case of "deliberate prosecutorial connivance to deprive a person of a preliminary hearing by delay until after indictment").

11.5. *Defense Rights at the Preliminary Hearing*

11.5.1. *Right to Counsel*

The Sixth Amendment right to counsel applies at every "critical stage" of the proceedings (*White v. Maryland,* 373 U.S. 59 (1963) (per curiam)), "at or after the time that adversary judicial proceedings have been initiated against [the individual] . . . – 'whether by way of formal charge, preliminary hearing, indictment, information, or arraignment'" (*Brewer v. Williams,* 430 U.S. 387, 398 (1977)). *See also Rothgery v. Gillespie County, Texas*, 554 U.S. 191, 198, 213 (2008); *Montejo v. Louisiana*, 556 U.S. 778, 786 (2009) (dictum). The right is triggered at "such time as the "'government has committed itself to prosecute, and . . . the adverse positions of government and defendant have solidified'"" (*Moran v. Burbine*, 475 U.S. 412, 432 (1986)). Under these principles it has long been clear that a defendant has a right to counsel at arraignment, and, if s/he is indigent, the right to appointed counsel under *Gideon v. Wainwright*, 372 U.S. 335 (1963). *See Hamilton v. Alabama*, 368 U.S. 52 (1961); *Michigan v. Jackson*, 475 U.S. 625, 627-28, 629, 636 (1986); *Missouri v. Frye*, 566 U.S. 133, 140 (2012) (dictum); *Gonzales v. Commissioner of Correction*, 308 Conn. 463, 68 A.3d 624 (2013). In *Rothgery v. Gillespie County, Texas, supra*, 554 U.S. at 198, 213, the Court explicitly recognized that the Sixth Amendment right to counsel is applicable to preliminary-arraignment-type proceedings (*id.* at 195) – that is, "a criminal defendant's initial appearance before a judicial officer, where he learns the charge against him and his liberty is subject to restriction" (*id.* at 213).

11.5.2. *Right To Cross-Examine Prosecution Witnesses and To Present Defense Witnesses; Right To Subpoena Witnesses; Right to Disclosure of Exculpatory and Impeaching Evidence*

In most jurisdictions, statutes, court rules, or judicial decisions give the defendant has the right to cross-examine the prosecution's witnesses at the preliminary examination. *See, e.g.,* FED. RULE CRIM. PRO. 5.1(e); HAWAI'I RULE CRIM PRO. 5(d)(2); N.M. DIST. CT. RULE CRIM. PRO. 5(B)(5); TENN. RULE CRIM. PRO. 5.1(a)(2); *Ex parte Wood*, 629 So.2d 808, 810 (Ala. Crim. 1993) ("'[a]ll jurisdictions grant the defense a right to cross-examine those witnesses presented by the prosecution at the preliminary hearing'"); *State v. Spears*, 634 So.2d 9, 10 (La. App. 1994) ("Although all of the procedural safeguards of a criminal jury trial need not be afforded at a preliminary examination, the defendant has a right to a hearing that ensures a fair and impartial determination of the issue of probable cause. The hearing is to be 'full-blown and adversary' and one in which the defendant is entitled to confront witnesses against him and to fully cross-examine the witnesses."); *Desper v. State*, 173 W. Va. 494, 501, 318 S.E.2d 437, 445 (1984) ("We . . . hold that in challenging probable cause at a preliminary examination conducted pursuant to Rule 5.1 of the West Virginia Rules of Criminal Procedure, a defendant has a right to cross-examine witnesses for the State and to introduce evidence; the preliminary examination is not entitled during the preliminary examination to explore testimony solely for discovery purposes. The magistrate at the preliminary examination has discretion to limit such testimony to the probable cause issue, and the magistrate may properly require the defendant to explain the relevance to probable cause of the testimony the defendant seeks to elicit."); *Sheriff of Washoe County v. Vasile*, 96 Nev. 5, 604 P.2d 809 (1980); *People v. Dodge-Doak*, 2022 WL 16858783 (Mich. App. 2022), summarized in § 11.3 *supra* (affirming a trial court's dismissal of the charges against a defendant where the preliminary hearing judge had "refused to allow defendant to call any defense witnesses" (2022 WL 16858783 at *1), had ordered cross-examination of the prosecution's sole witness – the child allegedly abused in a sexual-abuse case – "abruptly ended without warning . . . . [and had] repeatedly interrupted the cross-examination as well" (*id.* at *2)). The right to cross-examine at the preliminary examination may also be protected by the federal guarantee of confrontation incorporated in the Fourteenth Amendment (*Pointer v. Texas,* 380 U.S. 400 (1965); *Barber v. Page,* 390 U.S. 719 (1968); *cf. Olden v. Kentucky,* 488 U.S. 227 (1988) (per curiam); *but see, e.g., Sheriff v. Witzenburg*, 122 Nev. 1056, 145 P.3d 1002 (2006); *State v. Lopez*, 2013-NMSC-047, 314 P.3d 236 (N.M. 2013)), or by the Due Process Clause (see § 11.8.3 *infra*).

Local law also commonly accords the defense the right to present evidence at a preliminary examination. *See, e.g.*, the federal, Hawai'i and Tennessee criminal rules cited *supra*; *Ex parte Lankford*, 20 So.3d 843, 846 (Ala. Crim. 2009) (granting a writ of mandamus and ordering that the court of first instance set aside its order quashing the subpoenas issued by a defendant charged with sexual assault by which he sought to have the victim and her mother testify at a preliminary examination: "[a]ccording to Alabama law, Lankford had the right to subpoena witnesses for his preliminary hearing if their testimony was relevant to a determination of whether probable cause existed"); *State v. Spears, supra,* 634 So.2d at 10 ("[a]t the hearing, both the State and the defendant may produce witnesses, and the witnesses are subject to cross-examination"); *Beaird v. Ramey,* 456 P.2d 587 (Okla. Crim. App. 1969); *Desper v. State, supra; State v. Essman,* 98 Ariz. 228, 403 P.2d 540 (1965); *and see State v. Benedict,* 2022-NMCA-030, 511 P.3d 379, 385 (N.M. App. 2022) ("[W]e next address the State's argument that the court conducting the preliminary examination must 'view all evidence and draw all inferences in favor of the prosecution.' We disagree. ¶ Article II, Section 14 of the New Mexico Constitution requires that before a person 'shall be held to answer for a capital, felonious or infamous crime,' the prosecutor must either obtain an indictment by a grand jury or must file an information, which then must be followed by a preliminary examination before a magistrate or judge: 'No person shall be so held on information without having had a preliminary examination before an examining magistrate, or having waived such preliminary examination.' . . . ¶ The procedures required for a preliminary hearing in New Mexico do not command sole reliance on the evidence offered by the state. Rather, the rules of procedure adopted by our Supreme Court allow the defendant to subpoena and call witnesses on the defendant's behalf . . . ; to cross-examine the state's witnesses . . .; and to raise objections based on the Rules of Evidence . . . . These provisions require the district court to hear both the state's evidence and the evidence submitted by the defendant and 'determine probable cause from *all* the evidence.' ¶ Drawing all inferences from the evidence in the state's favor would conflict with the defendant's right to present evidence and to have disputes of fact and questions of credibility resolved by an impartial judge."). This right is arguably guaranteed by the federal Due Process Clause as well. *Cf. Jenkins v. McKeithen,* 395 U.S. 411, 429 (1969).

The defendant's right to call witnesses to testify at the preliminary examination is reinforced by the ancillary right to subpoena them (*see, e.g., Coleman v. Burnett,* 477 F.2d 1187, 1202-07 (D.C. Cir. 1973)), *in forma pauperis* under the Equal Protection principle of *Griffin v. Illinois,* 351 U.S. 12 (1956), if the defendant is indigent and makes an adequate showing that the witness's testimony will be material and helpful to the defense on the issue of probable cause (*see Washington v. Clemmer,* 339 F.2d 715, 718-19, 725-28 (D.C. Cir. 1964); *cf. United States v. Valenzuela-Bernal,* 458 U.S. 858, 866-71 & n.7 (1982)).

There is disagreement among the state courts as to whether the disclosure rights assured to defendants at the trial stage by *Brady v. Maryland,* 373 U.S. 83 (1963), and its progeny (discussed in § 18.9.1 *infra*) apply at a preliminary examination. For a holding that they do and for reference to the conflicting authorities, *see People v. Gutierrez,* 214 Cal. App. 4th 343, 153 Cal. Rptr. 3d 832 (2013). *See also Bridgeforth v. Superior Court,* 214 Cal. App. 4th 1074, 1077, 154 Cal. Rptr. 3d 528, 530 (2013) (dictum) ("due process requires the prosecution to disclose, prior to the preliminary hearing, evidence in its possession that is both favorable to the defense and material to the probable cause determination to be made at the preliminary hearing"). State law in some jurisdictions may give defendants a right to pre-preliminary-hearing discovery that extends beyond *Brady* material. *Compare People v. Kingsley,* 187 Colo. 258, 530 P.2d 501 (1975) (authorizing discovery of the names and prior statements of witnesses whom the prosecution will call at the preliminary hearing), *and Stafford v. District Court of Oklahoma County,* 595 P.2d 797 (1979) (authorizing discovery of the criminal records of witnesses whom the prosecution will call at the preliminary hearing) *with State v. Schaefer,* 308 Wis. 2d 279, 746 N.W.2d 457 (2008), *and Derby v. State,* 557 S.W.3d 355 (Mo. App. 2018) (foreclosing pre-preliminary hearing discovery).

Although *Gerstein v. Pugh,* 420 U.S. 103 (1975), holds that the rights discussed in this section are not necessary incidents of the preliminary determination required by the Fourth Amendment, *Gerstein* does not deny that they may be constitutionally obligatory in the "full preliminary hearing . . . procedure used in many States" (*id.* at 119). Rather, *Gerstein* says that "[w]hen the hearing takes this form, adversary procedures are customarily employed" and "[t]he importance of the issue to both the State and the accused justifies the presentation of witnesses and full exploration of their testimony on cross-examination" (*id.* at 120). Analogously, *Gerstein* recognizes no constitutional right to counsel at a Fourth Amendment preliminary hearing, *id.* at 122-23, but asserts that if the state chooses to conduct a full preliminary examination in lieu of a minimal preliminary hearing, then "appointment of counsel for indigent defendants" is required (*id.* at 120). In *Routhier v. Sheriff, Clark County,* 93 Nev. 149, 151-52, 560 P.2d 1371, 1372 (1977), the Nevada Supreme Court relied on Sixth Amendment precedent as well as state law to hold that a defendant had a right to a continuance of a preliminary hearing in order to locate, call, and cross-examine an informant whose identity was first disclosed at the hearing and who was involved in setting up the drug transaction for which the defendant was arrested.

11.5.3. *Right to Transcription of the Proceedings*

State law ordinarily requires that preliminary-hearing proceedings be transcribed. *See, e.g., Harris v. District Court of City and County of Denver,* 843 P.2d 1316 (Colo. 1993). An indigent defendant can assert a federal constitutional right to the transcription of the proceedings at state expense, since (a) the transcript would be an important aid to defense trial preparation as well as to impeachment of prosecution witnesses at trial (*cf. Coleman v. Alabama,* 399 U.S. 1, 9 (1970) (plurality opinion); *Britt v. North Carolina,* 404 U.S. 226, 228 (1971)); (b) a solvent defendant could employ a stenographer to make a transcript; and (c) the Equal Protection Clause of the Fourteenth Amendment, as construed in *Griffin v. Illinois,* 351 U.S. 12 (1956), forbids the states to deny an indigent, for the sole reason of indigency, an important litigation tool that a solvent individual could buy. *See Roberts v. LaVallee,* 389 U.S. 40 (1967); *Britt v. North Carolina, supra,* 404 U.S. at 228 (dictum); *Bounds v. Smith,* 430 U.S. 817, 822 & n.8 (1977) (dictum); *United States ex rel. Wilson v. McMann,* 408 F.2d 896 (2d Cir. 1969); *Peterson v. United States,* 351 F.2d 606 (9th Cir. 1965); *cf. Washington v. Clemmer,* 339 F.2d 715, 717-18 (D.C. Cir. 1964); *compare United States v. MacCollom,* 426 U.S. 317 (1976).

In localities where it is not routine practice to have preliminary hearings attended by a court reporter or stenographer, counsel should be sure to have a stenographer or recording device present and should move for payment of the cost by the state if the client is indigent.

11.5.4. *Restrictions on Prosecution Evidence*

In some jurisdictions, the prosecution's evidence at a preliminary examination is subject to the same general rules of admissibility that govern its evidence at trial (*see, e.g.,* N.M. DIST. CT. RULE CRIM. PRO. 5(B)(5); *State v. Sherry,* 233 Kan. 920, 929, 667 P.2d 367, 375 (1983)); in others, the trial rules apply with the exception that hearsay is admissible (*see, e.g.,* PA. RULE CRIM. PRO. 542(E); *but see Commonwealth v. McClellan,* 660 Pa. 81, 233 A.3d 717 (2020) (a bindover cannot be based solely on hearsay)) – or that some kinds of hearsay are admissible (*see, e.g.,* UTAH RULE EVID. 1102 (reliable hearsay); CAL. PENAL CODE § 872(b), *and Whitman v. Superior Court,* 54 Cal. 3d 1063, 820 P.2d 262, 2 Cal. Rptr. 2d 160 (1991); *People v. Olney,* 333 Mich. App. 575, 963 N.W.2d 383 (2020)); in still others, the magistrate may receive and base a bindover on any evidence s/he deems reliable (*State v. Brown,* 967 N.W.2d 797 (N.D. 2021)).

The jurisdictions also differ in regard to the admissibility of illegally obtained evidence. Some jurisdictions allow such evidence to be presented at a preliminary hearing. *See, e.g.,* FED. RULE CRIM. PRO. 5.1(e); *State v. Moats,* 156 Wis. 2d 74, 457 N.W.2d 299 (1990); *State v. Ayon,* 503 P.3d 405, 406, 2022-NMCA-003 (N.M. App. 2021), *cert. granted,* 2022-NMCERT-001 (case # S-1-SC-38937, January 11, 2022) ("the district court's authority at a preliminary hearing does not include the authority to determine the illegality of evidence"); *cf. State v. Lohnes,* 432 N.W.2d 77, 82 (S.D. 1988) ("In *State v. Reggio,* 84 S.D. 687, 176 N.W.2d 62 (1970), this court indicated that a probable cause determination at a preliminary hearing, based solely on illegally obtained evidence, would render the charge invalid. However, the *Reggio* court went on to assert that if there is other evidence to establish probable cause the charge will be upheld."). Other jurisdictions preclude it. *See, e.g., Grace v. Eighth Judicial District Court,* 132 Nev. 511, 513, 375 P.3d 1017, 1018 (2016) ("justice courts have express and limited inherent authority to suppress illegally obtained evidence during preliminary hearings"); *State v. Wilson*, 55 Hawai'i 314, 317, 519 P.2d 228, 230 (1974) ("We are of the opinion that in a . . . [preliminary hearing], the district court, a court of record, must adhere to the general rules of evidence which include objections to the admissibility of unconstitutionally seized evidence. Thus, the district court was correct in . . . excluding the unconstitutionally seized evidence although . . . [it lacked] authority [to entertain a motion to suppress as such]. To hold otherwise would allow the finding of probable cause that a felony had been committed upon illegally obtained evidence, a practice which violates the sanctions of the exclusionary rule. The district judge was bound by oath of office to uphold the Constitutions of the United States and the State of Hawaii. In our opinion the exclusionary rule is a sanction essential to upholding federal and state constitutional safeguards against unreasonable searches and seizures."); TENN. RULE CRIM. PRO. 5.1(a)(1), *and State v. Dixon*, 880 S.W.2d 696, 699 (Tenn. 1992) ("[A] general sessions court can suppress evidence incident to a preliminary hearing, but it cannot return the property suppressed if the district attorney general objects. . . . [A] ruling of the general sessions court cannot bar the State from submitting the evidence to the grand jury when it seeks an indictment for the same offense. . . . [T]he ruling of the general sessions court is not binding upon the criminal or circuit court if the grand jury returns an indictment against the accused. In other words, the criminal or circuit court must decide the admissibility of the evidence anew."); *cf. Massey v. Mullin*, 117 R.I. 272, 274, 366 A.2d 1144, 1145 (1976) ("We must now determine whether . . . a confession [taken in violation of *Miranda v. Arizona* (see § infra)] may be relied upon in determining that the 'proof of guilt is evident or the presumption great' and whether defendant is thus not entitled to bail as a matter of right. . . . [W]e hold that the denial of bail cannot be based on such a confession.") In still other jurisdictions, illegally obtained evidence must be excluded if, but only if, its illegality is not contestable. *Badillo v. Superior Court in and for City and County of San Francisco*, 46 Cal. 2d 269, 271-72, 294 P.2d 23, 24-25 (1956) ("In *Rogers v. Superior Court*, 46 Cal. 2d 3, 291 P.2d 929, 931, we held that a 'defendant has been held to answer without reasonable or probable cause if his commitment is based entirely on incompetent evidence', and accordingly, in such a case the trial court should grant a motion to set aside the information . . . , and if it does not do so, a peremptory writ of prohibition will issue to prohibit further proceedings. No problem is presented in applying this rule in cases involving searches and seizures in which the facts bearing on the legality of the search or seizure are undisputed and establish as a matter of law that the evidence is or is not admissible. In many cases, however, the evidence before the magistrate bearing on this issue may be in conflict or susceptible of conflicting inferences or consist only of the testimony of prosecution witnesses, and under these circumstances the court in ruling on a motion to set aside the information will frequently not be in a position to make a final determination as to the admissibility of the evidence. ¶ Accordingly, the information should not be set aside on the ground that essential evidence was illegally obtained if there is any substantial evidence or applicable presumption to support a contrary conclusion, and in such cases the ultimate decision on admissibility can be made at the trial on the basis of all of the evidence bearing on the issue.") *and People v. Butler*, 64 Cal. 2d 842, 415 P.2d 819, 52 Cal. Rptr. 4 (1966); *substantially in accord, State v. Mitchell*, 42 Ohio St. 2d 447, 450-51, 329 N.E.2d 682, 684 (1975) ("[I]n exercising the discretion inherent in a determination of probable cause, magistrates are aware that, at the trial level, questionable evidence will be tested. Therefore, evidence introduced at a preliminary hearing which is clearly excludable 'under the rules of evidence prevailing in criminal trials generally,' should, upon appropriate objection, be excluded by the magistrate in determining whether there is probable cause to believe that a crime has been committed by the accused. Evidence of doubtful constitutional validity may be accorded lesser weight in reaching such determination. But in neither event may such evidence be suppressed.").

Analytically, the first of these positions is assailable on constitutional grounds (federal or state, whichever of these constitutions renders the evidence illegally obtained) because it defies rationality to hold that evidence which cannot be used even to support a subsequent warrantless arrest or search (see § 25.42 *infra*) or a search warrant (see § 25.17.4 *infra*) can be used to support a bindover – which characteristically entails a longer period of detention than an initial warrantless arrest. As Justice Holmes put it in *Silverthorne Lumber Co. v. United States*, 251 U.S. 385, 392 (1920): "The essence of a provision forbidding the acquisition of evidence in a certain way is that not merely evidence so acquired shall not be used before the Court but that it shall not be used at all." In jurisdictions in which the recognized functions of the preliminary hearing include the weeding-out of prosecutions in which the evidence is too weak to justify a trial (see § 11.1.1 second paragraph *supra*), it is also assailable as inconsistent with this function. A preliminary-hearing process that permits a bindover to be based on evidence inadmissible at trial obviously fails to screen prosecutions in which there is no possibility of a sustainable conviction.

Where local rules or practice authorize the suppression or exclusion of illegally obtained evidence at preliminary hearings, pre-preliminary hearing discovery of materials needed to support claims of illegality should be available. *See Magallan v. Superior Court*, 192 Cal. App. 4th 1444, 121 Cal. Rptr.3d 841 (2011), summarized in § 18.7.3 *infra*.

11.6. *Procedures To Challenge Denial of Rights to or at a Preliminary Hearing*

11.6.1. *Before the Hearing*

Counsel who, prior to the stage of bind-over, is dissatisfied with the preliminary arraignment or preliminary examination procedures should apply to the court in which the case will ultimately be tried for an order to rectify the deficiencies. In most jurisdictions the appropriate form of action will be a prerogative writ proceeding – prohibition or mandamus – directed to the magistrate or to the prosecutor. For example, if a magistrate refuses to subpoena defense witnesses or refuses a defense request for free transcription of the testimony in the case of an indigent, counsel should seek mandamus to compel the magistrate to provide these services or prohibition to restrain the examination without them.

In some jurisdictions a bill in equity is used in lieu of the prerogative writs. In others, a simple motion in the court of record is entertained.

If the prosecutor obtains a continuance and if defense counsel suspects that the prosecutor is going to the grand jury, counsel may seek mandamus to compel the magistrate to proceed forthwith with the preliminary examination or prohibition to restrain the prosecutor from presenting the case to the grand jury before the examination has been had. If counsel's objective is to obtain a hearing promptly, s/he can file either a mandamus or a *habeas corpus* petition (see § 3.8.4 *supra*) complaining that the date set for the hearing – or the date to which the hearing is adjourned or continued – will result in excessive delay.

If a preliminary arraignment or a preliminary examination is being unduly delayed by the real or supposed unavailability of a magistrate to conduct it, counsel should also consider applying to one of the judges of the court of record to conduct the proceedings in the judge's capacity as a committing magistrate. See § 11.6.2 *infra*.

11.6.2. *After the Hearing or Bind-over*

If counsel is retained or appointed following the preliminary hearing stage, s/he should immediately ascertain from the client, the prosecutor, or court records whether both a preliminary arraignment and a preliminary examination have been held. (Since the client is unlikely to know what a "preliminary examination" is or to distinguish it from a preliminary arraignment, the best question to ask the client is whether there was a hearing at which people took the witness stand and testified.)

If any part of a preliminary hearing has been held, ordinarily counsel should have the stenographic notes transcribed or, if the client is an indigent, move for their transcription at state expense. See § 11.5.3 *supra*; § 11.8.7 *infra*. If the transcript shows defects in the hearing that counsel wishes to challenge or if there has been no hearing and no valid waiver or if there is no transcript of the hearing and no valid waiver of a transcript, counsel should decide whether s/he wants a preliminary hearing at this time. (See § 11.7.3 *infra*.) If s/he decides that s/he does want a preliminary hearing, one or more of several procedural devices may be available. First, in many jurisdictions courts of record are given statutory authority to conduct a "court of inquest" or their judges are empowered to sit as committing magistrates. Where this authority exists, a motion to the trial court to have one of its judges conduct a preliminary hearing that will afford the defendant the rights that s/he has heretofore been denied seems appropriate. See the discussion of the implications of *Manuel v. City of Joliet, Ill.*, 580 U.S. 357 (2017), in § 11.4 *supra*. Second, in jurisdictions where *habeas corpus* is traditionally available to review the magistrate's decision to bind a defendant over, the writ would seem equally appropriate to challenge denial of, or procedural defects in, the preliminary hearing. *See, e.g., Sheriff of Washoe County v. Vasile*, 96 Nev. 5, 604 P.2d 809 (1980). Third, a motion to dismiss the indictment or information may be the simplest and most effective procedure in some states. *See, e.g., State v. Essman*, 98 Ariz. 228, 403 P.2d 540 (1965). Elsewhere, a motion to quash the bind-over or the magistrate's transcript, to dismiss any outstanding charging paper, and to remand the case to the magistrate for preliminary hearing would seem appropriate. (*Gerstein v. Pugh*, 420 U.S. 103 (1975), described in § 11.2 *supra*, does not appear to permit an attack on a charging paper upon the sole ground that *Gerstein*'s requirement of a Fourth Amendment probable cause determination has not been satisfied. For that particular defect, standing alone, *habeas corpus* is the exclusive remedy. *See id.* at 119. If, however, any *other* federal constitutional rights have been infringed by proceedings at the preliminary arraignment or the preliminary examination (see §§ 11.4, 11.6 *supra*), a motion to dismiss or quash the charging papers is in order. *See Hamilton v. Alabama*, 368 U.S. 52 (1961); *Coleman v. Alabama*, 399 U.S. 1, 10-11 (1970) (plurality opinion).)

11.7. *Defensive Conduct of the Preliminary Arraignment*

11.7.1. *Pleading*

The general nature of the proceedings at preliminary arraignment is described in §§ 2.3.3, 2.3.4, 11.1.2 *supra*. A few points deserve further mention here.

In some jurisdictions, the defendant is asked to plead to the complaint at the preliminary arraignment. In other jurisdictions, s/he does not plead but simply elects to have or waive preliminary examination. Where pleading is required, local practice differs regarding the significance of a plea of guilty. It is sometimes treated merely as a waiver of preliminary examination, authorizing the defendant's bind-over without the presentation of evidence by the prosecution. Sometimes it is treated as a waiver of both preliminary examination and indictment in indictable cases (see § 2.4.3 *supra*; § 12.1 *infra*). Sometimes it is additionally treated as an indication by the defendant that s/he intends to plead guilty in the trial court to which s/he is bound over. The defendant may subsequently switch signals and plead not guilty in the court of record; but if s/he does so without good reason, the prosecutor and the trial judge will be displeased and will remember their displeasure at the time of sentencing in the event of a conviction. (These effects of a guilty plea to a complaint charging a felony or a misdemeanor must be distinguished from the effect of the defendant's plea of guilty to a summary offense that is a lesser included offense of the one charged in the complaint. Since a summary offense is within the dispositive jurisdiction of the magistrate (see §§ 2.2.4-2.2.5 *supra*), the defendant is convicted and sentenced by the magistrate upon this latter plea, and the greater charges are then dismissed.) Some jurisdictions do, while others do not, recognize special pleas (see §§ 14.5-14.6 *infra*) at preliminary arraignment. Where they are recognized, they are ordinarily required to be entered prior to a general plea of not guilty, or they are waived (*cf.* §§ 14.5, 14.7 *infra*), with the consequence either (1) that they may not later be made in the trial court or (2) that they may later be made only upon leave granted within the trial court's discretion. Motions to dismiss the complaint for failure to state an offense within the jurisdiction of the court (*cf.* § 20.4 *infra*) or on the ground of substantive unconstitutionality of the statute underlying the charge (*cf.* § 20.1 subdivision 10, *infra*), or for technical deficiencies (see § 11.7.2 *infra*) usually must also be made before a plea of not guilty is entered. Obviously, careful consideration of local practice is required prior to pleading.

Counsel who is first appointed at preliminary arraignment should request adequate time to interview the defendant and to do whatever investigation and research appear to be necessary before pleading. See §§ 3.14-3.18, 3.23.3 *supra*. In particular, counsel should not succumb to browbeating by a hurried magistrate who urges counsel to "go ahead and enter a safe plea of not guilty," since such a plea may, in fact, be far from safe. The decision whether to demand or to waive preliminary examination also requires thoughtful consideration. See § 11.7.3 *infra*.

Some courts appoint counsel for indigent defendants at preliminary arraignment only *after* the defendant (1) has pleaded, (2) has demanded or waived a preliminary examination, or (3) has done both. Counsel appointed at this juncture should immediately inform the court that s/he wants to consult with the client and will also need time to do additional research and investigation in order to advise the client whether to stand upon or to change the pleas and elections already made. If counsel then concludes that the defendant's pleas or elections were improvident, counsel should move to vacate them on the ground that the defendant's Sixth Amendment right to counsel at preliminary arraignment (see §§ 3.23.3, 11.5.1 *supra*) would be violated by holding the defendant to any decisions which s/he made prior to the appointment of an attorney. *See Hamilton v. Alabama*, 368 U.S. 52, 53-54 (1961).

11.7.2. *Technical Objections*

Objections to the form of a complaint may be made at preliminary arraignment by a motion to dismiss the complaint as insufficient or defective on its face. Also in some States the magistrate's jurisdiction depends on the validity of the arrest, with the result that a successful attack on the arrest (see § 25.7 *infra*) requires dismissal of the complaint.

These technical defenses should be raised very sparingly. In most instances the defects can be cured by the filing of a new complaint or by a rearrest, and the defendant gains nothing of substance. In fact, s/he may have to post new and higher bail for being vexatious. On the other hand, local rules may sometimes require that certain objections be taken or that certain motions be made at the preliminary arraignment in order to preserve the right to make the contentions involved subsequently at trial or on appeal.

11.7.3. *The Decision Whether to Demand or Waive Preliminary Examination*

Defense counsel should not ordinarily waive preliminary examination. It provides unique opportunities for discovery of the prosecution's case. See § 11.4 *supra*; § 11.8.2 *infra*. Waiver of the examination is usually appropriate only in one of the following situations:

(1) The chances of a defense victory are slim and the taking of evidence would benefit the prosecution because one or more of its witnesses will probably become unavailable by the time of trial (because of declining health, plans to leave the jurisdiction, or other circumstances) and the prosecution would have a credible argument that the witness's preliminary-examination testimony is admissible at trial on the ground of the witness's unavailability and the defendant's opportunity to cross-examine the witness amply at the preliminary examination. *See Crawford v. Washington*, 541 U.S. 36, 57 (2004) (prosecution may be able to introduce, at trial, recorded "preliminary hearing testimony" of a currently unavailable witness "if the defendant had an adequate opportunity to cross-examine" the witness on the pertinent subject matter at the preliminary hearing). *Compare People v. Fry*, 92 P.3d 970, 972 (Colo. 2004) (preliminary hearing testimony of an unavailable prosecution witness was not admissible at trial "[b]ecause preliminary hearings in Colorado do not present an adequate opportunity for cross-examination").

(2) The prosecution has a solid case, and the chances are less than slight that a preliminary examination will produce anything but high bail and intensification of the hostility of prosecution witnesses. Frequently, with the passage of time a complainant will mellow, but once s/he has testified under oath, s/he is unlikely to change the story and is impeachable if s/he does. Moreover, once s/he has testified for the prosecution, s/he may refuse to be interviewed by anyone representing the defendant's interests. See § 9.14 *supra*.

(3) The likely adverse publicity outweighs any possible gain from the examination.

(4) Counsel learns of a defect in the prosecution's case that, in all probability, would not be corrected before the case went to trial if not brought to the prosecutor's attention at the preliminary examination. This may happen especially in metropolitan areas where the prosecutor's office is handling an enormous caseload and relies primarily upon the police to make sure that all needed witnesses and essential elements of a case are produced at trial.

(5) The defendant is undercharged. If facts known to counsel suggest that the defendant is guilty of more, or more serious, offenses than those charged in the complaint, counsel may want to avoid a preliminary examination that could alert the prosecutor to the additional or more serious offenses.

Other exceptional reasons to waive may occasionally appear. When in doubt whether to waive or demand the examination, counsel should demand it.

11.8. *Defensive Conduct of the Preliminary Examination*

11.8.1. *The Nature of the Proceedings at Preliminary Examination*

The preliminary examination is in most respects conducted like a trial. The rules of evidence are ordinarily enforced (although counsel handling a federal matter should note FED. RULE EVID. 1101(d)(3)), often with some relaxation of the hearsay rule. (Indeed, in some jurisdictions magistrates may bind a defendant over on nothing but hearsay evidence.)

The prosecution must make a showing of probable cause of every element of the offense and of the defendant's identity as its perpetrator. The *corpus delicti* must ordinarily be proved before any admissions of the defendant may be received in evidence, but the magistrate has some discretion to allow variance from this order of proof. Compare § 26.17 *infra.*

Witnesses are questioned in the ordinary fashion, and real evidence is admitted as exhibits. Cross-examination of witnesses is permitted, although some magistrates tend to limit its scope to a narrower compass than would be allowed at trial. See § 11.8.3 *infra.* Sequestration of witnesses is allowed within the sound discretion of the magistrate.

There is modification of these rules in varying degrees in some jurisdictions, and local practice must be checked. In some localities, preliminary examination in misdemeanor cases is conducted for the prosecution by a police officer rather than a law-trained prosecutor; here, the proceedings are somewhat more informal, and the magistrate plays a greater role in questioning witnesses.

11.8.2. *Cross-examining for Discovery and Impeachment*

Defense counsel has three principal goals at the preliminary examination: (1) to secure the dismissal or reduction of the charges against the defendant if the prosecution does not meet its burden of proof; (2) to put the testimony of the prosecution witnesses on record in a way that makes them most impeachable at trial; and (3) to discover as much of the prosecutor's case as possible.

Once the prosecution has made out its *prima facie* case, there is no great likelihood that cross-examination will destroy it so completely as to warrant a dismissal. Therefore, counsel's focus narrows to the twin objectives of discovery and of nailing down impeachable prosecution testimony. As a practical matter, these are the major objectives of the defense from the outset of most preliminary examinations, since most magistrates will predictably find probable cause to bind most defendants over most of the time.

Frequently, counsel may find that s/he is working at cross-purposes in seeking to discover and to lay a foundation for impeachment simultaneously. S/he will obviously have to accommodate these objectives in particular situations with an eye to which objective is more important in dealing with an individual prosecution witness. If counsel vigorously cross-examines the witness, in an effort to get a contradiction or concession on record, the witness will normally dig in and give a minimum of information in an effort to save his or her testimonial position; and, more than likely, s/he will be uncooperative if counsel thereafter attempts to interview the witness prior to trial. On the other hand, if counsel engages the witness in routine examination, amiable and ranging, counsel may be able to pick up many clues for investigation and for planning of the defense. Of course, some witnesses resent any kind of cross-examination. If counsel thinks that this type of witness is lying or confused, counsel may wish to pin the witness down. Under no circumstances, however, should counsel educate the witness about the weaknesses of his or her testimony. To avoid mutual education by prosecution witnesses, counsel should ordinarily ask that all witnesses be excluded from the courtroom during one another's testimony. See § 34.6 *infra*.

The probable utility of cross-examining for impeachment depends almost as much on the prosecutor as on the witness. If the prosecutor is one who prepares witnesses as carefully for preliminary examination as for trial, the likelihood of getting anything out of the witness that will be useful to impeach him or her at trial is small. Most prosecutors, however, do not have the time to prepare witnesses thoroughly for the preliminary examination, with the result that the examination provides a unique opportunity to catch the prosecution witnesses, on record, with their guards down. On the other hand, the importance of using the preliminary examination for discovery depends largely upon the amount of funds available to conduct an independent investigation and the liberality of practice with respect to other criminal pretrial discovery devices in the locality. Investigation can be very expensive, and counsel must recognize that most clients simply cannot afford it. The investigative services made available to appointed counsel in indigent cases are generally woefully inadequate. As for other discovery procedures, it is fair to say that although there is a trend toward more liberal discovery, the trend has not yet gone very far – and *least* far in the area of defense access to the statements of prosecution witnesses. For a fuller discussion of pretrial discovery, see Chapter 18 *infra*. Counsel at the preliminary examination stage should therefore be careful to avoid undue optimism about what s/he will learn later if s/he lets this opportunity for some discovery go by.

11.8.3. *Resisting Limitations on Cross-examination*

Many magistrates allow defense counsel very grudging room for cross-examination at a preliminary examination on the reasoning that guilt is not at issue, that the prosecution needs only show a case the jury could believe, and that, therefore, nothing which cross-examination might disclose is relevant.

The theoretical answers to this reasoning are (a) that it would be plainly relevant if cross-examination forced the witness to withdraw his or her testimony on direct examination and (b) that the statute expressly permitting the defendant to cross-examine prosecution witnesses, call defense witnesses, or both at preliminary examination (as most statutes do) assumes that the magistrate is not to restrict the inquiry to a bare-bones hearing of the prosecution's evidence, untested for credibility. (Most of the cases cited in § 11.4 *supra* contain quotable language endorsing the right of the defense to conduct a probing cross-examination at the preliminary examination. See particularly the two *Coleman* opinions, *Hawkins*, and *Hodge*.)

Magistrates, however, like to push the hearing along and will often not be persuaded by these theories. Counsel should continue to attempt to cross-examine, as long as s/he can decently do so, in order to make clear for the record the extent of the limitations imposed on cross-examination. S/he should then respectfully ask the magistrate whether all cross-examination is going to be disallowed and, if not, what areas the magistrate is not going to let counsel go into. If the magistrate says that s/he cannot tell until counsel asks the questions, counsel should resume attempts to cross-examine. Eventually the magistrate will shut counsel off altogether. Counsel should then object to the denial of cross-examination on the grounds of the client's statutory right to a preliminary examination (§ 11.3 *supra*) and the statutory and constitutional rights to cross-examination and to confrontation (§ 11.5.2 *supra*; see §§ 18.9.2.3, 37.1 *infra*), effective representation by counsel (§ 11.5.1 *supra*; see § 18.9.2.1 *infra*), and a fair hearing (see §§ 18.9.2.3, 39.1 *infra*), as well as on the ground that the statute giving defendants a right to present testimony envisions that the magistrate will hear both sides of the case. The record should be clear that this objection has been overruled if it has. Counsel is now in a position to challenge the propriety of the bind-over by the procedures enumerated in § 11.6.2 *supra* if s/he can convince a higher court that upon one or another of these legal grounds, s/he had a right to cross-examine which was unduly restricted.

An unfortunate *dictum* in a plurality opinion of the Supreme Court appears to accept, without federal constitutional quarrel, a state-law practice permitting the magistrate "to terminate the preliminary hearing once probable cause is established" (*Adams v. Illinois*, 405 U.S. 278, 282 (1972)). This language, predictably, will be seized upon by lower courts as giving an examining magistrate virtually unlimited power to curtail defensive cross-examination. But the Supreme Court did not, in fact, have before it in the *Adams* case any instance of curtailment of the defensive conduct of a preliminary hearing. The plurality opinion was merely noting, as relevant to the question of the retroactivity of the constitutional requirement of appointed counsel at preliminary examination (see § 11.5.1 *supra*), that "because of limitations upon the use of the preliminary hearing for discovery and impeachment purposes, counsel cannot be as effectual as at trial" (405 U.S. at 282). So it is fair to urge that the *Adams dictum* must be read narrowly: as allowing magisterial discretion to curb cross-examination pursued "for discovery and impeachment purposes" only, "once probable cause is established" (*id.*), but not as authorizing the restriction of cross-examination designed to test the foundation of the probable cause showing itself, even if the cross-examination does also provide some discovery. For it seems plain that if, with one exception not presently relevant, a *parolee* has a right "to confrontation and cross-examination" at a preliminary parole-revocation hearing (*Morrissey v. Brewer*, 408 U.S. 471, 487 (1972)), a criminal defendant has rights that are at least as ample at a preliminary examination, which is "part of a criminal prosecution" (*id.* at 480). *See also Gagnon v. Scarpelli*, 411 U.S. 778, 781-82, 788-90 (1973); and see § 18.9.2.3 *infra*. (*Gerstein v. Pugh*, 420 U.S. 103 (1975), does not hold to the contrary. See § 11.5.2 *supra*.)

Certainly, counsel is on far firmer ground when s/he can justify his or her questions on cross-examination as going to probe the prosecution's showing of probable cause than when they have no justification except discovery. Only when there is no possibility of successfully urging that a line of questioning goes to probable cause and, therefore, that it is within the purview of the classic functions of preliminary examination (see § 11.1.1 *supra*) should counsel attempt to justify it on the basis of a right to discovery as such (see Chapter 18 *infra*; *cf.* § 11.4 *supra*), pointing out, if possible, why in the case at bar, unlike *Adams*, there are no effective "alternative procedures" for discovery (405 U.S. at 282).

11.8.4. *Calling Adverse Witnesses*

Because the prosecution needs do nothing more than make a *prima facie* case at the preliminary examination, it will frequently call only some of the witnesses whom it plans to use at trial. When persons whom defense counsel has identified as potential prosecution witnesses refuse to be interviewed by the defense, counsel may want to serve them with defense subpoenas for the slated date of the preliminary examination, approach them before court, and offer them the opportunity to talk with counsel – or with counsel's investigator – outside of the courtroom instead of having to appear in court. This cage-rattling technique can produce useful discovery. Similarly, issuing subpoenas *duces tecum* for the production of records, other documents and physical objects can provide a means for prying these materials out of the hands of uncooperative custodians at an earlier stage than the formal discovery process discussed in Chapter 18.

However, two cautions need to be observed here – one simple and obvious, the other more complex.

First, counsel should not subpoena any person or material that the prosecutor is otherwise unlikely to identify as a potential source of relevant information.

Second, counsel will seldom be advised to actually put an adverse witness on the stand, as distinguished from releasing him or her from the defense subpoena after out-of-court questioning. Most jurisdictions continue to follow the traditional rules of witness examination that prohibit a direct examiner from asking leading questions or impeaching his or her own witness, and most jurisdictions apply the same restrictions at preliminary hearings as at trials. Under these conditions, calling an unfriendly witness is a bad gamble: counsel will be handicapped against extracting any useful testimony, and anything useful that s/he does extract will be exposed to deconstruction or reconstruction by the prosecutor's use of leading questions and impeachment on cross. Consequently, counsel should ordinarily refrain from putting any adverse witness on the stand unless (a) the evidence rules applicable to preliminary examinations in counsel's jurisdiction do *not* forbid direct examiners to lead and impeach their own witnesses, or (b) the presiding magistrate is known to be liberal in granting defense requests to declare witnesses hostile (see § 39.29 *infra*). (Counsel's best chances for getting witnesses declared hostile are (i) situations in which a witness has publicly demonstrated strong personal animosity toward the defendant apart from the events giving rise to the criminal charge, and (ii) situations in which other prosecution witnesses have recounted incriminating hearsay declarations of the witness. In the latter situations, counsel can invoke the defendant's state-law right to contest the prosecutor's *prima facie* case and can also make some mileage out of the constitutional rights of confrontation and Due Process (see § 11.5.2 *supra*; §§ 18.9.2.3, 18.9.2.4 *infra*). Nevertheless, most magistrates will almost always exercise their discretion to refuse to allow defense counsel to use hostile-witnesses questioning techniques at a preliminary examination.)

11.8.5. *Calling Favorable Defense Witnesses*

Counsel should not present favorable defense testimony at a preliminary examination unless there is the strongest likelihood that the defendant will be discharged after it is presented. See § 11.1.1 *supra*. This is a very rare situation because the prosecution's burden of proving a *prima facie* case is not exacting, most magistrates are prosecution-friendly, and they will disregard any defense evidence on the theory that its credibility is a matter for the jury or the trial judge to determine.

Before making the rare decision to present defense testimony, counsel should always ask for the dismissal of the charge based upon the inadequacy of the prosecution's evidence. Argument on the question of dismissal at this point, even if dismissal is refused, will often reveal whether the judge would be inclined to dismiss the case on the basis of the defense that counsel is considering putting on. If not, counsel would be foolish to offer up his or her potential trial witnesses for pretrial cross-examination by the prosecution. *Cf.* § 11.8.2 *supra*.

11.8.6. *Objecting to Inadmissible Evidence*

To the extent that local practice makes the rules of evidence applicable to preliminary examinations (see § 11.8.1 *supra*), counsel will sometimes have the opportunity to object to prosecution evidence as inadmissible. Ordinarily s/he should object only if (a) there is a good chance that the prosecution will fail to make a *prima facie* case if the objectionable evidence is excluded; (b) counsel is sure s/he already knows everything s/he could learn from the evidence; or (c) the evidence is likely to be seriously damaging, and either (i) an objection is required under local rules in order to preserve a claim of its inadmissibility at trial (see § 11.7.2 *supra*), or (ii) there is substantial reason to believe that the witness may become unavailable to the prosecution by the time of trial and that the prosecution would be able to introduce the witness's preliminary hearing testimony at trial (see § 11.7.3 subdivision one *supra*). If the prosecution has a facially sufficient case, counsel will need investigative leads to defend against it. Helpful discovery can be obtained by permitting prosecution witnesses at preliminary hearings to make all the hearsay and other inadmissible statements that they want. Even more can often be obtained by cross-examining them on these statements. By allowing the testimony to come in, counsel can also lay a foundation for earlier objection at trial when the direct examination of a witness starts down an impermissible track. Referring to the transcript of the witness' testimony at the preliminary hearing, counsel will be able to demonstrate to the trial judge exactly where the prosecutor's line of questioning is headed. See § 40.4.2 *infra*.

The tactic of nonobjection can sometimes turn out to be a two-edged sword, enabling the prosecutor, as well as defense counsel, to learn previously unknown facts. This consideration will weigh more or less heavily against defense counsel's use of the tactic, depending upon how careless or careful the prosecutor is known to be in his or her investigation and preparation both before and after the preliminary examination.

11.8.7. *Obtaining a Transcript*

Many of the tactical suggestions just made have assumed that there will be a reporter or stenographer transcribing the testimony. Whether a court reporter routinely attends preliminary examinations depends on local practice. Counsel should not assume that a reporter will be in attendance but should inquire. If local practice does not provide for a court reporter, the expense of a stenographer should be considered by the defense. Alternatively, the magistrate can be asked to allow counsel to operate a recording device at the defense table. Either a court reporter's transcript or a defense recording will usually serve as an invaluable aid in counsel's preparation for cross-examination at trial. The added advantage of a transcript is its greater utility at trial to impeach a witness who alters his or her testimony. A defense-made recording of the witness's preliminary-examination testimony will be subject to prosecutorial quibbles about accuracy and intelligibility when offered for impeachment purposes at trial.

In some jurisdictions where preliminary hearing testimony is routinely recorded, it is nevertheless not transcribed unless specially ordered by a party. Again, counsel should inquire whether this is the situation and should order a transcript if necessary.

Where both recording and transcription are routine, the transcripts are usually forwarded several days or weeks after the hearing to the office of the clerk of court. Counsel may wish to examine the hearing transcript in the clerk's office before deciding whether to order a defense copy. *See, e.g.*, FED. RULE CRIM. PRO. 5.1(g).

If the client is unable to afford a transcript (or a stenographer, when testimony is not reported) counsel should request transcription (or reporting and transcription, as the case may be) at state expense. In the event that local law does not give counsel a right to what s/he wants, s/he should invoke the federal Equal Protection and Due Process doctrines summarized in §§ 5.2, 5.3, 11.5.3 *supra*. Procedures for enforcing an indigent client's rights under these doctrines and/or state law are discussed in § 11.6 *supra*.

11.9. *Continuances*

In a few jurisdictions, a continuance of the preliminary hearing of a defendant in custody may be made only with his or her personal assent. The more ordinary practice permits continuances in the discretion of the magistrate upon the application of either prosecution or defense. That discretion is doubtless now limited by *Gerstein v. Pugh*, 420 U.S. 103 (1975), and *County of Riverside v. McLaughlin*, 500 U.S. 44 (1991), see § 11.2 *supra*; and the citation of *Gerstein* and *McLaughlin* in opposition to a prosecution-sought continuance is appropriate *unless* local law can be construed to permit the judge to make a probable cause determination upon affidavits without a full evidentiary hearing.

The prosecutorial tactic of using a continuance to permit presentation of the case to the grand jury is discussed in § 11.4 *supra*, along with objections that can be made to this tactic. If defense counsel is ready for the hearing and if the prosecutor seeks a continuance during a period when the grand jury is in session, counsel should oppose the continuance except on a representation by the prosecutor in open court that s/he will not present the matter to the grand jury. If the prosecutor refuses to make such a representation and the continuance is nonetheless granted, counsel has made a record on which s/he can seek either mandamus against the magistrate to proceed forthwith or prohibition or an injunction against the prosecutor to forbid the prosecutor's presenting bills to the grand jury. See § 11.6.1 *supra*.

In other situations in which the magistrate grants the prosecution a continuance that defense counsel believes is excessive, counsel may challenge it for abuse of discretion by mandamus or by *habeas corpus* if the client is in custody. See §§ 3.8.4, 11.6.1 *supra*. Counsel should consider, alternatively, asking a judge of the court of record to assume jurisdiction as a committing magistrate and to conduct the examination. See *id.* and § 11.6.2 *supra*. Or counsel may be willing to agree to a continuance desired by the prosecution in exchange for the prosecutor's recommendation of favorable terms of bail and a promise not to go to the grand jury during the continuance.

The defense itself may want a continuance for various reasons – to investigate and prepare the case; to let a complainant's temper cool off; to demonstrate to the prosecutor that a defendant released on bail is behaving as a law-abiding citizen or has gotten a job or is starting to make restitution or that some other change of circumstances warrants the favorable exercise of the prosecutor's discretion to drop, reduce, or divert the contemplated charges (see §§ 8.2.2-8.2.4, 8.3.4, 8.4, 8.6 *supra*). When counsel is unprepared to conduct the preliminary examination and can show adequate justification for being unprepared, a defense request for a continuance may invoke the defendant's federal Sixth and Fourteenth Amendment rights to counsel (see §§ 3.23.3, 11.5.1, 11.7.1 *supra*) as well as the magistrate's state-law discretion. During the period of any continuance, the magistrate should be asked to release the defendant on bail or on some form of conditional release. See §§ 2.3.4, 3.8.3, 4.2-4.10 *supra*. If a defendant is not R.O.R.'d and cannot make bail, the magistrate may be asked to hold the defendant in the courthouse cellblock or to commit the defendant to jail rather than leave the defendant in the police lockup where s/he will remain in the hands of the investigating officers.

11.10. *Bind-over; Review*

The defendant may ordinarily be bound over to the grand jury or for trial for any offense shown by the evidence, even though not charged in the complaint. This practice, although traditionally accepted in many jurisdictions, should be subject to challenge on Due Process grounds, as depriving the defendant of fair notice and an opportunity to defend at the preliminary examination. *State v. Colvin*, 81 Ariz. 388, 307 P.2d 98 (1957); and see § 18.9.2.2 *infra*; *cf.* § 11.4 *supra*. "Few constitutional principles are more firmly established than a defendant's right to be heard on the specific charges of which he is accused" (*Dunn v. United States*, 442 U.S. 100, 106 (1979); *see also Cole v. Arkansas*, 333 U.S. 196 (1948); *Presnell v. Georgia*, 439 U.S. 14 (1978) (per curiam)); and this principle is not restricted to the trial stage of a criminal case (*see Jenkins v. McKeithen*, 395 U.S. 411, 429 (1969) (plurality opinion) (discussed in § 10.2 *supra*); *Morrissey v. Brewer*, 408 U.S. 471, 486-87 (1972) (preliminary hearing in parole revocation proceedings)).

In some jurisdictions, the bind-over is essentially unreviewable. In others, a motion to dismiss the consequent information may lie in a nonindictable case on the ground that the preliminary examination transcript fails to show probable cause to hold the defendant to answer or probable cause to charge a particular offense. In still others, *habeas corpus* or a motion to quash the bind-over or the magistrate's transcript is available to review the magistrate's finding of probable cause. *See, e.g., Commonwealth v. McClelland*, 660 Pa. 81, 233 A.3d 717 (2020); *Woodall v. Sheriff, Clark County*, 95 Nev. 218, 591 P.2d 1144 (1979).

Ordinarily the issue on the writ or motion is decided on the basis of the preliminary examination transcript, since the magistrate's order to commit the defendant for court was based on that record. In some States, however, the *habeas corpus* court will hold its own hearing on the question of probable cause.

The simple admission of inadmissible evidence at a preliminary examination is not usually sufficient to sustain the vacating of the bind-over on motion or *habeas corpus* unless the remaining admissible evidence fails to support a finding of probable cause. But the admission of unconstitutionally obtained evidence at the hearing may require that the bind-over be vacated: The analysis in § 20.3.3 *infra* regarding the applicability of constitutional exclusionary rules to the grand jury applies *a fortiori* to preliminary examinations.

Defense counsel's decision to proceed with a motion to dismiss or with *habeas* involves some of the same considerations as the decision to move to dismiss a complaint before the magistrate for technical reasons (see § 11.7.2 *supra*). Because the prosecution can rearrest and present evidence that it neglected or did not deem necessary at the first hearing, a ruling by a court of record invalidating a bind-over may give the defendant only a Pyrrhic victory, the results of which are (A) that s/he must go through the arrest process again and post new bail and (B) that the prosecution is alerted to defects in its case while there is still time for it to cure them before jeopardy attaches (see § 20.8 *infra*; see also §§ 17.5.2, 40.8.4 *infra*). As a matter of probabilities, though, the likelihood of rearrest is considerably less when counsel successfully overturns a bind-over than when s/he successfully urges some technical objection before the magistrate.

Counsel should be alert to the consideration that in some jurisdictions the scope of review of the magistrate's bind-over is broader on *habeas corpus* than on a motion to quash. When this is the case and when *habeas corpus* is available only to applicants in actual custody – that is, when state practice does not follow federal case law recognizing bail status as "custody" for *habeas corpus* purposes (see § 28.5.4 *infra*) – counsel may well be advised not to post bail at the preliminary hearing but to apply for bail in the *habeas* case after filing the petition for the writ.

11.11. *Discharge; Rearrest*

If it appears at the preliminary examination that there is no probable cause to believe that an offense was committed or no probable cause to believe that the defendant committed it, the magistrate "discharges" the defendant from custody. Following such a discharge, counsel should ask the magistrate to order the defendant's arrest record expunged or, alternatively, marked to reflect that the defendant was discharged for want of probable cause upon preliminary examination. See § 47.6 *infra*.

When the prosecutor disagrees with a magistrate's discharge (or if new evidence is discovered subsequent to the discharge), the prosecutor may order the defendant rearrested and presented for a second hearing, usually before a different magistrate. In some localities, by rule or practice, this second hearing is held before a higher ranking member of the judiciary – the chief magistrate or a judge of the court of record sitting as a committing magistrate. Although the rearrest practice is lawful, it is disfavored by many judges, and defense counsel may properly wear an air of abused innocence to the second hearing. Obtaining a transcript of the first hearing (see § 11.8.7 *supra*) is especially useful in these cases, since the prosecution can be made to look bad, whether its evidence is the same or different.

Chapter 12

Defensive Procedures Between Bind-over and the Filing of the Charging Paper

A. *Matters Relating to the Grand Jury*

12.1. *Introduction to Grand Jury Requirements and Procedures*

Most States, by constitution or statute, require the prosecution of some or all serious crimes by indictment. The Fifth Amendment to the federal Constitution similarly requires that prosecutions for any "capital, or otherwise infamous crime [in the federal courts be by] . . . indictment." The requirement is conceived principally as a protection to the defendant, and s/he may waive it. *See, e.g., People v. Myers*, 32 N.Y.3d 18, 20, 109 N.E.3d 555, 556, 84 N.Y.S.3d 406, 407 (2018) (upholding the validity of a defendant's waiver of the right to indictment "[b]ecause Steven Myers and the court supervising his waiver followed" the applicable procedure – under which defendants can "waive that right by signing a written instrument in open court in the presence of their counsel" – but the Court of Appeals "emphasize[s] . . . that the better practice . . . is for courts to elicit defendants' understanding of the significance of the right being waived, to minimize future challenges to the effectiveness of the waiver"). Indictments are the product of a grand jury. See § 2.4.3 *supra*.

Grand juries are convened, ordinarily at the outset of, or shortly preceding, each criminal term of court and are composed of a number of citizens (usually 15 to 23) selected by statutorily prescribed methods (see §§ 12.3, 32.3 *infra*) and possessing statutorily prescribed qualifications (usually age, residence, "good moral character"). There are also a few nonstatutory restrictions on juror selection practices and nonstatutory grounds of disqualification:

(1)   The Equal Protection Clause of the Fourteenth Amendment to the federal Constitution and parallel provisions of state constitutions forbid systematic exclusion of racial, ethnic, religious, or economic groups. See § 12.1.1, 12.3 *infra*.

(2)   Statutes or common-law judicial decisions in some, but not all, jurisdictions require that grand jurors be unbiased. *E.g.,* ARIZ. REV. STAT. § 21-211 and ARIZ. RULE CRIM. PRO. 12.2; *State v. Murphy*, 110 N.J. 20, 29-33, 538 A.2d 1235, 1239-41 (1988) ("We believe that the guarantee of an indictment by grand jury, enshrined in our State and federal constitutions, now means more than indictment by a body that may have prejudged the case. . . .¶ . . . We are satisfied that the procedures established in New Jersey by statute and by rule to implement the constitutional right to indictment contemplate indictment by an unbiased grand jury. ¶ . . . Accordingly, we now hold that, as an officer of the court, the prosecuting attorney has a responsibility to bring to the attention of the presiding judge any evidence of partiality or bias that could affect the impartial deliberations of a grand juror.").

(3)   The Fourteenth Amendment's Due Process Clause and parallel guarantees of state

constitutions may impose some, albeit not stringent, restrictions on service by grand jurors who have been prejudiced against a defendant through adverse newspaper publicity and the like. *See Beck v. Washington*, 369 U.S. 541, 546 (1962) (dictum). *Cf.* § 32.1 subdivision (1) *infra*.

12.1.1. *Constitutional Protections Against Discrimination in Grand Jury Selection*

The Fourteenth Amendment's Equal Protection Clause prohibits systematic exclusion of racial, ethnic, religious, or economic groups from jury service. *Coleman v. Alabama*, 389 U.S. 22 (1967), and cases cited (African Americans); *Turner v. Fouche*, 396 U.S. 346, 356-61 (1970) (same); *Hernandez v. Texas*, 347 U.S. 475 (1954) (Mexican-Americans); *Castaneda v. Partida*, 430 U.S. 482 (1977) (same); *Schowgurow v. State*, 240 Md. 121, 213 A.2d 475 (1965) (atheists); *Labat v. Bennett*, 365 F.2d 698 (5th Cir. 1966) (wage earners); *cf. Amadeo v. Zant*, 486 U.S. 214 (1988). This principle condemns the systematic exclusion of any "distinct class" of citizens shown to be viewed or treated differently from other classes in the local community (*Hernandez v. Texas, supra*, 347 U.S. at 478; *Castaneda v. Partida, supra*, 430 U.S. at 494-95). The prohibition applies to grand juries as well as trial juries. *Strauder v. West Virginia*, 100 U.S. 303 (1879); *Campbell v. Louisiana*, 523 U.S. 392 (1998).

In *Taylor v. Louisiana*, 419 U.S. 522 (1975), the Supreme Court held that the systematic exclusion of women from juries in criminal cases is forbidden by the Sixth Amendment as incorporated into the Due Process Clause of the Fourteenth; and in subsequent cases the Court has treated *Taylor* as overruling its antiquated holding in *Hoyt v. Florida*, 368 U.S. 57 (1961), that exclusion of women from criminal juries did not violate the Equal Protection Clause. *See J.E.B. v. Alabama* ex rel. *T.B.*, 511 U.S. 127, 134-35 (1994) (describing *Taylor v. Louisiana* as having "repudiated the reasoning of *Hoyt*," and observing that although "*Taylor* distinguished *Hoyt* . . . , [t]he Court now . . . has stated that *Taylor* 'in effect' overruled *Hoyt*" (quoting *Payne v. Tennessee*, 501 U.S. 808, 828 n.1 (1991))). Given the Court's application of the Equal Protection Clause in *J.E.B.* to prohibit a state actor's intentional discrimination on the basis of gender in using peremptory strikes in jury selection, and given the Court's record in other contexts of barring gender discrimination on Equal Protection grounds (*see, e.g., United States v. Virginia*, 518 U.S. 515 (1996); *Mississippi University for Women v. Hogan*, 458 U.S. 718, 723-28 (1982); *Sessions v. Morales-Santana*, 582 U.S. 47 (2017)), it is evident that women should now be held to be a "distinct class" whose exclusion from any jury selection process would render the resulting juries unconstitutional. *See also Gibson v. Zant*, 705 F.2d 1543 (11th Cir. 1983); *Machetti v. Linahan*, 679 F.2d 236 (11th Cir. 1982); *White v. Crook*, 251 F. Supp. 401 (M.D. Ala. 1966) (three-judge court).

Whether the systematic exclusion of particular age groups – for example, young people or the elderly – would also be condemned is a more difficult question, which the Supreme Court has reserved. *Hamling v. United States*, 418 U.S. 87, 137 (1974). *See* Donald H. Zeigler, *Young Adults as a Cognizable Group in Jury Selection*, 76 MICH. L. REV. 1045 (1978).

A grand jury whose composition is affected by systematic racial exclusion may be challenged even by a defendant who is not a member of the excluded class. *Campbell v. Louisiana*, 523 U.S. 392, 394 (1998) ("a white criminal defendant has standing to object to discrimination against black persons in the selection of grand jurors"). *See also Peters v. Kiff,* 407 U.S. 493 (1972). Regarding means of proving systematic exclusion claims, see § 12.3 *infra.*

12.1.2. *Grand Jury Procedures*

Once the jurors for a term have been selected, their names are published or made available through the office of the jury commissioners or the clerk of court. They meet in closed session, with no judicial officer in attendance. In most States, no one except the prosecutor, a stenographer, and the single witness testifying is permitted to be present during testimony to the grand jury; and the prosecutor and witnesses are also barred from the jury's deliberations. In some States, however, a witness can be accompanied and advised by counsel during his or her grand jury testimony. See §§ 12.6.1, 12.6.4.3 *infra.*

The grand jury is theoretically free, on its own initiative, to consider any matters of felony (and sometimes other matters) within its jurisdiction and to call any witnesses it pleases. But as a matter of actual practice, grand juries usually limit their consideration to cases presented by the prosecutor and to the witnesses whom the prosecutor suggests they call. The prosecutor drafts "bills" charging defendants with offenses, presents witnesses to the grand jury in support of the bills, and, at the conclusion of the testimony, asks the jury to return the bills as "true bills," or indictments.

The grand jury is supposed to indict a defendant if, upon the evidence presented to it, it finds that there are sufficient grounds to believe the defendant guilty of an offense. In some jurisdictions the test of sufficiency of the grounds is described as "probable cause" or "reasonable cause"; in others it is described as a *prima facie* case – that is, evidence which, if believed, unexplained and uncontradicted, would warrant the defendant's conviction by a trial jury.

Practice varies regarding the applicability of rules of evidence to the grand jury. In some jurisdictions the jurors are adjured by statute to receive only legally admissible evidence. In others they are left relatively unrestricted with regard to what they may hear. (For example, except with respect to privileges, the Federal Rules of Evidence are explicitly made inapplicable to federal grand jury proceedings by Rule 1101(d)(2).) In practice, with no judge and no defense counsel present, grand juries hear just about anything the prosecutor wants them to hear. (Sections 12.1.3 and 20.3 *infra* discuss possible grounds and procedures for obtaining judicial review of the admissibility, legality, and sufficiency of evidence received by the grand jury. Sections 12.6-12.8 *infra* discuss damage-control techniques that defense counsel can use during the grand jury proceeding itself.)

The grand jury has the subpoena power. Witnesses who refuse to testify before it are taken into court, ordered to testify by the judge, and, upon further refusal, punished by the judge for contempt.

The grand jury ordinarily takes its legal advice from the prosecutor, although it may also request instructions from the presiding judge of the felony court. (The judge's general "charge" to the grand jury at the beginning of a session usually consists of administrative instructions and civic exhortations, conveying no principles of substantive law except – in some localities – a reference to the probable-cause or *prima-facie*-case standard for indictment.)

Following their deliberations on the evidence, the jurors, by majority vote, return bills of indictment into the felony court, signed as "true bills" by their foreman. These are the indictments required by constitution and statute and constitute the charging papers on which felony defendants are subsequently put to trial. Although grand juries differ in their tempers, for the most part they simply rubber-stamp the prosecutor's work product and obligingly return as "true" all of the bills that the prosecutor presents, excepting those which s/he quietly lets it be known s/he does not want returned. In "no-billing" the latter cases, the grand jury serves the function of taking the heat off the prosecutor for not going forward with prosecutions that s/he prefers not to undertake but cannot overtly decline without arousing the ire of some political or personal constituency.

12.1.3. *Grounds for Challenging Defects in Grand Jury Proceedings*

In some jurisdictions, there is little or no judicial review of claims of impropriety in grand jury proceedings. In other jurisdictions, relatively robust review is provided. *See, e.g., People v. Gaworecki*, 37 N.Y.3d 225, 230, 175 N.E.3d 915, 919, 154 N.Y.S.3d 33, 37 (2021) (sustaining a trial court's order granting the defendant's motion to dismiss the manslaughter count of an indictment on the ground that the evidence before the grand jury was insufficient to establish a *prima facie* case that the defendant acted with the recklessness required for manslaughter or with the criminal negligence required for the lesser included offense of negligent homicide; "'[t]o dismiss [or reduce] an indictment on the basis of insufficient evidence before a Grand Jury, a reviewing court must consider whether the evidence viewed in the light most favorable to the People, if unexplained and uncontradicted, would warrant conviction by a petit jury'"); *State v. Miller*, 471 N.W.2d 380 (Minn. App. 1991) (affirming a trial court's dismissal of an indictment for causing death by criminal vehicular operation because the evidence before the grand jury was insufficient to show the requisite criminal gross negligence); *State v. Turner*, 300 Kan. 662, 663, 685, 333 P.3d 155, 157, 170 (2014) (upholding the dismissal of an indictment because of "constitutional violations and abuse of process in the grand jury proceedings": "(1) The DA violated Turner's Fifth Amendment right against self-incrimination by asking him numerous questions in front of the grand jury which required him to invoke the privilege over 100 times; (2) the State's chief investigator for the grand jury impermissibly commented on Turner's silence in violation of his Fifth Amendment right against self-incrimination; and (3) the State-sponsored testimony of the chief investigator violated Turner's due process rights by introducing irrelevant and unnecessary evidence about an unrelated murder case and suggesting that the grand jury should indict on the present case to help solve the prior murder case."); *Commonwealth v. Baker*, 11 S.W.3d 585, 588 (Ky. App. 2000) (upholding the inherent authority of a trial court to dismiss an indictment for "a flagrant abuse of the grand jury process that resulted in both actual prejudice and deprived the grand jury of autonomous and unbiased judgment": "A court may utilize . . . [this] supervisory power to dismiss an indictment where a prosecutor knowingly or intentionally presents false, misleading or perjured testimony to the grand jury that results in actual prejudice to the defendant."); *State v. Roers*, 520 N.W.2d 752 (Minn. App. 1994) (describing the court's earlier unreported decision affirming dismissal of an indictment because s grand juror had obtained information about the defendant out of court and discussed it with other grand jurors;

holding that dismissal would also have been within the trial court's discretion based upon prosecutorial misconduct including "(1) tailoring of the evidence so as to point to only one suspect, (2) improperly using Ryan Ford's mother to obtain information from respondent after respondent retained counsel, (3) improperly and frequently referring to the death of respondent's nephew throughout the grand jury hearing even though respondent had nothing to do with the death, (4) failing to remind a grand juror of her oath when it learned about her contact with respondent, (5) conducting a test that focused impermissibly on respondent, and (6) conducting two off-the-record discussions during the grand jury proceedings" (*id.* at 754); but that submission of the charges to a new grand jury is permissible: "Our decision today follows the federal courts' view that 'the better view is to allow reindictment upon dismissal if the new grand jury would not be affected by the prior government improprieties.'. . . Where governmental misconduct or gross negligence in prosecuting a case has not actually prejudiced the defendant, a defendant is not entitled to permanent immunity respecting alleged criminal conduct." *Id.* at 759-60.); *State v. Hardy*, 406 N.E.2d 313 (Ind. App. 1980) (sustaining a trial court order dismissing an indictment: "Under Indiana law, however, the presence and participation of an unauthorized person in the grand jury room is not, per se, grounds for the dismissal of an indictment. The defendant must show prejudice to his substantial rights, and such prejudice is not presumed. . . . ¶ . . . [Here] there was substantial evidence from which the court could have found the defendant to have sustained his burden of proving prejudice, namely, the presence and active participation of a prosecuting attorney who had requested the appointment of a special prosecutor to avoid a possible conflict of interest, and was therefore recused. We will not disturb the trial court's judgment."); *Crimmins v. Superior Court, In and For Maricopa County*, 137 Ariz. 39, 43, 668 P.2d 882, 886 (1983) (the prosecutor failed to present evidence that the defendant may have had the basis for a valid citizen's arrest of the complainant, offered inaccurate police testimony portraying the complainant as guiltless, and failed to instruct the grand jurors on the law authorizing citizen's arrest; "[T]he omission of significant facts, coupled with the omission of instruction on statutes which give the omitted facts their legal significance, rendered the presentation of the case against Crimmins less than fair and impartial. . . . We believe that the grand jury's inability to determine the case based on accurately depicted facts and the applicable law flawed their decision and entitles Crimmins to a new determination of probable cause. Petitioner was denied his right to due process and a fair and impartial presentation of the evidence by the manner in which the proceeding was conducted."); *State v. Jeannotte-Rodriguez*, 469 N.J. Super. 69, 78-79, 261 A.3d 1005, 1010 (2021) (affirming a trial court's order dismissing without prejudice an indictment charging that one defendant practiced medicine without a license and that she and two other defendants committed billing fraud by representing that she was a doctor; "[T]he prosecutor failed to adequately and accurately instruct the grand jury about what a medical assistant may do without encroaching upon the licensed practice of medicine. And, because the law does not clearly draw a line around a medical assistant's allowable activities, prosecuting someone for crossing the line may violate the right to fair warning. ¶ The prosecutor also improperly referred to additional evidence that he did not present to the grand jury, and presented a questionable analysis of the amount of money involved in the charged offenses." *Id.* at 78-79, 261 A.3d at 1010. A court may dismiss an indictment "when the evidence presented to the grand jury is insufficient to support the charge" and "in the case of 'prosecutorial misconduct . . . .'." (*id.* at 89, 261 A.3d at 1016).); *Hansen v. Chon-Lopez, Judge of the Superior Court in and for County of Pima*, 252 Ariz. 250, 501 P.3d 762 (Ariz. App. 2021) (reversing a trial court's denial of the defendant's motion to remand the case to the grand jury for a new finding of probable cause; "A grand jury's finding of probable cause can be challenged if the defendant was denied a substantial procedural right." *Id.* at 256, 501 P.3d at 768. "'The duties of fair play and impartiality imposed on those who attend and serve the grand jury are meant to ensure that the determinations made by that body are informed, objective and just.'... Consequently, the state has a duty to properly instruct the grand jury on the law, ... to present the evidence in a manner that is fair and impartial, and to introduce clearly exculpatory evidence ...." *Id.* at 258, 501 P.3d at 770. "[O]ur supreme court stated in *Trebus* [*v. Davis, Judge of the Superior Court in and for County of Pima*, 189 Ariz. 621, 623-24, 944 P.2d 1235, 1237-38 (1997)] that ... [the applicable] statute, combined with ... [a pertinent rule of court] and a defendant's right to due process, not only require the state to present clearly exculpatory evidence, they also require the state to inform the grand jury that a defendant has asked to appear or has submitted 'possible exculpatory evidence.'" 252 Ariz. at 258, 501 P.3d at 770. "It is undisputed that neither the prosecutor nor the detective told the grand jury Hansen had provided the prosecutor with a letter [detailing and attaching exculpatory information]. This was error under *Trebus* and its progeny. And, although the prosecutor summarized portions of the information in the letter, we cannot agree that this constituted a fair and impartial presentation of the evidence given the manner in which she characterized the potentially exculpatory information and what she chose to withhold." *Id.* at 259, 501 P.3d at 771.); *State v. Joao*, 53 Hawai'i 226, 230, 491 P.2d 1089, 1091-92 (1971) (the prosecutors vouched for the credibility of the state's only witness and failed to correct that witness's false testimony understating his criminal record; "We hold that the conduct of the prosecutors was contrary to those 'fundamental principles of liberty and justice which lie at the base of all our civil and political institutions' ... and therefore violated the due process clause of the Fourteenth Amendment of the Constitution of the United States, and article 1, section 4 of the Hawaii Constitution"; trial court order quashing the indictment is affirmed); *Herrera v. Sanchez*, 2014-NMSC-018, 328 P.3d 1176, 1182-85 (N.M. 2014) ("During ... [the defendant's voluntary] grand jury testimony, the prosecuting attorney prevented ... [her] from answering a grand juror's question regarding whether ... [s/he] ever told anyone that her husband was physically abusive to her. ... ¶ By preventing ... [the defendant] from answering a direct, relevant question from a grand juror, the prosecuting attorney interfered with the grand jury's statutory duty to make an independent inquiry into the evidence supporting a determination of probable cause. ... ¶ The prosecuting attorney [also] erred ... when she expounded upon this Court's prescribed jury instructions by telling the grand jury, 'She [the defendant]was directly appealing to you to consider the consequences of your verdict. That is absolutely inappropriate. Please do not let anything she said to you about, you know, implying what the right decision is influence your decisions. She was improperly seeking your sympathy.' ... ¶ ... Providing accurate, unbiased instructions to the grand jury is critical to the structural integrity of our grand jury system. We hold that the prosecuting attorney's failure to do so in this case warrants dismissal of the indictment regardless of whether Petitioner has demonstrated prejudice."); *People v. Graham*, 148 A.D.3d 1517, 1518-19, 50 N.Y.S.3d 196, 198-99 (N.Y. App. Div., 4th Dep't 2017) (despite defense counsel's failure to preserve a grand jury challenge by filing a pretrial motion to dismiss the indictment, the appellate court reaches the issue in "the interest of justice" on appeal of the defendant's conviction, and reverses the conviction because the prosecutor's failure to instruct the grand jury on "the defense of temporary and lawful possession" of a firearm "impaired the integrity of the grand jury proceeding"); *People v. Ball*, 175 A.D.3d 987, 987-88, 107 N.Y.S.3d 241, 243-44 (N.Y. App. Div., 4th Dep't 2019) ("[D]efendant asked the People to deliver to the grand jury foreperson a letter requesting, among other things, that the grand jurors be charged with respect to the . . . justifiable use of physical force in defense of premises and in defense of a person in the course of a burglary . . . . The People did not deliver the letter to the foreperson. ¶ . . . [W]e conclude that the court properly dismissed the indictment based on the People's failure to instruct the grand jury on the justification defense . . . , as requested in the letter. A court may dismiss an indictment on the ground that a grand jury proceeding is defective where, inter alia, the proceeding is so irregular 'that the integrity thereof is impaired and prejudice to the defendant may result' . . . ."). *See also, e.g., Morse v. Fusto*, 804 F.3d 538, 541, 547 (2d Cir. 2015) (upholding section 1983 relief for a defendant who, after his acquittal at trial, sued a Special Assistant Attorney General and an audit-investigator of the New York State Medicaid Fraud Control Unit for "depriv[ing] him of his constitutional right to a fair trial by intentionally manipulating the information contained on the spreadsheet summary charts before they were presented to the grand jury in order to create the false impression that Morse billed Medicaid for dental services that he did not provide"; "Notwithstanding the legally permissible one-sided nature of grand jury proceedings, everyone possesses the additional and distinct 'right not to be deprived of liberty as a result of the fabrication of evidence by a government officer acting in an investigating capacity.'"); § 20.3.1 subdivision (2) *infra*.

In most jurisdictions, the appropriate procedure for challenging improper prosecutorial conduct or other defects in grand jury proceedings is a motion to quash or dismiss the indictment. See § 20.3 *infra*. If the motion is denied, appellate review is ordinarily available by interlocutory appeal or by pretrial prerogative-writ proceedings (see Chapter 31 *infra*) or both. *See, e.g., Herrera v. Sanchez, supra*, 328 P.3d at 1180. The trial court should be asked to postpone arraignment on the indictment pending these appellate proceedings; if it fails to do so, a stay should be requested from the appellate court. Whether challenges to grand jury improprieties survive for post-trial review on an appeal from conviction is a dubious question in many States. Counsel is ordinarily advised to play it safe by pursuing whatever pretrial appellate remedies local practice provides.

12.2. *Deciding Whether to Waive Indictment*

12.2.1. *Advantages to Proceeding By Means of Indictment*

The various legal rules governing grand jury proceedings present a number of potential grounds for challenging the composition and conduct of any particular jury. See § 12.1.3 *supra*; §§ 20.3.1, 20.3.3 *infra*. In some jurisdictions, a defendant can also ask the trial judge review the grand jury transcript and dismiss an indictment on the ground that the prosecution's evidence is insufficient to meet the applicable probable-cause or *prima-facie-evidence* standard. See § 12.1.2 *supra*; § 20.3.2 *infra*. These defense opportunities will be lost if a defendant waives indictment and consents to be prosecuted by information. The defendant who waives also loses the slight chance that the grand jury may rebuff the prosecutor and no-bill the indictment.

Finally, s/he loses one rather significant trial advantage. Informations may be amended substantially by the prosecutor prior to or during trial. Indictments may not be amended so as to charge "an offense that is different from that alleged in the grand jury's indictment," without resubmission to the grand jury (*United States v. Miller*, 471 U.S. 130, 142 (1985) (dictum)). *See id.* at 142-45; *Ex parte Bain*, 121 U.S. 1 (1887); *Russell v. United States*, 369 U.S. 749, 770-71 (1962) (dictum). And, by reason of the prohibition against double jeopardy (see §§ 20.8, 40.8.4.2 *infra*), a prosecutor who finds at trial that the evidence is varying from the allegations of the indictment cannot stop the trial in order to resubmit the case to the grand jury. Consequently, an indictment imposes a much tighter check on the prosecution's proof at trial than does an information. Significant variance of the proof from the facts alleged in an indictment requires an acquittal (*see Sanabria v. United States*, 437 U.S. 54, 68-69 (1978), recognizing the principle and holding that double jeopardy bars a prosecutor's appeal from such an acquittal, even when the trial judge has taken an erroneously narrow view of the indictment's allegations), whereas a similar variance in an information case would ordinarily allow the defendant nothing more than a continuance. Similarly, the trial judge may not, in his or her charge, submit to the petit jury theories or grounds for conviction which an indictment does not support (*see Stirone v. United States*, 361 U.S. 212 (1960); *United States v. Miller, supra*, 471 U.S. at 138-40 (dictum); *United States v. Muresanu*, 951 F.3d 833 (7th Cir. 2020); *United States v. Phea*, 953 F.3d 838, 842 (5th Cir. 2020) (finding trial counsel ineffective for failing to object to jury instructions that permitted a conviction on a factual theory not charged in the indictment: these instructions amounted to a forbidden "constructive amendment of the indictment" – *i.e.*, an amendment that "'occurs when the trial court through its instructions and facts it permits in evidence, allows proof of an essential element of the crime on an alternative basis provided by the statute but not charged in the indictment.'"); *State v. Hicks*, 768 S.E.2d 373 (N.C. App. 2015)), although s/he may submit such theories or grounds in an information case, provided that the defendant has been given sufficient notice and preparatory opportunity to meet those theories or grounds at the trial (*see, e.g., State v. Ancira*, 2022-NMCA-053, 517 P.3d 292, 296-97 (N.M. App. 2022) (alternative ground)).

12.2.2. *Considerations Affecting Waiver*

The advantages mentioned in the preceding subsection suggest that generally a defendant should not waive indictment unless there is some affirmative reason for doing so. This is particularly true in the case of a defendant who is a member of a racial, ethnic, religious, or gender-defined minority that has traditionally been underrepresented on juries in the area. Frequently, in these cases, a systematic-exclusion claim is as strong as any defense that the defendant is likely to have.

Sound affirmative reasons for waiving indictment are presented in the following circumstances:

(1) *There is a substantial certainty of indictment; the next grand jury term will not begin soon; and the defendant is in jail or otherwise inconvenienced by the delay.* A proceeding by information needs not await the next term of the grand jury, which may be several weeks (or, in rural counties, months) after bind-over. This delay can be particularly oppressive to a defendant who has not made bail. The period of pretrial incarceration may or may not be credited against a subsequent sentence, depending on local practice. See § 4.19 second paragraph *supra*. In any event, some defendants who are bound over for the grand jury and detained in default of bail are being held on charges for which they will not be sentenced to imprisonment, with the result that the whole period of pretrial detention is wasted. In such a case, anything that speeds the process

up is advantageous. There may be other situations, too, in which a speed-up is desirable. A defendant on bail may be planning a move and want the case resolved quickly. In some jurisdictions a court-ordered mental examination is authorized only after the charging paper is filed. Defense counsel may want to have that examination made as early as possible, since the nearer to the time of the offense a psychiatric evaluation is made, the more persuasive its results may prove to be as the basis for a possible insanity or diminished-capacity defense or for favorable sentencing consideration. (See §§ 16.1.2, 16.3 *infra*).

(2) *The defendant intends to plead guilty at trial.* There are two considerations here. First, in a plea case, even more than in a case that goes to trial, waiver of the grand jury tends to speed up final disposition. Second, in negotiating with the prosecutor, a defendant's willingness to save the prosecution the trouble of going before the grand jury is worth something.

(3) *The grand jury proceeding or the indictment may occasion substantial adverse publicity.*

(4) *Counsel has reason to believe that testimony before the grand jury may alert the prosecutor to defects in the prosecution's case that have gone unnoticed through the stage of the preliminary hearing and are not otherwise likely to be noticed by the prosecutor prior to trial; or counsel apprehends that testimony before the grand jury may give the prosecutor other investigative leads or alert the prosecutor to additional charges.*

(5) *The prosecutor is known to call prospective defense witnesses before the grand jury to badger them or to get their testimony on record for purposes of impeachment at trial; and counsel apprehends that a potential defense witness or witnesses may be vulnerable to this tactic.*

Other affirmative reasons for waiver may occasionally appear.

12.3. *Challenge to the Array or to the Polls*

Unless compelling considerations call for waiving indictment, counsel should consider whether there is any available ground of attack on the selection procedure or composition of the grand jury. See § 12.1.1 *supra*; § 20.3.1 *infra*. Objections to the method of selection or to the qualifications of the jurors generally (including claims of systematic exclusion of a racial, ethnic, religious, economic, gender-defined, or other "distinct class" (§ 12.1.1 *supra*)) are made by a challenge to the array (that is, to the group of jurors collectively). Objections to a particular juror (on grounds of bias, lack of statutory qualifications, and so forth) are made by a challenge to the polls (that is, to specified individuals). Both sorts of challenges are ordinarily required to be made in writing and prior to the convening of the jury (or, in some jurisdictions, prior to indictment).

Counsel should therefore obtain from the court clerk's office or the office of the jury commission, as soon after bind-over as it is available, the list of grand jurors (or the roster of the grand jury "pool," "box," or "wheel") for the ensuing term. This list is often required by local law to be made accessible for inspection by counsel. *See, e.g., Alfaro v. Superior Court of Marin*

County, 58 Cal. App. 5th 371, 272 Cal. Rptr. 3d 404 (2020). If not, counsel should move the court having control over the grand jury to order the list disclosed on the grounds that "without inspection, a party almost invariably would be unable to determine whether he has a potentially meritorious jury challenge" (*Test v. United States*, 420 U.S. 28, 30 (1975)), and that the federal constitutional right against systematic exclusion of classes of citizens from the grand jury implies an ancillary right to a fair opportunity to discover and prove systematic-exclusion claims (*Coleman v. Alabama*, 377 U.S. 129, 133 (1964); *Amadeo v. Zant*, 486 U.S. 214 (1988); *cf. Ham v. South Carolina*, 409 U.S. 524 (1973)). *See also State v. Plain*, 898 N.W.2d 801, 828 (Iowa 2017) ("In at least four jurisdictions that lack a state statute establishing the right and procedures for obtaining the information necessary to enforce an individual's Sixth Amendment rights, courts have determined that the constitution mandates access even if statutes do not." ¶ "Like the courts in Missouri, Nevada, and New Jersey, we conclude the constitutional fair cross-section purpose alone is sufficient to require access to the information necessary to prove a prima facie case."). When race-based systematic exclusion is a potential issue, counsel's motion for disclosure of records necessary to evaluate the issue can point out that the Supreme Court has repeatedly emphasized the importance of guarding against the distorting influence of racial prejudice in criminal prosecutions. *E.g.*, *Vasquez v. Hillery*, 474 U.S. 254 (1986); *Turner v. Murray*, 476 U.S. 28 (1986); *Buck v. Davis*, 580 U.S. 100 (2017); *Peña-Rodriguez v. Colorado*, 580 U.S. 206 (2017); *Tharpe v. Sellers*, 138 S. Ct. 545 (2018); *Flowers v. Mississippi*, 139 S. Ct. 2228, 2242 (2019) ("[e]qual justice under law requires a criminal trial free of racial discrimination in the jury selection process"); *and see* Daniel S. Harawa, Lemonade: *A Racial Justice Reframing of The Roberts Court's Criminal Jurisprudence*, 110 CAL. L. REV. 681 (2022). The grand jury list usually notes the name and address of each prospective juror, and sometimes occupation. Thus individual jurors can be checked out if desired. In larger cities there are jury investigating services, but these tend to be costly, and checking out grand jurors is seldom worth the cost. The jurors are probably individually qualified as far as the statutory criteria go; the kind of bias that disqualifies is narrow; and if the juror's name has not come up in counsel's investigation of the case and the complainant, the juror is probably not technically challengeable.

The accepted method of proving claims of systematic exclusion has been described as follows:

> "The first step is to establish that the group [claimed to be excluded] is one that is a recognizable, distinct class, singled out for different treatment under the laws, as written or as applied. . . . Next, the degree of underrepresentation must be proved, by comparing the proportion of the group in the total population to the proportion called to serve [as jurors] . . . , over a significant period of time. . . . This method of proof, sometimes called the 'rule of exclusion,' has been held to be available as a method of proving discrimination in jury selection against a delineated class. . . . Finally . . . a selection procedure that is susceptible of abuse or is not racially neutral supports the presumption of discrimination raised by the statistical showing." (*Rose v. Mitchell*, 443 U.S. 545, 565 (1979), quoting *Castaneda v. Partida*, 430 U.S. 482, 494 (1977).)

The opinion in *Duren v. Missouri*, 439 U.S. 357 (1979), indicates that underrepresentation alone is not sufficient; it must also be shown that "this underrepresentation is due to systematic exclusion of the group in the jury-selection process" (*id.* at 364), as the result of "discriminatory purpose" (*id.* at 368 n.26). *See also Berghuis v. Smith*, 559 U.S. 314, 327 (2010). However, *Duren* recognizes that both systematic exclusion and discriminatory purpose may be inferred from a "significant discrepancy shown by the statistics" comparing a group's numbers in the general population with its numbers in jury pools and panels, and on juries (*Duren v. Missouri, supra,* 439 U.S. at 368 n.26). *See also Berghuis v. Smith, supra,* 559 U.S. at 327-33 (dictum); *Woodfox v. Cain,* 772 F.3d 358, 372-76 (5th Cir. 2014).

Counsel will therefore want to investigate both grand and petit jury lists, going back ten years or so, in order to demonstrate a pattern of discrimination. These are public records, available from the clerk of the criminal court or from the commissioners' office. If the clerk's or commissioners' records contain racial designations, the jury is probably challengeable upon the showing of even a relatively small discrepancy between the percentages of the racial minority group in the general population and on jury panels. *Avery v. Georgia,* 345 U.S. 559 (1953); *Whitus v. Georgia,* 385 U.S. 545 (1967); *Alexander v. Louisiana,* 405 U.S. 625 (1972); *cf. Foster v. Chatman,* 578 U.S. 488, 513-14 (2016) (recognizing the probative force of racial designations in the cognate context of *Batson* analysis (§ 33.3.2 *infra*)); *Adkins v. Warden,* 710 F.3d 1241, 1256 (11th Cir. 2013) (same); *and see Castaneda v. Partida, supra,* 430 U.S. at 493-95. When racial designations or similar indications of a selection process that "is not racially neutral" (*Rose v. Mitchell, supra,* 443 U.S. at 565) do not appear in the records, it is important to seek out other aspects of the procedure that are "susceptible of abuse" (*id.*). Any nonrandom method of culling or cutting prospective jurors would seem to be "susceptible of abuse" in this sense. *See id.* at 548 n.2, 566; *Henson v. Wyrick,* 634 F.2d 1080 (8th Cir. 1980); *and see Castaneda v. Partida, supra,* 430 U.S. at 497, describing the key-man system as "highly subjective." But in the absence of some form of identification of prospective jurors by nonneutral characteristics in the records available to jury-selection officials, a stronger statistical showing of underrepresentation is apparently required.

In any event counsel should conduct the most thorough statistical study practicable for a period going back at least a decade, comparing the proportion of minority individuals in the general population of the county or court district (as reflected in the latest federal census figures), with the proportions of minority individuals (a) who are on the jury rolls and (b) who have actually served as jurors. *See Alexander v. Louisiana,* 405 U.S. 625 (1972). If the jury records do not contain racial identifications, tax digests may. Sophisticated statistical methods for analyzing the data are available, and it is wise to consult a statistician for possible use as an expert witness. *See, e.g.,* NJP LITIGATION CONSULTING (Elissa Krauss & Sonia Chopra, eds.), JURYWORK: SYSTEMATIC TECHNIQUES, chs. 5 & 6 (2d ed. 2021-22); NATIONAL JURY PROJECT & NATIONAL LAWYERS GUILD, THE JURY SYSTEM: NEW METHODS FOR REDUCING PREJUDICE (David Kairys, ed. 1975); Michael O. Finkelstein, *The Application of Statistical Decision Theory to the Jury Discrimination Cases,* 80 HARV. L. REV. 338 (1966); David Kairys, *Juror Selection: The Law, A Mathematical Method of Analysis, and a Case Study,* 10 AM. CRIM. L. REV. 771 (1972); Peter W. Sperlich & Martin L. Jaspovice, *Statistical Decision Theory and the Selection of Grand Jurors: Testing for Discrimination in a Single Panel,* 2 HASTINGS CONST. L.Q. 75 (1975). Judicial receptivity to these statistical modes of proof is reflected in *Castaneda v. Partida, supra,* 430 U.S. at 496-97 n.17; *International Brotherhood of Teamsters v. United States,* 431 U.S. 324, 339-40 (1977); *Vasquez v. Hillery, supra,* 474 U.S. at 259-60; *cf. McCleskey v. Kemp,* 481 U.S. 279, 293-94 & n.13 (1987).

12.4. *Motions to Suppress*

Motions to suppress illegally obtained evidence are considered in greater detail in Chapters 24-27 *infra*. Although ordinarily made after indictment, in most jurisdictions they can be made earlier. The advantage of moving to suppress prior to the convening of the grand jury is that evidence suppressed at that time cannot be presented to the grand jurors. *Compare Silverthorne Lumber Co. v. United States*, 251 U.S. 385 (1920), *with United States v. Calandra*, 414 U.S. 338 (1974). The importance of forestalling its presentation is intensified in jurisdictions which follow the rule that an indictment will not be quashed on the grounds of the receipt of illegally obtained evidence by the grand jury. See § 20.3.3 *infra*. Counsel should accompany a preindictment motion to suppress with an application for a stay of all other proceedings in the case pending determination of the motion so that the prosecutor cannot go to the grand jury with the evidence while the question of its legality is under consideration by the court. For a *caveat* about a risk involved in filing suppression motions, see § 13.8 concluding paragraph *infra*.

12.5. *Requesting Recording of Grand Jury Proceedings*

In some jurisdictions the grand jury proceedings are routinely recorded, and a transcript of the notes of testimony is delivered to the defendant following indictment. There are slip-ups in the routine, however, and defense counsel may be wise to contact the prosecutor to obtain an express assurance that a stenographer will be present when the case against the client is presented.

In most jurisdictions the practice relating to disclosure of grand jury records to the defense has traditionally gone to the far extreme of illiberality. *Compare Henry v. Attorney General, Alabama*, 45 F.4th 1272 (11th Cir. 2022), *with Butterworth v. Smith*, 494 U.S. 624 (1990). Although the prosecutor makes free use of the grand jury transcript (if there is one), defense counsel has very limited access to it. Defense counsel is commonly forbidden to inspect it at all before trial except in a case in which the client is charged with perjury committed before the grand jury or in which counsel can show that grounds may exist for a motion to dismiss the indictment on account of matters occurring before the grand jury. See §§ 12.6-12.7, 20.3.1 subdivisions (2)-(4) *infra*. Even after a prosecution witness has testified at trial, defense inspection of the witness's transcribed grand jury testimony for purposes of impeachment is said to rest in the discretion of the trial court. This discretion, however, is increasingly being exercised in favor of permitting defense inspection at trial for impeachment purposes; in some jurisdictions (as in the federal courts), such at-trial inspection has become virtually a matter of right. *See* FED. RULE CRIM. PRO. 26.2(a), (f)(3). See also § 34.7.1 *infra*. A few jurisdictions are beginning to move in the direction of more liberal pretrial disclosure of grand jury minutes to the defense as well (see § 18.7.3 subdivision 9 *infra*), and constitutional arguments supporting the requirement of disclosure in some circumstances are available (see §§ 18.9.2.5-18.9.2.7 *infra*).

Depending upon the extent to which defense counsel anticipates that s/he will later be able to obtain access to transcribed grand jury testimony, s/he may or may not want to take steps to assure that stenographic notes are taken and transcribed in the first place. Frequently, the decision whether or not to have a stenographer record or transcribe particular grand jury proceedings is made by a budget-conscious prosecutor. Prosecutors usually like to have grand jury testimony transcribed, since they get far more use out of it than the defense does (both because of its greater accessibility to them and because, in the *ex parte* grand jury proceedings, the prosecutor can lead and cross-question witnesses without equal privileges for the defense). If the proceedings are not recorded, therefore, it is usually for financial reasons. Defense counsel who concludes that (notwithstanding the prosecutorial advantages just described) it would be in a client's interest to preserve a record of the grand jury proceedings, and whose client can afford it, may want to consider offering to pay for a stenographic transcript, either on condition that counsel receive a copy in the event of indictment or without condition. (The condition would be illegal in a number of jurisdictions whose statutes flatly prohibit disclosure of grand jury proceedings to any person without court order.) Alternatively, counsel may want to move the criminal court for an order requiring the recording and transcription of grand jury proceedings at public expense, under the theory of *McMahon v. Office of the City and County of Honolulu*, 51 Hawai'i 589, 590-91, 465 P.2d 549, 550-51 (1970) ("a defendant is under some circumstances constitutionally entitled to some part of the grand jury transcript"; "[w]e have no difficulty in requiring that presentations of evidence to grand juries . . . shall be recorded" because "[o]therwise there would be no remedy to make effective a constitutional right which may clearly exist").

In any event, if the defendant or prospective defense witnesses are subpoenaed to appear before the grand jury, counsel should contact the prosecutor and insist that a transcript of their testimony be made. The prosecutor will have one made anyway, if s/he wants one for later impeachment, so counsel loses little by the demand. A transcript will be necessary to support the defendant's claim that his or her privilege against self-incrimination was violated before the grand jury if it was. See § 12.6 *infra*. Counsel may also later wish to contend that the defendant or defense witnesses were called before the grand jury for the purpose of harassing and intimidating them; and either the transcript or the prosecutor's refusal to order a transcript will provide helpful support for that contention.

12.6. *Advising and Protecting Defendants Subpoenaed by the Grand Jury*

12.6.1. *Rights of Defendants Subpoenaed by the Grand Jury*

Statutes in a number of jurisdictions provide that grand jury witnesses are entitled to be represented by counsel. The statutes commonly provide that counsel may be present in the grand jury room while the witness is testifying but may not make objections or ask questions. *See, e.g.*, COLO. REV. STAT. § 16-5-204(4)(d); SMITH-HURD ILL. COMP. STAT. chap.725, § 5/112-4.1; KAN. STAT. ANN. § 22-3009(b); N.Y. CRIM. PRO. LAW § 190.52(2); 42 PA. CON. STAT. § 4549(c). Elsewhere, statutes or local practice give grand jury witnesses the right to confer with an attorney before testifying and to have the attorney standing by outside the grand jury room for consultation when the witness requests advice during his or her examination. *See, e.g.*, VERNON'S ANN. TEX. CODE CRIM. PRO. art. 20.17 (repealed, effective January 1, 2021, and replaced with new art. 20A.258, which provides equivalent protections); *Opinion of the Justices to the Governor*, 373 Mass. 915, 920, 371 N.E.2d 422, 424 (1977) ("It is recognized that a witness may need advice during his examination with respect to claiming the privilege against self-incrimination. Hence the practice in the Commonwealth (and many other jurisdictions) has been to break off the examination of a witness when he seeks legal advice and allow him to leave the room, consult with his counsel waiting in the corridor, and then return for continued examination. This may happen repeatedly in the course of the questioning.")

In a few jurisdictions a prospective defendant or a person who is a target of a grand jury investigation cannot be compelled to testify before the grand jury. *E.g.*, *People v. Avant*, 33 N.Y.2d 265, 307 N.E.2d 230, 352 N.Y.S.2d 161 (1973). Elsewhere (and so far as the federal Constitution is concerned), prospective defendants and targets of investigation can be subpoenaed to testify (*United States v. Wong*, 431 U.S. 174, 179-80 n.8 (1977)), and they need not be advised of their target status by the prosecutor (*United States v. Washington*, 431 U.S. 181 (1977)), although, like any other witness, they may decline to answer specific questions asked them on examination before the grand jury under a valid claim of the privilege against self-incrimination (*see United States v. Mandujano*, 425 U.S. 564, 571-76 (1976) (plurality opinion)). That privilege is given to witnesses, whether or not they are "suspects" (*Zurcher v. Stanford Daily*, 436 U.S. 547, 562 n.8 (1978) (dictum)), both by state constitutions and laws and by the Fifth Amendment to the Constitution of the United States (see § 18.12 *infra*), which is made applicable to state proceedings by the Fourteenth Amendment (*Malloy v. Hogan*, 378 U.S. 1 (1964)) and has been applied specifically to protect state grand jury witnesses (*Lefkowitz v. Turley*, 414 U.S. 70 (1973); *Lefkowitz v. Cunningham*, 431 U.S. 801 (1977); *Stevens v. Marks*, 383 U.S. 234 (1966)).

Although a plurality of the Supreme Court of the United States has said that grand jury witnesses need not be given *Miranda* warnings (see §§ 26.5, 26.7 *infra*) such as those which are required prior to police interrogation of persons in custody (*United States v. Mandujano, supra*, 425 U.S. at 578-81; *see Minnesota v. Murphy*, 465 U.S. 420, 431 (1984) (dictum)), the question remains open in the light of two concurring opinions in *Mandujano* (425 U.S. at 598-602, 609). *But see United States v. Williston*, 862 F.3d 1023, 1031-32 (10th Cir. 2017) (treating *Mandujano* as foreclosing a grand jury witness's right to full *Miranda* warnings; the "government's treatment of Williston during its investigation . . . more than complied with [his Fifth Amendment rights] because . . . [g]overnment representatives warned him three times that he could refuse to answer any grand-jury question if he felt the answer would incriminate him."); *cf. United States v. Otunyo*, 63 F.4th 948, 955 (D.C. Cir. 2023) (dictum) ("As a general rule, 'it is settled that forfeiture of the privilege against self-incrimination need not be knowing.' *Salinas v. Texas*, 570 U.S. 178, 190 (2013) (plurality opinion) [summarized in § 26.20 *infra*]."). Even the *Mandujano* plurality does not purport to decide whether a grand jury witness must be warned at least (1) that s/he may invoke the Fifth Amendment and refuse to answer any potentially incriminating question (*see id.* at 582 n.7) and (2) that s/he may have an attorney stand by outside the grand jury room and may interrupt his or her testimony to consult with that attorney whenever s/he wishes advice during the course of the examination (*see id.* at 581). *See also United States v. Washington, supra*, 431 U.S. at 186, 190. The contention that these latter warnings must be given to witnesses whom the grand jury has reasonable grounds to suspect of a crime – if not to all grand jury witnesses – is strongly supported by *Estelle v. Smith*, 451 U.S. 454 (1981) [§§ 16.6.1, 26.10.2 *infra*] (*see also Satterwhite v. Texas*, 486 U.S. 249 (1988)), and by the dictum in *Schneckloth v. Bustamonte*, 412 U.S. 218 (1973) [§ 25.18.1 *infra*], that in "trial-type situations" (412 U.S. at 238), like formal grand jury proceedings, a "waiver of trial rights . . . such as the waiver of the privilege against compulsory self-incrimination" (*id.*) and the right to counsel (*id.* at 237) "must meet the strict standard of an intentional relinquishment of a 'known' right" (*id.* at 238). *See also, e.g., Carnley v. Cochran*, 369 U.S. 506 (1962). This is particularly true when, as in the case of a witness whom the grand jury has cause to suspect, "the inquiring government is acutely aware of the potentially incriminating nature of the disclosures sought" (*Garner v. United States*, 424 U.S. 648, 657 (1976); *see also id.* at 660; *cf. Roberts v. United States*, 445 U.S. 552, 559 (1980); *Minnesota v. Murphy, supra*, 465 U.S. at 429-30; *but see id.* at 428-29), with the result that it is both practicable to require warnings and unfairly heedless of "the fundamental purpose of the Fifth Amendment – the preservation of an adversary system of criminal justice" (*Garner v. United States, supra*, 424 U.S. at 655) – to omit giving them. *See, e.g., State v. Cook*, 11 Ohio App.3d 237, 241, 464 N.E.2d 577, 581-82 (1983) ("In order to secure the Fifth Amendment privilege of a putative defendant-witness in the context of a grand jury proceeding, . . . the witness must be told that he has a constitutional privilege to refuse to answer any question that might incriminate him[,] . . . that any incriminating answers or statements he does make can be used against him in a subsequent prosecution[,] . . . [and] that he may have an attorney outside the grand jury room and may consult with him if he wishes."); *O'Neal v. State*, 468 P.2d 59, 71 (Okla. Crim. App. 1970) ("one being investigated by the grand jury is not just a witness and cannot be treated as such. The target of a grand jury investigation is not an ordinary witness; he is suspect and is entitled to be warned of his right against self-incrimination; and unless the witness is so warned and advised of his constitutional rights related thereto, any testimony revealed by him before the grand jury may not be used against him to prosecute a later charge arising out of that testimony . . . ."); *Commonwealth v. Woods*, 466 Mass. 707, 719-20, 1 N.E.3d 762, 772 (2014) ("Because grand jury testimony is compelled, it ought to be ameliorated with an advisement of rights where there is a substantial likelihood that the witness may become an accused; that is, where the witness is a 'target' or is reasonably likely to become one. Accordingly, we adopt a rule that where, at the time a person appears to testify before a grand jury, the prosecutor has reason to believe that the witness is either a 'target' or is likely to become one, the witness must be advised, before testifying, that (1) he or she may refuse to answer any question if a truthful answer would tend to incriminate the witness, and (2) anything that he or she does say may be used against the witness in a subsequent legal proceeding. . . . ¶ This rule is not a new constitutional rule, but rather an exercise of our power of superintendence 'to regulate the presentation of evidence in court proceedings.' . . . Therefore, this rule is only required to be applied prospectively to grand jury testimony elicited after the issuance of the rescript in this case.").

12.6.2. *Steps to Take if Counsel Enters a Case After the Client Has Already Testified Before a Grand Jury*

Counsel who enters a case after a client has already appeared and testified before a grand jury should move the court, at the earliest opportunity, for an order requiring transcription and disclosure to counsel of the stenographic notes of the client's grand jury appearance, so that counsel can determine whether there has been any infringement of the client's Fifth Amendment privilege, and what corrective measures may be advised. *See, e.g.,* FED. RULE CRIM. PRO. 6(e)(3)(E)(ii). Remedies that may be available include: (a) a motion to quash the grand jury's use of the client's testimony against him or her (*cf. Silverthorne Lumber Co. v. United States*, 251 U.S. 385 (1920)) if the grand jury proceeding is ongoing, or (b) a motion to quash any indictment based upon that testimony (*cf. United States v. Hubbell*, 530 U.S. 27, 38-40 (2000); and see

§ 20.3.1 subdivision (3) *infra*), or (c) a motion *in limine* (*see* §§ 17.5.3, 40.4.1 *infra*) to preclude the prosecution's use of the client's testimony (*see, e.g., Garrity v. New Jersey*, 385 U.S. 493 (1967)) or of any material derived from it (*cf. United States v. Hubbell, supra*) as evidence at a subsequent trial.

If the client is again summoned to testify before that or another grand jury, counsel should instruct the client to decline to answer any questions until the transcript of the client's earlier grand jury appearance has been furnished to counsel, on the grounds that without it counsel cannot make an intelligent decision regarding the extent to which the client now can and should claim privilege (*cf. Pillsbury Co. v. Conboy*, 459 U.S. 248 (1983)), and that any interrogation of the client before the grand jury under these circumstances would violate both the Fifth Amendment and Due Process. *Cf. Stevens v. Marks*, 383 U.S. 234 (1966); *Raley v. Ohio*, 360 U.S. 423 (1959).

12.6.3. *Steps to Take if Counsel Enters a Case Before Service of a Grand Jury Subpoena Upon the Client*

When counsel enters a case before the service of a grand jury subpoena upon a client, counsel's primary role at the grand jury stage lies in advising and assisting the client to claim such protections as the law gives the client against grand jury process. The available grounds for motions to quash grand jury subpoenas *duces tecum* or *ad testificandum* are reviewed in § 12.8 *infra*. They are lamentably few. The grounds upon which a duly subpoenaed witness may refuse to answer particular questions before the grand jury are also lamentably few. *See United States v. Calandra*, 414 U.S. 338 (1974). Basically, the latter grounds are:

(1) A claim of the Fifth Amendment privilege against self-incrimination (discussed in § 12.6.4 *infra*);

(2) A right not to answer questions based upon illegal electronic surveillance in violation of the Omnibus Crime Control and Safe Streets Act of 1968 [§§ 25.31, 25.32 *infra*] (*see Gelbard v. United States*, 408 U.S. 41 (1972)), and, therefore, to have proceedings conducted to determine whether, in fact, some illegal surveillance occurred and underlies the grand jury questioning (*see id.* at 52-58; 18 U.S.C. § 3504; *cf. Alderman v. United States*, 394 U.S. 165 (1969));

(3) A right not to answer questions that seek disclosure of associations protected by the First Amendment (*see Branzburg v. Hayes*, 408 U.S. 665, 708 (1972) (dictum); *cf. Gibson v. Florida Legislative Investigation Committee*, 372 U.S. 539 (1963); *DeGregory v. Attorney General*, 383 U.S. 825 (1966); *Liveright v. Joint Committee*, 279 F. Supp. 205 (M.D. Tenn. 1968)), or disclosure of information protected by any "valid [evidentiary] privilege . . . established by the Constitution, statutes, or the common law" (*United States v. Calandra, supra*, 414 U.S. at 346 (dictum)); and

(4) Possibly a right to relief against questioning pursued entirely for purposes of harassment (*United States v. Dionisio*, 410 U.S. 1, 12 (1973)), or demonstrably unrelated to any legitimate function of the grand jury inquiry (*see In re National Window Glass Workers*, 287 F.

219 (N.D. Ohio 1922)), particularly in cases in which the grand jury investigation may trench upon freedom of association or other First Amendment concerns (*see Branzburg v. Hayes, supra*, 408 U.S. at 707-08, 709-10 (concurring opinion of Justice Powell)).

Except for the Fifth Amendment, most of these grounds for refusing to answer grand jury questions are not factually presented in the ordinary criminal case. Counsel who does have a case presenting them should consult NATIONAL LAWYERS GUILD (GRAND JURY PROJECT), REPRESENTATION OF WITNESSES BEFORE FEDERAL GRAND JURIES (4th ed. 1999 & Supp. 2015).

12.6.4. *Advising a Client Under Grand Jury Subpoena*

12.6.4.1. *Immunity Statutes and Their Relationship to the Fifth Amendment Privilege*

Advising a client under grand jury subpoena concerning the Fifth Amendment privilege often requires examination of an applicable immunity statute. In most jurisdictions, immunity statutes permit the compulsion of testimony notwithstanding the fact that it is self-incriminating. They replace the privilege with a grant of immunity that, depending on the terms of the statute, may protect the witness against any prosecution on account of matters concerning which s/he is questioned or testifies (so-called transactional immunity) or may protect the witness only against the use of the witness's answers to prosecute him or her (so-called use immunity).

The latter, more limited, form of immunity – use immunity – was held insufficient to displace the privilege and hence inadequate to support compulsion of a witness's testimony in *Counselman v. Hitchcock*, 142 U.S. 547 (1892). *See Albertson v. Subversive Activities Control Board*, 382 U.S. 70, 79-81 (1965). It may still be held inadequate under some state constitutional privileges against self-incrimination. *See, e.g., State v. Gonzalez*, 853 P.2d 526, 530-33 (Alaska 1993); *State v. Thrift*, 312 S.C. 282, 296-301, 440 S.E.2d 341, 349-52 (1994). But in *Kastigar v. United States*, 406 U.S. 441 (1972), the Supreme Court overruled *Counselman's* requirement of "transactional immunity" as far as the federal Fifth Amendment is concerned. *See also United States v. Hubbell*, 530 U.S. 27, 38-40 (2000) (discussing *Kastigar*); *Lefkowitz v. Cunningham*, 431 U.S. 801, 809 (1977) (dictum). An immunity statute satisfies the Fifth Amendment, the Court held in *Kastigar*, if it provides "use and derivative-use immunity" (406 U.S. at 457), which the Court defined as "[i]mmunity from the use of compelled testimony, as well as evidence derived directly and indirectly therefrom" (406 U.S. at 453). *Kastigar* sustained a federal immunity-grant statute that, as construed, imposed a "total prohibition on use" of compelled self-incriminating testimony (*id.* at 460): – "a comprehensive safeguard, barring the use of compelled testimony as an 'investigatory lead,' and also barring the use of any evidence obtained by focusing investigation on a witness as a result of his compelled disclosures" (*id.*). *See also United States v. Hubbell, supra*, 530 U.S. at 38-39 (explaining that *Kastigar* upheld the constitutionality of the federal immunity statute "because the scope of the 'use and derivative-use' immunity that it provides is coextensive with the scope of the constitutional privilege against self-incrimination," and that *Kastigar* "particularly emphasized the critical importance of protection against a future prosecution "'based on knowledge and sources of information obtained from the compelled testimony'"). The Court in *Kastigar* emphasized that a criminal defendant "raising a claim under this statute need only show that he testified under a grant of immunity in order to shift to the government the heavy burden of proving that all of the evidence it proposes to use was derived from legitimate independent sources" (406 U.S. at 461-62). *See also United States v. Hubbell, supra*, 530 U.S. at 40, 45. The *Kastigar* opinion implies that not only the statute but also the Constitution "imposes on the prosecution the affirmative duty to prove that [its] . . . evidence [derives] . . . from a legitimate source wholly independent of the compelled testimony" (406 U.S. at 460). *See also United States v. Hubbell, supra*, 530 U.S. at 40, 45-46 (rejecting the government's attempt to shift the burden to the accused and explaining that *Kastigar* held that "the statute imposes an affirmative duty on the prosecution . . . 'to prove that the evidence it proposes to use is derived from a legitimate source wholly independent of the compelled testimony,'" and that *Kastigar* made clear "that the statutory guarantee of use and derivative-use immunity is as broad as the constitutional privilege itself" and "is coextensive with the constitutional privilege"); *Pillsbury Co. v. Conboy*, 459 U.S. 248, 255, 261 (1983). A witness's testimony compelled under an immunity statute may be used against the witness in a subsequent prosecution for perjury committed before the grand jury (*United States v. Apfelbaum*, 445 U.S. 115 (1980)); but, subject to this single exception, statements made by the witness after s/he has claimed the privilege and been granted immunity "may not be put to any testimonial use whatever against him in a criminal trial" (*New Jersey v. Portash*, 440 U.S. 450, 459 (1979) (holding that "a person's testimony before a grand jury under a grant of immunity cannot constitutionally be used to impeach him [as a witness] when he is a defendant in a later criminal trial" (*id.* at 459-60))).

Counsel should examine closely the terms and the judicial construction of any state immunity statute possibly relevant to the client's situation. Particularly if enacted prior to *Kastigar* or under the requirements of state constitutional holdings following *Counselman*, it may provide the client with full transactional immunity. This immunity would be binding upon the state that offers it in consideration for a witness's testimony, whether or not the federal Fifth Amendment obliged the state to go so far. *See Piccirillo v. New York*, 400 U.S. 548 (1971); *cf. Raley v. Ohio*, 360 U.S. 423 (1959). On the other hand, if the statute purports to grant only "use" immunity, counsel should examine the scope of that immunity to assure its conformance to the *Kastigar* requirements. Unless it conforms to those requirements, testimony may not be compelled under it.

12.6.4.2. *Mechanisms by Which Immunity Is Conferred*

In terms of the mechanism by which immunity is conferred, the immunity statutes may again be classified into two categories. One, the automatic or "immunity bath" statute, protects the witness who testifies in certain described proceedings (grand jury proceedings, legislative investigations, and so forth) relating to certain described subjects (gambling, narcotics, and so forth), whether or not the witness claims the privilege and even though the witness may volunteer incriminating information. The other, the "claim" statute, protects the witness only if s/he claims the privilege (again, in certain described proceedings relating to described subjects) and if s/he is then expressly granted immunity under the statute.

Defense counsel whose client is subpoenaed to appear before the grand jury in any situation in which the client's testimony may result in his or her indictment or may in any way incriminate the client with regard to any criminal offense (whether s/he has previously been bound over or charged by complaint or is merely under investigation) should ordinarily advise the client not to testify unless an "immunity bath" statute clearly applies and clearly provides full "transactional immunity" precluding future prosecution of the client for any and all matters relating to the testimony s/he may give. Under any other circumstances, testimony given before the grand jury in the absence of an explicit claim of the privilege may be used against the client (*see United States v. Washington*, 431 U.S. 181 (1977); *United States v. Mandujano, supra*, 425 U.S. at 572-76 (plurality opinion); *cf. Garner v. United States*, 424 U.S. 648, 653-56 (1976); *Minnesota v. Murphy*, 465 U.S. 420, 427-31 (1984)); and even apparently innocuous testimony can often turn out subsequently to assist the prosecution in constructing a case along some line or theory that neither the client nor counsel has sufficient information to anticipate at this early stage of the proceeding. Accordingly, the client should almost always claim the Fifth Amendment right to refuse to answer grand jury questioning and should avoid appearing before the grand jury if at all possible.

If the jurisdiction is one that forbids the calling of a prospective defendant (see § 12.6.1 *supra*) the prosecutor should be advised that counsel's client will not appear and should be asked to withdraw the subpoena. If the prosecutor refuses to do so, counsel should then move the court to quash it.

In a jurisdiction that allows the defendant to be called, counsel should advise the prosecutor that if the client is compelled to appear before the grand jury, the client will claim the Fifth Amendment in response to all questions bearing in any way upon any criminal charge. Counsel should ask the prosecutor, therefore, to discharge the client from the obligation to appear, since his or her compelled appearance would only harass and prejudice the client before the grand jury, without serving any legitimate purpose in furtherance of the jury's inquiry. If the client is not then excused from appearing, counsel should instruct the client to appear and claim the privilege. This claim may not subsequently be used against the client at any criminal trial (*United States v. Washington, supra*, 431 U.S. at 191 (dictum)), nor may the client be made by the state to suffer any "grave [adverse] consequences solely because he refused to waive immunity from prosecution and give self-incriminating testimony" (*Lefkowitz v. Cunningham, supra*, 431 U.S. at 807). *See, e.g., Gardner v. Broderick*, 392 U.S. 273 (1968); *Lefkowitz v. Turley*, 414 U.S. 70 (1973).

12.6.4.3. *Instructions to Give the Client*

As noted in § 12.6.1 *supra*, some States permit counsel for a grand jury witness to accompany the witness into the grand jury room and to advise the client during his or her testimony. Counsel should always take advantage of this right. In addition to protecting the client from incriminating questioning and other prosecutorial abuse, counsel stands to learn potentially useful information about the prosecution's theory of the case – and sometimes about specific pieces of prosecution evidence – by noting the prosecutor's questions and considering their drift. Prior to entering the grand jury room, counsel should advise the client that during his or her testimony s/he should pause briefly before answering each question, so as to give counsel time to determine whether there is a basis and reason for the client to refuse to answer.

In States which do not permit counsel to be present during a client's testimony, counsel should give the following instructions to the client. It is best to set them out in writing on a sheet of paper that the client can take into the grand jury room. A written prompt both reminds the client what s/he should say and gives the client confidence in saying it. As a stage prop, it also signals to the grand jurors that the client's hesitation to answer questions is a matter of routine protocol dictated by the client's legal adviser, not an indication of guilt or truculence.

> In answer to *every* question, say: "I RESPECTFULLY REQUEST PERMISSION TO LEAVE THE GRAND JURY ROOM TO CONSULT WITH MY LAWYER, SO THAT COUNSEL MAY ADVISE ME OF MY CONSTITUTIONAL RIGHTS IN REGARD TO ANSWERING THAT QUESTION."

> If permission to leave is granted, come out and tell me what the question was.

> If permission to leave is refused and you are directed to answer the question, say: "I RESPECTFULLY DECLINE TO ANSWER ON ADVICE OF COUNSEL, ON THE GROUNDS OF MY STATE AND FEDERAL PRIVILEGES AGAINST SELF-INCRIMINATION."

> *Never say anything other than these two things in the grand jury room* unless I instruct you specifically that you can.

Before the client enters the grand jury room, counsel should have determined whether any of the usual preliminary questions (name, current address, length of residence there) would be potentially incriminating. If not, the client should be told in advance that it is okay to answer those. But the client should be instructed to read the responses written on the card in answer to all other questions, even though the client may believe that the answer to a particular question would not, in fact, be incriminating.

The test of a valid claim of privilege is whether any conceivable answer the witness might give *could* furnish a link in a chain of evidence incriminating the witness, not whether a specific answer *would* do so. *Blau v. United States*, 340 U.S. 159 (1950); *Hoffman v. United States*, 341 U.S. 479 (1951); *and see Maness v. Meyers*, 419 U.S. 449, 461 (1975). *Cf. Hiibel v. Sixth Judicial District Court of Nevada*, 542 U.S. 177, 190-91 (2004) (rejecting a Fifth

Amendment challenge to a "stop and identify" statute because "[i]n this case petitioner's refusal to disclose his name was not based on any articulated real and appreciable fear that his name would be used to incriminate him, or that it 'would furnish a link in the chain of evidence needed to prosecute'" (quoting *Hoffman v. United States, supra*, 341 U.S. at 486), and also because "[a]nswering a request to disclose a name is likely to be so insignificant in the scheme of things as to be incriminating only in unusual circumstances," although the Court acknowledges that "a case may arise where there is a substantial allegation that furnishing identity at the time of a stop would have given the police a link in the chain of evidence needed to convict the individual of a separate offense" and the Court explains that "[i]n that case, the court can then consider whether the privilege applies, and, if the Fifth Amendment has been violated, what remedy must follow").

A witness who claims the privilege is not required to explain how the answer will incriminate him or her – or even to assert that it will (since that assertion is obviously incriminating). *Hoffman v. United States, supra*, 341 U.S. at 486-87. S/he needs only assert that it *may*. And counsel is not obliged to leave a client to make unassisted determinations of the applicability of the Fifth Amendment to particular questions that the client is asked in closed-door grand jury proceedings. Rather, counsel may properly instruct the client to make a routine claim of privilege – if the client's right to consult counsel about each question is refused – as a means of forcing the constitutional issue out of the grand jury room into open court, where an attorney can properly instruct and defend the client.

Counsel should emphatically warn the client not to *ad lib* in the grand jury room, to watch out for the trick questions that prosecutors often snap back disarmingly at witnesses who claim the privilege – "Would that really incriminate you?" or "Now how could that possibly incriminate you?" – and to answer these questions, like all others, by saying, "I respectfully decline to answer, on advice of counsel, on the grounds of my state and federal privileges against self-incrimination." The client should be told that if anyone offers the client immunity, s/he should say nothing; but, once again, answer the next question by saying: "I respectfully request permission to leave the grand jury room to consult with my lawyer, so that counsel can advise me of my constitutional rights in regard to answering that question."

Counsel should always accompany the client to the grand jury session and remain immediately outside the grand jury room, available for consultation. If immunity is offered, counsel should confer with the prosecutor and ask the statutory basis for the immunity. After inspecting the statute, counsel may conclude that it does not apply to the case or that it is constitutionally insufficient in the scope of immunity it allows and may then advise the client to persist in refusing to testify. If the prosecutor or the grand jury wishes to press the point, the client will be taken before a judge, in open court, for proceedings to compel the client's testimony. *See United States v. Mandujano, supra*, 425 U.S. at 575-76 (plurality opinion). The judge will ask what specific questions the client refuses to answer and will hear counsel's objections to those questions. If the objections are overruled, the client will again be ordered to testify prior to being held in contempt. Counsel who continues to think that s/he has valid objections to the client's compelled testimony should request that the final order to testify be stayed pending counsel's proceeding by appeal or prerogative writ (whichever local practice allows) to obtain review of the judge's order. If a stay is refused, the client should be instructed to state politely that s/he refuses to answer questions, on advice of counsel, because of his or her privilege against self-incrimination. As long as the client's manner is inoffensive, counsel is now in a strong position to urge that the question of the validity of the claim of privilege should be tested in civil, rather than criminal, contempt proceedings. *See Shillitani v. United States*, 384 U.S. 364, 371 n.9 (1966); *Young v. United States ex rel. Vuitton et Fils*, 481 U.S. 787, 801 (1987) (dictum). Either form of contempt commitment may be challenged by appeal or by *habeas corpus* in state and federal courts. See §§ 3.84, 4.13-4.14 *supra*. The trial judge should be asked to stay the contempt order pending appeal or to release the client on bail or recognizance pending appeal. *Cf. Pillsbury Co. v. Conboy*, 459 U.S. 248, 251 (1983). If the judge refuses, the same relief may be sought by motion on the appeal or in *habeas*. *In re Grand Jury Proceedings (Lewis, Applicant)*, 418 U.S. 1301 (Douglas, Circuit Justice, 1974); *cf. In re Roche*, 448 U.S. 1312 (Brennan, Circuit Justice, 1980). Many judges are reluctant to release recalcitrant grand jury witnesses from confinement pending appeal of contempt commitments because the purpose of these commitments is coercive and they believe that immediate coercion of the witness is necessary to enable the grand jury to go forward with its investigation. Counsel faced with a judge of this mind may find it useful to call the court's attention to a dictum of the Supreme Court of the United States in *United States v. Wilson*, 421 U.S. 309, 318 (1975): "A grand jury ordinarily deals with many inquiries and cases at one time, and it can rather easily suspend action on any one, and turn to another while [contempt] proceedings . . . are completed. . . . 'Delay necessary for a hearing would not imperil the grand jury proceedings.'"

Under no circumstances should the client be left to make his or her own unaided decision before the grand jury whether or not to claim the privilege against self-incrimination, or whether or not to testify under an immunity grant. S/he is always entitled to have the matter brought out into open court, through the procedures described in this section, so that counsel can address the complex issues involved. *Cf. Maness v. Meyers, supra*, 419 U.S. at 465-70; *Pillsbury Co. v. Conboy, supra*, 459 U.S. at 261-62.

12.7. *Advising Defense Witnesses Subpoenaed by the Grand Jury*

Some prosecutors will issue grand jury subpoenas for witnesses whom they expect to testify favorably to the defense, in order to nail the testimony of these witnesses down on record for possible use to impeach them at a subsequent trial. Defense witnesses may be compelled to testify unless they have a valid ground for invoking the privilege against self-incrimination on their own behalf or unless their testimony is otherwise privileged (under the lawyer-client, doctor-patient, priest-penitent, or other recognized privileges) or unless they are questioned on matters irrelevant to the grand jury's investigations.

Counsel should advise a witness with a claim of privilege other than self-incrimination to assert it and should support the witness in its assertion through the same procedures that are outlined in § 12.6.4.3 *supra* for protecting a client's claim of self-incrimination. A witness with a potential self-incrimination claim should be advised to secure a lawyer to represent him or her independently. Counsel should interview all potential defense witnesses before they testify and should prepare their testimony much as it would be prepared for trial. See § 29.5 *infra*. Counsel should also explain to the witness the nature of grand jury proceedings, in order to make the witness as comfortable as possible while testifying. If local practice allows a lawyer to accompany and advise a witness during his or her grand jury testimony, it is usually advisable for counsel to do so, or to arrange for another lawyer to do so. (The latter course will be necessary if counsel's representing both the client and the witness would raise potential conflict-of-interest problems.) In jurisdictions that do not permit lawyers to advise witnesses during grand jury proceedings – which is to say, in most jurisdictions – counsel nonetheless may wish to accompany the witness to the antechamber of the grand jury room and to stand by while s/he testifies, especially if the witness is apprehensive.

When counsel was not allowed to accompany a witness into the grand jury room, counsel will want to take whatever steps are permitted under local law to find out the questions the witness was asked and what s/he said to the grand jury. If local statutes do not prohibit a grand jury witness from disclosing matters occurring before the grand jury, counsel should interview the witness after s/he appears before the grand jury, for the purpose of learning both the testimony s/he gave (as an arm against future impeachment) and the questions s/he was asked (as a means for discerning the prosecution's theory of the case). If an applicable statute does purport to forbid grand jury witnesses to reveal what occurred during their grand jury appearances – as numerous state statutes do – counsel may want to interview the witness anyway, challenging the statute on the ground that it is unconstitutional as applied to defense counsel's interviewing of a potential defense witness because it precludes fair opportunity to prepare and present a defense. *Cf.* § 9.14 *supra*; §§ 18.9.2.1, 18.9.2.4, 39.1 *infra*. Of course, counsel undertaking such a challenge must advise the witness about the statute before the interview and should secure legal representation for the witness if the witness is going to talk.

In cases in which it is apparent that the prosecutor is subpoenaing defense witnesses simply for harassment – subpoenaing a witness repetitively, for example – counsel may move to quash the subpoenas as abusive, on the ground that the prosecution is using the grand jury to intimidate defense witnesses and deprive the defendant of a fair trial. *Cf. Webb v. Texas*, 409 U.S. 95 (1972), summarized in § 39.1 second paragraph *infra*.

12.8. *Resisting Grand Jury Process*

Motions to quash grand jury subpoenas *ad testificandum* may be made on the grounds that:

(1)   The person subpoenaed is a prospective defendant (in jurisdictions that recognize the "prospective defendant" rule (see § 12.6.1 *supra*));

(2)   The subpoena has no legitimate purpose in furtherance of an investigation within

the jurisdiction of the grand jury but is being used solely for "harassment" (*United States v. Dionisio*, 410 U.S. 1, 12 (1973) (dictum)); *cf. United States v. Mandujano*, 425 U.S. 564, 582-83 n.8 (1976) (plurality opinion) (dictum): a motion to quash a grand-jury subpoena as beyond the scope of the grand jury's "lawful authority" (*id.*) "must be denied unless the district court determines that there is no reasonable possibility that the category of materials the Government seeks will produce information relevant to the general subject of the grand jury's investigation" (*United States v. R. Enterprises, Inc.*, 498 U.S. 292, 301 (1991); *accord, United States v. Doe Corporation*, 59 F.4th 301 (7th Cir. 2023));

(3)   The grand jury is not pursuing a *bona fide* inquiry looking to indictment but is employing its subpoena power for some other purpose – for example, to gather evidence against a defendant who has already been indicted (*In re National Window Glass Workers*, 287 F. 219 (N.D. Ohio 1922)); *cf. United States v. Mandujano, supra*, 425 U.S. at 594 (concurring opinion of Justice Brennan); or

(4)   The prosecutor is forbidden by law or by ethical prescription to issue grand jury subpoenas for the person at issue. *See, e.g., State v. Gonzales*, 290 Kan. 747, 234 P.3d 1 (2010) (enforcing Kansas Rule of Professional Conduct 3.8(e), which is modeled on AMERICAN BAR ASSOCIATION, MODEL RULES OF PROFESSIONAL CONDUCT, Rule 3.8(e) (a prosecutor shall "not subpoena a lawyer in a grand jury or other criminal proceeding to present evidence about a past or present client unless the prosecutor reasonably believes: (1) the information sought is not protected from disclosure by any applicable privilege; (2) the evidence sought is essential to the successful completion of an ongoing investigation or prosecution; and (3) there is no other feasible alternative to obtain the information"); *accord, State v. G.L.L.*, 2020 WL 3604260 (N.J. Super. 2020).

(5)   The person subpoenaed possesses a testimonial privilege that precludes compelling him or her to answer any relevant questions s/he may be asked in the grand jury proceeding. *In re 2018 Grand Jury of Dallas County*, 939 N.W.2d 50, 52 (Iowa 2020) (because of the work product privilege, "we conclude that the State cannot subpoena an expert retained by the defense to testify before the grand jury regarding her opinions on the criminal matter being investigated"); *State v. Peters*, 213 Ga. App. 352, 444 S.E.2d 609 (1994) (affirming a trial court order quashing a grand jury subpoena on the ground that the person subpoenaed could properly claim the marital testimonial privilege). This ground is recognized only in some jurisdictions. In others, the person subpoenaed must appear before the grand jury and claim the applicable testimonial privilege question-by-question.

Grand jury subpoenas *duces tecum* seeking the production of documents, records, or writings are susceptible to a motion to quash predicated on the same grounds (*see, e.g., People v. Corr*, 682 P.2d 20, 29 (Colo. 1984) (ordering purported grand jury subpoenas quashed because they were "not bona fide grand jury subpoenas" but were "used for an improper purpose"; "It is apparent that what the Denver District Court labelled grand jury subpoenas were in fact obtained on the initiative of Strike Force investigators. They framed the requests to the court, served the subpoenas . . . , took the toll records to their offices, analyzed them, and incorporated them into the wiretap affidavit. The mere fact that the toll records later were referred to in grand jury testimony, although apparently never presented to the grand jury, is insufficient to establish through usage by the grand jury that the toll records were the product of a grand jury subpoena."); *Tiller v. Corrigan*, 286 Kan. 30, 182 P.3d 719 (2008) (on appeal of a trial court ruling refusing to quash subpoenas *duces tecum* issued to a women's health care clinic by a grand jury convened in response to a citizen petition and apparently aimed at investigating abortions, the Kansas Supreme Court remands with directions that the trial court (1) "determine and make specific findings on the record as to whether there is no reasonable possibility that the patients' records being sought will produce information relevant to the general subject of the grand jury's investigation" and, "[i]f not, the court should quash the subpoena or modify it to comport with the relevance standard" (*id.* at 42-43, 182 P.3d at 727); (2) consider whether the subpoena recipient has made "an initial showing that the subpoena is overly burdensome or intrudes on a privacy interest," in which case "the district court must balance the grand jury's need for the subpoenaed material against the burden or intrusion upon the subpoena recipient" (*id.* at 44-45, 182 P.3d at 728); (3) "satisfy itself that the grand jury has not engaged in an arbitrary fishing expedition and that the targets were not selected and subpoenas issued out of malice or with intent to harass . . . [and, i]f so, the court should quash the subpoenas" (*id.* at 46, 182 P.3d at 729); and (4) "consider the competing interests of the State and the patients" (*id.* at 48, 182 P.3d at 730), recognizing that the "constitutional privacy interests implicated by theses subpoenas present a unique circumstance requiring additional analysis" (*id.* at 46, 182 P.3d at 729).)) or on the ground that the materials sought are privileged or constitutionally protected against disclosure. *Hale v. Henkel*, 201 U.S. 43, 70-77 (1906). A motion to quash may invoke the state and federal privileges against self-incrimination (*see United States v. Dionisio, supra*, 410 U.S. at 11 (dictum); *Zurcher v. Stanford Daily*, 436 U.S. 547, 562 n.8 (1978) (dictum); *United States v. Judson*, 322 F.2d 460 (9th Cir. 1963)), under any of the following circumstances:

(1)   The production of the documents, records, or writings could (a) constitute an admission of their existence or possession in a context in which such an admission poses a substantial threat of incrimination (*United States v. Hubbell*, 530 U.S. 27, 37-38, 43-45 (2000); *United States v. Doe*, 465 U.S. 605 (1984); *Fisher v. United States*, 425 U.S. 391, 410-12 (1976) (dictum); *cf. United States v. Oriho*, 969 F.3d 917 (9th Cir. 2020)), or (b) constitute an implicit authentication of them, when the authentication poses such a threat (*id.* at 412-13 & n.12 (dictum); *Andresen v. Maryland*, 427 U.S. 463, 473 & n.7 (1976) (dictum); *United States v. Hubbell, supra*, 530 U.S. at 37-38), or (c) lead to the individual's being "compelled to take the witness stand and answer questions designed to determine whether he has produced everything demanded by the subpoena," the "answers [to which] . . . , as well as the act of production itself, may . . . communicate information about the existence, custody, and authenticity of the

documents" (*id.* at 38-40, 43-45; *compare Braswell v. United States*, 487 U.S. 99, 100, 108-10, 119 (1988) (a "custodian of corporate records" "is not entitled to resist a subpoena on the ground that his act of production will be personally incriminating" because "the custodian's act of production is not deemed a personal act, but rather an act of the corporation," and "[a]ny claim of Fifth Amendment privilege asserted by the agent would be tantamount to a claim of privilege by the corporation – which of course possesses no such privilege"); *In re Twelve Grand Jury Subpoenas*, 908 F.3d 525 (9th Cir. 2018)); or

(2)   The writings are "private books and papers" of the person who is ordered to produce them and their contents are potentially incriminating (*Boyd v. United States*, 116 U.S. 616, 633, 634-35 (1886)).

Boyd invoked the Fourth and Fifth Amendments to invalidate a federal statute which provided that in certain cases the court might issue a notice to a party opposing the government, requiring the production of any business book, invoice or paper that the government asserted would tend to prove specified allegations. "[A] compulsory production of a man's private papers to establish a criminal charge against him, or to forfeit his property, is within the scope of the fourth amendment to the constitution, in all cases in which a search and seizure would be, because it is a material ingredient, and effects the sole object and purpose of search and seizure." *Boyd v. United States*, 116 U.S. at 622. "Breaking into a house and opening boxes and drawers are circumstances of aggravation; but any forcible and compulsory extortion of a man's own testimony, or of his private papers to be used as evidence to convict him of crime, or to forfeit his goods, is . . . [forbidden]. In this regard the fourth and fifth amendments run almost into each other." *Id.* at 630. Despite its celebration by Justice Brandeis as a decision that would "be remembered as long as civil liberty lives in the United States" (*Olmstead v. United States*, 277 U.S. 438, 474 (1928) (dissenting opinion)), *Boyd* has fallen into a near-total amnesic abyss on the part of the late-Twentieth-Century Supreme Court. In a string of decisions, the Court has held that the Fifth Amendment privilege is not violated by compelling the production from an individual of his or her accountant's papers (*Fisher v. United States, supra*, 425 U.S. at 405-14) or his or her "business records" (*United States v. Doe, supra*, 465 U.S. at 606), or by "compelling a target of a grand jury investigation to authorize foreign banks to disclose records of his accounts, without identifying those documents or acknowledging their existence" (*Doe v. United States*, 487 U.S. 201, 202 (1988)), or by seizing an individual's business records under a valid search warrant (*Andresen v. Maryland, supra*, 427 U.S. at 470-77). It has also rejected a Fourth Amendment challenge to a subpoena compelling a bank to produce an individual's account records. *United States v. Miller*, 425 U.S. 435, 440-45 (1976). The opinions in the first two of these cases and in *Miller* do take pains to distinguish *Boyd* by pointing out that the writings in question were not the personal records or "private papers" of the persons whom they incriminated (*Fisher v. United States, supra*, 425 U.S. at 414; *United States v. Doe, supra*, 465 U.S. at 610 n.7; *United States v. Miller, supra*, 425 U.S. at 440); the Court in *Doe v. United States* does note that "petitioner asserts no Fifth Amendment right to prevent the banks from disclosing the account records, for the Constitution 'necessarily does not proscribe incriminating statements elicited from another'" (487 U.S. at 206; *see, e.g., Securities and Exchange Commission v. Jerry T. O'Brien, Inc.*, 467 U.S. 735, 742-43 (1984); *Couch v. United States*, 409 U.S. 322 (1973)); and *Andresen* rests squarely on the ground that a search warrant, unlike a subpoena, authorizes the seizure of documents but does not compel their possessor to take any action to produce them (*Andresen v. Maryland, supra*, 427 U.S. at 473-77). So *Boyd* arguably survives in drastically narrowed form, to the extent of forbidding subpoenas addressed to an individual for the production of his or her own private papers whose contents potentially incriminate the individual (*cf. G.M. Leasing Corp. v. United States*, 429 U.S. 338, 355-56 (1977) (treating *Boyd* ambiguously); *United States v. Ward*, 448 U.S. 242, 251-54 (1980) (same); *United States v. Doe, supra*, 465 U.S. at 610-11 nn.7, 8 (same)), or at least survives in the case of peculiarly private papers such as nonbusiness letters and diaries (*see, e.g., In re Grand Jury Subpoena Duces Tecum*, 741 F. Supp. 1059, 1061-72 (S.D. N.Y. 1990); *cf. Hill v. California*, 401 U.S. 797, 805-06 (1971) (reserving the question); *Fisher v. United States, supra*, 425 U.S. at 401 n.7 (same)). For discussion of Fourth and Fifth Amendment issues raised by document subpoenas and for critiques of regressive aspects of current doctrines bearing on those issues, *see* Caleb Lin, *Silence and Nontestimonial Evidence*, 58 AMERICAN CRIM. L. REV. 387 (2021); Donald A. Dripps, *"Dearest Property": Digital Evidence, and the History of Private "Papers" as Special Objects of Search and Seizure*, 103 J. CRIM. L. & CRIM. 49 (2013); Donald A. Dripps, *Perspectives on the Fourth Amendment Forty Years Later: Toward the Realization of an Inclusive Regulatory Model*, 100 MINN. L. REV. 1885 (2016); Robert P. Mosteller, *Simplifying Subpoena Law: Taking the Fifth Amendment Seriously*, 73 VA. L. REV. 1 (1987); Robert P. Mosteller, *Cowboy Prosecutors and Subpoenas for Incriminating Evidence: The Consequences and Correction of Excess*, 58 WASH. & LEE L. REV. 487 (2001); *and see United States v. Hubbell, supra*, 530 U.S. at 49-56 (Justice Thomas, dissenting, suggesting that the time may be ripe for reinvigoration of *Boyd*); *cf. Riley v. California*, 573 U.S. 373, 396-97 (2014), discussed in § 25.8.2 concluding paragraph *infra* (holding that the Fourth Amendment forbids warrantless searches of cell phones incident to arrest, in large part because "a cell phone search would typically expose to the government far more than the most exhaustive search of a house: A phone not only contains in digital form many sensitive records previously found in the home; it also contains a broad array of private information never found in a home in any form – unless the phone is."); *Carpenter v. United States*, 138 S. Ct. 2206 (2018) (citing *Boyd* for the proposition that the Fourth "Amendment seeks to secure 'the privacies of life' against 'arbitrary power'" (*id.* at 2214); noting that "the Court has drawn a line between what a person keeps to himself and what he shares with others" (*id.* at 2216); explaining that in *United States v. Miller*, "Miller had 'take[n] the risk, in revealing his affairs to another, that the information [would] be conveyed by that person to the Government'" (*Carpenter*, 138 S. Ct. at 2216); insisting that "this Court has never held that the Government may subpoena third parties for records in which the suspect has a reasonable expectation of privacy" (*id.* at 2221); and rejecting the notion that "private letters, digital contents of a cell phone – any personal information reduced to document form, in fact – may be collected by subpoena" unconstrained by the Fourth Amendment's requirement of a search warrant (*id.* at 2222); *Byrd v. United States*, 138 S. Ct. 1518, 1526 (2018) ("Few protections are as essential to individual liberty as the right to be free from unreasonable searches and seizures. . . . Ever mindful of the Fourth Amendment and its history, the Court has viewed with disfavor practices that permit 'police officers unbridled discretion to rummage at will among a person's private effects.'").

Subpoenas *duces tecum* seeking records that are protected by the lawyer-client, doctor-patient, or other privileges may also be quashed. *Continental Oil Co. v. United States*, 330 F.2d 347 (9th Cir. 1964); *People v. Desmond*, 98 A.D.2d 728, 729, 469 N.Y.S.2d 141, 142 (N.Y. App. Div., 2d Dep't 1983) ("When a privilege is claimed with respect to the production, pursuant to . . . a subpoena [duces tecum], of taped documents, the witness is, essentially, challenging the validity of the subpoena itself and a motion to quash made prior to the witness's appearance is an appropriate procedure" . . . . Consequently, the case must be remitted to Criminal Term in order to afford . . . an opportunity of establishing that the attorney-client privilege prevents disclosure"); *In the Matter of an Application to Quash a Grand Jury Subpoena*, 239 A.D.2d 412, 413, 657 N.Y.S.2d 747, 748 (N.Y. App. Div., 2d Dep't 1997) ("Although the Grand Jury's power to subpoena records as an exercise of its investigative powers is extensive, it is not unlimited . . . . The Grand Jury may not violate a valid privilege, whether derived from the Constitution, a statute, or the common law . . . . Here, the District Attorney issued a subpoena demanding production of Coney Island Hospital's quality assurance records. . . . [A statute] provides that these records shall be kept confidential and shall not be released except to the Department of Health or another hospital considering granting privileges to a physician. This provision does not except from confidentiality the release of quality assurance records to the Grand Jury. ¶ Accordingly, the Supreme Court should have granted the application to quash the Grand Jury subpoena duces tecum."); *cf. Losavio v. Robb*, 195 Colo. 533, 540, 579 P.2d 1152, 1157 (1978) ("[T]he precise issue before us is whether the trial court abused its discretion in quashing the subpoena for being 'unreasonable and oppressive.' The court correctly recognized that the general assembly has expressed a strong public policy. . . in favor of preserving the confidentiality of state income tax returns. Although this policy of confidentiality does not amount to a testimonial privilege, it should carry great weight in deciding whether a subpoena duces tecum is unreasonable or oppressive. ¶ We hold that in the face of this important public policy the party seeking the income tax return, in this case the grand jury, bears the burden to show a compelling need for it. Absent a compelling need, the subpoena duces tecum should be quashed."); *Fisher v. United States*, *supra*, 425 U.S. at 402-05 (dictum). It is a recognized ground for quashing or limiting a subpoena *duces tecum* that the subpoena is oppressively overbroad or indefinite. *See In re Certain Chinese Family Benevolent and District Ass'ns*, 19 F.R.D. 97 (N.D. Cal. 1956), and cases cited. And "[t]he Fourth Amendment provides protection against a grand jury subpoena *duces tecum* too sweeping in its terms 'to be regarded as reasonable.' *Hale v. Henkel*, 201 U.S. 43, 76 [(1906)]; *cf. Oklahoma Press Publishing Co. v. Walling*, 327 U.S. 186, 208, 217 [(1946)]" (*United States v. Dionisio*, *supra*, 410 U.S. at 11-12 (dictum)). *Accord, United States v. Calandra*, 414 U.S. 338, 346 (1974) (dictum); *Fisher v. United States*, *supra*, 425 U.S. at 401 (dictum); *United States v. Miller*, *supra*, 425 U.S. at 445-46 (dictum); *Donovan v. Lone Steer, Inc.*, 464 U.S. 408, 415 (1984) (dictum); *D'Alimonte v. Kuriansky*, 144 A.D.2d 737, 739, 535 N.Y.S.2d 151, 152 (N.Y. App. Div., 3d Dep't 1988); *cf. United States v. Doe*, *supra*, 465 U.S. at 607-08 n.3. Local law should be consulted regarding additional substantive grounds for attacking grand jury process and the procedures by which the attacks can be made.

Grand juries (and occasionally prosecutors in support of their own criminal investigations) sometimes seek and obtain a court order requiring that a named individual submit to fingerprinting, photographing, or blood-testing or provide exemplars for handwriting or voice comparison. These kinds of orders, compelling responses beyond the scope of traditional subpoenas *ad testificandum* or *duces tecum*, were virtually unknown before the late 1960's, probably because of doubts that they were consistent with the state and federal privileges against self-incrimination and also – more basically – because there existed no authority in law for courts to make them. But following the decisions of the Supreme Court of the United States in *Schmerber v. California,* 384 U.S. 757 (1966); *United States v. Wade,* 388 U.S. 218, 221-23 (1967); and *Gilbert v. California,* 388 U.S. 263, 266-67 (1967), holding the Fifth Amendment inapplicable to "non-testimonial" compulsions, prosecuting authorities were emboldened to begin to seek these orders; and orders compelling suspects to speak and write for voice and handwriting comparisons were sustained over constitutional objection in *United States v. Dionisio,* 410 U.S. 1, 12 (1973), and *United States v. Mara,* 410 U.S. 19 (1973). In both cases, the Supreme Court considered only Fourth and Fifth Amendment contentions made against the orders; the parties apparently did not ask, and the Supreme Court certainly did not answer, the question what authority empowered criminal courts to issue these unprecedented orders, constitutional or not. A basic rule of any legal system has always been supposed to require that a litigant applying to a court for the issuance of process must show something more than that the process, if issued, would not violate anybody's constitutional rights. S/he must show that there is some affirmative authority in law for the court to issue that kind of process and that s/he has some legal right to invoke the court's authority. *E.g., In re Sittenfeld,* 49 F.4th 1061 (6th Cir. 2022), summarized in § 47.3 *infra.* Prosecutors have not generally been thought exempt from these rudimentary requirements. *See, e.g., Goodwin v. Superior Court,* 90 Cal. App. 4th 215, 226, 108 Cal. Rptr. 2d 553, 561-62 (2001) ("There is wisdom in a procedure authorizing an ex parte order, on an adequate showing and before criminal proceedings are brought, compelling a suspect who is out of custody to attend a lineup. Further, there is no constitutional impediment to such a procedure. However, despite the best intentions of the Sheriff and respondent court, that procedure does not currently exist in California law. The court therefore lacked jurisdiction to grant the order at issue."); *State v. Sandstrom,* 225 Kan. 717, 728, 595 P.2d 324, 332 (1979), quoted in § 34.7.2 *infra; State v. Whitaker,* 202 Conn. 259, 267, 520 A.2d 1018, 1023 (1987) ("A number of courts facing prosecutorial discovery issues like the one at bar have declined to adopt a rule of mutual disclosure of witness statements in the absence of some previous authorization by statute or rule of practice."); *Commonwealth v. Perez,* 698 A.2d 640 (Pa. Super. 1997) (dictum); *Lynch v. Overholser,* 369 U.S. 705 (1962); *State v. Olson,* 274 Minn. 225, 143 N.W.2d 69 (1966). Therefore, counsel should oppose prosecutorial requests for these kinds of orders on the grounds that, whether or not it would be constitutional for the legislature to authorize them, the legislature has not done so; and in the absence of legislation, courts are not at liberty to entertain applications for orders alien to the common-law tradition. *Cf.* § 18.11 concluding paragraph *infra.* Although this contention appears to be foreclosed in the federal courts (*see United States v. Euge,* 444 U.S. 707 (1980), construing a general statutory grant of the subpoena power as authorizing the compulsion of handwriting exemplars), it remains open as a matter of state law when state grand juries or prosecutors ask state courts to issue these orders. For a challenge to the current Supreme Court caselaw holding that the compulsion of physical examinations and actions and of document production is not subject to regulation by the Fifth Amendment's guarantee against self-incrimination, *see* Rinat Kitai-Sangero, *The Protection of Free Choice and the Right to Passivity: Applying the Privilege Against Self-Incrimination to Physical Examinations and Documents' Submission*, 29 WILLIAM & MARY BILL OF RIGHTS J. 271 (2020).

12.9. *Advocacy to the Grand Jury*

In some jurisdictions, defense counsel is permitted to communicate directly with the grand jury by a letter or other written submission, which may urge the grand jury not to indict (giving supporting reasons), or may request that the jury call the defendant or defense witnesses to testify.

Letters urging against indictment may sometimes be quite fruitful, particularly when they offer constructive alternatives to criminal prosecution: for example, the representation that the client is prepared to enlist in the army; that military discipline will do more to shape up the client than a term in prison; and that an indictment would bar the client's acceptance by the armed services. On the other hand, it is ordinarily unwise to put defense testimony in before the grand jury because, in the absence of defense counsel and a judge, the prosecutor can rattle witnesses or shape their testimony by heavy-handed leading questions and then will have an almost unlimited right to use the grand jury transcript for impeachment. Also, at this point in time, defense counsel seldom knows enough about the prosecution's theory of the case to be sure that nothing which the prosecutor could extract from a defense witness by unrestricted interrogation will lead to evidence bolstering that theory.

In any event, before addressing any communication to the grand jury, counsel should consult local statutes, rules, and customs. In many jurisdictions *any* communication by counsel to the grand jurors is improper and may be punishable criminally or by contempt.

12.10. *Identifying Grand Jury Witnesses*

The secrecy of the grand jury does not extend beyond matters occurring in the grand jury room. Statutes or rules in many jurisdictions provide that a defendant is entitled to receive a list of grand jury witnesses at or after the time of indictment. See § 13.7 penultimate paragraph *infra*. Counsel should review these provisions and take whatever steps they require to obtain the list as promptly as possible. In other jurisdictions, copies of grand jury subpoenas, like other subpoenas, are kept in the office of the clerk or the bailiff of the court and are not embargoed. Inspecting them is a rapid, low-cost method of identifying prosecution witnesses. Elsewhere, if the defendant's case is being presented to the grand jury at a time when few other cases are on, it may be productive for counsel or an investigator to go to the corridor outside the courtroom where the grand jury is meeting and observe what witnesses are called in.

B. *Other Defense Activity During the Pre-filing Stage*

12.11. *Checklist of Additional Steps to Consider Taking During the Pre-filing Stage*

The routine procedures that immediately follow bind-over are the prosecutor's drafting and filing of an information or informations in a misdemeanor (nonindictable) case (see § 2.3.6 *supra*) or, in a felony (indictable) case, the prosecutor's presentation of a bill or bills to the grand jury and the jury's return of the bills as "true bills" or indictments (see §§ 2.4.3, 12.1.2 *supra*).

During the period between a bind-over and the filing of the charging paper, counsel representing a client in a felony case will be taking the various steps discussed in Part A of this chapter with regard to the grand jury, including, where applicable: (1) challenging the array of grand jurors, or individual grand jurors, on grounds of improper selection, disqualification, and so forth (§ 12.3 *supra*); (2) moving to suppress illegally obtained evidence before its presentation to the grand jury (§ 12.4 *supra*); (3) requesting recording of the grand jury testimony (§ 12.5 *supra*); (4) considering waiver of indictment (§ 12.2 *supra*); (5) discussing bills with the prosecutor (§ 12.13 *infra*); (6) advising the defendant and defense witnesses with respect to testifying before the grand jury (§§ 12.6-12.7 *supra*); (7) resisting grand jury process (§ 12.8 *supra*); (8) making some form of defense presentation to the grand jury (§ 12.9 *supra*); and (9) investigating grand jury witnesses (§ 12.10 *supra*).

In addition to these matters relating to the grand jury, counsel will need to attend to a number of other things during the immediate post-bind-over period:

A.   *Matters looking backward to the preliminary hearing* (§ 12.12 *infra*):

         1.   Arranging transcription of the notes of testimony of the preliminary hearing;

         2.   Obtaining review of the bind-over by *habeas corpus*, motion to quash the transcript, or other appropriate procedure;

         3.   Securing reopening of the preliminary hearing or a new preliminary hearing or attacking waiver of the preliminary hearing;

         4.   Obtaining review by *habeas corpus*, motion for reduction of bail, or other statutory bail-setting procedure, of the magistrate's setting or denial of bail at the preliminary hearing.

B.   *Matters looking forward to the information*: Discussing charges with the prosecutor (§ 12.13 *infra*).

C.   *Matters looking forward to trial*:

1.   Conducting defense investigation in light of new matter disclosed at the preliminary examination (§ 12.14 *infra*);

2.   Discussing with the client the prosecution's case presented at the examination (§ 12.14 *infra*);

3.   Considering whether the defendant needs to be committed for pretrial mental examination (§ 12.15 *infra*);

4.   Exploring the possibility of negotiating a plea with the prosecutor (§ 12.13 *infra*).

D.   *Matters relating to the timetable of the prosecution* (§ 12.16 *infra*).

E.   *Preparation for the possible issuance of a bench warrant upon the indictment* (§ 12.17 *infra*).

F.   *Matters looking forward to sentencing* (§ 12.18 *infra*):

1.   Placing the defendant in a job, rehabilitation program, or other situation in which s/he can make a good adjustment record;

2.   Advising the defendant in regard to other changes of life style that may increase his or her attractiveness to a sentencing judge.

G.   *Considering whether there are grounds for a motion to disqualify the prosecutor.* Possible grounds include the prosecuting attorney's personal bias against the defendant (*e.g., State v. Gonzales*, 2005-NMSC-025, 138 N.M. 271, 119 P.3d 151 (2005)); the prosecuting attorney's personal embroilment in the case (*e.g., Packer v. Superior Court*, 60 Cal. 4th 695, 711-12, 339 P.3d 329, 340-41, 181 Cal. Rptr. 3d 41, 55 (2014) ("We disagree . . . with the lower court rulings that no evidentiary hearing was warranted concerning the . . . substantial issue of whether the prosecutor had become so personally involved in the case """"as to render it unlikely that [petitioner] will receive fair treatment during all portions of the criminal proceedings."""" . . . In the Court of Appeal's view, petitioner 'presented no direct evidence that the prosecutor had any role in . . . [the conduct of three individuals – including two of the prosecuting attorney's adult children – who had been acquaintances of the defendant and were potential mitigation witnesses but who refused to cooperate with the defense or evaded contacts attempted by the defense] or the prosecution investigator's conduct [of allegedly discouraging those witnesses from assisting the defense]' or that the prosecutor's actions were motivated by a personal grievance against petitioner. The Court of Appeal acknowledged that the trial court 'could have reasonably inferred that the prosecutor was upset with [petitioner] and was grinding that personal axe by tampering with witnesses and taking positions in pretrial litigation unhelpful to the defense.' . . . ¶ . . . An evidentiary hearing . . . [is required in order to] address questions concerning whether the defense had manufactured a conflict, questions concerning defense discovery tactics, the prosecutor's pretrial conduct, the effect – if any – of . . . [the prosecuting attorney's] role as a prosecutor upon his children's potential penalty phase testimony, and the gravity of the prosecutor's conflict – if any – as it related to the fairness of petitioner's trial."); the prosecuting attorney's identity as the victim of the offense charged (*e.g.*, *In re Ligon*, 408 S.W.3d 888 (Tex. App. 2013)), or other conflict of interest (*e.g.*, *People v. Zimmer*, 51 N.Y.2d 390, 414 N.E.2d 705, 434 N.Y.S.2d 206 (1980)); the defendant's need to call the prosecuting attorney as a material witness in support of the theory of the defense (*e.g.*, *United States v. Prantil*, 764 F.2d 548 (9th Cir. 1985)); the prosecuting attorney's previous representation of the defendant during which the attorney had the opportunity to learn information bearing on the current charges or a defense to them (*e.g.*, *State ex rel. Burns v. Richards*, 248 S.W.3d 603 (Mo. 2008) (holding disqualification appropriate despite the absence of any affirmative showing that such information was actually learned)), and, in some jurisdictions, the "appearance of impropriety" arising from prior interactions between the prosecuting attorney and the defendant (*see, e.g.*, *People v. County Court, City and County of Denver,* 854 P.2d 1341 (Colo. App. 1992)). In appropriate cases, disqualification may extend to the entire prosecuting office. *E.g.*, *id.; State v. Gonzales, supra; State v. Marner, Judge*, 251 Ariz. 198, 199, 487 P.3d 631, 632 (2021) ("We hold that, in the interests of fairness to the defendant and public confidence in the judicial system, a trial court has broad discretion to vicariously disqualify a prosecutor's office based on an appearance of impropriety"); *State v. Nickels*, 7 Wash. App. 2d 491, 492, 434 P.3d 535, 537-38 (2019) ("[t]he standard set by the Washington Supreme Court is that when an elected prosecutor has previously represented a criminally accused person in a case that is the same, or substantially the same, as the one currently pending prosecution, the entire prosecutor's office should ordinarily be disqualified from further participation"); *People v. Dekraai,* 5 Cal. App.5th 1110, 210 Cal. Rptr. 3d 523 (2016) (affirming a trial court order disqualifying the entire prosecutor's office at the penalty phase of a capital case after finding that that office had a conflict of interest arising from its involvement with the sheriff's department in a number of improper practices in the defendant's case and others, including placing confidential informants in the jail cells of individuals awaiting trial in an effort to obtain incriminating statements and, at the hearing on defendant's motion, failing to disclose records revealing these practices); *People v. Doyle*, 159 Mich. App. 632, 406 N.W.2d 893 (1987), *relief expanded on rehearing*, 161 Mich. App. 743, 411 N.W.2d 730 (1987); *compare People v. Solis*, 2022 CO 53,

523 P.3d 427, 433 (Colo. 2022) (reversing a trial judge's ruling that the entire prosecutor's office was disqualified where one member of the prosecutor's staff had previously represented the defendant as a public defender, the Colorado Supreme Court states that "to determine if disqualification is necessary . . . we look to whether confidential information from . . . [the single disqualified prosecutor's] prior representation of . . . [the defendant] 'has been and can continue to be adequately screened'" and answers that question in the affirmative on the record of the case at bar); *United States v. Williams*, 68 F.4th 564 (9th Cir. 2023) ("'The doctrine of separation of powers requires judicial respect for the independence of the prosecutor.' . . . '[A]bsent a violation of . . . the Constitution, a [federal] statute, or a procedural rule,'. . . we do not dictate to the Executive branch who will serve as its prosecutors. . . . We run an even greater risk of offending separation-of-powers principles when disqualifying an entire office of Executive branch attorneys. Such sweeping interference is seldom warranted. Indeed, every circuit court that has reviewed an officewide disqualification has reversed." *Id.* at 571-72. "Before disqualifying an entire U.S. Attorney's Office, a district court must make specific factual findings that show that the office's continued representation would result in a clear legal or ethical violation. Because the record does not reveal pervasive misconduct or a blanket conflict here, we reverse the disqualification order." *Id.* at 574.).

12.12. *Matters Looking Backward to the Preliminary Hearing*

These were discussed in prior chapters. Concerning review of the magistrate's bail decision, see §§ 4.13-4.14 *supra*. Concerning transcription of the notes of testimony of the preliminary hearing, see §§ 11.5.3, 11.6.2, 11.8.7 *supra*. Concerning review of the bind-over, see § 11.10 *supra*. Concerning procedures for reopening the preliminary hearing or challenging a waiver of that hearing, see § 11.6.2 *supra*.

Procedures seeking review of the bind-over or reopening of the preliminary hearing or challenging a waiver of the hearing should be undertaken as early as possible and, in any event, before the presentation of the case to the grand jury. The doctrine that a supervening indictment moots all attacks on the preliminary hearing or bind-over, although assailable (see § 11.4 *supra*), remains strong in most jurisdictions. Under the practice prevailing in some localities, the filing of a petition for *habeas corpus* or other application for review may work an automatic *supersedeas* of all proceedings in the criminal case. When it does not, counsel should be careful to move in the review proceeding for an order restraining the prosecutor from presenting the case to the grand jury during the pendency of that proceeding.

12.13. *Discussions with the Prosecutor*

As indicated in § 8.2.2 *supra*, the prosecutor retains considerable discretion concerning the charges s/he will press or drop (or, in some jurisdictions, add) by information following the bind-over. S/he has still greater discretion regarding the charges s/he presents to the grand jury. *Id.* And s/he often has discretionary authority to divert the prosecution or to cooperate with the defense in presenting a diversion option to the court. See §§ 2.3.6, 3.19, 8.2.2-8.2.4, 8.4 *supra*. Accordingly, counsel will find it useful to discuss the case with the prosecutor at this stage and, in light of the evidence presented at the preliminary examination, urge the dropping or reducing or diversion of charges. The events surrounding the commission of the offense and apprehension of the defendant will often have cooled somewhat by this time; the complainant may have calmed down or been impressed at the preliminary hearing with the gravity of the defendant's situation; hence the time may be ripe for urging a favorable exercise of the prosecutorial discretion. See §§ 8.2.3, 8.4 *supra*.

If the prosecutor is indisposed to drop, reduce, or divert charges without a *quid pro quo*, plea negotiation is sometimes best begun at this time. See §§ 15.6-15.16.2 *infra*. The further along the process goes, the more work the prosecutor will have already done and the less s/he will save by dealing with the defense. Once the prosecutor has calendared the case for trial, s/he has made something of a psychological commitment to try it and has arranged his or her other affairs so as to leave the trial date free. Before this happens, s/he is likely to be more negotiable.

12.14. *Defense Investigation*

Matters learned at the preliminary examination may cast a new light on the nature of the prosecution's case and may open up new leads or establish new priorities for defense investigation. See § 9.2 *supra*. Shortly after the examination counsel should review the case and consider whether redirection or intensification of defense investigation is advised. This may also be a good time to pursue cross-examination of the client, confronting the client with items of prosecution evidence presented at the examination and pointing out that the magistrate apparently credited them. See § 6.14 *supra*.

12.15. *Commitment for Mental Examination*

In some jurisdictions a defendant may be committed for pretrial mental examination to determine competence to stand trial at any time following bind-over. Counsel dealing with a client who may be mentally ill or intellectually disabled should consider whether moving for such a commitment is advisable. See §§ 16.1.2, 16.3, 16.5-16.6 *infra*.

12.16. *The Timetable of Proceedings*

Questions relating to a criminal defendant's constitutional, statutory, and common-law rights to a speedy trial, including rights (a) to have the proceedings expedited; (b) to be released on recognizance if the proceedings are inordinately delayed; and (c) to have the proceedings dismissed with or without prejudice, by reason of the inordinate delay, are discussed in §§ 28.4-28.5.4 *infra*. Those sections should be consulted. Suffice it to say here that in some jurisdictions statutes require that an information be filed or an indictment be returned within a specified period of time after a bind-over (or after "commitment," which may be construed to mean either bind-over or arrest). In other jurisdictions, statutes require that a defendant must be tried within a specified time after bind-over or after commitment. Remedies under the statutes range from the release of the defendant from custody on his or her own recognizance to the dismissal of the prosecution with prejudice. Backstopping the statutes are constitutional provisions and the power of the court (sometimes expressly given by statute or rule, sometimes implied as "inherent") to dismiss charges for want of prosecution. Under these various guarantees of the right to speedy trial, counsel may (and sometimes must) make appropriate motions prior to the filing of the charging paper. These may be in the nature of a demand for expedition of the proceedings, or they may be an application for relief by way of discharge from custody or from prosecution. After considering §§ 28.4-28.5.4, counsel should consult local statutes, rules, and practice.

Conversely, there are cases in which the defense may want to slow the pace of proceedings. Prosecutors – particularly overloaded prosecutors – will often be amenable to calendaring post-bind-over proceedings at times later than those prescribed by the applicable statutes and rules, if the defendant files a waiver of his or her applicable speedy-trial rights. Mutually convenient dates and the terms of any waiver should be negotiated informally with the prosecutor. If the prosecutor persists in forging ahead on a schedule that is harmful to the interests of the defense, counsel should prepare motions or prerogative-writ papers seeking a continuance of the arraignment date and other proceedings in the trial court, for filing immediately after the return of an indictment or the lodging of an information. See § 3.23.3 *supra*; §§ 13.11 subdivision (3), 14.2-14.4, 28.1.2, 28.3 *infra*.

12.17. *Anticipation of a Bench Warrant*

Once an indictment is returned against a defendant who has not been previously arrested, a bench warrant authorizing his or her arrest will ordinarily be issued by the criminal trial court upon the prosecutor's request. See §§ 2.3.3, 2.4.4 *supra*. Therefore, when counsel represents an unarrested client and knows that the prosecutor is presenting the case to the grand jury, counsel should suggest to the prosecutor prior to indictment an arrangement to surrender the client, without warrant, in the event an indictment is returned.

The arrangements for surrender are similar to those at an earlier stage, discussed in §§ 3.11-3.13 *supra*, except that in the bench warrant phase it is easier to arrange for the client's surrender before a judge of the trial court instead of a magistrate if that seems advisable. Should the prosecutor be uncooperative, counsel may be able to block a warrant by appearing before the judge prior to indictment. Counsel should inform the judge about counsel's offers to surrender the client in the event of indictment and about the prosecutor's refusal and should request that the court notify counsel when a warrant is sought so that counsel may surrender the client in court. Alternatively, counsel may request that the judge issue a summons in lieu of a warrant when this is authorized by local law or practice.

A bench warrant may also be issued for a defendant previously released on bail if the grand jury indicts on new or additional charges. See § 4.16 *supra*. Prior to indictment or immediately after indictment, counsel should discuss with the prosecutor an arrangement under which the bench warrant will continue the amount and terms of bail already in effect and specify that the bond already posted will secure the defendant's appearance for trial. If the defendant was released on O.R (see §§ 3.8.1, 4.2 *supra*), counsel should request the prosecutor's cooperation in continuing the O.R. terms pending trial or – if the prosecutor is unwilling to do that – counsel should try to negotiate with the prosecutor an agreement that the bench warrant will set bail at a manageable figure and with manageable release conditions (see §§ 4.4-4.10 *supra*), and that the warrant will be served on the client in the courthouse, so that bail can be posted immediately without the client being taken into custody (*cf.* §§ 3.10, 3.12 *supra*). Failing such an agreement, counsel should ask the prosecutor where and when s/he will be applying for a bench warrant; and counsel should appear with the client to request the judge to release the client on recognizance or to set a favorable bail amount. If the prosecutor refuses even counsel's reasonable request for notice, counsel can report this stonewalling to the arraignment judge or duty judge and request that the court itself notify counsel when the prosecutor's warrant application is presented. Once notified, counsel should be present with the client and should be prepared to argue for his or her proposed terms of pretrial release. See §§ 4.2-4.10 *supra*. If s/he anticipates that the judge will not go for O.R., s/he should estimate as best s/he can the amount of bail the judge is likely to set, and, if possible, s/he should have the necessary security or bond arranged beforehand, so that the client can be released from the courtroom without spending any time in confinement. See § 3.12 *supra*.

12.18. *Anticipation of Possible Conviction and Sentencing; Assisting the Client to Make a Favorable Appearance at the Time of Sentence*

Even while working to prevent a client's being charged and convicted, counsel cannot afford to ignore the possibility that the client *may* be convicted and that some day, sooner or later, s/he will stand before the court for sentencing. To prepare for this contingency, counsel should begin at a very early stage of the case to think about things that can be done to improve the client's image at sentencing – while there is still time to do them. See § 7.2.4 *supra*. The client who comes before a sentencing judge on a presentence report showing that s/he has successfully completed four months of a six-month job-training program since arrest and release on bail or recognizance, for example, is a far more likely candidate for probation than the client who remains just as unemployed and unemployable during those four months as s/he was at the time of the offense. Counsel should, therefore, advise and assist the client at the earliest possible opportunity to find a situation in the community in which the client can make and document a good, solid record of adjustment prior to trial and sentencing. In particular, counsel should consider the possibilities of getting the client placed in:

(a)   a steady, responsible job (see § 9.6 *supra;* § 48.2 subdivision 3 *infra*);
(b)   a job-training program;
(c)   an out-patient psychiatric or psychological counseling program (see §§ 16.1.8, 48.8 *infra*);

(d)   a community-based rehabilitation program for alcoholics or drug addicts, if appropriate and if (i) the client's enrollment in such a program would not furnish unprivileged evidence against the client or otherwise prejudice the defense on the criminal charge in the event of a not guilty plea and trial, and (ii) counsel has determined by inquiries in the probation department or among local criminal lawyers that the particular program is well regarded by the court (see § 48.8 concluding paragraph *infra*); or

(e)   any other sort of counseling program – family counseling, vocational counseling, speech therapy, remedial reading – that responds to the basic problems that apparently got the client into trouble (see *id.*).

Counsel should also consider whether the client would look better to the probation department or the court if the client altered his or her place of residence, life style, or companions, and should advise the client accordingly with all possible tact. The client's family and various social service agencies may prove helpful in all of these regards, but counsel will find that sometimes there is simply no substitute for counsel's advising the client or for counsel's tracking down a job or placement opportunity for the client.

Chapter 13

Defense Procedures After the Filing of the Charging Paper and Before Arraignment

13.1. *Checklist of the Steps To Take During the Period Between the Filing of the Charging Paper and Arraignment*

During the period between the filing of the charging paper and arraignment, counsel will need to consider a number of matters, including:

A. *Matters relating to the client's arrest (§ 13.2 infra):*

    1. Entering an appearance as counsel for the defendant;

    2. Protecting the client against arrest on a bench warrant.

B. *Matters looking backward to the preliminary hearing (§ 20.2 infra):*

    1. *Habeas corpus* or a motion to quash the transcript or the information or for other relief on the ground of denial of a preliminary hearing or on the ground of defects in the procedures at preliminary hearing or on the ground of insufficiency of the evidence to support a bind-over;

    2. In a nonindictable case, a motion to quash the information as unsupported by the preliminary hearing transcript or bind-over.

C. *Matters looking backward to the grand jury: Motions to quash or to dismiss the indictment (§ 20.3 infra)* based on:

    1. Objections to the procedures used in selecting grand jurors, to the composition of the jury, or to the qualifications of jurors;

    2. Objections to procedural irregularities before the grand jury;

    3. Objections to the evidence before the grand jury on grounds of:

        a. Insufficiency;

        b. Inadmissibility or illegal procurement;

    4. Objections based on compelled self-incrimination of the defendant before the grand jury or on immunity grants.

D. *Matters relating to the face of the charging paper: Motions to quash or to dismiss on grounds of*:

    1.   Failure to charge an offense (§ 20.4 *infra*);

    2.   Objections to venue (§ 20.5 *infra*);

    3.   Technical defects (§ 20.6 *infra*);

    4.   A statute of limitations (§ 20.7 *infra*);

    5.   Double jeopardy (§ 20.8 *infra*);

    6.   Misjoinder (§ 20.9 *infra*);

    7.   Substantive unconstitutionality of the criminal statute on which the charge is based (§ 20.1 subdivision 10, *infra*);

    8.   Selective prosecution or enforcement (§ 20.1 subdivision 11, *infra*).

    9.   Violation of an Ex Post Facto prohibition. *See, e.g., Tipton v. Montana Thirteenth Judicial Court*, 392 Mont. 59, 421 P.3d 780 (2018).

E. *Matters looking forward to the arraignment and trial*:

    1.   Objections to the defendant's mental competency to plead; motions for commitment of the defendant for mental examination (§ 13.4 *infra*);

    2.   Discussions with the prosecutor (§ 13.5 *infra*);

    3.   Defense investigation (§ 13.6 *infra*);

    4.   Motions for state-paid investigative or consultative assistance and for other support services that the defendant cannot afford; arrangements for compensation of court-appointed counsel (Chapter 5 *supra*);

    5.   Defense discovery, including a motion for a bill of particulars, a demand for a list of witnesses, and the initiation of other pretrial discovery procedures (§ 13.7 *infra*);

    6.   Motions to suppress illegally obtained evidence (§ 13.8 *infra*);

    7.   Motions for a change of venue (§ 13.9 *infra*);

    8.   Challenges to the venire of trial jurors (§ 13.10 *infra*);

9.   If the client comes within the concurrent jurisdiction of the juvenile court, and if local law authorizes transfer of a juvenile's case to juvenile court, consideration of the advisability of seeking such a transfer (§ 21.7 *infra*).

F.   *Matters relating to the timetable for proceedings (§ 13.11 infra).*

G.   *Conferring with the client (§ 13.12 infra).*

In the drafting and presentation of the prearraignment motions discussed in §§ 13.3-13.4 and 13.7-13.11 *infra*, counsel should also consult §§ 17.3-17.11 *infra*, dealing with practice on pretrial motions generally.

13.2. *Entering Counsel's Appearance for the Defense; Guarding Against a Bench Warrant*

After the prosecution files the charging paper (an information or indictment), the next prosecutive step will be the arraignment of the defendant on that charging paper.

When a defendant is in custody, ordinarily the defendant, defense counsel who appeared at the preliminary hearing, or both of them will be notified of the arraignment date by the prosecutor, court clerk, or court administrator. If new counsel has entered a case following bind-over, s/he should immediately advise the prosecutor, jail authorities, and clerk of the criminal court that s/he is now representing the defendant and should ask to be informed as soon as any charging paper is filed. Once advised of the filing, s/he should enter an appearance for the defendant in the criminal docket number, so as to be sure that s/he will be notified of all subsequent proceedings.

When a defendant is on bond, the arraignment notice may be sent to the defendant, to defense counsel who appeared at the preliminary hearing, to the bonding company or other surety, or to all of them. Bonding companies are usually pretty faithful about relaying the notice to the defendant and to counsel, but they may slip up; and defendants themselves will sometimes fail to notify their lawyers of the receipt of notices from the court. Therefore, if counsel has received no notice within a short time after the end of a grand jury term when a bill against a client should have been presented – or within a short time after bind-over in a case that can be prosecuted by information – counsel should make inquiries of the client, the bonding company, and the clerk of the court, in that order.

When a defendant who has never been arrested is indicted, the prosecutor will usually obtain a bench warrant from a judge of the court in which the indictment has been filed. The bench warrant is executed by arrest; the defendant is brought immediately before the court; an arraignment date is set; the defendant is committed without preliminary examination; and bail is set by the presiding judge.

If counsel has not already forestalled the issuance of a bench warrant by the procedures advised in § 12.17 *supra*, s/he should undertake those procedures immediately after indictment or should arrange the surrender of the client (see §§ 3.11.1, 3.12-3.13 *supra*). If these efforts fail and the client is arrested, counsel must take the usual steps to protect the client in custody and to obtain the client's release on bail or recognizance as quickly as possible. See § 10.1 subdivisions I-VI *supra* and the references therein. If the case is one in which the defendant has been previously bailed, then surrendered or was rearrested after indictment because of the addition of charges by the grand jury, counsel should urge the court to release the defendant on recognizance or nominal bail on the additional charges, in light of the defendant's obligation, secured by the bail previously posted, to appear for trial on the original charges. See § 4.16 *supra*.

13.3. *Motions to Quash or Dismiss the Charging Paper*

There are numerous grounds for moving to quash or dismiss the information in a misdemeanor case or an indictment in a felony case. These are addressed in Chapter 20. Local statutes and rules need to be consulted to determine the deadline for filing such a motion and the formal requirements for the motion. See § 17.7 *infra*.

13.4. *Raising the Question of the Defendant's Competency to Plead or to Be Tried*

In some jurisdictions, objections to the defendant's mental competency to plead or to be tried are raised by a special plea at arraignment, while in others they may or must be raised by prearraignment motion. For discussion of this subject and the matters counsel should consider in determining whether to raise a claim of incompetency, see §§ 16.1.2, 16.3, 16.5-16.10 *infra*.

13.5. *Discussions with the Prosecutor – Negotiation and Discovery*

As the case progresses toward the trial stage, defense counsel will want to continue and intensify discussions with the prosecutor concerning possible dispositions without trial. See §§ 8.2.2-8.2.4, 8.4, 12.13 *supra*. Plea negotiation is discussed in §§ 15.8-15.13 *infra*. In addition to the possibility that negotiation will lead to agreement on a favorable disposition, counsel should keep in mind its discovery potential. Whether s/he offers to negotiate or not, counsel is often advised to discuss the prosecution's evidence with the prosecutor shortly before arraignment and to request inspection of the prosecutor's file or items in it: the police report, laboratory reports, statements of prosecution witnesses, the defendant's prison record and probation or parole records (vital documents that defense counsel often cannot obtain from their sources but that the prosecutor will usually have), the criminal records of the complainant and prosecution witnesses, and so on. At this stage the file is likely to be fuller and the prosecutor more knowledgeable than heretofore.

13.6. *Defense Investigation*

At arraignment the defendant will have to enter a plea to the charge. See §§ 14.1, 14.5-14.11 *infra*. Although the plea may later be changed under some circumstances (see §§ 14.7, 14.8, 15.7.2, 17.1 *infra*), leave to change it is ordinarily within the court's discretion. The initial plea entered at arraignment can be quite important, both for this reason and because the arraignment judge may be a particularly favorable one before whom to enter a guilty plea if the defendant is eventually going to plead guilty (see § 15.7.2 *infra*). Consequently, counsel's factual investigation of the case should be completed before the initial choice of plea at arraignment, if at all practicable. The plea decision will usually be preceded by negotiations with the prosecutor

(§ 13.5 *supra*), in which the bargaining position of the defense will depend in major part upon defense counsel's grasp of the facts of the case. See §§ 15.3-15.11 *infra*. The need to be knowledgeable in bargaining puts a premium on pushing defense factual investigation as far and fast as possible prior to arraignment. See Chapter 9. New investigative leads may be provided by the charging paper itself, by a bill of particulars, by a witness list, or through initial discovery proceedings. See §§ 13.7-13.8 *infra*.

13.7. *Defense Discovery: Motion for a Bill of Particulars, Motion for a List of Witnesses, and Other Devices*

Upon the filing of a charging paper that is insufficiently detailed to inform the defendant of the vital statistics of the offense charged, s/he may move for a bill of particulars, setting out in the motion the additional information that s/he seeks. *See, e.g., United States v. Montague*, 67 F.4th 520, 531-32 (2d Cir. 2023), quoted in § 20.4.3 *infra*. S/he is ordinarily entitled to:

(1)   The specific date and time of the offense;
(2)   Its street location;
(3)   The name of the complainant or victim; and
(4)   The means by which it is asserted that the defendant committed the offense.

See, e.g., State v. Hicks, 666 S.W.2d 34 (Tenn. 1984) ("motions seeking a particularization of the time and place of the alleged offense are routinely granted as being necessary in order for the defendant to know against what he must defend, what the prosecution intends to prove"); *State v. Huerta-Castro*, 2017-NMCA-026, 390 P.3d 185 (N.M. App. 2016) (the indictment contained six identical counts charging that the defendant "did cause [Child 1] to engage in sexual intercourse and/or caused the insertion of any object into the intimate part of [Child 1]" (*id.* at 190) and six identical counts containing the same allegations regarding Child 2; defense counsel moved for a bill of particulars; he "detailed the vagueness and the effect on his inability to formulate a defense. Specifically, Defendant could not ascertain from the charging document around what time of day things might have happened, or relating whether Defendant was at work, what day or week it was, or where he was during these times." (*id.* at 192); the trial court denied the motion; the Court of Appeals holds that "the district court's failure to order the State to produce a bill of particulars to address the insufficiency of the indictment to charge specific and distinct offenses violated Defendant's rights to due process and requires reversal of five of Defendant's convictions" (*id.* at 194). "'The object of a bill of particulars in criminal cases is to enable the defendant to properly prepare his defense, and, to achieve that fundamental purpose, it must state as much as may be necessary to give the defendant and the court reasonable information as to the nature and character of the crime charged[.]' . . . In cases involving child victims, allegations of criminal behavior often lack specificity as to the date, location, or details of a particular incident within the period of time for which a defendant is charged. . . . We recognize that because the State has a compelling interest in protecting child victims, our courts can be 'less vigorous in requiring specificity as to time and place when young children are involved than would usually be the case where an adult is involved.' . . . This flexibility does not, however, permit the State to proceed based on a lack of adequate notice of the conduct upon which an indictment is based." *Id.* at 191-92); *State v. Vumback*, 263 Conn. 215, 819 A.2d 250 (2003) (substantially the same, but holding the erroneous denial of a bill of particulars harmless because the defendant obtained through discovery and other sources adequate specification of the time of the offenses charged); *Dzikowski v. State*, 436 Md. 430, 449-50, 82 A.3d 851, 862 (Md. App. 2011) ("The State violated . . . [the applicable statute] when it filed a bill of particulars in which, rather than inform the petitioner of the conduct that was the basis for the reckless endangerment count, it instead simply directed the petitioner to discovery. In so doing, the State switched the burden to the petitioner to identify the facts underlying the indictment. Because a charging document must inform the defendant 'of the specific conduct with which he is charged,' . . . , logically, and . . . [under the applicable rule of criminal procedure], a bill of particulars, in supplementation of a short form indictment that fails to so inform, must specify the alleged conduct to which the subject charge relates. Discovery, even open-file discovery, that includes police reports and witness statements, is not the same and cannot substitute for a legally sufficient bill of particulars. While such discovery may contain the full facts of the case, when a defendant is charged using a short form indictment, it is not, and cannot be, a substitute, or satisfy a demand, for a bill of particulars. Discovery does not particularize or relate, from the perspective of the State, the factual information contained therein to the offense charged. It is this perspective and relation of factual information to the offense charged that satisfies the form and substance of a bill of particulars."); *State v. Larson*, 941 S.W.2d 847, 850-53 (Mo. App. 1997) ("Dr. Larson was charged by information with fifty counts of Class A misdemeanor animal abuse . . . . ¶ Dr. Larson filed a motion for bill of particulars claiming that the information was deficient. Specifically, he asserted that each charge identified neither the acts of abuse nor the specific animal. As a result, Dr. Larson claimed prejudice in the preparation of his defense and the inability to prevent multiple prosecution for the charged offenses. The trial court denied Dr. Larson's motion. ¶ . . . Where an information alleges all essential facts constituting the offense, but fails to assert facts necessary for an accused's defense, the information is subject to a challenge by a bill of particulars. . . . A bill of particulars clarifies the charging document. It prevents surprise and restricts the state to what is set forth in the bill. ¶ The information in Counts 1 through 50 did not sufficiently apprise Dr. Larson of which hog – male, female, dead, alive, white, black, red, Hampshire, Yorkshire or Duroc – he was charged with having abused. Without providing some reasonable description identifying each hog allegedly abused, Dr. Larson would be subject to multiple prosecutions with no way to disprove that the State of Missouri had already litigated criminal charges against him for abusing a particular hog. ¶ . . . The trial court, therefore, abused its discretion in not granting Dr. Larson's motion for a bill of particulars."); *People v. District Court for Second Judicial District*, 198 Colo. 501, 504, 603 P.2d 127, 129 (1979) ("In this case the theft charges lodged against the defendants are broad in scope, involving a number of people and acts allegedly committed over a long period of time. Consequently, the charges needed to be further clarified. The trial judge properly recognized, however, that the defendants' request for a bill of particulars was extensive and included some matters more properly the subject of discovery proceedings. Accordingly, the motion for the bill of particulars was granted but appropriately limited in its scope. Granting a bill of particulars did not constitute an abuse of discretion in this case."); *State v. Robinson*, 2020-01389 (La. 3/9/21), 312 So.3d 255 (Mem) (La. 2021) ("La. Const. Art. I, § 13 requires the State to inform the accused in a criminal prosecution of the nature and cause of the accusation against him. The State may provide that information in the indictment alone, or in its responses to a defense request for a bill of particulars. . . . The purpose of the bill of particulars is to inform the accused more fully of the nature and scope of the charge against him so that he will be able to defend himself properly and to avoid any possibility of ever being charged again with the same criminal conduct." *Id.* at 256. "[H]ere, the case is complex, and defendant is accused of a broad conspiracy to obstruct justice in two separate murder investigations. In addition, the State has alleged numerous means in the statute by which defendant may have committed the crimes. . . . [I]t is clear that the State has yet to provide defendant with enough information about the nature and cause of the accusations against him to comply with La. Const. Art. I, § 13, and to sufficiently inform him of the nature and scope of the charges so that he will be able to defendant himself properly. ¶ Accordingly, we grant defendant's application in part to remand to the district court, which is ordered to afford the State one final opportunity to expeditiously provide sufficient particulars." *Id.* at 257.); *Masingill v. State*, 7 Ark. App. 90, 92, 644 S.W.2d 614, 615 (1983), *petition for review dismissed without expressing a view on the merits,* 278 Ark. 641, 648 S.W.2d 62 (Mem) (1983) ("[T]he State's charges against appellant never revealed that any other person was involved in the alleged crime. In a criminal case, the Bill of Particulars must state the act relied upon by the State with sufficient certainty to apprise the defendant of the specific crime and to enable him to prepare his defense. . . . Here, the State withheld details of the crime to which appellant was entitled and in doing so clearly served to frustrate his defense preparation."); *cf. Hunter v. State*, 829 P.2d 64, 65 (Okla. Crim. App. 1992) ("Initially, we are very disturbed by the fact that the prosecution in the present case did not file the Bill of Particulars seeking the death penalty until seven days prior to trial. At present, there is no set time prior to trial within which the State must file a Bill of Particulars . . . However, both parties agree that the notice need only be given within a reasonable time prior to trial. We find that giving notice that the State intends to seek the death penalty seven days prior to trial is clearly unreasonable. By comparison, the State is required to give ten days notice of its intention to use evidence of other crimes. . . . It is our opinion the State knows or should know no later than the preliminary hearing whether or not they intend to seek the death penalty in a particular case. We find the notice in the present case simply inadequate. The defendant has the right to a fair trial; how can one properly prepare for a death case trial in one week. This Court adopts the standard that the State must file the Bill of Particulars prior to or at the arraignment of the defendant. The trial court may for good cause shown, extend this time but should use its sound discretion in so doing.").

Allowance of a bill of particulars is generally said to rest in the discretion of the court, and the standard jargon is that the bill does not lie to discover prosecution "evidence" (that is, means of proving facts, as distinguished from the operative facts of the offense themselves). But counsel should note the more liberal practice recognized in *Will v. United States*, 389 U.S. 90, 99 (1967); *State v. Haynes*, 2022-Ohio-4473, 2022 WL 17683758 (Ohio 2022) (reversing a conviction for error in denying the defendant a bill of particulars: Haynes was "indicted for the abduction of his grandchildren who lived and stayed with him after his unmarried daughter died of a drug overdose." 2022 WL 17683758, at*1. "The charges against Haynes were exceedingly vague. With regard to each child, the indictment alleged only that '[o]n or about December 21, 2017 to December 27, 2017,' Haynes 'did, without privilege to do so, knowingly, by force or threat, remove [his grandchild] from the place where [his grandchild] was found." 2022 WL 17683758, at *5. "Haynes requested a bill of particulars setting forth ¶ 1. [t]he exact nature of the offense(s) charged; ¶ 2. [t]he precise conduct of the Defendant alleged to constitute the offense(s) (i.e. principal offender, aider and abettor, etc.); and ¶ 3. [t]he exact time that the offense(s) allegedly took place." 2022 WL 17683758, at *2. On a subsequent motion to compel the prosecution to produce the bill of particulars, "Haynes argued ¶ The State . . . has refused to

. . . specify for the Defendant what conduct they believe the Defendant engaged in which they alleged to constitute the offenses of Abduction. In particular, the State . . . has refused to provide discovery to the Defendant or otherwise specify in a Bill of Particulars what force or threat was used to remove the children and what circumstances existed that created a risk of physical harm to the children. 2022 WL 17683758, at *2. "The Ohio Constitution explicitly provides that a defendant has the right to know the nature of the accusation being made by the state . . . . Historically, this right was satisfied by detailed indictments. But with the advent of short-form indictments, bills of particulars became necessary in some cases to give the accused specifics as to what conduct the state was alleging constituted the offense, so that the accused could mount a defense." 2022 WL 17683758, at *4. "Presently, the exact contours of that right are procedurally specified by . . . [Criminal Rule 7(E): ¶ 'When the defendant makes a written request within twenty-one days after arraignment but not later than seven days before trial, or upon court order, the prosecuting attorney shall furnish the defendant with a bill of particulars setting up specifically the nature of the offense charge[d] and of the conduct of the defendant alleged to constitute the offense.' ¶ See also . . . [Revised Code 2941.07 ('. . . the prosecuting attorney shall furnish a bill of particulars setting up specifically the nature of the offense charged and the conduct of the defendant which is alleged to constitute the offense') . . . ." 2022 WL 17683758, at *4. "A defendant is not entitled to a prosecutor's work product, such as his trial strategy . . . , but Haynes had a [constitutional] right to know when the offenses were supposed to have occurred and specifically what conduct he allegedly engaged in that the state was alleging constituted the offenses. . . . Not only did Haynes have a constitutional right to know, but the state had an obligation, based on a criminal rule, a statute, and multiple unequivocal decisions of this court, to produce a bill of particulars telling him what he had a right to know." 2022 WL 17683758, at *5. ¶ ". . . Despite that mandatory duty, the state, the trial court, and the intermediate court of appeals chose to rely on caselaw of intermediate courts of appeal holding that even though . . . [Rule] 7(E) plainly sets forth a mandatory duty to provide a bill of particulars, that duty evaporates when full discovery is provided. ¶ Neither Article I, Section 10, of the Ohio Constitution nor . . . [Criminal Rule] 7(E) nor . . . [Revised Code] 2941,07 contain this exception. None of our decisions has endorsed such an exception. ¶ To the contrary, we have made clear that a bill of particulars is not the same thing as discovery and that discovery and the bill of particulars serve different purposes. . . ." 2022 WL 17683758, at *5-*6.); *State v. Meadows*, 172 W. Va. 247, 254, 304 S.E.2d 831, 838 (1983) ("[w]e have recognized a bill of particulars as a discovery device."). In most jurisdictions the defendant may not demur to the facts stated in the bill or move to dismiss it on the ground of failure to state an offense (see § 20.4 *infra*); and in the event that the prosecution's proof at trial varies from the particulars contained in the bill, the defendant is usually given nothing more in the way of relief than a continuance (or mistrial and continuance if continuance without a mistrial is not feasible (*cf. People v. Petersen*, 190 A.D.3d 769, 770, 140 N.Y.S.3d 234, 236 (N.Y. App. Div., 2d Dep't 2021) (reversing a burglary conviction because "the People limited their theory of burglary in their bill of particulars, which incorporated the allegations of the criminal complaint, to the intent to commit property damage and/or theft," but the trial court "permitt[ed] the prosecutor to argue, during summation, and . . . permitt[ed] the jury to consider, the uncharged theory that the defendant intended to assault the complainant"))); only very rarely will a court dismiss a prosecution for variance of the proof from a bill of particulars. The bill is therefore a device of limited utility. *But see People v. Bradley*, 154 A.D.3d 1279, 1279-81, 63 N.Y.S.3d 159, 160-61 (N.Y. App. Div., 4th Dep't 2017) (reversing the defendant's convictions of criminally negligent homicide and reckless assault while operating a motor vehicle because the prosecution had responded to the defense's pretrial demands for a bill of particulars with respect to the element of recklessness by specifying that the "'[t]he ingestion of marihuana and a failure to take medication were both factors that contributed to the defendant's recklessness,'" but the prosecution's "evidence presented at trial varied from the limited theories alleged in the indictment, as amplified by the bill of particulars," in that the prosecution "presented evidence that defendant was reckless based upon not only marihuana use and failure to take medication, but also based upon, inter alia, his lack of sleep, failure to inform his doctors of his syncope events, and failure to control his alcohol consumption"; "Inasmuch as there was a variance between the People's trial evidence and the indictment as amplified by the bill of particulars, and that evidence was insufficient to support the theories of defendant's recklessness set forth in the bill of particulars, defendant was essentially tried and convicted on charges for which he had not been indicted . . . ."); *cf. People v. Faison*, 198 A.D.3d 1263, 1264, 154 N.Y.S.3d 180, 182 (N.Y. App. Div., 4th Dep't 2021) ("[W]e must reverse the murder conviction [and grant the defendant a new trial] because County Court's instructions created the possibility that the jury convicted him based on a theory different from that set forth in the indictment, as limited by the bill of particulars. . . . the People's theory of depraved indifference, as outlined in the bill of particulars, was limited to defendant's assaultive conduct, i.e., his infliction of head injuries by shaking or hitting the child, . . . [but] the court's instruction allowed the jury to consider, in addition to the specifically delineated assaultive conduct, defendant's 'inaction' after the assault ended.").

More significant is the defendant's right to a list of witnesses. The right is given by statute or rule in most jurisdictions and may entail (depending upon statutory phraseology) a right to the names of all witnesses who appeared before the grand jury or at the preliminary hearing or a right to the names of all witnesses whom the prosecution plans to use at trial. (The latter right is generally held not to include prosecution rebuttal witnesses. It is enforced at trial, during the prosecution's case in chief, by defense objection to any witness not named in the list. The court may exclude the testimony of the witness, or it may allow the witness to testify and may grant a defense continuance to meet the testimony, in the discretion of the judge. See § 18.7.2 *infra*.) The right to a witness list is given by statutes or rules of two sorts: those which require that the names of witnesses be endorsed on the charging paper (*e.g.*, MICH. COMP. LAWS ANN. § 767.40a, which requires "the prosecutor . . . to attach to the information a list of all witnesses the prosecutor might call at trial and of all known res gestae witnesses, to update the list as additional witnesses . . . [become] known, and to provide to the defendant a list of witnesses the prosecution . . . [intends] to call at trial" *People v. Everett*, 318 Mich. App. 511, 518, 899 N.W.2d 94, 100 (Mich. App. 2017); the statute also requires that the prosecutor "provide to the defendant, or defense counsel, upon request, reasonable assistance, including investigative assistance, as may be necessary to locate and serve process upon a witness" (§ 767.40a(5)) and those which authorize the defense to demand the names from the prosecutor (*see, e.g.*, WEST'S SMITH-HURD ILL. COMP. STAT. ANN. ch. 75, § 5/114-9; ILL. SUP. CT. RULE 412(a)(i); *and see People ex rel. Carey v. Strayhorn*, 61 Ill. 2d 85, 329 N.E.2d 194 (1975), holding section (c) of the predecessor statute, which exempted rebuttal witnesses from the prosecutor's disclosure obligation, invalid under *Wardius v. Oregon*, 412 U.S. 470, 472 (1973), summarized in § 18.9.2.7 *infra*); *State v. White*, 123 Ill. App. 2d 102, 259 N.E.2d 357 (1970) (reversing a conviction where the prosecutor, in response to a defendant's motion for a list of witnesses, provided 7 names before trial but then, during jury selection, handed defense counsel a list naming 24 witnesses (including the 7), and the trial judge overruled the defendant's objection to allowing the 17 new witnesses to testify and denied the defendant's request for a continuance and for an order that the prosecution make those witnesses available for interviewing); *Brown v. State*, 242 Ga. 536, 537-38, 250 S.E.2d 438, 439-40 (1978) ("Prior to the empaneling of the jury, the prosecutor presented the appellant with a list of supplementary witnesses. The appellant sought to have the witnesses disqualified . . . . In the alternative, she sought a continuance in order to interview the witnesses. The trial court denied the relief sought, but offered defense counsel an opportunity to interview the witnesses outside of the jury's presence. ¶ . . . We accept the Court of Appeals' finding that allowing the appellant an opportunity to examine the witnesses outside of the jury's presence was an inadequate means of curing the state's failure to comply with the defendant's demand for a list of witnesses. Therefore, we hold that a new trial is required."). Even under statutes of the former sort, it is often common for prosecutors to withhold a witness list unless defense counsel ask them for it. After checking local practice, counsel should demand the list from the prosecutor, move to dismiss the charging paper by reason of the absence of witnesses' names on it, or move the court for an order requiring the prosecutor to produce a list, as occasion warrants. *See, e.g., United States v. W.R. Grace*, 526 F.3d 499, 509-10, 516 (9th Cir. 2008) (en banc) (upholding trial court orders that required the prosecution to produce a final witness list (including all expert witnesses and excluding only potential rebuttal witnesses) before trial and that enforced this disclosure requirement by limiting the government's presentation of witnesses at trial to those disclosed as of the enforcement order's date and limiting the reports the government experts could rely upon to those ordered disclosed: "Other circuits that have addressed a district court's authority to require the government to disclose its witness list in advance of trial have agreed that the court may do so. *See United States v. Cannone*, 528 F.2d 296, 299 (2d Cir. 1975) ('The general discretion of district courts to compel the government to identify its witnesses is acknowledged widely . . . .'). Some have invoked the court's 'inherent power, exercisable under appropriate circumstances, to assure the proper and orderly administration of criminal justice.' . . . Others have not explained the source of authority, but simply have stated that it is within a district court's discretion to order the government to produce a witness list under appropriate circumstances. . . . ¶ . . . [W]e . . . hold that the district court had authority to order and enforce the pretrial disclosures of government witnesses and evidentiary documents and that the district court did not abuse its discretion in doing so here.").

In addition to the motion for a bill of particulars and the demand for a witness list, defense counsel may, in some jurisdictions, proceed before arraignment with the various discovery devices discussed in Chapter 18 *infra*.

13.8. *Motions for the Suppression of Illegally Obtained Evidence*

Substantive and procedural matters relating to these motions are discussed in Chapters 24-27 *infra*. The motions may ordinarily be made during a part or all of the period after arraignment and prior to trial. But where they are also authorized before arraignment, there may be good reason to make them at that time. *First*, the motions are often a valuable informal discovery technique. Hearings on suppression motions can provide considerable information about the prosecutor's case. Any investigative leads unearthed in this manner are most useful if they come sufficiently early so that the defense has ample time to follow them up thoroughly.

Second, in many cases – particularly those in which the principal charges are for possession crimes – the defense will stand or fall entirely on a motion to suppress. If this is lost, the defendant is advised to plead guilty. Of course, s/he usually may plead not guilty at arraignment, move to suppress thereafter, and, in the event the motion is lost, change the plea to guilty. But there are some advantages to having the decks cleared for an initial guilty plea at arraignment if counsel thinks this advised (for example, when the arraignment judge turns out to be a favorable sentencer). For this reason, it is often sensible to make the suppression motion before arraignment and, if necessary, move to continue arraignment pending disposition of the motion.

Counsel considering whether to file a suppression motion should be aware that some judges may be irritated by being put to the extra work of conducting suppression proceedings and may reflect their irritation at sentencing if the motion is denied and the defendant is convicted, particularly when in hindsight they regard the motion as having been frivolous. In federal practice, the circuits are split on the question whether the defendant's filing of a suppression motion justifies the prosecution's refusal to request a sentencing reduction otherwise available under the Sentencing Guidelines to defendants who plead guilty. *See United States v. Longoria*, 958 F.3d 372, 376 (5th Cir. 2020) (citing the conflicting decisions).

13.9. *Motion for a Change of Venue*

Motions for a change of venue, discussed in §§ 22.1-22.3 *infra*, are ordinarily made following arraignment. In some jurisdictions, however, they may or must be made before arraignment. Local practice should be checked.

13.10. *Challenges to the Venire of Trial Jurors*

Matters relating to the selection of trial jurors (sometimes called petit jurors or traverse jurors) are discussed in Chapters 32 and 33 *infra*. It is sufficient to note here that challenges to the venire or to the array of trial jurors, raising contentions of improper selection methods or standards or of the disqualification of the jurors on a ground common to all of them, are required in some jurisdictions to be made within a designated time after the filing of the charging paper. Local practice must be consulted.

13.11. *Matters Relating to the Timetable for Proceedings*

Questions of the timing of the various stages of the criminal proceeding following filing of the charging paper are discussed in Chapter 28 *infra*. These sections deal with procedures and grounds for defense efforts to speed the proceeding up or to slow it down. Several matters, particularly, require consideration by defense counsel at the prearraignment stage. These include:

(1) Counsel will sometimes have grounds to move to dismiss the charging paper because it was not filed within a period of time limited by statute or rule following bind-over or commitment. See § 12.16 *supra*. The motion ordinarily must be made prior to plea.

(2) Counsel may wish to expedite trial or to lay a foundation for a motion to dismiss the prosecution because of lack of expedition of the trial. State statutes or rules frequently limit the

time within which a defendant must be tried following bind-over or "commitment" or the filing of the charging paper. (In some jurisdictions, more than one of these periods is limited.) The statutes and rules, however, are usually qualified (explicitly or by judicial construction) by a principle known as the "demand rule," which obliges a defendant to invoke the statutory rights by a motion to bring the case on for trial. In the absence of such a motion, no motion to dismiss the prosecution for delay beyond the statutory periods prescribed for trial will subsequently lie. See § 28.5.2 *infra*. In some jurisdictions, the period nominally prescribed by statute as running from bind-over or commitment or the filing of the charging paper is held by judicial construction to be tolled during the period of a defendant's failure to demand trial, with the result that the period actually runs from the date of demand. This version of the demand rule requires counsel's attention in the days immediately following indictment or information.

(3) Counsel may, on the other hand, want to consider a motion for continuance of the arraignment in order to allow time for preparation for matters that will arise at arraignment. See Chapters 14, 15.

13.12. *Conferring with the Client*

Arraignment is a stage at which the defendant will be required to enter pleas and to make various objections and motions. See Chapter 14 *infra*. Failure to raise available claims through the proper use of these procedures will ordinarily forfeit the claims irrevocably. Also, like any other court appearance, arraignment is a theater in which the defendant and defense counsel will be performers whose behavior will make a more or less favorable impression on the judge and the prosecutor. If the defendant is pleading guilty, s/he will have an elaborate role to perform. See §§ 14.1, 15,16.1, 15.17, 48.11.4 *infra*. How s/he plays it will affect both the validity of the plea and the judge's attitude when exercising the discretion – often quite considerable discretion – authorized by law or local practice in the choice of sentence and in ancillary decisions such as whether to suspend sentence or admit the defendant to postconviction diversion programs. See Chapter 48 *infra*. Even if the client is not pleading guilty, his or her demeanor at arraignment may affect the sentence s/he will receive after conviction at a trial. (This is most likely when the arraignment judge will also be the sentencing judge. But it can also happen if the defendant's demeanor at arraignment arouses a particularly sympathetic or antipathetic reaction on the part of a prosecutor who will later be making a sentencing recommendation.) And counsel's own demeanor will have to be thoughtfully planned. Often, arraignment is the first occasion on which the defendant will see his or her lawyer performing in court. The lawyer's *persona* may well need to be very different than that which the lawyer has displayed in previous interactions with the client. It will have to implement the defense theory of the case (see Chapter 7 *supra*), which may require counsel to be more accommodating toward the judge or prosecutor than the client would expect from a gung-ho defense attorney unless the client understands beforehand why counsel is behaving as she is.

Before arraignment, therefore, counsel needs to have an extended sit-down with the client to:

(a)   Discuss all of the options regarding pleas, objections, and motions that can be made at arraignment; decide which options counsel will pursue; and get both the client and counsel as comfortable as possible with those choices. See §§ 1.3, 6.5-6.6, 6.14 *supra*; §§ 15.2-15.7, 15.14-15.17 *infra*.

(b)   Forewarn the client about everything that is likely to happen in court – including the nature of counsel's own performance – in sufficient detail so that there will be no surprises.

(c)   Prepare the client to play the client's role, and rehearse that role sufficiently to maximize the likelihood that s/he will play it well. See §§ 29.6-29.7, 48.11.4 *infra*.

Chapter 14

Arraignment and Defensive Pleas

14.1. *Arraignment Procedure Generally*

Arraignment is the stage of proceedings when a misdemeanor or felony defendant ordinarily appears for the first time in the court that has jurisdiction to try the case. The defendant has been notified of the arraignment date as indicated in § 13.2 *supra*.

A judge presides at arraignment. The charging paper (indictment or information) is handed to the defendant and is usually read to the defendant by the clerk. In metropolitan courts with a heavy docket, it is often customary for defense counsel to waive reading of the charging paper in open court. The defense loses nothing by going along with this custom; it may irk the judge if counsel does not. Counsel who is being appointed to represent the defendant for the first time at this arraignment will want to study the written charging paper in detail and discuss the charges with the client. See §§ 14.2-14.4 *infra*. Counsel who has been representing the client before the arraignment will have already discussed the charges with the client and made all necessary plans for how to handle the defense response to them at the arraignment. See § 13.12 *supra*.

The defendant is ordinarily asked to enter a plea to the charging paper. S/he may enter one or more of a variety of pleas. See §§ 14.5-14.11 *infra*. If s/he pleads not guilty, a trial date is set. If s/he enters a special plea requiring a hearing or an argument before trial on the merits, a date is ordinarily set for that purpose.

If the defendant indicates a wish to plead guilty, s/he is ordinarily advised by the judge:

–   that s/he has the right to have a trial; the rights to be represented by counsel, call witnesses, and cross-examine the prosecution's witnesses at trial; and the right to jury trial (if applicable);

–   that a plea of guilty waives all these rights; and

–   that upon the plea the defendant will be convicted and may be sentenced by the court in its discretion to a term of imprisonment of as much as x years (specifying the maximum) and to a fine of as much as y dollars (specifying the maximum).

In some jurisdictions, local law or practice may require that the judge also inform defendants that, if they are not a United States citizen, a conviction may result in removal or exclusion from the United States. *See, e.g.*, FED. RULE CRIM. PRO. 11(b)(1)(O). See generally § 15.6.1 subdivision (E) *infra*. If mandatory minimum sentences or other special sentencing consequences apply to convictions of the particular offenses charged, local law or practice may require the judge to inform the defendant of these. The defendant will be asked whether s/he understands the judge's warnings.

Ordinarily the judge will then proceed to interrogate the defendant to determine whether his or her plea is voluntary. The defendant will be asked:

- whether s/he is pleading guilty of his or her own free will, because s/he is guilty, and for no other reason, and

- whether anyone has made any threats or any promises to the defendant to induce the guilty plea or has promised that the defendant will receive any sentence less than the maximum in this case.

Some judges will reiterate that it is the judge's duty to decide what the sentence should be and that the judge will not be a party to, and will not honor, any promises on sentence but will sentence the defendant solely in light of his or her background and the nature of the offense. Some judges also will ask the defendant whether s/he is guilty of the charge of *x* (reading each charge) and then ask the defendant to describe briefly in his or her own words what s/he did (that is, to confess in factual detail in open court).

Most judges will also ask:

- whether the defendant has consulted his or her lawyer;

- whether the lawyer has advised the defendant concerning the consequences of the guilty plea; and

- whether the defendant is satisfied with the services of the lawyer.

This interrogation is sometimes conducted by the prosecuting attorney instead of the judge. In other courts defense counsel is expected to conduct it. Courts differ considerably regarding the extent of the inquiry that they conduct or require. Some ask a few perfunctory questions of the defendant or defense counsel; others cross-examine the defendant at length. (In federal practice, FED. RULE CRIM. PRO. 11 requires the judge to address the defendant personally and to make specified inquiries. Some States have similar requirements by statute or court rule.) If the defendant gives satisfactory answers, his or her formal plea of guilty is taken. S/he may then be sentenced at once, or a sentencing date may be set, with or without presentence investigation by the probation officer of the court and with or without a subsequent evidentiary hearing on sentence. (Again, local practice differs considerably regarding the extent to which a pre-sentence work-up is mandatory or discretionary following a guilty plea; and in any given jurisdiction, the requirements may depend on the grade or nature of the offense.)

If the jurisdiction in which counsel is practicing provides for defendants' participation in court proceedings via videoconferencing in some circumstances, the defendant may be able to assert a right to be physically present in court when entering a guilty plea. *See, e.g., United States v. Bethea*, 888 F.3d 864, 865, 867 (7th Cir. 2018) (granting the defendant's request to vacate a guilty plea which he made "via videoconference" due to "his health issues and limited mobility," because "the plain language of [Federal] Rule [of Criminal Procedure] 43 requires all parties to be present for a defendant's plea and . . . [therefore] a defendant cannot consent to a plea via videoconference. ¶ Our decision is supported by the unique benefits of physical presence. As the Sixth Circuit explained, '[b]eing physically present in the same room with another has certain intangible and difficult to articulate effects that are wholly absent when communicating by video conference.' . . . Likewise, the Fourth Circuit reasoned that 'virtual reality is rarely a substitute for actual presence and that, even in an age of advancing technology, watching an event on the screen remains less than the complete equivalent of actually attending it.' . . . ¶ . . . 'Without this personal interaction between the judge and the defendant – which videoconferencing cannot fully replicate – the force of the other rights guaranteed' by Rule 43 is diminished."). *Cf.* § 34.1 *infra* (relating to a defendant's right to be present during the trial) and § 48.11.4 *infra* (relating to a defendant's right to address the court at sentencing).

14.2. *Rushed Proceedings; Making the Record Clear; Continuances*

Counsel should expect that arraignment will be a hectic proceeding. Especially in metropolitan courts, dozens of cases are scheduled for arraignment in a morning. Defendants and their lawyers are moving back and forth from the bench. The judge is frequently impatient. Sometimes the prosecution will request a continuance to continue its investigation, and this will be granted before the defendant or counsel reaches the bench.

Counsel will have to keep composure in this confusion. If s/he does not understand what the judge is doing, or has done, with counsel's case, s/he should respectfully ask the court for an explanation. The record should be clear on whether the arraignment has been held or continued and, if continued, on whose motion. Defense objections to a prosecution-sought continuance should be noted. If defense counsel is confronted by something unexpected, s/he should ask for time to confer with the client or for a continuance to a later hour or date. S/he should resist being harried or pressured into snap judgments on previously unconsidered matters. *Cf.* § 11.7.1 paragraph 3 *supra.* In requesting consultation time or a continuance, counsel should state that s/he has not had adequate time to prepare for the arraignment and that proceeding under those circumstances would violate the defendant's Sixth Amendment right to counsel. See § 3.23.3 *supra*; § 14.3 *infra*.

14.3. *Appointment of Counsel at Arraignment*

If a defendant is called for arraignment and appears without counsel, s/he is usually advised by the judge of the right to counsel and to have counsel appointed if s/he is indigent. If s/he says s/he wants a lawyer and swears under oath that s/he cannot afford one (or executes a form pauper's affidavit), the court will appoint a lawyer. Sometimes a lawyer is appointed from among the members of the bar who are in the courtroom on other matters. The judge may say something like: "Counselor, will you talk with this defendant and advise the defendant on arraignment?" Such a request leaves it unclear whether the lawyer is being asked to represent the client and, if so, whether for the arraignment only or for the whole case. Counsel's first job is to clarify his or her own role. S/he should ask the court whether s/he is being appointed to represent the defendant as the defendant's attorney. Counsel should not accept an appointment to "talk to this defendant." Either s/he represents the defendant or s/he does not. Further, s/he should ask the court whether the appointment is to represent the defendant generally in the matter, at this and later stages, or only for the arraignment. If the latter, counsel should express the understanding that this means that the court will appoint other counsel to represent the defendant at subsequent stages if subsequent proceedings are advised. Counsel should make a clear request on behalf of the client for the assurance of adequate representation throughout the case. As an attorney s/he has an obligation to accept appointment, but s/he has neither the obligation nor the right to be used to create the appearance of representation without its reality.

Counsel's second job, therefore, is to request adequate time to interview the defendant privately and to prepare for the arraignment. This is as important as at a preliminary arraignment, and counsel's position should be the same. See §§ 3.15-3.16, 3.23.3 *supra*. Ample opportunity for lawyer-client consultation is guaranteed by the Sixth Amendment to the federal Constitution (*see Geders v. United States*, 425 U.S. 80 (1976); *Martin v. United States*, 991 A.2d 791, 793-96 (D.C. 2010); *cf. Perry v. Leeke,* 488 U.S. 272, 278-85 (1989)), and counsel must insist on it. Ordinarily a continuance of the arraignment to a later day should be requested. If the request is denied and counsel is forced to proceed, s/he should make an objection for the record on the ground that s/he is unprepared, has just been appointed, is not being afforded sufficient time to acquaint himself or herself with the case, and that thereby the defendant's Sixth Amendment right to counsel at the arraignment (*Hamilton v. Alabama*, 368 U.S. 52 (1961); *Rothgery v. Gillespie County, Texas*, 554 U.S. 191, 198, 213 (2008); *Gonzales v. Commissioner of Correction,* 308 Conn. 463, 68 A.3d 624 (2013)) is being violated. See § 3.23 *supra*. If the defendant is nevertheless compelled to plead, counsel should advise the defendant to stand mute, whereupon the court will enter a not guilty plea. See § 14.10 *infra*. After counsel has had time to investigate the case further, s/he may want to move to withdraw that plea, again asserting the client's Sixth Amendment right, in order to make other pleas or to raise defenses or objections customarily waived by a not guilty plea. See §§ 14.5-14.6 *infra*. Should counsel be relieved from representing the defendant after entry of the plea and the appointment of another lawyer, counsel should inform that lawyer of the circumstances under which the plea was taken.

14.4. *Continuances*

Arraignment may be continued, in the discretion of the presiding judge, on motion of either the prosecution or the defense. Defense counsel should request a continuance whenever s/he is unprepared to proceed (see §§ 14.2-14.3 *supra*) or needs additional time for some purpose (for example, to complete negotiations with the prosecutor, see §§ 15.8-15.13 *infra*). Whenever a defense motion is pending that, if granted, would terminate the proceedings or affect the choice of a defensive plea (see §§ 14.5-14.6 *infra*), counsel should either move to continue the arraignment or ask leave to withhold entry of a plea until the motion is decided.

Local practice varies with regard to whether motions for continuances of arraignment are made (a) in writing prior to the arraignment date; (b) by telephone, more or less informally, to the judge or clerk prior to the arraignment date; or (c) in open court when the case is called for arraignment. In localities in which more than one of these procedures is permitted, counsel should nevertheless ordinarily try to give the court at least some advance notice of a request for continuance. The court will appreciate this courtesy and may be more sympathetic to the request. It is also important to attempt to obtain the prosecutor's agreement to, or acquiescence in, a defense motion for continuance, if possible.

If an application for a continuance is denied, counsel should ordinarily object and then have the client stand mute (see § 14.10 *infra*). Only if s/he is adequately prepared to enter special pleas or to decide to forgo them and enter a not guilty plea, should s/he do so. See §§ 14.5-14.6 *infra*. Standing mute is the only safe course if counsel is unprepared and is forced, over objection, to plead. The judge will then instruct the clerk or counsel to enter a plea of not guilty. Should subsequent developments suggest a guilty plea, the plea of not guilty entered at arraignment can ordinarily be withdrawn and a guilty plea can be entered, with leave of court, at a later stage. This leave is usually easy to obtain. Should special pleas later appear advised, a motion to withdraw the not guilty plea for the purpose of pleading specially is in order. See § 17.1.1 *infra*.

14.5. *Special Pleas*

In some jurisdictions, particularly those that maintain the old common-law forms of criminal procedure, certain defensive contentions must be raised by special pleas at arraignment. In other jurisdictions these contentions are raised by motion, before or at arraignment or a specified time prior to trial on the merits, as prescribed by statute or rule of court.

Where special pleas are used, they must ordinarily be made prior to the entry of a general plea (guilty or not guilty). Usually a defendant may plead both generally and specially at arraignment, but s/he must enter the special pleas *first*. Several States are quite strict in holding that a general plea waives the right to present any defensive contention raisable but not raised by a prior special plea. Except where the grounds for the special plea are not then available or discoverable (*cf. O'Connor v. Ohio*, 385 U.S. 92, 93 (1966); *Smith v. Yeager*, 393 U.S. 122, 126 (1968); *Reed v. Ross*, 468 U.S. 1 (1984); *Amadeo v. Zant*, 486 U.S. 214 (1988)), it is probable that these sorts of enforced waivers can be made to stick. *See Davis v. United States*, 411 U.S. 233 (1973); *Francis v. Henderson*, 425 U.S. 536 (1976); *cf. Wainwright v. Sykes*, 433 U.S. 72 (1977); *Engle v. Isaac*, 456 U.S. 107 (1982); *but see Humphrey v. Cady*, 405 U.S. 504, 517 (1972); *Blackledge v. Perry*, 417 U.S. 21 (1974); *cf. Menna v. New York*, 423 U.S. 61 (1975) (per curiam), discussed in *Abney v. United States*, 431 U.S. 651, 659-62 (1977). On the other hand, where – as is common – the arraignment or trial judge is given broad discretion to permit the withdrawal of a general plea in order to allow the belated entry of special pleas, the irregular, unfavorable exercise of that discretion in particular cases may not foreclose federal constitutional claims against subsequent appeal or collateral attack. The mere existence of judicial discretion to enforce or relax a state procedural rule does not open the door to federal challenge. *Beard v. Kindler*, 558 U.S. 53 (2009); *Engle v. Isaac, supra*, 456 U.S. at 135 n.44. But a showing that the discretion has been exercised erratically or inexplicably does. *See Barr v. City of Columbia*, 378 U.S. 146, 149-50 (1964); *James v. Kentucky*, 466 U.S. 341, 345-49 (1984); *Johnson v. Mississippi*, 486 U.S. 578, 587-89 (1988); *Williams v. Georgia*, 349 U.S. 375, 382-89 (1955), *reaffirmed in Shuttlesworth v. City of Birmingham*, 376 U.S. 339 (1964) (per curiam). Counsel who seeks and is denied leave to enter an untimely special plea under these discretionary practices should therefore be sure that the special plea and the grounds for it are preserved in the record for appeal, and should document the irregularity with which the discretion has been exercised in other cases. Reported appellate decisions may or may not suffice to make the point that a discretionary procedural bar is being whimsically applied in counsel's State. If they do not, counsel may be able to establish the point by putting transcripts of other cases into the record or by presenting affidavits from experienced criminal trial practitioners.

14.6. *Checklist of Special Pleas and Other Matters That Must Be Presented at Arraignment*

In the various jurisdictions, counsel may find that one or more of the following special pleas must be used to raise the indicated claims. Local practice should be consulted.

A. *Plea to the jurisdiction*. This plea challenges the jurisdiction of the court over the subject matter or the person of the defendant.

B. *Pleas in abatement*. These pleas are used to attack the face of the charging paper for substantive or technical inadequacy. They raise points like those that are considered in connection with the motions discussed in §§ 20.4-20.7, 20.9 *infra*.

C. *Plea of limitations*. The contention that prosecution is barred by a statute of limitations is sometimes raised by a special plea. In other localities it is raised by a plea in abatement, by pretrial motion, or by demurrer or motion at trial. See § 20.7 *infra*. Unless state law treats the bars created by a criminal statute of limitations as jurisdictional (*see, e.g., People v. Williams*, 21 Cal. 4th 335, 981 P.2d 42, 87 Cal. Rptr. 2d 412 (1999); *Cunningham v. District Court of Tulsa County*, 432 P.2d 992 (Okla. Crim. App. 1967)), a defendant's failure to use the appropriate procedure for claiming the bar will forfeit the claim (*see Musacchio v. United States*, 577 U.S. 237, 246-48 (2016)).

D. *Special pleas in bar*. These include:

    1. Pardon (that is, a grant of executive clemency);

    2. Double jeopardy (technically, *autrefois convict, autrefois acquit*, or former jeopardy; see § 20.8 *infra*);

    3. Immunity (see § 12.6.4 *supra*).

E. *Plea of not guilty by reason of insanity* (that is, lack of criminal responsibility by reason of mental disease under *M'Naghten* or its modern-day counterparts *at the time of the offense charged*). In some jurisdictions the defendant is automatically committed for pretrial mental examination upon the entry of this plea. See §§ 16.11-16.13 *infra*.

F. *Plea of incompetency to be tried* (that is, *present* mental disorder rendering the defendant incapable of appreciating the nature of the proceedings or of consulting with counsel in his or her defense). In some jurisdictions the defendant is automatically committed for pretrial mental examination upon the entry of this plea. See §§ 16.5, 16.7-16.10 *infra*. The contention is sometimes made by an objection to pleading on the ground that the defendant is mentally incompetent to plead.

In addition to these special pleas, some jurisdictions require the filing of certain notices or motions at arraignment. The principal ones are:

G. *Notice of intention to present the defense of insanity* (that is, lack of criminal responsibility) *or other psychiatric defenses.* In a number of jurisdictions the notice procedure is used in lieu of, or in addition to, a special plea of not guilty by reason of insanity. Unlike the traditional special plea, the notice is frequently required to state the names and addresses of the witnesses whom the defendant intends to call in support of the insanity defense. A few jurisdictions require similar notice of intention to present expert testimony in support of other mental defenses, such as diminished capacity. *See, e.g., People v. Morris*, 173 A.D.3d 1220, 1222-23, 104 N.Y.S.3d 155, 157-58 (N.Y. App. Div., 2d Dep't 2019) (the statute requiring the defense to file a pretrial notice of intent to present psychiatric evidence applied to the defendant's intended use of psychiatric evidence "for the purpose of negating intent," but the trial court was wrong to preclude the evidence on the ground that "[t]he defendant failed to provide the People with timely notice of his intent to offer this evidence": the trial court should have exercised the statutorily-authorized discretion to permit late-filing because "[t]he evidence that the defendant previously had suffered auditory hallucinations had high probative value to corroborate the defendant's testimony that he entered the home with the intent to aid a woman who was yelling, rather than to damage the house," and "the preclusion of testimony regarding those portions of the defendant's conversation with the responding officer which involved his past auditory hallucinations, and his resultant hospitalization . . . deprived the jury of the full context of the interaction"). The constitutionality of these several requirements is governed by the principles discussed in the following paragraph. See also § 16.6.1 *infra*.

H. *Notice of intention to present the defense of alibi.* This notice also is ordinarily required to contain specified details: the names and addresses of alibi witnesses and the place where the defendant contends that s/he was at the time of the offense. State courts have generally sustained the constitutionality of notice-of-alibi statutes against attacks based upon the state privileges against self-incrimination. In *Williams v. Florida*, 399 U.S. 78 (1970), the Supreme Court upheld a notice-of-alibi provision challenged under the Fifth and Fourteenth Amendments. However, *Wardius v. Oregon*, 412 U.S. 470 (1973), holds "that the Due Process Clause . . . forbids enforcement of alibi rules unless reciprocal discovery rights are given to criminal defendants" (*id.* at 472); and a strong argument can be based on *Brooks v. Tennessee*, 406 U.S. 605 (1972), that the Fifth Amendment also forbids enforcement of alibi rules unless local practice provides the defendant with sufficient discovery, *prior* to the time when the alibi notice is required to be filed, to permit defense counsel to make an advised decision whether or not to rely upon an alibi defense. See §§ 18.11-18.12 *infra*. Both *Williams* and *Wardius* reserve the question of the constitutionality of the sanction commonly prescribed by notice-of-alibi statutes: exclusion of the defendant's alibi evidence at trial if s/he fails to file timely notice. *See Williams, supra,* 399 U.S. at 83 n.14; *Wardius, supra,* 412 U.S. at 472 n.4. The treatment of similar issues in *United States v. Nobles,* 422 U.S. 225, 241 (1975), and *Taylor v. Illinois,* 484 U.S. 400 (1988), strongly suggests that the exclusionary sanction will be sustained. *See also Estelle v. Smith,* 451 U.S. 454, 466 n.10 (1981); *Michigan v. Lucas,* 500 U.S. 145, 149-53 (1991); *Nevada v. Jackson,* 569 U.S. 505, 508-11 (2013) (per curiam). But where, as is usual, the statutes give the trial judge discretion to relieve defendants of this sanction, a failure to allow relief in particular cases may be challenged under the principle of *Barr v. City of Columbia,* 378 U.S. 146 (1964), and cognate cases (see § 14.5 *supra*), because the right to present alibi evidence is unquestionably protected by the Sixth Amendment against arbitrary or unreasonable restriction by the states. *Cf. Chambers v. Mississippi,* 410 U.S. 284, 302 (1973), discussed in §§ 18.9.2.4, 39.1 *infra; Holmes v. South Carolina,* 547 U.S. 319 (2006); *Rock v. Arkansas,* 483 U.S. 44, 52-53 (1987); *Taylor v. Illinois, supra,* 484 U.S. at 406-09 (dictum). *And see State v. Bradshaw,* 195 N.J. 493, 507-08, 950 A.2d 889, 898 (2008) (adopting the following "balancing test for preclusion of a defendant's undisclosed alibi testimony" as a matter of state law under New Jersey's Criminal Rule 3:12-2, which provides that, in the event a defendant fails to give notice of his or her alibi, the court may preclude the witness from testifying "or make such other order or grant such adjournment, or delay during trial, as the interest of justice requires": "[I]n reaching a fair determination for the appropriate sanction for the breach of the alibi rule, the trial court should consider: (1) the prejudice to the State; (2) the prejudice to the defendant; (3) whether other less severe sanctions are available to preserve the policy of the rule, such as a continuance or a mistrial to permit the State to investigate the alibi; and (4) whether the defendant's failure to give notice was willful and intended to gain a tactical advantage. Absent a finding that the factors on balance favor preclusion, the interest of justice standard requires a less severe sanction.").

I. *Motions to suppress illegally obtained evidence* (see § 13.8 *supra;* §§ 17.4-17.11 *infra;* Chapters 24-27 *infra*).

J. *Election or waiver of jury trial* (see § 32.2 *infra*).

K. *Motions to dismiss or to quash the indictment or the information.* As noted in § 14.5 *supra,* many jurisdictions have abolished or limited special pleas and now provide that some or all of the contentions discussed in §§ 20.2-20.9 *infra* should be raised by motions to dismiss or to quash the charging paper. Like the special pleas, these motions may be required to be filed prior to the entry of a general plea; or some other deadline for their filing, before or shortly after arraignment, may be fixed by statute or rule of court.

In some jurisdictions there are rather strict technical rules governing the order in which special pleas and motions must be made. Local practice should be consulted.

If the client comes within the concurrent jurisdiction of the juvenile court and if local law authorizes transfer of a juvenile's case to juvenile court, it may be necessary for counsel to file a motion for transfer at arraignment or to take some other action at arraignment to seek a transfer. Here again, local practice should be consulted. For discussion of the strategic considerations that counsel should take into account in determining whether to seek a transfer to juvenile court, see § 21.7 *infra*.

14.7. *General Pleas – the Plea of Not Guilty*

The general pleas are not guilty, guilty, and *nolo contendere* (or *non vult*). The plea of not guilty (at common law, a general plea in bar) raises what is known in the jargon as "the general issue." That is, it requires the prosecution to prove its case on the facts beyond a reasonable doubt and permits the defendant to show any defense to the charge that is not required to be set up by special plea, motion, or notice. As noted in §§ 14.5-14.6 *supra*, these latter matters must ordinarily be pleaded *before* the entry of a general plea of not guilty, or they are waived.

A not guilty plea at arraignment may later be withdrawn by leave of court to permit the defendant to enter a guilty plea, and courts are liberal in granting leave at any time prior to the close of trial. Therefore, unless a case presents some issue that must be raised by special plea, motion, or notice, it is ordinarily safe to enter a not guilty plea at arraignment as a holding operation, leaving the defendant the option of pleading guilty later at some more advantageous time. See § 15.7.2 *infra* on considerations of timing in entering a guilty plea.

14.8. *The Guilty Plea*

A plea of guilty is an admission by the defendant that s/he is legally guilty of the charges to which the plea is entered. The consequence is that a judgment of conviction may be entered on the plea and the defendant sentenced to the penalties provided by law for the offense. The plea ordinarily waives all rights to make any defense against conviction and thus forecloses an appeal raising even claims that error was committed in judicial proceedings prior to the entry of the plea (for example, pre-plea rulings on motions attacking the composition or procedure of the grand jury, motions to suppress evidence, motions for the provision of state-paid defense resources to an indigent defendant). *See, e.g., Wise v. State*, 708 N.W.2d 66 (Iowa 2006); *People v. New*, 427 Mich. 482, 398 N.W.2d 358 (1986); *State v. Mathieu*, 2018-964 (La.App. 3 Cir. 11/6/19), 283 So.3d 1041 (La. App. 2019); *but see Dos Santos v. State*, 307 Ga. 151, 156, 834 S.E.2d 733, 738-39 (2019) ("Defendants who plead guilty to criminal charges in Georgia courts have the right to timely pursue post-conviction remedies, including a motion to withdraw the guilty plea and an appeal.").

In most jurisdictions a strictly limited number of contentions may be raised on appeal or by *certiorari* or on collateral attack (see § 49.2 *infra*) following a guilty plea. See the subdivisions of the following paragraph. Some of these contentions may also be extinguished if, in addition to pleading guilty, the defendant expressly waives the rights to challenge the ensuing conviction by appeal or collateral attack. *Compare Khadr v. United States*, 67 F.4th 413 (D.C. Cir. 2023), *and Portis v. United States*, 33 F.4th 331 (6th Cir. 2022), *and United States v. Rakhmatov*, 2021 WL 6621136 (2d Cir. 2021), *with Garza v. Idaho*, 139 S. Ct. 738, 748 (2019), *and United States v. Yung*, 37 F.4th 70 (3d Cir. 2022); *and United States v. Watson*, 48 F.4th 536 (7th Cir. 2022). In some jurisdictions, a statute, rule or court decision also authorizes the appeal of pre-plea rulings on suppression motions and similar matters, notwithstanding a guilty plea. *See, e.g.*, FED. RULE CRIM. PRO. 11(a)(2) (amended in 1983 to permit defendants to enter a conditional plea of guilty or *nolo contendere*, with the assent of the court and prosecutor, that reserves the right to appellate review of specified rulings on pretrial motions; this statutory amendment resolved the previously open question of the propriety of conditional guilty pleas in the federal courts (*see United States v. Morrison*, 449 U.S. 361, 363 n.1 (1981))); N.D. RULE CRIM. PRO. 11(a)(2); *Mahaffy v. State*, 486 P.3d 170 (Wyo. 2021); *Christensen v. Commonwealth*, 2023 WL 2033445 (Ky. 2023). But counsel should make very sure that post-plea review is expressly authorized by statute or authoritative judicial decision in the particular jurisdiction before s/he advises a guilty plea in the expectation that any ground of legal defense will survive it. The Supreme Court of the United States has gone very far in according finality to guilty pleas and in holding them effective waivers of all defense claims. *Brady v. United States*, 397 U.S. 742 (1970); *McMann v. Richardson*, 397 U.S. 759 (1970); *Parker v. North Carolina*, 397 U.S. 790 (1970); *North Carolina v. Alford*, 400 U.S. 25 (1970); *Tollett v. Henderson*, 411 U.S. 258 (1973); *see also Corbitt v. New Jersey*, 439 U.S. 212, 218-25 (1978); *United States v. Goodwin*, 457 U.S. 368, 377-80 & n.10 (1982); *Mabry v. Johnson*, 467 U.S. 504, 508-09 (1984); *and see United States v. Chavez-Diaz*, 949 F.3d 1202 (9th Cir. 2020); *United States v. Dominguez*, 998 F.3d 1094 (10th Cir. 2021); *United States v. Williams*, 29 F.4th 1306 (11th Cir. 2022); *United States v. Spaeth*, 69 F.4th 1190 (10th Cir. 2023). Essentially, these decisions hold that a voluntary and understanding guilty plea entered by an adequately counseled defendant is conclusive upon the issue of guilt unless the applicable state law provides otherwise (*see Lefkowitz v. Newsome*, 420 U.S. 283 (1975); *Lo-Ji Sales, Inc. v. New York*, 442 U.S. 319, 324-25 (1979); *Shea v. Louisiana*, 470 U.S. 51, 53 (1985); *cf. Berkemer v. McCarty*, 468 U.S. 420, 424-25 & n.2 (1984)).

In the absence of a controlling statute or court decision authorizing appellate review of pre-plea issues despite a guilty plea, most state courts will not consider these issues, with the result that the only issues that survive a plea of guilty are:

(a)   whether the plea itself was voluntary (*e.g., Machibroda v. United States*, 368 U.S. 487 (1962); *Fontaine v. United States*, 411 U.S. 213 (1973); *Godinez v. Moran*, 509 U.S. 389, 400 (1993) (dictum)) and made with an understanding of the charge (*e.g., Bradshaw v. Stumpf*, 545 U.S. 175, 182-83 (2005) (dictum); *United States v. Ruiz*, 536 U.S. 622, 629 (2002) (dictum); *Marshall v. Lonberger*, 459 U.S. 422, 436 (1983) (dictum); *Smith v. United States*, 309 F.2d 165 (9th Cir. 1962)), including all of its critical elements (*see Henderson v. Morgan*, 426 U.S. 637, 647 n.18 (1976)), and with an understanding of the possible penalty (*Marvel v. United States*, 380 U.S. 262 (1965); *Crespin v Ryan*, 46 F.4th 803, 809 (9th Cir. 2022) (to escape a death sentence, a capitally-charged 16-year old defendant pleaded guilty to first degree murder pursuant to a plea bargain providing for a sentence of LWOP; years later, the United States Supreme Court held that the death penalty could not constitutionally be imposed on a juvenile of that age (see § 48.15 *infra*); later still, it held that the mandatory imposition of LWOP on a juvenile of that age was also federally unconstitutional (see § 48.7 subdivision (2)(d)(ii) *infra*); in federal *habeas corpus* proceedings, the Ninth Circuit vacates the defendant's sentence on the ground that it was made without an understanding of the penalty authorized upon conviction because "a defendant cannot voluntarily and intelligently waive a constitutional right of which he is unaware" or be aware of a right that has not yet been legally established); *United States v. Johnson*, 850 F.3d 515, 518, 522-23 (2d Cir. 2017); *Chapin v. United States*, 341 F.2d 900 (10th Cir. 1965); *and see State v. Engle*, 74 Ohio St. 3d 525, 660 N.E.2d 450 (1996) (the defendant's plea was not made knowingly or intelligently, and must be set aside, where the record showed that "all the parties, including the judge and the prosecutor, shared the impression that appellant could appeal rulings other than a pretrial motion" (*id.* at 527, 660 N.E.2d at 452), so that "[t]here can be no doubt that the defendant's plea was predicated on a [mistaken] belief that she could appeal the trial court's rulings that her counsel believed had stripped her of any meaningful defense" (*id.* at 528, 660 N.E.2d at 452)); *cf. Lane v. Williams*, 455 U.S. 624, 630 & n.9 (1982) (reserving the question whether and under what circumstances a failure to inform a defendant of a mandatory parole term will invalidate a guilty plea); *Hill v. Lockhart*, 474 U.S. 52, 56-57 (1985) (dictum that failure to inform a defendant that his eligibility for parole is restricted because of a prior conviction would not invalidate a guilty plea));

(b)   whether an adequate inquiry into voluntariness and understanding was conducted on the record before the plea was accepted (*McCarthy v. United States*, 394 U.S. 459 (1969); *Boykin v. Alabama*, 395 U.S. 238 (1969); *United States v. Tien*, 720 F.3d 464, 470 (2d Cir. 2013); *United States v. Fuentes-Galvez*, 969 F.3d 912 (9th Cir. 2020); *United States v. McIntosh*, 29 F.4th 648 (10th Cir. 2022); *see also United States v. Timmreck*, 441 U.S. 780, 784 (1979) (stating in dictum that a violation of FED. RULE CRIM. PRO. 11 would be raisable on direct appeal, while holding that such a violation is not raisable in collateral attack proceedings in the absence of a showing of prejudice resulting in a miscarriage of justice); *United States v. Lockhart*, 947 F.3d 187 (4th Cir. 2020) (en banc) (the defendant's guilty plea is vacated on direct appeal because the trial court's failure to advise him that he was subject to a mandatory minimum sentence of 15 years imprisonment violated Rule 11 and constituted plain error; the prosecutor, during a plea colloquy, had stated that conviction on the offense charged carried a maximum penalty of ten years, and the defendant had reason to believe that he would be sentenced to less than that maximum); *United States v. Murphy*, 942 F.3d 73 (2d Cir. 2019) (the trial court's acceptance of a guilty plea is vacated when it appears from the record that the prosecutor, judge and defense counsel were all of the erroneous view that the crime charged was a strict-liability offense; the defendant's ignorance that *scienter* was an element of the offense renders the plea invalid); *United States v. Jawher*, 950 F.3d 576 (8th Cir. 2020) (the trial court's acceptance of a guilty plea is vacated when the plea colloquy discloses that the judge, in inquiring whether the defendant admitted each element of the offense, omitted the *mens rea* element and thus left the defendant unaware of that element); *United States v. Heyward*, 42 F.4th 460, 464 (4th Cir. 2022) ("Antwan Heyward pleaded guilty to 'knowingly' possessing a firearm after being convicted of 'a crime punishable by imprisonment for a term exceeding one year.' . . . Two years later, the Supreme Court held that 'the word "knowingly" applies both to the defendant's conduct *and* to the defendant's status.' . . . Heyward was not advised of the second knowledge requirement before pleading guilty, and his lawyer made no objection to that omission. Because Heyward is the rare defendant who can make the 'difficult' showing that, had he been properly advised, 'there is a reasonable probability that he would not have pled guilty,' . . . we vacate his conviction and remand for further proceedings."); *United States v. Pierre*, 2022 WL 1198222, at *2 (5th Cir. April 22, 2022) ("Pierre argues that his plea was not knowing and voluntary and thus should be vacated because, among other things, it was conditioned on the government agreeing not to pursue a sentencing enhancement under a provision that could not apply to him. We agree with Pierre and hold that that the district court plainly erred by accepting his plea under these circumstances."); *Lejeune v. McLaughlin*, 99 Ga. 546, 546-47, 789 S.E.2d 191, 192-93 (2016) ("This Court has, for many years now, held that for a plea to be constitutionally valid, a pleading defendant must be informed of his three '*Boykin* rights.' . . . And, in . . . [2014] this Court [further] held that for a plea to be knowingly and voluntarily entered, a pleading defendant was required to know of his 'essential constitutional protections,' including his right against self-incrimination."); *State v. Brinkman*, 2021-OHIO-2473, 165 Ohio St. 3d 523, 527, 530, 180 N.E.3d 1074, 1078, 1081 (2021) (reversing a conviction based on a guilty plea because, in the colloquy preceding the plea, the presiding judge failed to advise the defendant "that by pleading guilty he was waiving his constitutional rights to confront the witnesses against him and to have the state prove his guilt beyond a reasonable doubt"; "the trial court's failure to strictly comply with Crim. R. 11(C)(2)(c) before accepting Brinkman's guilty plea renders his plea invalid."); *People v. Johnson*, 160 A.D.3d 516, 518, 76 N.Y.S.3d 18 (N.Y. App. Div., 1st Dep't 2018) (vacating the defendant's guilty plea because the judge advised the defendant that "she faced an adult sentencing range of 5 to 25 years in State prison when, as a 15-year-old juvenile offender, she in fact faced a minimum sentence of one to three years and a maximum sentence of 3⅓ to 10 years in the custody of the Office of Children and Family Services"; "Defendant's belief that she was avoiding a much greater risk than she actually was casts doubt on a finding that she had a clear understanding of her guilty plea."); § 14.1 *supra* (describing the procedure that judges usually follow when accepting a guilty plea)), so that it appears that the defendant knew and understandingly waived his or her "privilege against compulsory self-incrimination . . . [,] right to trial by jury . . . [, and] right to confront one's accusers" (*Boykin v. Alabama, supra*, 395 U.S. at 243); *see Lejeune v. McLaughlin, supra*, 299 Ga. at 547, 789 S.E.2d at 193; *Bautista v. State*, 163 N.E.3d 892 (Ind. App. 2021);

(c)   whether any promise made to the defendant as a part of a plea bargain has been violated (*Santobello v. New York*, 404 U.S. 257 (1971); *Blackledge v. Allison*, 431 U.S. 63 (1977); *Mabry v. Johnson, supra*, 467 U.S. at 509 (dictum); *United States v. Wilson*, 920 F.3d 155 (2d Cir. 2019); *United States v. King-Gore*, 875 F.3d 1141 (D.C. Cir. 2017); *United States v. Warren*, 8 F.4th 444 (6th Cir. 2021) (holding that the prosecutor's comments to the sentencing judge that the Government did not know certain aggravating features of the defendant's priors at the time when it entered into a plea agreement and that it likely would have made a different recommendation if it had known about those features violated the terms of the agreement stipulating that neither party would suggest in any way that a departure or variance from a specified sentencing range was appropriate); *United States v. Malone*, 51 F.4th 1311 (11th Cir. 2022); *United States v. Thomas*, 58 F.4th 964 (8th Cir. 2023) (finding a breach of a "no further prosecution" clause in a plea agreement in an earlier prosecution); *United States v. Diaz-Menera*, 60 F.4th 1289, 1298 (10th Cir. 2023) ("[t]o determine whether the government violated the plea agreement, we 'examine the nature of the promise' and evaluate that promise 'in light of the defendant's reasonable understanding' of such promise."); *compare United States v. Benchimol*, 471 U.S. 453 (1985) (per curiam));

(d)   whether the defendant was mentally competent to plead (*e.g.*, *Godinez v. Moran*, 509 U.S. 389, 400-01 (1993) (dictum); *Taylor v. United States*, 282 F.2d 16 (8th Cir. 1960));

(e)   whether s/he pleaded guilty without counsel and without an effective waiver of the right to counsel (*see, e.g.*, *Osbey v. State*, 425 S.C. 615, 825 S.E.2d 48 (2019)) or was inadequately represented by counsel in connection with the plea (*see Tollett v. Henderson*, 411 U.S. 258 (1973); *Hill v. Lockhart*, 474 U.S. 52, 56-57 (1985) (dictum); *Arvelo v. Secretary, Florida Department of Corrections*, 788 F.3d 1345, 1348 (11th Cir. 2015) ("[T]he Supreme Court has expressly held that a defendant does not waive an ineffective assistance of counsel claim simply by entering a plea. Instead, because 'voluntariness of the plea depends on whether counsel's advice was within the range of competence demanded of attorneys in criminal cases,' courts must continue to apply the familiar two-part test provided by *Strickland v. Washington*, 466 U.S. 668 (1984) . . . . Therefore, we decide (1) whether counsel's representation fell below an objective level of reasonableness, and (2) if so, whether a defendant suffered prejudice as a result. . . . ¶ In cases like this one, where a petitioner faults his lawyer for failing to pursue a motion to suppress prior to entering a plea, both the deficient performance and prejudice prongs of *Strickland* turn on the viability of the motion to suppress."); *Brock-Miller v. United States*, 887 F.3d 298, 308 (7th Cir. 2018) ("In the plea bargaining context, a reasonably competent lawyer must attempt to learn all of the relevant facts of the case, make an estimate of the likely sentence, and communicate the results of that analysis to the client before allowing the client to plead guilty"); *Day v. United States*, 962 F.3d 987, 992-93 (7th Cir. 2020) (the defendant was advised by a federal public defender to accept a favorable plea deal offered by the Government; the defendant subsequently substituted retained counsel who ignorantly advised him not to accept the offered deal, who prepared for trial belatedly, and who then, after realizing the strength of the Government's case, advised him to plead guilty without any deal and throw himself on the mercy of the court; the Seventh Circuit finds private counsel incompetent and remands for a hearing on the issue of prejudice: "To prove *Strickland* prejudice in the plea-bargaining context, the defendant must show a reasonable probability that he would have accepted the government's plea offer but for the ineffective advice of his attorneys *and* that the court would have accepted the agreement and imposed a less severe sentence." The District Court's postconviction finding of no prejudice "because the plea agreement would not bind the court to a particular sentence" was erroneous: "[T]he proper inquiry is not whether the sentencing court is bound by a plea agreement, but whether it is reasonably probable that the court 'would have accepted its terms,' and the resulting sentence 'would have been less severe' than the one that was actually imposed. . . . ¶ . . . Few court observers would contend that the government's views as reflected in its plea stipulations and Guidelines recommendations have no influence on a judge's real-world sentencing decisions."); *United States v. Galanis*, 759 Fed. Appx. 88, 91 (2d Cir. 2019) ("In the context of plea offers, counsel performs deficiently when he fails to (1) 'communicate formal offers from the prosecution to accept a plea on terms and conditions that may be favorable to the accused,'. . . or (2) 'inform the defendant of the strengths and weaknesses of the case against him, as well as the alternative sentences to which he will most likely be exposed'"); *United States v. Thomas*, 999 F.3d 723 (D.C. Cir. 2021) ("We remand the case to the district court so it may consider . . . [the] claims that . . . [Thomas] received ineffective assistance of counsel due to counsel's failure to (1) argue for or present facts supporting a *Smith* variance [that is, "'a downward departure . . . where the defendant's status as a deportable alien is likely to cause a fortuitous increase in the severity of his sentence. . .'" (*id.* at 736) or object to the district court's reasons for rejecting one, (2) raise mitigating facts contained in the Government's sentencing exhibits, (3) review the sentencing exhibits with Thomas, and (4) submit character letters Thomas's family and friends had written" (*id.* at 739)); *Mahrt v. Beard*, 849 F.3d 1164, 1170-71 (9th Cir. 2017) (dictum) (the rule of *Tollett v. Henderson*, *supra*, which allows a defendant to "'attack the voluntary and intelligent character of the guilty plea' based on pre-plea ineffective assistance of counsel," applies not only to "ineffective assistance rendered [by a lawyer] when providing incompetent advice concerning the guilty plea itself" but also to "pre-plea ineffective assistance of counsel . . . [that] prevent[ed] . . . [the defendant] from making an informed choice whether to plead," including "pre-plea ineffective assistance by failing to file a motion to suppress"); *United States v. Gardner*, 2022 WL 422167, at *1-*2 & n.1 (5th Cir. 2022) (the defendant is entitled to further consideration by the district court, "including any evidentiary hearing, as the court deems proper," of his pre-sentencing motion to withdraw his guilty plea on the ground that "he pled guilty to illegal possession of drugs without moving to suppress their seizure on his counsel's advice that he would raise the legality of the search in his objections to the presentence investigation report": the court explains that "Gardner's allegations may bear both on application of the factors [for determining whether to "'permit withdrawal [of a guilty plea] before sentencing,'" set out in *United States v. Carr*, 740 F.2d 339, 343-44 (5th Cir. 1984) – which include whether "'close assistance of counsel was available'" –] and also "on an eventual claim for ineffective assistance lodged under 28 U.S.C. § 2255 [see § 49.2.3.1 *infra*]," and that ""nothing in this opinion forecloses any of Gardner's rights under 28 U.S.C. § 2255"); *accord, Sunseri v. State*, 137 Nev. 562, 495 P.3d 127 (2021); *Johnson v. Uribe*, 682 F.3d 1238 (9th Cir. 2012), *as amended on denial of rehearing in* 700 F.3d 413 (9th Cir. 2012); *Anderson v. United States*, 981 F.3d 565 (7th Cir. 2020); *but see Clayton v. Crow*, 2022 WL 11485471, at *11 (10th Cir. 2022) (rejecting a challenge to a guilty plea presumably entered in reliance on counsel's unfounded promise or prediction of a favorable sentencing outcome because the defendant failed to prove that he would not have entered the plea but for counsel's bad advice; in postconviction proceedings, the defendant presented affidavits by himself, his wife, and his brother-in-law, all asserting that he would not have pleaded guilty if counsel had not made the improvident promises, but the Tenth Circuit dismisses these assertions as conclusory and insists that a defendant "must provide *some* explanation why he or she would rationally take the risk of going to trial" (*id.*). "This usually involves discussion of factors such as unmade but available legal and evidentiary arguments and affirmative defenses, the weight of the evidence against the defendant, the risk of an unsympathetic jury, and sentencing exposure." *Id.*). *Cf. People v. Dodson*, 30 N.Y.3d 1041, 1042, 89 N.E.3d 1254, 1254-55, 67 N.Y.S.3d 574, 574 (2017) (when the defendant, "[a]t a sentencing hearing following his guilty plea, . . . asked for a new attorney to advise him on whether to move to withdraw his plea before sentence was imposed" and supported the request with "specific allegations regarding counsel's [inadequate] performance[,] . . . the [trial] court had a duty to inquire into defendant's request for new counsel before it proceeded to sentence defendant"; because the trial court failed to do so, the Court of Appeals reverses and remands the case so that the defendant can be "afforded the opportunity to decide whether to make a motion to withdraw his guilty plea upon the advice of counsel"); *Davis v. Commissioner of Correction*, 319 Conn. 548, 549, 568, 126 A.3d 538, 540, 550 (2015) (defense counsel deprived his client of effective assistance at sentencing, and prejudice must be presumed, because "defense counsel agreed with the prosecutor's [sentencing] recommendation that the trial court should impose the maximum sentence allowed under a plea agreement even though that agreement contained a provision entitling defense counsel to advocate for a lesser sentence"); *State v. Mamedov*, 288 Ga. 858, 708 S.E.2d 279 (2011) (affirming the grant of postconviction relief in a case in which the defendant entered a guilty plea while represented by counsel who had a conflict of interest arising from counsel's simultaneous representation of a more culpable codefendant whose family paid counsel for representing both men); *Commonwealth v. Dew*, 210 N.E.3d 904, 906 (Mass. 2023) (ordering a Muslim, African-American defendant's guilty plea vacated and a new trial granted where the plea was entered on advice of court-appointed defense counsel who, unbeknownst to the defendant, had strong anti-Muslim and anti-black prejudices; the Massachusetts Supreme Judicial Court holds that there was a "conflict of interest inherent in counsel's bigotry")), or, in cases in which the defendant waived counsel, whether the waiver of counsel was effective (*see Williams v. Kaiser,* 323 U.S. 471 (1945); *Rice v. Olson,* 324 U.S. 786 (1945); *Uveges v. Commonwealth of Pennsylvania,* 335 U.S. 437

(1948); *Commonwealth of Pennsylvania ex rel. Herman v. Claudy*, 350 U.S. 116 (1956); *United States v. Johnson*, 24 F.4th 590 (6th Cir. 2022) (the defendant's election to proceed *pro se* after a defective *Faretta* colloquy (see § 1.4 *supra*) was not an effective waiver of the right to counsel); *United States ex rel. Durocher v. LaVallee,* 330 F.2d 303 (2d Cir. 1964); *compare Iowa v. Tovar*, 541 U.S. 77 (2004)));

(f)   whether the court had subject-matter jurisdiction of the offense (*see, e.g., People v. Thiam*, 34 N.Y.3d 1040, 139 N.E.3d 366, 115 N.Y.S.3d 745 (Mem) (2019); *Ashwell v. State*, 226 So.3d 69, 72 (Miss. 2017) ("It is well settled that '[a] plea of guilty does not waive (1) the failure of the indictment to charge a criminal offense or, more specifically, to charge an essential element of a criminal offense, and a plea of guilty does not waive (2) subject matter jurisdiction.'"); *Johnson v. State*, quoted in subdivision (g) *infra*);

(g)   whether, substantively, the statute proscribing the offense to which the defendant pleaded guilty is unconstitutional (*see, e.g., Class v. United States*, 138 S. Ct. 798, 803-05 (2018); *Haynes v. United States*, 390 U.S. 85, 87 n.2 (1968); *State v. Albano,* 67 Hawai'i 398, 688 P.2d 1152 (1984); *State v. Small*, 2005 Ohio 3813, 162 Ohio App.3d 375, 833 N.E.2d 774 (2005); *McKenzie v. State*, 103 So.3d 84 (Ala. Crim. App. 2010); *Johnson v. State*, 916 N.W.2d 674, 680 (Minn. 2018) ("Johnson argues that he was convicted under a statute that is unconstitutional as applied to him. Johnson's argument therefore attacks the subject-matter jurisdiction of the district court. And, by pleading guilty, Johnson did not forfeit his right to make this jurisdictional argument."); *Armijo v. State*, 678 P.2d 864, 866, 867 (Wyo. 1984) (the defendant's pre-plea "Motion to Preserve All Constitutional Questions and . . . Motion to Dismiss . . .[a] Count . . . of the Information" charging him with violating a statute that he contended was unconstitutional sufficed to sustain his right to challenge the statute's constitutionality on appeal despite his guilty plea: "Little purpose would be served by requiring a defendant to insist upon a trial in order to preserve his opportunity to challenge the constitutionality of the statute, and we do not insist upon that."); *but see, e.g., State v. Norris*, 2007 UT 5, 152 P.3d 305, 306 (Utah 2007) ("an unconditional guilty plea does waive a defendant's right to challenge the constitutionality of a statute");

(h)   whether the charging paper fails to allege facts that constitute the criminal offense to which the plea is entered (*see, e.g., People v. Hightower*, 18 N.Y.3d 249, 961 N.E.2d 1111, 938 N.Y.S.2d 500 (2011); *People v. Dreyden*, 15 N.Y.3d 100, 931 N.E.2d 526, 905 N.Y.S.2d 542 (2010); *Ashwell v. State*, quoted in subdivision (f) *supra*); *State v. Blount*, 209 N.C. App. 340, 343, 703 S.E.2d 921, 924 (2011) ("it is well established that a defendant may challenge the sufficiency of the indictment despite having knowingly and voluntarily pled guilty to the charge"); *Barker v. State*, 342 Ga. App. 505, 506, 803 S.E.2d 792, 794 (2017) ("Barker did not challenge the indictment, and '[g]iven that [Barker] pled guilty to the crime charged, his only possible challenge to the indictment would be the sufficiency thereof'"); *compare State v. Jones*, 140 Idaho 755, 758-59, 101 P.3d 699, 702-03 (2004) ("Jones argues the information filed against him failed to expressly allege the element of 'willfulness' . . . .Willfulness is a necessary element of felony injury to a child because it is named in the statute and without willful intent the information would describe a non-crime. . . . ¶ Although the failure of an information to charge an offense is never waived, defects 'which are tardily challenged are liberally construed in favor of validity.'. . . When an objection to the information was not timely raised before trial – as in the instant case [where the defendant pleaded guilty pursuant to a plea bargain] – the sufficiency of the charging document will 'be upheld unless it is so defective that it does not, by any fair or reasonable construction, charge an offense for which the defendant is convicted.'"); *accord, United States v. Ruelas*, 106 F.3d 1416, 1419 (9th Cir. 1997) ("[a]lthough Ruelas may raise a defective indictment claim at any time, we liberally construe the indictment in this case because he did not object to it before he pleaded guilty");

(i)   whether some basic procedural precondition for the entry of a guilty plea, such as the defendant's appearance in court in person, was disregarded (*see United States v. Bethea*, 888 F.3d 864 (7th Cir. 2018));

(j)   whether some constitutional right precluded the defendant's prosecution for the offense to which s/he pleaded guilty (as distinguished from the procedures used in the prosecution or in the investigation of the offense underlying it) (*see Blackledge v. Perry*, 417 U.S. 21 (1974); *Menna v. New York*, 423 U.S. 61 (1975) (per curiam); *Haring v. Prosise*, 462 U.S. 306, 320 (1983) (dictum));

(k)   in jurisdictions that require that a factual basis for a guilty plea must be established on the record before the plea is accepted, whether the record shows the requisite basis (*see, e.g., United States v. Bain*, 925 F.3d 1172 (9th Cir. 2019); *United States v. Prado*, 933 F.3d 121 (2d Cir. 2019); *United States v. Murphy*, 942 F.3d 73 (2d Cir. 2019); *State v. Johnson*, 142 Ariz. 223, 689 P.2d 166 (1984)); and

(l)   whether there are any issues relating to sentence (*see, e.g., State v. Russell*, 598 S.W.3d 133 (Mo. 2020)).

Courts frequently have discretion to permit the withdrawal of a valid guilty plea (that is, a voluntary and understanding plea made by a competent, adequately counseled defendant), but most are reluctant to do so. See § 17.1.2 *infra*. The entry of a guilty plea at arraignment may, therefore, be irrevocable.

A plea of guilty may be entered to the offense charged in the charging paper or, with the prosecutor's agreement, to any lesser included offense. See § 42.4 *infra*. Sometimes leave of court is required for a plea to a lesser offense, and in a few jurisdictions the prosecutor is required to file a statement of reasons for agreeing to a guilty plea to a lesser offense.

A number of jurisdictions disallow a plea of guilty to a specific degree of homicide. The defendant may plead guilty to homicide (or to murder) "generally," leaving to the court the determination of the degree of the offense.

Some jurisdictions forbid a plea of guilty to a capital charge. If an offense is punishable capitally, the defendant's guilty plea to it may be taken (with agreement of the prosecutor), but the defendant may thereupon be sentenced only to some punishment less than death. (This practice is plainly unconstitutional under *United States v. Jackson*, 390 U.S. 570 (1968). *See Funicello v. New Jersey*, 403 U.S. 948 (1971) (per curiam); *Atkinson v. North Carolina*, 403 U.S. 948 (1971) (per curiam); *compare Corbitt v. New Jersey*, 439 U.S. 212 (1978).)

In jurisdictions where sentencing is done by a jury following trial and conviction on a not guilty plea, the effect of a guilty plea may be to waive jury sentencing and authorize sentencing by the court.

Considerations involved in the decision to plead guilty and in guilty plea negotiation are discussed in Chapter 15 *infra*. The colloquy ordinarily employed by judges when they accept a guilty plea is described in § 14.1 *supra*.

14.9. *Nolo Contendere or Non Vult*

The pleas of *nolo contendere* or *non vult contendere* mean that the defendant does not contest the charge. They have the same effect as a guilty plea for the purpose of the criminal proceeding: that is, they authorize conviction and sentence without more ado. They differ from the guilty plea in that they do not constitute an admission of guilt and are, therefore, inadmissible in any collateral proceedings (other than collateral proceedings challenging conviction on the plea). Hence they are used principally in cases in which there are, or may be, civil proceedings arising out of the same set of facts on which the criminal prosecution is grounded (such as vehicular homicide, fraud, and antitrust cases). The *nolo* plea usually may be entered only with leave of court and agreement by the prosecutor. Neither leave nor agreement is likely to be given unless defense counsel can point to the pendency or probability of a related civil action.

14.10. *Standing Mute*

In some jurisdictions the defendant is permitted to stand mute at arraignment. Defense counsel announces that the defendant is standing mute, and the judge thereupon enters a plea of not guilty. The device is most useful in cases in which defense counsel is unprepared to plead and when counsel's motion for a continuance has been overruled and counsel's objection to proceeding has been noted for the record. See §§ 14.3-14.4 *supra*. Standing mute in this situation dramatizes the point that defendant waives nothing and particularly does not waive the special pleas and defenses that a not guilty plea might forfeit. See §§ 14.5-14.6 *supra*.

14.11. *Pleading to Priors*

In most jurisdictions recidivist sentencing statutes authorize more severe penalties for a second or subsequent conviction of some or all offenses. See §§ 15.6.1 subdivision (A)(2),

48.13.1 *infra*. In many jurisdictions the previous offenses upon which the prosecutor will rely to support invocation of the stiffer recidivist penalties are not charged at the initial stages of a criminal prosecution but are made the subject of a supplemental information filed after a verdict of guilty. See § 48.13.1 *infra*. In other jurisdictions, however, the previous offenses (called in the jargon "the priors") are charged in the initial charging paper, and the defendant is required to plead to them, as well as to the offense presently charged, at the time of arraignment. By pleading guilty to the priors, s/he admits that s/he was, in fact, previously convicted, as alleged. By pleading not guilty, s/he contests that issue, which is then submitted to the jury on the proof of the previous convictions by the prosecutor and any proof the defendant may offer (mistaken identity, and so forth).

The result of pleading not guilty to the priors is, therefore, that the jury which is trying the defendant's guilt on the present charge learns in the prosecution's case in chief about the defendant's prior convictions. *See Spencer v. Texas*, 385 U.S. 554 (1967). Since there is ordinarily no real contest to be made about the defendant's record, it is usually wise to plead guilty to the priors (or to stipulate the priors, as local practice may have it). This obviates the need for proof of the priors at trial and should preclude the prosecutor from presenting evidence of prejudicial priors to the jury. *Cf. Old Chief v. United States*, 519 U.S. 172 (1997). Before pleading to the priors, however, counsel should review the terms of the applicable recidivist statute to determine whether s/he can plausibly argue that it does *not* call for alleging and proving the defendant's earlier convictions to the jury, but rather is one of those statutes which make prior convictions solely a matter for post-verdict trial by the sentencing judge. *See, e.g., State v. Skipper*, 2004-2137 (La. 6/29/05), 906 So.2d 399 (La. 2005). This argument would support a motion to strike the allegations of priors from the charging paper, thus obviating the need for the defendant to plead to them.

A different procedure for contesting priors should be used when the defendant admits their factual accuracy but disputes their legal validity or the legal propriety of their use as the basis for enhanced penalties under the recidivist statute. This sort of collateral attack on previous convictions must be entertained by all courts if a prior is challenged on federal right-to-counsel grounds. *Burgett v. Texas*, 389 U.S. 109 (1967); *see Baldasar v. Illinois*, 446 U.S. 222 (1980); *United States v. Addonizio*, 442 U.S. 178, 187 (1979) (dictum); *Lewis v. United States*, 445 U.S. 55, 60 (1980) (dictum); *cf. United States v. Mendoza-Lopez*, 481 U.S. 828 (1987); see § 48.9 *infra*. If its invalidity is asserted to rest on other grounds, the State's practice may, or may not, permit such an attack. But in any case in which the attack is permitted, it raises issues of law for the court, not the jury, and so it would appear to be appropriately presented either by a motion to quash or strike the particular allegations of priors that are contested or by a simple objection to presenting that portion of the charging paper to the jury or to the court for purposes of sentencing. When collateral attack in this form is not permitted, counsel will have to use some sort of postconviction remedy to vacate the earlier convictions (see § 49.2.3 *infra*; *cf. Johnson v. Mississippi*, 486 U.S. 578 (1988)), and s/he should undertake to do so before arraignment on the present charge, if possible. Sometimes a continuance of the arraignment will be advised, but ordinarily the postconviction proceeding against the previous convictions will be protracted and therefore render continuance of arraignment on the present charge impracticable. In this situation counsel should explain that s/he is asking the court to entertain a collateral attack on the priors; that the attack presents only a question of law; that counsel does not want the priors to go to the jury because they will prejudice the defendant on the guilt issue; and that the defendant will stipulate to the priors or enter a guilty plea to them, with the reservation of all rights subsequently to challenge their legal validity and the validity of their use in this proceeding.

14.12. *Dismissal of Charges on Motion of the Prosecution*

The prosecutor may move at arraignment to dismiss charges in the interest of justice or for want of evidence or because the defendant has agreed to cooperate and testify against others. See §§ 8.22-8.2.3 *supra*. Or the prosecutor may agree to have the criminal charges diverted. See §§ 2.36, 8.2.2, 8.4 *supra* .This is another stage at which discussion with the prosecutor may invoke a favorable exercise of the prosecutorial discretion. See §§ 8.2.2, 8.2.3, 8.2.4, 8.4, 8.6, 12.13 *supra*.

Prosecutors will frequently insist that the defendant sign a stipulation of the validity of his or her arrest (or that there was probable cause for the arrest) or a waiver of any legal claims in connection with the arrest as the condition of an "interest of justice" dismissal. If the prosecution's case is known to be very weak, defense counsel can afford to resist the execution of such a stipulation or waiver, and the prosecutor will often back down. See § 8.3.3 *supra*. But if the prosecution has any strength, the signing of a stipulation or a waiver is usually a small price to pay for dismissal, since the client is unlikely to persist in any desire to sue the police (a desire usually voiced very loudly when the prosecutor offers to drop charges but soon forgotten), and even more unlikely to win a suit if s/he sues. Local law should, however, be carefully consulted in regard to the form of the stipulation or waiver, and consideration must be given to which of the client's various possible concerns with the arrest is paramount. A stipulation that there was probable cause for the arrest, for example, may preclude the client from subsequently having the arrest record expunged, but it may not bar a damage action for false arrest on grounds other than lack of probable cause. A waiver of the right to bring a civil-rights action in connection with the arrest will bar the damage action (*see Town of Newton v. Rumery*, 480 U.S. 386 (1987)) but not preclude expungement.

Other sorts of conditions or concessions may also be demanded by a prosecutor as the *quid pro quo* for dismissing charges. See §§ 8.5-8.6 *supra*; § 15.13 *infra*. These should be thoroughly discussed with the client, with due appreciation for the truism that what looks like a good deal now (such as an agreement to make restitution to a complainant in installments over a period of time) may begin to gall the client seriously as time passes. Plea bargaining is discussed in Chapter 15 *infra*.

Chapter 15

Guilty Pleas: Preparing for and Conducting Plea Negotiations; Counseling the Client About a Plea Offer

A. *Introduction*

15.1. *Overview of the Chapter*

This chapter examines the processes by which counsel prepares for and conducts plea negotiations with the prosecutor and advises the client about a bargained plea. The chapter leads off with a discussion (in § 15.2) of the relative roles of counsel and client in deciding whether the client should plead guilty rather contesting a criminal charge. Part B (§§ 15.3-15.7) discusses the benefits and costs to a defendant of resolving a criminal charge by pleading guilty. It then reviews the factors that counsel should consider in developing an advantageous plea bargain to propose to the prosecutor or in assessing a plea offer from the prosecutor and advising the client whether to take an available deal. Part C (§§ 15.8-15.13) focuses on plea negotiations, explaining the steps that counsel should take to prepare for negotiation, techniques to use in negotiating, strategic considerations to keep in mind, and matters to consider in memorializing a plea agreement. Part D (§§ 15.14-15.17) addresses a variety of matters that counsel should consider when counseling a client about a plea offer and when preparing a client for the entry of a guilty plea in court.

Some other aspects of guilty pleas are covered in other chapters. Section 14.1 *supra*, dealing with the arraignment process, describes the procedures that judges ordinarily follow when taking a guilty plea. Section 14.8 *supra* explains that guilty pleas commonly extinguish the availability of appellate and collateral review of most pretrial rulings; this section also identifies the relatively limited number of claims that can be raised on appeal or by *certiorari* or on collateral attack after a guilty plea. Section 17.1.2 *infra* describes the procedures that may be available for withdrawing or vacating a guilty plea.

15.2. *The Roles of Client and Counsel in Deciding Whether to Accept a Guilty Plea*

The decision whether to plead guilty or to contest a criminal charge is ordinarily the most important single decision in any criminal case. This decision must ultimately be left to the client's wishes. Counsel cannot plead a client guilty or not guilty against the client's will. *McCoy v. Louisiana*, 138 S. Ct. 1500 (2018). *See, e.g.*, *Florida v. Nixon*, 543 U.S. 175, 187-88 (2004) ("A guilty plea . . . is an event of signal significance in a criminal proceeding. By entering a guilty plea, a defendant waives constitutional rights that inhere in a criminal trial, including the right to trial by jury, the protection against self-incrimination, and the right to confront one's accusers. . . . While a guilty plea may be tactically advantageous for the defendant, . . . the plea is not simply a strategic choice; it is 'itself a conviction,' . . . and the high stakes for the defendant require 'the utmost solicitude,' . . . . Accordingly, counsel lacks authority to consent to a guilty plea on a client's behalf . . .; moreover, a defendant's tacit acquiescence in the decision to plead is insufficient to render the plea valid . . . ."); § 1.3 *supra*.

It is also the case, however, that counsel may – and, indeed, must – give the client the benefit of counsel's professional advice on this crucial decision, and often the only way for counsel to protect the client from disaster is by using a considerable amount of persuasion to convince the client that a plea which the client instinctively disfavors is, in fact, in his or her best interest. This persuasion is most often needed to convince a client that s/he should plead guilty in a case in which opting for a trial would be destructive.

The limits of allowable persuasion are fixed by the lawyer's conscience. Of course, s/he must make absolutely clear to the client that if the client decides to plead not guilty despite counsel's advice, counsel will defend the client vigorously and will raise every defense that the client legitimately has. Counsel also must acknowledge the limits of his or her own predictive capacities. In describing both the likely benefits of a guilty plea and the likely consequences of going to trial, s/he must not make probabilities sound like certainties. Although s/he may emphasize the risks of going to trial in a way that accurately portrays the danger involved, s/he should avoid language that makes it seem as though *counsel* is threatening the client. And it should go without saying that counsel must scrupulously stick to the facts and probabilities as s/he sees them, without exaggeration. *See, e.g., Tovar Mendoza v. Hatch*, 620 F.3d 1261, 1272 (10th Cir. 2010) (defendant's "reliance on [defense counsel's] . . . blatant and significant misrepresentations about the amount of time [defendant] . . . would spend in prison [if defendant accepted the plea offer] rendered his no contest plea unknowing and violative of Tovar's due process rights"). Beyond this, the question of how much s/he should bend the client's ear in a particular case must rest on counsel's judgment. Counsel's appraisal of the case is probably far better than the defendant's, and counsel's difficult and painful responsibilities include making every reasonable effort to save a client from his or her own ill-informed or ill-estimated choices. When there is reason to believe that the defendant's insistence on a trial is the product of mental or emotional disability, counsel should retain a mental health expert to conduct a competency examination. *See* W. Bradley Wendel, *Autonomy Isn't Everything: Some Cautionary Notes on McCoy v. Louisiana*, 9 St. Mary's J. Legal Malpractice & Ethics 92 (2018). This had best be done without court process, if possible (see § 16.3 *infra*), but a motion for a court-ordered confidential examination is a last resort if necessary (see *id.*, last two paragraphs).

B. *The Decision Whether To Plead Guilty or Go to Trial; Factors to Consider in Developing and Evaluating a Potential Plea Bargain*

15.3. *Overview of the Cost-Benefit Analysis Involved in Deciding Whether to Plead Guilty or Go to Trial*

The determination of the advisability of a guilty plea usually requires a complex cost-benefit analysis that takes into account: (i) the likelihood of winning the case at trial; (ii) the chances that the judge, in the event of conviction, would penalize the defendant at sentencing for going to trial and – in the judge's opinion – wasting the court's time and (if the defendant testifies) perjuring himself or herself on the witness stand; and (iii) a number of specific advantages that, in any particular case, could be gained through a guilty plea. Even a reasonable prospect of winning at trial might be bartered away if the benefits of a plea are substantial enough or if the severity of the sentence which is likely to be imposed in the event of a conviction is daunting. On the other hand, a defendant could reasonably opt for trial even in the face of overwhelming prosecution evidence when a guilty plea is unlikely to produce any sentencing advantages or other benefits.

In order to determine what plea bargain to seek from the prosecutor and in order to assess whether to recommend to the client to take a prosecutor's plea offer (and precisely what to say to the client about its likely benefits and costs), counsel will have to research the above issues – the chances of winning at trial; the possible consequences of going to trial and losing; and the roster of potential benefits of a guilty plea in the client's individual circumstances – thoroughly enough to be able to make a well-informed, reliable judgment. *See, e.g., Lafler v. Cooper*, 566 U.S. 156, 174 (2012) (accused was denied effective assistance of counsel because defense counsel advised the accused to reject a plea offer based on counsel's erroneous view of the law, resulting in the accused's rejecting the plea, "being convicted at trial, . . . [and] receiv[ing] a minimum sentence 3½ times greater than he would have received under the plea"); *United States v. Rodriguez-Vega*, 797 F.3d 781, 786-88 (9th Cir. 2015) (counsel inadequately advised the defendant about the plea offer, thereby denying her of effective assistance of counsel, by informing her that she faced the "'potential' of removal" rather than advising her "that her conviction rendered her removal virtually certain, or words to that effect"; although the defendant "received notice that she might be removed [*i.e.*, deported] from a provision in the plea agreement and the court's plea colloquy under Federal Rule of Criminal Procedure 11[,] . . . [t]he government's performance in including provisions in the plea agreement, and the court's performance at the plea colloquy, are simply irrelevant to the question whether *counsel's* performance fell below an objective standard of reasonableness"); *Pidgeon v. Smith*, 785 F.3d 1165, 1167-68, 1172-73 (7th Cir. 2015) (counsel deprived his client of effective assistance by "incorrectly advis[ing] . . . Pidgeon" that a guilty plea was necessary in order to avoid a life sentence under the State's "persistent repeater law," when actually Pidgeon's prior conviction "did not qualify as a serious felony offense, meaning that Pidgeon did not face the possibility of life imprisonment"); *Kovacs v. United States*, 744 F.3d 44, 48, 50 (2d Cir. 2014) (counsel "rendered ineffective assistance by giving erroneous advice concerning the deportation consequences of pleading guilty . . . , with the result that [Kovacs] is at risk of detention and deportation if he reenters the United States"); *Heard v. Addison*, 728 F.3d 1170, 1172 (10th Cir. 2013) (defense counsel "provided ineffective assistance in failing to advise [Heard] . . . of viable defenses to the charges against him" when counseling Heard about a plea offer); *Dando v. Yukins*, 461 F.3d 791, 799-802 (6th Cir. 2006) (defense counsel was ineffective in recommending a "no contest" plea to the client without first "adequately investigat[ing] the availability of a duress defense and the related possibility that Dando suffered from Battered Women's Syndrome"); *Maples v. Stegall*, 427 F.3d 1020, 1022, 1034 (6th Cir. 2005) (defense "counsel provided ineffective assistance by advising [the defendant] . . . that his guilty plea reserved his speedy trial claim for appeal, when in reality it did not").

Section 15.4 discusses the range of factors that counsel should consider to assess the likelihood of winning at trial. Section 15.5 discusses the risk that a judge might penalize a defendant at sentencing for opting in favor of trial instead of pleading guilty. Section 15.6 examines the kinds of benefits that a guilty plea might obtain. Section 15.7 identifies a number of additional factors that may bear on the advisability of a guilty plea in a particular case.

15.4. *Assessing the Likelihood of Winning at Trial*

The threshold determination of the chances of acquittal at trial will require more than a simple weighing of the relative strengths of the prosecution's and defense's theories of the case and supporting evidence. Counsel's calculus will have to incorporate a host of variables that are difficult to predict, such as the probable resolution of debatable issues of admissibility of specific evidentiary items, the odds of a prosecution or defense witness being unavailable at the time of trial, and the effect of the judge's application of a variety of presumptions and other legal doctrines.

15.4.1. *The Strength of the Case for the Prosecution*

The first step is to analyze the strength of the prosecution's case from a dual perspective:

(a)   How likely is the prosecution to establish a *prima facie* case (that is, to survive a defense motion to dismiss at the conclusion of the prosecutor's case-in-chief (see § 38.1 *infra*))?

and

(b)   How likely is the prosecution to persuade the trier of fact to return a guilty verdict at the conclusion of the trial?

These two questions need independent consideration because the first is usually easier to answer than the second (judges being more predictable in their assessment of the sufficiency of evidence than in their assessment of its weight, and juries being less predictable than judges) and because, if the prosecution is unlikely to establish a *prima facie* case, all potential problems and uncertainties relating to defense evidence fall out of the calculus.

Counsel should begin by examining the charging instrument and listing all of the elements that the prosecution will need to prove in order to sustain each of the counts. Then, on the basis of the information that counsel has learned through discovery and investigation, counsel should analyze the prosecutor's ability to prove each of these factual elements with the witnesses, documents, and exhibits believed to be available to the prosecutor.

If counsel has learned through investigation that a prosecution witness will be out of town or otherwise unavailable on the trial date, counsel will need to predict whether the prosecutor will be able to obtain a continuance in order to secure the witness's presence, or whether the judge is likely to grant a defense motion to dismiss the case for want of prosecution. See § 28.4 *infra*. If counsel has learned through investigation that a prosecution witness is reluctant to come to court, counsel will need to predict whether the prosecutor will be able to compel the witness's attendance by successfully serving and enforcing a subpoena. Similarly, if counsel can predict that certain documents the prosecution needs will go missing – for example, in some jurisdictions, tape recordings of 911 calls, which the prosecution must turn over to the defense, are routinely erased before the time when the prosecutor gets around to requesting them from the police – counsel will have to evaluate whether the loss or destruction of those documents will cause the judge to grant a defense motion for sanctions such as dismissal of the case or preclusion of the testimony of prosecution witnesses about matters that would have been reflected in the lost document. See § 34.7.1.1 *infra.*

In analyzing the strength of the prosecution's case, counsel will need to consider both doctrinal rules relating to presumptions and permissive inferences, and the realistic likelihood that a trier of fact will find them persuasive. For example, on a charge of criminal possession of stolen property, the prosecutor may be able to survive a motion for a directed verdict by relying on the formal doctrine that a person who is in possession of recently stolen goods is presumed to know that the goods were stolen; but triers of fact are often unwilling to convict if nothing more than that is proven. See § 41.4.4 *infra.*

Analysis of the strength of the prosecution's case must also take account of factors that could discredit its witnesses or evidence. For example, when a prosecution witness has made statements to the police (recorded in police reports) or in pretrial hearings (the preliminary examination or a suppression hearing) or to the defense investigator (either an oral statement or, preferably, a written, signed statement), counsel will be able to use these statements to impeach the witness's inconsistent testimony at trial. See § 37.4 *infra.* If a prosecution witness has prior convictions, counsel may be able to impeach the witness's credibility with those. See § 37.5 *infra.* Or counsel may be able to undercut a prosecution based on forensic-science evidence by criticizing the methodology or competence of the prosecution's experts or debunking their purported field of specialization as fundamentally unreliable. See § 37.14 *infra.*

In addition to measuring the prosecution's probable case against the applicable burdens of proof – the *prima-facie*-evidence standard for surviving a motion to dismiss (see § 38.1 *infra*) and the beyond-a-reasonable-doubt standard for conviction (see §§ 41.2-41.3, 42.5 subdivision (4) *infra*) – counsel needs to consider other evidentiary doctrines that can undercut that case. These include the missing-witness doctrine (see § 29.4.7 *infra*) and the rules relating to accomplice testimony (see §§ 41.2.2 subdivision (2), 42.3 subdivision (5) *infra*), and uncorroborated confessions (see §§ 41.2.2 subdivision (1), 42.3 subdivision (5) *infra*).

Counsel will not be in a position to conduct this kind of thorough evaluation of the prosecution's case until s/he has completed all or most of the defense investigation (see Chapter 9 *supra*) and the formal discovery process (see Chapter 18 *infra*). Counsel's analysis of the prosecution's theory of the case and of the persuasiveness of the evidence available to the prosecutor will be heavily dependent on counsel's study of police reports and witness statements. These documents usually set the upper boundary of what the prosecutor will be able to prove convincingly at trial, because they can be used to impeach prosecution testimony that goes beyond them. They may also contain inconsistent statements that could turn the tide in favor of the defense at trial. Also, information about prior convictions of prosecution witnesses has to be obtained through defense investigation and discovery before counsel can make a sufficiently confident assessment of the prosecution's trial evidence to support the serious consideration of a guilty plea.

15.4.2. *The Strength of the Case for the Defense*

In much the same way that counsel evaluates the prosecution's case, counsel will need to assess the strengths and weaknesses of the defendant's. After identifying all viable defense theories of the case (see Chapter 7), counsel should itemize the facts that must be proven to sustain each theory, the witnesses and exhibits available to prove each of these facts, their persuasiveness, and their vulnerabilities.

In analyzing the prosecution's charges, counsel will have already drawn up a list of the elements that the prosecution has to prove in order to make out a *prima facie* case. If counsel can successfully attack the prosecutor's proof on one or more of these elements, a motion for a directed verdict of acquittal at the close of the prosecution's evidence will be a central feature of the defense. Assuming contingently that the judge denies the defense motion, counsel will need to consider whether any of the loopholes in the prosecution's case can be widened to the point of acquittal through the presentation of defense witnesses. For example, a tenuous prosecution case on *mens rea* might be successfully undermined by the defendant's testimony that s/he did not possess the requisite mental state. Conversely, counsel's assessment of the odds of acquittal will need to weigh the danger that the presentation of defense evidence could strengthen an otherwise weak prosecution case. If the prosecution's case was doubtful in regard to both the identity and criminal *mens* of the perpetrator, the defendant's testimony disputing only the *mens* will foreclose a mistaken-identity defense in the endgame. See § 39.2 *infra*.

In addition to potential attacks on the prosecution's proof of the elements of the offenses it has charged (and their lesser included offenses, see § 42.4 *infra*), counsel will need to consider the availability of defenses such as alibi and self-defense. (For discussion of the differing burdens of proof that apply to defense theories, depending upon whether they are labeled "affirmative defenses," see § 41.3 *infra*.) In some cases, counsel will also need to consider mental defenses such as incompetency and insanity. See Chapter 16. Assessing each possible theory of defense requires an analysis that is essentially a mirror-image of the one used to evaluate the prosecution's case: Counsel must itemize the elements of the defense, enumerate the facts necessary to establish each of these elements, identify the witnesses and exhibits necessary to prove each of the facts, and then assess their persuasiveness.

Here, too, counsel will have to take account of practical contingencies, such as the likelihood that defense witnesses will fail to show up for court. If counsel anticipates that a defense witness may be out of town on the trial date or may be reluctant to testify, counsel will need to gauge the likelihood that the problem can be alleviated by securing a continuance or judicial enforcement of a subpoena.

Counsel also must consider whether any defense witnesses can be impeached with prior inconsistent statements or a prior record or other discrediting material. In this regard, counsel will need to be particularly concerned about the question of how the defense case will look if the defendant has priors and does – or, alternatively, does not – testify. If s/he takes the stand, state law usually allows the prosecutor to impeach him or her with prior convictions, prior bad acts, or both. See § 36.4.2 *infra*. If s/he does not take the stand, the trier of fact is supposed to obey the legal rule that no adverse inferences can be drawn from the defendant's failure to testify. The reality, however, is that fact-finders – not only juries but even judges in a bench trial – may well believe that the defendant's refusal to testify indicates guilt or at least the existence of detrimental information that the defendant is trying to conceal. In a bench trial, counsel must also consider the possibility that the judge may already know about, or will learn about, the defendant's prior record even if s/he does not take the stand, as a result of: (1) the judge's having presided over a prior hearing in the case or a prior case of the defendant's; (2) sloppy administrative procedures that counsel will not be able to correct (such as court jackets that indicate the docket numbers of the defendant's other cases); or (3) courthouse leaks (such as a bailiff mentioning the repeated court appearances of the defendant).

15.4.3. *Circumstances That May Prejudice the Trier of Fact Against the Defendant*

In comparing the strengths of the competing cases for the prosecution and for the defense, counsel will need to factor in numerous variables that may undermine the objectivity of the trier of fact.

The most significant of these factors is the risk that jurors or the judge conducting a bench trial may feel distaste for, or outrage over, a particularly violent or repugnant crime. Hard drug offenses, violent sex crimes, and crimes involving gruesome injuries to the victim are likely to be viewed by fact-finders as peculiarly abhorrent. While many fact-finders have the capacity to appraise a defendant's case objectively even in the face of graphic, grisly evidence, there are others whose objectivity and ability to apply a reasonable-doubt standard will be overwhelmed by sheer disgust or by the fear of setting free a probable perpetrator of atrocities s/he may repeat.

The fact-finder's objectivity will frequently also be compromised in cases involving a particularly vulnerable victim, such as a young child or a senior citizen. The courtroom demeanor, behavior, and physical characteristics of the victim, the defendant, and potential prosecution and defense witnesses may well sway the fact-finder's judgment. And counsel's calculus must include the additional biases that may arise in cases involving interracial crimes.

The problem of the prejudice that is likely to attach to a defendant with a prior record was mentioned in the preceding subsection. It is sufficiently important to require further discussion here. Local evidence rules may limit the impeachment of a testifying defendant to admission of a documentary record setting out the name[s] of the previous crime[s] of which s/he has been convicted, or they may authorize more or less detailed factual information about the prior[s]. Counsel must consider the probable impact of the name[s] or admissible facts of the crime[s] not only upon the trier's assessment of the defendant's credibility but upon the trier's impression of the defendant as a criminal *type* deserving less than the benefit of the doubt. (Sometimes the name of the crime is worse than the facts. When unscrupulous medical clinics staged automobile accidents to set up exaggerated insurance claims, the individuals to whom they paid a few dollars for crowding into the back seats of rear-ended vehicles were subsequently convicted of the crime of federal "health care fraud.")

In a bench trial, counsel also must consider whether the judge has prior knowledge of inadmissible evidence as a result of having presided over a pretrial suppression hearing or other pretrial proceeding. If, for example, a judge has suppressed a confession or tangible evidence in a pretrial hearing but then refuses to recuse himself or herself (see §§ 22.4-22.7 *infra*), s/he may be unable to put the illegal but incriminating evidence wholly out of mind.

The potential prejudicial impact of media reports of a crime is an additional factor for consideration. Newspaper, television and social-media accounts may have informed the fact-finder of damaging information that would be inadmissible in evidence at the trial on a not-guilty plea. Counsel cannot rely on theoretical rights to exclude biased jurors (see §§ 22.2, 32.4, 33.3.1 *infra*) and to recuse biased judges as fully effective protection against these dangers. In a bench trial, counsel also must bear in mind that many judges are highly sensitive to criticism in the media and are more likely to convict when an acquittal could expose them to adverse publicity.

Another danger that present legal rules signally fail to avert is that complainants and their supporters may pack the courtroom with manifestly grieving or outraged countenances. *See, e.g., Carey v. Musladin*, 549 U.S. 70 (2006). Pervasive enactment of "victim's rights" legislation (*see, e.g.*, Douglas E. Beloof & Paul G. Cassell, *The Crime Victim's Right to Attend the Trial: The Reascendant National Consensus*, 9 LEWIS & CLARK L. REV. 481 (2005); Anna Roberts, *Victims, Right?*, 42 CARDOZO L. REV. 1449 (2021); *but see League of Women Voters of Pennsylvania v. DeGraffenreid*, 265 A.3d 207 (Pa. 2021) (invalidating a typical victim's rights package embodied in a constitutional amendment on the ground that it violated the state constitutional requirement that an amendment submitted to voters for a single vote be restricted to matters that are sufficiently interrelated to be viewed as a single subject)) has intensified this problem.

To inform an assessment of the probable effects of these factors, counsel should gather as much information as is practicable about the views and biases of local judges and juries. If the defendant's case is not eligible for jury trial (see § 32.1 *infra*) or if counsel is considering advising the defendant to elect a bench trial (see § 32.2 *infra*), counsel should try to get a sense of individual judges' proclivities and attitudes by talking with attorneys who have previously appeared before those judges. (How early in the pretrial process the identity of the trial judge will be ascertainable depends on local court structures and practices. In some circumstances, counsel may be able to steer the trial to a favorable judge or away from an unfavorable one. See § 22.7 *infra; see also* § 15.7.2 *infra.*) When jury trial is an option, counsel should not only search media sources for whatever coverage they may have given to counsel's individual case but for what they may reveal about local attitudes toward similar crimes and defendants; and counsel should talk with experienced criminal defense attorneys about what to expect from the relevant jury pool.

15.4.4. *Relative Ability, Experience, and Personableness of the Lawyers*

Counsel's assessment of the fact-finder's likely reactions to the evidence at trial also has to take into account the relative abilities, experience, and personableness of the prosecutor and counsel himself or herself. Factors such as these may have a considerable effect on whether counsel will be able to exclude prejudicial prosecution evidence or persuade the judge to admit favorable defense evidence; how the jurors will react to the lawyers' opening statements and closing arguments; and how the jurors perceive and evaluate each side's witnesses and the case as a whole.

15.4.5. *The Possibility of a Divided Jury*

Counsel also will need to consider whether the nature of the evidence or the law or the character of the parties to the alleged offense is sufficiently controversial to set a jury at loggerheads, with the result that the jury may deadlock or bring in a compromise verdict of guilty on a lesser included charge. A hung jury is ordinarily a defense victory: Even if the prosecutor is disposed to invest resources in a retrial, the defense bargaining position becomes considerably stronger after a first jury has failed to find the prosecution's case persuasive.

15.5. *Assessing the Likelihood That the Judge Will Penalize the Defendant at Sentencing Because the Defendant Opted in Favor of a Trial Instead of a Guilty Plea*

There are various factors that may cause a judge at sentencing to consciously or unconsciously penalize a defendant for having opted in favor of a trial instead of a guilty plea.

The judge may be irritated that the defendant has (in the judge's opinion) wasted the court's time by demanding a trial. This is especially true when the prosecution's evidence of guilt is overwhelming and/or the defendant lacks a viable theory of defense. Conversely, if the defendant does present a viable albeit ultimately unsuccessful defense, many (although not all) judges will be tolerant of the defendant's insistence on a trial.

The judge is particularly likely to covertly punish the defendant for insisting on a trial if the defendant takes the witness stand at trial and tells a story that the judge believes is perjurious. In most situations in which the defendant testifies to an exonerating version of the events relating to the offense charged, the jury (or the judge in a bench trial) will have to find the defendant's testimony incredible in order to convict. So, in such cases, there is always at least some risk that the judge will conclude at sentencing that an enhanced penalty is appropriate. Even when the defendant does not take the stand, the defense presentation of testimony by friends or relatives of the defendant may cause the judge to covertly penalize the defendant at sentencing for having committed what the judge views as subornation of perjury.

Most judges make it a practice to encourage the attorneys to conduct a final round of plea negotiations immediately before trial. Some judges go even further, inquiring about the precise terms of the plea bargains that have been offered or asking in a general way whether the lawyers for each side have made a plea offer that they regard as reasonable. If the judge believes that the prosecutor's plea offer was reasonable, s/he is likely to feel even more strongly that the defendant has wasted the court's time by insisting on a trial. Conversely, when prosecutor's best plea offer seems unreasonable, the judge is likely to direct his or her irritation at the prosecutor rather than the defendant. In these cases, defense counsel should consider bringing the prosecutor's obstinacy to the attention of a judge who has prompted negotiations but not has not explicitly inquired why they are stalling. However, this strategy can backfire and should ordinarily not be used unless the defendant is prepared to accept an offer that the judge is likely to believe *is* reasonable. For if the judge pressures the prosecutor into offering a more favorable plea which the defendant then refuses to accept, the judge will be doubly irritated at the defendant's apparent disingenuousness and lack of gratitude for the judge's intervention on his or her behalf.

The extent to which judges participate directly in plea negotiations between the prosecution and defense counsel varies widely from jurisdiction to jurisdiction and from locality to locality. Some jurisdictions prohibit or radically restrict judicial involvement in plea bargaining. *See, e.g.*, FED. RULE CRIM. PRO. 11(c)(1), *discussed in United States v. Davila*, 569 U.S. 597 (2013); *United States v. Rankins*, 675 Fed. Appx. 231, 234 (4th Cir. 2017) (the trial court violated FED. RULE CRIM. PRO. 11(c)(1), which "prohibits judicial involvement in plea discussions," by making "statements likely to induce Rankins to enter into a plea agreement"); *State v. Buckalew*, 561 P.2d 289 (Alaska 1977); *State v. Anyanwu*, 681 N.W.2d 411 (Minn. App. 2004). Others recognize its legitimacy in varying degrees. *See, e.g.*, *State v. McMahon*, 94 So.3d 468 (Fla. 2012); *State v. Davis*, 155 Vt. 417, 584 A.2d 1146 (1990); *State v. Jabbaar*, 2013-Ohio-1655, 991 N.E.2d 290 (Ohio App. 2013); N.Y. Advisory Committee on Judicial Ethics, Opinion 17-110 (October 19, 2017), N.Y. LAW J., December 18, 2017, at 3, col. 1, *available at* http://www.nycourts.gov/legacyhtm/ip/judicialethics/opinions/17-110.htm. Counsel should ascertain the local rules and practices in this regard and should ask experienced criminal defense attorneys about:

(a)   particular presiding judges' attitudes toward brokering negotiations, and

(b)   each available judge's predilections regarding what constitutes an appropriate disposition in cases like the defendant's,

before deciding whether, when, and how to engage a judge in counsel's dealings with the prosecutor.

If a defendant opts for trial and is convicted, and if it appears at or before sentencing that the judge is inclined to penalize the defendant for exercising his or her constitutional right to go to trial rather than plead guilty – and especially if the judge has made any statements on the record that manifest such a mindset – counsel should consider whether to raise the issue and seek recusal or some other sort of relief. *See, e.g.*, *People v. Hodge*, 154 A.D.3d 963, 965-66, 63 N.Y.S.3d 448, 450-51 (N.Y. App. Div., 2d Dep't 2017) (even though the "defendant failed to preserve for appellate review his contention that the sentencing court penalized him for exercising his right to a jury trial," the appellate court reaches the issue "in the interest of justice," rules for the defendant, and reduces the sentence; in concluding that the sentence imposed by the trial court "raises the inference that the defendant was penalized for exercising his right to a jury trial," the appellate court cites the lower sentence offered the defendant as part of a plea agreement, the disparity between the defendant's sentence and that of a codefendant who pled guilty, and the "sentencing court['s] [having] admonished the defendant for putting the elderly complaining witness through the 'ordeal' of a trial even though the defendant was caught 'red-handed'"); *State v. Nakamitsu*, 140 Hawai'i 157, 166-67, 398 P.3d 746, 755-56 (2017) (dictum) (comments that the judge made at sentencing to "Nakamitsu and his counsel regarding Nakamitsu's decision to proceed with trial" indicate that "the sentence was 'likely to have been improperly influenced by the defendant's persistence in his innocence'"; "[i]f the district court erroneously relied on Nakamitsu's refusal to admit guilt in imposing its sentence, that reliance would have violated Nakamitsu's constitutional right to due process and his right against self-incrimination"). *See also People v. Wesley*, 428 Mich. 708, 711, 411 N.W.2d 159, 161 (1987) (affirming the general principle that "a sentencing court cannot, in whole or in part, base its sentence on a defendant's refusal to admit guilt," but finding that "[h]ere, the trial court made clear when stating its reasons for exceeding the sentencing guidelines that defendant's assertion of innocence was not the reason for imposing the harsh sentence"). In considering such a strategy, counsel needs to carefully assess whether raising the issue could backfire by angering the judge and causing him or her to impose a severe sentence while saying things on the record to justify the sentence's severity and to ostensibly refute any improper motivation on the judge's part. See § 22.7 *infra* (discussing tactical considerations in deciding whether to seek recusal of the judge and in framing a recusal request).

15.6. *Assessing Whether a Guilty Plea Would Produce Any Significant Advantages at Sentencing and/or By Averting Collateral Consequences of a Conviction*

No intelligent plea decision can be made by either lawyer or client without a full understanding of the possible consequences of a conviction. These consequences include (a) the potential sentence the judge might impose in the event of a conviction at trial or a guilty plea, and (b) the potential collateral consequences of a conviction at trial or by means of a guilty plea (*see generally* NATIONAL REENTRY RESOURCE CENTER, NATIONAL INVENTORY OF THE COLLATERAL CONSEQUENCES OF CONVICTION, *available at:* https://niccc.csgjusticecenter.org/database/results/?jurisdiction=&consequence_category=&narro w_category=&triggtrigg_offense_category=&consequence_type=&duration_category=&page_n um_ber=1; Michael Pinard & Anthony C. Thompson, *Offender Reentry and the Collateral Consequences of Criminal Convictions: An Introduction*, 30 N.Y.U. REV. L. & SOC. CHANGE 585 (2006)). In some cases, the collateral consequences may be so severe that even the faintest ray of hope at trial is magnified in significance. If, for example, a conviction of the offense charged will result in the automatic revocation of the defendant's parole from a prior prison sentence on which s/he owes long years of back time or will subject a noncitizen defendant to removal or exclusion from the country, the defendant may have little to lose by denying guilt and going to trial, even with a weak defense. The direct and collateral consequences of a conviction are the baseline for identifying the plea offer that counsel will seek from the prosecutor and measuring the worth of any bargain that results from plea negotiations.

So, in order to prepare for plea bargaining, counsel will need to research all of the potential consequences the client may suffer in the event of a conviction and to determine precisely what concessions could be extracted from the prosecutor that would reduce the severity of the sentence likely to be imposed and/or would avert or minimize the potential collateral consequences. Section 15.6.1 describes the subjects that counsel should research in order to acquire an adequate understanding of the potential consequences of a conviction. Section 15.6.2 discusses the types of concessions that counsel might seek to obtain from the prosecutor in plea negotiations to avert or reduce the consequences of a conviction.

15.6.1. *Identifying the Possible Consequences of a Conviction*

To take account of all of the potential consequences of a conviction, counsel will need to research:

(A)   *The maximum penalties authorized by law upon the conviction, including*:

(1)   The maximum sentences prescribed by statute for each of the charged

offenses, which will ordinarily take the form of imprisonment, a fine, restitution and other special monetary assessments (*see, e.g.*, 18 U.S.C. §§ 3013, 3014, 3663, 3663A, 3664; *Hughey v. United States*, 495 U.S. 411 (1990); *Stacy v. United States*, 70 F.4th 369 (7th Cir. 2023); *United States v. Salti*, 59 F.4th 1050 (10th Cir. 2023); *United States v. Graves*, 908 F.3d 137 (5th Cir. 2018); *United States v. Johnman,* 948 F.3d 612 (3d Cir. 2020); *United States v. Elbaz*, 52 F.4th 593 (4th Cir. 2022); *United States v. Wells*, 55 F.4th 784 (9th Cir. 2022); *United States v. Norton*, 48 F.4th 124 (3d Cir. 2022); *United States v. Carson*, 55 F.4th 1053 (6th Cir. 2022); *United States v. Lillard*, 57 F.4th 729 (9th Cir. 2022); *see United States v. Richardson*, 67 F.4th 268, 272 (5th Cir. 2023) (in making "loss-amount calculations [for purposes of restitution,] . . . '[t]he Government first must carry its burden of demonstrating the actual loss to [the victim] by a preponderance of the evidence,' after which 'the defendant can rebut the Government's evidence'"); *accord, United States v. Workman*, 71 F.4th 661 (8th Cir. 2023); *United States v. Love*, 2023 WL 3243991, at *2 (9th Cir. 2023) ("restitution for multiple wrongdoers may be apportioned by relative culpability"); *and see United States v. Ruiz-Lopez*, 53 F.4th 400 (6th Cir. 2022) (discussing the Circuit split regarding the question whether restitution can be ordered based on facts other than those required to establish the elements of the conviction offense); WEST'S REV. NEB. STAT. ANN. § 29-2280 – 2983; *State v. McCulley*, 305 Neb. 139, 939 N.W.2d 373 (2020)), or some combination of these sanctions. In cases involving more than a single charge, counsel will need to determine whether sentences of imprisonment can run consecutively (as is frequently the case (*but see, e.g., People v. Torrez*, 2013 COA 37, 316 P.3d 25, 35 (Colo. App. 2013) (statute creates a "substantive right . . . 'to the imposition of concurrent sentences' when two or more convictions are based on identical evidence"))), and whether the judge who will preside at sentencing ordinarily imposes consecutive rather than concurrent sentences in the absence of prosecutorial support for concurrent sentencing as part of a plea bargain. In jurisdictions with "sentencing guidelines" and other such systems of determinate-sentencing formulas, identifying the maximum sentence will often require a multi-variable analysis of the "baseline" sentence for each offense or category of offenses, any applicable aggravating and/or mitigating circumstances that may affect the baseline sentence, the rules on concurrent and consecutive sentencing for multiple convictions, and a variety of other possibly applicable factors. See § 48.12 *infra*.

(2)   Provisions that enhance or modify the basic sentence when a defendant's conviction of a designated offense or class of offenses is accompanied by the finding of specified features in addition to the elements of the root offense, or under specified circumstances arising after sentencing. For example:

(a)   Repeat-offender sentencing provisions (sometimes called "recidivist" or "second offender" or "persistent violator" or "habitual criminal" laws, including "three strikes" laws). *See, e.g., United States v. Moore*, 71 F.4th 392 (5th Cir. 2023); *United States v. Cardwell*, 2023 WL 4243927 (8th Cir. 2023); CAL. PENAL CODE §§ 667, 1170.12; and see § 48.13.1 *infra*. The point made in § 48.9 *infra* about the critical importance of getting the defendant's record of priors straight applies in this context as well as in the context of guidelines-based sentencing enhancement provisions (§ 48.12 *infra*). *See Brock-Miller v. United States*, 887 F.3d 298 (7th Cir. 2018). Statutes authorizing or requiring enhanced sentences for repeat offenders are frequently cast in terms posing difficult issues of construction – whether, for example a defendant's prior conviction constitutes "a crime of violence" (*compare Taylor v. State*, 122 So.3d 742 (Miss. App. 2011), *with Brown v. State*, 102 So.3d 1087 (Miss. 2020)) – and may generate specialized canons of construction such as the "categorical approach" and the "modified categorical approach" used in determining whether an offense is "a violent felony" for purposes of the federal Armed Career Criminal Act (*e.g., Descamps v. United States*, 570 U.S. 254 (2013); *United States v. Williams*, 64 F.4th 149 (4th Cir. 2023); *United States v. Henderson*, 64 F.4th 111 (3d Cir. 2023); *United States v. Eldridge*, 63 F.4th 962 (2d Cir. 2023); *United States v. Jenkins*, 68 F.4th 148 (3d Cir. 2023); *see also Commonwealth v. Ashford*, 486 Mass. 450, 159 N.E.3d 125 (2020) (explicating the similar analysis used in applying Massachusetts's Armed Career Criminal Act); *and cf. State v. Wetrich*, 307 Kan. 552, 555, 412 P.3d 984, 987 (2018) (dealing with the classification of felony convictions as "person felonies" or "nonperson felonies" for purposes of a sentencing scheme in which "crimes classified as person felonies are given the most weight in the criminal history calculus"). The phrase "crime of violence" or its equivalent may also be used in other contexts – for example, in provisions which define an offense such as possession of a firearm during or in furtherance of a crime of violence (*see, e.g., United States v. Morris*, 61 F.4th 311 (2d Cir. 2023); *United States v. Graham*, 67 F.4th 218 (4th Cir. 2023); *United States v. Patterson*, 68 F.4th 402 (8th Cir. 2023)) or which prescribe secondary consequences of a conviction (*see, e.g., United States v. Hankton*, 51 F.4th 578, 594-95 (5th Cir. 2022); – and the construction of the phrase in the latter contexts may influence its construction in the recidivist-sentencing context. This is particularly important in jurisdictions where the courts tend to apply the void-for-vagueness doctrine somewhat more strictly to provisions defining offenses than to sentencing provisions. *See* §§ 20.1 subdivision 10, 48.7 subdivision (1)((b) *infra*.

(b)   Provisions authorizing or requiring more severe punishment if a designated crime or class of crimes is committed by certain means (for example, with a firearm (*see, e.g., Lora v. United States*, 143 S. Ct. 1713 (2023); *cf. United States v. Holden*, 70 F.3d 1015 (7th Cir. 2023); *and see United States v. Alaniz*, 69 F.4th 1124 (9th Cir. 2023), *and Atkinson v. Garland*, 70 F.4th 1018 (7th Cir. 2023) (discussing the implications of the Supreme Court's Second Amendment analysis in *New York State Rifle & Pistol Association, Inc. v. Bruen*, 142 S. Ct. 2111 (2022))) or with certain consequences (for example, if the personal injuries inflicted upon the victim or if the amount of damage to property sustained by or taken from the victim was particularly great;) or upon certain categories of victims (for example, children below a specified age), or in certain locations (for example, within a certain distance of a school or school bus stop). *See, e.g., People v. Ahmed*, 53 Cal. 4th 156, 264 P.3d 822, 133 Cal. Rptr. 3d 856 (2011) (describing the enhancement provisions of California's Determinate Sentencing Act); WEST'S TENN. CODE ANN. §§ 40-35-114, 40-35-210. These provisions may be couched in terms like those of ACCA-type legislation (see the preceding subparagraph), requiring classifications of offenses that give rise to similar rules of statutory construction. *Compare United States v. Taylor*, 142 S. Ct. 2015 (2022), *with United States v. Buck*, 23 F.4th 919 (9th Cir. 2022)).

(c)   "Sexually violent predator" (sometimes called "sexual psychopath") laws that provide for civil commitment after conviction of a specified sexual offense. See § 48.13.2 *infra*.

(d)   Special indefinite sentencing legislation applicable to the defendant, like "youthful offender" or "youth corrections" legislation. *See, e.g.,* WEST'S FLA. STAT. ANN. §§ 958.021 *et seq.*; N.Y. CRIM. PRO. LAW §§ 720.10 *et seq. See also People v. Z.H.*, 192 A.D.3d 55, 62 & n.1, 137 N.Y.S.3d 866, 873 & n.1 (N.Y. App. Div., 4th Dept. 2022) ("we urge future courts [when deciding whether to grant a defendant's request at sentencing for a "youthful offender" sentence] to consider whether a defendant may be facing discrimination based on protected characteristics such as race or gender and to take an intersectional approach by considering the combined effect of the defendant's specific characteristics and any bias that may arise therefrom": "For example, prosecutors are far less likely to exercise their discretion to dismiss in cases against black girls, such as defendant, than they are in cases against white girls (see Samantha Ehrmann et al., *Girls in the Juvenile Justice System* at 13, Juvenile Justice Statistics, National Report Series Bulletin [April 2019], Office of Juvenile Justice and Delinquency

Prevention, available at
https://ojjdp.ojp.gov/sites/g/files/xyckuh176/files/pubs/251486.pdf
[accessed Dec. 8, 2019]; Kim Taylor-Thompson, *Girl
TalkBExamining Racial and Gender Lines in Juvenile Justice*, 6
Nev LJ 1137, 1137 [2006] ['Prosecutors dismiss seven out of
every ten cases involving white girls as opposed to three out of
every ten cases for African American girls'])").

(e) general indefinite sentencing provisions that authorize corrections
officials to prolong confinement beyond a term set by the
sentencing judge. *See State v. Dames*, 2020-Ohio-4991, 2020 WL
6193967, at *1-*2 (Ohio App. 2020).

(f) provisions authorizing civil commitment of mentally ill and
dangerous inmates who are due to be released from prison upon
expiration of the term of confinement to which they have been
sentenced. *See, e.g.*, 18 U.S.C. § 4246; *United States v. Williams*,
53 F.4th 825 (4th Cir. 2022).

(B) *Any applicable mandatory minimum penalties. See, e.g., United States v. Stitt*, 139
S. Ct. 399 (2018); *Stokeling v. United States*, 139 S. Ct. 544 (2019); *Quarles v.
United States*, 139 S. Ct. 1872 (2019); *Shular v. United States*, 140 S. Ct. 779
(2020); *United States v. White*, 24 F.4th 378 (4th Cir. 2022); *United States v.
Jackson*, 55 F.4th 846, 849 (11th Cir. 2022) (for purposes of the mandatory
minimum sentence prescribed by the federal Armed Career Criminal Act in cases
of prior convictions for certain crimes defined in the Controlled Substances Act,
"the version of the controlled-substances list in effect when the defendant was
convicted of his prior state drug offense," rather than the list in effect at the later
time of ACCA sentencing is controlling). Note that similar questions of temporal
reference arise in several sentencing contexts: *see, e.g., United States v. Baker*,
2022 WL 17581659, at *2 (6th Cir. 2022), cited in § 48.12 *infra*. If imposition of
a mandatory minimum requires a finding of a fact other than the existence of a
prior conviction, the Sixth Amendment and the Due Process Clause require that
this finding be made by a jury, based on proof beyond a reasonable doubt, not by
a judge. *Alleyne v. United States*, 570 U.S. 99, 111-12 & n.1, 113-17 (2013);
Robinson v. Woods, 901 F.3d 710 (6th Cir. 2018). See § 48.6 subdivision (4)
infra, discussing the *Apprendi* doctrine.

(C) *Applicable statutes, rules, and regulations governing probation (sometimes called
"supervised release"), relating to eligibility for probation, duration of the
probationary period, conditions that may be imposed upon the allowance of
probation, and grounds for revocation.* These must be considered with regard
both to the offense presently charged and to any offense or offenses for which the
defendant was on probation at the time of this offense. Conviction on the present
offense may result in revocation of a prior probation and in a prison sentence for
the prior offense that exceeds the maximum for the present offense. *See Black v.*

Romano, 471 U.S. 606, 616 (1985). If probation on the present offense is a possibility, counsel should review the rules governing administration of probationary supervision. Although these are often oppressive and galling, there are at least some outer boundaries on a court's power to set conditions of probation. *See, e.g., United States v. Green*, 618 F.3d 120, 122-24 (2d Cir. 2010) ("A condition of supervised release must provide the probationer with conditions that 'are sufficiently clear to inform him of what conduct will result in his being returned to prison'"; "it violates due process if 'men of common intelligence must necessarily guess at its meaning and differ as to its application.'"; "The condition of supervised release that prohibits Green from the 'wearing of colors, insignia, or obtaining tattoos or burn marks (including branding and scars) relative to [criminal street] gangs' . . . does not provide Green with sufficient notice of the prohibited conduct. The range of possible gang colors is vast and indeterminate."); *accord, United States v. Carlineo*, 998 F.3d 533 (2d Cir. 2021); *United States v. Sandidge*, 863 F.3d 755, 757-79 (7th Cir. 2017) (the court of appeals – which had previously ruled that the district court's "special condition [of supervised release] prohibiting 'mood-altering substances' was impermissibly vague and overbroad," and remanded the case to the district court for resentencing – holds that the "revised condition[ ] of supervised release," imposed by the district court at resentencing, which prohibited "the 'excessive use of alcohol,' defined [by the district court] as including 'any use of alcohol that adversely affects [the] defendant's employment, relationships, or ability to comply with the conditions of supervision'" is impermissibly vague because it "raises concerns about fair notice to defendants trying to comply and leaves room for arbitrary enforcement by supervising agents"; the court of appeals modifies the condition by inserting the "limiting" adverb "materially" before "affects".); *compare United States v. Cabral*, 926 F.3d 687 (10th Cir. 2019) (when imposing the standard federal supervised-release condition that the defendant must notify third parties if a probation officer determines that s/he poses a risk to them, the district court must provide adequate guidance to the probation officer regarding what constitutes a risk; by leaving the matter in the unconstrained discretion of a probation officer, the sentencing judge violated the doctrine forbidding delegation of judicial functions to a non-judicial officer), *with United States v. Hollingsworth*, 2023 WL 2771497 (11th Cir. 2023); *People v. Acuna*, 195 A.D.3d 854, 855, 145 N.Y.S.3d 831, 832 (Mem) (N.Y. App. Div., 2d Dep't 2021) (vacating a probation condition that "required the defendant to consent to a search by a probation officer of his person, vehicle, and place of abode, and the seizure of any illegal drugs, drug paraphernalia, gun/firearm or other weapon or contraband found": state law "'quite clearly restricts probation conditions to those reasonably related to a defendant's rehabilitation,'" and "[t]he defendant was not under the influence of any substance or armed with a weapon when he committed the crimes at issue, and his criminal history did not include offenses involving substance abuse or weapons. As such, the consent to search condition of probation was improperly imposed because it was not reasonably related to the defendant's rehabilitation, or necessary to ensure that the defendant will lead a law abiding life."); *State v. Chapman*, 2020-Ohio-6730, 163 Ohio St. 3d 290, at 290, 293-94,

170 N.E.3d 6, 7, 10 (Ohio 2020) (striking down the community-control release condition that a defendant convicted of failing to pay child support to the mothers of his eleven children "'make all reasonable efforts to avoid impregnating a woman'" during his probationary period: the validity of a condition of community-control release "looks to whether . . . [it] reasonably relates to the offense at issue, furthers the twin goals of rehabilitation and justice, and does not cause a greater deprivation of liberty than is necessary to achieve those penological goals."); *United States v. Malenya*, 736 F.3d 554, 559-61 (D.C. Cir. 2013) (probation conditions prohibiting the "'possess[ion] or use [of] a computer or . . . access to any on-line service without the prior approval of the United States Probation Office'" violated the governing statute's requirement that "conditions of supervised release . . . 'involve[ ] no greater deprivation of liberty than is reasonably necessary'"; "We have often noted the ubiquity of computers in modern society and their essentialness for myriad types of employment. . . . A ban on computer and internet usage, qualified only by the possibility of probation office approval, is obviously a significant deprivation of liberty."; "It is unclear if *any* computer or internet restriction could be justified in Malenya's case, but the condition in its current form is surely a greater deprivation of liberty than is reasonably necessary to achieve the goals referenced in [the statute] . . . ."); *United States v. Blair*, 933 F.3d 1271 (10th Cir. 2019) (holding impermissible a condition of supervised release that forbade a defendant convicted of child pornography to access the internet except as authorized by his probation officer); *United States v. Eaglin*, 913 F.3d 88 (2d Cir. 2019) (invalidating conditions of probation that prohibited a defendant convicted of failing to register as a sex offender – on the basis of decade-old statutory rape convictions – from accessing the internet without prior court permission or from viewing or possessing adult pornography); *accord, United States v. Ellis*, 984 F.3d 1092 (4th Cir. 2020) ("[T]here is no evidence connecting the internet to any criminal conduct. Mr. Ellis's only federal offense – failing to register as a sex offender – did not involve the internet. Mr. Ellis's violations of his supervised release – travelling without permission, dishonesty with the probation officer, failing to cooperate with treatment – did not involve the internet." *Id.* at 1102-03. "[T]he district court heard no evidence about how . . . pornography use may or may not influence Mr. Ellis's behavior. The government put forward no individualized evidence linking pornography to Mr. Ellis's criminal conduct or rehabilitation and recidivation risk." *Id.* at 1099. "We find, on this record, the conditions banning legal pornography and internet access cannot be sustained as 'reasonably related' [to the nature and circumstances of the offense, the history and characteristics of the defendant, and the statutory goals of deterrence, protection of the public, and rehabilitation] under 18 U.S.C. § 3583(d)(1) and are overbroad under 18 U.S.C. § 3583(d)(2) [providing that conditions be no greater [a] deprivation of liberty than is reasonably necessary" to achieve those statutory goals]." *Id.* at 1095.); *People v. Morger*, 2019 IL 123643, 160 N.E.3d 53, 57, 61, 442 Ill. Dec. 480, 484, 488 (2019) (relying on *Packingham v. North Carolina, infra*, to strike down, as "unconstitutionally overbroad," a state statute mandating that a sentencing order of probation for "a sex offense, as defined in the SORA [Sex Offender

Registration Act]," include a probationary condition "ban[ning] . . . the [probationer's] use of social media . . . , whether or not a minor was involved [in the sex offense] and whether or not the use of social media was a factor in the commission of the offense"); *Janny v. Gamez*, 8 F.4th 883 (10th Cir. 2021) (an encyclopedic opinion collecting the federal cases holding that probation or parole conditions which require releasees to reside in religious halfway houses and other facilities where the rules require participation in religious exercises of instruction violate the First Amendment); *In re Ricardo P.*, 7 Cal. 5th 1113, 1115-16, 446 P.3d 747, 749, 251 Cal. Rptr. 3d 104, 107 (2019) (striking down a probation condition which "required Ricardo to submit to warrantless searches of his electronic devices, including any electronic accounts that could be accessed through these devices," even though "there was no indication Ricardo used an electronic device in connection with the burglaries" that resulted in the convictions and sentencing order, and which was imposed as a probation condition by the sentencing judge "in order to monitor [Ricardo's] compliance with separate conditions prohibiting him from using or possessing illegal drugs": "We hold that the record here, which contains no indication that Ricardo had used or will use electronic devices in connection with drugs or any illegal activity, is insufficient to justify the substantial burdens imposed by this electronics search condition. The probation condition is not reasonably related to future criminality and is therefore invalid"); *In re Edward B.*, 10 Cal. App. 5th 1228, 1231, 1236, 217 Cal. Rptr. 3d 225, 228, 232 (2017) (invalidating a probation condition that prohibited the defendant from "associating with known gang members and gang associates"; the court explains that although "Edward is well advised to keep his distance from gang members and gang associates," the record does not show "a reasonable connection between the condition and the offense or between the condition and future criminality. . . . Any connection between Edward's offense [grand theft from the person] and gang activity is speculation. And in the absence of evidence of gang affiliation or association with gang members or risk of gang involvement on Edward's part, the gang condition is not tailored to his future criminality."); *Commonwealth v. Feliz*, 481 Mass. 689, 691, 119 N.E.3d 700, 703-04 (2019) (construing the state constitution to hold that "prior to imposing GPS monitoring on a given defendant [as a condition of probation], a judge is required to conduct a balancing test that weighs the Commonwealth's need to impose GPS monitoring against the privacy invasion occasioned by such monitoring"); *United States v. Parkins*, 935 F.3d 63, 64-65, 67 (2d Cir. 2019) (vacating a "condition of supervised release requiring 300 hours of community service per year" (which would have amounted to "a total of 695 hours") and remanding for resentencing because "the pertinent policy statement issued by the Sentencing Commission must be read to advise that courts should generally refrain from imposing more than a total of 400 hours of community service as a condition of supervised release," and "[w]e further conclude that Parkins's condition of supervised release requiring 300 hours a year is not reasonably related to any of the relevant sentencing factors and involves a greater deprivation of liberty than is reasonably needed to achieve the purposes of sentencing": "While community service can provide educational or vocational training, Parkins's service consists primarily, if not entirely, of distributing uncooked meals in the St. John's food pantry. In any event, the district court did not find that Parkins was in need of any of the training that community service might provide, and there is no reason on this record to believe that 695 hours of community service is required for Parkins to achieve the benefit such service offers. ¶ The government argues that the community service will keep Parkins occupied in productive activities, thus preventing him from returning to the 'negative influences' that 'led him astray.' . . . But this argument lacks a limiting principle that would allow an evaluation of how much community service is 'greater than necessary' to keep Parkins off the street. And Parkins's job driving for Uber seems at least equally suited to keeping him occupied, and confers the not-incidental benefit of allowing him to provide for his young daughter. Moreover, it appears evident that, as Parkins argues, his productive occupation is disrupted by the amount of community service he must perform."); *United States v. Hamilton*, 986 F.3d 413, 416 (4th Cir. 2021) (holding that a condition of supervised release imposed upon a defendant convicted of possessing child pornography that he "must not work in any type of employment without the prior approval of the probation officer" is overbroad and lacking a sufficient nexus to the nature and circumstances of the offense); *People v. Martin*, 51 Cal. 4th 75, 82, 244 P.3d 496, 500, 119 Cal. Rptr. 3d 99, 104 (2010) ("when under a plea agreement a defendant pleads guilty to one or more charges in exchange for dismissal of one or more charges, the trial court cannot, in placing the defendant on probation, impose conditions that are based solely on the dismissed charge or charges unless the defendant agreed to them or unless there is a 'transactional' relationship between the charge or charges to which the defendant pled and the facts of the dismissed charge or charges"). *See also Packingham v. North Carolina*, 582 U.S. 98 (2017) (striking down, on First Amendment grounds, a state statute that made "it a felony for a registered sex offender to gain access to a number of websites, including commonplace social media websites like Facebook and Twitter" (*id.* at 101); the Court explains that the statutory prohibition "from using these websites . . . bars access to what for many are the principal sources for knowing current events, checking ads for employment, speaking and listening in the modern public square, and otherwise exploring the vast realms of human thought and knowledge," and that "[e]ven convicted criminals – and in some instances especially convicted criminals – might receive legitimate benefits from these means for access to the world of ideas, in particular if they seek to reform and to pursue lawful and rewarding lives." (*id.* at 108)); *Paroline v. United States*, 572 U.S. 434, 456 (2014) (*dictum*) (restitution orders in criminal cases may come "'within the purview of the Excessive Fines Clause'").

Statutes or rules of court may make certain conditions mandatory whenever a sentence of probation or supervised release is imposed (*e.g.*, 18 U.S.C. § 3563(a)); these conditions can be challenged only on grounds of unconstitutionality. *Compare People v. Morger, supra, with United States v. Langley*, 17 F.4th 1273 (9th Cir. 2021) (per curiam). Other conditions are prescribed in the discretion of the sentencing judge; these may be challenged on grounds of unconstitutionality (*see, e.g., United States v. Eaglin, supra; United*

States v. Green, supra; United States v. Hall, 912 F.3d 1224 (9th Cir. 2019) (per curiam); *Fazili v. Commonwealth*, 71 Va. App. 239, 835 S.E.2d 87 (2019)), dissonance with any general rules pertaining to the administration or purposes of supervised release (*see, e.g., United States v. Ellis, supra; People v. Acuna, supra; In re Ricardo P., supra; United States v. Mike*, 632 F.3d 686, 698 (10th Cir. 2011); *State v. Valin*, 724 N.W.2d 440 (Iowa 2006)), or abuse of discretion (*see, e.g., United States v. Fernandez*, 776 F.3d 344 (5th Cir. 2015) (per curiam); *United States v. Moore*, 449 Fed. Appx. 677 (9th Cir. 2011) (per curiam); *State v. Rieger*, 286 Neb. 788, 839 N.W.2d 282 (2013); *State v. Robinson*, 146 Ohio App. 3d 344, 766 N.E.2d 186 (2001) (per curiam)). *Compare United States v. Voyles*, 2022 WL 3585637 (6th Cir. 2022) (finding no abuse of discretion in a district court's imposition of sex-offender restrictions on a defendant convicted of theft of government property: these restrictions were reasonably related to the rehabilitation of the defendant and the protection of the public because jailers had found in the defendant's cell, during his pretrial detention, a graphic note expressing a desire to commit violent sexual offenses against children).

(D)   *Applicable statutes, rules, and regulations authorizing and governing home confinement and similar restrictions less onerous than imprisonment. See, e.g.,* 18 U.S.C. § 3624(c)(2) as amended by section 602 of the First Step Act of 2018 [S. 756, 115th Cong., 2d Sess. 3649].

(E)   *Applicable statutes, rules, and regulations governing parole, relating to eligibility for parole, duration of the period of parole, conditions that may be imposed upon the granting of parole (see, e.g., United States v. Stiteler*, 2023 WL 4004573 (2d Cir. 2023) (finding no abuse of discretion in sentencing a defendant convicted of making harassing phone calls to one year of post-incarceration supervised release with a condition requiring that he "submit to a search of his person, property, vehicle, place of residence or any other property under his control, based upon reasonable suspicion, and permit confiscation of any evidence or contraband discovered"*), and grounds for revocation, with an eye particularly to the minimum term in prison required to be served before parole eligibility, and the requirements of the "parole plan" demanded by the parole authorities as a condition of admission to parole. See, e.g., Stradford v. Secretary Pennsylvania Department of Corrections*, 53 F.4th 67 (3d Cir. 2022). In some jurisdictions six months must be added to the professed minimum prison time because it invariably requires six months or more for the prisoner to work out a satisfactory parole plan – job, acceptable living quarters, community "sponsor" – demanded as the precondition of release. Owing to parole eligibility standards or parole plan requirements, it is also possible to predict that for some defendants the possibility of parole is illusory. A frequently encountered example is the policy of some parole boards to deny parole to any prisoner who has a detainer lodged against him or her for trial on other charges or for service of sentence on other convictions in any jurisdiction. Parole issues must be considered with regard both to the present offense and to any offense or offenses for which the defendant was on parole at the time of this offense. In some jurisdictions there are early-release provisions that are alternatives to, or substitutes for, traditional parole. *See, e.g.,* 18 U.S.C. § 3624(g) as amended by section 102 of the First Step Act of 2018, *supra.*

(F)   *In cases in which the defendant is not a U.S. citizen, the immigration laws, regulations, and practices that bear on the question whether a conviction of any of the charged crimes could result in removal or exclusion.* A noncitizen may be subject to removal or exclusion if s/he is convicted of any one of a wide range of crimes, including those classified by the Immigration and Nationality Act as "aggravated felonies"; "crimes involving moral turpitude"; certain types of controlled substance offenses; certain types[of firearms offenses; and certain crimes of domestic violence, stalking crimes against children, or violations of protection orders. *See generally Pugin v. Garland,* 2023 WL 4110232 (U.S. 2023); *Barton v. Barr,* 140 S. Ct. 1442 (2020); *Alfred v. Garland,* 64 F.4th 1025 (9th Cir. 2023) (en banc); *Tetteh v. Garland,* 995 F.3d 361 (4th Cir. 2021); *Rad v. Attorney General,* 983 F.3d 651 (3d Cir. 2020); *but see, e.g., Thok v. Garland,* 2023 WL 4520320 (8th Cir. 2023); *Cordero-Garcia v. Garland,* 44 F.4th 1181 (9th Cir. 2022); *Walcott v. Garland,* 21 F.4th 590 (9th Cir. 2021); *Hylton v. U.S. Attorney General,* 992 F.3d 1154 (11th Cir. 2021); *and see Hernandez v. Garland,* 66 F.4th 94 (2d Cir. 2023). And convictions of some offenses may also make a removable alien ineligible for discretionary relief. *See generally Pereida v. Wilkinson,* 141 S. Ct. 754 (2021). For detailed discussion of the relevant rules and practices, *see* MANUEL D. VARGAS, REPRESENTING IMMIGRANT CRIMINAL DEFENDANTS IN NEW YORK STATE (5th ed. 2011); Manuel D. Vargas, *Immigration Consequences of Guilty Pleas or Convictions,* 30 N.Y.U. REV. L. & SOC. CHANGE 701 (2006). *See also, e.g.,* FED. RULE CRIM. PRO. 11(b)(1)(O) (the plea colloquy in federal criminal cases must include a judicial warning to a defendant who is "not a United States citizen" that a conviction may result in the defendant's being "removed from the United States, denied citizenship, and denied admission to the United States in the future"); *People v. Peque,* 22 N.Y.3d 168, 176, 3 N.E.3d 617, 621, 980 N.Y.S.2d 280, 284 (2013) ("deportation is a plea consequence of such tremendous importance, grave impact and frequent occurrence that . . . due process compels a trial court to apprise a defendant that, if the defendant is not an American citizen, he or she may be deported as a consequence of a guilty plea to a felony"). Immigration laws are in a state of flux and there is always the risk that statutory amendments, regulation changes, or agency interpretations or policies could result in an expansion of the categories of crimes that are a basis for removal or exclusion. Accordingly, if counsel's client is not a citizen, it is essential that counsel research the possible immigration consequences of a conviction and consider whether a guilty plea might entail, increase, avoid or reduce the risk of any such consequences. *See Padilla v. Kentucky,* 559 U.S. 356, 364 (2010) ("The[ ] changes to our immigration law have dramatically raised the stakes of a noncitizen's criminal conviction. The importance of accurate legal advice for noncitizens accused of crimes has never been more important."); *Rodriguez-Penton v. United States,* 905 F.3d 481, 487 (6th Cir. 2018) ("Counsel has an obligation to 'advise a noncitizen client that pending criminal charges may carry a risk of adverse immigration consequences.'. . . This obligation is not met if counsel either fails to mention the risk of deportation or specifically discounts such a risk."); *Lee v. United States*, 137 U.S. 1958 (2017) ("Everyone agrees that Lee received objectively unreasonable representation" from his defense attorney, who "assured . . . [Lee that] the Government would not deport him if he pleaded guilty [to a "count of possessing ecstasy with intent to distribute"] when in fact "[t]he conviction meant that Lee [who is "a lawful permanent resident" and "not a United States citizen"] was subject to mandatory deportation from this country." (*id.* at 1962); the Court concludes that counsel's erroneous advice, which led to Lee's pleading guilty, was prejudicial even though Lee "had no real defense to the charge," and thus conviction and deportation were likely if Lee opted for trial, and even though the guilty plea "carried a lesser prison sentence than he would have faced at trial" (*id.*); the Court explains that "common sense (not to mention our precedent) recognizes that there is more to consider than simply the likelihood of success at trial. The decision whether to plead guilty also involves assessing the respective consequences of a conviction after trial and by plea. . . . When those consequences are, from the defendant's perspective, similarly dire, even the smallest chance of success at trial may look attractive." (*id.* at 1966); "But for his attorney's incompetence, Lee would have known that accepting the plea agreement would *certainly* lead to deportation. Going to trial? *Almost* certainly. If deportation were the 'determinative issue' for an individual in plea discussions, as it was for Lee; if that individual had strong connections to this country and no other, as did Lee; and if the consequences of taking a chance at trial were not markedly harsher than pleading [guilty], as in this case, that 'almost' could make all the difference. Balanced against holding on to some chance of avoiding deportation was a year or two more of prison time. . . . Not everyone in Lee's position would make the choice to reject the plea. But we cannot say it would be irrational to do so." (*id.* at 1968-69)). *See also, e.g., United States v. Akinsade*, 686 F.3d 248, 251, 255-56 (4th Cir. 2012) (counsel committed ineffective assistance by misinforming the client that the charge to which the client was pleading was not a deportable offense); *Hernandez v. State*, 124 So.3d 757, 762-63 (Fla. 2013) (even if the accused was warned by the judge during the plea colloquy of the risk of deportation and the accused explicitly affirmed his understanding, defense counsel nonetheless can be found to be ineffective under *Padilla v. Kentucky, supra,* for "failing to warn [the accused] . . . of the clear immigration consequences of his plea": "an equivocal warning from the trial court is less than what is required from counsel and therefore cannot, by itself, remove prejudice resulting from counsel's deficiency"); *Commonwealth v. DeJesus*, 468 Mass. 174, 174-75, 9 N.E.3d 789, 791 (2014) (counsel committed ineffective assistance by advising his noncitizen client that a guilty plea to possession with intent to distribute cocaine would make him "'eligible for deportation'" when in fact "applicable immigration law . . . makes deportation or removal [for this crime] . . . automatic or 'presumptively mandatory'"); *State v. Nunez-Diaz*, 247 Ariz. 1, 444 P.3d 250 (2019) (applying *Padilla and Lee* to the case of an undocumented immigrant). *Cf. United States v. Juarez*, 672 F.3d 381, 384, 385-90

(5th Cir. 2012) (counsel, who advised the client to plead guilty to lying about United States citizenship and illegal re-entry after deportation following a conviction of an aggravated felony, committed ineffective assistance because counsel "failed to independently research and investigate the derivative citizenship defense" which "is a defense to the alienage element of both crimes to which Juarez pled guilty").

(G)   *Forfeiture statutes condemning automobiles and other paraphernalia used to commit drug, liquor, gambling, and like offenses, or the proceeds of offenses (see, e.g.,* 21 U.S.C. § 853; *compare United States v. Monsanto,* 491 U.S. 600 (1989), *with Honeycutt v. United States,* 581 U.S. 443 (2017)); *United States v. Kousisis,* 66 F.4th 406, 427 (3d Cir. 2023) ("the government must prove its forfeiture allegations by a preponderance of the evidence"); BALDWIN'S OHIO REV. CODE ANN. §§ 2981.01-2981.14; *State v. O'Malley,* 2022-Ohio-3207, 169 Ohio St. 3d 479, 206 N.E.3d 662 (2022). "In a civil-forfeiture proceeding, the Government bears the burden 'to establish, by a preponderance of the evidence, that the property is subject to forfeiture.'. . . Property is subject to forfeiture if it either facilitated the transportation, sale, receipt, possession, or concealment of a controlled substance [or other designated criminal materials], or was intended to do so, or constitutes proceeds of . . . [specified criminal] activities. . . . And when pursuing forfeiture on either of those theories, the Government must show a 'substantial connection between the property and the offense.'" *United States v. McClellan,* 44 F.4th 200, 205 (4th Cir. 2022). Regarding the "rigid procedure [prescribed by FED. RULE CRIM. PRO. 32.2] to ensure that any forfeiture order is correct before it becomes final at sentencing," *see United States v. Maddux,* 37 F.4th 1170, 1175 (6th Cir. 2022). *And see Frein v. Pennsylvania State Police,* 47 F.4th 247 (3d Cir. 2022) (firearms belonging to a husband and wife which were lawfully seized under a search warrant issued in connection with the investigation of their son's assassination of a state trooper and wounding of another but which were not used in evidence could not be retained by officials after the son's conviction became final). *Compare United States v. Wright,* 49 F.4th 1221, 1226 (9th Cir. 2022) (an individual from whom currency was seized at the time of his arrest for armed robbery was not entitled to recover it despite (1) the dismissal of the prosecution against him as a result of sanctions imposed upon the prosecutor for discovery violations, and (2) the government's failure to institute forfeiture proceedings, because "the government adequately demonstrated [at the hearing on his motion for return of the currency] that the money . . . was stolen, overcoming the presumption that . . . [he] is entitled to lawful possession").

(H)   *Civil disabilities imposed by state law,* including:

    (1)   Loss of any outstanding occupational license (taxi operator license, professional license, license to operate a bar, and so forth) and ineligibility for future licensing.

    (2)   Loss of a driver's license (frequent under traffic and drug legislation) and ineligibility for future licensing. *But see Parham v. District of Columbia,*

2022 WL 17961250 (D. D.C. 2022) (finding that an ordinance automatically disqualifying applicants from obtaining or renewing a driver's license if they owe more than $100 in parking, traffic, or other fines and fees violates due process because "D.C. does not afford any opportunity for Plaintiffs to be heard prior to disqualifying them from renewing their driver's licenses" (2022 WL 17961250, at *9) and instances of erroneous ticketing demonstrate a significant risk of such error).

(3)   Loss of public office or employment and ineligibility for future public office or employment.

(4)   Loss of voting rights (*see Richardson v. Ramirez*, 418 U.S. 24 (1974); *compare Hunter v. Underwood*, 471 U.S. 222 (1985) *with Harness v. Watson*, 47 F.4th 296 (5th Cir. 2022) (en banc), *and Thompson v. Alabama*, 65 F.4th 1288 (11th Cir. 2023); *and see Jones v. Latimer*, 15 F.4th 1062 (11th Cir. 2021)).

(5)   Sex offender registration requirements and other types of criminal registration requirements. *See, e.g., Gundy v. United States*, 139 S. Ct. 2116 (2019); *Smith v. Doe*, 538 U.S. 84 (2003); *Duarte v. City of Lewisville, Texas*, 858 F.3d 348 (5th Cir. 2017); *Doe v. DeWine*, 910 F.3d 842 (6th Cir. 2018); *John Does 1-7 v. Abbott*, 945 F.3d 307 (5th Cir. 2019); *Doe v. Settle*, 24 F.4th 932 (4th Cir. 2022); *McGuire v. Marshall*, 50 F.4th 986 (11th Cir. 2022); *Hope v. Commissioner of Indiana Department of Correction*, 66 F.4th 647 (7th Cir. 2023); *In the Interest of Justin B.*, 419 S.C. 575, 799 S.E.2d 675 (2017). Rare judicial decisions imposing constitutional restrictions on such requirements include *Doe v. Pennsylvania Board of Probation & Parole*, 513 F.3d 95 (3d Cir. 2008) (equal protection restriction); *Hendricks v. Jones ex rel. State ex rel. Oklahoma Department of Correction*, 349 P.3d 531 (Okla. 2013) (same); *ACLU of New Mexico v. City of Albuquerque*, 139 N.M. 761, 137 P.3d 1215 (N.M. App. 2006) (same); *Does #1-#5 v. Snyder*, 834 F.3d 696 (6th Cir. 2016) (federal *ex post facto* restriction, distinguishing *Smith v. Doe, supra*); *Doe v. Rausch*, 461 F. Supp. 3d 747 (E.D. Tenn. 2020) (same); *Doe #1 v. Lee*, 518 F. Supp. 3d 1157 (M.D. Tenn. 2021) (same); *Does 1-9 v. Lee*, 2023 WL 2335639 (M.D. Tenn. 2023) (same); *Wallace v. State*, 905 N.E.2d 371 (Ind. 2009) (state constitutional *ex post facto* restriction, disagreeing with the federal ruling in *Smith v. Doe, supra*); *Cornelio v. Connecticut*, 32 F.4th 160 (2d Cir. 2022) (a convict's challenges to provisions of Connecticut's sex offender registration statute that required him to disclose his email address and other internet communication identifiers and periodically to verify his residence stated tenable claims under the First Amendment); *Meredith v. Stein*, 355 F. Supp. 3d 355 (E.D.N.C. 2018) ("In determining that an individual must register as a sex offender because his out-of-state conviction is 'substantially similar' to a reportable conviction, North Carolina provides neither prior notice nor a hearing. In fact, North Carolina provides nothing at all. Rather, each county sheriff's office can decide unilaterally whether any out-of-state

offense is 'substantially similar' to any reportable North Carolina conviction. The sheriff's deputies responsible for making the determinations do not need to consult with legal counsel, even though substantial similarity has been described as a 'question of law.' . . . No evidentiary hearings are held. The registrants are given no opportunity to provide input. The substantial similarity determinations are final and result in individuals being forced to register within days or face felony prosecution; there is no opportunity to appeal. There is no statute, regulation, policy, or ordinance outlining the determination process, listing factors that are considered, or identifying who is responsible for making the determinations." *Id.* at 365. "Thus, plaintiff has adequately demonstrated that North Carolina's process of determining whether out-of-state offenses are 'substantially similar' to reportable convictions in North Carolina violates his procedural due process rights under the Fourteenth Amendment." *Id.* at 366.); *E.B. v. Verniero*, 119 F.3d 1077, 1111 (3d Cir. 1997) (as applied retroactively to individuals convicted of specified sexual offenses, the New Jersey version of Megan's Law violated due process insofar as it placed the burden of proof on a convict in judicial proceedings seeking review of a prosecutor's determination that the convict was subject to certain public notification provisions; rather, "the Due Process Clause requires that the state prove its case by clear and convincing evidence in a Megan's Law proceeding"); *Taylor v. Pennsylvania State Police of the Commonwealth*, 132 A.3d 590 (Pa. Commonwealth Ct. 2016) (petitioner stated tenable claims under the state *ex post facto* and due process clauses, the latter claims challenging the statute's irrebuttable presumption of recidivism and the abridgment of the petitioner's state constitutional interest in his reputation by registration and notification requirements not narrowly tailored to meet a compelling governmental interest); *Rogers v. State*, 468 Md. 1, 37-38, 226 A.3d 261, 283 (2020) (in a case involving human trafficking of a minor, the court holds that "sex offender registration under the current statutory scheme is sufficiently punitive, *i.e.,* serving as more than a mere civil regulation, to require determination of a fact necessary for placement on the Registry – such as the victim's age – be made beyond a reasonable doubt by the trier of fact during the adjudicatory phase of the criminal proceeding prior to sentencing"; and if the defendant elects a jury trial on the issue of guilt, the predicate fact for registration must be found by a jury under the Sixth Amendment rule of *Apprendi v. New Jersey*, 530 U.S. 466 (2000), summarized in § 48.7 subdivision (4) *infra*). *And see Doe as Next Friend of Doe # 6 v. Swearingen*, 51 F.4th 1295 (11th Cir. 2022).

(6) Restriction or abrogation of the right to possess firearms or other weapons (*see, e.g., Evans v. Wisconsin Department of Justice*, 2014 WI App 31, 353 Wis.2d 289, 844 N.W.2d 403 (Wis. App. 2014); *Wolak v. Pennsylvania State Police*, 898 A.2d 1176 (Pa. Commonwealth Ct. 2006)).

(I) *Liabilities under federal law or regulations*, including:

(1)   Ineligibility for military service (including National Guard service, which, in turn, is the precondition for certain employments).

(2)   Ineligibility for public office or employment.

(3)   Restriction or abrogation of the right to possess firearms or other weapons (*see, e.g., Folajtar v. Attorney General*, 980 F.3d 897 (3d Cir. 2020); *State ex rel. Suwalski v. Peeler*, 2021-Ohio-4061, 167 Ohio St. 3d 38, 188 N.E.3d 1048 (2021), *abrogated on another issue in State v. Brasher*, 2022-Ohio-4703, 2022 WL 17970382 (Ohio 2022); *but see Range v. Attorney General*, 69 F.4th 96 (3d Cir. 2022) (en banc)).

(J)   *Privately imposed sanctions*:

(1)   Higher insurance rates (particularly in traffic cases).

(2)   Hurdles to employment, admission to professions, admission to educational institutions, financing, residential opportunities, credit, and so forth.

(K)   *Other collateral consequences of conviction. See* NATIONAL REENTRY RESOURCE CENTER, NATIONAL INVENTORY OF THE COLLATERAL CONSEQUENCES OF CONVICTION, *available at:* https://niccc.csgjusticecenter.org/database/results/?jurisdiction=&consequence_ca tegory=&narrow_category=&triggtrigg_offense_category=&consequence_type= &duration_category=&page_num_ber=1.

In addition to knowing each of the consequences that may follow conviction, counsel must undertake to calculate the likelihood of the actual occurrence of each.

15.6.2. *Determining the Concessions that Could be Obtained from a Prosecutor to Avert or Reduce the Consequences of a Conviction*

After conducting the research described in section 15.6.1 *supra* regarding the possible consequences of a conviction, counsel will need to identify the concessions that conceivably could be extracted from a prosecutor, as part of a plea bargain, to avert or reduce the severity of these consequences. The types of concessions that are most common are:

(1) *A prosecutor's agreement to accept a guilty plea that reduces the maximum possible term of incarceration.* Depending upon the sentencing laws of the jurisdiction, the sentencing practices of the judge presiding over the case, and the specific circumstances of the case, this may involve:

(a)   *A plea of guilty to some lesser offense[s] included within the offense[s] charged.* A guilty plea to a lesser offense is the classic form of "copping a plea" and the one that most defendants think of first. It usually produces a guaranteed reduction of the statutory maximum sentence to which the defendant is exposed, limiting the "max" to the penalty authorized by law for the lesser offense. It also usually – but not invariably – lessens the sentence that the defendant will actually receive. Approval of the court for a plea of guilty to a lesser included offense is not often required and, where required, is ordinarily routinely given. There is little or no way the prosecutor can renege once the plea is entered. This sort of agreed disposition is therefore less risky than some others. However, its value to the defendant varies greatly, depending upon judicial sentencing patterns – and, in particular, upon the relationship between the maximum sentence authorized by law and the actual sentences customarily given for the greater and the lesser included offenses. Assume, for example, the common phenomenon of a judge who (A) never sentences first offenders to more than a third of the statutory maximum term for armed robbery and (B) assumes that any defendant who pleads guilty to simple robbery is really guilty of armed robbery and is copping a plea. Counsel representing a first offender before this judge is not likely to see a great difference in the sentence if the client pleads guilty to simple robbery rather than going to trial and being convicted of aggravated robbery. If counsel wants to make a deal that means much in terms of time served, s/he will have to consider other possible forms of plea bargaining.

(b) *A plea of guilty to less than all of the offenses charged, with dismissal of the others on a nolle prosequi.* "Knocking off" indictments or counts also ordinarily produces a guaranteed reduction of the maximum sentencing power of the court. But this is so only when state law or the constitutional law of double jeopardy (see § 48.7 subdivision (3) *infra*) does not bar cumulative punishment for the several offenses. Counsel, therefore, must research this issue. Counsel should also be aware of local judicial practice with regard to consecutive or concurrent sentencing for convictions on related offenses. Some courts invariably give concurrent sentences for these offenses, so counsel has gained nothing by a dropping of some charges. It is also significant that the *nolle prosequi* often requires leave of court, and leave is not always routinely given. Furthermore, the prosecutor may sometimes renege on a *nol pros*; local law and the prosecutor's habits should be checked out.

(c) *A plea of guilty to offenses charged in a new indictment or information that are less serious than the offense[s] presently charged but are not lesser included offenses.* On this plea, the prosecutor *nol prosses* the original indictment or information. Although the *nol pros* requires leave of court, the court may have no choice but to grant it if the new offenses selected for the plea bar prosecution of the original charges under the principles of double jeopardy. See § 20.8 *infra*.

(d) *Affecting the application of the jurisdiction's sentencing guidelines to the defendant's case by means of a plea of guilty to a reduced charge.* In jurisdictions that employ sentencing guidelines and similar types of determinate-sentencing formulas, it will usually be the case that pleading guilty to a lesser offense or to less than all of the offenses charged will limit the potential maximum sentence by affecting the determinations of the "base offense level" and "combined offense level." In some such jurisdictions, however, such a guilty plea may have no practical effect on the ultimate sentence, either because (i) a lesser included offense, although having a lower maximum sentence, falls within the same guidelines category as the higher charge; or (ii) the guidelines or local practice allow a judge at sentencing to consider the criminal conduct underlying a dismissed or bargained-away charge when determining what guideline range applies.

(2) *A prosecutor's agreement, as part of a plea bargain, to support (or not to oppose) a particular sentence, or otherwise to assist the defense in securing a more favorable sentence:*

    (a)   In jurisdictions that do not employ sentencing guidelines, defense counsel commonly seek one or more of the following types of agreements from the prosecutor which may influence the judge's sentencing decision:

        (i)   The prosecutor's commitment to recommend a specific sentence or to make a specified form of recommendation or statement to the sentencing judge. Commitments of this type might specify:

            (A)   The recommendation of a specific sentence.

            (B)   The recommendation of a sentence not more than X.

            (C)   The recommendation of a suspended sentence, with or without probation. The suspension may be unconditional or may be conditioned on the defendant's doing specified things (such as, for example, enrolling in a community-based treatment program) or refraining from doing specified things.

            (D)   The recommendation that sentences on several present charges be concurrent or that they be made concurrent with sentences on previous convictions, including sentences on which the defendant's probation or parole may be revoked by reason of the present conviction.

            (E)   The recommendation that a term of imprisonment be served in a specialized facility (minimum-security prison, residential drug program, and so forth).

            (F)   The recommendation that the defendant be sentenced under specialized sentencing provisions (*e.g.*, a "youthful offender" provision or the like).

> (G)   A general recommendation of leniency or announcement to the court that the defendant is "cooperating."

It is important to recognize that, in most jurisdictions, *sentencing recommendations are only recommendations.* They are the riskiest form of agreement because the judge may not go along with them. *See, e.g., United States v. Santeramo*, 681 Fed. Appx. 762 (11th Cir. 2017). Some judges invariably do; some never do; some do or do not, depending on the case. Negotiating for a sentencing recommendation is effective only if counsel has sufficient information about the judge who will be – or about all of the judges who may be – the sentencing judge. In some cases it may be possible to meet with the judge in chambers, in a formal or informal pretrial conference, to sound out his or her reaction to a proposed sentencing recommendation by the prosecutor. *See, e.g., Cripps v. State*, 122 Nev. 764, 137 P.3d 1187 (2006); see § 18.14 subdivision (1) *infra*. Defense counsel may wish to suggest such a conference when the judge's attitude toward sentencing recommendations is uncertain. *See, e.g., State v. Warner*, 762 So.2d 507 (Fla. 2000).

In some localities, a formal or informal practice of "conditional" plea bargaining has developed. Under this practice the prosecution and defense negotiate (i) the terms of the sentence that the defendant will receive if s/he pleads guilty (an "on the nose" bargain) or (ii) the rules that will be followed in sentencing the defendant if s/he pleads guilty (for example, that the sentence will be no more than X [nor less than Y]; that the prosecution will inform the court that the defendant is cooperating with the authorities and will ask the court to consider this circumstance in mitigation, or any other arrangement among those described in this section. The parties' agreement is then submitted to the sentencing judge for approval. If the judge agrees (i) to impose the bargained sentence or (ii) to observe the bargained sentencing rules, the defendant pleads guilty and the judge performs as agreed. If the judge does not agree, then the deal is off, and the case goes to trial (or to renegotiation). *See, e.g., People v. Clancey*, 56 Cal. 4th 562, 570, 572-77, 299 P.3d 131, 135, 137-40, 155 Cal. Rptr. 3d 485, 490, 492-95 (2013). If this procedure is customary in counsel's jurisdiction, counsel should ordinarily follow it. If it is not, counsel should consider suggesting it to the prosecutor and the judge for use on an *ad hoc* basis. The extent of a trial judge's power to reject a negotiated plea co-sponsored by the prosecution and the defense differs from jurisdiction to jurisdiction. In some jurisdictions, that power is unrestricted; in others, it is constrained to some extent. *See, e.g., United States v. Walker*, 922 F.3d 239 (4th Cir. 2019), *vacated and remanded on an unrelated point, Walker v. United States*, 140 S. Ct. 474 (2019) (noting that under federal practice a district judge's refusal to accept a bargained plea is reviewable for abuse of discretion but finding no abuse in the case at bar: "[A] district court is not entitled to base its decision on arbitrary or irrational factors" (*id.* at 249) but "should carefully weigh whether the plea agreement adequately reflects the defendant's misconduct and serves the objectives of sentencing" (*id.* at 250). "Importantly, a district court should also weigh whether the plea agreement is in the public interest." *Id.* "Of additional importance, a court should always consider any danger the defendant might pose to the public." *Id.* "At bottom, the court should articulate a rational justification for its decision after weighing all the relevant circumstances. . . . And, in so doing, the court must accord due respect to the prosecutorial prerogatives involved in charging decisions, thus ensuring that the separation of executive and judicial powers is not infringed." *Id.*).

        (ii)   The prosecutor's agreement to make no recommendation on sentence and to take no position on the question, leaving defense counsel free to argue the matter to the court. This sort of agreement is usefully made to break the stalemate in negotiation that occurs when the prosecutor and defense counsel are agreed that the defendant should receive some consideration for a guilty plea but are far apart on the sort of sentence that should be imposed.

        (iii)   The prosecutor's agreement not to "press the priors," that is, not to invoke the provisions of recidivist sentencing legislation of various sorts (including habitual-criminal and sexual predator provisions). The prosecutor may or may not have authority under local practice to decide unilaterally whether the stiffer penalties of recidivist law will be invoked. Counsel should determine whether the judge has any power to invoke the priors *sua sponte*.

(b)   In jurisdictions that employ sentencing guidelines and similar sorts of determinate-sentencing formulas, a prosecutor's agreement to one or more aspects of sentencing can have a significant effect on the ultimate determination of sentence by the judge. Depending on the nature of the local guidelines and local practice, counsel might seek to obtain:

        (i)   A prosecutorial "agree[ment] that a specific sentence or sentencing range is the appropriate disposition of the case, or that a particular provision of the Sentencing Guidelines, or policy statement, or sentencing factor does or does not apply." FED. RULE CRIM. PRO. 11(c)(1)(C). Under some guidelines, "such a recommendation or request binds the court once the court accepts the plea agreement" (*id.*).

        (ii)   A prosecutorial commitment to "recommend, or agree not to oppose the defendant's request, that a particular sentence or sentencing range is appropriate or that a particular provision of the Sentencing Guidelines, or policy statement, or sentencing factor does or does not apply" (FED. RULE CRIM. PRO. 11(c)(1)(B)). It is usually the case that "such a recommendation or request does not bind the court" at sentencing (*id.*).

        (iii)   Prosecutorial support for a downward departure from the presumptive guidelines sentence. In some jurisdictions, there is a well-established process for obtaining such prosecutorial support if a defendant agrees to cooperate with the government by providing information and/or agreeing to testify against others. In such systems, a downward departure usually is not a guarantee even when the defendant has followed through with the contemplated cooperation because (A) the judge is not required to follow the prosecutor's recommendation and (B) the prosecutor often has latitude to treat the defendant's assistance as insufficient to satisfy the agreement. *Cf. Ricketts v. Adamson*, 483 U.S. 1 (1987).

(3) *A prosecutor's agreement to have specified favorable information included in the corrections department's intake summary (or, in federal cases, the "risk assessment report" required by 18 U.S.C. § 3632(a) as added by section 101 of the First Step Act of 2018 [S. 3649]).* This information may affect prison officials' discretion in determining the conditions of a defendant's confinement; and in regimes such as the one introduced by the federal First Step Act, it may affect the length of time that a defendant has to spend in a penal facility before eligibility for supervised release or release into a residential reentry center or home confinement.

(4) *In cases in which the defendant would be in danger of abuse by vindictive codefendants or is particularly vulnerable to attacks by predators in certain jail or prison facilities, counsel may be able to obtain a commitment or at least a recommendation from the prosecutor that s/he be housed elsewhere.* The prosecutor may also be willing to join in a request to the sentencing judge to sign off on this arrangement and include it in the defendant's commitment papers as speaking from the judge to the correctional officials who will be determining the location and conditions of the defendant's confinement.

(5) *A prosecutor's agreement, as part of a plea bargain, to secure the dropping of other charges against the defendant in other jurisdictions, federal or state.* The prosecutor may or may not be able to deliver on this agreement. Counsel should ordinarily get personal assurances from the other prosecutors involved. S/he should also be familiar with prosecutorial policies, or s/he may be making a bad deal. For example, the federal government very infrequently prosecutes for a federal offense following state conviction on a charge based upon the same incident (see § 20.8.7 *infra*), so an agreement to have federal charges dropped is often worth little.

(6) *In the case of a defendant who is not a citizen, a prosecutor's agreement to accept a plea to a charge that does not expose the defendant to the risk of removal or exclusion, along with dismissal of all charges that have those potential consequences.* See § 15.6.1 subdivision (E) *supra*.

(7) *A prosecutor's agreement to accept a plea to a charge that does not expose the defendant to certain collateral consequences (such as mandatory sex offender registration, or ineligibility for a professional license of a certain type).* See § 15.6.1 subdivision (G) *supra*.

15.7. *Other Factors That May Bear on the Advisability of a Guilty Plea*

15.7.1. *The Presence or Absence of Debatable or Dubious Legal Points Relating to Substantive or Evidentiary Matters on Which the Judge Might Commit Reversible Error in a Pretrial Ruling or in the Course of a Trial*

In comparing the costs of guilty plea and of a trial, counsel must keep in mind that guilty pleas foreclose appellate review of most pretrial rulings. See § 14.8 *supra*. If the trial court has ruled against the defense on a pretrial issue that has a reasonable prospect of prevailing on appeal, and if that ruling is not among the very few which will be appealable after a guilty plea, counsel has to consider whether the better course of action would be to go to trial in order to preserve the issue. Of course, this calculus must take into account not only how likely it is that the issue will be good for a reversal on a post-trial appeal (or prerogative writ proceeding) but how much time the client might have to serve before an appellate ruling is handed down, and also any other harms that may attend the trial and a possible retrial (embarrassment, stress, whatever).

The advisability of a guilty plea depends, as well, upon the presence or absence of legal issues that will require rulings by the judge at trial, and the likelihood that the judge may commit reversible error in one or more of those rulings. Counsel will want to pay attention particularly to any unsettled issues of construction of the statute under which the client is charged – issues that can generate challenges to jury instructions (see § 42.5 *infra*) or, in a bench trial, to the trial judge's conclusions of law (see § 46.3 *infra*) – and debatable issues of the admissibility of significant pieces of prosecution or defense evidence. Like a hung jury (see § 15.4.5 *supra*), an appellate reversal usually produces a significant improvement of the client's prospects in the endgame.

15.7.2. *The Possibility of Using a Guilty Plea to Steer the Case Before a Favorable Sentencing Judge*

Despite systemic attempts to achieve some uniformity in sentencing, individual judges continue to differ enormously in their sentencing patterns and attitudes. Often the most significant thing that counsel can do to affect a client's sentence is to have the sentence imposed by the right judge or not imposed by the wrong judge. Experienced criminal lawyers in a locality (and the prosecutor if s/he is trustworthy and cooperative) will usually be able to advise counsel about who are the right and wrong judges in particular sorts of cases.

The judge who presides over the entry of a guilty plea ordinarily assumes jurisdiction over future stages of the case and becomes the sentencing judge. For this reason, plea negotiation with the prosecutor may profitably include consideration of bringing the case on for arraignment – and entry of a guilty plea – at a time when the arraignment judge is a favorable sentencer. If this cannot be done at the initial arraignment (as it can in localities where the prosecutor controls the calendar call at arraignment), a continuance by agreement may be in order. Alternatively, the defendant may plead not guilty at arraignment, with an eye to changing the plea at a later time. Sometimes judges will receive a plea at other than regular arraignment sessions, and this possibly should be explored with the prosecutor. Or the prosecutor may have sufficient control over calendaring for trial so that the case can be listed for trial before a favorable judge, with the understanding that the defendant will withdraw his or her initial not guilty plea and will plead guilty on the trial date.

In the absence of a negotiated plea, counsel whose client is pleading guilty will have to make such decisions concerning timing as counsel can effectuate unilaterally. Whether the plea should be entered at arraignment will depend on whether there is a chance that a more lenient judge will sit on post-arraignment motions or at trial. Similar sentencing considerations may determine whether to ask for a jury trial or to waive a jury; different judges will be sitting in different jury and nonjury courts. Knowledge of individual judicial predilections and of court calendars is indispensable.

15.7.3. *Considerations That May Arise in a Case in Which the Defendant Is Detained Pending Trial*

When the defendant is detained pending trial, it may be possible to include in the plea agreement a prosecutorial commitment to support post-plea release of the defendant pending sentencing, either on the defendant's own recognizance or with a bond the defendant can afford. *Cf.* §§ 4.2, 4.7-4.11 *supra.* Such an arrangement not only speeds up the client's release from galling pretrial confinement but gives him or her the chance to demonstrate good behavior in the community during the presentencing period and thereby "earn" a sentence of probation. See §§ 4.19, 7.24, 12.18 *supra.*

Even when a guilty plea will not serve to secure the defendant's liberty pending sentencing, a defendant who is detained before trial may nevertheless have an interest in pleading guilty in order to cut down on the period of detention prior to sentencing. This will obviously be the case when a sentence of probation is expected or in misdemeanor cases in which the period of pretrial detention pending a trial may exceed the likely length of the sentence that would be imposed upon conviction. It may even be the case when a longer incarcerative sentence is likely, if the period of time spent in pretrial detention is not automatically credited against the length of a sentence.

Although reducing the duration of incarceration in this way is a valid consideration, counsel who discusses it with the client will want to be sure that the discomfort of being in jail does not overwhelm the client's judgment and push him or her into a hasty decision to forgo a trial in which s/he may have a winning defense.

15.7.4. *The Potential Advantages of a Guilty Plea in a Case in which the Prosecutor Has Under-Charged the Defendant*

Occasionally, counsel will encounter a case in which the charges filed by the prosecution are significantly less serious than those that counsel's independent interviewing and investigation reveal could be proved at a trial. If the client pleads not guilty and thereby puts the case on the prosecution's trial-preparation agenda, s/he could end up facing graver charges. See §§ 8.2.2, 12.13 *supra.* Under these circumstances, a quick plea of guilty may be advisable in order to bar the subsequent filing of aggravated charges. The constitutional prohibition against double jeopardy (see § 20.8 *infra*) bars a defendant's prosecution upon greater charges following his or her conviction of a lesser included offense (*e.g., United States v. Dixon,* 509 U.S. 688 (1993); *Heath v. Alabama,* 474 U.S. 82, 87-88 (1985) (dictum)), except (a) "where the State is unable to proceed on the more serious charge at the outset because the additional facts necessary to sustain that charge have not occurred or have not been discovered despite the exercise of due diligence" (*Brown v. Ohio,* 432 U.S. 161, 169 n.7 (1977); *Illinois v. Vitale,* 447 U.S. 410, 419-21 & n.8 (1980); *compare Garrett v. United States,* 471 U.S. 773, 789-92 (1985)); or (b) the state files the more serious charge at the outset, but the defendant elects to seek adjudication of the lesser charge first and succeeds in obtaining such an adjudication over the prosecutor's objection (*see Ohio v. Johnson,* 467 U.S. 493 (1984); *cf. Jeffers v. United States,* 432 U.S. 137, 151-54 (1977) (plurality opinion)); or (c) the adjudication of the lesser charges is effected pursuant to a plea bargain that the defendant later breaches (*see Ricketts v. Adamson,* 483 U.S. 1 (1987)).

15.7.5. *Cases in Which a Client Manifests Strong Discomfort With One or the Other of the Options of Entering a Guilty Plea or Going to Trial*

Another factor to consider is whether the defendant does not "feel" guilty and is agreeing to a guilty plea only with considerable reluctance. Given the fact that the decision is the client's to make and that it is the client who will have to live with the sentencing consequences of that decision, the comfort of the client should be a major factor. Moreover, if the client is unhappy with the plea, his or her discomfort may be sufficiently apparent to the judge during the plea colloquy that the judge may be unwilling to accept the plea. As indicated in § 14.1 *supra,* the judge may interrogate the defendant extensively before allowing the entry of a guilty plea. (Problems of the latter sort may be avoided or ameliorated in jurisdictions that allow an "*Alford* plea." See § 15.16.1 *infra.*)

Conversely, the client may have concerns that make him or her uncomfortable with the prospect of undergoing a trial, regardless of its outcome. Some defendants have psychological or emotional problems that render them unable to cope with the nervous stress that attends a trial, particularly a lengthy trial. Some defendants fear a spouse's or family member's reactions to hearing the testimony that will emerge at trial, particularly when the offense is a sex offense or involves extreme violence. Some defendants are worried about the bad publicity that a trial may generate. In these situations, counsel will need to play the role of a dispassionate but not uncompassionate adviser, helping the client to examine his or her feelings with a measure of objectivity but not underrating their importance.

C. *Plea Negotiations*

15.8. *Defense Counsel's Obligations in Plea Negotiations*

"Plea bargaining" and "bargain justice" conjure up shabby images in many minds, ranging from a sluggardly or exploitative defense practice to politicking and graft. Undoubtedly, there are some corruptions of plea bargaining. But the negotiated resolution of criminal matters is no more to be scorned for that reason than are all contracts because some contracts are fraudulent. There is absolutely nothing wrong with defense counsel's settling a criminal case with authorization from the client and after fair dealings with the prosecutor.

What is involved in settlement, and in the antecedent negotiation, is an attempt to come to agreement on a disposition that serves and reconciles, as far as possible, the legitimate interests of the prosecution and the defendant, without the wasted effort and needless vagaries of trial. In criminal – as in civil – matters, negotiation is the essence of lawyering. Experienced criminal lawyers know that one of defense counsel's most important functions, perhaps the most important, is working out with the prosecutor the best possible disposition of a client's case in situations in which there is no realistic prospect of acquittal. Not only may the lawyer properly do this, but s/he violates the obligation of competent representation if s/he fails to pursue plea-bargaining opportunities that could produce a better outcome for the client than a trial (*see* AMERICAN BAR ASSOCIATION, STANDARDS FOR CRIMINAL JUSTICE MONITORS AND MONITORING, DEFENSE FUNCTION (4th ed. 2017), Standard 4-6.1, *Duty to Explore Disposition Without Trial* ("(a) Defense counsel should be open, at every stage of a criminal matter and after consultation with the client, to discussions with the prosecutor concerning disposition of charges by guilty plea or other negotiated disposition. Counsel should be knowledgeable about possible dispositions that are alternatives to trial or imprisonment, including diversion from the criminal process. ¶ (b) In every criminal matter, defense counsel should consider the individual circumstances of the case and of the client, and should not recommend to a client acceptance of a disposition offer unless and until appropriate investigation and study of the matter has been completed. Such study should include discussion with the client and an analysis of relevant law, the prosecution's evidence, and potential dispositions and relevant collateral consequences."); *id.*, Standard 4-6.2, *Negotiated Disposition Discussions* ("(a) As early as practicable, and preferably before engaging in disposition discussions with the prosecutor, defense counsel should discuss with and advise the client about possible disposition options."); *Missouri v. Frye*, 566 U.S. 133, 143-46 (2012); *Williams v. Jones*, 571 F.3d 1086, 1090-91 (10th Cir. 2009); *Johnson v. Uribe*, 682 F.3d 1238 (9th Cir. 2012), *as amended on denial of rehearing in* 700 F.3d 413 (9th Cir. 2012); *Ebron v. Commissioner of Correction*, 307 Conn. 342, 53 A.3d 983 (2012) or fails to conduct an adequate investigation of the possibility of a favorable plea bargain (*see United States v. Jenks*, 2022 WL 1252366, at *2, *3 (10th Cir. April 28, 2022) (requiring a hearing on a postconviction claim of ineffective assistance of counsel based upon allegations that "without consulting a DNA expert to perform any tests or interpret the government's DNA test results, Petitioner's trial counsel told Petitioner that the government's evidence was weak, that he would win at trial, and that he should reject every offer to enter a plea agreement": "We can think of no reasonable professional judgment that would justify failing to accurately discover and convey to the defendant the results of DNA testing, which are likely to be critical to the prosecution's case.")).

15.9. *Opening Discussions with the Prosecutor*

From the outset of proceedings, counsel will have been discussing the case with the prosecutor. See §§ 8.1.1, 8.1.4, 8.2.2-8.24, 8.4, 8.6, 12.13, 13.5 *supra.* Initial discussions should have focused principally on learning what the prosecutor was willing to disclose about the prosecution's case. But counsel should also have learned something about the prosecutor's attitude; counsel should have tried to affect that attitude in favor of the client; and in the course of urging a favorable exercise of the prosecutor's broad charging discretion, counsel should have asked specifically and ascertained what the prosecutor regards as a satisfactory disposition of the case. Counsel can ordinarily do this much without making any offer to plead the client guilty or even intimating that the client might be receptive to a plea agreement. Counsel can, therefore, proceed this far without explicit authorization by the client.

15.10. *When Negotiation Should Begin*

Exactly when negotiation in a stricter sense should begin – that is, when defense counsel should begin to raise the possibility of a guilty plea if some mutually satisfactory terms of settlement can be agreed upon – depends on a variety of circumstances.

Obviously, the paramount consideration is whether the defendant will derive any specific benefits as a result of pleading early in the process. One common example of a situation in which an early plea is often essential is when the crime was committed by a group of perpetrators. If all of the perpetrators have been arrested, the one who first cooperates to "break" the case and implicate the others will very likely receive the most consideration from the prosecution. If some members of the group have not yet been identified, or have not yet been apprehended, the defendant who seeks to win governmental consideration by dislosing their names and/or whereabouts also will need to move quickly in order to provide that information before the police acquire it through independent investigation.

The defense may also gain collateral advantages from prompt commencement of plea negotiations with the prosecutor. Plea negotiation is one of the most profitable methods of informal discovery. Most prosecutors will disclose their case to some extent in order to persuade defense counsel that a guilty plea is advised. Indeed, some prosecutors will disclose facts about their case *only* if a guilty plea is being discussed. And counsel wants to begin discovery as early as possible. See Chapters 7 and 18.

Conversely, there may be reasons for delaying plea negotiations. One of the most important reasons for delay exists when counsel knows that the defendant is being sought for other crimes for which s/he has not yet been arrested. If counsel delays the negotiation and the defendant does end up being arrested for the other crimes, then counsel can negotiate for a plea that covers both the current case and the new cases. If counsel had gone ahead and worked out a plea bargain to cover only the current case, the prosecutor might insist on a second plea agreement (and often a far less favorable overall deal) when the new case[s] entered the system.

Moreover, even in cases in which an early plea might be beneficial, counsel is frequently in no position to negotiate at the outset of the case. Adequate factual investigation and legal research are the necessary preconditions for intelligent negotiation. And negotiation involves offering something, even if the something is only a possibility. Offering something *does* require authorization from the client. Counsel frequently will have nothing to offer at an early stage.

The client's attitude should play a major part in determining whether counsel initiates plea negotiations early in the process. Some clients will expect their attorney to begin promptly to discuss a plea with the prosecutor. The police, in their immediate post-arrest interrogation of a defendant, often stress the value of cooperation, in order to obtain a confession of the offense for which the arrest was made, to encourage the defendant to confess to – and hence to "clear" – other unsolved crimes, and to persuade the defendant to finger any accomplices or help "break" other crimes. These suggestions by the police set a tone that may make the defendant quite anxious to clinch a quick deal; and, particularly if s/he is system-savvy, s/he will expect counsel to jump into bargaining with both feet.

On the other hand, many clients persist long after arrest in vigorously protesting innocence and expounding plausible tales (some true, some not), which, if true, render the suggestion of a guilty plea inconceivable. Counsel cannot broach the subject of a possible guilty plea to such clients, for the purpose of obtaining their authority to negotiate, without appearing to call the client a liar. At this early stage in the process, counsel has not yet established the rapport needed to probe the client's position tactfully yet skeptically to see whether the client will stick to it in the face of all of the hard questions and hard facts that counsel will eventually have to put to the client. See §§ 6.8, 6.14, 12.14 *supra.*

Accordingly, the best approach in gauging how early to initiate plea negotiation is ordinarily to be guided by the client's outlook in the initial interview. If the client admits guilt and feels that s/he has been caught red-handed, counsel may raise the question of a possible guilty plea and suggest that – if the client wishes – counsel will explore the prosecutor's attitude toward some sort of a plea bargain at the same time that counsel looks further into the facts of the case. Counsel should explain that:

1. Of course, counsel will make no commitments and will not indicate to the prosecutor that the client has any interest in pleading guilty.

2. Counsel does not as yet have any idea of the prosecutor's position. But counsel will undertake to find out what the prosecutor might be willing to accept in the way of a reduced sentence.

3. After counsel learns what the prosecutor is offering, counsel will relay that offer to the client so that the client can evaluate whether the offer is even worth considering. Counsel will at that point give the client his or her advice, but the final decision will be the client's.

4. Even if the client authorizes counsel to initiate discussions with the prosecutor, counsel intends to investigate the facts thoroughly in order to determine whether the prosecution's case is strong or weak. Counsel will not even consider a plea, or advise the client to consider a plea, unless counsel's investigation shows that the prosecutor's case is strong and likely to result in conviction at trial.

5. Counsel is starting out with the attitude that "if this case can be fought, we are going to fight it." Counsel's only reason for bringing up the possibility of a plea is that s/he does not want to overlook any opportunity for getting the most favorable deal for the client if the client later decides that s/he would do better with a plea than with a trial.

Even with a client who acknowledges guilt, counsel is wise not to seem too attracted to a possible plea disposition at the outset, lest the client get the impression that counsel is anxious to sell out the client in order to save counsel work. But if counsel's mention of talking to the prosecutor elicits a positive reaction from the client, counsel might as well start talking early.

On the other hand, if the client denies involvement in the offense or speaks of contesting guilt and if there appear no pressing reasons to begin negotiation, counsel can let the matter go until defense investigation and research have given counsel a thorough, detailed grasp of the case. After counsel has investigated the facts and had a chance to study and make some tentative evaluation of the matters discussed in §§ 15.3-15.7 *supra,* s/he should raise with the client the question of a possible guilty plea. At this stage, counsel is not yet prepared to tell the client with any certainty what the advantages of a guilty plea will be, but s/he is in a position to suggest that there may be some advantages, depending on the prosecutor's attitude toward negotiation. Even though counsel may have come to the unilateral conclusion that the case is plainly one for a not-guilty plea and trial, s/he owes it to the client to give the client the option of having negotiation with the prosecutor explored as an alternative. Of course, if counsel and the client are agreed at this stage that the case should be fought out on the guilt issue, no matter what sort of disposition the prosecutor might agree to – or if the client is adamant against any thought of a guilty plea notwithstanding counsel's belief that negotiations looking to a plea might profitably be considered – the matter is ended. There remains nothing for counsel to do but prepare for trial and perhaps raise the issue with the client again later in light of subsequent developments.

15.11. ***The Conditions Precedent for Effective Defense Negotiation – Things to Know about the Law, the Case, and the Motivations of the Prosecutor***

Thorough investigation must precede any serious negotiation. Counsel must know enough about the prosecution and defense cases – that is, about the facts, their likely provability in court, and the likely responses of a judge or jury to them – to make, at least provisionally, the sort of evaluation suggested in § 15.4 *supra.*

Counsel should also have a comprehensive working knowledge of:

(1) *The identity of every lesser offense included within the offense charged against the defendant* (see § 15.6.2 subdivision (1)(a) *supra*; § 42.4 *infra*) and the consequences of conviction (see § 15.6.1 *supra*) for each lesser included offense.

(2) *The identity of every other offense that might be charged against the defendant on the basis of the facts of the case,* or on the basis of some of those facts (see § 15.6.2 subdivision (1)(c) *supra*), and the consequences of conviction for each of these offenses.

(3) *Legal doctrines relating to:*

    (a) *The authority of the court to suspend sentence and the consequences of different forms of suspended sentences* (see § 15.6.2 subdivision (2)(a)(i)(C) *supra*; § 48.6 subdivision (F) *infra*);

    (b) *The potential applicability of specialized sentencing provisions, such as "youthful offender" laws* (see § 15.6.2 subdivision (2)(a)(i)(F) *supra*; § 48.6 subdivision (B) *infra*), *and the procedures for, and consequences of, sentencing the defendant under those laws* – procedures and consequenes which may be more favorable to the defendant than the ordinary sentencing provisions in some aspects or circumstances and less favorable in others;

(c) *Merger or grouping of offenses and concurrent or consecutive sentencing in the event of conviction of more than one offense* (see § 15.6.2 subdivision (2)(a)(i)(D) *supra*; § 48.6 subdivision (H) *infra*).

(4) *The defendant's previous criminal record, including probation or parole status at the time of the present offense, and all other charges presently pending or contemplated against the defendant in any jurisdiction* (see §§ 15.6, 15.6.2 subdivision (3) *supra*; § 48.6 subdivision (I) infra*).

(5) *In jurisdictions that use sentencing guidelines and similar sorts of determinate-sentencing formulas, the guideline categories that may apply to the case based on the charged offenses, the circumstances of the crime, the defendant's previous criminal record, and other specified factors; and the guideline categories applicable to lesser included offenses and to alternative offenses that might be charged on the basis of the underlying factual scenario giving rise to the prosecution* (see § 15.6.2 subdivision (2)(b) *supra*; § 48.6 subdivision (C) *infra*).

(6) *If a client is not a citizen, the potential immigration consequences of a plea to the charged offense[s], any lesser included offenses, and all alternatively chargeable offenses* (see §§ 15.6.1 subdivision (E), 15.6.2 subdivision (4) *supra*).

(7) *The identity of, and conditions at, the various places of confinement to which the defendant might be committed at the court's discretion* (or assigned by state correctional officials at the court's recommendation) in the event of an incarcerative disposition (see § 48.6 subdivision (D) *infra*), including specialized rehabilitative and training programs available at these various institutions.

(8) *The defendant's family resources and the local community resources available to the defendant*, which may offer assistance in making some nonincarcerative disposition of the case that has affirmative rehabilitative or restitutionary potential, including:

 (a) Employment opportunities for the defendant;

 (b) Educational and job-training opportunities for the defendant;

 (c) In-patient or out-patient medical or psychiatric treatment facilities for the defendant;

 (d) Alternative places of residence for the defendant, including places out of the locality;

 (e) Present or potential financial resources of the defendant to make restitution to the complainant, in an appropriate case. (Note that federal practice permits a defendant who pleads guilty to include in a plea agreement an enforceable commitment to pay restitution even though the law governing the pled offense would not otherwise authorize a restitution order. 18 U.S.C. § 3663(a)(3); *Doe v. United States District Court*, 51

F.4th 1023 (9th Cir. 2022).)

(9) *Any plea-bargaining or presentencing practices that are used in the locality, and whether they are standard operating procedure.* In some courts, for example, it is a common practice, when defense counsel and the prosecutor are considering the possibility of a plea agreement, for the defendant to submit to a "proffer interview" by the prosecutor or by a probation officer, to put on record the factual information that will be treated as established for the purposes of supporting the plea and consequent sentencing. The proffer interview is recorded and is filed for the record if a plea bargain is reached. If not, the proffer interview and the facts elicited by it and otherwise not provable by the prosecution are inadmissible against the defendant (except in a prosecution for perjury when the statement was made under oath). *See, e.g.*, FED. RULE EVID. 410; *United States v. La Luz-Jimenez*, 226 F. Supp. 3d 79 (D. Puerto Rico 2017); *United States v. Deantoni*, 171 F. Supp. 3d 477 (E.D. Va. 2016); *cf. State v. McGee*, 282 Neb. 387, 395-96, 803 N.W.2d 497, 505 (2011).

Counsel should know, in addition, whether the client is able and willing to cooperate with the prosecution in:

(10) *Incriminating other persons or turning state's evidence.*

(11) *Confessing guilt of uncleared offenses and thereby assisting in their clearance by the police.*

It is also helpful, if possible, for counsel to know:

(12) *Any more or less formally articulated policies of the prosecutor's office bearing on the sort of case involved.*

(13) *Previous similar cases in which plea negotiations favorable to the defense have been worked out.* (Argument from precedent is often quite effective in negotiation.)

Armed with this information, counsel is in a position to draft a set of possible settlement terms that entail less onerous consequences or have more rehabilitative promise than does conviction of the charged offense[s]. Counsel should consider the availability and potential of each of the concessions that could be obtained from a prosecutor to avert or reduce the consequences of a conviction (see § 15.6.2 *supra*), as well as the possibility of enlisting the prosecutor's aid in using a guilty plea to steer the case to a favorable judge for sentencing (see § 15.7.2 *supra*) and/or to expedite the release of a defendant who is currently detained pending trial (see § 15.7.3 *supra*).

Counsel should also consider what the defendant can offer the prosecutor, including:

(A)   A plea of guilty to one or another offense.

(B)   Voluntary submission to treatment programs, changes of residence (for example, moving out of a certain neighborhood or moving out of the jurisdiction), and other matters that could not be compelled by law.

(C)   Voluntary financial restitution or submission to community service.

(D)   Cooperation to incriminate or convict other persons.

(E)   Cooperation to clear uncleared crimes.

(F)   A waiver of claims to damages for unlawful arrest and other violations of the defendant's rights in the initial stages of the criminal proceeding (see § 8.3.3 *supra*).

15.12. *Techniques of Plea Negotiation*

The process of negotiation with a prosecutor is in many ways like negotiation aimed at settling a civil case. Ordinarily, the prosecutor must be impressed with the discrepancy between what s/he wants and what s/he is likely to get or with the inconvenience involved in getting what s/he wants before s/he will settle for less than what s/he wants. The major difference in criminal negotiation is that it is the prosecutor alone, not a client, who decides what the prosecutor wants. The prosecutor's personal sense of justice may affect this calculus, and the prosecutor's prediction of a judge or jury's likely reaction to the evidence almost always constitutes a major factor in determining what s/he will regard as an acceptable negotiated outcome. *See* Anna Offit, *Prosecuting in the Shadow of the Jury,* 113 Nw. U. L. Rev. 1071 (2019). Counsel lobbying for a favorable plea bargain can therefore pitch any or all of the considerations mentioned in §§ 8.2.3, 8.4, and 8.6 *supra. See* Bruce Frederick & Don Stemen, The Anatomy of Discretion: An Analysis of Prosecutorial Decision Making (Vera Institute 2012). In negotiating with the prosecutor, defense counsel must also bear in mind that criminal cases, more than most civil cases, tend to attract media coverage, so the prosecutor could be concerned about justifying any "deals" to the public. Counsel often does well to suggest a face-saving rationale that the prosecutor can articulate to defend an agreed-upon disposition. An additional problem is that prosecutors rely heavily on the police and need their cooperation. When the police feel that they have done a good job in building a case, they may be chagrined to see the prosecutor dismiss or compromise it. This latter consideration may suggest the desirability of counsel's doing a bit of lobbying with the investigating officer after counsel has begun plea negotiations with the prosecutor. Conversely, where the police have engaged in demonstrable misconduct – using excessive force in making the client's arrest (see § 25.7.4 last paragraph *infra*) or in conducting a search or seizure (see § 25.21 last paragraph *infra*), the prosecutor may be motivated to offer a favorable plea bargain in order to avoid litigation airing these abuses. See generally §§ 8.2.3, 8.3.3 *supra.* In a case in which the complainant's wishes are likely to be significant to the prosecutor, a discussion with the complainant also may be advised. See generally § 8.5 *supra.* In both cases, of course, extreme caution must be observed in counsel's decision to involve these parties in the affair. Often the prosecutor will not consult them, and their involvement may stir up trouble for the defense.

Some prosecutors will request – and some of them may insist – that the defendant submit to a proffer interview as a part of the negotiation process. See § 15.11 subdivision (9) *supra.*

Defense counsel should ordinarily not agree to this procedure if they can avoid it. Under questioning, the defendant may make damaging factual statements or a bad impression that will jeopardize the chances for a favorable plea bargain. It is safer for negotiation to proceed on the basis of either (1) counsel's representations to the prosecutor of the defense version of the facts, or (2) a written statement of the relevant facts prepared by counsel for the defendant's signature (which may be notarized if the prosecutor wishes). If the prosecutor adamantly will not bargain without a proffer interview and if defense counsel and the defendant are of the view that a guilty plea is likely to produce a better outcome than a trial, counsel should prepare the defendant for the interview with the same care with which s/he would prepare the defendant to testify in court. See § 29.6 *infra*.

Like any negotiation, plea negotiation involves the art of agreeing with the other side's position on all points that are not essential to counsel as a means of getting the other side to agree with counsel's position on essential points. This means, analytically, that counsel must figure out what the prosecutor really wants and how to give the prosecutor what s/he wants without sacrificing what counsel wants. For example, a prosecutor who says that s/he thinks "this defendant ought to be taken off the streets" does not necessarily want incarceration; s/he may be saying that s/he wants the defendant out of the community so as not to give the complainant, the police, and this prosecutor any further trouble. S/he may be quite satisfied with a suspended sentence and probation if the defendant will move to a different neighborhood or county, whereupon probationary supervision can be shifted to that jurisdiction.

The multitude of possible offenses that could be charged in any factual situation (including offenses of which the defendant is not technically guilty) and the large range of sentencing alternatives for those offenses under the laws of most jurisdictions (see § 15.6.1 *supra*) ordinarily give counsel plenty of possibilities for effective compromise if s/he reviews them thoroughly and uses imagination. Similarly, the range of informal accommodations must be viewed with imagination. A prosecutor who adamantly refuses to make a formal sentencing recommendation to the court, for instance, may be willing to make an informal recommendation to the probation officer who is writing up the pre-sentence report on the case – and the latter recommendation may be just as valuable to the defense as the former.

At the personal level, it is important to minimize the extent of counsel's disagreements with the prosecutor without giving in to the prosecutor on substantive matters. It is particularly important for counsel to appear not to be standing in personal opposition to the prosecutor, even when counsel's position is opposed to the prosecutor's position. (Bruce Green has suggested in a provocative article that every criminal defendant should have two lawyers – a trial lawyer and a settlement lawyer – with the aim, *inter alia,* of reducing the adversarial animosity that impedes effective plea negotiation. Bruce Green, *The Right to* Two *Criminal Defense Lawyers*, 69 MERCER L. REV. 675, 687-688 (2018). Because this isn't about to happen soon for any but the wealthiest of defendants, an attorney representing those less affluent has to work hard at *being* both of those two lawyers.) One way for defense counsel to avoid a clash of personalities with the prosecutor is for counsel to establish a personal posture that is not completely identified with counsel's bargaining position, by associating the bargaining position with the client and appearing to play the role of an honest broker between the client's interests and the prosecutor's. Thus, the "I-really-see-the-case-the-way-you-do-because-any-sensible-lawyer-would-know-that-what-you-say-makes-sense-but-you've-got-to-help-me-to-sell-it-to-my-client-by-giving-me-something-more-to-take-to-the-client-that-s/he-can-live-with" approach is frequently productive. This use of the absent client as a third force in negotiation allows defense counsel to hold firm to his or her position while establishing a broad base of personal and professional agreement with the prosecutor. It also avoids arousing any instincts that the prosecutor may have toward combative gamesmanship – that is, the game of "beating" defense counsel in flea-market haggling. However, when possible, counsel should never say that the client *does not* or *will not* accept the prosecutor's position, since this may simply redirect the prosecutor's combativeness toward the client. The better formulation is a "What-worries-my-client-is- . . ." or an "I-just-don't-think-I-can-sell-that-to-my-client-unless- . . ." approach or their equivalents.

Keeping on the prosecutor's good side and avoiding clashes that may arouse the prosecutor's ire at either the defendant or defense counsel is indispensable because, as a practical matter, the prosecutor ordinarily has the upper hand in the bargaining process. Although defense counsel may be able to appeal to some judges to lean on a prosecutor who stands adamant on an outrageous bargaining position (see § 15.5 *supra*; § 18.14 subdivision 1 *infra*), the prosecutor can usually get away with either stonewalling or playing very rough at the bargaining table. *See, e.g., Weatherford v. Bursey*, 429 U.S. 545, 561 (1977) ("there is no constitutional right to plea bargain; the prosecutor need not do so if he prefers to go to trial"); *Ricketts v. Adamson*, 483 U.S. 1, 9 n.5 (1987), citing *Mabry v. Johnson*, 467 U.S. 504 (1984) (same); *Bordenkircher v. Hayes*, 434 U.S. 357 (1978) (finding no constitutional objection to a prosecutor's filing a recidivist charge, carrying a mandatory life sentence, for the admitted purpose of inducing the defendant to accept the prosecutor's offer of a plea bargain involving a five-year sentencing recommendation); *United States v. Goodwin*, 457 U.S. 368, 377-80 (1982) (reaffirming *Bordenkircher*); *Alabama v. Smith*, 490 U.S. 794, 802 (1989) (same). The prosecutor is under heavy pressure to settle most cases in order to reduce the prosecution's trial docket to manageable proportions, and that pressure is defense counsel's greatest asset as long as counsel does nothing to give the prosecutor the impression that this case deserves "special treatment." But if the prosecutor gets riled, s/he usually has sufficient resources to make any particular case unpleasantly "special" for the defendant.

15.13. *The Plea Agreement with the Prosecutor*

In some jurisdictions, agreements between defense counsel and the prosecutor are not reduced to writing. The reputation and integrity of each attorney are the only guarantees that each will keep his or her word. *See Mabry v. Johnson*, 467 U.S. 504 (1984). In theory, of course, a guilty plea entered in consideration of an oral prosecutorial promise that is not fulfilled must be set aside. *E.g., Santobello v. New York*, 404 U.S. 257 (1971); *Blackledge v. Allison*, 431 U.S. 63 (1977). But proof of the facts necessary to bring the theory into play is not easy; postconviction litigation over broken plea bargains can consume years; and the relief, if any, that the client ultimately gets may be nothing more than the right to stand trial. Therefore, if counsel does not know the particular prosecutor, s/he should check out the prosecutor's reputation by inquiry among knowledgeable members of the bar *before* a guilty plea is entered. And unless local practice strongly disfavors written plea agreements or the prosecutor adamantly refuses to consider one, counsel should press to reduce any plea bargain to writing.

Some States and localities have developed a practice under which the terms of plea bargains are set out in writing and filed with the court. *See, e.g., People v. West,* 3 Cal. 3d 595, 477 P.2d 409, 91 Cal. Rptr. 385 (1970). (This practice is often but not always incidental to the "conditional" plea bargaining process described in § 15.6.2 *supra.*) Such a procedure for memorializing the plea agreement should ordinarily be followed if the prosecutor and the court can be persuaded to accept it. Defense counsel should always offer to draft the written instrument for the prosecutor's review rather than *vice versa,* since the drafter of a document has the advantages of initiative, inertia, and a working familiarity with the draft during any negotiations that may be required to secure its approval or arrange for its revision into final form. The drafter's ability to shape the terms of the agreement, make initial choices about the terms to be included, and craft specific implementing language is an invaluable advantage. The courts ordinarily "treat plea agreements like contracts . . . [,] use 'traditional principles of contract law' to interpret them, and . . . enforce them according to their literal terms" (*United States v. Warren,* 8 F.4th 444, 448 (6th Cir. 2021), summarized in § 14.8 *supra*). *See also, e.g., United States v. Wilson,* 920 F.3d 155 (2d Cir. 2019) ("[w]e review interpretations of plea agreements *de novo* and in accordance with principles of contract law"); *Commonwealth v. Martinez,* 637 Pa. 208, 231, 147 A.3d 517, 531 (2016) ("plea agreements clearly are contractual in nature . . . [and] this Court utilizes concepts closely associated with contract law when evaluating issues involving plea agreements"); *Grider v. State,* 976 N.E.2d 783, 786 (Ind. App. 2012) ("we will look to principles of contract law when construing plea agreements to determine what is reasonably due to the defendant"); *State v. Peterson,* 296 Kan. 563, 567, 293 P.3d 730, 734 (2013) ("A plea agreement is a contract between the State and the accused, and the exchanged promises must be fulfilled by both parties. . . . The State's breach of a plea agreement denies the defendant due process."); *State v. King,* 218 N.C. App. 384, 388, 721 S.E.2d 327, 330 (2012) (a "plea agreement is 'in essence a contract[,]' and thus the law of contracts governs judicial interpretation of plea agreements"); *People v. Donelson,* 2013 IL 113603, 989 N.E.2d 1101, 1106, 371 Ill. Dec. 173, 178 (2013) ("As we have frequently stated, . . . a plea agreement has often been compared to an enforceable contract, and this court has applied contract law principles in appropriate circumstances. ¶ Where a plea rests in any significant degree upon promise or agreement of the prosecutor, so that it can be said to be part of the inducement or consideration for the plea, that feature of the agreement must be fulfilled."); *State v. Cheatham,* 44,247 (La.App. 2 Cir. 5/13/09), 12 So.3d 1047, 1051-52 (La. 2009) ("A plea bargain agreement is considered to be a contract between the State and the criminal defendant. . . . If the State is a party to a plea bargain agreement, the bargain must be enforced."); *United States v. Petties,* 42 F.4th 388, 393 (4th Cir. 2022) ("Plea agreements are 'grounded in contract law,' and we employ 'traditional principles of contract law' as a guide to their interpretation. . . . But we give plea agreements 'greater scrutiny' than we apply to ordinary commercial contracts because of the context: a defendant's waiver of his constitutional right to trial, induced by the government's commitments in the plea agreement. . . . As a result, the law governing the interpretation of plea agreements is an 'amalgam of constitutional, supervisory, and private [contract] law concerns,' which 'require holding the Government to a greater degree of responsibility than the defendant' for any 'imprecisions or ambiguities' in those agreements."); *accord, State v. Obas,* 320 Conn. 426, 442, 130 A.3d 252, 262 (2016) (consequently, "ambiguous language of a plea agreement must be construed against the state," *id.* at 446, 130 A.3d at 264) *and United States v. Thomas,* 58 F.4th 964, 971, 973 (8th Cir. 2023); *State v. Patten,* 981 N.W.2d 126, 131 (Iowa 2022) ("A plea agreement is 'akin to [a] contract[ ],' . . . but one that carries significant constitutional implications . . . . Therefore, 'we are compelled to hold prosecutors and courts to the most meticulous standards of both promise and performance.' . . . We require 'strict, not substantial, compliance with the terms of plea agreements.' . . . '[V]iolations of either the terms or the spirit of the agreement,' . . . even if seemingly minor, 'are intolerable and adversely impact the integrity of the prosecutorial office and the entire judicial system . . . .'"); *State v. King*, 361 Or. 646, 648, 398 P.3d 336, 338 (2017) ("As this court observed in *State v. Heisser*, 350 Or. 12, 23, 249 P.3d 113 (2011), principles of contract law generally inform the determination of whether a plea agreement has been performed. However, contract principles that apply in a commercial setting do not necessarily suffice for an analysis of a plea agreement, because the rights of criminal defendants 'not ordinarily found in contracts between private parties * * * may override contractual principles.'"); *State v. Thrift*, 312 S.C. 282, 292-93, 440 S.E.2d 341, 347 (1994) ("The United States Supreme Court in *Santobello v. New York*, 404 U.S. 257 . . . (1971), held that where a guilty plea rests on a promise or agreement which can be said to be a part of the inducement or consideration, then the agreement must be fulfilled. The Fourth Circuit recently addressed this same issue in *United States v. Ringling*, 988 F.2d 504 (4th Cir. 1993). In *Ringling*, the court held that a plea bargain rests on contractual principles, and that each party should receive the benefit of the bargain. *Id.* The court further stated that a plea agreement analysis must be more stringent than a contract because the rights involved are fundamental and constitutionally based. *Id.* The court also noted that the government had to be held to a higher degree or responsibility than the defendant for imprecisions or ambiguities. *Id.*"); *In re Timothy N.*, 216 Cal. App. 4th 725, 734, 157 Cal. Rptr. 3d 78, 85 (2013) ("'[P]lea agreements are interpreted according to the general rule 'that ambiguities are construed in favor of the defendant. Focusing on the *defendant's* reasonable understanding also reflects the proper constitutional focus on what induced the *defendant* to plead guilty.'"); *Commonwealth v. Moose*, 2021 PA Super 2, 245 A.3d 1121, 1130 (Pa. Super. 2021) (en banc) ("Although a plea agreement occurs in a criminal context, it remains contractual in nature and is to be analyzed under contract-law standards. . . . ¶ Any ambiguities in the terms of the plea agreement will be construed against the Government."); *State v. Karey*, 2016-0377 (La. 6/29/17), 232 So.3d 1186, 1190 (La. 2017) ("[a]s a general matter, in determining the validity of agreements not to prosecute or of plea agreements, the courts generally refer to analogous rules of contract law, although a defendant's constitutional right to fairness may be broader than his or her rights under the law of contract"); *State v. Yoon*, 66 Hawai'i 342, 348, 662 P.2d 1112, 1116 (1983) ("To be sure, '[c]ourts have frequently looked to contract law analogies in determining the rights of defendants aggrieved in the plea negotiation process. . . . Yet, '[w]hile [such] analogies . . . are important to the determination of questions regarding the effects of a plea bargain, [they] are not solely determinative of the question.' . . . ¶ An unfulfilled plea agreement, we are taught, implicates other considerations of constitutional dimension. For one, the acceptance of a plea by a court following plea bargaining 'presuppose[s] fairness in securing agreement.' agreement." . . . And, 'it is also clear that a prosecutor's [broken] promise may deprive a guilty plea of the 'character of a voluntary act.'").

A plea agreement contemplating that the defendant will serve as an informer or a witness against accomplices or will otherwise assist the prosecution in any way other than the mere entry of a plea of guilty should be detailed and unambiguous regarding (1) the specific actions that the defendant is to take, (2) the investigations or cases in which (or the persons against whom) s/he is to take those actions, (3) the circumstances under which s/he is to take the actions, and (4) the duration of the defendant's obligations to act. See § 8.6 *supra*. If the defendant is to testify against accomplices, the agreement should specify precisely the proceedings in which s/he is required to testify, and should not leave unclear the scope of the defendant's duties in the event that proceedings against an accomplice later take varying twists (for example, prosecution of the accomplice on multiple charges involving separate trials; reprosecution of the accomplice following a mistrial or the appellate reversal of an initial conviction). Unclarity about the defendant's responsibilities in these eventualities must be avoided, since a defendant who subsequently disagrees with the prosecutor's interpretation of his or her responsibilities does so at the risk that the entire plea bargain will be set aside and s/he will then be prosecuted for the most serious offenses originally charged, if the courts should happen to prefer the prosecutor's interpretation to the defendant's. *See Ricketts v. Adamson,* 483 U.S. 1 (1987).

When writing up a plea agreement, counsel will also need to take particular care regarding another aspect of any commitment made by the defendant to divulge factual information that could incriminate him or her in either the present offense or other offenses. Almost invariably, in cases in which the defendant has agreed to divulge information or to testify against accomplices, the prosecution will want to delay the defendant's sentencing until after the information has been provided or the testimony has been given. By holding the sentencing over the defendant's head, the prosecutor guarantees compliance on the part of the defendant. Defense counsel must be concerned, however, with ensuring that the information or testimony will not be used against the defendant subsequently if, for any reason, the plea agreement falls apart. In theory, in many jurisdictions incriminating statements made by a defendant or defense attorney to the prosecutor during plea negotiations are inadmissible as prosecution evidence if the negotiation fails. *See, e.g.,* FED. RULE EVID. 410; MINN. RULE EVID. 410; § 21.6 *infra*. But slip-ups can occur that remove some statements from the protection of this rule, so counsel should include explicit inadmissibility provisions in any plea agreement. And counsel should be careful to advise the client not to communicate personally with the prosecutor or the court during the course of the negotiations. *See United States v. Bauzó-Santiago,* 867 F.3d 13 (1st Cir. 2017).

Language such as the following should be included in the written agreement:

The parties hereby agree that any statements, testimony, evidence, information, or leads of any sort that:

(a) are capable of incriminating the defendant in the present offense or any other offense; and that

(b) have been or are now or hereafter given by the defendant or the defendant's attorney to any of the following entities or individuals during the negotiation of this plea agreement or following its negotiation but before the agreement is fully executed by the defendant's sentencing:

(i)   the prosecutor or any other prosecuting authority of any jurisdiction;

(ii)   any police or criminal investigating authority of any jurisdiction;

(iii)   any law enforcement authority of any jurisdiction;

any court of any jurisdiction;

    (v)   any probation department or other agency of any such court;

    (vi)   any agent or successor of any entity designated in items (i) through (v),

are expressly understood to have been given in consideration of this agreement and shall not be used against the defendant in any way, directly or derivatively, by or before any entity or individual designated in items (i) through (vi), except:

(1) with the defendant's express consent, in the course of proceedings undertaken to secure the defendant's conviction and sentencing pursuant to this plea agreement; or

(2) for the sole purpose of upholding and enforcing that conviction and sentencing after they have been obtained according to the terms of this plea agreement and so long as neither of them has been vacated.

In no event shall any such statements, testimony, evidence, information, or leads be used against the defendant in connection with any criminal charge other than the charge[s] to which the defendant is presently agreeing to plead guilty.

Unless an agreement of this sort has been made with the prosecutor, counsel ordinarily should not divulge, or permit the defendant to divulge, any incriminating information to anyone during, or after, plea bargaining. *See Hutto v. Ross,* 429 U.S. 28 (1976) (per curiam).

If counsel is unable to obtain such an agreement but counsel and the client conclude that a guilty plea with a cooperation condition is nonetheless necessary or advisable, and if counsel is worried that the prosecutor may not live up to his or her end of the bargain after the defendant's testimony against accomplices has been given, then counsel should try to talk the prosecutor into going ahead with sentencing promptly after the guilty plea rather than delaying the sentencing until the defendant has testified. Counsel may urge that the defendant has no love for the accomplices and can be counted on to testify against them without the coercion applied by keeping the defendant's own sentencing pending. Counsel may point out that the defendant will be more impeachable as a prosecution witness if those charges are still pending than if they have already been disposed of; and that even after sentencing, the sentence and the plea bargain are subject to rescission at the prosecutor's option if the defendant reneges on his or her promise to testify. *See Ricketts v. Adamson, supra*, 483 U.S. at 8-12. If the prosecutor is adamant about delaying the sentencing, counsel should suggest alternative means of ameliorating the prejudice to the defendant. For example, if the defendant is in custody, counsel can suggest that the prosecutor join in a motion to release the defendant on his or her own recognizance or an affordable bail pending the delayed sentencing. *Cf.* §§ 4.2, 4.7-4.11 *supra.*

Counsel should ordinarily include in the written plea agreement a provision that only the factual information explicitly recited in or referenced by this agreement is to be considered by the court in sentencing. Absent such a provision, the defendant is at risk of being sandbagged with adverse information contained in a presentence investigation report, other materials of record, or live witness testimony. *See United States v. Bentley*, 49 F.4th 275 (3d Cir. 2022), and cases cited; *United States v. Ubiles-Rosario*, 867 F.3d 277, 288-89 (1st Cir. 2017); *State v. Rardon*, 327 Mont. 228, 115 P.3d 182 (2005); *cf. United States v. Habbas*, 527 F.3d 266, 269-72 (2d Cir. 2008).

Plea agreements may include a provision by which the defendant waives certain appeal rights. The effect of the waiver depends largely upon the specific language used; some claims on appeal may be extinguished while others are preserved (*United States v. Moran*, 70 F.4th 797 (4th Cir. 2023)); any waiver provision should be carefully drafted with a recognition that after conviction and sentence new facts may emerge and/or the client may have second thoughts about forgoing appellate review. *See Garza v. Idaho*, 139 S. Ct. 738, 744 (2019) ("an appeal waiver does not bar claims outside its scope[;] . . . '[a]lthough the analogy may not hold in all respects, plea bargains are essentially contracts'" whose exact wording determines their effects). *See also People v. Bisono*, 36 N.Y.3d 1013, 1017-18, 164 N.E.3d 239, 241, 140 N.Y.S.3d 433, 435 (2020) ("The waivers of the right to appeal were invalid and unenforceable . . . . It is well-settled that 'a waiver of the right to appeal is not an absolute bar to the taking of a first-tier direct appeal' . . . . [I]n each case, among other infirmities, the rights encompassed by an appeal waiver were mischaracterized during the oral colloquy and in written forms executed by defendants, which indicated the waiver was an absolute bar to direct appeal, failed to signal that any issues survived the waiver and, in the Queens and Orleans Counties cases, advised that the waiver encompassed 'collateral relief on certain nonwaivable issues in both state and federal courts' . . . . Viewing these deficiencies in the context of the record in each case and considering the totality of the circumstances, including in several cases defendants' significant mental health issues . . . , we cannot say that 'defendants comprehended the nature [and consequences] of the waiver of appellate rights'").

In some cases there may be reasons why it would be beneficial to a defendant to have the record of his or her plea agreement sealed: for example, when it contains a commitment to provide confidential information against persons from whom the defendant fears recrimination. In these cases, counsel should include in the plea negotiation a request that prosecutor cooperate in filing a joint motion for sealing. Conversely, there are cases in which the defendant's interests are best served by having the plea agreement accessible for his or her use: for example, when the agreement does *not* include a commitment to testify or to provide confidential information against others who might suspect that it does. Here, counsel can invoke the right of public access to court records as a ground for requesting that the agreement not be sealed. *See United States v. Bacon*, 950 F.3d 1286 (10th Cir. 2020). *Cf. In re Leopold to Unseal Certain Applications for Electronic Surveillance Applications and Orders*, 964 F.3d 1121 (D.C. Cir. 2020); *Application of Los Angeles Times Communications LLC to Unseal Court Records*, 28 F.4th 292, 296 (D.C. Cir. 2022) ("[t]he common law right of access attaches to 'judicial records,' which this court has characterized as documents intended to 'influence a judge's decisionmaking . . .'"); *Emess Capital LLC v. Rothstein*, 841 F. Supp. 2d 1251 (S.D. Fla. 2012), and cases cited; *A.B. v. Walmart Stores, Inc.*, 2015 WL 1526671 (S.D. Ind. 2015), and cases cited.

If a memorandum reciting the terms of the plea agreement is not filed with the court, counsel should make such a memorandum for his or her own files. A contemporaneous, detailed memo will enhance counsel's credibility if it ever becomes necessary for counsel to establish what was and was not agreed upon as the basis for the plea. Unfortunately, counsel may end up having to prove the specifics of the plea bargain years later, in response to attacks by either a faithless prosecutor or an ungrateful client.

D. *Counseling the Client*

15.14. *Advising the Client Whether to Plead Guilty*

In advising a client whether to accept or reject a plea bargain, counsel should ordinarily begin by emphasizing that the final decision is entirely the client's and that counsel's job is merely to give the client advice on the basis of counsel's legal knowledge and experience in criminal practice [and/or with the local criminal court – and the particular judge who is handling the case – if counsel does have such experience]. See §15.2 *supra.* (The narrower and more specific the basis upon which counsel can claim specialized insight the better. Clients may resent claims which make it sound as though what counsel is saying is simply that his or her judgment or analytic capability is superior to the client's.) Counsel should stress that the ultimate decision is up to the client to make on the basis of his or her own independent judgment. See §§ 1.3, 15.2 *supra.*

Counsel should then explain to the client all of the factors that militate for and against a plea, covering each of the considerations in §§ 15.3-15.7.4 *supra* that is relevant. Essentially, counsel will need to explain to the client:

1. The realistic probability of winning a favorable outcome at trial, with a full explanation of the comparative strengths of the cases for the prosecution and the defense, as well as extraneous factors that might influence the result. (See § 15.4 *supra.*)

2. Any realistic probability that the judge might penalize the defendant at sentencing because the defendant opted in favor of a trial instead of a guilty plea. (See § 15.5 *supra.*)

3. The sentencing advantages that counsel expects or predicts the defendant will obtain through a guilty plea, including the specific terms of any agreement that counsel has reached with the prosecutor. Counsel should inform the client of the maximum sentence that s/he can receive (a) if s/he pleads guilty and, alternatively, (b) if s/he is convicted after a trial, and should give counsel's best estimate of the sentence that the client will actually receive on each hypothesis, making clear the limits of counsel's ability to predict what the judge will do. (See § 15.6 subdivisions (A)-(D) *supra.*)

4. The risks of collateral consequences that might flow from a guilty plea and, alternatively, from conviction after a trial. (See § 15.6 subdivisions (E)-(I) *supra.*) In any case in which the client is not a citizen and in which a conviction of any of the charges in the charging instrument or their lesser included offenses could result in removal or exclusion, counsel must carefully explain these immigration

consequences along with any benefits that pleading guilty might have in averting that risk. See § 15.6.1 subdivision (E) *supra.*

5.   The prospects of using a guilty plea to steer the case before a favorable judge for sentencing if that is a consideration in play. (See § 15.7.2 *supra.*)

6.   Any other special aspects of the case or the defendant that might cause a guilty plea to be particularly advantageous or detrimental. (See §§ 15.7.1, 15.7.3-15.7.4 *supra.*)

In discussing all of these complex matters, counsel must take pains to phrase the explanations in language that will be comprehensible to the client. Counsel should periodically check with the client to make sure that the client is, in fact, understanding counsel's explanations.

One of the most difficult decisions for a defense attorney to make is whether to employ the lawyer's considerable persuasive powers to influence the client's choice between a guilty plea and a trial. Clients who have criminal charges hanging over their heads are often experiencing extreme stress and anxiety, and therefore they may defer unduly to the lawyer's persuasion rather than thinking independently. The best rule of thumb is to use persuasion only when the cost-benefit analysis clearly and unequivocally points to a certain result, and otherwise to restrict one's role to furnishing the client with the information (including counsel's objective predictions of alternative outcomes) necessary for the client to make a fully informed, independent decision.

The client should be given adequate time to think about the decision. For this reason it is often advisable to meet with the client to discuss the plea several days (or, in cases where the plea will expose the client to severe penalties, several weeks) before the decision must be conveyed to the prosecutor. Counsel might also consider encouraging the client to talk the decision over with his or her spouse or partner or other members of the family or some other trusted personal advisor.

15.15. *Making a Record of the Advice Given to the Client*

It is one of the unhappy realities of criminal practice that defense attorneys need to take certain precautions to guard against later accusations of ineffectiveness or misconduct. Criminal defendants faced with lengthy prison sentences occasionally resort to unwarranted accusations of ineffectiveness or misconduct on the part of their lawyers as a last-ditch effort to overturn their convictions. Among the most common claims of ineffectiveness or misconduct of defense counsel are allegations that counsel coerced the client to plead guilty or gave the client inadequate advice concerning the significance and consequences of the plea or concerning the client's rights. If counsel wishes to guard against the risk of these attacks, counsel should make file notes of all conversations with the client leading up to the client's decision to plead guilty. This record should reflect that counsel gave the client all of the explanations and advice described in § 15.14 *supra.* The file record should also reflect when it was that the client communicated his or her decision to counsel, what that decision was, and that counsel immediately inquired whether the client clearly understood that the decision had to be the client's own and not the lawyer's.

15.16. *Special Problems in Counseling the Client Whether to Plead Guilty*

15.16.1. *The Guilty Plea and the Innocent Client*

Views differ on whether a lawyer may properly advise (or even permit) a guilty plea by a client who protests his or her innocence. Fortunately, the moral problem arises infrequently. If the case is such that a guilty plea is advised, the client probably (although not invariably) is guilty; and if counsel discusses the evidence critically with the client and subjects the client to the sort of cross-examination that in every case will be necessary to prepare adequately for trial (see §§ 6.14, 12.14 *supra*; §§ 29.5.3-29.6 *infra*), the client will usually admit guilt.

Should the client continue to assert innocence, counsel should consider the feasibility and desirability of a plea entered in accordance with *North Carolina v. Alford,* 400 U.S. 25 (1970), known in many jurisdictions as an *"Alford* plea." In *Alford,* the Court held that "an express admission of guilt . . . is not a constitutional requisite to the imposition of criminal penalty [sic]" (*id.* at 37), and therefore that a plea of guilty may constitutionally be accepted from a defendant who protests his or her innocence, as long as (i) the "defendant intelligently concludes that his interests require entry of a guilty plea" and (ii) "the record before the judge contains strong evidence of actual guilt" (*id.*). In the wake of *Alford,* several jurisdictions have adopted procedures permitting defendants to plead guilty without an admission of guilt, provided that the defendant concedes on the record that the prosecution's evidence is sufficient to support a guilty verdict and that the defendant is therefore entering a plea of guilty as a tactical choice. The *Alford* plea colloquy was held adequate, notwithstanding the absence of a prosecutorial proffer of the proof against defendant, because the trial court ensured that the defendant understood the nature of the proceedings and the rights he was waiving, and elicited the defendant's explanation that he was pleading guilty because he feared a conviction of a higher charge.

Alford pleas, however, are not accepted in all jurisdictions. And even in jurisdictions that permit such pleas, some judges will not accept a guilty plea without an admission of guilt. *But cf. State v. Beasley,* 2018-Ohio-16, 152 Ohio St. 3d 470, 472-73, 97 N.E.3d 474, 476-77 (2018) (although local rules give trial judges the "discretion to accept or reject a no-contest plea," the trial court in this case abused its discretion by employing "a blanket policy of not accepting no-contest pleas").

If *Alford* pleas are permitted in counsel's jurisdiction and are accepted by the judge presiding over the case, then counsel will need to make two final decisions before advising the client to enter an *Alford* plea. The first of these is a tactical decision whether the nature or tone of an *Alford* plea would vitiate whatever benefits counsel hopes to gain for the client through the entry of a guilty plea. Judges who view a full confession of guilt as "the first step toward rehabilitation" are unlikely to give substantial credit for an *Alford* plea. Moreover, whatever sentence-related benefits the client would receive from the plea may ultimately be diminished or even lost altogether if admission of the crime and an expression of remorse are necessary in order to qualify for a community treatment program that is a condition of probation (*e.g.*, a sex offender treatment program that requires an admission of guilt as a prerequisite for participation) or in order to eventually qualify for parole. *See Carroll v. Commonwealth*, 54 Va. App. 730, 733, 742-49, 682 S.E.2d 92, 93, 98-101 (2009) (upholding the trial court's finding that the defendant, who had pled guilty with an *Alford* plea, "violated the conditions of his probation by refusing to admit that he committed the crime charged during court-ordered sex offender treatment"); *In the Matter of Silmon v. Travis*, 95 N.Y.2d 470, 474, 477, 741 N.E.2d 501, 503, 505, 718 N.Y.S.2d 704, 706, 708 (2000) (rejecting a challenge to the Parole Board's denial of parole to a defendant, whose conviction was by means of an *Alford* plea, on the ground that he has never "accept[ed] responsibility for the crime"). *See also McKune v. Lile*, 536 U.S. 24, 29, 31, 43-45 (2002) (holding that the adverse consequences that a state prisoner suffered – denial of visitation rights and other privileges, and transfer to a maximum-security unit – as a result of refusing to participate in a sex offender treatment program, which required that he "admit having committed the crime for which he is being treated," were not so severe as to violate the Fifth Amendment privilege against self-incrimination); *but see Lacy v. Butts*, 922 F.3d 371 (7th Cir. 2019), summarized in § 16.6.1 *infra*, distinguishing *McCune*.

The second decision facing counsel is a question of conscience: whether to take advantage of the *Alford* procedure and urge the client to enter a guilty plea notwithstanding the client's emphatic protestations of innocence. The fact that the *Alford* procedure is not unconstitutional does not mean that counsel is morally free to press it on a client. A defense attorney can reasonably adopt the position that s/he should urge a client to follow the *Alford* procedure only if the client's guilt is clear – that is, if counsel concludes that the client's denials, however fervid, are face-saving or self-deluded – and if the tactical advantages of the plea are equally clear.

15.16.2. *Clients Who Are Unrealistic About the Chances of Winning at Trial*

Counsel will sometimes encounter a client who unrealistically believes that s/he will win at trial notwithstanding counsel's best explanation of the reasons why conviction is a virtual certainty. The first step in convincing the client of the realities of the situation should be to review with the client all of the written statements that counsel or counsel's investigator has taken from prosecution witnesses (see § 9.13 *supra*) and all of the other prosecution evidence known to counsel, in its most convincing form (graphic photos, highlighted lab reports, and so forth). If this fails to convince the client, then counsel should consider conducting a moot court version of the trial, including the defendant's direct and cross-examination, to show the defendant the precise manner in which the evidence would emerge at trial. See §§ 6.14, 12.14 *supra*; §§ 29.5.3-29.6 *infra*.

15.17. *Preparing the Client for the Entry of the Plea in Court*

If the client decides to plead guilty, counsel should give the client a detailed explanation of what to expect in court when the client enters the plea. This preparation has three functions. First, it helps to set the client at ease, so that s/he will make a better impression in court. Second, it helps to reduce the likelihood that the client will say something that precludes the judge from finding that all of the criteria for a "knowing, intelligent, and voluntary" plea have been satisfied. Finally, it guards against the client's mentioning aggravating facts about the offense that need not be stated.

Section 14.1 *supra* describes the procedure that judges commonly follow when accepting a guilty plea. As that section explains, jurisdictions (and also individual judges within a jurisdiction) vary considerably with regard to the number and types of questions the judge asks the defendant and defense counsel. If counsel is not already familiar with the practices of the judge who will preside over the entry of a guilty plea, counsel should consult other defense lawyers who have experience with that judge's guilty-plea practices.

Both in order to prepare the client for the judge's questions and to ensure that the client fully understands the implications and consequences of a guilty plea, counsel should discuss at least the following subjects with the client in considerable detail:

1.   The nature of a criminal trial and the rights that a defendant has at trial, including the rights to representation by counsel, trial by jury (assuming the charged crime is eligible for a jury trial), cross-examination of the prosecution's witnesses, and presentation of defense witnesses.

2.   The effect of a guilty plea in waiving all of these rights and also waiving appellate review of most (possibly all) pre-plea issues (see § 14.8 *supra*).

3.   The potential sentencing consequences of conviction of the offense[s] to which the defendant is pleading guilty (see § 15.6.1 *supra*), including the extent to which the judge is (or, more likely, "is not") bound by any promises that the prosecutor has made to support (or not to object to) a particular sentence (see § 15.6.2 subdivision (2) *supra*).

4.   Any potentially applicable rules relating to probation and parole (see § 15.6.1 subdivision (C) and (D) *supra*; § 48.6 subdivision (E) *infra*).

5.   Collateral consequences that might flow from the conviction (see § 15.6.1 subdivisions (E)-(I) *supra*), particularly exposure to enhanced sentencing in the event of any subsequent criminal convictions (*see, e.g., United States v. Lopez*, 907 F.3d 537 (7th Cir. 2018)), and any potential immigration consequences if the defendant is not a citizen (see § 15.6.1 subdivision (E)).

It is usually advisable for counsel not only to explain these subjects but also to ask the precise questions that are commonly put to a defendant by the judge who will be presiding over the plea. Counsel should carefully explain any terms and concepts that are likely to be unfamiliar to the client.

Unless an *Alford* plea is contemplated, counsel also will need to prepare the client for his or her or her admission of guilt of the crime to which s/he is pleading guilty. (Judges vary substantially in the language that they use in asking the client to admit or deny guilt. Here again, it is extremely useful to learn the formulation used by the specific judge who will be presiding over the entry of the plea, so that the client can be prepped with the right code words.) Counsel should keep in mind that there are some clients who will admit guilt to their lawyers and will agree to a plea of guilty when speaking with their lawyers but who never really accept the notion of their guilt as anything but a highly private affair – a secret between themselves and counsel – not for public announcement. Thus when the judge questions them about their version of the offense, they deny guilt. This, of course, will prove embarrassing to all concerned, and it may cause the judge to refuse to take the guilty plea. Avoidance of the situation is possible if counsel advises the client before the plea hearing that a public admission of guilt in court will be required.

If the client was released on his or her own recognizance or on bail pending trial, and if there is any risk that the judge will modify the prior order and set a new, higher bail pending sentencing after a guilty plea, it is essential that counsel alert the client to this risk and provide counsel's best estimate of its likelihood and the likely amount of the increased bail. The client will need advance warning in order to try to obtain the money or security needed to meet the new bail requirement or, if that is not feasible, to make whatever arrangements are needed regarding his or her family, employers, and other personal responsibilities while s/he is detained pending sentencing. To the extent necessary, counsel should assist the client in arranging and posting the new bail. See §§ 4.7-4.11 *supra*.

Chapter 16

Representing Clients Who Are Mentally Ill or Intellectually Disabled

A. *Introduction and Overview*

16.1. *Stages at Which a Defendant's Mental Problems May Be Relevant*

As explained in § 1.3 *supra*, a defense attorney's obligation to "maintain an effective and regular relationship with all clients" (AMERICAN BAR ASSOCIATION, STANDARDS FOR CRIMINAL JUSTICE MONITORS AND MONITORING, DEFENSE FUNCTION (4th ed. 2017), Standard 4-3.1(f), *Establishing and Maintaining an Effective Client Relationship*) is not in any way "diminish[ed]" when a "client appears to have a mental impairment or other disability that could adversely affect the representation" (*id.*, Standard 4-3.1(c)). *See also* ABA MODEL RULES OF PROFESSIONAL CONDUCT, Rule 1.14(a) (2015) ("When a client's capacity to make adequately considered decisions in connection with a representation is diminished, whether because of minority, mental impairment or for some other reason, the lawyer shall, as far as reasonably possible, maintain a normal client-lawyer relationship with the client."). As long as the client is competent, s/he must be allowed to make those fundamental decisions that are reserved for the accused in a criminal case. See § 1.3 *supra*. *See, e.g., Cooke v. State*, 977 A.2d 803, 809, 843 (Del. 2009) ("Here, defense counsel pursued a 'guilty but mentally ill' verdict over Cooke's vociferous and repeated protestations that he was completely innocent and not mentally ill. This strategy deprived Cooke of his constitutional right to make the fundamental decisions regarding his case."; "We conclude that defense counsel's strategy infringed upon the defendant's personal and fundamental constitutional rights to plead not guilty, to testify in his own defense, and to have the contested issue of guilt beyond a reasonable doubt decided by an impartial jury.").

There are, however, some clients who are not competent to make decisions affecting their own welfare; and counsel may need to take special measures in these cases. If counsel reasonably believes that mental illness or an intellectual disability has so severely "diminish[ed]" the client's "capacity to make adequately considered decisions in connection with the representation . . . [that] a normal client-lawyer relationship with the client" cannot be maintained, and if counsel furthermore "reasonably believes" that the client "is at risk of substantial physical, financial or other harm unless action is taken and [that the client] cannot adequately act in the client's own interest," then counsel may take "reasonably necessary protective action, including consulting with individuals or entities that have the ability to take action to protect the client and, in appropriate cases, seeking the appointment of a guardian ad litem, conservator or guardian." ABA MODEL RULES OF PROFESSIONAL CONDUCT, Rule 1.14(a), (b). *See also* Christopher Slobogin, *The American Bar Association's Criminal Justice Mental Health Standards: Revisions for the Twenty-First Century*, 44 HASTINGS CONST. L. Q. 1 (2016) (explaining the implications of ABA CRIMINAL JUSTICE MENTAL HEALTH STANDARD 7-1.4 for defense attorneys); W. Bradley Wendel, *Autonomy Isn't Everything: Some Cautionary Notes on McCoy v. Louisiana*, 9 ST. MARY'S J. LEGAL MALPRACTICE & ETHICS 92 (2018).

Even when a mentally ill or intellectually disabled client is competent for purposes of steering his or her own course, the client's limitations may present special difficulties for defense counsel. And whether or not a client's impairments impact the attorney-client relationship, they may also give rise to claims and defenses that would not otherwise be available. *See* Slobogin, *supra* at 4 ("Defense attorneys may fail to adjust their style of communication to take into account impairments of their clients, . . . or may focus solely on narrow legal issues when a more holistic approach might prove both more beneficial to their clients and less likely to miss key aspects of the relevant legal or psychological problems."). The following subsections identify the stages of a case at which a client's mental illness or intellectual disability is likely to be relevant for one purpose or another.

16.1.1. *The Initial Interview and Subsequent Client Counseling*

If a client has mental problems, counsel will usually need to take special pains and precautions in evaluating the client's perceptions, recollections, and interpretations of pertinent facts; in eliciting information when interviewing the client; in preparing the client to testify or to participate in other court proceedings (including interviews with court personnel); and in explaining and talking through with the client all of the matters that bear on decisions which the client must make (such as whether to plead guilty or contest guilt) and decisions which the client and counsel collaborate in making (such as whether certain witnesses should be called to testify). Mental illness and mental limitations potentially affect every aspect of the client's comprehension and behavior, often in subtle and nonobvious ways, and so potentially affect every aspect of the client's interaction with counsel. *See generally* Slobogin, *supra* at 4, 8, 19-20, 21-22, 27-28, 33-34.

In the initial interview and subsequent meetings with a mentally ill or intellectually disabled client, counsel should be constantly attentive to the areas and dimensions of the client's impairment. See § 6.3 *supra*. Counsel should make file notes of whatever limitations or dysfunctions s/he observes on the client's part. If counsel decides at some point to apply for court funds for retention of a psychiatrist or psychologist (see § 16.3 *infra*), counsel's previous observations will be an important source of the facts necessary to support the application.

If counsel feels that s/he is unable to interact effectively with the client, counsel should consider retaining a mental health professional to assist in understanding and communicating with the client as well as for other purposes in the case. See § 16.2 *infra*.

A defendant's incompetence to participate understandingly is a bar to any court proceeding. So, in theory, counsel may raise the issue of the defendant's competence as early as preliminary arraignment, by a motion to postpone proceedings pending a mental examination. However, the risks involved in projecting mental-health issues into a case (see § 16.3 *infra*) before counsel's investigation and research have progressed sufficiently to support an evaluation of those risks and possible countervailing benefits will ordinarily make such a motion unwise, particularly inasmuch as the client's role in preliminary-arraignment and preliminary-examination proceedings is relatively limited. Only if (1) the client is floridly psychotic and visibly unable to play those roles, or (2) state law requires special pleas based on mental impairment to be raised at preliminary arraignment or permanently forfeited (see § 11.7.1 *supra*), would an objection to proceeding in these early stages be strategically sound.

16.1.2. *Considering the Possibility of a Mental Examination Prior to Arraignment*

If a client appears to be mentally ill or intellectually disabled, counsel should give some thought, very early in the case, to the possibility of having the client undergo a mental evaluation. *See United States v. Melhuish*, 6 F.4th 380 (2d Cir. 2021); *Jones v. Ryan*, 52 F.4th 1104 (9th Cir. 2022) (9th Cir. 2021), quoted in § 7.2.4 *supra*. Such an evaluation should obviously be considered if the client is demonstrating symptoms of mental disorder so severe as to impede counsel's ability to communicate with the client or if a history of mental illness plainly flags the probable availability of the defenses of lack of criminal responsibility or (when recognized) diminished capacity. But it is also a good idea to seek the aid of a mental health professional in any serious case in which the nature of the crime or the history or behavior of the defendant suggests that s/he is having significant trouble in getting along in his or her present mental or emotional condition. If the client has been having trouble functioning normally, counsel wants to know about it early, for several reasons. It may signal a condition that is serious enough to affect the client's capacity to stand trial. See §§ 16.7-16.10 *infra*. It may affect the reliance that counsel should place on the client's judgment or perceptions. It may be a factor counsel can cite in plea negotiations with the prosecutor to advocate for diversion or a favorable plea offer. See § 16.1.6 *infra*. It may suggest the possibility of a psychiatric defense on the issues of guilt or degree of the offense charged (see §§ 16.11-16.13 *infra*) or the possibility of developing mental health material useful to the client at the sentencing stage (see § 16.1.8 *infra*).

As explained in § 16.3 *infra*, one of the ways to have the client examined is to invoke the provisions of law authorizing a defendant's pretrial commitment to a state mental facility for evaluation or the appointment of mental health experts to examine the defendant on behalf of the court. Some jurisdictions provide for a court-ordered pretrial mental examination at any time following bind-over; in others, a motion for an examination can be made as soon as the charging paper has been filed in the trial court. See § 12.2.2 subdivision (1) *supra*. However, a court-ordered examination entails significant risks. These are discussed in § 16.3 *infra*, together with other possible, less risky ways to obtain a mental evaluation.

16.1.3. *Defense Investigation*

In any case in which a client appears to be mentally ill or intellectually disabled, counsel should begin immediately to gather any institutional or agency records concerning the mental health of the defendant. These include hospital records generated by emergency or out-patient treatment or by periods of hospitalization; records compiled by private psychiatrists or psychologists or community mental health centers where the defendant was evaluated and/or had therapy; psychiatric or psychological reports contained in a court file or in probation or corrections or parole files if the client was charged in any prior criminal or juvenile delinquency cases; and school records (particularly special education records). *See* DAVID FREEDMAN, COGNITIVE AND FUNCTIONAL ASSESSMENT: A PRACTITIONER'S GUIDE TO TESTING (March 2019), referenced in § 16.4 *infra*. In order to obtain these records, counsel will need release forms signed by the client, authorizing counsel or counsel's investigator to inspect and copy each of these kinds of confidential records. Counsel should also proceed promptly to obtain the services of a defense expert to examine the defendant (see §§ 16.2-16.4 *infra*), and should provide the expert with all available records and background information bearing on the defendant's mental state. *See Jacobs v. Horn*, 395 F.3d 92 (3d Cir. 2005) (finding defense counsel ineffective for failing to provide a psychiatric consultant with adequate background information, failing to "question any of . . . [the defendant's] family members or friends regarding his childhood, background, or mental health history, . . . [failing] to obtain any medical records demonstrating mental deficiencies," and failing to inform the consultant that the prosecution was seeking the death penalty (*id.* at 103), with the consequence that the defendant's potential diminished-capacity defense was critically impaired); *Wilson v. Sirmons*, 536 F.3d 1064, 1085 (10th Cir. 2008) finding defense counsel ineffective where he hired a mental health expert "only three weeks prior to trial and met with him only two days before he testified," so that the expert "did not have time to conduct additional testing to confirm a diagnosis of schizophrenia, nor could the defense team gather collateral evidence that might provide insight into Mr. Wilson's psychology"); *Jones v. Ryan*, 52 F.4th 1104, 1118-19 (9th Cir. 2022) ("Counsel should have obtained a defense mental health expert well before the start of the guilt phase of Jones's [capital] trial, but instead, he waited to make this request until after Jones had already been convicted. . . . ¶ Obtaining the court-appointed, independent expert's short and cursory evaluation did not satisfy this duty."); AMERICAN BAR ASSOCIATION, STANDARDS FOR CRIMINAL JUSTICE MONITORS AND MONITORING, DEFENSE FUNCTION (4th ed. 2017), Standard 4-4.1(d), (e), *Duty to Investigate and Engage Investigators* ("(d) Defense counsel should determine whether the client's interests would be served by engaging   forensic   experts, or other professional witnesses . . . , and if so, consider, in consultation with the client, whether to engage them. Counsel should regularly re-evaluate the need for such services throughout the representation. ¶ (e) If the client lacks sufficient resources to pay for necessary investigation, counsel should seek resources from the court, the government, or donors.").

16.1.4. *Arraignment*

In some jurisdictions, a plea of incompetency to be tried or (less frequently) a plea of not guilty by reason of insanity must be entered by the accused at arraignment. See § 14.6 subdivisions (E) and (F) *supra*. In a number of jurisdictions, defense counsel must file a notice at (or within a specified number of days after) arraignment of an intention to present a defense of insanity or other psychiatric defenses. See § 14.6 subdivision (G) *supra*.

16.1.5. *Pretrial Motions and Other Pretrial Pleadings*

There are a number of pretrial motions and other pleadings that may be required by a client's mental problems.

Counsel may want to file a motion with the court seeking court funds for retention of a defense expert. See § 16.3 *infra*.

Depending upon the results of the examination and the facts of the case, the client's mental problems may provide a basis for:

(a) A suppression motion challenging a confession or other incriminating statement (i) on the due process ground that it was not """"the product of a rational intellect and a free will"""" (*Mincey v. Arizona*, 437 U.S. 437 U.S. 385, 398 (1978); see §§ 26.4.2-26.4.3 *infra*) or (ii) on cognate state-law grounds (see § 26.12 *infra*), or (iii) on the ground that the defendant's capacity to make a "knowing and intelligent" waiver of *Miranda* rights was critically impaired (see § 26.8.2 subdivisions (2), (3) *infra*); or (iv) on the ground that the defendant's waiver of *Miranda* rights was involuntary because interrogators overbore his or her limited powers of resistance (see § 26.8.1 *infra*). *See generally* William C. Follette, Richard A. Leo, & Deborah Davis, *Mental Health and False Confessions*, in ELIZABETH KELLEY (ed.), REPRESENTING PEOPLE WITH MENTAL DISABILITIES 95 (2018).

(b) A suppression motion challenging the seizure of tangible evidence through a purportedly consensual search, on the ground that the defendant's mental problems were exploited in obtaining the consent (see § 25.18.1 *infra*).

(c) An objection to proceeding to trial, on the ground of the defendant's incompetence to be tried (see § 14.6 subdivision (F) *supra*; §§ 16.7-16.10 *infra*).

(d) A plea of not guilty by reason of insanity (or an equivalent notice, see § 14.6 subdivisions (E) and (G) *supra*) or (in jurisdictions that recognize some form of diminished-capacity defense) a plea or notice raising that defense (see § 14.6 subdivision (G) *supra*; §§ 16.11-16.12, 39.25 *infra*).

Also, in some jurisdictions a statute or court rule provides a basis for moving for dismissal or diversion in the "interests of justice" (or some linguistic equivalent, see § 21.1 *infra*), which counsel may invoke in a case in which a mentally ill or intellectually disabled defendant is receiving services through the mental health system or from a private mental health professional.

16.1.6. *Plea Negotiations with the Prosecutor*

Depending on the seriousness of the charge and the nature of the client's mental problem, counsel may be able to persuade the prosecutor that the case should be treated therapeutically rather than criminally. For example, a prosecutor may be willing to agree to a diversion arrangement (particularly when the offenses charged do not suggest that the defendant will be a danger to others) which enrolls the defendant in a facility or program that will provide appropriate supervision and/or treatment. See §§ 2.3.6, 3.19, 8.2.2-8.2.4, 8.4 *supra*. Even if the prosecutor is intent upon a conviction, s/he may be willing to agree to a bargained disposition involving no jail time or prison time, if s/he is persuaded that a term of probation conditioned upon mental health services will address the defendant's needs and make it unlikely that the defendant will be arrested for other offenses in the future.

16.1.7. *Trial*

The insanity defense is available as a defense at trial in most jurisdictions. See §§ 16.11-16.13 *infra*. Some jurisdictions recognize a defense of "diminished capacity," which permits the defendant to use evidence of impaired mental capacity to show that s/he was incapable of forming the requisite *mens rea* for the charged offense(s). See § 39.25 *infra*. In a smaller number of jurisdictions, expert testimony is admissible to show that the defendant's psychological proclivities make it unlikely that s/he would commit a crime of the kind charged. See *id.* When the prosecution's case includes confessions or other incriminating statements, the "defendant may introduce evidence of mental retardation, defect, and/or diminished capacity at the guilt stage of trial as part of the circumstances surrounding the making of a confession for jurors to consider in determining the weight or probative value given the statement" (*State v. Doyle*, 56 So.3d 948, 949 (La. 2011)).

16.1.8. *Sentencing*

Counsel can sometimes use the defendant's mental problems as a mitigating factor at sentencing. It is especially persuasive to be able to show that the defendant has been successfully attending a community-based program arranged by counsel to deal with the mental problems. A client who begins some form of therapy program early in the case has the advantage of appearing before the sentencing judge in the posture of a person on the road to voluntary reform and rehabilitation. See §§ 7.2.4, 12.18 *supra*. An opinion from a mental health professional working with the client that the client is not dangerous in society or that imprisonment would interrupt a productive course of outpatient therapy will probably be very important to the judge and may make the difference between a prison sentence and probation. Even if incarceration is indicated, the judge may be persuaded that a short county jail sentence, which will allow early resumption of the client's therapy program, is preferable to a prison term. Potential uses of neuroscientific evidence at sentencing are discussed in Christopher Slobogin, *Neuroscience Nuance: Dissecting the Relevance of Neuroscience in Adjudicating Criminal Culpability*, 4 JOURNAL OF LAW & THE BIOSCIENCES 577 (December 2017); John H. Blume & Emily C. Paavola, *Life, Death, and Neuroimaging: The Advantages and Disadvantages of the Defense's Use of Neuroimages in Capital Cases – Lessons from the Front*, 62 MERCER L. REV. 909 (2011); Deborah W. Denno, *The Myth of the Double-Edged Sword: An Empirical Study of Neuroscience Evidence in Criminal Cases*, 56 BOSTON COLLEGE L. REV. 493 (2015); Deborah W. Denno, *How Courts in Criminal Cases Respond to Childhood Trauma,* 103 MARQUETTE L. REV. 301 (2019). *And see generally Symposium, Criminal Behavior and the Brain: When Law and Neuroscience Collide*, 85 FORDHAM L. REV. 399 (2016); Deborah W. Denno, *Neuroscience and the Personalization of Criminal Law*, 86 U. CHI. L. REV. 359 (2019); Owen D. Jones, *The Future of Law and Neuroscience*, 63 WILLIAM & MARY L. REV. 1317 (2022); Jane Campbell Moriarty, *Neuroimaging in US Courts, available at* https://ssrn.com/abstract=4150892. Mental disorders and their symptoms are catalogued in AMERICAN PSYCHIATRIC ASSOCIATION, DIAGNOSTIC AND STATISTICAL MANUAL OF MENTAL DISORDERS (5th ed. 2013) [DSM-5]; *see also* DAVID FREEDMAN, COGNITIVE AND FUNCTIONAL ASSESSMENT: A PRACTITIONER'S GUIDE TO TESTING (March 2019), referenced in § 16.4 *infra*. Concerning intellectual disability, *see* AMERICAN ASSOCIATION ON INTELLECTUAL AND DEVELOPMENTAL DISABILITIES, INTELLECTUAL DISABILITY: DEFINITION, DIAGNOSIS, CLASSIFICATION, AND SYSTEMS OF SUPPORTS 131 (12th ed. 2021); James W. Ellis, Caroline Everington & Ann M. Delpha, *Evaluating Intellectual Disability: Clinical Assessments in* Atkins *Cases,* 46 HOFSTRA L. REV. 1305, 1359 (2018). Concerning Traumatic Brain Injury, *see* Alison J. Lynch, Michael L. Perlin & Heather Cucolo, *"My Bewildering Brain Toils in Vain": Traumatic Brain Injury, the Criminal Trial Process, and the Case of Lisa Montgomery*, 74 RUTGERS U. L. REV. 215 (2021).

B. *Retention of a Defense Psychiatrist or Psychologist*

16.2. *Reasons for Retaining a Mental Health Expert: The Many Functions a Defense Expert Can Perform in a Criminal Case*

16.2.1. *Using a Mental Health Expert as a Witness at a Pretrial Hearing or Trial*

In any case in which counsel presents a mental defense at trial (see §§ 16.11-16.12, 39.25 *infra*), counsel will probably need to call a mental health professional to testify as an expert witness. Counsel also may need to call a mental health expert as a witness at a suppression hearing in which the client's mental problem bears upon a ground for suppressing a statement or tangible evidence (see § 16.1.5 *supra*).

In most cases in which a mental health expert serves as a testifying witness, s/he will be crucial in ways that go beyond presenting factual information based on his or her examination of the defendant and explaining its medical and psychological significance in light of his or her specialized knowledge of a scientific field. S/he can make the defendant's mental life accessible to the fact-finder (whether that is a judge at a suppression hearing, a jury at trial, or a judge at a bench trial), organizing and presenting the defendant's perceptions and actions as a comprehensible and coherent story and "pedigreeing" that story by showing that it has an extensive scientific foundation and wasn't made up to order. *See United States v. Laureys*, 866 F.3d 432 (D.C. Cir. 2017) (finding defense counsel constitutionally ineffective for failing to obtain expert mental health testimony in a case in which the defendant was convicted by a jury of attempted coercion and enticement of a minor and travel with intent to engage in illicit sexual conduct, arising from an online encounter with an undercover detective with whom Laureys enthusiastically envisioned sexual encounters with a nine year-old girl: "Laureys has steadfastly maintained his innocence, despite the existence of a chat transcript in which he discussed child sex in graphic detail, because he insists that he was only engaging in fantasy and that his actual intent was to engage in an adult sexual encounter while fantasizing about a child. Such a defense might seem unimaginable to the average juror absent a clinical presentation regarding, for instance, the prevalence of fantasy in internet chat rooms, or the use of fantasy chat as a coping mechanism to deal with inappropriate or unlawful sexual urges."). S/he can provide concepts and contexts to frame information – ways of thinking about mental disorders, their manifestations, their predisposing and precipitating factors, and their prognosis. Where predictions are needed (for example, regarding the defendant's likely response to treatment), s/he can make them; but s/he can also provide the basis for predictions without speaking to them explicitly (*e.g.*, by testifying about the availability of treatment sources and inspiring confidence in them). She can present information obtained from third parties that would otherwise be inadmissible hearsay – and information from records that lack sufficient authentication for admission as independent exhibits – by testifying that s/he relied on these sources of information in forming his or her opinion, and then relating the information in detail. See § 33.13 *infra*.

16.2.2. *Potential Functions of a Mental Health Expert Other Than Testifying at a Pretrial Hearing or Trial*

Beyond the functions that a mental health professional can perform as an expert witness, s/he can assist the defense in a wide range of ways to prepare a criminal case for trial or sentencing.

One such function has already been mentioned: If counsel is experiencing difficulties in communicating with the client, a mental health professional can serve as a facilitator. See § 16.1.1 *supra*. A mental health professional can help counsel understand what the client is saying, thinking, and feeling. S/he can help counsel to understand the client's sensitivities, resistances, and motivations. If there are matters the client finds it difficult to hear or consider, a mental health professional will usually be better able than counsel to talk with the client about these matters. For example, in what is likely to be a flashpoint for some clients in cases involving mental defenses, a mental health professional can help the client get a fix on what terms like "mental defenses" and "being mentally ill" do and don't imply, and to accept the implications of using a defense of this sort to seek a favorable outcome in the case. If there are subjects that the client is blocked against discussing – or simply too embarrassed to discuss – with counsel, a mental health professional is trained and experienced in cutting through precisely those barriers. Sometimes it is only with the professional's assistance that – even after the client has been gotten to open up to counsel about closeted thoughts, feelings, experiences and events – the client can be persuaded to testify about these intensely disturbing matters in open court.

During the pretrial investigation of the case, a mental health expert can help counsel to identify what records might be available to document the client's history of mental problems (e.g., hospital records, school records, other institutional records, see § 16.1.3 *supra*) and how to find them. Once those records have been obtained, the expert can help counsel to understand the records (*see, e.g., McWilliams v. Dunn*, 582 U.S. 183, 198-99 (2017)): – the abbreviations and partial illegibilities; what recorded observations and events mean; how commonplace or rare those observations and events are; the implications of those observations and events; the implications of material in the records as potential evidence or potential investigative leads; the presence of potential analytic pitfalls in relying on those implications; and – often most important – what the *absence* of particular events or information from the records may signify. (*See* Sir Arthur Conan Doyle, *Silver Blaze*, in 1 SHERLOCK HOLMES, THE COMPLETE NOVELS AND STORIES 455, 472 (Bantam Classic edition 1986):

[The inspector]:	"Is there any point to which you would wish to draw my attention?"
[Sherlock Holmes]:	"To the curious incident of the dog in the night-time."
[The inspector]:	"The dog did nothing in the night-time."
[Sherlock Holmes]:	"That was the curious incident. . . .")

As counsel develops a theory of the case (see § 7.2 *supra*) and considers possible story lines to present in a pretrial suppression hearing or a trial or at sentencing (see § 7.3 *supra*), an expert can help to identify narratives that explain and connect events. S/he can provide a sounding board for trying out the plausibility of logical inferences and gauging whether a story line is plausible, given the information already known, the information that the expert predicts can be gathered, the realities of life for individuals with a mental condition like the client's, and the practices and practical constraints of the mental health system. S/he can also provide a different angle of vision – a different interpretive perspective – on people, events, and other aspects of the case. *Cf. United States v. Laureys*, 866 F.3d 432, 438 (D.C. Cir. 2017) (defense counsel deprived his client of effective assistance of counsel by leading a potential mental health expert "to believe that counsel was interested in establishing only . . . [a] diminished capacity defense" – which "counsel had arrived at through his own online research" but which the expert did not support – and thereby causing the expert to "bow[ ] out of the proceeding altogether, leaving . . . [the defendant] without the benefit of the clinical testimony that . . . [the expert] could have offered, which . . . would have informed the jury's assessment of . . . [a defense that the defendant "lacked the requisite intent" rather than that he was incapable of forming such an intent] and helped buttress . . . [the defendant's] own testimony"; "[C]ounsel focused . . . [the expert] on an *invalid* diminished capacity defense *to the exclusion of all other possible defenses.*").

Even if the expert is not going to testify, s/he can help counsel to prepare a case for a suppression hearing or trial. S/he can recommend, identify, and enlist other professionals, including other potential testifying experts. S/he can help counsel anticipate and prepare to answer the prosecution's case by predicting what experts (or what kinds of experts) the prosecutor might recruit and what they are likely to say on the witness stand. S/he can educate counsel about possible lines of attack on prosecution experts and their credentials, theories, analyses, and conclusions (including writings by the prosecution experts, and authoritative texts with which the experts or their writings might be impeached). At the hearing or trial, the expert can observe the testimony of prosecution experts and advise counsel on what subjects to cover in cross-examination and how to handle them. *See, e.g., McWilliams v. Dunn, supra*, 582 U.S. at 198-99; and see §§ 30.2, 37.14 *infra*.

If the case is a high-profile one that is being covered by the media, the expert can help counsel to present or defend the case in any media forum that is expected or desired. If the media are not yet paying attention to the case and if counsel wishes them to, the expert can help counsel strategize about how to accomplish that goal. If, as is usually the case, counsel would like to deflect or defuse media attention, the expert can help counsel figure out how best to do so.

The expert can assist counsel's plea bargaining efforts by providing information about the client or available programs that counsel can cite when trying to persuade the prosecutor to divert the case or to agree to a favorable plea and sentence. See § 16.1.6. If the prosecutor seems open to these options but wants more reassurance, counsel might arrange for the expert to meet with the prosecutor. See §§ 2.3.6, 3.19, 8.2.2-8.2.4, 8.4 *supra*.

Finally, the expert can help counsel to prepare for sentencing by identifying appropriate community-based therapeutic programs for the client and perhaps arranging for the client's admission to a particular program. At capital sentencing hearings, expert testimony by mental health professionals has become commonplace. *See, e.g., Williams v. Stirling*, 914 F.3d 302 (4th Cir. 2019). They can often play an equally crucial role in non-capital sentencing proceedings by (a) presenting expert testimony if evidentiary sentencing hearings are held upon convictions of charges like the client's in counsel's jurisdiction; or (b) preparing a written report and sentencing recommendation for counsel's submission to the court (or a probation officer, see § 48.1 *infra*) and perhaps also by appearing at sentencing to answer any questions the judge may have, in cases where sentencing proceedings are non-evidentiary.

16.3. *Retaining a Mental Health Expert*

Ordinarily, counsel should begin the task of finding a psychiatrist or psychologist as soon as counsel detects any indications that the client has significant mental problems. *See, e.g., Sasser v. Kelley*, 321 F. Supp. 3d 900 (W.D. Ark. 2018). As explained in §§ 16.1.2-16.1.3 and 16.2.2, the expert may be able to play an invaluable role at even the earliest stages of the case. Also, psychiatrists and psychologists often have such crowded schedules that appointments for evaluations must be scheduled several weeks in advance.

Counsel cannot arrange a mental health evaluation without the client's agreement. Unless the client is obviously incompetent, s/he should have the final say on whether s/he will be subjected to an evaluation. See §§ 1.3, 16.1 *supra*. Counsel can attempt to be persuasive, however, and may be most effective if s/he can get the client to understand that psychiatrists work with "sane" people and not just with people who have "mental illnesses"; that psychiatrists are very useful in helping "well" people with adjustment problems; and that many people who are not at all "sick" see psychiatrists.

There are essentially four ways of obtaining a mental evaluation of the defendant: (i) retaining a private psychiatrist or psychologist at his or her regular rate of compensation (which is usually billed on an hourly basis); (ii) arranging for a private examination on an informal basis, either *pro bono* or for a sliding-scale fee adjusted to the income of the defendant and/or any family members who are willing to provide financial assistance; (iii) requesting that the court appoint a state-paid psychiatrist or psychologist for the defense; and (iv) invoking statutory provisions that authorize or trigger a defendant's examination by a state psychiatrist or psychologist or other purportedly "neutral" expert, on either an in-patient or out-patient basis. Since the cost of a private examination at the usual rates charged by a psychiatrist or psychologist is prohibitive for most clients and their families, counsel usually will need to consider one of the other alternatives.

The major problem with requesting a court-ordered mental examination by a state-employed or "neutral" expert is that the resulting report will be provided not only to defense counsel but also to the judge and the prosecutor. If the report contains unfavorable facts about the defendant's mental condition or background, it may provide the prosecutor with bases for (i) seeking rescission of bail on the ground of the defendant's supposed dangerousness (see §§ 4.3.1, 4.15.2 *supra*), or an increase of the amount of bail to a prohibitive figure by a judge who prefers not to have a mentally questionable defendant running free until trial; (ii) refuting the defense position on mental issues raised at a suppression hearing or at trial, and/or (iii) arguing for a harsher sentence than the defendant might otherwise have received. See § 16.5 *infra*. In addition, in some jurisdictions and depending upon subsequent developments in the case, the court may rule that the defendant's statements about the offense, made during the defense-requested examination and recounted in the report, can be used by the prosecution as evidence of guilt at trial (see §§ 16.6.1, 18.12 *infra*) or can be used to impeach the defendant's inconsistent trial testimony (see §§ 18.12, 39.13.1 *infra*).

A request for court funds to hire a defense expert may also be problematic, although less so. First of all, unless the judge permits counsel to make the request on an *ex parte* basis (see § 5.4 *supra*), the very act of seeking court funds for a mental health expert will tip off the prosecution to the fact that the defendant has mental problems and may lead to the prosecutor's seeking a court-ordered examination, directing its own investigative efforts into troubling aspects of the defendant's background, opposing pretrial release or a community-based disposition because s/he does not want "a possible nut wandering around loose" or doing all of these things. Even when applications for state-paid expert assistance are received *ex parte*, it is difficult to keep the prosecutor from learning that the defendant is being attended by a mental-health expert: the expert's visits to a jailed defendant will be logged at the detention facility; discussions among counsel and the court about scheduling are likely to reveal that court dates are being set in ways that accommodate the client's evaluation by a mental health expert; the local low-cost forensic-science community may well be small, close-knit, and loose-lipped. In addition, in some jurisdictions judges will not grant a defense motion for court funds until after a court-ordered examination has shown that the defendant does indeed have mental problems warranting the appointment or retainer of a defense expert. In such jurisdictions the request for the defense expert will activate an order for a mental examination by a state-employed or "neutral" expert, with all of the problems described in the preceding paragraph.

Thus, if retaining a mental health professional at his or her ordinary rates is beyond the client's means, counsel will want to investigate the resources available in the community for nonofficial, cost-free or *pro bono* examination. These include: hospital clinics (which often offer individual or group therapy as well as evaluation at nominal or no cost); hospitals with psychiatric residencies; community mental health centers; the county medical society; social welfare agencies; the psychiatry and psychology departments of private universities and of the local branch of the State University; and private psychiatrists and psychologists who have been involved in the past with the criminal justice system or who might welcome the chance to render service or obtain experience in a criminal case. ACLU chapters often have substantial numbers of mental-health professionals among their members; the chapter chairperson may be able to provide useful referrals or leads.

If counsel is unable to arrange for the informal examination of an indigent client by a private psychiatrist or psychologist, then counsel will have to apply for state funds to hire a defense expert. Counsel should move the court *ex parte* for funds "to retain [or for court appointment of] a psychiatrist [or psychologist] as a defense consultant to examine the defendant and advise counsel regarding the defendant's mental state for purposes of assisting counsel to prepare the defense" (see §§ 5.1.2-5.4 *supra*). This form of retainer or appointment will assure that information revealed by the client to the expert and information conveyed between counsel and the expert is shielded by attorney-client privilege (*see, e.g., People v. Lines*, 13 Cal. 3d 500, 507-16, 531 P.2d 793, 797-804, 119 Cal. Rptr. 225, 229-36 (1975); *United States v. Alvarez*, 519 F.2d 1036, 1045-47 (3d Cir. 1975); *Neuman v. State*, 297 Ga. 501, 503-09, 773 S.E.2d 716, 719-23 (2015); *see also Elijah W. v. Superior Court*, 216 Cal. App. 4th 140, 146, 150-60, 156 Cal. Rptr. 3d 592, 595, 599-606 (2013)) and the work-product privilege (see § 18.10.2 *infra*). If the motion is denied, counsel should file whatever objections may be necessary to preserve a claim of error, including state and federal constitutional error (see §§ 17.6, 17.11 *infra*), in its denial; and counsel may want to pursue available avenues of pretrial appellate review (see Chapter 31 *infra*). *See Stephen A. Saltzburg, The Duty to Investigate and the Availability of Expert*

Witnesses, 86 FORDHAM L. REV. 1709 (2018).

If all of the previously described methods for obtaining a defense mental health expert have failed, then counsel must weigh the potential benefits of a court-ordered examination against all of the risks that this process entails. If the benefits clearly outweigh the risks, counsel should request the court-ordered examination, stating on the record that (1) s/he is making this request only because the court has denied the defendant's application for state funds for a defense expert, and (2) the defendant is preserving his or her objections to that denial notwithstanding counsel's subsequent motion for a court-ordered examination.

16.4. *Selecting a Mental Health Expert: Choosing Between Psychiatrists and Psychologists; Choosing Among Specialties*

This section sets forth some very rough generalizations about the suitability of various types of mental health experts for criminal cases. In selecting an expert for a particular case, counsel is well advised to consult other defense lawyers who have retained a mental health expert in a similar type of case. If other lawyers are unable to make a recommendation, counsel should ask a faculty member of a university psychiatry or psychology department or a reputable local psychiatrist or psychologist to list experts with the specialized qualifications necessary to handle the case effectively.

In a case in which counsel raises an incompetency claim (see §§ 16.7-16.10 *infra*) or an insanity defense (see §§ 16.11-16.13 *infra*), it is usually advisable to retain a psychiatrist.

In a case involving an intellectually disabled client, counsel should almost invariably retain a psychologist. An assessment of the defendant's comprehension and functioning levels will necessitate the I.Q. tests that psychologists administer. For this same reason, in any case in which counsel intends to challenge the defendant's comprehension of *Miranda* rights, counsel should usually retain a psychologist, preferably one with some expertise in the specialized area of comprehension of *Miranda* rights.

If counsel's primary goal is to obtain a report about the client's mental problems for use at sentencing or perhaps in negotiating with the prosecutor, counsel should usually turn to a psychologist, preferably one who has familiarity with treatment programs that might be appropriate for an individual with the client's type of mental problem. As a general rule, psychologists tend to go deeper into an individual's family history, social background, and emotional problems than many psychiatrists. There are two exceptions to this general rule, however. Counsel will need to retain a psychiatrist in any case in which the client is presently taking or appears to require psychotropic medication: Psychiatrists have the medical training necessary to calculate and prescribe psychotropic drugs. A psychiatrist also should be retained in cases in which counsel's sentencing proposal will recommend admission to a residential mental health facility: Most facilities of this sort will be more swayed by a psychiatrist's recommendation than a psychologist's.

In some cases counsel will need to obtain a neurological evaluation of the defendant, which can be conducted by either a neurologist or a psychiatrist with a speciality in neurology.

(There are also some psychologists specializing in neurological matters who have the requisite qualifications but these are not common, and counsel should have a recommendation for the particular psychologist from a trusted source before choosing this alternative.) A neurological evaluation is necessary to ascertain whether a client's disturbed behavior is due to brain damage caused by prenatal problems, birth trauma, or childhood head injuries. Such an explanation of the client's behavior, especially when coupled with an assessment that the malady is treatable through medication (as it often is), can be highly persuasive in a sentencing argument. *See United States v. Fields,* 949 F.3d 1240, 1256 (10th Cir. 2019) ("we have noted 'that evidence of mental impairments "is exactly the sort of evidence that garners the most sympathy from jurors,"' . . . and that '[o]rganic brain damage is so compelling . . . because "the involuntary physical alteration of brain structures, with its attendant effects on behavior, tends to diminish moral culpability, altering the causal relationship between impulse and action"'").

In cases involving sex offenses, counsel should seek out an expert in assessment and treatment of sex offenders. Frequently, behavioral psychologists are especially skilled in developing modes of treatment for sex offenders.

There is a comprehensive discussion of the kinds of evaluations that may be useful in particular categories of cases, and of the ways to prepare and arrange for them, in DAVID FREEDMAN, COGNITIVE AND FUNCTIONAL ASSESSMENT: A PRACTITIONER'S GUIDE TO TESTING (March 2019), *available at* https://fdprc.capdefnet.org/litigation-guides/mental-health. To access this useful resource, counsel will have to obtain access to the password-protected private side of the Federal Death Penalty Resource Counsel sector of the CapDefNet website.

C. Mental Health Examinations

16.5. Opposing a Court-Ordered Mental Health Examination

In some jurisdictions, the defense's raising of a claim that the defendant is incompetent to plead or to be tried – which, depending on the jurisdiction, may be raised by a special plea at arraignment or by a prearraignment motion (see §§ 12.15, 14.5 subdivision (F) *supra*) – automatically triggers a court order for a psychiatric examination. Such orders often are for an in-patient examination at a state mental institution or specialized facility. The commitment period generally ranges from 30 to 90 days, although theoretically required by the federal Constitution to be "strictly limited" to a duration reasonably necessary for evaluating the defendant's competency (*cf. McNeil v. Director*, 407 U.S. 245, 250 (1972)). Usually, the court also has the option of ordering an out-patient examination by one or more psychiatric experts appointed by the court. At the conclusion of the examination, the mental health professional who examined the defendant sends a report to the judge, and a copy is provided to defense counsel and the prosecutor.

As explained in § 16.3 *supra*, it will usually be in the defendant's interest to oppose a court-ordered mental examination because the prosecutor will receive a copy of the report and will be able to use any unfavorable information in it to argue for the client's detention pending trial, to refute at pretrial suppression hearings or at trial any defense contentions based on the defendant's mental problems, and to urge a harsher sentence. As that section also explains, there is an additional risk in some jurisdictions that any statements the defendant makes to the evaluator about the offense can be used by the prosecution at trial as evidence of guilt or to impeach the defendant if s/he testifies. See § 16.6 *infra*. Some prosecutors retain psychiatric consultants who specialize in diagnosing criminal defendants as having antisocial personality disorder or other stigmatizing mental conditions which the prosecutor then finds a way to convey to the judge and, in jury trials, to the jurors, with devastating results. *See, e.g.*, Gabriella Argueta-Cevallos, Note, *A Prosecutor with a Smoking Gun: Examining the Weaponization of Race, Psychopathy, and ASPD Labels in Capital Cases,* 53 COLUMBIA HUMAN RIGHTS L. REV. 624 (2022); Brock Mehler, *The Supreme Court and State Psychiatric Examinations of Capital Defendants: Stuck inside of Jurek with the Barefoot Blues Again*, 59 U. MO. KAN. CITY L. REV. 107, 115-16 (1990). Therefore, defense counsel will usually want to oppose a court-ordered mental examination and, if counsel needs an evaluation of the client, to seek it through the alternative methods discussed in § 16.3.

Statutes and rules authorizing mental health examinations sometimes specify the factual circumstances under which a competency examination may be ordered (for example, the existence of reasonable grounds for believing that the defendant is incompetent). In these jurisdictions, counsel can defeat an examination order by contesting the sufficiency of the requisite evidentiary showing. *See, e.g., United States v. Rinaldi*, 351 F.3d 285 (7th Cir. 2003); *United States v. Lapi*, 458 F.3d 555 (7th Cir. 2006);*United States v. Visinaiz*, 96 Fed. Appx. 594 (10th Cir. 2004). In other jurisdictions, statutes, rules or established practice give trial judges discretion to order an examination whenever they deem it appropriate. Counsel can argue that such discretion is not unrestricted: that the authorization for an examination is logically limited by the examination's function (*see United States v. Taveras*, 233 F.R.D. 318 (E.D. N.Y. 2006)) and therefore comes into play only when there is a substantial factual showing that the defendant may be incompetent. In the absence of any statutory or other doctrinal standards that can be invoked, counsel will have to rely on commonsense arguments to persuade the judge that there simply is no need for a court-ordered examination. If counsel is able to arrange an examination through some other means (see § 16.3 *supra*), s/he can argue to the court that this is a better way of proceeding. If counsel is able to arrange a private mental health evaluation, she can point out that this will save the state the expense of a period of commitment and a state-conducted evaluation. In cases of this sort as well as those in which counsel seeks state funds to retain a defense mental health expert to evaluate the defendant, counsel can argue that providing for the defendant's evaluation by a defense consultant *before* any court-ordered commitment or examination would spare the state potentially needless costs and complications. In any case in which the court is inclined to have the defendant evaluated at all, it will be because there is some indication of significant mental disorder. And "when the defendant's mental condition is seriously in question," *Ake v. Oklahoma*, 470 U.S. 68, 82 (1985), requires the appointment of a *defense* mental-health expert for defendants who cannot afford to retain one. *Ake*'s command cannot be satisfied through examination by a court-appointed neutral expert; what is required is that the defendant be afforded "access to a competent psychiatrist who will conduct an appropriate examination and assist in evaluation, preparation, and presentation of the defense" (*id.* at 83). *See, e.g., United States v. Sloan*, 776 F.2d 926 (10th Cir. 1985); *Powell v. Collins*, 332 F.3d 376, 392 (6th Cir. 2003) ("Today, we join with those circuits that have held that an indigent criminal defendant's constitutional right to psychiatric assistance in preparing an insanity defense is not satisfied by court appointment of a 'neutral' psychiatrist – *i.e.*, one whose report is available to both the defense and the prosecution."); *Moore v. State*, 390 Md. 343, 379-83, 889 A.2d 325, 346-48 (2005); *De Freece v. State*, 848 S.W.2d 150 (Tex. Crim App. 1993); *State v. Sharrow*, 2017 VT 25, 205 Vt. 300, 303, 306, 175 A.3d 504, 505, 507 (2017) ("a defendant whose competency has been called into question has a constitutionally based right to hire, with state funding, a defense-retained mental health expert to assist in his or her defense in order to guard against the possibility of an erroneous determination of competency"; in contrast, the prosecution does not have either a constitutional or state statutory right to an evaluation of the defendant by a "mental health expert of the State's choosing, following a court-ordered competency evaluation by a neutral mental health expert"). *See also McWilliams v. Dunn*, 582 U.S. 183 (2017) (explaining that the Court "need not, and do[es] not" reach the question whether "*Ake* clearly established that a State must provide an indigent defendant with a qualified mental health expert retained specifically for the defense team, not a neutral expert available to both parties" (*id.* at 197) because, even if "[w]e . . . assume that Alabama met the *examination* portion of . . . [*Ake*'s] requirement by providing for [State Department of Mental Health neuropsychologist] Dr. Goff's examination of McWilliams" (*id.* at 198-99), "[n]either Dr. Goff nor any other expert helped the defense evaluate Goff's report or McWilliams' extensive medical records and translate these data into a legal strategy. Neither Dr. Goff nor any other expert helped the defense prepare and present arguments that might, for example, have explained that McWilliams' purported malingering was not necessarily inconsistent with mental illness (as an expert later testified in postconviction proceedings . . .). Neither Dr. Goff nor any other expert helped the defense prepare direct or cross-examination of any witnesses, or testified at the judicial sentencing hearing himself." (*id.* at 199); the Court observes that "language in *Ake* . . . seems to foresee th[e] . . . consequence" that "a neutral expert available to both parties" would not suffice (*see id.* at 197), and the Court notes that "[a]s a practical matter, the simplest way for a State to meet th[e] . . . [*Ake*] standard may be to provide a qualified expert retained specifically for the defense team," which "appears to be the approach that the overwhelming majority of jurisdictions have adopted." (*id.*)). For a fuller discussion of *McWilliams*, see § 5.4 *supra*. Thus, the court's initiation of a court-ordered examination will almost certainly lead to the need for appointment of a defense expert as well. It would be more economical and orderly to have the defense expert examine the defendant initially, so that the whole process of a court-ordered examination can be avoided unless the defense decides to raise mental health issues in the first instance.

In the event that the judge orders a mental health examination over counsel's objections, counsel will ordinarily want to argue that the examination should be conducted on an out-patient basis and not in a state mental institution or other specialized facility. In a number of jurisdictions, the applicable statute or court rule or common-law rules permit the commitment of defendants to a state institution only upon medical affidavits making a *prima facie* showing of the defendant's incompetency, or when "there is reason to believe" that the defendant is incompetent. Counsel should scrutinize the affidavits or other evidence mounted in favor of the preliminary determination of incompetency, pointing out (a) any reasons for doubting unfavorable evidence (for example, when the affidavits contain multiple hearsay, as they often do), and (b) any evidence indicating that an out-patient examination would serve as well as an institutional commitment. In jurisdictions whose statutes or court rules expressly state a presumption in favor of out-patient examinations, counsel should stress the legal effect of that presumption, arguing that the professed preliminary showing of incompetency is insufficient to rebut the presumption.

Even if the evidence makes out the requisite initial showing of incompetency, the judge usually possesses discretion not to commit the defendant for an in-patient examination. Counsel can argue that it would be an inappropriate exercise of judicial discretion to commit a defendant involuntarily to a mental hospital if there are community mental health facilities available for the defendant's diagnosis on an out-patient basis. *Cf. State v. Page,* 11 Ohio Misc. 31, 228 N.E.2d 686 (C.P., Cuyahoga Cty. 1967).

In those cases in which the court announces its intention to order an in-patient examination, counsel can insist upon a hearing that satisfies the requirements of procedural due process. *Cf. Vitek v. Jones,* 445 U.S. 480, 491-94 (1980); *Jones v. United States,* 463 U.S. 354, 361-62 (1983) (dictum). This would appear to include both a full adversary hearing on whatever issues of fact are decisive of the propriety of a commitment order under state law (*Vitek v. Jones, supra,* 445 U.S. at 494-96) and a right to challenge the findings supporting such an order on the ground that there is "no basis" for them in fact (*see Schware v. Board of Bar Examiners,* 353 U.S. 232, 239 (1957)).

In some jurisdictions, orders committing the defendant for an in-patient examination are reviewable by interlocutory appeal (*see, e.g., United States v. Rinaldi,* 351 F.3d 285 (7th Cir. 2003); *United States v. Visinaiz,* 96 Fed. Appx. 594 (10th Cir. 2004)); in others, they may be challenged by prerogative writs such as prohibition or mandamus (see Chapter 31 *infra*). The committing court should be requested to stay its commitment order pending review by the writs. If it refuses to do so, a stay should be sought from the appellate court in which the application for the writ is filed. When no other form of review of commitment orders is recognized by local practice, *habeas corpus* should be used (see §§ 3.8.4, 4.14 *supra*), and the *habeas* court should be asked to stay the defendant's commitment *pendente lite.*

In most jurisdictions it is settled that a court may raise the issue of the defendant's competency to stand trial *sua sponte* or on the suggestion of the prosecution if there is a sufficient factual foundation to doubt that s/he is competent. *See, e.g., In re Davis,* 8 Cal. 3d 798, 505 P.2d 1018, 106 Cal. Rptr. 178 (1973); *State v. Locklair,* 341 S.C. 352, 535 S.E.2d 420 (2000) (alternative ground); *Sibug v. State,* 445 Md. 265, 126 A.3d 86 (2015); *Pate v. Robinson,* 383 U.S. 375, 385 (1966) (under Illinois statutory law, "[w]here the evidence raises a 'bona fide doubt' as to a defendant's competence to stand trial, the judge on his own motion must impanel a jury and conduct a sanity hearing"); *Speedy v. Wyrick,* 702 F.2d 723 (8th Cir. 1983). In such cases, the same procedures follow that apply when the defense raises the issue. If the defendant's competency is not called into question by the court or any party, the prosecution can ordinarily not obtain a court-ordered exam. *See, e.g., Caruthers v. Wexler-Horn,* 592 S.W.3d 328 (Mo. 2019) (the defendant's intention to present a diminished-capacity defense (revealed when defense counsel listed a mental health expert as a trial witness) did not authorize the trial court to order the defendant to submit to an examination at the State's instance); *but see* FED. RULE CRIM. PRO. 12.2, explicitly providing that "[i]f a defendant intends to introduce expert evidence relating to a mental disease or defect or any other mental condition of the defendant bearing on either (1) the issue of guilt or (2) the issue of punishment in a capital case," s/he must give pretrial notice to this effect (Rule 12.2(b), and the court then "may, upon the government's motion, order the defendant to be examined under procedures ordered by the court" (Rule 12.2(c)(1)(B)). The rule goes on to provide that: " No statement made by a defendant in the course of any examination conducted under this rule (whether conducted with or without the defendant's consent), no testimony by the expert based on the statement, and no other fruits of the statement may be admitted into evidence against the defendant in any criminal proceeding except on an issue regarding mental condition on which the defendant . . . has introduced evidence . . . requiring notice. . . ."

16.6. *Procedural Protections at a Mental Health Examination*

16.6.1. *Fifth and Sixth Amendment Protections*

In *Estelle v. Smith,* 451 U.S. 454 (1981), the Court held that the Fifth Amendment privilege against self-incrimination is applicable to a criminal defendant's "statements . . . uttered in the context of a psychiatric examination" (*id.* at 465). Specifically, *Smith* ruled that a defendant's Fifth Amendment rights were violated by the admission of opinion testimony of a psychiatrist called by the prosecution to prove the defendant's probable future dangerousness at the penalty stage of a state capital trial, when the psychiatrist's opinion was based upon his questioning of the defendant during a pretrial competency examination ordered *sua sponte* by the trial court, without notice to the defendant or an effective waiver of the privilege. *See Penry v. Johnson,* 532 U.S. 782, 793-94 (2001) (describing the ruling in *Smith*); *Petrocelli v. Baker,* 869 F.3d 710 (9th Cir. 2017). Because "[d]efense counsel . . . were not notified in advance that the psychiatric examination would encompass the issue of their client's future dangerousness, . . . and . . . [the defendant] was denied the assistance of his attorneys in making the significant decision of whether to submit to the examination and to what end the psychiatrist's findings could be employed," the Court also held that "the psychiatric examination on which . . . [the court-appointed psychiatrist] testified at the penalty phase proceeded in violation of . . . [the defendant's] Sixth Amendment right to the assistance of counsel" (451 U.S. at 470-71). *See also People v. Guevara,* 37 N.Y.3d 1014, 174 N.E.3d 1240, 152 N.Y.S.3d 866 (2021) (reversing a conviction on the ground that the testimony of a prosecution expert psychologist who denied defense counsel admittance to a court-ordered examination of the defendant violated the Sixth Amendment).

Although the *Smith* case involved a capital sentencing hearing, the rules it established are fully applicable to noncapital cases. *See, e.g., United States v. Chitty,* 760 F.2d 425, 430-32 (2d Cir. 1985); *Brown v. Butler,* 815 F.2d 1054 (5th Cir. 1987). The rules are not limited to evidence used at sentencing: they also apply to prosecution evidence offered on the issue of guilt. *See Estelle v. Smith, supra,* 451 U.S. at 462-63 (the Court observes that it could "discern no basis to distinguish between the guilt and penalty phases of [a] . . . capital murder trial so far as the protection of the Fifth Amendment privilege is concerned"). *See, e.g., People v. Pokovich,* 39 Cal. 4th 1240, 1246, 1253, 141 P.3d 267, 271, 276, 48 Cal. Rptr. 158, 163, 169 (2006); *United States v. Garcia,* 739 F.2d 440 (9th Cir. 1984); *People v. Branch,* 805 P.2d 1075, 1082-83 (Colo. 1991) ("To be sure, *Smith* involved a prosecution for a capital offense, but its rationale, we believe, is equally applicable to those situations in which the trial court orders a competency examination when formal criminal charges are pending against a defendant. If a trial court is constitutionally required to employ adequate procedural safeguards to protect a defendant against the risk of making uncounseled inculpatory statements during a court-ordered competency examination before such statements may be used against him at the sentencing phase of a capital case, there is all the more reason to require a trial court to employ the same procedural safeguards in order to protect a defendant against the risk of making similarly uncounseled inculpatory statements that might be used against him at the guilt phase of a criminal prosecution. . . . ¶ A trial court, therefore, must provide a defendant with adequate procedural safeguards calculated to ensure protection not only of the defendant's privilege against self-incrimination in connection with a court-ordered competency examination but also of his right to counsel. Discharge of this responsibility requires a trial court to advise a defendant that he has the right not to say anything to the psychiatrist during the competency examination, that his statements to the psychiatrist can be used against him at the guilt phase of the trial as rebuttal or impeachment evidence, that he has the right to confer with counsel prior to submitting to the competency examination, and that the court will appoint an attorney for the defendant at state expense if the defendant is unable to retain counsel prior to the competency examination. A trial court's failure to adequately advise a defendant of his Fifth and Sixth Amendment rights and to provide him with the opportunity to confer with counsel prior to the commencement of the competency examination precludes the prosecution from using such statements as substantive evidence during its case-in-chief at the guilt phase of the trial. . . . These same procedural deficiencies will not prohibit the prosecution from utilizing such statements, so long as they are otherwise voluntary, either to rebut the defendant's evidence of lack of capacity to form the requisite culpable mental state or to impeach the defendant's testimony offered in defense of the charges.").

Smith therefore supports the defendant's right to claim the Fifth Amendment and refuse to talk to a psychiatrist in any court-ordered mental examination unless the order for the examination explicitly provides that nothing disclosed by the defendant during the examination and no results of the examination may subsequently be used against the defendant for any purpose except to determine competency to stand trial (*see Estelle v. Smith, supra*, 451 U.S. at 468; *State v. Johnson*, 276 Ga. 78, 576 S.E.2d 831 (2003), and cases cited), and that the same restriction applies to "any evidence derived directly and indirectly" from the defendant's disclosures and examination results (*see Kastigar v. United States*, 406 U.S. 441, 453 (1972)). Counsel should either insist upon the inclusion of such a provision in the judicial order for an examination or advise the defendant not to say a word to the examiner under any circumstances, whichever seems more appropriate to the needs of the particular situation.

A more difficult question is whether the defendant is entitled to such a restrictive order if the defense acquiesces in or affirmatively seeks the mental examination. For, although defense counsel will almost always oppose the ordering of such an examination (see § 16.5 *supra*), s/he may find it necessary to accept an examination in jurisdictions where a statute or court rule authorizes the court to order one, and s/he may even need to request an examination in situations in which the court has denied a motion for appointment of a defense mental health expert (see § 16.3 *supra*). The defendant in *Estelle v. Smith* had "neither initiate[d] a psychiatric evaluation nor attempt[ed] to introduce any psychiatric evidence" (451 U.S. at 468), and *Smith* was distinguished on this ground in *Buchanan v. Kentucky*, 483 U.S. 402 (1987), in which the Supreme Court held that when a defendant had *both* "joined in a motion for [a pretrial psychiatric] . . . examination" (*id.* at 423) *and* presented an expert witness at trial "to establish

. . . a mental-status defense" (*id.* at 404), the prosecutor could constitutionally use the results of the examination to impeach this witness. *See also Penry v. Johnson, supra*, 532 U.S. at 795 (discussing *Buchanan*); *Kansas v. Cheever*, 571 U.S. 87, 93-96 (2014) (discussing *Estelle v. Smith* and *Buchanan*). *Buchanan* poses the thorny problems: (a) whether *Smith*'s prohibition of prosecutorial use of pretrial psychiatric examination results continues to govern cases in which the examination was unopposed or sought by the defendant or was ordered in response to the defendant's raising of a claim of incompetency or some other psychiatric issue before trial *but the defendant presents no evidence in support of any psychiatric issue at the trial or sentencing,* and (b) whether the exception to the *Smith* prohibition recognized by *Buchanan* is limited to the use of pretrial examination results *to rebut expert psychiatric evidence presented by the defendant at a trial or sentencing,* or whether the defendant's raising of a psychiatric issue at the trial or sentencing opens the door to the prosecutor's use of the results generally.

Regarding problem (a), the argument appears substantial that, unless and until the defendant actually presents evidence in support of a psychiatric plea or defense, *Smith* prohibits the prosecutor's use of any information produced by a pretrial psychiatric examination of the defendant, even one requested or invited by the defense. This is so because the logic of *Smith* was not that Smith's Fifth Amendment rights were violated by the competency examination conducted in that case – to the contrary, the Supreme Court acknowledged that the competency examination had been "validly ordered" by the trial judge *sua sponte* (*Estelle v. Smith, supra,* 451 U.S. at 468) – but rather that the Fifth Amendment came into play "[w]hen [the psychiatrist] . . . went beyond simply reporting to the court on the issue of competence and testified for the prosecution at the penalty phase on the crucial issue of . . . future dangerousness, [so that] his role changed and became essentially like that of an agent of the State recounting unwarned statements made in a postarrest custodial setting" (*id.* at 467; *see id.* at 465; *Johnson v. Winstead,* 900 F.3d 428, 434 (7th Cir. 2018)). *See also Allen v. Illinois,* 478 U.S. 364 (1986), upholding compulsory psychiatric examination of an individual subject to civil commitment proceedings so long as that individual "is protected from use of his [or her] compelled answers in any subsequent criminal case in which [s/]he is the defendant" (*id.* at 368). Under this logic it should make no difference that the defendant originally moves for the examination or triggers it by a pretrial plea of incompetency unless such a motion or plea can properly be treated as a waiver of the Fifth Amendment privilege. But it cannot. Under *Pate v. Robinson,* 383 U.S. 375 (1966), and *Drope v. Missouri,* 420 U.S. 162 (1975), every person accused of a crime has a federal constitutional right to an adequate psychiatric evaluation and judicial determination of competency to stand trial; and it would impermissibly place the defendant "'between the rock and the whirlpool'" (*Garrity v. New Jersey,* 385 U.S. 493, 498 (1967)) to treat the defendant's invocation of this right as a waiver of the Fifth Amendment privilege. *See Simmons v. United States,* 390 U.S. 377, 389-94 (1968), reaffirmed in *United States v. Salvucci,* 448 U.S. 83, 89-90 (1980); *Brooks v. Tennessee,* 406 U.S. 605, 607-12 (1972); *Lefkowitz v. Cunningham,* 431 U.S. 801, 807-08 (1977); *State v. Melendez,* 240 N.J. 268, 282, 222 A.3d 639, 647 (2020) ("Like the defendants in *Garrity,* claimants in a civil forfeiture action who are defendants in a parallel criminal case also face an untenable choice: to forfeit their property or incriminate themselves. To defend against a forfeiture complaint, claimants who are also criminal defendants must file an answer that states their interest in the property. In other words, to assert their constitutional right not to be deprived of property without due process, they have to link themselves to alleged contraband and give up their constitutional right against self-incrimination. Alternatively, they can refuse to answer and lose their property. ¶ We need go no further than the reasoning in *Garrity* to find that a defendant's choice to file an answer under those circumstances is not freely made. It is fraught with coercion. A criminal defendant's statements in an answer to a civil forfeiture complaint thus cannot be considered voluntary. As a result, they cannot be introduced in the State's direct case in a later criminal proceeding."); *cf. Jeffers v. United States,* 432 U.S. 137, 153 n.21 (1977) (plurality opinion); *United States v. Goodwin,* 457 U.S. 368, 372 (1982) (dictum); *Spaziano v. Florida,* 468 U.S. 447, 455 (1984) (dictum); *McDonough v. Smith,* 139 S. Ct. 2149, 2158 (2019); and *compare United States v. Jackson,* 390 U.S. 570, 581-83 (1968), *with Middendorf v. Henry,* 425 U.S. 25, 47-48 (1976), *and Corbitt v. New Jersey,* 439 U.S. 212, 218-20 & n.8 (1978); *compare Jackson v. Denno,* 378 U.S. 368, 387-89 & nn.15, 16 (1964), *with Spencer v. Texas,* 385 U.S. 554, 565 (1967), *and Jenkins v. Anderson,* 447 U.S. 231, 236-37 (1980). *And see Lacy v. Butts,* 922 F.3d 371 (7th Cir. 2019) (holding that an Indiana monitoring program which required incarcerated sex offenders to complete a questionnaire listing all of their sex crimes and to fill out workbooks describing those crimes – whether previously charged or uncharged – in detail violated the Fifth Amendment privilege because inmates who elected not to participate in the program were penalized by the denial of good-time credits: "[T]hrough its denial of the opportunity to earn good-time credits and its revocation of credits already earned, as a means of inducing participants to furnish information, [this program] *compels* self-incrimination in contravention of the Fifth Amendment." *Id.* at 377 (original emphasis).); *but see Chavez v. Robinson,* 12 F.4th 978 (9th Cir. 2021).

To treat the defendant's request for a psychiatric examination as a waiver of the privilege is the more impermissible because the very purpose of the examination is to obtain information that is necessary in order to assess the merits of potential psychiatric defenses and the defendant's capability to participate in judgments relating to those defenses: A forced choice between forgoing such information and forgoing a constitutional right has none of the qualities of a valid waiver. *Compare Brooks v. Tennessee, supra,* 406 U.S. at 607-12, *with Town of Newton v. Rumery,* 480 U.S. 386 (1987). In discussing *Smith* and *Buchanan,* the Supreme Court has suggested that the justification for finding a waiver of the Fifth Amendment "'[w]hen a defendant asserts the insanity defense and introduces supporting psychiatric testimony'" is that in this situation "'his silence may deprive the State of the only effective means it has of controverting his proof on an issue that he has interjected into the case'" (*Powell v. Texas,* 492 U.S. 680, 684 (1989) (per curiam), quoting *Estelle v. Smith, supra,* 451 U.S. at 465). *Accord, Kansas v. Cheever, supra* at 94 ("The rule of *Buchanan,* which we reaffirm today, is that where a defense expert who has examined the defendant testifies that the defendant lacked the requisite mental state to commit an offense, the prosecution may present psychiatric evidence in rebuttal. . . . Any other rule would undermine the adversarial process, allowing a defendant to provide the jury, through an expert operating as proxy, with a one-sided and potentially inaccurate view of his mental state at the time of the alleged crime."; "When a defendant presents evidence through a psychological expert who has examined him, the government likewise is permitted to use the only effective means of challenging that evidence: testimony from an expert who has also examined him."). No similar justification exists for finding waiver when the defendant has merely sought a mental examination for the purpose of determining whether to interject psychiatric issues into the case and has then elected not to. *See Wilkens v. State,* 847 S.W.2d 547, 550 (Tex. Crim. App. 1992) ("The trial court ordered the examinations for competency and insanity at appellant's request. Appellant did not waive his Fifth

Amendment privilege merely by requesting appointment of a court-appointed psychiatrist and psychologist and submitting to a competency and sanity examination" although he did subsequently waive it under *Buchanan* by presenting evidence in support of an insanity defense.). So nothing in *Buchanan* undermines the trenchant analysis in *United States v. Alvarez,* 519 F.2d 1036, 1046-47 (3d Cir. 1975) ("The issue here is whether a defense counsel in a case involving a potential defense of insanity must run the risk that a psychiatric expert whom he hires to advise him with respect to the defendant's mental condition may be forced to be an involuntary government witness. The effect of such a rule would, we think, have the inevitable effect of depriving defendants of the effective assistance of counsel in such cases. A psychiatrist will of necessity make inquiry about the facts surrounding the alleged crime, just as the attorney will. Disclosures made to the attorney cannot be used to furnish proof in the government's case. Disclosures made to the attorney's expert should be equally unavailable, at least until he is placed on the witness stand. The attorney must be free to make an informed judgment with respect to the best course for the defense without the inhibition of creating a potential government witness."). Thus *Smith*'s ban upon the use of evidence obtained from a pretrial psychiatric examination of a defendant to prove guilt or enhance penalty should apply "whether the defendant or the prosecutor requested the examination and whether it was had for the purpose of determining competence to stand trial or sanity" (*Gibson v. Zahradnick,* 581 F.2d 75, 80 (4th Cir. 1978); *State v. Berget,* 2013 S.D. 1, 826 N.W.2d 1, 28-37 (S.D. 2013); *see Battie v. Estelle,* 655 F.2d 692, 700-03 (5th Cir. 1981); *and see Collins v. Auger,* 577 F.2d 1107, 1109-10 (8th Cir. 1978)). It follows that orders for any of these sorts of examinations are required to contain a provision restricting the use of their products to the purposes for which the examination was ordered, and defense counsel should demand such a provision. *See, e.g., Park v. Montana Sixth Judicial District Court, Park County,* 289 Mont. 367, 371, 374, 961 P.2d 1267, 1269-70, 1272 (1998) (approving a trial court order which required a defendant to submit to examination by a prosecution expert for possible use if the defendant presented expert testimony in support of an affirmative defense (acting under the influence of extreme mental or emotional stress for which there was a reasonable explanation or excuse) but "restricted the State's experts from disclosing to the State any incriminating statements made by Park during their examination, and stated that the experts could only testify regarding their conclusions in rebuttal to Park's expert testimony"); *State v. Goff,* 128 Ohio St. 3d 169, 170, 942 N.E.2d 1075, 1077 (2010) ("a court order compelling a defendant to submit to a psychiatric examination conducted by a state expert in response to the defendant raising a defense of self-defense supported by expert testimony on battered-woman syndrome . . . does not violate a defendant's right against self-incrimination. However, we . . . hold that to preserve a defendant's right against self-incrimination, the examination of the defendant and the subsequent testimony from the state's expert must be limited to information related to battered-woman syndrome and whether the defendant's actions were affected by the syndrome. Since the examination and testimony of the expert in this case were not so limited, we hold that the defendant's rights under Section 10, Article I of the Ohio Constitution and the Fifth Amendment to the United States Constitution were violated"); *State v. Jocumsen,* 148 Idaho 817, 229 P.3d 1179 (Idaho App. 2010) (finding an *Estelle v. Smith* violation when materials generated by a pretrial competency evaluation were included in a presentence investigation report considered by the sentencing judge after the defendant recovered competence and pleaded guilty); *In re Hernandez,* 143 Cal. App. 4th 459, 471-72, 49 Cal. Rptr. 3d 301, 309-10 (2006), discussing the rule of *Tarantino v. Superior Court,* 48 Cal. App. 3d 465, 122 Cal. Rptr. 61 (1975), which requires that statements made by a defendant during a court-ordered competency examination be shielded by a "judicially declared immunity reasonably to be implied from the code provisions" (48 Cal. App. 3d at 469, 122 Cal. Rptr. at 63); *People v. Diaz*, 3 Misc. 3d 686, 777 N.Y.S.2d 856 (N.Y. Sup. Ct., Kings Cty. 2004); *United States v. Beckford*, 962 F. Supp. 748, 765 (E.D. Va. 1997) (on a pretrial motion by the prosecution for disclosure of mental-health examination materials and information generated by the defense and for examination of the defendants by prosecution experts, the court adopts "procedures [that] will ensure that Government examinations of the defendants will be ordered only if a defendant provides notice of intent to use mental health or condition in mitigation . . . [;] that the results of examination will be disclosed, if, and only if, a defendant chooses to introduce testimony or other evidence relating to issues of his mental health at the capital sentencing hearing, thus preventing the Fifth and Sixth Amendment infringements prohibited by *Estelle* . . . [; and that] the jury will not be exposed to any mental health evidence unless the defendant first opens that door during the penalty phase.); *cf.* FED. RULE CRIM. PRO. 12.2 as applied in *United States v. Taveras*, 233 F.R.D. 318, 322 (E.D. N.Y. 2006) ("Defendant in the instant matter has protected his right to introduce expert evidence of his mental condition as a mitigating factor at sentencing, but not during the guilt phase. . . . If the court orders the defendant to be examined by a government expert before trial, the government is prohibited from learning the results of the examination until after the defendant is found guilty of a capital charge and the defendant confirms his intent to offer expert mental health evidence at sentencing. Fed. R. Crim. P. 12.2(c)(2). Neither statements made during the government examinations, nor testimony of the expert based on such statements, nor 'other fruits of the statement' may be admitted against the defendant unless he presents his own expert evidence first. Fed. R. Crim. P. 12.2(c)(4). Leakage of information from a government expert to the prosecuting attorneys during the course of trial of guilt – or the allegation that this has occurred – might require a hearing and could provide a ground for appeal or a petition for habeas corpus. This risk can be avoided by postponing the government's examination to the period after a finding of guilt, but before the penalty phase begins."). An alternative form of protection, available under some circumstances, is a provision forbidding the examiners to question the defendant about matters relating to the crime, as distinguished from matters bearing on his or her mental condition at subsequent stages of the case (such as at the time of sentencing, when the defense intends to rely upon the defendant's current mental state as a mitigating factor). *See, e.g., United States v. Johnson*, 383 F. Supp. 2d 1145, 1152 (N.D. Iowa 2005).

Regarding problem (b), it is noteworthy that *Buchanan* describes the "narrow" issue it decides as "whether the admission of findings from a psychiatric examination . . . proffered solely to rebut other psychological evidence presented by . . . [the defendant] violated his . . . [constitutional] rights" (*Buchanan v. Kentucky*, 483 U.S. at 404; *see also id.* at 424-25). It treats this issue as "one of the situations that we distinguished from the facts in *Smith*" (*id.* at 423). *See also Kansas v. Cheever, supra* at 93-94 (discussing *Buchanan*). The *Smith* opinion itself, in noting that the prosecution might be permitted to use evidence obtained by a pretrial psychiatric examination of the defendant in rebuttal, appeared to limit this possibility to cases in which the defense (i) presents expert psychiatric evidence and (ii) addresses the evidence to the specific issue on which the prosecution offers its rebuttal evidence. *Estelle v. Smith, supra*, 451 U.S. at 466 n.10; *see also id.* at 465-66; *Powell v. Texas, supra*, 492 U.S. at 683-84, 685 n.3; *Kansas v. Cheever, supra* at 97; *Gholson v. Estelle*, 675 F.2d 734, 741 & n.6 (5th Cir. 1982); *Battie v. Estelle, supra*, 655 F.2d at 701-02. There are pre-*Smith* cases allowing the prosecution greater latitude in rebuttal – for example, permitting the prosecution to use the defendant's statements made during the psychiatric examination to impeach the defendant's trial testimony, by analogy to *Harris v. New York,* 401 U.S. 222 (1971) (see § 26.19 *infra*). *People v. Brown,* 399 Mich. 350, 249 N.W.2d 693 (1976); *People v. White,* 401 Mich. 482, 257 N.W.2d 912 (1977). But in the light of *Smith* these decisions are assailable under the settled principle that a defendant's statements obtained in disregard of the Fifth Amendment may not be used even to impeach the defendant's inconsistent testimony at trial (*Mincey v. Arizona,* 437 U.S. 385, 397-98 (1978); *New Jersey v. Portash,* 440 U.S. 450, 458-60 (1979); *Hemphill v. New York*, 142 S. Ct. 681, 692-93 (2022) (dictum); *United States v. Leonard,* 609 F.2d 1163 (5th Cir. 1980)). *See, e.g., Wilkens v. State, supra,* 847 S.W.2d at 553 ("a defendant has a separate Fifth Amendment privilege at the punishment phase of a capital murder case which is not waived by his testifying at guilt/innocence. Therefore, appellant's waiver of his Fifth Amendment privilege at the guilt/innocence phase concerning psychiatric testimony [by experts whom the trial court had appointed at defense counsel's request] on the issue of sanity did not carry over to the punishment phase. Under the dictates of *Smith* such psychiatric testimony would not have been admissible at the guilt/innocence phase absent appellant's waiver in that proceeding; likewise, it was not admissible at the punishment phase on the issue of future dangerousness absent some waiver by appellant."); *State v. Goff, supra; People v. Pokovich, supra,* 39 Cal. 4th at 1253, 141 P.3d at 276, 48 Cal. Rptr. at 169 ("the Fifth Amendment's privilege against self-incrimination prohibits the prosecution from using at trial, for the purpose of impeachment, statements a defendant has made during a court-ordered mental competency examination"); *People v. Williams*, 197 Cal. App. 3d 1320, 1322, 1325, 243 Cal. Rptr. 480, at 480, 482 (1988) (alternative ground) ("when a court-appointed psychiatrist examines a defendant for the purpose of testifying in the sanity phase of a bifurcated trial, defendant's constitutional privilege against self-incrimination is violated by allowing the psychiatrist to testify in the guilt phase that defendant confessed his guilt during the examination, when defendant has not placed his mental state at issue in the guilt phase of the trial"); *Gibbs v. Frank*, 387 F.3d 268 (3d Cir. 2004). Notably, the Federal Criminal Rules Advisory Committee has opted to preclude the government's use against a defendant of any information generated by court-ordered mental examinations for any purpose other than to rebut a mental health issue opened by the defense. *See* FED. RULE CRIM. PRO. 12.2(c)(4) ("No statement made by a defendant in the course of any examination conducted under this rule (whether conducted with or without the defendant's consent), no testimony by the expert based on the statement, and no other fruits of the statement may be admitted into evidence against the defendant in any criminal proceeding except on an issue regarding mental condition on which the defendant: ¶ (A) has introduced evidence of incompetency or evidence requiring notice [of intent to assert a defense of insanity or intent to adduce diminished-capacity evidence]. . . , or ¶ (B) has introduced expert evidence in a capital sentencing proceeding . . . .").

16.6.2. *State Law Prohibitions Against Using Statements Made During a Mental Health Examination as Proof of Guilt at Trial*

Apart from the Fifth Amendment protections enunciated in *Estelle v. Smith,* there are statutes, court rules, and common-law decisions providing that statements made during a competency evaluation, during a sanity evaluation, or both cannot be used to prove the accused's guilt at trial. *See, e.g.,* MICH. COMP. LAWS ANN. §§ 330.2028(3), 768.20a(5); *United States v. Alvarez,* 519 F.2d 1036 (3d Cir. 1975); *Lee v. County Court,* 27 N.Y.2d 432, 267 N.E.2d 452,

318 N.Y.S.2d 705 (1971). The scope of this prohibition varies from jurisdiction to jurisdiction and may depend, within any given jurisdiction, on: the nature of the examination (that is, whether it was ordered to determine the defendant's competence to stand trial or the defendant's sanity at the time of the offense); whether the examination was ordered on defense motion or on motion of the prosecution or by the court *sua sponte;* whether it was ordered before or after the defendant tendered a claim of incompetency or a plea raising some psychiatric defense, such as not guilty by reason of insanity; whether the defendant raises some such defense at trial; and whether, if s/he does, s/he calls defense mental health experts to support it. Compare the approaches taken in *Seng v. Commonwealth*, 445 Mass. 536, 839 N.E.2d 283 (2005); *People v. Spencer,* 60 Cal. 2d 64, 383 P.2d 134, 31 Cal. Rptr. 782 (1963); *In re Spencer,* 63 Cal. 2d 400, 406 P.2d 33, 46 Cal. Rptr. 753 (1965); *People v. Arcega,* 32 Cal. 3d 504, 651 P.2d 338, 186 Cal. Rptr. 94 (1982); *People v. Williams*, 197 Cal. App. 3d 1320, 243 Cal. Rptr. 480 (1988); *Parkin v. State,* 238 So.2d 817, 820 (Fla. 1970); *People v. Stevens,* 386 Mich. 579, 194 N.W.2d 370 (1972); *State v. Whitlow,* 45 N.J. 3, 210 A.2d 763 (1965); *State ex rel. LaFollette v. Raskin,* 34 Wis. 2d 607, 150 N.W.2d 318 (Wis. 1967).

D. *Incompetency To Stand Trial*

16.7. *The Standard for Determining Competency*

The criminal procedure statutes of virtually every State codify the common-law rule that a criminal defendant may not be tried for a crime while s/he is incompetent to stand trial. The prevailing test of incompetency in most jurisdictions is the relatively simple one whether the defendant (a) by reason of mental disease or disorder is (b) unable at the time of plea or trial to (i) understand the nature and purpose of the proceedings or (ii) consult and cooperate with counsel in preparing and presenting the defense. *E.g., Sibug v. State*, 445 Md. 265, 126 A.3d 86 (2015). This is the test in federal prosecutions (*Dusky v. United States,* 362 U.S. 402, at 402 (1960) ("it is not enough for the district judge to find that 'the defendant (is) oriented to time and place and (has) some recollection of events,' but . . . the 'test must be whether he has sufficient present ability to consult with his lawyer with a reasonable degree of rational understanding – and whether he has a rational as well as factual understanding of the proceedings against him'")) and it is probably the federal constitutional test as well. *See Indiana v. Edwards*, 554 U.S. 164, 170 (2008); *Cooper v. Oklahoma*, 517 U.S. 348, 354 (1996); *Pate v. Robinson*, 383 U.S. 375 (1966); *Drope v. Missouri,* 420 U.S. 162, 171-72 (1975); *see also* Christopher Slobogin, *The American Bar Association's Criminal Justice Mental Health Standards: Revisions for the Twenty-First Century*, 44 HASTINGS CONST. L. Q. 1, 20-21 (2016) (explaining that the ABA's Criminal Justice Mental Health Standards concerning a defendant's "competence to proceed" employ "the test set out in the Supreme Court's decision in *Dusky v. United States*" and that "[w]hile the test is the same in every proceeding, the Standards recognize that context matters. Thus, for example, in the guilty plea context the Standards highlight 'the nature and complexity of the charges and the potential consequences of a conviction.' When the defendant is contemplating waiving counsel, the relevant standard provides that the court should determine whether the defendant 'has a rational and factual understanding of the possible consequences of proceeding without legal representation, including difficulties the defendant may experience due to his or her mental or emotional condition or lack of knowledge about the legal process.'").

"Where the evidence raises a 'bona fide doubt' as to a defendant's competence to stand trial, the judge on his own motion must impanel a jury and conduct a sanity hearing." *Pate v. Robinson, supra,* 383 U.S. at 385. Although this passage in the *Pate* opinion refers to Illinois law, it is now commonly understood as stating a federal due process requirement. *See, e.g., Drope v. Missouri, supra,* 420 U.S. at 172-73; *Griffin v. Lockhart,* 935 F.2d 926 (8th Cir. 1991); *Maxwell v. Roe,* 606 F.3d 561 (9th Cir. 2010); *State v. Sides,* 376 N.C. 449, 852 S.E.2d 170 (2020); *People v. Wycoff,* 12 Cal. 5th 58, 493 P.3d 789, 283 Cal. Rptr. 3d 1 (2021); *Goad v. State,* 137 Nev. 167, 488 P.3d 646 (Nev. App. 2021); *and see Anderson v. Gipson,* 902 F.3d 1126, 1133 (9th Cir. 2018) ("[s]ince *Pate* courts, including the Ninth Circuit, have generally adopted the 'bona fide doubt' [regarding a defendant's competence] standard as to when a trial court is required to order a competency hearing before proceedings may continue").

Under the conventional formulation of the competency standard, courts usually will not find a defendant incompetent unless s/he is floridly psychotic. However, in cases in which a finding of incompetency would be in the client's interest, counsel can argue that the second half of the incompetency standard – inability to confer and cooperate with counsel – should be extended to encompass: (a) defendants whose mental disorder affects their ability to recall the events of the period when the offense is alleged to have been committed (*see Wilson v. United States,* 391 F.2d 460 (D.C. Cir. 1968); *State v. McIntosh,* 146 Wis. 2d 870, 433 N.W.2d 32 (Table), 1988 WL 126494 (Wis. App. 1988) ("We conclude that McIntosh did not receive a fair trial [on a charge of homicide by negligent use of a vehicle] because the critical evidence – whether his brakes failed – could not be extrinsically reconstructed without his testimony, [he had amnesia regarding the facts of the relevant time period,] and the strength of the state's case was not such as to negate his reasonable hypothesis of innocence."); *United States v. No Runner,* 590 F.3d 962, 965 n.2 (9th Cir. 2009) (dictum) ("courts have uniformly held that amnesia regarding the alleged crime does not constitute incompetence per se but may establish a basis for a finding of incompetence in a particular case."); *Commonwealth v. Lombardi,* 378 Mass. 612, 615-16, 393 N.E.2d 346, 348-49 (1979) ("[A] defendant's amnesia is a factor to be considered in dealing with the fundamental question whether the defendant can receive a fair trial. . . . ¶ The real question . . . is whether a trial of the defendant would be unfair in a due process sense because of his amnesia. Such a question of fundamental fairness can only be determined on a case by case basis. Where the amnesia appears to be temporary, an appropriate solution might be to defer trial for a reasonable period to see if the defendant's memory improves. That alternative appears to be foreclosed here because the defendant's amnesia has been found to be permanent. Where the amnesia is apparently permanent, the fairness of proceeding to trial must be assessed on the basis of the particular circumstances of the case. A variety of factors may be significant in determining whether the trial should proceed, including the nature of the crime, the extent to which the prosecution makes a full disclosure of its case and circumstances known to it, the degree to which the evidence establishes the defendant's guilt, the likelihood that an alibi or some other defense could be established but for the amnesia, and the extent and effect of the defendant's amnesia."); *cf. People v. Palmer,* 31 P.3d 863, 867-68 (Colo. 2001) (superseded by statute on an unrelated issue) ("[A] majority of courts have concluded that amnesia, in and of itself, does not constitute incompetency to stand trial. . . . ¶ . . . A more difficult question is whether the defendant's lack of memory is even relevant to a competency determination. Courts have split on this issue. One view holds that if the defendant has the present ability to understand the proceedings against him, to communicate with his lawyer, and generally to conduct his defense in a rational manner, then his loss of memory is irrelevant to a competency determination. . . . Another line of cases, in contrast, holds that amnesia is relevant to the issue of competency, but is only determinative if a defendant suffers a loss of memory so severe that it renders him unable to understand the proceedings against him or to assist in his own defense. . . . We find this latter approach more convincing.")); (b) defendants whose mental disorder impairs their ability to testify intelligibly in their own defense (*see Lopez v. Evans*, 25 N.Y.3d 199, 202, 206, 31 N.E.3d 1197, 1199, 1202, 9 N.Y.S.3d 601, 602, 605 (2015) (holding on state constitutional grounds that "when a parolee lacks mental competency to stand trial, it is a violation of his or her due process rights to conduct a parole revocation hearing" because "[a]n incompetent parolee is not in a position to exercise rights, such as the right to testify and the opportunity to confront adverse witnesses . . . that are directly related to ensuring the accuracy of fact-finding"); (c) defendants whose mental disorder precludes their participation in a rational fashion in certain crucial decisions, such as whether to plead guilty in return for a bargained disposition or whether to invoke the defense of insanity at the time of the crime (see § 16.13 *infra*); and (d) defendants whose physical disability prevents them from assisting in their own defense. *See generally* Melinda G. Schmidt, N. Dickon Reppucci & Jennifer L. Woodard, *Effectiveness of Participation as a Defendant: The Attorney-Client Relationship*, 21 Behav. Sci. & L. 175 (2003).

Supreme Court decisions involving constitutional claims by condemned inmates that they are incompetent to be executed can be invoked to shed some light by analogy on what is required to satisfy the mental-disease-or-disorder component and the inability-to-understand component of the standard test for incompetency at the pretrial and trial stages. *Madison v. Alabama*, 139 S. Ct. 718 (2019), recognizes that questions of competency turn on the "particular effect" of any cognitive impairment – specifically, the individual's ability or "inability to rationally understand" whatever information is necessary to perform the defendant's task at any stage – not on the diagnostic label or etiology of the impairing condition. The "standard has no interest in establishing any precise cause: Psychosis or dementia, delusions or overall cognitive decline are all the same . . . so long as they produce the requisite lack of comprehension. . . . ¶ In evaluating competency to be executed, a judge must therefore look beyond any given diagnosis to a downstream consequence." (*Id.* at 728-29.) *See also State v. Linares*, 2017-NMSC-014, 393 P.3d 691, 697, 698 (N.M. 2017) ("A defendant may be incompetent to stand trial due to mental retardation . . . [although] mental retardation, in and of itself, is not conclusive evidence that a defendant is incompetent. . . . ¶ The evidence adduced at the mental retardation hearing supports the conclusion that Linares is incapable of consulting with her attorney with a reasonable degree of rational understanding, that she holds a fundamentally incoherent view of the nature of the proceedings that were to be brought against her, and that she would not comprehend the reasons for punishment if she were convicted. Accordingly, substantial evidence supports the district court's determination that Linares is incompetent."). *Madison* treats *Panetti v. Quarterman*, 551 U.S. 930 (2007), as the governing precedent and describes *Panetti* as holding that "the issue is whether a 'prisoner's concept of reality' is 'so impair[ed]' that he cannot grasp the . . . [relevant legal proceeding's] 'meaning and purpose' . . . ." (*Madison*, 139 S. Ct. at 723.). Both the facts and the reasoning in *Panetti* add some useful insight here. In challenging his competency for execution, Panetti claimed that he suffered from psychotic delusions that "recast . . . [his] execution as 'part of spiritual warfare . . . between the demons and the forces of the darkness and God and the angels and the forces of light . . .' . . . [and that] although . . . [he] claims to understand 'that the state is saying that [it wishes] to execute him for [his] murder[s],' he believes in earnest that the stated reason is a 'sham' and the State in truth wants to execute him 'to stop him from preaching'" (*Panetti*, 551 U.S. at 954-55). The lower federal courts found these delusions irrelevant because the "'test for competency to be executed requires the petitioner know no more than the fact of his impending execution and the factual predicate for the execution'" (*id.* at 942). The Supreme Court declared this test unconstitutionally narrow. Although it did "not attempt to set down a rule governing all competency determinations" (*id.* at 960-61), it did observe that in the seminal case of *Ford v. Wainwright*, 477 U.S. 399 (1986), "[w]riting for four Justices, Justice Marshall . . . indicat[ed] that the Eighth Amendment prohibits execution of 'one whose mental illness prevents him from comprehending the reasons for the penalty or its implications . . .' [whereas] Justice Powell, in his separate opinion, asserted that the Eighth Amendment 'forbids the execution only of those who are unaware of the punishment they are about to suffer and why they are to suffer it'" (*Panetti*, 551 U.S. at 957). The *Panetti* Court concluded that "the principles set forth in [each of these] *Ford* [opinions] are put at risk by a rule that deems delusions relevant only with respect to the State's announced reason for a punishment or the fact of an imminent execution . . . as opposed to the real interests the State seeks to vindicate" (*id.* at 959). "A prisoner's awareness of the State's rationale for an execution is not the same as a rational understanding of it." *Id.* The same conception of rational understanding plainly should apply at earlier stages of a criminal case as well. *United States v. Nissen*, 550 F. Supp. 3d 1002, 1017 (D. N.M. 2021) ("In determining a defendant's competency, 'it is not enough . . . that the defendant is oriented to time and place and has some recollection of events.' *Dusky v. United States*, 362 U.S. [402] at 402 [(1960)]. Nor is it enough that 'the defendant can make a recitation of the charges . . . for proper assistance in the defense requires an understanding that is "rational as well as factual."' *United States v. Hemsi*, 901 F.2d 293, 295 (2d Cir. 1990) (quoting *Dusky v. United States*, 362 U.S. at 402)."). A defendant who knows that s/he is being haled into court to be prosecuted on a criminal charge but who delusionally believes that the charge is the work of a conspiracy between the state and the devil (or ISIS, or Wall Street) will not make the cut for competence.

Useful information about competency evaluations can be found in John T. Philipsborn & Melissa Hamilton, Jill Molloy & Sarah L. Cooper, *Competence to Stand Trial Assessment: Practice-Based Views on the Role of Neuroscience*, 15 U. St. Thomas J. L. & Public Policy 259 (2021).

16.8. *Results of a Finding of Incompetency*

If a defendant is found incompetent to stand trial, s/he will be confined in a mental health facility (*see, e.g.*, *United States v. Shawar*, 865 F.2d 856 (7th Cir. 1989); *United States v. Brennan*, 928 F.3d 210 (2d Cir. 2019); *United States v. Quintero*, 995 F.3d 1044 (9th Cir. 2021); *cf. United States v. Ceasar*, 30 F.4th 497 (5th Cir. 2022) – usually a state hospital and, in cases of violent offenses, a secure ward of that hospital. In *Jackson v. Indiana,* 406 U.S. 715 (1972), the Court imposed the following due process restrictions upon the duration of the confinement:

"[A] person charged by a State with a criminal offense who is committed solely on account of his incapacity to proceed to trial cannot be held more than the reasonable period of time necessary to determine whether there is a substantial probability that he will attain that capacity in the foreseeable future. If it is determined that this is not the case, then the State must either institute the customary civil commitment proceeding that would be required to commit indefinitely any other citizen, or release the defendant. Furthermore, even if it is determined that the defendant probably soon will be able to stand trial, his continued commitment must be justified by progress toward that goal." (*Id.* at 738.)

Substantial delays in transferring an incompetent defendant from jail to a mental health facility for evaluation of his or her prospects for restoration to competency are impermissible under *Jackson* (*see, e.g., United States v. Donnelly*, 41 F.4th 1102 (9th Cir. 2022); *Stiavetti v. Clendenin*, 65 Cal. App. 5th 691, 280 Cal. Rptr. 3d 165 (2021); *cf. Medina v. Superior Court of Orange County*, 65 Cal. App. 5th 1197, 281 Cal. Rptr. 3d 1 (2021); *and see Carr v. State*, 303 Ga. 853, at 853, 815 S.E.2d 903, 906 (2018) (invalidating a statute that required automatic commitment of defendants charged with violent crimes and found incompetent to stand trial: "Because the nature of *automatic* commitment for all those defendants does not bear a reasonable relation to the State's purpose of accurately determining the restorability of individual defendants' competence to stand trial, that aspect of . . . [the statute] violates due process. . . . In such cases, the trial court should proceed as it does in determining how to evaluate mentally incompetent defendants accused of nonviolent offenses. To ensure that the nature of commitment to the department is appropriate for the particular defendant, the court should consider all relevant evidence and make a finding as to whether the evaluation . . . should be conducted on an inpatient or outpatient basis. A defendant who is not already lawfully detained should be committed to the department only if the court finds that such confinement is reasonably related to the purpose of accurately evaluating whether that particular defendant can attain competency. A hearing on this issue should be held at the same time or promptly after the court initially determines the defendant's competency to be tried.")): courts have rejected institutional claims that overcrowding of the only available facilities can justify protracted pre-commitment confinement (*see, e.g., Oregon Advocacy Center v. Mink*, 322 F.3d 1101 (9th Cir. 2003); *Disability Law Center v. Utah*, 180 F. Supp. 3d 998 (D. Utah 2016); *Advocacy Center for Elderly and Disabled v. Louisiana Department of Health and Hospitals*, 731 F. Supp. 2d 603 (E.D. La. 2010); *J.K. v. State*, 469 P.3d 434 (Alaska App. 2020); *State v. Hand*, 192 Wash. 2d 289, 295-99, 429 P.3d 502, 505-07 (2018)). If, upon evaluation, it appears that there is no substantial probability that the defendant will become competent to be tried in the foreseeable future and if s/he is not civilly committed, s/he must be released. *Harris v. Clay County*, 40 F.4th 266 (5th Cir. 2022); *State ex rel. Deisinger v. Treffert*, 85 Wis. 2d 257, 269, 270 N.W.2d 402, 408 (1978). *See also Sharris v. Commonwealth*, 480 Mass. 586, 106 N.E.3d 661 (2018), requiring the dismissal of criminal charges when a defendant found incompetent to be tried is released under *Jackson; accord, Gonzales v. State*, 15 So.3d 37 (Fla. App. 2009).

Thus in cases in which the hospital concludes that restoration to competency is not probable and in which the state refrains from seeking civil commitment, the defendant will be released. However, the state ordinarily does institute civil-commitment proceedings unless the offense currently charged is minor and the defendant has no significant prior record. Even low-grade priors like panhandling or turnstile-jumping or drunk-and-disorderly can, if recurrent, provoke a state's attorney to view the defendant as a nuisance who should be gotten off the streets. And in some jurisdictions statutes *mandate* the initiation of civil commitment proceedings if a defendant is found to be incompetent to stand trial.

Of course, even when the state elects to seek civil commitment, it will not necessarily succeed in committing the defendant. Under typical civil commitment statutes, an individual is subject to commitment only if s/he is mentally ill or intellectually disabled *and* if these conditions render the individual dangerous to self or others. *See, e.g.,O'Connor v. Donaldson*, 422 U.S. 563, 576 (1975) ("a State cannot constitutionally confine without more a nondangerous individual who is capable of surviving safely in freedom by himself or with the help of willing and responsible family members or friends"). And under *Addington v. Texas,* 441 U.S. 418, 425-33 (1979), a state bears the burden proving illness and dangerousness by "clear and convincing" evidence or an equivalent standard (*id.* at 433). Individuals whose incompetency is based on factors other than mental disease or defect – such as amnesia or physical disability – will probably be deemed ineligible for civil commitment. And there are many mentally ill and intellectually disabled people who, although incompetent to stand trial, are not dangerous to self or others.

If the state seeks and succeeds in obtaining an order of involuntary civil commitment, the commitment will, as a practical matter, continue until such time as (a) the institutional psychiatrists believe that the defendant has recovered from his or her mental illness or at least has ceased to be physically dangerous to self or others, or (b) the institution runs out of beds and is glutted with inmates sicker than the defendant. In theory, "even if . . . involuntary confinement was initially permissible, it could not constitutionally continue after that [initial] basis [– illness plus dangerousness –] no longer existed" (*O'Connor v. Donaldson, supra*, 422 U.S. at 575; *see, e.g., Van Orden v. Schafer*, 129 F. Supp. 3d 839, 867-70 (E.D. Mo. 2015)). But unless counsel is prepared for long-haul monitoring of the hospital's continuing justification for confining a defendant, it will probably be bed pressure rather than the Constitution that eventually determines a release date.

In federal practice, 18 U.S.C. § 4246(e) authorizes the conditional discharge of persons involuntarily committed as incompetent to stand trial. The procedure to be followed in proceedings to revoke such a discharge under § 4246(f) is discussed in *United States v. Perkins*, 67 F.4th 583 (4th Cir. 2023), which, *inter alia*, holds that the government's burden of proof on the issues of failure to comply with a required treatment regimen and of dangerousness is a preponderance of the evidence.

16.9. *Strategic Considerations in Deciding Whether to Raise a Claim of Incompetency*

Counsel should ordinarily be very hesitant to raise a claim of incompetency in a case in which the client is not facing a lengthy sentence of imprisonment if convicted. As explained in § 16.8 *supra,* the consequence of a finding of incompetency may well be civil commitment to a mental hospital. Because mental problems are often of long duration – and because the hospital will probably get away with confining the client until its staff gets around to asking itself whether there are sicker people who need the client's bed – a finding of incompetency to be tried is often a one-way ticket to indefinite warehousing in an oppressive state institution. Defendants facing heavy felony charges may be advised to accept prolonged hospitalization as an escape from the risk of an even longer prison sentence. But in less serious felony cases and in most misdemeanor cases, the cost-benefit calculus tips the other way.

There are also other adverse consequences that can flow from raising a claim of incompetency. "The 'collateral consequences of being adjudged mentally ill' include potential limits on the right to vote, serve on a jury, obtain a driver's license, and own a gun." *United States v. Bergrin*, 885 F.3d 416, 420 (6th Cir. 2018). In the event that the defendant is found to be only temporarily incompetent, with the prospect of regaining capacity to stand trial, s/he may be held for months in the mental hospital and then returned to court to face the original charge; then, if s/he is convicted and sentenced to a term of incarceration, the length of the sentence will not be proportionately reduced to give "credit" for the months s/he spent in the mental hospital. And in the event that the defendant is not found incompetent at all, the incompetency proceedings – the mental examination and the incompetency hearing – may provide the prosecution with information about the defendant's background and psychic make-up that the prosecutor can use: (i) to urge that the defendant should be held in custody pending trial (*i.e.*, that an initial order setting bail should be rescinded or that the amount of bail should be increased); (ii) to counter claims that defense counsel might make at a suppression hearing when challenging incriminating statements or tangible evidence seized by "consent" searches, on theories that rely in whole or part upon the defendant's vulnerable mental condition; (iii) at trial, to impeach the defendant's credibility as a witness, refute defenses of diminished capacity or insanity, and sometimes affirmatively prove guilt; and (iv) at sentencing, to argue for a harsher sentence on the ground that the defendant's mental problems render him or her too dangerous to leave at large in the community. See § 16.3 *supra*. There are legal doctrines that the defense can invoke to ward off these consequences (see § 16.6.1 *supra*) but they are full of legal and practical wrinkles that may render their protection less than fully effective in any particular case.

Counsel also must take into account that competency proceedings can consume several months, since there will probably be at least two mental examinations (one by defense experts and one by prosecution experts), and the court proceedings will be repeatedly continued because the experts' reports are not ready or the attorneys or experts have scheduling conflicts. This delay is yet another factor rendering an incompetency claim inadvisable in cases in which a client is in custody pending trial or is likely to be committed for an in-patient evaluation, especially if the case is a misdemeanor or low-grade felony.

A claim of incompetency may be advisable even in a misdemeanor or low-grade felony, however, in the rare case where counsel can feel confident that the client faces little or no risk of civil commitment if found incompetent. This circumstance would arise when: (i) the finding of incompetency would rest upon some physical condition or non-organic mental problem (such as amnesia) that could not serve as a "mental disease or defect" rendering the client eligible for civil commitment under state statutory standards; or (ii) even though the finding of incompetency is based on a mental disease or defect, the defense psychiatrist or psychologist is certain that there is no basis for a finding that the defendant is so "dangerous" to self or others as to require civil commitment. In these unusual circumstances counsel can feel reasonably safe that a finding of incompetency would spare the defendant from facing trial on the charged offenses without exposing him or her to the peril of civil commitment. However, even in these situations, the incompetency claim should not be pursued unless the defense psychiatrist or psychologist is confident that the defendant will not be classified as likely to regain capacity and thereby subjected to a period of hospitalization followed by return to court to face trial on the charges.

In more serious felony cases and in any misdemeanor or low-grade felony cases that meet the preceding, rare conditions, counsel will want to consider the following matters before finally determining whether to raise an incompetency claim:

(1) The advantages to the defense of having the defendant examined and of conducting a hearing on the issue of the defendant's competency, including:

    (a) The possibility of putting into the record, in a form that may make it admissible at a subsequent trial, evidence favorable to psychiatric defenses, such as insanity and diminished capacity.

    (b) The possibility of early disclosure to the judge, who may preside at trial and sentencing, of evidence of mental illness that may attract the judge's sympathy.

    (c) The possibility of using the hearing for discovery of some portion of the prosecution's case.

(2) The disadvantages of having the defendant examined and of conducting a hearing on the issue of the defendant's competency (see §§ 16.3, 16.5-16.6 *supra*), including:

    (a) Advance disclosure to the prosecutor of evidence – or of leads to evidence – that may subsequently be used by the defense to support mental-impairment defenses at trial or mental-impairment theories in connection with suppression motions, giving the prosecutor opportunities to cross-examine defense experts, learn their weaknesses, and make a record for their subsequent impeachment.

    (b) Disclosure to the court and to the prosecutor of evidence – or of leads to evidence – that the prosecution can use affirmatively to rebut mental-impairment defenses at trial or mental-impairment theories presented by the defense on suppression motions; or to impeach the defendant if s/he testifies at trial, or to prove the prosecution's case on the guilt issue.

    (c) Disclosure to the court and to the prosecutor of matters respecting the defendant's character and mental condition that may be prejudicial at sentencing in the event of conviction; or on such other matters as the allowance or amount of bail pending trial or appeal.

    (d) The possibility that if counsel decides not to present psychiatric defenses at trial, the jury may nevertheless learn from allusions to the pretrial hearing by witnesses, the judge, the prosecutor, or court attendants – or from newspaper accounts of the hearing or from courthouse gossip – that there is some question whether the defendant may be mentally ill.

(e) The delay of other proceedings occasioned by the hearing.

(f) The risk that the court, on a motion by the prosecution, will order the defendant to be forcibly medicated in an effort to render him or her competent. *See, e.g., United States v. Abney*, 760 Fed. Appx. 171 (4th Cir. 2019). The potential harm of forced medication and the high bar that a prosecutor must meet to obtain an involuntary-medication order under *Sell v. United States*, 539 U.S. 166 (2003), are discussed in *United States v. Berry*, 911 F.3d 354 (6th Cir. 2018). Divergent lower-court interpretations of the *Sell* standard are discussed in Blake R. Hills, Sell v. United States: *Has the Split Between the Lower Courts Created a Substantial Likelihood of Injustice?*, 38 QUINNIPIAC L. REV. 83 (2019).

(3) The likelihood of success in convincing the court that the defendant is not competent to stand trial.

(4) The benefits of success, including:

(a) The possibility of avoiding a trial on the merits of the charges against the defendant either because the defendant is unlikely ever to recover competency to be tried or because the prosecution is likely to drop the charges rather than try a "stale" case after the defendant finally recovers competency.

(b) Other advantages of delaying the trial, including the abatement of prejudicial publicity or community sentiment that may make it difficult for the defendant to get a fair trial or a reasonable plea bargain at the present time.

(c) The potential advantages of a pretrial finding of incompetency for the defendant's presentation of psychiatric defenses at trial if the finding can be brought to the attention of the trial jury, for example, by calling as defense witnesses any hospital personnel who may examine or treat the defendant following his or her commitment upon such a finding.

(d) The acquisition of additional evidence supporting psychiatric defenses at trial, which may emerge during the defendant's commitment for examination, observation, and treatment, particularly inasmuch as the hospital personnel who encounter the defendant in this setting *begin* with the assumption that s/he is mentally disordered and may interpret their observations in this light.

(5) The costs of success (see § 16.8 *supra*) including:

(a)   Delay of the trial until the defendant is subsequently found competent.

(b)   Possible incarceration of the defendant in a mental institution during the period of this delay; and, in some cases, lifelong institutionalization.

(c)   The possibility that, if and when the defendant is found to have recovered his or her competency and is returned to court for the resumption of criminal prosecution, the course of diagnosis and treatment which s/he has received during the period of pretrial hospitalization will have generated information about the defendant's mental condition that the prosecution can use as evidence – or to lead to evidence – to rebut mental-impairment defenses at trial or mental-impairment theories presented by the defense on suppression motions; or to impeach the defendant if s/he testifies at trial, or to prove the prosecution's case on the guilt issue.

(d)   The effect upon the defendant's record of a formal adjudication of incompetency.

(6)   The defendant's attitude toward taking the position that s/he is incompetent.

If counsel has significant, reliable information indicating that a client may be incompetent to stand trial, counsel should evaluate the potential benefits and costs of pursuing the subject further; and if s/he decides on balance not to do so, s/he should make notes to the files recording that decision and explaining in detail the reasons for it. Inability to justify the decision may expose counsel to claims of ineffective assistance. *See, e.g., Jermyn v. Horn*, 266 F.3d 257, 283, 300-03 (3d Cir. 2001); *Harris v. United States*, 2023 WL 3302978, at *4-*7 (11th Cir. 2023).

16.10. *Procedures for Raising and Litigating a Claim of Incompetency*

If counsel concludes that a claim of incompetency to plead or be tried may be in the defendant's interest, s/he will need to develop sufficient evidence to convince the presiding judge that there is a *bona fide* doubt concerning the defendant's competence. See the third paragraph of this section. This is often possible on the basis of a history of mental disorder shown through medical records or lay testimony, without having the defendant clinically examined for the purpose. However, because of the numerous problems and pitfalls involved in raising the issue of competency, it is ordinarily wise for counsel to retain a psychiatrist or psychologist to examine the defendant, determine whether s/he is arguably incompetent under the standards described in § 16.7 *supra*, and advise counsel regarding the potential benefits and costs of raising the claim, outlined in § 16.9. *Cf. Blakeney v. United States*, 77 A.3d 328, 342-43, 345 (D.C. 2013) ("The test for determining when defense counsel is obligated to raise the issue of the defendant's competency with the court cannot be stated with precision. . . . That a defendant suffers from a severe mental disorder does not necessarily mean he is incompetent; the latter is a 'much narrower concept.' . . . [W]e hold that criminal defense counsel must raise the issue of the defendant's competency with the court if, considering all the circumstances, objectively reasonable counsel would have reason to doubt the defendant's competency. Failure to do so is constitutionally deficient performance."); *Humphrey v. Walker*, 294 Ga. 855, 874-75, 757 S.E.2d 68, 83 (2014). Procedures for obtaining a defense mental health expert are described in § 16.3 *supra*. For an overview of the relevant forensic-science materials, *see* John T. Philipsborn, *Lawyering Competence to Stand Trial with an Eye on Neuroscience*, 43-NOV THE CHAMPION 18 (2019).

Assuming that the examination results in a report attesting to the defendant's incompetency and assuming that counsel concludes that an incompetency claim is the proper strategy, counsel then will proffer the report to the court together with whatever written pleading, motion, or "suggestion" of present incompetency is required by local practice in order to raise the claim. In many jurisdictions the judge will, at this point, routinely grant a prosecutorial request that the defendant be ordered to submit to an examination by a prosecution psychiatrist or psychologist. *But see State v. Sharrow*, 205 Vt. 300, 175 A.3d 504, 505 (2017) ("This case comes before the Court on interlocutory appeal. The sole issue is whether, under . . . [the applicable statute], the State may compel a defendant to submit to a competency evaluation conducted by a mental health expert of the State's choosing, following a court-ordered competency evaluation by a neutral mental health expert. We hold that the State may not compel such an evaluation. . . ." *Id.* at 302-03, 175 A.3d at 505. "[O]ur conclusion that the court lacks the authority to order a defendant to submit to a competency evaluation conducted by an expert retained by the State is consistent with underlying constitutional principles. . . . [W]here – as is the case here – an indigent defendant's mental health is at issue, 'due process requires that the State provide the defendant with the assistance of an independent psychiatrist.' . . . Additionally, in the context of a competency hearing, the U.S. Supreme Court has recognized that '[f]or the defendant, the consequences of an erroneous determination of competence are dire. . . .' ¶ . . . [A]s other courts that have addressed this issue have noted, '[t]he policy reasons behind prohibiting the [State] from obtaining its own competency evaluation are clear.'. . . Specifically, ordering 'an examination for the sole purpose of ascertaining competency, especially if ordered against a defendant's wishes,' creates the risk that the State 'would gain the inherent and possibly unfair advantage of gleaning insight as to the defense strategy.'" *Id.* at 306-08, 175 A.3d at 508-09.); *State v. Garcia*, 128 N.M. 721, 998 P.2d 186 (N.M. App. 2000) (holding that after a court has ordered a competency examination by a neutral ("court") expert, it may in its discretion refuse to order a follow-up examination by a prosecution expert.).

After all of the mental examinations are completed and the reports filed, the judge will convene an evidentiary hearing on the issue of competency. The defense has a due process right to an adversarial hearing unless the examinations have dispelled any significant doubt of incompetency. *Pate v. Robinson,* 383 U.S. 375 (1966); *Drope v. Missouri,* 420 U.S. 162 (1975). *See, e.g., Taylor v. Davis*, 164 F. Supp. 3d 1147 (N.D. Cal. 2016), *postconviction relief granted in* 213 F. Supp. 3d 1232 (N.D. Cal. 2016), *aff'd*, 747 Fed. Appx. 577 (9th Cir. 2018) ("Due process requires a trial court to conduct a competency hearing if it has a 'bona fide doubt' concerning the defendant's competence. . . . ¶ . . . A good faith doubt about a defendant's competence arises 'if there is substantial evidence of incompetence.'"). State law may go further and require a hearing whenever the court has ordered a competency evaluation, whatever the results of that evaluation may be. *See Johnson v. State*, 254 So.3d 1035 (Fla. App. 2018). The jurisdictions differ as to who bears the burden of proof at the hearing, with some placing the burden upon the state once the issue has been raised, and others assigning the burden to the defense. *See Cooper v. Oklahoma*, 517 U.S. 348, 360-62 & nn.16-18 (1996) (citing state statutes and caselaw). In the latter jurisdictions, the quantum of the burden imposed on the defense is a "preponderance of the evidence" (*see id.* at 361 n.17). The Supreme Court held in *Cooper* that imposing upon the accused the heavier burden of "clear and convincing evidence" would violate the Due Process Clause (*see id.* at 362-69). Although the Court has not yet addressed the distinct question of what burden must be placed upon the state when a finding of incompetency is sought against a defendant who opposes it and when the result is involuntary hospitalization, the reasoning of *Cooper* and the Court's decision in the civil commitment context in *Addington v. Texas*, 441 U.S. 418 (1979), strongly suggest that the burden must be placed upon the state to prove incompetency by "clear and convincing evidence." *See Jones v. United States*, 463 U.S. 354 (1983) (distinguishing *Addington* in cases in which a defendant has been found not guilty by reason of insanity because, in such cases, commitment is warranted by "the proof . . . [adduced at trial that the defendant] committed a criminal act as a result of mental illness" (*id.* at 366-67) – a circumstance justifying "the widely and reasonably held view that insanity acquittees constitute a special class that should be treated differently from other candidates for commitment" (*id.* at 370); *and see Foucha v. Louisiana*, 504 U.S. 71, 80 (1992).

The prosecution may seek an order requiring that a mentally incompetent defendant be involuntarily medicated in order to render him or her capable to stand trial. In *Sell v. United States*, 539 U.S. 166, 179-80 (2003), the Supreme Court held that such orders are permissible consistently with Due Process if, "but only if the treatment is medically appropriate, is substantially unlikely to have side effects that may undermine the fairness of the trial, and, taking account of less intrusive alternatives, is necessary significantly to further important governmental trial-related interests. ¶ This standard will permit involuntary administration of drugs solely for trial competence purposes in certain instances. But those instances may be rare."). The prosecution "must establish the four [*Sell*] factors by clear and convincing evidence, and not just by a preponderance of the evidence" (*United States v. James*, 938 F.3d 719 (5th Cir. 2019)). In federal prosecutions, an involuntary-medication order can be challenged by an immediate interlocutory appeal (see § 31.1 *supra*); in state prosecutions, that may or may not be so, but the order may be challenged by an action in federal court. The federal filing should be captioned in the alternative as a petition for habeas corpus under 28 U.S.C. § 2241 and as a civil-rights action for injunctive relief under 42 U.S.C. § 1983 and 28 U.S.C. §§ 1331 and 1343(3). *See Bean v. Matteucci*, 986 F.3d 1128 (9th Cir. 2021).

E. *Insanity*

16.11. *The Standard for Acquittal on the Ground of Insanity at the Time of the Crime (a/k/a the Verdict of Not Guilty by Reason of Insanity, Colloquially Called NGI)*

The traditional *M'Naghten* rule, which is still employed in a number of States, provides "that to establish a defence on the ground of insanity, it must be clearly proved that, at the time of the committing of the act, the party accused was labouring under such a defect of reason, from disease of the mind, as not to know the nature and quality of the act he was doing; or, if he did know it, that he did not know he was doing what was wrong" (*M'Naghten's Case,* 8 Eng. Rep. 718, 722 (1843)). *See also* Christopher Slobogin, *The American Bar Association's Criminal Justice Mental Health Standards: Revisions for the Twenty-First Century*, 44 HASTINGS CONST.

L. Q. 1, 22-23 (2016) (explaining that the ABA's Criminal Justice Mental Health Standards "opt for a 'liberal' version of the *M'Naghten* test"). Other States employ the American Law Institute (ALI) test, which provides that "[a] person is not responsible for criminal conduct if at the time of such conduct as a result of mental disease or defect he lacks substantial capacity either to appreciate the criminality [wrongfulness] of his conduct or to conform his conduct to the requirements of law" (AMERICAN LAW INSTITUTE, MODEL PENAL CODE § 4.01 (1962), 10 U.L.A. 490-91 (1974)). *See generally Kahler v. Kansas*, 140 S. Ct. 1021 (2020) (surveying varying formulations of the insanity defense and collecting an array of federal and state statutes and British and American caselaw); *Clark v. Arizona*, 548 U.S. 735, 749-52 & nn.12-22 (2006) (same); ABRAHAM S. GOLDSTEIN, THE INSANITY DEFENSE (1980 ed.); DONALD H. J. HERMANN, THE INSANITY DEFENSE: PHILOSOPHICAL, HISTORICAL, AND LEGAL PERSPECTIVES (1983); RITA J. SIMON AND DAVID E. AARONSON, THE INSANITY DEFENSE, at *2: A CRITICAL ASSESSMENT OF LAW AND POLICY IN THE POST-HINCKLEY ERA (1988); Richard A. Wise & Denitsa R. Mavrova Heinrich, *Toward a More Scientific Jurisprudence of Insanity*, 95 TEMPLE L. REV. 45 (2022); Deborah W. Denno, *How Experts Have Dominated the Neuroscience Narrative in Criminal Cases for Twelve Decades: A Warning for the Future*, 63 WILLIAM & MARY L. REV. 1215 (2022). The *Clark* decision rejects a due process challenge to Arizona's "fragment[ary]" *M'Naghten* rule which asks only the "moral incapacity" question "whether a mental disease or defect leaves a defendant unable to understand that his action is wrong" and not the "alternative" "cognitive incapacity" question "whether a mental defect leaves the defendant unable to understand what he is doing" (*id.* at 747, 756); the *Kahler* decision rejects a due process challenge to Kansas's refusal to recognize any insanity defense that goes beyond the traditional concept of "diminished capacity" (see § 39.25 *infra*), the Court noting that Kansas does allow defendants to "raise mental illness after conviction to justify either a reduced term of imprisonment or commitment to a mental health facility" (140 S. Ct. at 1024); the upshot of these cases is that the federal Constitution imposes no significant substantive constraint upon a state's power to craft insanity-defense standards. *But see* Matthew Hughes, *Comment, A New Argument for the Next* Kahler v. Kansas: *Due Process Demands More Than Cognitive Capacity*, 15 LIBERTY U. L. REV. 27 (2020).

In all jurisdictions the defense bears the burden of introducing sufficient evidence to raise the issue of insanity. The requisite quantum of evidence varies among jurisdictions. Some States provide that the defense can raise the issue by merely presenting "some evidence," or enough evidence to raise a reasonable doubt, whereupon the burden shifts to the prosecution to prove sanity beyond a reasonable doubt, just as the prosecution must prove every other element of the offense beyond a reasonable doubt. In other States the defense bears the burden of persuasion and must prove insanity by a preponderance of the evidence. Constitutional challenges to placing the burden on the defense have been consistently rejected. *Rivera v. Delaware,* 429 U.S. 877 (1976) (per curiam); *see Patterson v. New York,* 432 U.S. 197, 201-05 (1977) (dictum); *Jones v. United States,* 463 U.S. 354, 368 n.17 (1983) (dictum).

16.12. *Strategic Considerations in Deciding Whether to Raise an Insanity Defense*

The primary consideration militating against the raising of incompetency claims in misdemeanors and low-grade felony cases (see § 16.9 *supra*) – the risk of institutionalization in a mental hospital for many years more than the defendant could serve if convicted at trial and sentenced to a term of incarceration – also may render an insanity defense highly inadvisable. Indeed, the risks are even greater in the context of insanity defenses. A defendant who is found incompetent to stand trial and who is then subjected to involuntary civil commitment proceedings is entitled to a hearing at which the state must show by clear and convincing evidence both that the defendant is mentally ill and that s/he is dangerous to self or others. See § 16.8 *supra*. In a number of States the statutes provide for civil commitment of an insanity acquittee as an automatic consequence of the finding of insanity made at trial, even though that finding is usually made under the far weaker "preponderance of the evidence" standard and does not involve an express finding of dangerousness. *But cf. People v. Daryl T.*, 166 A.D.3d 68, 84 N.Y.S.3d 458 (N.Y. App. Div., 1st Dep't 2018) (describing New York's procedure, under which a verdict or plea that a defendant is "not responsible by reason of mental disease or defect" gives rise to a hearing at which the prosecution "bear[s] the burden of proving 'to the satisfaction of the court,' i.e., by a fair preponderance of the credible evidence, that the defendant has a dangerous mental disorder or is mentally ill" (*id.* at 77, 84 N.Y.S.3d at 464); the court holds that defense counsel "rendered ineffective assistance when he conceded at the plea proceeding that defendant was a danger to himself and society, and waived defendant's right to an initial hearing [on the issue of dangerousness] before reviewing the psychiatric examination reports which had not yet been prepared for the court. Further, at the proceeding that followed the issuance of the reports, counsel simply relied on the psychiatrists' reports and deferred to the court's discretion. He did not call any witnesses or seek to cross-examine the psychiatrists who prepared the reports. Nor did counsel consult an expert on defendant's behalf who might have offered a contrasting opinion." (*id.*, 84 N.Y.S.3d at 464-65).).

In *Jones v. United States,* 463 U.S. 354 (1983), the Court sustained the constitutionality of a statute that provided that defendants who "successfully invoke[ ] the insanity defense" are automatically "committed to a mental hospital" (*id.* at 356). Under such a statutory scheme, an insanity acquittee is theoretically "entitled to release when he has recovered his sanity or is no longer dangerous" (*id.* at 368). *See, e.g., Foucha v. Louisiana*, 504 U.S. 71 (1992), holding Due Process violated by a state statute that permitted the continuing confinement of an insanity acquittee even after a hospital review committee had concluded that the acquittee's mental illness was in remission); *see also Kansas v. Crane*, 534 U.S. 407, 412-13 (2002); *Richard S. v. Carpinello*, 589 F.3d 75, 82-85 (2d Cir. 2009); *State v. Edwards*, 2022-00983 (La. 11/1/22), 348 So.3d 1269, 1272 (La. 2022) (a person acquitted by reason of insanity "must be conditionally discharged despite the State's clear and convincing evidence of his dangerousness because, under the law as amended to comply with *Foucha* , . . . [such a person] must be *both* dangerous *and* mentally ill" in order to justify his or her continued detention). But once in an institution, the acquittee is likely as a practical matter to be confined at the discretion of the institution's medical staff, since they will both create and evaluate the record on which any subsequent determination of recovery or dangerousness is going to be based, and their observations and findings are bound to be given great deference by the courts. *See, e.g., State v. Klein*, 156 Wash. 2d 103, 124 P.3d 644 (2005).

Even in the States that extend the usual procedural protections in civil commitment proceedings to insanity acquittees, an insanity acquittal still poses greater risks than a finding of incompetency to stand trial. A defendant who is found incompetent to stand trial cannot have the pending criminal charge used against him or her in the determination of "dangerousness" for civil commitment purposes, since s/he has never been convicted of the charge and must be presumed innocent. In contrast, "[a] verdict of not guilty by reason of insanity establishes two facts: (i) The [defendant] . . . committed an act that constitutes a criminal offense, and (ii) he committed the act because of mental illness" (*Jones v. United States, supra*, 463 U.S. at 363). And in *Jones,* the Court concluded that "[t]he fact that a person has been found, beyond a reasonable doubt, to have committed a criminal act certainly indicates dangerousness" (*id.* at 364), even when the criminal act is "a nonviolent crime against property" (*id.* at 365). The Court's conclusions on this point were made solely in the context of reviewing the reasonableness of a finding of legislative fact underlying a challenged statute (*see id.* at 364-65), and the Court's deference to legislative judgment in *Jones* would not necessarily justify a finding of fact in an individual case that the evidence shows a particular defendant to be "dangerous." *Cf. id.* at 365 n.14. However, notwithstanding this argument for distinguishing *Jones,* there is considerable risk that lower courts will follow the reasoning of *Jones* and find in individual cases that a criminal conviction satisfies the criterion of "dangerousness" for purposes of civil commitment.

Thus, the suggestion in § 16.9 *supra* that counsel could consider a claim of incompetency to stand trial with somewhat less trepidation in cases in which a defense psychiatrist is confident that the defendant will not qualify for civil commitment as "dangerous" to self or others, is inapplicable in the NGI context. Even in jurisdictions that do not provide for automatic commitment but require a finding of dangerousness to support confinement of an insanity acquittee, the risk that the defendant's conviction alone will suffice to establish dangerousness is too great.

In assessing the advisability of an insanity defense, counsel also must consider whether a finding of "not guilty by reason of insanity" could result in any of the collateral consequences that may stem from a criminal conviction. *See, e.g., Halvonik v. Maryland Department of Safety and Correctional Services*, 2015 WL 7301702, at *1, *3 (Md. Ct. Special App. 2015), *cert. denied*, 446 Md. 705, 133 A.3d 1110 (Table) (2016) (the defendant, who pled guilty to sexual offenses but was deemed "not criminally responsible" and placed on probation for five years, nonetheless "was required [by state law] to register as a sex offender" and "the required registration was for life"). For discussion of the various types of collateral consequences that can result from a criminal conviction, see § 15.6.1 *supra*.

16.13. *Defending Against the Judicial Interposition of an Insanity Defense*

In some jurisdictions the court can raise the issue of insanity *sua sponte. E.g., Hendrix v. People*, 10 P.3d 1231 (Colo. 2000); *and see generally* Justine A. Dunlap, *What's Competence Got to Do with It: The Right Not to Be Acquitted by Reason of Insanity*, 50 OKLA. L. REV. 495, 508-10 (1997). In jurisdictions of this sort defense counsel may have to defend against the judge's interposition of the insanity defense, in order to avoid an insanity acquittal with the probable consequence of prolonged institutionalization in a mental hospital. This often requires addressing a test that "balance[s] . . . the public's interest in not holding criminally liable a defendant lacking criminal responsibility and the defendant's interest in autonomously controlling the nature of her defense" (*Hendrix, supra*, 10 P.3d at 1241). In urging that the balance should be struck in favor of the defendant's autonomy interest, counsel can analogize to decisions recognizing the weight of that interest in related contexts: *Faretta v. California*, 422 U.S. 806 (1975), discussed in § 1.4 *supra*; *McCoy v. Louisiana*, 138 S. Ct. 1500 (2018), discussed in § 15.2 *supra*; *and see* § 1.3 second paragraph *supra*. *Hendrix*, for example, cites *Faretta*, *inter alia*, in concluding that "an individual's interest in autonomously controlling the nature of her defense, provided that interest is premised on a choice that satisfies the basic rationality test, will predominate over the broader interest of society unless pressing concerns mandate a contrary result" (10 P.3d at 1243). In jurisdictions that have not resolved the issue, counsel can take the position that "the trial judge may not force an insanity defense on a defendant found competent to stand trial *if* the individual intelligently and voluntarily decides to forego that defense" (*Frendak v. United States*, 408 A.2d 364, 367 (D.C. 1979) (emphasis in original); *accord, United States v. Marble*, 940 F.2d 1543 (D.C. Cir. 1991); *United States v. Read*, 918 F.3d 712 (9th Cir. 2019); *State v. Brown*, 2005 VT 104, 179 Vt. 22, 32-36, 890 A.2d 79, 88-91 (2005) (citing caselaw from other States); *State v. Jones*, 99 Wash. 2d 735, 664 P.2d 1216 (1983); *State v. Glenn*, 148 Hawai'i 112, 126, 468 P.3d 126, 140 (2020); *Farrell v. People*, 54 V.I. 600, 614 (Virgin Islands 2011) ("in the absence of a statute or precedential local case law addressing this issue, this Court adopts the majority approach, which prohibits an unpled insanity defense from being imposed on a defendant unless the trial court ascertains that the defendant did not voluntarily and intelligently waive the defense")). *See also* Christopher Slobogin, *The American Bar Association's Criminal Justice Mental Health Standards: Revisions for the Twenty-First Century*, 44 HASTINGS CONST. L. Q. 1, 33 (2016) (noting that some jurisdictions treat "the decision about raising the insanity defense . . . as a tactical one to be made by the [defense] attorney," and explaining that ABA CRIMINAL JUSTICE MENTAL HEALTH STANDARD 7-6.3 "instead provides that this decision is controlled by the defendant if he or she is competent to make it"). However, counsel should be prepared for an inquiry into the defendant's competency to intelligently waive an insanity defense, which is not necessarily the same as competency to stand trial. *See Frendak v. United States, supra*, 408 A.2d at 367; *Phenis v. United States*, 909 A.2d 138, 154-60 (D.C. 2006).

Even if a judge is permitted to foist an insanity defense on an unwilling defendant, it does not follow that the consequence of the defense once established should be automatic involuntary civil commitment in those jurisdictions where such commitment is the usual fate of insanity acquittees. The *Jones* case discussed in § 16.12 *supra* attached importance to the fact that "automatic commitment under [the challenged statute was provided] . . . only if the *acquittee himself* advances insanity as a defense . . ." (*Jones v. United States*, 463 U.S. 354, 367 (1983) (emphasis in original); *see also id.* at 367 n.16). Counsel in jurisdictions with statutes that are ambiguous on the subject can argue that they should be construed as imposing the same limitation, under the doctrine calling for statutory construction that avoids unnecessary constitutional issues (*e.g., In re M.F.*, 298 Ga. 138, 780 S.E.2d 291 (2015); *State v. Dahl*, 874 N.W.2d 348 (Iowa 2016)); and, if the statute is not so construed, counsel can distinguish *Jones* in arguing that the statute is unconstitutional for all of the reasons advanced in the dissenting opinions in that case (463 U.S. at 371-87).

Made in United States
Troutdale, OR
10/01/2024